BELIEF

BELIEF

WHAT IT MEANS TO BELIEVE AND
WHY OUR CONVICTIONS ARE SO COMPELLING

JAMES E. ALCOCK

Prometheus Books

59 John Glenn Drive
Amherst, New York 14228

Published 2018 by Prometheus Books

Cover image © Ratana21 / Shutterstock
Cover design by Liz Mills
Cover design © Prometheus Books

Inquiries should be addressed to
Prometheus Books
59 John Glenn Drive
Amherst, New York 14228
VOICE: 716–691–0133 • FAX: 716–691–0137
WWW.PROMETHEUSBOOKS.COM

22 21 20 19 18   5 4 3 2 1

Library of Congress Cataloging-in-Publication Data Pending

Printed in the United States of America

For Karen and Erik

CONTENTS

PART IV: KNOWING OURSELVES

PART V: BELIEF IN A WORLD BEYOND

PART VI: VETTING BELIEF

FOREWORD

Jim Alcock leads a busy life. His full-time job is as professor of Social Psychology at York University in Toronto. He also maintains a private practice. He contributes chapters and articles to books and journals. He and his wife, Karen, travel extensively and frequently.

So for him to write a book is quite an achievement. Considering the amount of scholarship and research that has gone into the present book, it is more than an achievement—it is a miracle.

"Psychology" covers a number of subareas. Every generation of psychologists complains about the lack of an overarching and integrated set of principles that unifies all these separate categories of psychology. This book, however, ties together fields of psychology that rarely, if ever, overlap. Every psychologist and psychology student should read it. Unless the situation has changed drastically since I retired in 1998, typical undergraduate psychology majors receive an overview of the various fields of psychology in the Introductory Psychology class. After that they choose courses from a menu of offerings, which could include Sensation and Perception, Cognition, Comparative Psychology, Individual Differences, Learning, Memory, Motivation, Social Psychology, Statistics, Child Psychology, and so on. If they continue on to a graduate degree, they will end up in one of the many special subdivisions of psychology. These could include Occupational Psychology, Clinical Psychology, Animal Psychology, Testing and Assessment, Cognitive Science, Social Psychology, or others.

I believe that all psychology majors should be required to take a course that provides an integrated overview of all the areas of psychology. This book would be an ideal text for such a course. While not actually claiming to put forth such an integrated framework, this book shows how a single concept, in this case "belief," can be illuminated by using the findings from all areas of psychology and related disciplines. At the same time, the focus on belief enables us to gain an integrated sense of psychology as a whole.

Jim says that he has written this book for a general audience. He writes so clearly that anyone, regardless of background, will be able to not only read it but also to enjoy it and learn from it. The fact that he has aimed for a general audience does not mean that he has oversimplified or skimped on what he includes, though. Indeed, his coverage of belief is exhaustive. I know of no other treatment of this topic that is so comprehensive and authoritative.

In other words, Jim has written a book on belief that can be read and enjoyed by a general audience, but that is, at the same time, a book that can, and should, be read by psychologists and professionals such as philosophers and social scientists. In fact, everyone can benefit from this book.

Ray Hyman
Professor of Psychology Emeritus,
University of Oregon,
and founding member of the
Committee for Skeptical Inquiry

ACKNOWLEDGMENTS

I extend my grateful appreciation to all those who have provided feedback and guidance with regard to various portions of the book, including Ray Hyman, Timothy Moore, Guy Proulx, and Tomasz Witkowski. My deepest gratitude goes to the three people who carefully read through the entire manuscript and provided detailed and incisive feedback that helped me improve the book in a number of important ways. They are, in no particular order:

- Psychologist Loren Pankratz, whose extensive comments and thoughtful insights, and in particular those that reflect his impressive breadth of psychological knowledge and experience, have been invaluable;
- Author Gary Bauslaugh, whose acumen as a writer and keen insight into the human condition have helped shape my presentation of important concepts, and have been of particular value in making this psychological material more accessible to a lay audience;
- My wife, Karen Hanley, who not only provided astute guidance and constant encouragement during the long preparation of this book, but also applied her keen editorial professionalism to careful review of the manuscript throughout the editing process.

Thanks also to Emily Duncan Nadeau for her assistance in the initial literature search and to Laura Galin-Corini for her help with the formatting of the extensive set of endnotes.

I also wish to thank my literary agent, Nancy Rosenfeld, and Prometheus Books editor in chief Steven Mitchell, both of whom were key to the successful publication of this book. In addition, I thank all those at Prometheus Books who were involved in making this book a reality, including Sheila Stewart, Hanna Etu, Liz Mills, Laura Shelley, Catherine Roberts-Abel, Bruce Carle, and Cheryl Quimba.

PART I

THE POWER OF BELIEF

Believing is the most mental thing we do.
—Bertrand Russell[1]

Our heads are chockablock with beliefs, beliefs about ourselves, our families, our friends; beliefs about our society and peoples around the world; beliefs about what things are and how things work; beliefs about politics, religion, and the environment. Beliefs provide a moral compass, guide our relationships, and motivate our behaviors in affairs large and small. Our thoughts and feelings, our actions and reactions, respond not to the world as it actually is—for we never know reality directly—but to the world as we believe it to be. Because of our beliefs, we brush our teeth or don't bother; we vote for Jennifer and not for John; we eat certain foods and avoid others; we worship one deity or another or none at all; and we rely on scientific medicine or homeopathy to cure our ills. Beliefs propel us to work tirelessly toward a desired goal or to abandon all hope and sink into despair; they lead us to worry when we need not, or to relax when to do so is unwise. Faulty beliefs—arising from misapprehension about the cause of a disease, misperception of an enemy's actions, misunderstanding of a lover's motives, misconceptions about which, if any, gods are real—lead to inappropriate, maladaptive, and sometimes fatal actions.

Beliefs have inspired humans to conquer diseases, to explore unchartered lands, to construct beautiful edifices, and to look beyond their personal needs and work for the welfare of others, fighting for equality, defending freedom, helping the sick, and assisting the poor. Beliefs have also led to war, terrorism, suicide, martyrdom, and human sacrifice to appease the gods. Nothing speaks to the ultimate power of belief more than the willingness to give up one's life because of it, because of a belief to die for.

CHAPTER 1

BELIEF TO DIE FOR

Those who can make you believe absurdities can make you commit atrocities.

—Voltaire[1]

War. Terrorism. Mass suicide. Martyrdom. Human sacrifice to appease the gods. As we know all too well, *Homo sapiens* is no stranger to violence. There are many motivations, including jealousy, revenge, superstition, greed, lust, honor, and self-aggrandizement, but underlying most violence is belief: belief that someone has insulted you or your group, has stolen your lover, or occupies territory that rightfully belongs to you. Belief that the gods will punish you if you do not offer a human sacrifice. Belief that your martyrdom will be rewarded in a glorious afterlife. Belief that sacrificing your own life will help or protect your family and community. Belief that taking your own life is the only escape from present or future agony.

On average, more than a million people around the world take their own lives each year, one person every forty seconds.[2] Suicide is the second-leading cause of death for young people between fifteen and twenty-four years of age, accounting for almost a quarter of all deaths.[3] And although more women than men attempt suicide, four times as many men actually succeed because they typically choose deadlier means, such as firearms.[4]

Suicide is at times the product of psychosis that renders the individual unable to distinguish between reality and horrible fantasy, but it is most often hopelessness, depression, and the "slings and arrows of outrageous fortune" that lead people to knock on death's door. A man diagnosed with an incurable and debilitating degenerative disease jumps from a bridge to avoid a future filled with misery and drear. A grief-stricken parent, overwrought by news that her children were killed in a car accident, takes a lethal dose of sleeping pills to end her suffering. And upon hearing jackboots in the corridor, a captured spy bites his cyanide capsule in the belief that he is about to be tortured to death. Just as Shakespeare's Romeo tragically took his own life in the mistaken belief that Juliet was dead, these decisions, too, would be in grievous error if the beliefs underlying them were false—if the degenerative disease were a misdiagnosis, the report of the children's death were erroneous, and the boots were those of a liberating army.

> To be, or not to be, that is the question—
> Whether 'tis Nobler in the mind to suffer
> The Slings and Arrows of outrageous Fortune,
> Or to take Arms against a Sea of troubles,
> And by opposing, end them?
> To die, to sleep—
> No more; and by a sleep, to say we end
> The Heart-ache, and the thousand Natural shocks
> That Flesh is heir to? 'Tis a consummation
> Devoutly to be wished.
>
> —Hamlet, Act III, Scene I

To be or not to be: Belief is fundamental to the decision to end one's life. Believing that life is not and never will be worth living and that there is no other means to escape pain, sorrow, humiliation, or future suffering can bring one directly to Hamlet's contemplation. It was the belief that they faced execution or banishment to the Gulag that motivated hundreds of former Soviet citizens, sent back to the Soviet Union after their liberation from the Nazis in 1945, to take their own lives, and in some cases, those of their children as well.[5]

To sleep, perhaps to dream: Of course, suicidal contemplation will be influenced by belief about what happens when one dies. It is one thing if death is simply the end, a "fade to black." It is quite another if you believe that you have a soul that will survive death, and that you will be judged and punished for having taken your own life. Depending on your religion, the consequences might be an eternity of hellfire and brimstone or reincarnation as a lower life form. Judaism,

Christianity, Islam, and Hinduism all traditionally condemn suicide, although Hinduism makes an exception for fasting to death. Buddhism and Jainism are somewhat more tolerant in this regard, but they too discourage such acts.

> To die, to sleep.
> To sleep, perchance to dream—ay, there's the rub,
> For in that sleep of death what dreams may come
> When we have shuffled off this mortal coil,
> Must give us pause. There's the respect
> That makes calamity of so long life.
>
> —Hamlet, Act III, Scene I

Suicide was not condemned in the early days of Christianity, and in some circumstances, it was even considered a virtuous act—for example, if carried out in order to avoid being raped.[6] The desire to escape religious persecution, combined with a belief in the promise of a glorious afterlife, motivated many early Christians to catch the fast train to heaven by taking their own lives. One Christian sect, the Circumcellions, actually glorified suicide, and its members would sometimes even go so far as to pay others to kill them. They were not alone. Members of a contemporaneous sect, the Donatists, equally impatient to be freed from their dreary mortal existence, sought quick entry to heaven through mass suicides carried out by burning themselves to death or jumping from cliffs.[7]

Mass suicides threatened the sustainability and growth of Christianity, and this contributed to a gradual change in attitude toward self-destruction. It is not easy to build a religious movement when new recruits are killing themselves. In the fourth century, St. Augustine publicly condemned suicide and martyrdom as sins and crimes, and thus began the Christian church's equation of suicide with sin to be punished in the afterlife.[8] Later, in the thirteenth century, Thomas Aquinas preached that suicide was such a terrible sin that it could never be forgiven because it was directed against God himself. Because of the church's hardening attitude, burial in hallowed ground was forbidden for anyone who had died by suicide. The bodies of suicide victims were often desecrated, and their families were forced to live in shame.

Church law fed into criminal law, and the stigma associated with suicide became so great in many parts of Europe during the Middle Ages that the possessions of suicide victims, along with those of their family members, were confiscated by the state. Attempted suicide became a crime that ultimately—and ironically—was punished by being put to death. Attempted suicide continued to be a crime in England and Wales until 1961 and in Canada until 1974, but even today, it continues to be a criminal offense in many countries. There is currently no law against attempting suicide in the United States.

ASSISTED SUICIDE

As lives are being extended by modern medicine, growing numbers of people are confronted by debilitating physical or mental deterioration in their later years. Imagine spending most of your life in good physical and mental health only to be diagnosed with a neurodegenerative disease that will leave you unable to feed yourself, to look after personal hygiene, or even to walk or talk. While many people would choose not to live out their lives in that manner, those unfortunate enough to suffer from degenerative disorders foresee a time when physical incapacitation will deprive them of the ability to take their own lives even should they wish to do so. Because of this, a growing number of people support the legalization of physician-assisted suicide. Still, many others continue to believe that such action goes against divine will.

While such medical assistance remains illegal in most countries, it is now lawful in a few parts of the world, including Switzerland, Belgium, the Netherlands, and a few states in the United States. Canada enacted a new law in 2016 to allow physician-assisted suicide, but only for people who are "suffering intolerably" and whose death is "reasonably foreseeable."[9] Because physician-assisted suicide could not be provided legally in their home nations, 172 people went to Zürich, Switzerland, as so-called "suicide tourists" in 2012 alone.[10]

SUICIDE AND TRANSFORMATION

While it continues to be generally condemned by the traditional religions, some modern religious cults have promoted suicide in the belief that it results in a transformation of the person's soul. Consider, for example, the *Order of the Solar Temple*, founded in Geneva in 1964 and with congregations in Switzerland, Canada, and a few other countries. A core belief was that an apocalyptic catastrophe was about to strike the world and members of the order could escape the catastrophe by liberating their souls, allowing them to move to a higher spiritual plane. Because of this belief, fifty-three members of the sect dressed themselves in ceremonial robes and committed suicide in October 1994. Another sixteen followed suit the next year, and yet another five in 1997.[11]

That is but one of a number of modern transformational suicides. In March 1997, thirty-nine members of Heaven's Gate, a California religious cult, committed collective suicide. They did so in the belief that life on earth was about to be "recycled" by extraterrestrial beings but that, through their suicides, their souls would be "replanted" in new, superhuman bodies.[12] In November 1978, 913 members of the Peoples Temple, an American religious sect led by Jim Jones that had moved to live in a commune in Guyana, committed "revolutionary suicide," with the expectation that this would take their souls to a better place. They lined up by the hundreds to drink a soft drink laced with cyanide. In this case, though, the primary motivation was not so much spiritual transformation but obedience to their crazed leader's directive that this was the only escape from a perceived threat to their way of life.[13] Belief to die for—and those who did not share the belief were helped on the way to Paradise with a bullet in the head or a forced injection of cyanide.

SUICIDE AS PROTEST: SACRIFICE FOR THE COLLECTIVE GOOD

People sometimes take their own lives in the altruistic belief that their sacrifice will help improve the lives of their families or communities. For example, in Vietnam in June 1963, Thich Quang Duc, a Buddhist monk, set himself on fire and burned to death to protest the Vietnamese government's mistreatment of Buddhists. Before doing so, he wrote, "Before closing my eyes to go to Buddha, I have the honor to present my words to President Diem asking him to be kind and tolerant toward his people and enforce a policy of religious equality."[14] Setting oneself afire in a public square certainly draws attention, but such a horrific act and the almost unimaginable pain that goes with it make one wonder why a person would choose to die in this way. Yet, self-immolation only rarely reflects a suicidal tendency or psychopathology. Instead, the motivation is to express protest and to incite action from sympathizers in the belief that this will benefit others, either through concessions from those in power, or through a public uprising in pursuit of justice.[15]

Indeed, such demonstrations of self-sacrifice can trigger cataclysmic social and political change. Think back to Tunisia in December 2010, when twenty-six-year-old street vendor Tarek Bouazizi set himself on fire to protest harassment by municipal officials. His self-immolation catalyzed public anger against government officials and triggered widespread demonstrations that ultimately forced the country's president, who had been in power for twenty-three years, to step down. This Tunisian revolution triggered the "Arab Spring" that resulted in the overthrow of governments in a number of Arab nations.[16]

SUICIDE, MURDER, AND HONOR

In 1996, Captain Ernie Blanchard, chief of public affairs for the United States Coast Guard, shot himself in the head after expressing feelings of mortification when complaints were leveled about sexist jokes that he had made in his address to the Coast Guard Academy. That same year, when told that reporters wanted to interview him about why he had worn military medals that he had not earned, chief of US naval operations Admiral Mike Boorda shot himself in the chest, in the very spot where he had worn the medals.[17]

Choosing to take one's life rather than face humiliation and shame is viewed as a cowardly escape in much of the world. On the other hand, it is considered an honorable action in some cultures. Consider Japan, for example: Following Japan's surrender in 1945, several senior military leaders, along with some members of the Imperial Guard, committed suicide by *seppuku* (ritual disemboweling), both in atonement for their military failures and to salvage their honor.[18] This has a long history: Prior to about 1600, the besmirching of a samurai's honor rarely led to a duel with the antagonist. Instead, the samurai regained honor by committing *seppuku*.[19]

Such suicides are not restricted to members of the military. In contemporary Japan, *Inseki-Jisatsu* ("responsibility-driven suicide") is not uncommon, reflecting the strongly held belief that this is the only honorable way to express regret for failed duty. People believe that if they fail to act in this "responsible" manner, their lives will be forever filled with shame and humiliation. For example, in 2004, a Japanese high school principal took his own life in order to "take responsibility" after a student was crushed to death by a poorly secured schoolyard soccer goalpost that had been blown over by the wind.[20] Then in 2006, another Japanese school principal committed suicide after it was reported that his school had bypassed required courses in order to allow students to focus on competitive university-entrance examinations.[21]

In some other cultures, honor suicide results from a clash of traditional and modern values and norms. So-called "virgin" suicides are typically committed by teenage girls who have "shamed" their families by the way they dress or by their obvious interest in a young man, and usually follow urgings by family members to spare the family from dishonor.[22]

The belief that "honor demands it" promotes not only honor suicide, but "honor killings" of family members as well. The United Nations estimates that about five thousand women are murdered each year around the world—most of them in the Middle East—by family members who believe that the family has been dishonored.[23] As one example: In the West Bank in September 2013, a young woman was choked to death by her father after more than fifty members of her extended family accused her of "disgraceful and outrageous acts" and posted a petition in five local mosques demanding that her father "reinstate the cultural and religious morals in his family." This was only one of twenty-seven "honor crimes" in Palestine in 2013.[24] In each case, the perpetrators believed that they were "doing the right thing."

In many South Asian societies, people believe that a man's honor is directly related to the chastity and purity of his female family members.[25] In light of this belief, in Pakistan in 2016, Qandeel Baloch, a fashion model who had provoked controversy by posting pictures of herself with a Muslim cleric on social media, was strangled to death by her brother. He later explained that he was proud of what he did and that her murder was necessary to preserve the family's honor.[26]

Amnesty International has described the perceived importance of honor killings among the Pashtuns of Pakistan:

> [B]y being perceived to enter an "illicit" sexual relationship, a woman defiles the honor of her guardian and his family. She becomes kari (black) and forfeits the right to live. . . . In most communities, there is no other punishment for kari but death. A man's ability to protect his honor is judged by his family and neighbors. He must publicly demonstrate his power to safeguard his honor by killing those who damaged it and thereby restore it.[27]

Such beliefs about honor are carried to Western countries by the diaspora. Thus, in Canada in June 2009, four members of an Afghani immigrant family, three of them teenaged girls, were found dead in an automobile submerged in a canal. The teenagers' parents and brother were subsequently convicted of first-degree murder in what was labeled an "honor killing," apparently triggered by a forbidden relationship between the eldest daughter and a young Pakistani man. The father later stated, "There is nothing more valuable than our honor."[28]

While people typically associate honor killings with Middle Eastern or Asian societies, Western history is itself replete with killings resulting from threats to honor. In times gone by, duels in Europe and the Southern United States led to the deaths of many thousands of people. Dueling during the reign of Henry IV in France resulted in more than four thousand deaths over an eighteen-year period, and eight thousand pardons for "dueling murders" were issued during the reign of Louis XIII, where "personal honor, pride and revenge took precedence over other values including life itself."[29] During the reign of George III in Britain, sixty-two dueling deaths were recorded.[30]

In the United States, dueling was also at one time an accepted means of defending one's honor, particularly in the South, where chivalry reigned. Dueling was so common during the first half of the nineteenth century that the US Navy lost two-thirds as many officers in duels as it did in sea battles.[31] Two US senators, as well as a signer of the Declaration of Independence and several newspaper editors, congressmen, and other notables, all lost their lives in duels. One of the most famous American duels occurred on July 11, 1804, when Vice President Aaron Burr shot and killed Alexander Hamilton, the former Secretary of the Treasury.

While pride and defense of honor were the immediate motivators underlying dueling, it was the (generally accurate) belief that refusing to take part in the duel would bring unacceptable and long-lasting social humiliation. Once again, it was belief to die for.

MURDER AND MISTAKEN BELIEF

Belief that honor has been besmirched is not the only cultural motivation that justifies murder. For example, from the fifteenth to the eighteenth century, many thousands of people in Europe, most of them women, were burned at the stake or otherwise tortured and killed in the belief that they were witches. Such belief was widespread among both the intelligentsia and the proletariat, and many events, interpreted through such belief, appeared to bear witness to the reality of witches and their malicious and diabolical powers, thereby justifying their extermination.

Fear, rooted in mistaken belief, continues to be a motivation for murder even in modern times. For example, in Pakistan in February 2007, Dr. Abdul Ghani Khan, chief surgeon at the main government hospital in a tribal area of Pakistan, was killed by a remote-controlled roadside bomb as he was touring the region to reassure people about the value of vaccinating their children against polio. Residents, suspicious of the nature of the vaccine and the motivations of the polio teams, had warned him against coming to the area. Dr. Khan met his death because the villagers believed that the vaccinations were intended to harm them.[32]

BELIEF AND REFUSAL OF TREATMENT

Some people refuse lifesaving medical intervention for themselves or their children because of their religious beliefs. As just one of many examples, a twenty-two-year-old British woman gave birth to twins at the Royal Hospital in Shrewsbury, England, in November 2007. She died from loss of blood only a few hours later, after refusing a blood transfusion that would have saved her life. Her refusal reflected her belief as a Jehovah's Witness that it is a grievous sin to accept a blood transfusion.[33]

It is not just religious belief that leads to refusal of lifesaving treatment. Numerous people have eschewed or delayed modern medical treatment that might have saved their lives in the mistaken belief that noninvasive "alternative" therapies would cure their cancers without the stress and side effects associated with conventional treatment. And in recent years, a growing number of parents have refused to have their children vaccinated, in the mistaken belief that vaccines pose a dangerous risk. As a result, they put their children, and possibly also their neighbors' children, at risk of serious illness and even death. Of course, unlike refusal of treatment because of religious motivation, those who turn to alternative medicine or who refuse to vaccinate their children do so in the belief that their actions are beneficial, rather than a pathway to death.

SUICIDE AS A WEAPON

Soldiers are expected to put their lives at risk when danger threatens their nation. While accepting the risk, they usually go into battle with a reasonable hope of survival. At times, however, deliberate self-destruction has become an instrument of war. In October 1944, as the Second World War was drawing to a close, the Japanese Air Force unleashed a new weapon—*kamikaze* (literally "divine wind"). Volunteer pilots in the kamikaze squadron deliberately crashed their aircraft into American warships, causing extensive damage and heavy casualties. More than 80 percent of kamikaze pilots were university students,[34] and they died by the thousands.[35] During the Battle of Okinawa alone, two thousand kamikaze pilots crashed their airplanes into three hundred US ships, killing themselves and five thousand American service members.[36] Around the same time, not to be outdone, the Japanese Navy began to employ the *Kaiten* torpedo, manned by two onboard pilots who had no means of escape. After aiming their weapon at the target ship, the two pilots then embraced before shooting each other in the head. And the Japanese Army introduced *banzai*, suicide attacks in which waves of infantrymen rushed headlong into the guns of superior enemy forces with virtually no hope of survival.

The *kamikaze* attack, the *Kaiten* torpedo, the *banzai* charge were intended not just to destroy but, more importantly, to spread terror among enemy soldiers. The attacks were directed exclusively at military targets; soldiers were fighting soldiers. But in early 1945, the government of Japan went even further and undertook the *kamikazefication* of its civilians—men, women, and children—urging them to become "home-front warriors" and to emulate the spirit of sacrifice of the kamikaze pilots in a fight to the death with the invaders.[37]

What would motivate healthy young men to volunteer for missions leading to certain death? A careful study of the diaries, wills, and letters written home by young kamikaze pilots provides significant insight.[38] These young men recognized that Japan was about to lose the war. Japanese military forces were facing disaster: ammunition, fuel, and supplies were becoming scarce, and most of the major battleships and almost all the aircraft carriers of the Japanese Imperial Navy had been sunk. Meanwhile, Japan was facing the ever-advancing Allied Forces, which possessed hundreds of battleships, a large number of aircraft carriers, thousands of aircraft, and large quantities of fuel, bombs, and ammunition. In the face of this, well aware that their deaths would not stop the enemy advance, these young men believed that their actions would bring such terror to the enemy that it would be forced to make concessions during armistice negotiations and that further casualties would be avoided.

Another important theme also emerged from their writings. They believed that dying for their country was an ultimate demonstration of respect for their parents, especially for their mothers, who would be praised and honored for their sons' courage. In addition, the empowering sense of solidarity they felt with their fellow kamikaze pilots was a strong influence. The thought of sacrificing their lives together in a "convoy of death" assuaged their fears somewhat, and a strong sense of responsibility and their contempt for cowardice further bolstered their determination.

Just the threat of suicide can be a powerful weapon in some circumstances. The best-known example is that of Mahatma Gandhi, whose hunger strikes exerted powerful pressure against the British Raj during his Quit India campaign. The British recognized that were he to die from starvation, his death would trigger massive and possibly unmanageable civil revolt. Note, however, that this technique would not have been successful against the Nazis.

TERRORISM

Terrorism refers to politically motivated acts of violence directed against anonymous and innocent members of the public. Its goal is to frighten and demoralize the citizenry as a means of bringing about desired social or political outcomes.[39] Although this typically involves relatively small groups of people inciting terror through small-scale attacks against helpless and unsuspecting members of the public, terrorism has also been used as a weapon of the state, as is addressed in a later chapter.

Terrorist attacks are obviously intended to kill others, even though the terrorists generally have no specific grievances toward their hapless victims. Terrorists play to their audience, and it is those who witness the attack firsthand or through the media who are the primary targets of influence.[40] Whether it is suicide terrorism—a young woman boards a bus in Jerusalem and then blows herself up—or the military-style Al Qaeda attack on a gas plant in Algeria in 2013, or videotaped terrorist beheadings, the major goal is to horrify through the media.[41] Without an audience, the value and benefits of such terrorist acts would be greatly reduced.[42]

One person's terrorist is another person's martyr: A drive along the Rani Jhansi Road on the Northern Ridge of New Delhi brings one to the Mutiny Memorial, a now-neglected monument erected by the British during the days of the Raj. It honors the heroism of the defenders of the city against insurgents during the so-called Sepoy Mutiny of 1857, when Indian soldiers serving under colonial rule rose up against their British masters. An inscription on the monument states:

> City finally evacuated by the enemy Sept 20.

In 1972, on the twenty-fifth anniversary of India's freedom from British rule, the Mutiny Memorial was renamed *Ajitgarh* ("Place of the Unvanquished"), and a new plaque was installed in front of the memorial (see figure 1-1), which states:

> The "enemy" of the inscriptions on this monument were those who rose against
> colonial rule and fought bravely for national liberation in 1857. In memory of
> the heroism of these immortal martyrs for Indian freedom, this plaque was
> unveiled on the 25th anniversary of the nation's attainment of freedom.

Just as those enemy rebels to the British are "immortal martyrs for Indian freedom" to Indian citizens, so too are modern "terrorists" typically viewed as "heroes" and freedom fighters by people in their own communities.[43] This is sometimes difficult for us to appreciate. Understandably, people in the west reacted with disgust and dismay to the 2001 terrorist attack on the World Trade Center in New York. The terrorists were readily viewed as deranged and cowardly killers who had attacked innocent civilians rather than fighting soldiers, and Westerners found it difficult to understand how they could be viewed as heroes by their own people. It is not easy to see the situation from the other's point of view, and so it was not surprising that there was an overwhelming outcry against American television personality Bill Maher after he stated on his ABC network program, *Politically Incorrect*:

> We have been the cowards, lobbing cruise missiles from 2,000 miles away.
> That's cowardly. Staying in the airplane when it hits the building, say what you
> want about it, it's not cowardly. Stupid maybe, but not cowardly.[44]

Not surprisingly, he was publicly rebuked by President Bush, his show was subsequently canceled, and his contract with the ABC network was not renewed.

THE 'ENEMY' OF THE INSCRIPTIONS ON THIS
MONUMENT WERE THOSE WHO ROSE AGAINST
COLONIAL RULE AND FOUGHT BRAVELY FOR
NATIONAL LIBERATION IN 1857.
    IN MEMORY OF THE HEROISM OF THESE
IMMORTAL MARTYRS FOR INDIAN FREEDOM,
THIS PLAQUE WAS UNVEILED ON THE 25TH
ANNIVERSARY OF THE NATION'S ATTAINMENT
OF FREEDOM.   28 AUGUST 1972

ਇਸ ਯਾਦਗਾਰ ਦੇ ਸ਼ਿਲਾ-ਲੇਖ ਵਿਚ 'ਵਰੁ' ਸ਼ਬਦ ਦਾ ਪ੍ਯੋਗ ਉਨ੍ਹਾਂ
ਬਹਾਦਰਾਂ ਲਈ ਕੀਤਾ ਗਿਆ ਹੈ, ਜਿਨ੍ਹਾ ਨੇ ਵਿਦੇਸ਼ੀ ਰਾਜ ਦੇ ਵਿਰੁਧ
ਅੰਦੋਲਨ ਚਲਾਇਆ ਤੇ ੧੮੫੭ਵਿਚ ਕੌਮੀ ਮੁਕਤੀ ਲਈ ਬਹਾਦਰੀ ਨਾਲ ਲੜੇ

Figure 1-1: The Ajitgarh (Indian Mutiny Memorial; photos by the author).

TERRORISM OLD AND NEW

Terrorism has a long history. As sociologist Gustav Le Bon noted a century ago:

> Terrorization has always been employed by revolutionaries no less than by kings, as a means of impressing their enemies, and as an example to those who were doubtful about submitting to them.[45]

Terrorism has evolved. There is a substantial difference between the "old" terrorism of decades past and the "new" terrorism of recent years.[46] The old terrorism attempted to cause costly damage in human and economic terms in an effort to force a government to change its policy, or to push the population to revolt against their government.[47] For example, Basque separatists and the Irish Republican Army both employed terrorist attacks, but these were aimed primarily, although not exclusively, at government institutions and at individuals closely associated with the government and the military. The goal was not to *destroy* the opponent but only to persuade it to yield, and there was no intention to send the people carrying out the attacks to their deaths.

The "new" terrorism is different. The focus has shifted toward blanket violence directed at ordinary citizens,[48] and the aim is no longer to attain concessions, to win independence, or to revolutionize the system of government. Instead, it has the utopian goal of *eliminating* the current system of government and establishing a new, religiously based world order, a global caliphate operating under Sharia law.[49] This new terrorism cannot be appeased; it has no specific demands that can be negotiated in order to bring the conflict to an end. And it has become a truly global enterprise. Islamist terrorist organizations, such as Al Qaeda and Daesh (also known as ISIS), strive to recruit both Muslims and converts from around the world, and, rather than being centrally organized and directed, this new terrorism encourages others of shared belief anywhere in the world to take up the cause on their own.[50]

SUICIDE TERRORISM

Suicide terrorism, in which terrorists sacrifice their own lives in bringing death and destruction to others, is relatively new, but the tactic has become more and more frequent in recent years. Such attacks are extremely difficult to prevent. The threat of capture and punishment is one of society's main deterrents to violence, but such deterrence is not possible when perpetrators willingly choose to die in service of their beliefs.

Although employed to a limited degree by the Vietcong during the Vietnam War, this tactic came to prominence in the hands of Hezbollah in the Middle East and later became the weapon of choice of terrorist groups in Sri Lanka and Turkey. No weapon in the history of terrorism has produced so many casualties at so little cost.[51] The bombers' deaths carry an added convenience for the terrorist group in that they are not left alive to be interrogated.[52]

There were relatively few terrorist attacks during the 1970s and 1980s, but their frequency steadily increased over time to the point that between 2000 and 2004 there were 472 suicide attacks carried out in twenty-two different countries, killing more than seven thousand people and injuring tens of thousands more.[53] In 2005, in that one year alone, there were 460 such attacks.[54] In 2012, there were more than 6,700 terrorist attacks around the world, causing 11,000 deaths and more than 21,000 injuries.[55] These were spread across eighty-five countries, but more than half of the attacks and casualties occurred in just three countries—Iraq, Pakistan, and Afghanistan. In 2013, terrorist attacks around the world increased by 43 percent compared to the previous year, resulting in 17,891 deaths.[56] The cumulative total from October 1980 to September 2015 was 5,305 suicide attacks carried out by 123 militant organizations, causing approximately 40,000 deaths.[57] Most were carried out by Islamist jihadists.[58]

There is somewhat of a parallel between the kamikaze attacks of the Second World War and modern-day suicide bombings. Compare, for example, the Japanese tactics of World War II with those that were carried out by the Palestinians in the 1980s.[59] Both the Japanese and the Palestinians were unable to respond in a conventional military manner to the overwhelming military might of their adversaries. If other military means were available, the notion of sending people to their inevitable deaths might have quickly lost appeal within the very community that spawned the volunteer bombers.

In light of the prohibition against suicide in Islam, the reader may wonder how devout Muslims can rationalize suicidal terrorism. Some do so by referring to *sacred explosions* rather than suicides.[60] In the words of one Palestinian terrorist, "We do not have tanks or rockets, but we have something superior, we are exploding Islamic bombs."[61]

Research shows that terrorist groups did experience some success in achieving their political objectives through the use of suicide bombers against foreign occupiers in the latter part of the twentieth century. The retreat of French and American military forces from Lebanon in 1983[62] and the withdrawal of Israeli forces from the Gaza Strip and West Bank in 1994 and 1995 stand out in this regard.[63] This led some researchers to view foreign occupation as the primary driver of suicide terrorism.[64] That explanation has lost its currency, however, because a large majority of suicide attacks in recent years have not been directed against foreign occupiers but against domestic targets.[65] Moreover, recent research clearly shows—and this may surprise the reader—that militant groups for the most part *rarely* achieve their primary goals, and that the groups that employ suicide attacks are actually the *least* successful of such organizations.[66] Given that fact, it is only by understanding the roots of terrorism that we can make sense of why suicide attacks continue.

ROOTS OF SUICIDE TERRORISM

It is unlikely that you could imagine any scenario that would persuade you to strap a bomb to your body, mingle in a crowd, and blow yourself—and many innocent people—to bits. It seems equally difficult to understand how suicide terrorists come to believe that they have a worthy cause to murder and cripple innocent individuals while sacrificing their own lives. Possible explanations readily come to mind: Perhaps suicide-bombers are mentally ill? Or perhaps they are simple-minded, gullible victims of persuasive indoctrination? Or maybe they have a powerful need to prove themselves and welcome the prospect of becoming posthumous heroes? Or perhaps they are religious fanatics who believe that their sacrifice will please their God and lead to glorious rewards in a life yet to come?

It is important to distinguish between suicide terrorists and other violence-wielding terrorists, who do not so willingly go to their graves. While the former can at best hope for a reward in an afterlife, the latter want to survive to taste the fruits of victory. Thus, suicide terrorism is essentially an altruistic action carried out in the belief that it will benefit others who live on. Psychopaths and bullies and those out to sate their greed do not become suicide terrorists, for there is nothing in it for them, but they may be attracted to membership in terrorist organizations that wield power, practice violence with relative impunity, and enjoy the "spoils of war."

Why do people become suicide terrorists? "The dead don't tell tales," but it is fortunate for our understanding that researchers have had the opportunity to interrogate suicide terrorists apprehended before their bombs went off, as well as suicide-terrorists-in-training who were detained before they could commence their deadly missions. Based on that information, a picture emerges of a variety of factors that might underlie the attraction to suicide terrorism.

PERSONAL FACTORS

Mental Illness and Social Deviance

One way to "make sense" of suicide attacks is to assume that the terrorists must be mentally ill, emotionally unstable, or socially deviant. Research shows that this is barking up the wrong tree, for these explanations are not supported by the evidence. A number of researchers have concluded that suicide bombers are typically psychologically normal, stable individuals with unremarkable personalities. Only rarely are they social misfits or criminals, and overall there is no common pattern of personal characteristics that would help identify them. That is, because terrorists do not differ sufficiently from everyone else, profiling that might prevent terrorist attacks is next to impossible.

Political scientist Robert Pape reviewed all 315 suicide terrorist attacks that occurred worldwide between 1980 and 2003.[67] None of the 462 attackers were mentally ill or deviant within their societies or had significant criminal histories, nor were they hopeless and despairing. Only rarely were they poor or unemployed. They typically came from working- or middle-class families and were generally educated and capable individuals who fit well into their societies and could have expected to be successful in their lives.

In the late 1990s, Pakistani journalist Nasra Hassan reached a similar conclusion after interviewing nearly 250 people involved in militant Palestinian camps, including volunteers for suicide missions, their trainers, and the families of dead bombers. None of these martyrs-in-waiting were uneducated, desperately poor, simple-minded, or depressed. On the contrary, they held well-paying jobs and were considered model youths within their communities.[68]

There is a selection factor at play: Individuals with mental or emotional problems do not suit the purposes of terrorist groups because they cannot be relied upon to act as directed, and so such groups do their best to weed them out. (On the other hand, it has been estimated that almost a third of "lone-wolf" terrorists have a history of mental or emotional problems,[69] problems that may leave them more susceptible to ideological influences.)

Religious Zealotry

Religious beliefs are particularly powerful, and European history is filled with accounts of Christian martyrs who chose execution over renunciation of their faith in the belief that torture and death were but a small burden to endure on their way to eternal happiness with their God. Islamic faith is also a powerful motivator. Many people have come to believe that Islamist terrorists are highly indoctrinated religious zealots brainwashed in madrasas to believe that their deaths will propel them to exalted martyrdom. This notion is reinforced by a history of calamitous terrorist events carried out by Islamic extremists, including the destruction of the World Trade Center in New York in 2001, the London bus bombing in February 1996, the Madrid train bombings in 2004, the 2014 massacre of the *Charlie Hebdo* journalists in Paris, the 2015 terrorist attacks in a concert hall, stadium, restaurant, and bar in Paris, and the attacks in London and Manchester in 2017.

Psychologist Ariel Merari's 2003 study of 261 suicide bombers from around the world revealed that all the groups that carried out suicide attacks, with one major exception, believed in a militant Islamic ideology, and three-quarters of the attackers were single Muslim males under the age of thirty.[70] (The one exception was a secular group, the Tamil Tigers of Sri Lanka, who until recently led the world in terms of the number of suicide terrorist attacks. Their ideology was Marxist, not religious, although most of them came from Muslim societies.[71]) Similarly the Palestinian terrorists in Hassan's investigation also were all deeply religious,[72] and they followed a regime of spiritual exercises, religious lectures, and fasting. Then, as "living martyrs," they paid off all debts, prepared a will, and made a final video. After the bombing, festivities were organized to celebrate the honor that had been bestowed on their families by their martyrdom, even though the celebration was colored by grief.

Yet, Islam and Islamic beliefs have endured for centuries, but modern terrorism in the name of Islam has a history only a few decades long. Even though Islamic zealots have directed so many disastrous terrorist attacks in recent history, it is overly simplistic to attribute all of the blame for modern-day terrorism to those seeking religious hegemony and martyrdom. For example, Pape's study of terrorist attacks, discussed above, found not only that significant numbers of the bombers were not religious, but that those who were devout were *not* motivated by the belief that martyrdom leads to a life in paradise in the company of virgins.[73] Nor was it a matter of their minds having been twisted by propaganda, for few had been exposed to anything other than mild indoctrination. The assumption that attendance at a madrasa increases the likelihood of joining a militant group is simply not justified by available data.[74] Few Muslim suicide bombers had received a traditional religious education in a madrasa. This is not surprising, for students in madrasas are typically drawn from a lower echelon of society and lack the social, linguistic, and technical skills needed to carry out suicidal missions. Instead, the majority of the terrorists had gone to university, and the professions most represented in Al Qaeda have been engineer and physician.[75]

It is also important to remember that terrorism is not the monopoly of Muslims, for all religious groups have been associated with terrorism at one time or another. What's more, political violence has been conducted in the name of all sorts of beliefs, not just religious ones, such as in the struggle for economic fairness and the quest for freedom and human rights.[76]

Rite of Passage

French criminologist Florent Gathérias draws a comparison between typical suicide terrorists and adolescents in search of their identity. He notes:

> Paradoxically this behavior corresponds to the rite of passage from adolescence into an idealized adult by a quasi-romantic vision of their place and position in the society to which they want to belong.[77]

Similarly, Pape concludes that suicide terrorists, adolescents among them,

> resemble the kind of politically conscious individuals who might join a grassroots movement more than they do wayward adolescents or religious fanatics.[78]

So we see that suicide bombers are not the savage, bloodthirsty, religiously zealous demons that they are often seen to be. Instead, they sacrifice their lives for a higher purpose, in an act that they view as altruistic, and in the belief that they are serving their people and their God.

GROUP FACTORS

Social psychological research has repeatedly found that situational factors, including group influence, generally play a larger role in determining behavior than do personal characteristics.[79] This reflects the extraordinary *power of the situation*. For example, many otherwise compassionate and helpful people will act "out of character" in some circumstances and fail to assist a person in serious need of help, or will follow orders to harm a stranger. Failure to appreciate the influence of the situation is so widespread that psychologists refer to it as the *Fundamental Attribution Error*: We ignore or downplay situational circumstances and instead attribute people's behaviors to their personalities.[80] Thus, when behavior is strange or abhorrent—such as when a suicide bomber launches an attack—it seems natural to attribute it to strange and abhorrent traits of the individual.

The research, however, teaches a different lesson. Terrorism is fundamentally a *group* phenomenon with shared beliefs and values. It is a powerful tool used in the service of particular goals,[81] and the perception that one's group is being oppressed and humiliated provides an important motivation to attack the enemy by whatever means one can. Think back to the various resistance organizations that fought against Nazi occupation during the Second World War and the terrorist tactics that they used against the occupying enemy.

Islamic extremists believe that their religion is under attack. In the eyes of Al Qaeda and Daesh (ISIS), the United States and its allies have invaded Muslim homelands and have attempted to humiliate or even exterminate Islam.[82] The resulting resentment and anger feeds a lust for revenge, and revenge is a powerful motivator that strengthens the appeal of terrorism.[83] The result is *jihad*, a holy war.[84] When the struggle is viewed by the community as one of good-versus-evil, sacrificing one's life can appear highly justified.[85] Feeling powerless in the face of perceived humiliation and injustice produces anxiety, but becoming part of a force to fight back in defense of one's group and one's religion brings a sense of power and a decrease in anxiety.[86] Becoming a suicide terrorist turns one from feeling personally insignificant into someone who plays an important and honored role in the group's battle against the perceived enemy.[87]

Social identity refers to how we define ourselves in terms of the groups and categories to which we belong. Who are you? A student, professor, homemaker, or plumber? Scot, American, Canadian, or Australian? Liberal, Republican, Democrat, or member of the Labor Party? Atheist, born-again Christian, Jew, Muslim, or Hindu? We have multiple social identities, and situational factors determine which one is most salient at a given moment.

At times, some people so strongly identify with a particular group that they no longer see themselves as unique individuals, but instead only as constituents of the group,[88] resulting in *identity fusion* and a "visceral feeling of oneness" with the group.[89] When this happens, the individual becomes willing to do whatever the group asks, even if this involves going to extreme lengths, such as sacrificing one's life. Once established, such fusion remains relatively stable.[90] This helps explain why people volunteer to be suicide terrorists instead of letting others in the group do the heavy lifting, thereby remaining alive to enjoy whatever benefits accrue. Almost all suicide terrorists are managed by the groups to which they belong, either face-to-face or virtually, over the internet.[91] They are deployed in a rational and calculated manner in order to promote group goals. They are inspired, recruited, trained, and provided with explosives for specific assignments.[92]

The suicide terrorist's primary social identification is with the terrorist group. Even when terrorist organizations such as Daesh encourage sympathizers around the world to become lone-wolf suicide terrorists, those who respond to the call do so because they are identifying with the organization, even if they have never had direct contact with it. Commitment to the group and pressure from the group are important, and commitment typically increases over time.[93] Terrorists are all the more determined when motivated by religious values that are part of the group's identity,[94] and, as a result, they will ignore their own rewards and costs.[95] Interviews with frontline Daesh fighters have identified the crucial importance of powerful, nonnegotiable, spiritual values in motivating terrorism.[96] Such values promote self-sacrifice, especially when combined with identity fusion and the belief that the group's spiritual superiority outweighs any material disadvantage relative to the enemy. This leads to increased dedication to group goals and eliminates any personal cost-benefit analysis.

Violence-promoting ideologies are not the monopoly of religious groups, but militant Islamic ideology adds one important element to the picture: martyrdom. The Koran differentiates between suicide, which is forbidden, and martyrdom, which is promoted through the promise of honor and earthly delights in heaven.[97] Not all martyrdom involves violence toward others; hunger strikes, for example, are also a form of martyrdom. Terrorism is also a means of restoring honor and dignity to the group and endowing the individual with a strong feeling of social significance. Thus,

> a terrorism-justifying ideology is critical in setting up a belief system that glorifies violence against the group's detractors and portrays it as an effective and worthy way of making a supreme contribution to one's community, that merits vast veneration in the eyes of others.[98]

Terrorist ideology not only promotes cruelty and violence toward others but also considers such actions as reasonable and justifiable in response to an injustice against one's group, be it ethnic or religious.[99] Terrorists come to view actions that are normally considered evil to be honorable and good when directed at certain target groups.

Given the power of social identification to turn individuals into cogs in a group machine, we must be careful to distinguish between the influence of being in a group united by religion and the influence of the religion itself. An attack that is perceived as directed at one's religion is often regarded as an attack on one's group, one's community, one's society. In such cases, it is the threat to the group, rather than religion per se, that motivates a violent response.

Researchers interviewed a nationally representative sample of more than 1,100 Palestinian adults, more than 700 Palestinian Muslim university students, and close to 200 randomly selected Israeli settlers living in the West Bank and Gaza.[100] Their focus was on the relationship between religion and popular support for suicide attacks. By way of comparison, data from representative surveys of Mexican Catholics, Indonesian Muslims, British Protestants, Russian Orthodox adherents, Jews in Israel, and Indian Hindus were also analyzed. They found no evidence of a relationship between religious devotion per se and support for suicide attacks.

On the other hand, while frequency of prayer (a generally reliable index of religious devotion) was *not* related to support for suicide attacks, frequency of *attendance* at religious gatherings *did* predict such support. That is most interesting, because participation in religious gatherings provides more than religion. It also provides an important source of belonging and social identity. The researchers concluded that it is *coalitional commitment*—identification with a group, sharing its beliefs, and committing oneself to its causes—that is significant, rather than actual religious beliefs and devotion. The seeming connection between religion and suicide terrorism is only a by-product of the way that religion brings people together into communities of "parochial altruists" willing to sacrifice their own lives in the service of the group interests.

Community Support

A necessary condition for suicide terror is the belief shared by the community that other more peaceful strategies have failed, making violence necessary.[101] The suicide bombers' community must be sympathetic, helping them to avoid being apprehended before they can carry out an attack and providing fertile soil for the development of future suicide terrorists.[102] Community attitudes reinforce the terrorists' belief that they will be remembered as heroes and martyrs rather than murderers or misguided youth.

Merari reported that the families of young Palestinian men who had died as suicide terrorists, while grieving their loss, nonetheless expressed pride in their martyrdom:

> The great majority of the would-be suicides . . . would not have assumed a self-destructive mission for the reasons they stated had it not been for the atmosphere in the Palestinian community at the time. . . . It was social encouragement of these particular acts—suicide attacks—that infused the stated motives with their power and legitimacy; without public support, they probably would have seemed bizarre to the suicides themselves.[103]

Without community support, the appetite for suicide terrorism withers eventually. This is what occurred with the *Shahidka* (also known as the "Black Widows") of Chechnya, who carried out a number of suicide bombing attacks against Russia. Most of these women were teenagers motivated by a desire to seek revenge against Russian occupiers whom they considered responsible for the deaths of their husbands.[104] However, the Shahidka attacks dwindled for several reasons: the deaths of some of their leaders, the belief that resistance to Russian authority was doomed to failure, and the lack of community support for the practice. Unlike parents in some Middle Eastern societies, Chechen parents did not take pride in their children's deaths, and as a result many Chechens came to oppose suicide bombings.[105]

Group Dynamics

Many organizations sometimes act in ways that serve an unstated, implicit, and perhaps even unrecognized purpose—the survival of the organization and the enhancement of its influence and status. Terrorist groups are no different in this regard, and research has found that improving the group's status is sometimes the leading rationale for launching suicide bombings.[106] When a community honors martyrdom, group status is bolstered by serving up martyrs, and this then attracts new members. Suicide attacks directed against infidels and heretics by groups such as the Taliban and Daesh increase their status and appeal so long as the attacks are supported by the community.[107]

HISTORICAL FACTORS

One must not overlook the important role that historical conflict plays in modern-day terrorism. Individuals have short memories, but communities and nations do not. Some societies have experienced such long-standing conflict that their children are brought up to hate the "enemy." Such deeply ingrained antagonism—hate-filled belief "bred in the bone"—nourishes violence and provides a basis for leaders to incite others to commit acts of destruction, including suicidal acts against the enemy. The conflict that infects the Middle East, often punctuated by terrorism, cannot be understood without taking into account the historical context of the founding of Israel in territory claimed by others.

Every child in Ireland learns about the Battle of the Boyne in 1690, when King William III, the Protestant head of the Dutch Royal House of Orange, was invited by powerful Protestant political figures in England to seize the throne from his father-in-law King James II, a devout Roman Catholic. James escaped to France but subsequently attempted to take back the throne with the help of Irish soldiers. His forces were defeated on the banks of the Boyne River in Ireland. To this day, Irish Catholics remember that defeat. Irish Protestants in Northern Ireland have not forgotten either, and so the Protestant Orange Order leads a ceremonial march on July 12 to honor that historic Protestant victory. The memory of defeat at the Battle of the Boyne provided a historical foundation for the terrorist activities of the Irish Republican Army, which carried out numerous acts of terrorism directed at Protestant and British institutions in Northern Ireland. Loyalist Protestant paramilitaries responded with terrorist acts of their own. Known as the "Troubles," the conflict ended only with the St. Andrews Agreement of 2006, followed by the election of a government in 2007 that shared power between the two sides. More recently, the decision in 2017 by Prime Minister Teresa May to shore up her minority government through an agreement with the Northern Ireland Democratic Unionist Party, which was involved in setting up Protestant paramilitary forces in the 1980s, is seen by some as threatening the peace agreement.

Another vivid historical example of a belief in historical injustice is the Battle of Kosovo Polje, fought on June 28, 1389, between some 80,000 Christian Serbian knights and an invading Muslim army from the Ottoman Empire. The Serbs were defeated and their land was surrendered to the Muslim invaders. But the battle was not forgotten, and on its 600th anniversary on June 28, 1989, more than one million Serbs went in pilgrimage to Kosovo Polje to honor their fallen heroes from centuries ago. In 1999, Christian Serbs in Kosovo sought much-delayed revenge through "ethnic cleansing," involving the brutal killings of thousands of their Muslim compatriots.

SOCIETAL FACTORS

Societies vary in terms of how individualistic or collectivist they are, with nations such as the United States being at the individualist extreme and many Asian societies at the collectivist end. People with a collectivist orientation are more likely to be willing to participate in terrorism when it is called for by the group. A collectivist orientation also tends to be associated with reduced anxiety about death, which further contributes to a willingness to sacrifice one's life.[108]

Societies change over time. Globalization is rapidly changing the lives of people around the world. This seemingly uncontrollable change is perceived by some as an attack on traditional and fundamentalist beliefs and values, engendering fear that a cherished way of life will disappear. This contributes to the foundation underlying terrorism,[109] which is in part a response to an "engine of modernity that is stealing the identity of the oppressed,"[110] and the greatest danger comes from those societies where people feel unable to keep up, even though they might feel superior to those who can.

Feeling alienated from the larger society is another root of terrorism. Europe, as it struggles to accommodate waves of immigrants, has left large numbers of Muslim newcomers feeling alienated from the larger society, providing ample opportunity for radicalization and conversion to *jihadi* extremism. While the great majority of Muslims living in Western countries condemn violence and do not become radicalized, radical Islam offers common ground for Western Muslim youth who feel excluded and disenfranchised from the society in which they live.

Eurojihad—Islamic radicalization and terrorism based in Europe itself[111]—is a product of the bonding, whether face-to-face or online, of disenchanted youth who experience the same sense of alienation. Such association provides increased self-confidence, a sense of purpose, and a new value system that justifies violence against perceived enemies. Such alienation can be experienced even by people who appear to be well integrated within a society. For example, a terrorist attack in Glasgow in 2007 was carried out by a group of seemingly successful individuals, including practicing physicians.[112]

Despite overwhelming differences in the personal and family circumstances among alienated youths around the world, radical Islam provides a common purpose, leading many to convert to Islam. At least forty-eight European converts were involved in terrorist attacks in ten different European countries between 1990 and 2010, and many were given important leadership roles in major attacks.[113] This is summed up by American terrorism expert Jessica Stern, who, based on her interviews with Muslim, Jewish, and Christian terrorists, concluded:

> They start out feeling humiliated, enraged that they are viewed by some [other group] as second-class. They take on new identities as martyrs on behalf of a purported spiritual cause. . . . The weak become strong. The selfish become altruists, ready to make the ultimate sacrifice of their lives in the belief that their deaths will serve the public good. Rage turns to conviction. . . . They know they are right, not just politically, but morally. They believe that God is on their side.[114]

Through this radicalization, alienation is replaced by idealism. Indeed, anthropologist Scott Atran argues that most suicide terrorists in modern times are inspired by idealism—by a global jihadism that fills a void in Islamic communities created by corrupt politicians and their discredited Western ideologies.[115]

Pro aris et focis. For God and country (literally, *"For our altars and our hearths"*): This ancient Latin phrase was first used by the Roman soldier and lawmaker Tiberius Gracchus more than two millennia ago. To this day, it is the motto of several military institutions, either in its original Latin form (e.g., Victoria Rifles of Canada) or in its English equivalent (e.g., the American Legion). Interestingly, "For God and country—Geronimo, Geronimo, Geronimo" was the signal radioed to headquarters by US military personnel to confirm the killing of Osama bin Laden in 2011.

Figure 1-2A: *Pro Aris et Focis* (© Her Majesty the Queen in Right of Canada represented by the Canadian Heraldic Authority).

Figure 1-2B: "For God and Country."

This sentiment is at the heart of modern terrorism. As we have seen, the research indicates that suicide bombers themselves typically are not trying to escape misery or attain paradise; they are not of low intellect; they are not mentally ill; they are not religious zealots; they have not been brainwashed to "do the dirty work" by manipulative others who remain comfortably alive. (Just how they are recruited to become suicide bombers is discussed in a later chapter.) But what about the morality of it all? How do suicide terrorists justify the murder of innocents, children among them? Some may reduce their discomfort by persuading themselves that "they are all the enemy, and they kill our children with their bombs." Some may dehumanize the victims in their own minds, so that the usual moral constraints do not apply.[116] And some may come to believe that noble ends justify horrible means.[117]

Suicide terrorists are not motivated by blind rage but are inspired by their devotion to their group and community, and, if they are religious, by commitment to their God.[118] As a member of Hamas explained, the focus of volunteer bombers when preparing for a bombing is directed both at serving Allah and the prophet Mohammed and at helping bring about a better future for their people.[119] *Pro aris et focis*.

***

Our beliefs guide us, motivate us, and define the world for us. Nothing demonstrates their hold over us as much as a willingness to die for them. But what does it mean to "believe"? And how is it that some beliefs are so powerful that they are impervious both to reason and to evidence that challenges them? To answer these questions, to understand the nature of beliefs and why they are often so compelling, one must first understand how our minds—our brains—construct and sustain them. It is to this that we now turn.

PART II

THE BELIEF ENGINE

Man is made by his belief. As he believes, so he is.
—Bhagavad Gita, 500 BCE

Many beliefs are shared by everyone in a society. For example, we all believe that humans and other animals need food and water to survive. But many beliefs stand in dramatic opposition to one another. Consider the origin of our planet: Do you believe, along with the vast majority of modern scientists, that the universe came into existence approximately 14 billion years ago, bursting out of nothingness in a Big Bang? Or do you believe, as do many fundamentalist Christians, that the universe was created only a few thousand years ago, shaped directly by the hand of an invisible, all-seeing, all-knowing supernatural being? Or do you manage to have your cake and eat it too, believing that the universe was created through a Big Bang some 14 billion years ago, but a Bang detonated by . . . well, an invisible, all-seeing, all-knowing supernatural being?

How is it that reasonably intelligent people growing up in roughly the same cultural milieux, attending the same schools and exposed to the same media, come to harbor with great conviction such widely different beliefs? And why do *you* believe as you do? Where is your evidence? If you are a Fundamentalist Christian, the answer is easy: The Bible tells you so, and that is evidence enough for you. On the other hand, if you believe that the universe began with a Big Bang 14 billion years ago, it is unlikely that you have directly examined and understood the scientific data that support this belief. Unless you are an astrophysicist, your belief no doubt also relies upon authority, in this case the secular authority of scientists.

Of course, most of our beliefs do not involve such heady matters as the beginnings of the universe, but even many of those that are more prosaic were not hammered into being on the anvil of rational enquiry. We like to think that we consciously *choose* to believe one thing and not another, and while some beliefs are indeed based on a logical analysis of available information, most come into being without much awareness or consideration of actual evidence. They develop, often spontaneously and involuntarily, through a combination of a number of mental processes, many of which are nonconscious.[1]

There is nothing fundamentally different about the nature of beliefs that we consider rational and those we deem irrational. Belief in fairies, ghosts, or leprechauns can be held as strongly as beliefs about more mundane matters, and believers will cite evidence in support of such beliefs. We are all likely to have at least some beliefs that others might judge as foolish, but we are adept at finding justification for them. We can point to the paucity of evidence supporting other people's "irrational" beliefs, but, truth be known, we rarely have good supporting evidence for most of our own. As psychologist Patrick Boyer points out,

> It is a hallmark of genuine belief that we generally care little for its origin, for the ways in which it became a denizen of our mental household. For instance, most of us believe that salt is white and steel is tough, but we do not generally know how we acquired these beliefs; nor do we care.[2]

Even though we might like to think that we choose our beliefs, we all know that we cannot arbitrarily choose to believe just anything or change a belief simply on a personal whim. Psychologist and philosopher William James made this point in 1897:

> Can we, by just willing it, believe that Abraham Lincoln's existence is a myth, and that the portraits of him in McClure's magazine are all of someone else? Can we, by any effort of our will, or any strength of wish that it were true, believe ourselves well and about when we are roaring with rheumatism in bed, or feel certain that the sum of the two one-dollar bills in our pocket must be a hundred dollars? We can say any of these things but we are absolutely impotent to believe them.[3]

Where do our beliefs come from? They are generated and maintained through a complex and generally automatic process in our brains that I call the *Belief Engine*.[4] This metaphor is in reference to Charles Babbage's "analytical engine," the immense, steam-powered precursor of the modern computer that he conceived in the early nineteenth century.[5] It was intended to generate solutions to complex algebraic equations based on numerical data entered through punch cards. (Unfortunately, Babbage was unable to raise sufficient funding, and so it was never completed.)

Figure Part II-1: Trial model of a part of the Analytical Engine built by Babbage, Science Museum London (Wikimedia Creative Commons, Bruce Barral, CC-BY-SA 2.5).

Our brains act somewhat analogously to this analytical engine, albeit in a much more sophisticated manner. The Belief Engine chugs away in the background, taking in information from the world outside, scrutinizing its source, checking its compatibility with existing beliefs, subjecting it at times to logical analysis, and then effortlessly generating new beliefs and maintaining or modifying old ones. Most often, this occurs without the awareness of the "oper-ator"—you or me. And, like a computer, our Belief-Engine brains comprise both hardware and software. We come into this world equipped with the basic hardware, although it continues to develop further over a number of years after birth. The "software," the programming, comes through interaction with our environment (parents, teachers, siblings, friends, the media, and the experiences of everyday life) and through the development of the thinking skills that we acquire as we grow up.

In order to understand the nature and importance of beliefs in our lives, it is first necessary to understand how they are generated and maintained. There are a number of important aspects to the Belief Engine, including *perceiving*, *remembering*, *learning and feeling*, and *thinking*. These processes are explored in the next four chapters.

CHAPTER 2

WHEN SEEING IS BELIEVING

We see the sun, the moon and the stars revolving, as it seems to us, round us. That is all false. We feel that the earth is motionless. That is false, too. . . . We touch what we think a solid body. There is no such thing. We hear harmonious sounds; but the air has only brought us silently undulations that are silent themselves. . . . Sensation and reality are two different things.
—Camille Flammarion (1842–1925)[1]

It is often said that "seeing is believing," but experience teaches us the unreliability of that maxim. For example, think about the full moon as it comes over the horizon. While it definitely looks so much larger than when overhead, no one believes that it actually changes size as it moves across the sky, despite what our eyes tell us.

But why do our eyes fool us in this way? Humans have pondered this for millennia. In 350 BCE, Aristotle explained the phenomenon in optical terms, offering reassurance that the eyes are not deceived, but accurately observe an image of the moon that has been magnified by the earth's atmosphere acting as a lens. That explanation made sense to many, and some believe it even today, but it is wrong.

In the eleventh century, Arab mathematician Al-Hassan Ibn al-Haytham (965–1040) determined that the seeming magnification of the moon at the horizon is only an illusion. In his *Book of Optics*, he described how our brains automatically adjust the apparent size of an object based on its perceived distance from us, and he concluded that our brains treat the moon at the horizon as though it is farther away than when overhead. When the moon is overhead, we have no way of judging its distance, and so the brain creates a perception based only on the size of the moon's image on the retina. On the other hand, when the

47

moon is at the horizon, its distance is more obvious and the brain assumes that the moon must be very large to create an image of that size on the retina. Further distance information is provided by the fact that objects of known size, such as trees and buildings, appear very small in the distance. (Recent research, however, indicates that the explanation for the illusion is actually slightly more complicated than this, but nonetheless, it is only an illusion; it is "all in our heads."[2])

Figure 2-1: Harvest moon.

Despite how large a full moon at the horizon seems to be, the illusion is quickly dispelled when you observe the moon through a pinhole in a piece of paper. With the paper screening out everything except the moon itself, it appears of normal size. One can accomplish the same thing by turning one's back to the moon, bending down, and observing it through one's legs, which interrupts the brain's process for judging distance.

The moon illusion is not the only trick that our senses play on us. We have all been amused by perceptual illusions, among which the *Shepard tabletop illusion* and the *checker-shadow illusion* are two of the very best:

- *The Shepard tabletop illusion*: The two tabletops in figure 2-2 are identical in size and shape, but because of cues that suggest perspective, they appear to be very different. Even after you confirm with a ruler that they are indeed identical, the illusion will still overwhelm your perception, and it is all but impossible to overcome it.

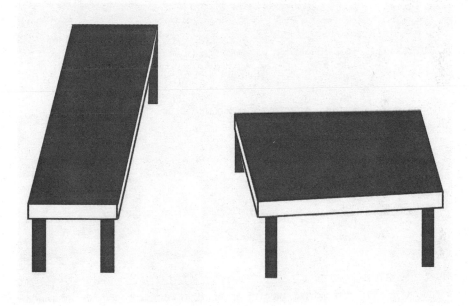

Figure 2-2: Shepard tabletop illusion.

- *The checker-shadow illusion*: Similarly, because the brain learns that objects in shadows appear darker than they actually are, when we see something in shadow, the visual system compensates so that we perceive lighter tones, presumably closer to its actual color. This leaves us vulnerable to error: Consider the squares marked A and B on the chessboard (figure 2-3): as impossible as it may seem, both squares are of exactly the same color, but because one appears to be in shadow, the brain compensates for the shadow, and so it ends up appearing to be a lighter color.

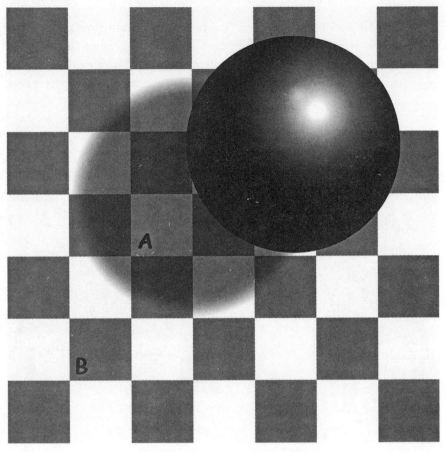

Figure 2-3: Checker shadow illusion (Shutterstock / Peter Hermes Furian).

Another illusion with which we are all familiar is the illusion of movement that occurs at times when sitting on a stopped train and the train next to us begins to move. It certainly feels for a moment as if we are the ones in movement. Some movement illusions have been exploited for entertainment purposes. We see movement, lots of it, whenever we watch a movie or observe moving images on an electric sign, but nothing is actually moving. The apparent movement is only an illusion (known as the *phi phenomenon*). For example, suppose that you are watching a video of a horse race on your laptop. You seem to "see" images of the animals running around a track, but what creates this perception is the successive illumination of pixels on the screen. Nothing actually moves, but your perceptual system does not know that, and so it reacts to the series of successive images by constructing a perception of the images in motion. The same principle is involved with movies, as well as with an older form of entertainment, the flipbook. When the flipbook's pages are turned quickly, this produces what appears to be a moving image because the image on every successive page is slightly different from the one before. By viewing the pages in quick succession, the eyes see what they would see if the image were actually moving.

And then there is the illusion of the hole in the hand: Roll up a sheet of paper, close one eye, and look through the hole with the other. Now open the other eye as well, and move the palm of your empty hand back and forth closely along the length of the roll of paper. If you do this just right, it will seem as though you are looking through a hole in your moving hand. To understand why this happens, perform this even more basic exercise: With one eye closed, extend your arm, and make a hole with your thumb and forefinger, and use that to frame some object in the distance. Now close that eye and open the other eye. What do you see through that same hole? Something quite different, no doubt. This is because the two eyes see things differently. This provides an important cue for depth perception, but it would be very confusing if we were to constantly see two different images. As a result, the visual system suppresses one of the images, preventing it from reaching consciousness. Now, going back to the hole in the hand: your brain fused together the two images that were seen separately by each eye.

PERCEPTION AND BELIEF

How we perceive objects and events is fundamental to the formation of our beliefs about the world. Look around you; what do you see? A book? A picture on the wall? The sky? People? Now listen carefully; what do you hear? The clicking of a computer keyboard? Traffic noise? Someone's stomach gurgling? And what do you feel? The pressure on your fingers as you grasp this book? A light breeze from an open window? Yet, how can you be sure that it is a picture that you see, traffic noise that you hear, or a book that you feel between your fingers? Frivolous question, one might think, but it only appears so because our perceptual system is so automatic that it *seems* as though we see and hear and feel the world as it actually is. After all, we can generally trust our senses, and firsthand experience does not often let us down.

Yet perception is tricky and, occasionally, as we have seen with the illusions discussed above, let us down it does. There are times when we perceive things quite differently than they really are, there are times when we fail to perceive things that are right in front of us, and there are times when we perceive things that are not there at all.

Perception is a vital part of the Belief Engine; it is the source of new information and exerts a powerful influence on our beliefs. When we see a horse galloping down the street, we then *believe* that a horse is galloping down the street. Conversely, our beliefs can influence what we see. Someone with a belief in ghosts may "see" a transparent, human form when catching a glimpse of an animal moving through the woods, while someone else sees only an amorphous shadow.

How do we actually "see" anything? At one time, most people believed in the "emission theory." That is, they believed that rays of light are emitted from the eyes that go out and "examine" the environment. Today, we know that this is preposterous. Or at least, most of us do, but not everyone, for, astonishingly, nearly 50 percent of college students in a study carried out in the United States in 2002 believed that something leaves the eyes in order for us to see.[3]

Of course, our eyes do not send out beams to scan the environment, but neither do they behave like a video camera passively recording whatever is going on in front of them. That is, they do not actually "see" that picture on the wall. Instead, they are stimulated by a mixture of different wavelengths of light that strike the retinas, triggering signals that are sent to a region in the back of the brain. There they are translated into colors, textures, and forms that are then compared with past experience, and finally an image is *constructed* in the brain. This is key to understanding perception: *it is a construction.* We "see" a construction corresponding to the picture on the wall, not the picture itself, and the two are not identical. What we perceive is less like a photograph that faithfully captures the scene and more like a representative painting that we have created of what is "out there" (see figure 2-4). A range of physiological and psychological factors influence the construction of the image, the "painting," and in some circumstances the representation can differ significantly from reality. For example, we see color, even though color does not actually exist in the world outside our brains. It is only a subjective experience resulting from the brain's conversion of particular wavelengths of light into particular hues, for nothing is actually red or yellow or green in the world outside. Think of those who are color-blind. To them, the world looks somewhat different than it does to the rest of us. It is not that they do not "see" all the colors, it is just that their visual systems do not *construct* them.

Figure 2-4: Photograph versus painting (photo and painting by Sharon Stewart).

The experience of sound is also a subjective phenomenon that exists only inside our heads. In light of this, the seventeenth-century philosopher George Berkeley (1685–1753) posed the question of whether there is any sound when a tree falls in the forest and no one is there to hear it. The falling tree creates ripples in the ocean of molecules that make up the atmosphere, and just as ripples appear when a stone is thrown into a lake, those ripples spread out and reach our ears. Our brains then *construct* the sound of a falling tree based on the vibrations of our eardrums as those waves of molecules beat against them. This experience of sound is not a part of the world outside. So to answer Berkeley, if a tree falls and there is no one there to hear it, the atmospheric ripples will still be created, but without the presence of a brain to transform them into the experience of sound, all is silence.

We take speech and hearing for granted, but they are truly remarkable. Think of this: if you want to say something to a friend, you automatically translate your words into movements of your lips, mouth, and vocal cords, which in turn produce ripples in the air. Those ripples cause your friend's eardrums to vibrate, sending signals to her brain, resulting in the very words that originated in your brain being accurately reproduced in hers. What a monumental feat of evolution that we can manipulate the air and achieve this kind of communication. A visitor from another planet where there is neither speech nor hearing would be confounded to see that even with your backs turned from one another, you and your friend can exchange thoughts without any obvious channel of communication. It would appear as though you were using some kind of extrasensory perception.

Just as with vision and hearing, our other senses also involve constructions. Pressure receptors in the skin detect deformations resulting from contact with objects, and from this the brain generates sensations of touch. Feedback from our muscles tells our brains where our hands, feet, heads, and torsos are located in space. Sweetness, saltiness, or bitterness are not intrinsic qualities of foods themselves but are constructed when molecules of fructose, sodium chloride, or other chemicals interact with specific gustatory receptors in the tongue, sending signals to the brain that lead to the subjective experience of taste. Odors do not exist outside our heads. Particular molecules drift off flowers or lemon meringue pie and stimulate olfactory receptors, which send signals to the brain, where the subjective perception of fragrance is constructed. Our brains do not always produce the same constructions, and genetic differences account for some of the variations in people's preferences.[4] For example, do you like the taste of cilantro (coriander)? About 10 to 15 percent of people dislike it, claiming that it tastes like soap. This reaction is the result of a particular genetic variation that affects the way our nervous systems create taste and smell.[5] The "soapiness" is only a subjective experience, and not a quality of the herb itself.

It is from this maelstrom of sensory information—the ever-shifting lights and hues, sounds, and other sensations—that our brains build an image of an ordered and stable world and of our place in it.

LEARNING TO PERCEIVE THE WORLD

How are our brains able to create the various subjective experiences associated with sensory input? Although we are born with the basic apparatus, the senses—vision, hearing, taste, touch, and smell—have not yet sorted themselves out at birth. While adults, with rare exceptions, "see" only the sights around them, "smell" only odors, and "hear" only sounds, the newborn is confronted by a confusion of sensory information. Odors smell, but the infant may hear, taste, and feel them as well. The newborn's world is, according to developmental psychologist Daphne Maurer,

> a melee of pungent aromas—and pungent sounds, and bitter-smelling sounds, and sweet-smelling sights, and sour-smelling pressures against the skin.[6]

The eminent psychologist and philosopher William James (1842–1910) made a similar point more than a century ago:

> The baby, assailed by eyes, ears, nose, skin, and entrails at once, feels it all as one great blooming, buzzing confusion.[7]

The infant gradually overcomes this sensory jumble. The senses sort themselves out and, by two or three months of age, a baby perceives color vision almost at an adult level, allowing discrimination among many colors.[8] For a small number of children, this sorting out remains incomplete, resulting in a degree of sensory confusion that endures into adulthood, at which point it is referred to as *synesthesia*.[9] In this case, two senses, and rarely three, are involved. Upon hearing a particular sound, a synesthetic individual may also experience a specific taste, or while reading, a particular word or letter will always appear to be in a specific color. Thus, seven may always appear in blue and six in red. These associations remain stable over time.[10] This condition is not quite as rare as one might think. It affects about four percent of the population, and tends to run in families, although an actual genetic basis has not been established.[11]

Sorting out the senses is not the only challenge for newborns. Fortunately, they come well equipped for the task of learning about the world. They are highly curious and motivated to explore, and this leads to endless opportunities to learn. (In contrast, autistic children typically demonstrate limited curiosity and tend instead to focus on only a narrow range of stimuli, limiting their opportunity to learn about the world.) Their learning has a direct effect on the organization and development of the brain, and modification and multiplication of neural connections occur because of it. For example, the brain of a child taught to play a musical instrument responds by developing more neural connections devoted to functions associated with musical skill.[12] This is known as brain plasticity.[13] Plasticity continues, to a lesser degree, into adulthood, and it is because of it that recovery is possible following brain damage. Lost physical functioning as a result of a stroke can often gradually be regained through retraining, as other neural pathways develop to take over the function of those that have been put out of commission.

Just about everything about perception has to be learned, although some rudimentary perceptual processes are present at birth. We are born with *shape constancy*, that is, we perceive objects as keeping their shapes even when their images on our retinas alter as we move around while looking at them.[14] We are also born with *size-distance constancy*; our brains automatically take distance into account in judging an object's size.[15] (Recall the moon illusion.) As a result, when someone walks away from us and the image on the retina becomes smaller and smaller, we do not perceive the person as shrinking. Instead, our brains recognize that this is a person of fixed size moving away.

There is also some evidence that babies come into this world predisposed to recognize human faces. This is suggested by the fact that newborns' eyes are more likely to follow a moving pattern that is face-like rather than one that is not. It is not yet clear whether this means that they have the ability to actually recognize faces at that early age.[16]

How does the infant come to see the world as being external to the brain? This might seem to be another frivolous question, but when one stops to think about it, it is not. Even though we understand that our actual perception of the world occurs deep within our brains, everything that we see certainly *seems* to be "out there" rather than inside our heads. This perception of externality develops as the infant's brain, based on experience, gradually constructs a model of the outside world. For example, when the infant moves a foot against the side of the crib, the combination of observing the foot touch the crib and the feeling of contact with the crib contributes to perceiving the crib as being "out there." When the baby begins to creep about and make contact with various objects, this adds to the "map" of an external world. As this model develops, it gradually comes to dominate the child's perceptual experience, and images inside the head become the model of the world outside.

SEEING FOR THE FIRST TIME

Given that the infant must, to a large extent, learn how to perceive the world, what happens when vision is restored to an adult who has been blind from birth? Could such a person make much sense of the visual world? Philosopher William Molyneux put this question to philosopher John Locke in 1694:

> Suppose a man born blind, and now adult, and taught by his touch to distinguish between a cube and a sphere of the same metal. . . . Suppose then the cube and the sphere placed on a table, and the blind man made to see; query, Whether by his sight, before he touched them, he could now distinguish and tell which is the globe, which the cube? To which the acute and judicious proposer answers: "Not. For though he has attained the experience of how a globe, how a cube, affects his touch; yet he has not yet attained the experience, that what affects his touch so or so, must affect his sight, so or so."[17]

Upon consideration of this question, Locke responded:

> I agree with this thinking gentleman, whom I am proud to call my friend, in his answer to this problem; and am of the opinion that the blind man, at first sight, would not be able with certainty to say which was the globe, which the cube, whilst he only saw them; though he could unerringly name them by his touch, and certainly distinguish them by the difference of their figures felt.[18]

This question can now be answered more directly, for through the marvels of modern medicine, a number of people, blind since birth, usually as result of cataracts, have had their sight restored in adulthood.[19] What do they see? Not the world that we see, not right away at least. At first, they do not know how to make sense of the overwhelming avalanche of visual information, although they do show some ability to transfer what they have learned through touch.[20] They have to learn to control the movement of their eyes and to focus on selected parts of the visual landscape. They have to learn to make sense of changes in the visual field brought about by movement of their eyes, heads, or bodies, and to distinguish this movement from movement "out there." They have to learn to associate visual information with their knowledge of objects that they have built up with their other senses.

Yet, there are limits to recovery, despite brain plasticity. Even when cataracts are removed from newborns after a relatively brief period of only weeks or months of visual deprivation, changes have already occurred in the visual processing region of the brain that result in some permanent visual deficits. Neurons that would normally be associated only with vision have become responsive to sound to some degree, resulting in enhanced activity in the visual region in response to sound and a deficit in terms of vision.[21]

PERCEPTION IS ORGANIZING

Older children and adults see the world as a more or less orderly collection of separate "things." We see trees, dogs, automobiles, people, paperclips, and shoes, all of them distinct entities. We know that Carla's legs and arms are part of Carla, but that her mittens are not. We can look at a specific animal that we have never seen before and recognize it as a dog or cat—that is, as a member of a class of things that have very similar properties. We know about relationships between objects. Corks float but nails do not. We know about gravity, or rather we can apply that term to the observation that unsupported objects invariably fall downward. We know about daytime and nighttime, and fall and spring, and good and bad. Newborns are bereft of all such knowledge. They have no concept of "mom" or "dad," or of "trees," "redness," "love," "nature," or "religion." They even must learn where their bodies end and the crib blanket begins. They do not understand that objects continue to exist when they cannot be seen at the moment, and so an object that goes out of sight no longer exists for them. They have to learn to distinguish humans from animals and chairs from tables. They learn quickly, however, and, by four months of age, they have begun to treat objects as stable entities that continue to exist even when they have moved out of view.[22] Yet, it is only at about ten months that the infant understands that a solid object cannot pass through another solid object.[23]

There is so much organization to be acquired. In the visual system, for example, colors, texture, and form need to be organized to produce coherent images of things "out there"—this pattern of light corresponds to a teakettle, that one to a tree. Of course, this is another task, to learn to see the similarities among teakettles and group them together. Infants begin developing this categorization skill by the second half of the first year of life and become able to distinguish one class of objects from another—for example, dogs from cats and animals from furniture. Gradually, a whole set of categories (*schemas*, in psychological parlance) form, and the infant soon realizes that what was learned about one baby bottle applies to other baby bottles as well; there is no need to learn about each new bottle individually.

Once the child has built up a large collection of schemas, less and less is encountered in the everyday world that is completely new. Whatever the child learns about dolls, dogs, or doorknobs is now applied respectively to all dolls, dogs, and doorknobs. Gradually, the child learns to make distinctions within each schema and then establishes subcategories. Baltimore orioles are not the same as robins. Dogs that growl should be avoided, while dogs that wag their tail are friendly.

This ability to categorize is vital for day-to-day living and even for survival. Were we not able to rely upon our schemas, we would have to learn afresh in every new situation instead of applying knowledge accumulated in similar situations in the past. We take this ability for granted, and most of the time adults have no difficulty matching what comes in through the senses to the appropriate schema.[24] When we see a door, whether in Toledo, Toronto, or Timbuktu, we have a good idea of how to open it, as well as some expectation about what is on the other side.

It is important to note that people who share a common environment develop very similar sets of schemas, but that we also develop particular schemas specific to our own particular experiences. Biologists looking at a specimen through a microscope perceive a lymphocyte because they have developed a schema for lymphocytes. The rest of us see only a mélange of colors. Similarly, the jazz aficionado may perceive complex and exciting musical developments in a piece of music that is cacophony to those less knowledgeable and who lack the relevant schema.

Schemas become so much a part of automatic perceptual organization that one need not perceive all of an object in order to classify it correctly. The child gradually becomes able, in the words of psychologist Jerome Bruner, to "go beyond the information given."[25] That is, the growing child becomes capable of perceiving and reacting on the basis of only partial information, filling in the gaps based on the relevant schemas.[26] When we see a dog's head sticking out from a car window, we perceive, and will remember, having seen a dog. When we hear the drone of an airplane, we do not need to see the entire airplane to perceive it flying above our heads. While very young infants do not know that when a ball rolls behind a screen, the same ball should come out the other side, a six-month-old is aware of this, having acquired a schema for rolling objects that allows her to "fill in the gap" when the ball cannot be seen and to predict when it will emerge.[27]

Dividing people into different schemas gradually leads to distinctions between "in-group" (*our* people) and "out-groups" (all those other people). In addition, through experience, children recognize that people in their in-group vary in all sorts of ways from one another, while the schemas for other groups appear much more homogeneous. Gradually, the child will "prejudge" a person based on fixed notions (stereotypes) about the group or category to which the individual belongs. Such prejudgments provide the basis for prejudice and discrimination based on group membership. This all begins in childhood.

Top-Down versus Bottom-Up Processing

We often process sensory information in a *top-down* manner; that is, we assume the "big picture" and set about to fill in the details. We use top-down processing when doing a jigsaw puzzle after having examined the picture on the cover of the box. If we know that there are mountains, a house, a horse, and a stream, we will likely begin by looking for pieces that clearly correspond to those features, so that we can begin to construct the mountains or the stream and then build up the rest of the scene around it. On the other hand, if we have lost the box and have no idea about the nature of the scene, we now have to pursue a *bottom-up* approach and carefully examine the individual pieces without any notion in advance of what picture they will form when put together correctly.

Look at figure 2-5 and what do you see? Some will see a woman in a hoop skirt dancing with a man with a cane, while others will see a seal balancing a ball on its nose facing a trainer holding a whip or stick. This difference is the result of top-down processing. You first react to the picture as a whole, and then iden-tify the parts that make up the picture in light of your interpretation. You can imagine what happens when this drawing is shown to a group of people for a few moments and they are later asked to recall what they saw. Without the picture in front of them, about half will report having seen the woman in the hoop skirt, and the other half the seal, and all will be surprised to hear others report some-thing so different from what they have seen.

Figure 2-5: Top-down versus bottom-up (J. R. Nation, L. T. Benjamin, and J. R. Hopkins, *Psychology* [New York: Macmillan, 1987], p. 118, fig. 4-24, "Demonstration of preceptual set").

Sometimes information coming in from the outside world is so vague that it can easily be associated with any one of a number of schemas. This can result in what psychologists refer to as *pareidolia*, a meaningful perception of a visual image built up on the basis of ambiguous input where in reality there is no meaning. There are many examples: the reports from time to time of the face of Jesus appearing in a tortilla chip, a face on Mars,[28] and one that we are all familiar with—the "man in the moon." A good historical example is provided by the 1954-series Canadian one-dollar bill bearing a portrait of Queen Elizabeth. So many people "saw" the face of the devil in the Queen's hair that the bills were later withdrawn from circulation.

Pareidolia generally occurs without conscious effort, although sometimes the suggestions of others will promote the interpretation of an ambiguous stimulus in a particular way. Once one perceives a clear distinct image, it is often difficult to jettison it.

Figure 2-6: Canadian 1954 dollar bill.

Reading involves complex perceptual processing, much of which is top-down. Psychologists have used eye-tracking computers to learn how people visually inspect words during reading. At one time, it was believed that we processed the letters in each word serially from left to right, and at other times it was considered that we viewed the word as a whole. At present, research supports a *parallel letter-recognition model.*[29] We recognize several of the letters of a word simultaneously, and this information leads us to recognize the complete word.

In the fall of 2003, the following passage began to circulate widely on the internet:

Aoccdrnig to rscheearch at Cmabrigde Uinervtisy it deosn't mttaer in waht oredr the ltteers in a wrod are, the olny iprmoetnt tihng is taht the frist and lsat ltteers be at the rghit pclae. The rset can be a toatl mses and you can sitll raed it wouthit a porbelm. Tihs is bcuseae the huamn mnid deos not raed ervey lteter by istlef, but the wrod as a wlohe.

Figure 2-7: Jumbled words.

It is remarkable that we can quickly extract meaning from what at first glance appears to be meaningless combinations of letters that we have never seen before. (Note that the actual content of this message is misleading. The reference to Cambridge is someone's invention, and it is not true that we use only the first and last letters of the word when reading. In fact, someone has carefully chosen the arrangement of letters to retain a degree of readability.)

Top-down processing is often based on partial information or expectation, and again we fill in the gaps. You hear a dog's bark and, as a result, your dog schema is activated, and then, when you catch a glimpse of an animal in your garden, you are likely to "fill in the gaps" and perceive a dog. Psychologists refer to this selection of a schema based on expectation as *priming.* If partial information or expectation is misleading, we will select the wrong schema. This can result, for example, from size-distance confusion, and newspaper reports have from time to time told of urban dwellers who, because of their expectations, have misperceived an ordinary house cat as a wild animal.[30] In one such case, in November 2014, it was reported that a tiger had been spotted near Disneyland Paris, resulting in a search for the animal that involved more than two hundred police, firefighters, and soldiers. Ultimately, the "tiger" turned out to be a large house cat.[31] When "primed" to expect a tiger, this mistake is relatively easy to make because of size-distance constancy. The size of the retinal image of a house cat that is twenty feet away can be the same as that of a tiger at some greater distance. Catching a quick look at a cat when "primed" to see a tiger may lead your brain to interpret the image as a large animal far away rather than a smaller animal up close.

Such size-distance confusion can lead to the opposite error as well, as when a woman in Wyoming mistakenly perceived a ninety-pound mountain lion lying on her back porch to be a large house cat.[32] The late Canadian polymath and experienced bird-watcher Lister Sinclair once described to me his own surprising size-distance error.[33] As he and his friends scanned the skies with their binoculars while on a bird-watching jaunt, someone excitedly announced having spotted a species of bird that was extremely rare in that area. It was far away, but Sinclair and the other birders (now primed to apply that same schema) confirmed the initial identification and excitedly noted the rare sighting in their birding books. Their excitement turned to shock as they watched the bird approach over the next several minutes. The "bird" turned out to be a Cessna airplane.

Expectations have even at times led scientists to see things that are not there. For example, in 1903, physicist René Blondlot, at the University of Nancy in France, reported the discovery of a new form of radiation that he named *N rays*, after his university. He announced that these "rays" are emitted by all substances, except wood, and when focused by a prism, they can be observed as very faint beams of light. Over the next three years, one hundred other scientists published close to three hundred articles describing the properties of this newly discovered radiation. Ultimately, however, the scientific community determined that N-rays do not exist, and that those who had claimed to have observed them had deceived themselves.

PERCEPTION IS SELECTIVE

Perception is a highly complex and dynamic process that constantly samples information from the outside world. It focuses on some data while ignoring others, compares that data with what is stored in memory, takes into account our expectations about the situation we are in, and then, in an instant, constructs meaningful images, sounds, and feelings that appear in our consciousness. We are continually flooded with so much incoming information—visual, auditory, olfactory, gustatory, touch—that we cannot consciously monitor all of it at once. Our brains automatically filter this information flow and allow into consciousness only what seems relevant at the moment. For example, as you read this, you are probably not aware of the pressure of your chair against your body—until now, when you think about it. Or the sound of the ventilation system—again until now, when your attention is drawn to it. When playing soccer, your focus will be on the ball and to some extent on the other players, but not on what spectators are doing. If you are absorbed in a book while someone else is watching television nearby, you may completely tune out the television program.

Yet, the attentional system is very responsive to sudden changes in the environment. We are usually immediately aware when someone enters the room or when there is a sudden drop in temperature or a cell phone buzzes. And while engrossed in conversation with friends at a noisy cocktail party and not paying attention to the din of chatter that fills the room, you are nonetheless likely to immediately recognize your name if someone mentions it across the room. This is known as the *cocktail party effect*. Your brain has been monitoring the incoming data and has just popped some important information, your name, into consciousness.

We miss a great deal of information in our day-to-day lives, although we are rarely aware of it. Psychologists have produced a number of surprising demonstrations of what is referred to as *change blindness*. In one study, college students were observed as they individually approached a counter and spoke to a clerk.[34] The clerk then bent down behind the counter, ostensibly to retrieve something, and a *different* clerk stood up in his place. Even though the second person looked quite different from the first, most of the students failed to notice the change. Change blindness occurs when a significant change in the visual field (in this case, the change of clerk) coincides with some sort of visual disruption (in this case, disappearing behind the counter). To detect the change, the individual would have to note the disparity between the present scene and the scene remembered from a moment ago. Change blindness is the result either of a failure to store the initial information or a failure to make a comparison with it.

In other even more striking research, individual students walking across a university campus were stopped by a stranger asking directions.[35] The interaction was temporarily interrupted by two people carrying a door, who excused themselves while walking between the questioner and the student. That was the visual disruption. As the people with the door continued on their way, the questioner, now concealed by the door, went with them. In the questioner's place was another person (who had arrived on the scene concealed by the door) poised waiting for an answer to the question. Even though the two questioners clearly differed in terms of clothing, appearance, and voice, only about half of the students detected the change. Of course, we do not normally experience such changes in our everyday lives, and so we have not learned to expend resources watching for them.

Inattentional blindness is a related phenomenon. In this case, people fail to notice an unexpected addition to the scene that they are observing. For example, in a well-known study that became a hit on the internet, observers watched a video of people playing basketball, some of whom were dressed in white and the others in black.[36] Viewers were instructed to count the number of passes of the ball, but only those made by the players in white. Thus, their attention was focused on the white outfits while ignoring the black ones. Most observers completely failed to notice when someone in a black gorilla suit walked among the players waving at the camera! They had "tuned out" black in order to focus their attention on white.

While such demonstrations are amusing, the underlying phenomenon is no laughing matter, for its effects can be deadly. Inattentional blindness is likely a major cause of accidents—think of an automobile driver engaged in conversation on a cellular telephone who fails to notice the flashing lights and the bell while approaching a railway crossing.

PERCEPTION AND EMOTION

Strong emotions can influence how an experience is interpreted. Suppose that you are staying overnight in an old house, and, as you lie in bed in the dark, you hear noises above you that sound like footsteps upstairs. Your anxiety soars, for you are alone in the house, and you contemplate the possibility that there is an intruder—or perhaps a ghost. You turn on the lights, and now, as you listen, you realize that what you hear is just the creaking of water pipes cooling down for the night. Your anxiety level drops, but turn off the lights again and it may be hard once more to resist the "perception" that you hear footsteps. Anxiety can determine which schema comes in to play.

Emotional responses can be triggered by events around us even before we are consciously aware of them. In such a case, perceptual information triggers a reaction in the amygdala, the brain's fight-or-flight center, before it reaches the cortex, where we become conscious of it. Once we become aware, this ongoing emotional reaction may influence our perception. That is, when something in the environment provokes fear even before we are aware of the trigger, that fear response may itself lead us to interpret the event as being more dangerous than it actually is. For example, imagine that you are walking through the woods and you glimpse a slender, curved object on the ground. This "snake-like" information goes directly to the amygdala, leaving you in a frightened state by the time, an instant later, that you are consciously able to perceive the object. Now, with heart pounding, you evaluate whether the object really is a snake, and that interpretation will either augment the fear response and lead to evasive behavior, or will serve to reduce the anxiety.[37] If you recognize the object as a stick, you will begin to calm down. On the other hand, your anxiety might "prime" a snake schema so that you mistakenly identify the stick as a snake and then take action to avoid it. Or perhaps the emotional arousal leads to immediate avoidance— running away to avoid the "snake" before cognitive processing is complete. Such avoidance results in the memory of having encountered a snake, even if it was only a piece of wood.

PERCEPTION WITHOUT AWARENESS

As noted above, while our attention focuses only on a subset of incoming information, our brains continue to "unconsciously" monitor other information, so that if there is a sudden change or threat, we can quickly switch our attention to it. Because of this nonconscious monitoring, we are able at times to respond to subtle cues of which we are not even aware. For example, you may react to subtle changes in a person's appearance or demeanor without really being aware of having detected anything. If George has less color in his cheeks or is not quite as jovial as he usually is, you may have a "feeling" that there is something wrong with George, even though you "cannot quite put your finger on it." More about this in a later chapter.

We are not always conscious of how our thoughts, feelings, and actions are influenced by stimuli around us. We may notice the stimulus but not be aware of its effects. Advertising is a good example. Someone purchasing a particular brand of soft drink is unlikely to relate that choice to a billboard that she saw an hour earlier, and yet we know that advertising billboards generally increase sales.

Still, the idea of perception without awareness has been carried too far at times. In the latter part of the twentieth century, considerable public concern was directed to the possibility that advertisers and others were influencing people through *subliminal perception*, that is, presenting information at such a low level that although it reached the brain, it was not consciously detected. It was then assumed that this information could influence the person's thoughts, feelings, and behavior without the person being aware.

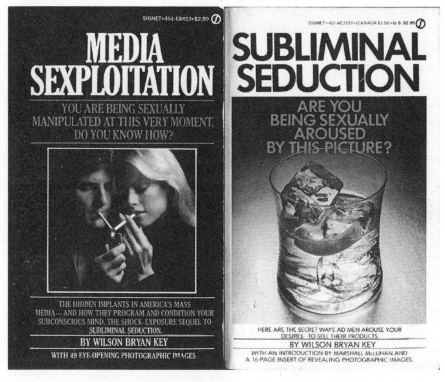

Figure 2-8: Subliminal seduction (New York: Signet, 1977/1974).

Several books and articles were published in the early 1970s that generated a kind of moral panic. They claimed that subliminal messages were being inserted by unscrupulous manipulators into magazine pictures and popular music, messages that people were literally unable to see or hear even if they tried, but which nonetheless had powerful influences on thoughts and actions. Many such messages were described as being sexual in nature,[38] but in some cases, they were supposedly satanic. It was further claimed that because we have no way of vetting subliminal information, given that it is perceived nonconsciously, its effects are much stronger than the effects of stimuli of which we are aware.

There is no empirical evidence that an individual's behavior can be affected in this way by subliminal stimuli,[39] and no reason to think that it can be. People have to be at least partially aware of a stimulus before they can be influenced by it.[40] Similarly, claims that commercial "subliminal" audio tapes can help people learn a language, improve their psychological well-being, lose weight—or even increase breast size—have been shown to be nonsense.[41]

"Stairway to Heaven" was released in 1971 by the popular British rock band Led Zeppelin and soon became one of the most popular rock tunes of all time. It was written by guitarist Jimmy Page in a single afternoon. Then, in 1982, a prominent Baptist minister in the United States alleged that a "subliminal" satanic message had been built into the song. Jimmy Page and Led Zeppelin insisted that this claim was nonsense. To complicate matters, it was further claimed that the message had been recorded *backward* in the song. Supposedly, as people listened to the record played normally, their brains were not only able to detect the subliminal message but somehow able to reverse it as well so that it registered, nonconsciously of course, in a forward direction and then influenced their beliefs and actions. This supposed influence was said to be greater than that of a normal message because, again, listeners were not consciously aware of it and were therefore unable to resist it. That would be an extraordinary perceptual accomplishment if true, one that would certainly raise questions as to how such an ability could have evolved naturally, given that reversed speech does not exist in the natural environment.

There is no evidence that there actually are any backward-recorded messages in the song. Yet, remember, perception is a construction, and under the right circumstances, we can come to "hear" messages that are not actually there. If you were to listen to the portion of "Stairway to Heaven" played backward that was identified by the minister as carrying a subliminal message, it is unlikely that you would distinguish any words among the static, even after several repetitions. But here is where it gets interesting. Were you to listen to the passage again, with the words that the minister "detected" in front of you (beginning with "Oh here's to my sweet Satan"), you would be astonished at how clearly you now actually "hear" the words. (The reader should be able to find this backward passage on any of a number of sites on the internet.) The effect is so strong that it is difficult for many people to resist the notion that the words actually are there.

Each year, I give this demonstration in my class. (To be certain that it had not been doctored, the passage I use was made for me by someone with the equipment necessary to play a record—a "vinyl" in today's terms—backward and record it.) With the minister's "words" in front of them, my students are startled to hear those words clearly in what was originally nothing but noise. Once, I made up a set of words of my own, and after the class had failed to detect anything but static in the backward presentation, I provided half of them with the minister's words and the other half with mine. Each "heard" the message provided to them, and later had difficulty in "hearing" the other message.

What is going on? One *hears* what one first *sees* in this case. When first listening to the backward passage, the brain attempts to find words by matching the sounds against existing sound patterns (words), but they do not correspond to any words with which it is familiar. When guided by a specific set of words, the brain distorts the sounds to fit with these word schemas, which then "pop" into consciousness and we "hear" words that are not actually there.

Hearing words or sounds that are not there is referred to as *apophenia*, the auditory analogue to pareidolia. A common example of apophenia occurs when a person is taking a shower and mistakenly thinks that she hears the doorbell or telephone ringing. The white noise produced by the shower contains a broad spectrum of sounds, including those that make up the sound of ringing bells. The ear picks out certain sounds from the spectrum, and we "detect" a pattern corresponding roughly to a bell.

Remember, there is no backward subliminal message in "Stairway to Heaven," and remember as well that even if someone were to insert hidden messages into music, whether forward or backward, there is no evidence that such messages can influence beliefs or behavior.[42] Perhaps the most remarkable aspect of the whole episode is that the minister went to the trouble of finding a way to play records backward, and then listening, presumably for many hours, in search of patterns of sound that corresponded to his assumption that Satan's army was at work.

Led Zeppelin was not the only band accused of satanic tinkering. In 1985, two boys shot themselves with a twelve-gauge shotgun after a long bout of drinking alcohol and smoking marijuana. One died immediately, but the other succeeded only in destroying half his face. It was later learned that they had been listening at the time to the song "Better by You, Better than Me" on a Judas

Priest album, and it was claimed that they were persuaded to shoot themselves by a subliminal message, "*do it*," hidden in the song. This resulted in the band being sued in 1990. The suit failed largely because of expert psychological testimony from my colleague, psychologist Timothy Moore, who informed the court that there is no empirical evidence or theoretical reason to believe that an individual's behavior can be affected by subliminal stimuli.[43]

Incidentally, in response, some bands did then produce albums with backward and hidden messages to make fun of the whole hullabaloo. Following the "Stairway to Heaven" controversy, Electric Light Orchestra released an album, *Secret Messages*, in 1983. Some of the songs were recorded with backward "subliminal" messages to mock Christian fundamentalists' claims about satanic messages in music. The British release of the album carried a parody warning.

IMAGERY

If you close your eyes and imagine that you are looking at a horse and buggy, you no doubt can see it in your "mind's eye." This is *imagery*, a mental event that occurs in the absence of actual sensory stimulation, based on previous perceptual experiences.[44] Imagery is similar in some ways to perception, but very different in others.[45] Perceptions seem to occur "out there," while images are inside our heads; perceptions are detailed and accompanied by vivid sensory elements, while images are generally more diffuse, incomplete, and less vivid. Perceptions are constant, whereas images soon dissipate. Perceptions are not under voluntary control, but images are, and so we can change them at our whim. Think again of the horse and buggy. If you choose, you can also "see" Santa Claus sitting in the buggy with a gaggle of children cheering him from the street.

Eidetic imagery is a particular form of imagery that, unlike voluntary imagery, is initiated by actual sensory stimulation and then persists long after the stimulation has ceased. It is somewhat like an after-image—think of the after-image that persists for a few moments after someone has snapped a flash camera near you. However, unlike the after-image, it does not move with the eyes—it stays in one place and can be scanned, just as a book stays in one place as you move your eyes to read. It also differs from an after-image in that, while it may occur immediately after the stimulation, it can also occur sometime later. Eidetic imagery is not an exact reproduction of the sensory stimulation;

our schemas influence the form it takes. That is, it too involves a constructive process, resulting in the inclusion of information that was not actually observed.

Eidetic imagery is virtually nonexistent in adults, but does occur, although even then only rarely, in children between the ages of six and twelve years.[46] Its rarity is generally a good thing, for imagine what life would be like if, while looking at something, its image stayed with you when you turned your head to look at something else.

People sometimes describe themselves as having "photographic memories," but such skill does not involve actual eidetic imagery and is not "photographic." It is just good visual memory reflecting a superior ability to organize and retain data with impressive efficiency.[47]

REALITY TESTING

The brain in some circumstances cannot distinguish between external perceptual information and information originating in other parts of the brain itself. Dreams and nightmares are good examples, and, with few exceptions, we are not aware during a dream that it is only a dream.

Young children cannot distinguish between fantasy and reality. They have to learn how to "reality test," to distinguish perceptions based on information from the outside world from perceptions generated within the brain. This ability develops gradually, but by the time they are three years old, they can distinguish between thoughts about an object and the actual object.[48] Yet even then, they may still be unsure about the separation between inside and outside the brain, and whether thinking about events can cause them to occur. For example, many children of that age, after *imagining* that a particular object is inside what they know to be an empty box, subsequently believe that it is in fact now inside the box.[49]

We teach children to reality test. When they wake from a nightmare, we tell them that it was not real, that it was "only a dream." Gradually, the child's reality testing becomes virtually automatic, based partly on instruction, partly on direct experience, and partly on logical analysis. On the other hand, young children are often taught to believe in such impossible beings as Santa Claus and the Tooth Fairy, and depending on the family and the society in which they are reared, they may come to interpret strange events in terms of ghosts, poltergeists, or demons. Moreover, where religion is concerned, a child may be taught to ignore logic and to accept certain impossibilities on faith. For example, when I was young child I learned that at the beginning, Adam, Eve, Cain, and Abel were the only people on earth, After Cain killed his brother, there were only three people left, and yet somehow, he married. This puzzled me, but when I raised this question with my religious aunt, I was sharply chided and instructed not to ask such questions and to accept that God works in mysterious ways.

Of course, older children and adults usually have no difficulty in reality testing, in distinguishing between external perceptual information and imagery. Yet there are times when even adults are not able to distinguish perceptions originating in the brain from material coming from the outside world, and, as a result, mistake images originating inside the brain for external reality. We usually refer to such images as *hallucinations*.

Perception is a process of construction, and sometimes our constructions are significantly distorted representations of reality. At times, we can even "see," "hear," "taste," or "feel" things that are not there, while at other times we can completely fail to take notice of things that are. Think back to the moon illusion, the ninety-pound mountain lion, the gorilla in the basketball game, and the switch of desk clerks.

We also have an extraordinary ability to detect patterns in sensory information. Indeed, we are the best pattern detectors in existence (although computers are rapidly gaining on us). The fact that not all of the patterns that we detect actually correspond to reality does not reflect a weakness in our perceptual processing, but rather is an unavoidable consequence of our ability to respond to partial information and fill in the gaps automatically through the use of schemas.

In consequence, we need to be cautious when basing a belief entirely on what our senses tell us. *Seeing* should not always lead to *believing*, and this is especially so when in strange situations or during times of emotional turmoil. As author Anaïs Nin wrote, quoting the Talmud, "We don't see things as they are; we see them as we are."[50] That is, not only do our perceptions inform our beliefs, but our beliefs also influence our perceptions, and at times we perceive only what we expect to perceive rather than what is there.

CHAPTER 3

BELIEVING WHAT WE REMEMBER

*Life is all memory, except for the one present moment that goes
by you so quickly you hardly catch it going.*
                                                    —Tennessee Williams[1]

s Tennessee Williams observed, we "live" in only a brief moment of time
sandwiched between memories of what has already occurred and anticipation of what is to come. Even if you close your eyes and think about what you
read just a moment ago, you are remembering the past. The reality of it has gone,
and only its traces remain.

Beliefs are tied to memory. Whatever you believe about the world and about
yourself at this moment—without consulting books or the internet—comes
from your memory. Just who are you anyway? Mother, flute player, student,
senior citizen, football player? Rebecca, George, Robin? Your answers to these
questions come from your memory. In a real sense, who you are—your self-
identity—is who you *remember* yourself to be. It is your memory that provides
you with a sense of continuity in your life. It is your memory that allows you to
recognize your family, your friends, and your possessions. It is your memory that
enables you to find your way home, to recognize yourself in the mirror, to dress
yourself, and to choose the words to express your thoughts. And when memory
fails, *really* fails, as it does with advanced Alzheimer's disease, one sinks into an
infantile and isolated world, largely cut off from others and bereft of the ability
to recognize and appreciate all that was once held dear.

MEMORY AND THE BRAIN

On December 2, 2008, eighty-two-year-old Henry Gustav Molaison died from respiratory failure in Manchester, Connecticut. Psychologists remember him because he had "died," in a way, fifty-five years earlier. When only seven years old, he struck his head and lost consciousness after being knocked to the pavement by a child on a bicycle. He seemed unharmed when he regained consciousness after five minutes, but a few years later, he began having seizures, which his family thought were related to the accident (although there was also a family history of epilepsy). By age twenty-seven he was suffering from attacks and blackouts so severe that he could not lead a normal life even with medication.

Figure 3-1: Young Henry Molaison.

With the goal of reducing or eliminating the seizures, a neurosurgeon removed the small portions of his brain thought to be causing them, including large portions of the amygdala and hippocampus. The good news was that, as a result of the surgery, Henry's epilepsy was all but cured, and he suffered only one or two seizures a year from that point onward. The bad news was that he lost the ability to form new memories and, in addition, he lost the memories of much that he had experienced in the prior decade. He could remember nothing at all from the two years prior to surgery. His experience of life, as reflected in his memory, came to a stop on the day he underwent the operation.

After that, nothing ever changed in his world. His family never changed. His town never changed. The president of the United States never changed. He was never again able to recognize a new face. He became distressed each time that he was informed that his father was dead. He could remember how to get to the house in which his family had previously lived, but not to the one to which they had moved ten months before his surgery. He could read the same magazine day after day with no idea that he had encountered it before. He continually underestimated his own age and quickly forgot people's names when they were introduced to him. He described his life as akin to awaking from a dream each morning. His world was frozen in time.

Out of this tragedy emerged "H. M." (as he was referred to in the psychological literature), probably the best-known patient in the history of neuroscience. His loss of the ability to create new memories provided a rare opportunity for psychologist Brenda Milner at the Montreal Neurological Institute, who soon began a life-long study of Henry that led to fundamental discoveries about the anatomical basis of memory. Prior to this, no one had been able to identify the regions of the brain responsible for memory, and it was therefore assumed to be a higher-order function not tied to any particular brain area. And yet, here was Henry, whose memory had been perfectly normal prior to the surgery, but was forever altered after some particular brain tissues were snipped away.

As a result of Henry's misfortune, Milner was able to show that memory is a separate and distinct brain function, associated with particular anatomical sites in the brain. She also discovered that perceptual and intellectual functions are to some degree separate from the ability to form memories. And the fact that Henry lost memory for events almost immediately after they occurred—for example, he was able to carry on a conversation, but a minute or two later would be unable to remember having had the conversation—pointed to an anatomical distinction between short-term ("working") memory and long-term memory. It was apparent that Henry's problem was an inability to convert immediate, short-term memory into enduring long-term memory.

LONG-TERM MEMORY

So-called "long-term" memory takes different forms.[2] First, there is *semantic* memory. This is memory for general knowledge—words, concepts, and "facts" that are independent of our personal experience: Paris is the capital of France; dogs have fur; 2 x 2 = 4; and a Percheron is a horse. We take for granted that we can tap into semantic memory in the same way that we can flip open a dictionary or consult the internet, but we rely upon nonconscious processes to be our search engine. Think of your mother's maiden name. It likely "pops" into your mind immediately. No surprise there, perhaps. But *how* did it pop into your mind? Occasionally, the words we seek do not come to mind immediately, resulting in frustration because we know that we "know" the words that we are looking for. "Who was the actor who played the fat man in the movie *Casablanca*?" "I know for certain that I know, but I cannot think of his name; it will come to me!" ("Ah yes, I remember now, it was Sydney Greenstreet.") This is the *tip-of-the-tongue phenomenon*, and as people age, it often causes more frequent irritation, particularly with regard to names. We learn through experience that struggling to find the word usually does not help, and that the better strategy is to divert our attention to something else. The sought-after material then usually comes to mind when we least expect it, demonstrating the continuing operation of our nonconscious search engine.

Episodic memory involves our particular history of personal experience. It is tied to a specific brain system that allows us to go back in time and re-experience earlier events.[3] You recall the what, where, and when of past events in your life— your high school graduation dance, a trip to the dentist last week, or learning about an election outcome on TV. Episodic and semantic memory are handled somewhat differently in the brain,[4] to the extent that for some brain-damaged individuals, one type of memory is relatively impaired while the other is not.[5] A particular brain region, the hippocampus, is involved in encoding incoming information whether the memory is semantic or episodic, yet damage to the hippocampus interferes with episodic memory, but not with semantic memory. In addition, neuroimaging shows that the patterns of brain activation triggered by memory tasks involving semantic or episodic memory are somewhat different.[6] Nonetheless, semantic and episodic memory do influence each other, and some memories involve features of both.

Autobiographical memory involves not only the recall of past events, but also the recognition that it is *you* who has experienced those events. Autobiographical memories are organized in a more or less chronological sequence that provides a personal narrative of your life, and it is this unfolding continuity of personal experience that underlies your sense of self.[7] You remember where you lived when you were in grade 6; you remember that you went on a holiday with your parents when you were fourteen; you remember passing your driver's test at age sixteen; you remember your first kiss. The grade 6 student, the kid on a holiday, the sixteen-year-old taking a driver's test, the young lover—those are all the same person at different points in time, and they are all "you." If dementia robs you of this ribbon of memory, you will no longer know who you are.

Autobiographical memory was once considered to be part of episodic memory, but it is now recognized that, although related, the two differ somewhat.[8] Autobiographical memory involves information about oneself drawn from *both* semantic and episodic memory. For example, you remember your birthdate and where you were born, and perhaps even some details surrounding your birth, and so these memories are part of your autobiographical memory. Yet, no one can remember the actual experience of being born, for autobiographical memory only begins to take form at about two years of age, when the infant establishes a sense of being a unique individual.[9] As result, any knowledge about your birth is *not* remembered experience, not a part of episodic memory. You have acquired that information from others, and so it comes from semantic memory.

There is another distinction between autobiographical and episodic memory as well. Autobiographical memory also includes *procedural* learning, such as remembering how to ride a bicycle or operate a chainsaw.[10]

CONSTRUCTING MEMORY

Until not so many years ago, experimental psychologists, in common with lay people, viewed memory simply as a very sophisticated recording process, and any errors were treated as defects in the process. A mountain of research now clearly contradicts that view. We now know that errors of memory are commonplace, not rare, and rather than being caused by defects, they reflect the fundamental character of the memory process. Memory is not some sort of cerebral video recorder that captures events around us as we experience them. As solid and reliable as most of our personal memories seem to be, episodic and autobiographical memories are not direct and faithful records of our past.

Just as our perceptions are constructed, so too do our episodic and auto-biographical memories involve dynamic mental reconstructions of events that come into being only at the time that we recall them. They are based in part on information stored in the brain, and in part on situational factors at the time of recall. Memory of an event can be influenced and distorted by the circumstances in which we recall it, including our knowledge of other events that have occurred since, our current emotional state, and even the questions asked of us that lead to the recall.[11] And in some circumstances, we can "remember" having experienced events that never occurred at all.

Thus, memories can be altered without our awareness as they are being constructed, and such alterations then can lead to changes in related beliefs. Yet, when we access autobiographical memory, it certainly does not feel as though we are "constructing" anything. The memories seem to come into our minds full-blown, even if some of the details may be a bit hazy at times.

MEMORY AND IMAGINATION

It is probably difficult to accept that something you clearly remember having experienced could be a distorted reconstruction of what actually happened, or even a complete fiction. Such departures from reality occur more frequently than we realize.

Before exploring this further, try this little exercise: After reading the following, close your eyes and try to visualize what is described in as much detail as you can: *Think of a restaurant where you have recently dined. Try to remember as much as you can about the scene—who was with you, the food that you ordered, the decor of the restaurant. Now, add some imagination. Imagine that while you are dining, a musician strolls over to your table and plays a song on a Spanish guitar. Study her features in your mind's eye. She is tall, slender, dark, and striking. Her black hair falls to her waist and she smiles as she sings. Note her gold necklace and the heart-shaped tattoo on her left wrist.*

Were you able to visualize that scene and blend memory and imagery together? And when you formed a picture of that restaurant scene, from what perspective did you view it? Most people will answer that they saw the scene from a little above and slightly behind where they were sitting. That is how we remember most scenes from our past, whether about being in a canoe or at a friend's wedding ceremony. This is a direct outcome of the constructive nature of memory, and the memory does not correspond to our actual perceptual experience. This occurs because our brains are constructing an image that best captures and summarizes the event. If your eyes acted as a video recorder, your memory of being in the restaurant would include your nose in front, and eyeglasses if you wear them, and it would continually shift hither and yon as your eyes moved around the room—down to your plate, up to meet the eyes of your friend or partner, and to the left when the waiter walks by.

As for the guitar player, remember what she looked like, for we will come back to her later. But for the moment, is it not fascinating just how similar memory and imagination can be? Yet, you can tell the difference because you can reality test. The restaurant was real, but the guitarist was fantasy, and you know that because you invented her. We shall see later how reality testing can fail us, and how our beliefs can be changed when fantasy is mistaken for reality.

PHOTOGRAPHS, MEMORY, AND BELIEF

Think back to an important occasion in your life, such as your high school graduation or your wedding. When we think of past events, the first thing that comes to mind is often some sort of visual picture of the event. Yet, our brains are not very good at storing pictorial information, and so, as we build up the image of the event in our minds, we may be adding elements that were not there and ignoring others that were. As psychologist Stanley Milgram wrote:

> The limit in human functioning is simply that although we can see things very well, we cannot store what we see so that we can reliably bring up the image for repeated viewing. Instead, visual images are incompletely stored in memory— often in a highly schematized form—and subject to decay and distortion.[12]

The advent of photography provided people with the means to keep visual records of themselves and others, and of important events. Photographs became the authoritative anchor points for memories. Was your cousin at your birthday party when you turned ten years old? Look at the pictures. Did you have light or dark hair as a child? Look at the pictures. Milgram pointed out that although collections of family pictures are now taken for granted, this is a relatively recent feature of family life. Until the beginning of the nineteenth century, only people with a talent for drawing or painting could make for themselves a visual record of what they witnessed, and only the rich could afford paintings of themselves and their families. Ordinary people went through life without recorded images to remind them either of events gone by or of how their appearances and those of their family members had changed over the years.

Not surprisingly, research shows that our memories for past events are strongly affected by photographs taken at the time of those events. Milgram again:

> Photographs are often treated as compelling and incontrovertible evidence that the events depicted in them actually happened.... The pictures constitute a reality of their own and invoke emotions, attitudes and convictions. Photographs, therefore, not only depict realities; they create a new plane of reality to which people respond.[13]

Figure 3-2: The family album (photo by the author).

So, pictures—our pictures, other people's pictures, pictures in the media— have come to be viewed as accurate representations of people or events in the past. Family histories are often neatly summarized in a series of photographs. And once again, Milgram:

Through the family photo album, the family constructs a type of fairy tale. Only the happy moments tend to be shown. Families construct a pseudo-narrative which highlights all that was life-affirming and pleasurable, with a systematic suppression of life's pains. However imperfect, for most contemporary families the album is the only narrative available of its history, having supplanted the family Bible—where, in earlier times, a record of births, deaths and marriages was maintained.[14]

This is changing, of course. In this era of ubiquitous cell-phone cameras, few people now keep family albums, and, unless some effort is made to sort and store such digital images, there may be few family photographs for future generations to see.

While photographs anchor autobiographical remembrances and can contribute to more accurate recall, they can also lead to erroneous recollections because we focus only on what was recorded and fail to consider what was not captured in the picture. The photograph is to some extent posed, for even the decision of what to exclude when taking the picture changes the context in which the content is viewed.[15] As well, in days gone by we did not have to worry very much about doctored photographs. In this modern digital age, however, just about anyone can readily manipulate photographic images in a manner that is next to impossible to detect. People can be inserted into pictures of events where they were never present, or their images removed from pictures of events they attended. Research has demonstrated that when presented with doctored photographs of events in their personal past, people's memories of those events often change to be consistent with the pictures.[16]

CONTAMINATING INFLUENCES ON MEMORY RECONSTRUCTION AND BELIEF

Errors and distortions in memory affect our beliefs. If you remember having heard Ernest make a racist comment, you are likely to believe he is a racist. Yet, if your memory was in error and it was Betty who made the comment, then your belief is also in error. In light of the way that memory works, false memories are a normal and even frequent occurrence in everyday life.[17] However, we rarely notice them because we only infrequently have the motivation or the opportunity to subject autobiographical memories to any kind of vetting. Occasionally, we may be surprised to find that, when discussing some long past event with a friend whom we have not seen for many years, the friend's memory of the event is at considerable variance with our own. Even then, we are more likely to discount the friend's memory than to question our own. Some people are more prone than others to develop false memories, but, at present, the reason for this is not understood.[18]

There are a number of influences that can distort or corrupt memory:

Priming: Just as priming plays a role in perception, it can similarly influence our memories. For example, if someone asks you whether you think Janet looked a little worried when you saw her last, your memory of Janet may be influenced by the question, so that you now recall that she did look a little troubled about something, even though you had not thought so at the time.

Retroactive falsification: When an event is recalled a number of times in succession, the details tend to become more consistent with one's interpretation of the event. For example, suppose you describe a recent experience with a rude waiter. You recall that your partner had complained about the soup not being hot enough, and that you sarcastically suggested to the waiter that the chef should learn how to cook. The waiter then snarkily advised you to dine somewhere else next time. As you relate this account, your listener responds by suggesting that your sarcasm may have provoked the rude response, thereby challenging the "rude waiter" theme of your story. Now, the next time you tell the story, you may unwittingly or perhaps even deliberately reduce the likelihood of such a challenge by leaving out the bit about your sarcasm. Each new reconstruction influences the following one, and over several retellings, you may actually forget all about your sarcasm. This is *retroactive falsification*, and it can occur completely without awareness. Deliberately tailoring your story to align with your listeners' knowledge and opinions ("audience-tuning") can also alter your subsequent memory of the events.[19]

Misinformation effect: The *misinformation effect* occurs when misleading information acquired *subsequent* to an experience leads to alterations in memory and belief about the experience.[20] For example, in one study participants were presented with a series of photographs portraying a thief stealing a woman's wallet and then putting it in his *jacket* pocket. Subsequently, the participants listened to a recording that described the series of photos, but the recording indicated that the thief had put the wallet into his *pants* pocket. A substantial proportion of the participants later recalled that the photographs had shown the thief putting the wallet into his pants pocket.[21] The subsequent misinformation had become part of their memories.

The misinformation effect can be produced in various ways, even simply by the questions that elicit the recall. For example, psychologist Elizabeth Loftus showed research participants a video of a traffic accident involving a collision between two automobiles.[22] After watching the video, some were asked to estimate the speed of the cars when they "hit each other," while others were asked to estimate their speed when they "smashed into each other." A week later, all the participants were questioned again. Those whose initial questioning involved the word "smashed" reported having observed significantly higher speeds, compared to those who had initially been questioned using the word "hit." Participants were also asked whether they remembered having seen any broken glass at the accident scene. Even though there was no broken glass, twice as many of the participants who had been asked about the "smashed" cars recalled seeing broken glass compared to those who had been asked the question using the word "hit." Memory of the actual event was modified as the result of a question subsequently asked.

In a similar experiment, some participants were asked, "Did you see the broken headlight?" while others were asked, "Did you see a broken headlight?"[23] The two questions produced substantially different responses. The question with "a" in it resulted in many more "I don't know" responses than did the question with "the." Why should that be so? "Did you see *the* broken headlight?" implies that there *was* a broken headlight to be seen, and that was enough to lead many participants to incorporate a broken headlight into the construction of their memories. You can imagine the difficulty that this poses for testimony in court, where lawyers' questions may influence the answers that witnesses provide.

Children are particularly vulnerable to the misinformation effect. Repeatedly *telling* children that they have had a particular experience that did not actually occur, or even just repeatedly *asking* about a nonevent, is enough to lead many to come to remember that they had had the experience.[24] In one demonstration, preschool children aged three to six were interviewed once a week for six weeks, both about some actual events (as reported by their parents) and about others that had not occurred (such as having had their fingers caught in a mousetrap).[25] In each interview, the interviewer read out the details of all the supposed events and asked the child to remember what actually happened. On the eleventh week, the children were questioned by a new interviewer, who asked about each event and whether it had actually occurred. More than half the children told the interviewer that at least one of the invented events had actually occurred to them, and they described details, such as having been treated at a hospital, that had not been in the original story. A number of other studies have confirmed just how suggestible young children can be.

Imagination inflation: Close your eyes again and recall that scene in the restaurant with the Spanish guitar player. Take a couple of seconds and recall her features. Does that memory of her seem any less vivid than your memory of the waiter who actually served you, or the faces of other strangers in the room, or maybe even people at your table? How can you be sure that she was not there? Of course, you remember deliberately making her up. Yet, perhaps a year from now if someone mentions Spanish guitar players, the woman who you invented will come to mind and you may not recall that she was an illusion of your own creation. Research has demonstrated that something *imagined* in the context of a particular memory is sometimes later "remembered" as having actually happened. As result of this *imagination inflation*, the "memory" may carry with it all the corresponding emotional and physical reactions that would occur were the memory accurate.[26]

As psychologists Eryn J. Newman and Maryanne Garry point out:

> When people spend just a short time imagining an event they originally rated as unlikely, they become more confident that it occurred.... [Imagining encourages] elaboration about the event—as people add details, people and sensory information, the imagined event feels more like a real memory.[27]

This poses a significant risk of memory contamination in therapy settings. When a therapist simply suggests to a client that an unfortunate event might have occurred in her childhood—as some careless therapists do—this can be enough for imagination inflation to occur and for the imagined event to take on an air of reality. It is similarly a problem in the courtroom.

Source-monitoring errors: Distortions in memory can also come about because of source-monitoring errors in which information is recalled but, with the passage of time, its dubious source has been forgotten. No longer being able to evaluate the information in terms of the reliability of the source, an individual may now believe information that earlier was not considered credible.[28] (This is sometimes referred to as the *sleeper effect*.)[29] For example, you mention to your friend that diet colas are bad for your teeth, and your friend challenges you about where you learned this. You remember having "heard it somewhere," but have forgotten that it was your neighbor, Joe, who told you this. You have no confidence in anything he tells you, and had you remembered that the statement came from him, you would have discounted it completely.

Memory and emotion: Think back to some notable events in your life—a wedding, the birth of a child, the death of a parent, a serious accident or illness, or a natural disaster. Such emotionally laden events often create the most vibrant and indelible memories, and they are generally held with great confidence. While strong emotion surrounding an event generally enhances its recall, it negatively affects the memory for other events that were peripheral at the time.[30] Such *memory narrowing* is even more likely to occur when the strong emotion is negative, such as fear, anger, or anxiety.[31] You may remember the tornado but forget who warned you to take shelter.

Confidence: We tend to trust other people's memories when they are confident in them. This trust is misplaced, for researchers have repeatedly found that confidence in a memory is at best a poor predictor of its accuracy.[32] Memories can be held with great confidence even when they are false.

What all this tells us is that while we take for granted that our memories are more or less accurate records of our past experience, this is not always the case. We need to understand that there are times when our memories can be greatly at variance with what actually occurred. The problem is, of course, that erroneous memories are often as vivid and realistic as those that are accurate.

IMPLANTING MEMORIES

Extensive research by psychologist Elizabeth Loftus has demonstrated that it is not difficult to "implant" memories of events that never occurred, even in emotionally healthy individuals.[33] In one of her studies, Chris, a fourteen-year-old boy, was given descriptions (supplied by his parents) of three events that had actually happened to him when he was a young child.[34] Mixed in with these accounts was one false event of having become lost in a shopping mall while the family was on a shopping trip when he was five years old. He was told that he was crying uncontrollably before being rescued by an elderly man and brought back to his family. Chris was then asked to write down everything he could remember about each of the four events, and to do this once a day for five days.

And what happened? Over the course of five days, Chris began to "remember" more and more detail about having been lost in the mall and about the man who had rescued him. A few weeks later, he was asked to rate his memories of the four events, and, in terms of the clarity of the memories, he provided the second-highest rating for the lost-in-the-mall episode. When asked to describe having been lost, he provided a host of details about how he felt at the time and about the appearance of the man who rescued him. When informed that one of the four events had never occurred and asked to guess which one, he picked one of the real memories. When subsequently informed that he had never been lost in a mall, he had difficulty in accepting that his memory of it was an illusion.

"RECOVERING" MEMORIES

When police in the movies are faced with a witness who is unable to recall some crucial detail, hypnosis is often employed in the effort to recover the missing memory. In reality, hypnosis provides a fertile field for imagination inflation. It typically results in a mélange of fantasy and reality so intertwined that they cannot be distinguished. Going forward, the "recovered" material will be remembered as though it had really occurred.[35] (Hypnosis is explored in detail in chapter 11.)

Hypnosis is one of the most common approaches to "memory recovery" in a therapeutic setting. Rather than a pathway to truth, however, it most often leads directly to what the therapist expects to find—such as fragmentary accounts of sexual abuse in childhood constructed in response to specific questioning. Through imagination inflation, these accounts are subsequently mistaken for genuine memory.

"Guided imagery" (a technique in which the therapist leads the client to generate mental images of a supposedly forgotten event or situation, along with the sounds, taste, odors, and emotions that accompanied it) is as effective as hypnosis in inducing false memories. This was demonstrated in a study in which participants were led to believe that they were endowed with very good visual exploration skills, and it was suggested that this was probably because they had been born in hospitals where there were colored mobiles above their cribs.[36] In order to "confirm" that this was the case, two memory-recovery techniques were used. Half of the participants were hypnotized and then told to "go back" to when they were one day old and to remember what they could see. (Recall that autobiographical memory does not reach back beyond about two years of age.)

The other participants were subjected to "guided imagery," through which they were encouraged to imagine their experience as a one-day-old in order to help their recall of being a newborn in a hospital. Both techniques led to supposed memories of being one day old, and many "remembered" the mobile, and some recalled their cribs, nurses, and physicians. When asked later about the memories, half of the participants believed that they were genuine, while only 16 percent recognized them as fantasies. This demonstrates just how easy it is to create vivid and complex false memories.

In the latter part of the twentieth, and into the early years of the twenty-first century, a wave of "recovered" memories of childhood sexual abuse swept through Canada, the United States, and a few other countries. Many psychotherapists of various professional stripes jumped on the recovered-memory bandwagon and began to look for evidence of forgotten childhood sexual abuse in their clients. People who sought psychotherapy for a range of problems, such as depression, anxiety, insomnia, obesity, smoking, alcoholism, marital problems, or employment difficulties ended up being convinced through their therapy that their problems were the result of childhood sexual abuse of which they had had no memory.

In keeping with the now-discredited Freudian notion of "repressed memory," the therapists believed that the traumatic nature of childhood sexual abuse resulted in memories that were so deeply buried that the victims became completely unaware that they had occurred. It was only by bringing these "repressed" memories to the surface and dealing with them that they could help their clients overcome the emotional problems that flowed from them. And so, well-meaning therapists regularly elicited reports of sexual abuse that were sometimes so horrific that they were beyond credibility. In addition, many therapists told their clients that, to free themselves of the emotional consequences of abuse, they must confront the abuser and take appropriate legal action. As a result, innocent people ended up in prison.

In some cases, once one person has made an accusation of childhood sexual abuse toward an individual, other people who had childhood contact with that person begin to seek for hidden memories, and subsequently conclude, "remember," that they too had been abused, even when they had not. The convergence of accusations against a specific individual lends credibility to presumed guilt.

The claim that traumatic memories of sexual abuse are "repressed," pushed down deep into some unconscious part of the brain, leaving the individual with no recollection of the abuse, is not supported by good research evidence and makes no sense from what we know about memory in general.[37] Indeed, the real problem with genuine traumatic memories is one of trying to get rid of them, for they often haunt people forever. Children who have experienced such terrible events as seeing their parents murdered are unable to "repress" these memories, and no one is ever able to forget torture or concentration-camp experiences.[38] In response, some therapists argue that sexual trauma is different from other trauma, that memories of it are repressed while memories of other trauma are not. That claim is not supported by research either. Moreover, the many survivors of childhood sexual abuse that occurred in Canadian residential schools for indigenous children might wish the repression hypothesis were true, for they report being unable all their lives to rid themselves of the unwanted memories of their experiences.[39]

REALITY TESTING AND MEMORY

Memory and imagination both result in mental constructions, but those based on memory usually come to mind without any mental effort. Reality testing is vital in distinguishing imagined history from real history. It is based in part on whether we "actively" construct a scene (as with imagination) or "passively" reconstruct it (as with memory). When reality testing fails, imagination is mistaken for reality.

Although we usually do not think that we have any difficulty distinguishing imagination from actual memory, recent research indicates that normal individuals vary substantially in terms of their ability to assess whether a remembered event was imagined or actually occurred, and that these differences are linked to structural differences in a particular region of the prefrontal cortex of the brain, the *paracingulate sulcus*.[40] These structural characteristics are laid down prior to birth. Thus, our ability to reality test depends significantly on prenatal developmental processes affecting the brain. As a consequence, some people are more likely than others to suffer a breakdown in reality testing in certain circumstances.

Some activists in the repressed-memory "movement" make efforts to discourage reality testing. For example, *The Courage to Heal*,[41] a best-selling self-help guide to digging out hidden memories of childhood sexual abuse, specifically undermines reality testing by advising the reader that any doubts about having been abused in childhood reflect unconscious attempts to avoid the truth:

If you think you were abused, and your life shows the symptoms, then you were.[42]

and

Survivors often doubt their own perceptions. Coming to believe that the abuse really happened, and that it really hurt you, is a vital part of the healing process.[43]

Some years ago, while I was addressing a number of senior judges on the topic of the unreliability of recovered memories, one of the judges pointed out that when such memories are reported in court, they always appear clear and detailed, and it was his belief that such clarity suggests that they are genuine. At that point, I asked him and the other judges to close their eyes for a moment and to imagine that they were on their way overland to the North Pole. I asked them to try to picture the scene as vividly as possible. After a few minutes, I then asked them to open their eyes and to tell me each in turn what they had seen in their mind's eye. One described being on a snowmobile, smelling the exhaust smoke, and being tossed up and down as the vehicle bounced over moguls in the snow. Another described being on skis and feeling blinded by the brightness of the sun reflecting off the snow. The judge who had raised the question related a very vivid scene in which he was on a dogsled mushing a team of dogs over endless fields of blinding snow. He could hear the squeal of the runners on the snow and the yelping of his dogs as he cracked his whip, and he could see icicles, formed from his own frozen breath, clinging to the fur of his parka hood.

I pointed out that these accounts were all very detailed and vivid, just as he believed real memories to be, and I asked him how he could be so sure that his own recollection was not real. His response reflected confidence in his reality testing. He knew that he had actively constructed the scene in his mind's eye, and, in addition, he knew that he had never traveled to the North Pole. I reminded him that I had made no suggestion of dog sleds or any other method of travel, and that perhaps he was actually retrieving a repressed memory, and that if this were a therapeutic context, the reassurance from a therapist that the memory was genuine might be persuasive. The point was taken. Clarity and detail are not infallible guides to accuracy.

NONBELIEVED MEMORIES

Suppose that you remember having been at an event with your friends many years ago, but now, after a reunion with those friends, you have come to realize that your memory is in error and that you were not actually present. You had incorporated the event into your own autobiographical memory after having heard it described in detail many times in the past. Now, however, even though you no longer believe the memory to be real, you can still recall vivid features of the event. It seems somewhat counterintuitive that one would continue to "remember" something while recognizing it to be false. Yet, this is not an uncommon occurrence. In one survey, 20 percent of respondents reported having had such an experience.[44] They had ceased to believe in their recall because of social feedback and contradictory evidence, but that did not remove it from their autobiographical memory, although it did change its truth status.

MEMORY AND JUSTICE

The vulnerability of memory has been a special problem for the justice system, which depends to a substantial degree on people's testimony about what they have experienced or witnessed. As psychologist Charles Brainerd points out,

> The determinative evidence about who did what, where, when, and to whom
> reduces to what witnesses and suspects report; memory reports in other words.
> It follows that the study of accuracies and inaccuracies in human memory is
> bedrock science for the reliability of legal evidence.[45]

As we have seen, autobiographical memory is not only vulnerable to error through the misinformation effect and imagination inflation, but can be significantly corrupted through memory techniques such as hypnosis. This problem is slowly beginning to be acknowledged by the courts. For example, in 2007, the Supreme Court of Canada declared hypnotically recovered memories to be inadmissible as evidence.[46] In the United States, the admissibility of such evidence varies from state to state, and as law professor Brent Paterline has noted:

> Even with all the scientific studies that show that human memory is fragile and
> malleable; many courts in the United States still regard hypnotic memories as

a permanent record of past events. In many jurisdictions, hypnotic memories are treated as if they were a videotape of past events, faithfully storing everything we say and do.[47]

Eyewitness testimony: "Pluris est oculatus testis unus, quam auriti decem." ("Better one eyewitness than ten who only know a thing from hearsay.") So declared the classical scholar Erasmus (1466–1536).[48] On the face of it, that would seem to make sense. If we have doubts about a piece of gossip, those doubts usually vanish if we can see a thing for ourselves. Still, as we have seen, our brains can lead us to erroneous perceptions, and for many people seeing is believing.

The most common cause of wrongful convictions is faulty memory in the form of an erroneous eyewitness report.[49] Witnesses often make mistakes in identifying the people whom they think they observed committing a crime. For one thing, the circumstances surrounding the incident are likely to make accurate identification difficult, given that criminal activities are typically unexpected, fast-paced, and invoke strong emotions. Moreover, witnesses tend to pay more attention to significant aspects of the scene, such as an injured person or a weapon, while ignoring other possibly key details.[50] Add to this the misinformation effect. Memory of the event can be contaminated by subsequent information, such as newspaper reports, as well as by leading questions posed by investigators and lawyers. In addition, relentless questioning can lead to imagination inflation, which again can produce fallacious memories.[51]

Law professor Brandon Garrett reviewed the cases of the first 250 people in the United States who were exonerated on the basis of DNA evidence. Almost one-third of them had been sentenced to life in prison, and seventeen were facing execution. About two-thirds of these convictions had relied heavily on eyewitness testimony. Garrett noted that, while the eyewitnesses expressed great confidence in identifying the perpetrator at the time of the trial, the trial transcripts clearly showed that in 57 percent of the cases, these same witnesses had initially had significant difficulty in identifying the individual.[52]

Confidence in eyewitness memory increases when memory is presumed to be consistent with other evidence. Consider this experiment: Participants watched a video of what appeared to be a terrorist planting a bomb, and at one point the perpetrator's face was clearly shown.[53] Subsequently, they were shown a set of pictures of six people who resembled the bomber. Even though none of the pictures was of the bomber, every participant identified one of the pictures as being that of the perpetrator. The participants were then randomly assigned to several conditions. Some were advised that there was evidence that corroborated their identification, while others were told that there was evidence that exonerated the accused perpetrator, and still others were given no feedback. When feedback was given, some participants received it immediately after the initial identification, and for others it was provided forty-eight hours later in a second session. Participants were then asked a number of questions concerning their confidence in their choice, how good a look at the perpetrator they had had, and how much they focused their attention on the perpetrator. Whether it was provided immediately or forty-eight hours later, feedback indicating that there was evidence that corroborated their identification increased participants' confidence in their memories compared with those who received no feedback.

FLASHBULB MEMORIES

But surely, vivid memories of momentous events are permanent and accurate, are they not? It is likely that everyone has experienced at some point in their lives a so-called *flashbulb memory* of some dramatic and emotionally laden public event.[54] Our recollections of the event itself, where we were at the time, and how we learned about it are so striking that it is like a flash photograph permanently seared into our brains. Thus, older readers will feel confident that they remember exactly where they were when they heard the news on November 22, 1963, that John F. Kennedy had been assassinated or when they learned of the assassination of Martin Luther King in Memphis on April 4, 1968. Beatles fans may believe that they "know for certain" where they were at the time and how they heard about the murder of John Lennon on December 8, 1980. Others may have such memories of the explosion of the *Challenger* space shuttle on January 28, 1986, or the destruction of the Berlin Wall on November 9, 1989. And most of us can vividly recall the events of September 11, 2001, and where we were at the time and how we heard about them.

Even though people are very confident that those memories are accurate, can we be so sure? Consider this research: In 1986, when the *Challenger* exploded shortly after taking off, psychologist Ulrich Neisser seized the opportunity to assess the accuracy of flashbulb memories.[55] On the day following the tragedy, he administered a questionnaire to his students asking them to state what they were doing and who they were with when they heard about it. Then, almost three years later, he was able to contact a large majority of the students and again ask them the same questions. In addition, he asked them to state their confidence in the accuracy of their memory. He then compared what each student wrote with what that same student had written the day after the explosion. He was surprised to find that, compared to what they had written three years earlier, half of them were wrong with regard to two-thirds or more of what they now reported, and a quarter of the students were wrong about everything. Only 7 percent had perfect scores. (See figure 3-4 for an example of two accounts from the same student, written almost three years apart.) Although the students generally reported high confidence in their memories, there was no relationship between confidence and accuracy.

Figure 3-3: Flashbulb memories

And what would you expect the students whose reports had changed dramatically to say when confronted with what they had written two-and-a-half years earlier? So confident were they in their present memories that many of them simply stated that what they had written earlier was obviously false, although they could not understand why they had written a false account the first time. Such was the power of their current "memory."

> January 1986: "I was in religion class and some people walked in and started talking about [it]. I didn't know any details except that it had exploded and the school teacher's students had all been watching which I thought was so sad. Then after class I went to my room and watched the TV program talking about it and I got all the details from that."

> September 1988: "When I first heard about the explosion I was sitting in my freshman dorm room with my roommate and we were watching TV. It came on a news flash and we were both totally shocked. I was really upset and I went upstairs to talk to a friend of mine and then I called my parents."

Figure 3-4: Shift in memory.

The 9/11 attack provided another opportunity to study flashbulb memories, and again there was evidence of significant forgetting. Beginning just a week after the attack, a number of researchers collaborated in a large-scale, longitudinal survey of several thousand individuals across the United States, asking them to describe exactly where they were at the time of the attacks and how they had heard about them.[56] Follow-up surveys were carried out after one year, two years, and ten years. The researchers reported that rapid forgetting occurred in these "flashbulb memories" within the first year, and participants no longer remembered the events as they had initially reported them. The recollections did not change much over the next nine years after that. Despite the significant forgetting and distortion that occurred during the first year, the respondents' confidence in the accuracy of their memories remained extraordinarily high and did not decline, even over the ten-year period.

Various studies of flashbulb memory combine to show that information gathered at the time is modified and updated subsequently in response to news reports and other peoples' recollections of an event, so that as time goes on what people remember bears less and less correspondence to what they would have recalled in the immediate aftermath of the event.[57] Studies of veterans of the First Gulf War were asked about their war experiences one month after their return home. When asked again two years later, 70 percent of these veterans recalled a traumatic event that they had not recalled initially, while 46 percent failed to mention a traumatic event that they had reported upon their return.[58]

This and other research indicates that so-called flashbulb memories, despite being held with strong confidence, do not reflect some special kind of memory. Like other memories, they are subject both to forgetting and to distortions over time.[59] And given that many flashbulb memories involve important public events, extensive media treatment of such events has a considerable influence in shaping and changing the memories. Neisser referred to these memories as "phantom" flashbulbs; we *think* that they are burned into our memories with great accuracy, but they are not.

COLLECTIVE MEMORY

Our autobiographical memories contribute importantly to our self-identity and self-esteem. We remember ourselves as having acted honestly or cowardly or bravely, and in turn we see ourselves as honest or cowardly or brave. Our memories often shift to minimize inconsistency with how we want to see ourselves, and so, over time, a cowardly act may change into a memory of caution and discretion, and a dishonest act may morph into an "honest mistake." In this way, self-esteem is maintained.

Similarly, just as our own identities are anchored in our autobiographical memories, so too is group identity anchored in collective memories.[60] And just as individual memories are sometimes significantly in error, groups and communities share collective memories that are also subject to distortion. When people converse about shared past events, one person's recollections may be quite different from another's, and so they influence or even reshape each other's memory. This mutual social influence can lead to the development of a collective memory that departs considerably from the individual memories that gave rise to it.[61]

Indeed, when historians collect accounts of important past events, what people remember collectively is often at considerable variance with "the facts," which have often been distorted in a direction that makes people feel better, boosts their collective self-esteem, and supports their positive sense of identity. Thus, it was much more comfortable for the British who served in India during the Raj to remember their actions as altruistic efforts intended to bring India into the modern era. The historian, on the other hand, who is focused on a search for objective evidence, is likely to provide quite a different account about the attitudes and actions of British colonial rulers:

> History and collective remembering represent two ways of relating to the past, and the pictures they provide are often related. . . . In a nutshell, one could say that history is willing to change a narrative in order to be loyal to facts, whereas collective remembering is willing to change information (even facts) in order to be loyal to a narrative.[62]

Consider the overwhelming human and material damage during the Blitz of 1940–41, when the Luftwaffe carried out seemingly endless bombing raids over London. There were more than 20,000 deaths, and a million homes were destroyed.[63] When people who lived through the Blitz are asked to describe what it was like, they typically recall a time when Londoners were resolute in the face of danger from the skies. In their memories, they rallied behind Winston Churchill in defiance of Hitler and "remained calm and carried on." Yet, when historian Angus Calder reviewed newspaper accounts, personal diaries, and correspondence of the time, he found that rather than keeping calm and carrying on, the citizens of London were in a state of despair.[64] They were exhausted, frightened, and in mourning over the loss of loved ones and the destruction of their city. Morale was so low that Churchill was frequently booed when he toured bombed-out parts of the city. Like so many other group recollections, the collective memory of the Blitz in London is a highly distorted one. There is no pride in remembering that you and your fellow citizens were frightened and despairing, but there is considerable emotional benefit to recalling that everyone kept calm and carried on.

A group's collective memory can often influence behavior long into the future. Indigenous peoples around the world will not forget colonization and the treatment meted out by colonizers, Jews will not forget the Holocaust, and African-Americans will not forget the abomination of slavery.

Our memories generally serve us well. Yet, episodic memory is highly susceptible to error, and some circumstances make errors more likely. Memories inform our beliefs, and distorted or corrupted memories result in distorted or corrupted beliefs. Most of the time, this may be of little consequence. It really does not matter much if you remember spending a week in Berlin last year when it was really only four days, or if you recall that you broke off with your high school sweetheart when in fact it was the other way around. Yet, in some circumstances, the consequences are serious, such as when errors and bias in memory while giving testimony in court result in egregious miscarriages of justice and ruined lives.

The lesson for us all is that no matter how clear our memory of an event may seem, and no matter how confident we are in its accuracy, we are likely to be sorely mistaken at times. Although they are hard to resist, our memories should not be treated as unshakable foundations for our beliefs.

CHAPTER 4

BELIEVING WHAT WE LEARN AND FEEL

Wisdom . . . comes not from age, but from education and learning.

—Anton Chekhov[1]

Anyone who experienced anxiety while watching the movie *Jaws* will recall that, as the movie progressed, there was no need to actually see the great shark in order to feel tense and anxious. One just had to hear the repeated musical chords that always indicated that the shark was nearby. Our nervous systems had quickly learned to respond with anxiety to those specific chords.

We are constantly learning. But *how* do we learn? Direct experience is a great teacher and a primary source of our beliefs. Taste a spicy vindaloo for the first time, your mouth feels afire, and you acquire a belief about vindaloos. Kick a beverage machine when it fails to deliver a can of pop, and, if it immediately surrenders the can, you acquire a belief about how to deal with recalcitrant pop machines. We also learn by observation. A person from a rural area coming to the city and encountering an escalator for the first time stands back and watches how other people step onto it before trying it for himself. And, of course, as we grow from childhood to adulthood, more and more of our learning comes from books, newspapers, and television.

THE WAY WE LEARN

Vindaloo Sets the Mouth Afire: Classical Conditioning

Most readers will know of Russian physiologist Ivan Pavlov (1849–1946), whose work on digestion led to a Nobel Prize in 1904. Pavlov made a very important but serendipitous discovery about learning while studying salivation in dogs. Salivation is, of course, an automatic (or, in psychological parlance, an *unconditioned*) response to food. That is, present food to an animal or human, and salivation follows automatically. No surprise there. However, Pavlov *was* surprised to observe that, over time, dogs began to salivate even *before* food was presented, and he discovered that the salivation was being triggered by particular cues that had been repeatedly paired with the food. These cues—for example, the noise made by the food cart as it was trundled along the corridor—signaled that food was about to arrive. He reasoned that these originally neutral cues had become *conditioned* stimuli, with a power similar to that of the *unconditioned* stimulus (food) to elicit salivation.

Figure 4-1: Ivan Pavlov.

This "conditioning" process, whereby a neutral stimulus becomes capable of triggering an automatic bodily response is known as *classical* (or "Pavlovian") conditioning, and it occurs with a wide range of physiological responses and emotional reactions. Just as Pavlov's dogs came to salivate at the sound of the food cart in the corridor, so too do our own salivary and gastric juices begin to flow as soon as we sit down at the dinner table, preparing our digestive system for action even before our first bite of food.

Many other physiological processes are similarly subject to classical conditioning. For example, if someone were to blow a puff of air at your eye, your eyelid would automatically close (*unconditioned* response) whether you wanted it to do so or not. Now, if a bell were rung just before the puff of air, and if this pairing were repeated a few times, you would soon blink (*conditioned* response) at the sound of the bell, again *whether you wanted to or not.*

Classical conditioning involves two important concepts, *similarity* and *temporal contiguity*.

- **Similarity:** Learning would be of limited value if what we have learned in a particular situation was restricted only to that situation. It works mostly to our advantage that conditioned responses generalize to other similar objects or situations. A fear response conditioned to a particular Rottweiler will also be triggered by other Rottweilers, and perhaps by other large dogs as well. The downside of this, of course, is that the generalization may go too far. Just because one Rottweiler was ferocious does not mean that they all pose a risk.
- **Temporal contiguity:** At the most basic level, all animals "learn" when two stimuli occur closely together in time, leading to associations being set up in the brain between these events. Conditioning of physical responses, such as the eye blink, occurs most readily when the interval between the cue (the bell) and the unconditioned stimulus (the puff of air) is about one-half a second.

Although in Pavlov's day conditioning was viewed only as a mechanical, reflexive process, we now know that it is much more complex, even in animals. While temporal contiguity is critical in producing learning, also important is the *information value* of the pairing. Animals and humans alike use the information available to them to respond adaptively to situations in which they find themselves.[2] For example, if you hear a car door slam a moment before your telephone rings, this random pairing does not carry any information value, and so your brain does not set up an association between the two. If an animal learns that when a light turns on, shock follows, it will do what it can to avoid the shock whenever the light comes on. Yet, when the researcher then presents a tone at the same time as the light, the animal does *not* learn that the tone predicts the shock, despite it also being a reliable indicator that the shock is coming. The tone is ignored because it has no information value since the animal already has a reliable predictor of shock, the light.[3] In the words of psychologist Robert Rescorla,

> Pavlovian conditioning is not a stupid process by which the organism willy-nilly forms associations between any two stimuli that happen to co-occur. Rather, the organism is better seen as an information-seeker using logical and perceptual relations among events, along with its own preconceptions, to form a sophisticated representation of its world.[4]

Conditioned emotional responses

"I always cry at weddings:" Our emotional reactions are also subject to conditioning. Recall the earlier reference to the movie *Jaws* and the anxiety that automatically occurred in response to those particular musical chords. Automatic triggering of conditioned emotional responses occurs across a wide range of settings.[5] A student who is overcome by anxiety as he begins to write his exam, or an airplane passenger who shakes in fear despite telling herself that flying is safer than driving, or the warm feelings elicited by a romantic song, and, yes, those spontaneous tears at weddings are all examples of conditioned emotional responses. And if being in a church, temple, or synagogue was associated with calm and pleasant feelings in childhood, those settings may elicit similar feelings in adulthood, even if one's faith has lapsed.

Classical conditioning and beliefs

While it may appear to adults that infants and children spend much of their time engaging in mindless, repetitive activities, every new situation provides an opportunity for learning. Classical conditioning underlies much of the infant's development of belief about the world because we are neurologically "hardwired" to associate events that occur closely together in time. Infants learn that hitting the side of the crib brings pain and that crying brings mummy or daddy, and this leads to beliefs about the effects of hitting things and how to summon mummy or daddy. The growing child gradually learns to recognize complex patterns in the constant barrage of incoming sensory information she experiences, to perceive relationships among objects, people, and events. This leads to beliefs about "what causes what." Regularities come to be the rule: Drop an object, it falls; clap hands, noise follows. Eventually, such beliefs become so well-established that violations of them—an object that floats in midair without support or hand-clapping that makes no sound—are surprising and even disturbing.

Even as adults, we continue to develop classically conditioned beliefs tied to temporal contiguity and similarity. You taste rice wine for the first time and do not like it (temporal contiguity), and you form the belief that rice wines in general (similarity) are unpalatable. You gobble some ice cream and a moment later feel a sharp pain in your forehead, and, because of the temporal contiguity, you believe that it was the ice cream that caused the pain. We should never underestimate the importance of temporal contiguity in the formation of our beliefs. People are repeatedly warned that cigarette smoking is a major cause of cancer, but the pleasure of smoking is immediate and any negative consequences are far in the future. There is no temporal contiguity. If cancer developed soon after having a cigarette, no one would smoke.

The conditioning of *emotional* responses, whether positive or negative, also feeds our beliefs. If we experience nervousness when confronted by a homeless person asking for change, this may lead to a conditioned response that extends to homeless people in general. As a result, to provide consistency with the emotional response we may come to believe that homeless people are threatening or unpleasant. Similarly, conditioned emotional reactions fuel prejudiced beliefs, whether racist, homophobic, sexist, or religious. A conditioned anxiety response may develop in someone who feels nervous or uncomfortable when first in the presence of a woman wearing a niqab. That anxiety may feed into negative beliefs about people who dress in that manner.

Acquiring prejudiced beliefs can also occur much more subtly. Suppose a child is playing with children from a disadvantaged minority group when her parent, who harbors prejudice toward that group, yells at the child and then rushes out and drags her into the house. If this is traumatic for the child, a conditioned emotional response is likely to develop, especially if this is repeated in other similar circumstances. The parent's behavior in this case is the unconditioned stimulus that triggers anxiety, and the children of the target group become the conditioned stimulus. Subsequently, the simple sight or presence of children from that group will elicit a degree of anxiety. At a cognitive level, the child may interpret her anxiety as being *caused* by "those people," and negative and even hostile beliefs about that group grow.

Figure 4-2: A target of discrimination.

Extinguishing conditioned responses and overcoming the beliefs that go with them

Recall the old saying that if you fall off your horse (or motorcycle), you should get right back on it and ride again or else you will become more and more fearful of it. This common-sense advice reflects the fact that such anxiety when left on its own does not simply fade, but can actually increase over time.

We can "undo" classical conditioning. The link between the sound of the bell and the blinking response mentioned earlier can be eliminated if the bell is presented a number of times without the puff of air. Note, however, that there is an important asymmetry with regard to learning and unlearning. It takes much longer to eliminate a conditioned response than it does to establish it in the first place. This is adaptive, of course, for imagine what life would be like if it were otherwise. Suppose that after being attacked by a Rottweiler, resulting in a conditioned fear response to that dog, the same dog ignores you the next day. If this were enough to sever the link between that dog and fear, it would leave you vulnerable to an attack whenever the dog is next in a foul mood.

Psychologists have developed procedures to extinguish fear responses such as, for example, a phobia of driving after having been in a serious car accident. Since such phobias are learned, they can be unlearned. This is done through a process known as *systematic desensitization*. The psychologist establishes with the client a hierarchy of frightening stimuli going from weakest (for example, sitting in a car with the engine off) to strongest (for example, driving on a busy highway). After training the client in a relaxation technique, desensitization begins by pairing the least frightening item in the hierarchy with relaxation a number of times until the anxiety diminishes. The intervention then moves to the next higher stimulus, and continues in this way until thinking about driving on a highway does not produce anxiety. The intervention then moves from imagination to reality, systematically pairing relaxation with actual sitting in the car, then starting the car, then driving a short distance, and eventually driving on a highway. This is an extremely effective method for eliminating the fear response.

Conditioned responses sometimes are spontaneously extinguished through experience. Someone who takes a job on a fishing boat may initially feel terror as the boat pitches about during a storm. If when back on shore, the individual refuses to go out fishing again, a conditioned fear response associated with boats is likely to persist. On the other hand, if reason triumphs over emotion and he goes back to sea, that fear is likely to gradually extinguish with experience.

Social phobias involve intense anxiety in the presence of others that often feeds into such beliefs as "I cannot relate to people" or "no one likes me" or "everyone is against me." When clinical psychologists tackle such problems, they must deal both with the conditioned emotional responses and with the beliefs that have been engendered by them. Phobias often become so potent that they set up self-fulfilling prophecies. The conviction that "I cannot relate to people" increases anxiety when faced with social interactions, thereby confirming the belief.

Classically conditioned compensatory responses

Imagine a person who, when offered heroin by a friend, has always refused it in the belief that using it only once is enough to cause addiction. Finally yielding to persuasion, he tries it and enjoys the experience, and is later relieved to find that he has no compulsion to take it again. He thinks that his prior belief about the powerful addictive nature of heroin was erroneous. With this new confidence, he takes heroin again, and for a second time he does not experience any craving for more. His new belief that he can use the drug without becoming dependent soon traps him, and he ends up an addict.

Our beliefs about addiction are often poorly informed, and rarely are people told about how classical conditioning can trap them. How does addiction come about? Among the many automatic physiological responses that are subject to classical conditioning are those that are associated with drugs. Although we are unaware of it, repeatedly ingesting a drug stimulates the body's neuroendocrine system to secrete chemicals that to some extent counter the primary effects of the drug. This *compensatory response* gradually becomes strong enough that it can completely cancel out the primary effects of the drug.

When someone takes a drug such as heroin for the first time in a quest for pleasure, the emotional result is likely to be positive, but over the course of a few such experiences the compensatory response produced by the neuroendocrine system strengthens to the point that it neutralizes the pleasurable feelings. This pushes the individual to take a higher dosage to obtain the desired "high." Tolerance for the drug is now developing, and this leads down a slippery slope toward addiction.

The compensatory response that neutralizes the pleasure is aversive if unopposed by the drug. It does not cease being produced immediately when one stops taking the drug, and in the absence of the drug, the consequences of the compensatory response are the well-known withdrawal symptoms that addicts strive to avoid. The drug has become compulsory medicine.

This automatic, unlearned compensatory response reacts readily to classical conditioning and is easily conditioned to respond to the surroundings in which the drug is typically taken. Addicts are of course unaware of this process. Their belief is that they simply need to stave off withdrawal symptoms by regularly ingesting the drug. That belief can be deadly. To understand why this is so, consider the effects of morphine on pain. While the administration of morphine brings about a decrease in pain, a compensatory response develops that can be classically conditioned. This is clearly evident in research. If a specific cue (a particular sound, for example) is presented a number of times just prior to each morphine administration, soon, when the cue is presented without the morphine, the compensatory response will occur on its own. Because the response is now unopposed by morphine, the result is *increased* sensitivity to pain.[6] Similarly, insulin administration leads to reduced blood sugar levels, but when a tone is presented on a few occasions just prior to its administration, subsequent presentation of the sound—by itself—triggers an *increase* in blood sugar.[7] Of course, we do not usually encounter sound cues just prior to ingestion of a drug, at least not on a repeated basis, but there are other cues in the environment that are regularly present when a drug is taken that can inadvertently create a conditioned compensatory response.

Alcohol is also associated with a compensatory response. In one study, healthy male social drinkers consumed vodka and tonic in a distinctive setting on only two occasions.[8] Subsequently, *in that same distinctive setting*, they were given a placebo, a drink that looked and tasted like vodka and tonic but contained no alcohol. While one might expect that the drink would have no physiological effect, there indeed was an effect—and it was *opposite* to the effects of alcohol. Alcohol leads to relaxation of the peripheral blood vessels, resulting in warming in the fingers, but ingestion of the placebo triggered a compensatory response which led to decreased finger temperature. Similarly, while heart rate increases after alcohol ingestion, it decreased following consumption of the placebo. Through classical conditioning, the compensatory process was elicited not only by the appearance and taste of the nonalcoholic beverage, but also by the environmental cues that had accompanied the alcoholic drink, such as the distinctive features of the room in which it was consumed.

This brings us to psychologist Shepard Siegel. He was puzzled about why so many overdose deaths of heroin addicts result from dosages that are no different from those they regularly take.[9] He found that the explanation lies in the classical conditioning of the compensatory response. When an addict takes the drug in the same environment day after day, situational cues (such as sitting in a living room chair) become conditioned stimuli for the compensatory process that reduces or neutralizes the drug's effect. Now, when the addict takes the same dose in a different situation, where the usual environmental cues are absent, the conditioned compensatory response is not fully elicited, and so the effects of the drug are now largely unattenuated. A tolerable dose in the usual setting becomes an overdose when taken in other than that setting.[10]

Siegel provided a striking example of this destructive power of the conditioned compensatory responses. A man was being treated with morphine to control severe pain caused by pancreatic cancer. Gradually, tolerance to the drug developed, and the dosage was increased to a high level, administered through four injections a day. Siegel described the outcome:

> The patient stayed in his bedroom (which was dimly lit and contained apparatus necessary for his care) and received injections in this environment. For some reason, after staying in this bedroom for about a month, the patient left his bed and went to the living room (which was brightly lit and different in many ways from the bedroom/sickroom). He was in considerable pain in the living room, and as it was time for his next scheduled morphine administration, he was administered his usual dose of the drug. The patient quickly displayed signs of opiate overdose (constricted pupils, shallow breathing) and died a few hours later.[11]

Because of the significant change in environmental cues, the conditioned compensatory response was not triggered in full, and his usual dosage became an overdose.

It is often assumed that after withdrawal symptoms subside, the addict will forever have a persistent craving for the drug and that there will be a continuing risk of re-addiction. Conditioned reactions can be extinguished, however, and this occurs over time when the drug is no longer taken. A large study was conducted years after a group of heroin-addicted Vietnam War veterans had stopped using narcotics, and contrary to popular belief about heroin addiction only 4 percent reported any craving.[12] Additional research showed that these veterans, who had been dependent on drugs but had successfully withdrawn from them, could occasionally use the drug without becoming re-addicted—again contrary to what people generally believe.[13] This speaks to conditioned compensatory responses once again. After the compensatory response has been extinguished, occasional drug use is not enough to escalate it to a level that will lead to withdrawal symptoms.

The point here is that our bodies learn without our awareness, leaving us with beliefs that make us vulnerable to addictive processes that we mistakenly believe we can control.

Kick the Pop Machine: Operant Conditioning

A second form of automatic learning also involves an association between two events occurring closely together in time, but in this case the first event is the individual's action, which is then followed within a short interval by some desirable ("reinforcing") outcome. Psychologists refer to this is as *operant* conditioning. Pavlov himself recognized the power of operant conditioning to shape a dog's behavior. He wrote,

> You lift the dog's paw, saying "give me your paw," or even "paw," and then give the dog something to eat. After repetition of this procedure the dog gives its paw at these words; it does so without any word of command when it has a keen appetite.[14]

There are all sorts of reinforcers that influence human behavior: food, shelter, sex, money, cars, friendship, status, attention. A baby cries (behavior), and mum comes running (reinforcement). Kick the recalcitrant soft-drink machine (behavior), and a can of cola drops (reinforcement). Reinforced behaviors are more likely to be repeated in future because they work, or at least seem to do so. Just as with classical conditioning, temporal contiguity is important. Too much delay between action and outcome and conditioning will not occur. And as with classical conditioning, stimulus generalization occurs. What you learn with one cola machine will extend to others.

The reinforcement may also come in the form of a reduction of an unpleasant state (e.g. fear, anxiety, or pain). Whatever works to reduce your anxiety—listening to music, praying, having a cup of tea—is reinforced as you begin to calm down, making it more likely that you will repeat the behavior the next time that you feel nervous. Beliefs form that align with your actions. Pray that you will get the job that you have applied for, and when you do you may now believe that it was prayer that was responsible.

Through anxiety reduction, operant conditioning can also strengthen the effects of a classically conditioned fear response. Someone who has developed a fear of Rottweilers (classical conditioning) will experience anxiety the next time a Rottweiler is encountered, but the anxiety will diminish as she walks away from a dog. This avoidance is operantly reinforced by anxiety reduction, making it more likely that the person will keep her distance from such dogs in the future. This in turn makes it unlikely that the classically conditioned fear response will gradually extinguish even through repeated exposure to dogs that do not bite.

Recall the asymmetry mentioned earlier: Conditioning, whether classical or operant, can occur quickly, while it generally takes much longer to "unlearn" an association. As a result, only occasional "reinforcement" of the association is enough to maintain it, and indeed, *intermittent* reinforcement actually produces the most resistance to extinction. Think of it this way: Rover bites you once, and for several weeks you are very chary whenever Rover is nearby. Then, as time passes and Rover does not bite, your anxiety level drops back to normal in the dog's presence. That is, the fear response has gradually extinguished. Now suppose that just as you are becoming relaxed around Rover, he bites you again. Your brain immediately learns that even a long series of uneventful encounters does not mean that Rover will not attack. And now that association between the dog and anxiety will be much less likely to fade away over time.

We regularly employ operant conditioning to influence others—animals and humans—even if we are not aware of it. Parents shape their children's behavior in part through their control over reinforcements. Smile when the child behaves in a desirable manner, withhold access to social media when the child misbehaves, and lend the seventeen-year-old the car only after she has cleaned up her room.

Belief and the power of coincidence

Our learning depends on two events occurring closely together in time, but events very often occur close together simply by chance. Yet, most of the time we do not notice the co-occurrence. A white panel truck passes in the street just after your cell phone has rung. A sparrow flies against your windowpane and falls to the ground just after you put bread in your toaster. A helicopter passes overhead just as you feel a twinge of pain in your hip. As noted earlier, conditioning occurs only when the concurrence of two events has information value.

What we consider to be a "coincidence" is not just any concurrence of two events, but ones that are both unexpected and that seem to have information value, to have some meaning for us.[15] Psychiatrist Carl Jung (1875–1961) was fascinated by coincidences and believed that *meaningful* coincidences occur much more often than can be explained by chance. For one event to "cause" another, Jung said, energy must be expended, but he argued that meaningful coincidences do not involve energy because no causality is involved.[16] Yet, somehow, the two events do not occur just by chance, and there is something tying them together. To account for this, he introduced the concept of *synchronicity*, a sort of framework in nature that somehow ties events together. Yet synchronicity is merely a label and does not explain anything. It is only based on Jung's belief that there must be more to meaningful coincidences then coincidence alone.

But what are *meaningful* coincidences? Meaningfulness is in the eye of the beholder, for something that seems a very meaningful coincidence when it happens to us may seem commonplace when it occurs to someone else. For example, if a brick falls from a building and strikes someone in the crowd below, this does not seem to us to be a meaningful coincidence, for after all, it is likely that someone would be hit. Yet if the brick falls and hits you or your friend on the shoulder, this is a rare and personal event and you may search for meaning. "Why me?" A religious person may interpret this as divine retribution for some earlier transgression.

This is what psychologist Ruma Falk refers to as *egocentric bias*: other people's coincidences do not seem so striking to us.[17] Why should this be so? Suppose that your friend Ann tells you about a strange coincidence that she experienced. A childhood friend with whom she had not spoken for years telephoned out of the blue and said that he was prompted to call because he had been thinking about her father and wondered how he was doing. The next day, Ann learned that her father, who resided back home in her country of origin, had died that same night. Ann of course views the coincidence as meaningful, and believes that more than chance must be involved. Yet because the coincidence evokes no emotion for you, you can consider it dispassionately, and you are not surprised that such an event happened to *some*body. After all, such circumstances can occur just by chance from time to time.

Not all coincidences result from chance, however, and some may have a hidden cause,[18] and we can often imagine various other possibilities that might account for other people's coincidences. It might be a coincidence when you find to your surprise that your former lover is seated next to you on an airplane, but it is at least possible that she is stalking you and has somehow arranged to have a seat next to yours. Of course, paranoid individuals often suspect hidden causes of any meaningful coincidences.

Superstitious conditioning

Operant conditioning occurs when a desired outcome follows shortly after a particular action. You kick the cola machine and a can of pop appears, leaving you to believe that this action was effective. Suppose, however, that the kick had nothing to do with the appearance of the can, and it would have appeared anyway. In such a case, your belief about the effectiveness of the kick is in error.

During the 1940s, psychologist B. F. Skinner studied operant conditioning in pigeons as they learned to adapt to the world around them.[19] Imagine this: a pigeon is in a cage, and in one wall of the cage is a chute through which grain can be presented to the bird. In one of Skinner's experiments, food was delivered on a random time schedule and nothing that the pigeon did affected that.[20] Skinner observed that if the pigeon happened to be doing something specific when the food was delivered, such as standing on one foot, it would subsequently repeat that behavior on a frequent basis, as though that action had caused the food to be produced. Skinner referred to this behavior as *superstitious conditioning*. Three-quarters of his pigeons spontaneously developed various superstitious behaviors. Because the food was being presented at random times, there were other occasions when by coincidence, the same incidental behavior was again reinforced by another delivery of grain.

Despite our relative cognitive prowess, we are similar to pigeons in that we are also subject to superstitious conditioning. Superstitious conditioning is not to be confused with superstition in general. While it is indeed a prime source of superstition, it can occur with other behaviors as well, where no "magical" explanation is assumed.[21] More about this in a later chapter.

Watching Others

Much of our learning occurs vicariously simply through watching other people do things and observing the consequences of their actions. If while traveling abroad you want to use the subway in a major city but are confused by how to get through the turnstile, you watch someone else navigate the system. When you see someone insert a ticket into a slot, pull the ticket out when it emerges from another slot, and then push through the turnstile, you now know what to do. And when you observe that your employer compliments those workers who stay past quitting time in order to complete their day's assignment, this teaches you that you can please her by staying until the work is done. Such *social learning* is in part automatic, but it often involves rational analysis as well. You may even silently verbalize an observed sequence of actions in order to help remember it.

So many of our beliefs are acquired through this kind of social learning that we are probably not even aware of all that we have learned in that manner. For example, although few people have actually thrown a hand grenade, just about everyone has "learned" more or less how to do so by watching war movies. If you faced death as a horde of armed assailants rushed toward you and you discovered a hand grenade lying about, you would likely pull the pin, count to five or so, and throw it at your attackers in the belief that it would explode and prevent them from harming you.

Young children are especially receptive to this kind of observational learning. In general, this is a great benefit, but not all that is learned in this manner is positive. For example, when a young child walking with her mother feels her mother's hand stiffen whenever someone approaches with a dog and then relax again as they put distance between themselves and the dog, the child may automatically learn to be nervous when around dogs, and this can be the seed for both an anxiety reaction and a belief about dogs that extends far beyond childhood. Or suppose that whenever a little Caucasian boy goes to the grocery store with his father, dad always lines up at a counter with a white cashier at checkout time, even if it means waiting longer than at an adjacent counter where the cashier is a person of color. Beliefs about racial and ethnic differences and the seeds of racial prejudice can take root on this basis alone, without a word being spoken.

Read the Book

In addition to learning directly through personal experience, we also learn *intellectually*, by acquiring information from many authoritative sources and employing reason to reach novel conclusions about how the world works. Language provides a powerful means for social transmission of knowledge in the absence of direct experience. Indeed, the majority of the beliefs that each of us holds has been passed down from generation to generation, and this is essential because none of us could possibly have enough time in one lifetime to learn all that we need to know to live successfully. This social transfer provides us with massive amounts of information accumulated over thousands of years, and so we do not have to figure out for ourselves that the motion of the moon causes ocean tides, or that dirty hands may carry germs that cause disease, or that jellyfish are dangerous and should be avoided.

Many of a person's most important beliefs are acquired in early childhood at a time when a combination of unfettered trust and lack of critical acumen render the child like a sponge, eager to soak up new information. Religious beliefs, political beliefs, beliefs about health and illness, and beliefs about how the world works are handed down from parent to child. Whether it is belief in the benefits of dental hygiene, the dangers of the evil eye, the roundness of the earth, or the power of some divinity, the young child lacks the reasoning ability to be able to critically evaluate what is being taught. This leads to the establishment of fundamental "core" beliefs—the earth goes around the sun; a god created the world. These become well entrenched and are often held without question. Of course, many other beliefs are systematically acquired as part of our formal education.

In adult life, we continue to learn through listening to others whose opinions we respect, as well as through sources such as books, newspapers, and television. Yet, as we all know, one person's facts can be another person's fictions, and the sources that we choose to follow and to believe are usually those whose expressed opinions mesh with our own. In this way, our beliefs are strengthened, and it is easy to ignore or discredit other sources with whom we disagree.

You probably believe, as almost everyone does, that American astronauts have walked on the moon. Yet there are those who insist that the moon landings never occurred and that the television broadcasts were faked as part of a massive United States governmental conspiracy. Such a position seems silly, or paranoid, or both, but what evidence do *you* personally possess to persuade dissenting others that the moonwalks occurred? Yes, they have been widely documented in books and television programs, but that is not compelling evidence in and of itself, for lots of nonsense has also been presented as fact by the media at times. Or perhaps you are old enough to remember having watched live on television as Neil Armstrong took his first steps on the moon. That television footage might seem to be good evidence, but on the other hand, you may also have seen—again on television—fictional astronauts being evaporated from the "transporter deck" of the *Starship Enterprise* only to reappear moments later on a planet's surface. As realistic as those scenes might have seemed, you did not mistake them for reality. So how can you be so certain that Neil Armstrong's moonwalk did not take place on a Hollywood soundstage?

Or another example: Although many people in the West view Mao Zedong as a sociopath who callously caused the deaths of 70 million of his compatriots during peacetime, he continues to be revered in China, where few people have any knowledge of his crimes.[22] But how can we be so sure that Mao was responsible for the deaths of millions? For most of us, it is because we have read about it in a book, newspaper, or magazine that we consider reliable, or because we have been taught by educators and others whom we trust. And how is it that most of the Chinese citizenry believes otherwise? Because they too have read books that they consider reliable and have been taught to believe by educators and others whom they trust that Mao was a great man who always worked on behalf of the Chinese people.

Frustrating, isn't it? When it comes right down to it, our beliefs in those moonwalks or in Mao's murderous deeds are based on trust. We trust the reporters, the television networks, the politicians, the historians, and all the others who have confirmed for us that the moonwalks actually happened and that Mao was a mass murderer. The past is the past and we cannot go back in time and observe for ourselves. "Our faith," as William James observed over a century ago, is "faith in someone else's faith, and in the greatest matters this is most often the case."[23]

Not everyone trusts the same sources. We choose whom to believe. For some, particular books, magazines, and television programs are authority enough, while others rely on the credentials, academic or otherwise, of those who wrote the books or magazines and made the programs. As philosopher Elton Trueblood noted in 1942,

> when we rely on authority, we are not guilty of credulity. There is a reason for our reliance. We trust the men and institutions presenting the most reason for being trusted. We must use reason to determine which authority to follow.[24]

It is more and more difficult in our internet culture to discern which sources are reliable. This has become particularly evident in the United States following the 2016 presidential election. Those who are drawn to and depend upon Fox News as their major source of information and analysis are often exposed to quite different interpretations of political events compared with those who rely upon, say, CNN. The confusion grows when prominent politicians, even the president of the United States, label critical and unflattering news reports as "fake news."

EMOTION AND BELIEF

> *The orator persuades by means of his hearers, when they are aroused to emotion by his speech; for the judgments we deliver are not the same when we are influenced by joy or sorrow, love or hate.*
>
> —Aristotle[25]

Learning does not occur in a vacuum. We are not passive receivers of information and we actively seek out information to satisfy our many needs. We may yearn to find meaning in life. We may yearn for a sense of identity. We may yearn for recovery from disease. We may yearn to be in touch with deceased loved ones. We may yearn for information that supports and defends important beliefs.

Beliefs influence emotions

Whether correct or false, our beliefs have a major impact on our emotions,[26] and emotional reactions in a given situation are generally determined by our beliefs about that situation.[27] For example, we may react with anger to an innocent remark because we immediately believe that it was said with sarcasm or malice.

We become most vulnerable to fallacious beliefs when they satisfy important needs and yearnings. Particular beliefs that improve our mood or reduce anxiety are as a result generally very resistant to information that challenges them. Belief in the effectiveness of magical remedies can provide relief from despair, at least for a while, in cases where scientific medicine has been ineffective in battling a serious disease. Religious belief that assures one a happy afterlife can assuage anxiety about mortality or grief following the loss of a loved one.

Emotions influence beliefs

The relationship between belief and emotion works both ways, and our beliefs can be shaped by our emotions. Our emotional reactions serve as an important source of information. Feeling frightened when in a risky situation will amplify the belief that one is in danger. Feeling jealous strengthens the belief that one's relationship is threatened. In a sense then, "feeling is believing" in such cases.[28] Once emotion takes over, as psychologists Gerald Clore and Karen Gasper explain,

> the system no longer operates as a scientist carefully weighing the pros and cons of the belief implied by the emotion. Instead the emotional person acts like a prosecutor or defense lawyer seeking by any means to find evidence for the belief.[29]

We also tend to interpret ambiguous information in such a way that it lines up with our feelings and desires. This is referred to as *motivated cognition*. For example, if it feels good to believe that your nation is fair and honorable, then any information that challenges that belief will produce discomfort, and so, most likely without being aware of it, we either discount the information or look for a way to reinterpret it so that it is consistent with what we want to believe.

Emotions also motivate us to act upon our beliefs. You may believe that you have a responsibility to help the poor, but it may take the emotional reaction elicited by seeing poverty up close to motivate you to turn your beliefs into action.[30]

We acquire our beliefs both through personal experience and by paying attention to what others say, do, or write. Much of our experiential learning is automatic and tied to events that occur closely together, and this leaves us open to making erroneous associations as a result of simple coincidence. And when we learn from others, we trust their accuracy, reliability, and honesty, which leaves us open both to error and to manipulation. It is only through using our intellect, through critical thinking, that we can attempt to separate fact from fiction. It is to that intellectual aspect of the Belief Engine that we now turn.

CHAPTER 5

THINKING AND BELIEVING

A great many people think they are thinking when they are
merely rearranging their prejudices.

—William James

Descartes famously observed, "I think, therefore I am." The converse is also true: *We are; therefore we think.* Indeed, we cannot stop thinking. Try to clear your mind of thought for a few minutes. Except perhaps for advanced meditators, this is all but impossible. We constantly plan; we mull; we ruminate; we churn things over in our minds. Some of our thinking is intuitive: we reach conclusions without really knowing exactly how we reach them. And some of our thinking involves reason and critical analysis: we consider the source of information, whether the information makes logical sense, and whether it is consistent with what we already believe.

THEORY OF MIND

Not only do we think, but we believe that other people think too, and this allows us to make inferences about their feelings and intentions. We are not born with this belief, but it develops quickly during early childhood. Before this can happen, however, one has to learn to distinguish between animate and inanimate objects, and most infants can do this by five months of age. Researchers know this because, by that age, infants show surprise when they see odd movements of inanimate objects but show no such surprise when animate objects move similarly.[1] This distinction leads to viewing animate objects as being capable of both initiating actions and of reacting to events around them, while inanimate objects cannot do so. The growing child builds on this distinction and eventually comes to believe that other animate beings—humans, dogs and cats, and so on—have internal mental processes similar to his own. Psychologists refer to this belief as *theory of mind*.

A cross-cultural study of infants in China, Fiji, and Ecuador revealed that children even as young as eighteen months were able to demonstrate some basic aspects of theory of mind; that is, they could understand another person's perspective of a situation.[2] That research employed a *false-belief test*, in which the young child watched as an adult came into the room and hid a pair of scissors inside a box. After that person left the room, another person entered and took the scissors, and put them in his pocket. He then paused and asked aloud, "Hmm . . . I wonder where they'll look for the scissors." The children reacted to that question by looking toward the box, indicating that they expected the first person to look where he had left the scissors. They apparently understood that that person would have the "false" (that is, erroneous) belief that the scissors were still in the box.

Another study involved identical-looking blindfolds, some of which were "trick" blindfolds that were transparent despite looking opaque.[3] A group of eighteen-month-olds wore the blindfolds for a short period. Half of them were given the normal blindfolds and the rest, the trick ones. The blindfolds were then removed, and the infants were observed while an adult wearing a blindfold placed an object in a specific location. With the blindfolded adult still in the room, a puppet then moved the object to a different location. The infants' eye movements were monitored when the adult removed her blindfold. The findings were clear: the eye movements of those infants who had been given the true blindfold indicated an expectation that the adult would have been unable to see the puppet move the object and so would believe that it would be where she had left it (false belief). However, those who had worn the transparent blindfold looked toward where the object had been moved, apparently reflecting their belief that the adult could see through her blindfold and would have observed the relocation of the object. This demonstrates a rather amazing capacity of these young children to make inferences about what another person has observed, and about how such an observation will alter that person's beliefs. By the time children reach two years of age, they are not only able to predict people's behavior to some degree but are also on their way to some understanding of their motivations as well.[4]

As theory of mind takes root, the developing child more frequently attributes motivations and intentions to others' actions. This is of enormous importance for the development of a mature understanding of the social world, and it would be difficult to function successfully in social networks without being able to make inferences about how other people think, about how they interpret our actions, and about how they are likely to respond. As they grow and learn, young children begin to develop abstract theories about causality, about "what causes what." These ideas develop relatively quickly and increase in accuracy as they are modified in the light of accumulating experience and information.[5]

Theory of mind reflects the evolution of the human brain, distinguishing humans from almost all other members of the animal kingdom. It so powerfully affects our perception of living things that people sometimes attribute human-like motivations and beliefs even to organisms that are neurologically incapable of having them,[6] and at times this is extended even to inanimate objects. Such anthropomorphic thinking can come readily to all of us in some circumstances. Consider this example. Many years ago, I acquired an electronic chess-playing instrument, *Chess Challenger Seven*, consisting of a chessboard with a small keyboard and a digital readout. Using the keyboard, the player entered each move in chess notation, and, after a few moments, *Chess Challenger* responded by indicating a move on the digital screen. This little machine presented an impressive challenge to an average chess player, but a colleague who was an accomplished player scoffed at the idea that an electronic device could offer any serious competition. He offered to demonstrate its weakness and began to play with the device set at its highest level of difficulty. After a few moves, his demeanor began to change, and he started to refer to the device as though it had intention: "I see what it's trying to do here . . ." As time went on, his language became even more personalized: "Look, he tried to trap me here . . ." When I pointed out that he was now referring to the machine as if it were a person, he expressed surprise at his own discourse. Although he ultimately won the match, he came away impressed by the "ability" of the apparatus.

In a similar vein, is it not difficult at times to treat the disembodied voice of your automobile GPS as merely computer-generated words? Have you never felt a small pang of guilt when you failed to follow the voice's instruction and were "admonished" to "make a U-turn as soon as possible"? This is not surprising. As noted earlier, although we learn early in childhood to distinguish animate from inanimate objects, inanimate objects did not until rather recently play chess or tell us which way to turn when driving. Perhaps today's children, growing up with a variety of electronic devices, will in adulthood have quite a different reaction to the commanding voice of the GPS. But will they be able to resist extending theory of mind to the robots that will undoubtedly play a major, human-like role in their lives?

TELEO-FUNCTIONAL REASONING

Young children think of both animate and inanimate objects as existing for some presumed purpose.[7] This is referred to as *teleo-functional reasoning* ("teleo" from the Greek *telos*, meaning "goal").[8] A personal example: While walking through the woods with my son Erik when he was quite young, I pointed to the buds of a particular shrubbery and mentioned that deer like to eat them. Months later while in a different park, he spotted similar shrubs and announced, "There must be deer here." When asked why, he pointed at the shrubbery. In his young mind, the purpose of the shrubbery's existence was to feed the deer, and so there must be deer about.

Adults also lapse at times into such thinking, although when caught doing so they usually struggle to avoid admitting it. For example, physical scientists from top-ranked universities in the United States demonstrated teleo-functional thinking when they were required to make decisions under time pressure that hindered cognitive analysis. They agreed, for example, that "trees produce oxygen so that animals can breathe," and that "germs mutate in order to become drug-resistant."[9] It is also interesting that teleo-functional reasoning becomes more prominent in Alzheimer patients, perhaps as a result of the degradation of their ability to think critically.[10]

DUAL-PROCESS THINKING

Just as we learn about the world both experientially and intellectually, it has long been recognized that thinking takes two analogous forms. That is, we employ a *dual-systems* approach to information-processing. William James referred to these two forms of thinking as *associative thinking* and *true reasoning*, but many psychologists now use the terms *System 1 thinking* and *System 2 thinking*, respectively. *System 1 thinking* refers to experiential, intuitive thought. It developed early in our evolutionary history and is tied to an "old" part of the brain, the limbic system, which underlies our emotional reactions. *System 2 thinking* refers to rational thinking and is related to the frontal lobes, a more recently evolved part of the brain.[11]

SYSTEM 1: EXPERIENTIAL, INTUITIVE THINKING

System 1 thinking is rapid, automatic, nonverbal, and involves little effort. It is intuitive and occurs without any sense of deliberate control. It is often imbued with emotion.[12] We can think of it as based on "experientially acquired knowledge" that comes to mind quickly and without effort.

Nobel Prize–winning psychologist Daniel Kahneman, in his best-selling book *Thinking Fast and Slow*,[13] offers, among others, these examples of System 1 thinking:

- Read the large letters on a billboard.
- Answer to 2 + 2 =?
- Orient to the source of a sudden sound.
- Look at a person's face and recognize that she is angry.

As Kahneman points out, most of these examples, which illustrate "thinking fast," involve involuntary reactions. You cannot *not* read the large letters on a billboard once you glance at it. You cannot *not* know the answer to "What is 2 + 2?" And, even if you voluntarily restrain yourself from turning toward it, you cannot *not* have your attention drawn to a sudden loud noise.

System 1 thinking allows us to carry on well-learned behaviors without conscious attention. For example, consider a long road trip on a super highway. An experienced driver need not pay close attention to all the details of the relatively unchanging roadway. She may be engaged in conversation with a passenger or be lost in daydreaming for much of the trip, and yet stay safely on the road even while occasionally changing lanes and passing other cars. The intuitive System 1 is in charge, but if traffic conditions become more complicated—for example, if one lane is closed off making it necessary to slow down and merge into traffic in the other lane—System 2 thinking will take over.

Our "intuitions" are part of System 1. Intuitions are generally very compelling and can trump rational thought at times, particularly in situations where we lack control and when the outcome is unpredictable. Intuition operates largely out of conscious awareness, and often we are only aware of the final product—an impression, a feeling, a hunch about something—without understanding how it came about.

On the other hand, people learn to rely on intuition in situations where they have considerable knowledge and experience, for an intuitive, non-rational "gut reaction" can provide a rapid and efficient means for processing information.[14] For example, an experienced painter may be able to look around a room and quickly come up with a good estimate of how much paint is needed without the need for measuring the total surface area and then calculating precisely how much paint to buy. An experienced physician, when presented with atypical symptoms, may have a hunch about what is causing them and as result order particular tests that turn out to be very important, tests that a less experienced physician might not consider. Intuitive thinking also underlies creativity, compassion, and aesthetic appreciation and can solve some problems that are beyond our ability to solve through reason.[15]

Intuitions provide for rapid responding that helps us survive. A pedestrian who sees a bus careening toward him while crossing the street has no time to reason about what to do; he intuitively recognizes the danger and his body reacts with a powerful fear response that includes pronounced arousal in the autonomic nervous system, providing a burst of energy to get out of harm's way.

A Basketful of Biases

The intuitive processes associated with System 1 thinking involve heuristics ("rules of thumb") that we use to analyze information when trying to solve problems.[16] The downside of this is that heuristics often introduce biases into our thinking, and this can result in erroneous conclusions that are often resistant to logical analysis.[17] Among the more prominent of these heuristics:

- The *availability heuristic.* Our judgment of the likelihood of an event is biased by how readily we can bring the event to mind. For example, if we are contemplating the dangers of riding a bicycle in the city, we will be more likely to ignore statistics and assess it as being dangerous if a recent fatal bicycle accident is "available" to come to mind.
- The *simulation heuristic.* Our evaluation of the probability of events is influenced by how easily we can imagine them. What is the risk involved

in letting ten-year-old Julie go to the grocery store on her own? We can immediately imagine all sorts of terrible things that might happen, even though they rarely occur, and this biases our assessment.

- The *representativeness heuristic*. This is a bias based on how similar a particular person or event is to a particular category of people. For example, Alice loves reading, wears glasses but not makeup, and has three cats. If you had to decide, is it more likely that she is a schoolteacher or a fashion model? The information is insufficient to make a reasonable assessment, but because her description better fits the stereotype of a schoolteacher than that of a fashion model, you may be likely to assume that she is the former. That is, she seems to be more *representative* of schoolteachers than she is of models.

Apart from these heuristics, there are other biases that can also distort our thinking. These include:

- The *introspection illusion*.[18] This is a cognitive bias based on the belief that we are capable of accurate insight into our mental states and therefore can understand why we think about something as we do. On the other hand, we are likely to consider other people's introspections as unreliable. However, research suggests that our "insights" into our own mental states are based only on inferences that we draw about ourselves, in the same way that we make inferences about other people's mental states based on their actions. In other words, we simply do not have direct access to the workings of our minds.[19]

  This introspection illusion contributes to a belief in free will, for we can quickly produce explanations for our behavior that reflect deliberate choices, even though these explanations often are misplaced. For example, we know that billboards that advertise soft drinks or hamburgers boost sales, and that companies would not advertise in that manner otherwise. However, it is unlikely that anyone enters a fast-food restaurant thinking that she has been influenced by a billboard. That is, we are unaware of or ignore the myriad influences that help determine our behavior even while we think that we are making a free choice.

- The *confirmation bias* ("tunnel vision"). This is the tendency to focus selectively on new information that is consistent with what one already believes, while downplaying the value of information that does not fit. This has been a particular problem in police investigations when a specific individual is suspected of having committed a crime, leading detectives to give more weight to evidence that is consistent with that suspicion and to discount or ignore evidence that points in another direction. This confirmation bias has played an important role in many miscarriages of justice. Consider the example of a man wrongly convicted of the murder of a neighbor girl and then eventually exonerated by new evidence, but only after spending several years in prison.[20] During the investigation, police had found a cigarette butt at the crime scene, but because the prime suspect did not smoke, it was dismissed as being unrelated to the murder. On the other hand, actions on the suspect's part, such as not joining the search for the girl who had gone missing, were taken as a reflection of his culpability.

Hunches Gone Wild

Our intuitions, or "hunches," when backed up by considerable experience, can be remarkably accurate at times, but they can also lead us wildly astray. Sometimes, this can be deadly. Take, for example, what happens when an aircraft pilot becomes confused when unable to see the visual horizon. The instruments may indicate that the aircraft is in a deep dive, but misleading information from the vestibular system in the inner ear may lead to the intuition that it is actually climbing. Going with intuition and ignoring the instruments, the pilot "corrects" for the apparent climb and thereby accentuates the dive. This is what apparently happened on July 16, 1999, when John F. Kennedy Jr. was piloting a small plane on his way to a wedding at Martha's Vineyard with his wife and elder sister as passengers. They never arrived; their airplane crashed into the Atlantic Ocean. The crash was later attributed to pilot error presumably caused by such spatial disorientation.

Hunches gone wild and the Gambler's Fallacy

Over a long number of repetitions of an event, such as rolling dice or tossing a coin, the average of the results moves closer and closer to what is expected on the basis of mathematical theory. For example, if you toss a "fair" coin, you cannot predict how it will land on any given toss, but if it is a fair coin and you toss it a million times, you would be safe in your expectation that heads would come up very close to half of the time. Yet this expectation results in fallacious thinking when not dealing with large numbers. If a fair coin is tossed only twenty times and comes up heads each time, people often intuitively feel that it must soon come up tails in order to balance out. This particular kind of erroneous intuition is known as the *Gambler's Fallacy*. If a fair coin has landed heads twenty times in a row, it makes no rational sense to think that there is now a high probability that it will come up tails because tails are overdue. The coin does not know about probabilities. It has no memory of the earlier tosses, and so the chances of coming up tails on the next toss are unchanged by whatever has happened in the earlier tosses. Yet, even though we are aware that coins or dice or roulette wheels do not have memories, intuition often overwhelms logic and it *feels* as though a particular outcome is overdue.

This fallacy has also been referred to as the *Monte Carlo fallacy* because of what occurred in a celebrated roulette game in a casino in Monte Carlo on August 18, 1913. In roulette, bettors gamble on whether the ball will land on red or black after the wheel is spun. On the occasion in question, the ball fell on black a number of times in succession, and as the succession of blacks increased, gamblers began to shift their bets to red on the assumption that the sequence of blacks must soon come to an end, that red was "overdue." It did eventually land on red, but only after twenty-six spins. In the meantime, millions of dollars were lost by those who had switched to red.

Researchers have found that even regular gamblers—those who gamble twenty hours a week or more—fall prey to the Gambler's Fallacy despite their experience.[21] They are not alone. People working in financial markets are prone to a similar bias, reacting as though continued increases or decreases in the value of stocks must soon lead to a reversal in the trend. Related to this is the fallacy of the *hot hand*. The term derives from basketball, where players and fans alike tend to share the fallacious belief that the likelihood that a player will quickly score again is greater following a successful shot than following a missed shot.[22]

Hunches gone wild and rare events

"Rare" events are not always as rare as we think, and improbable (but not impossible) events are almost certain to occur sooner or later. Consider this: When a woman won the New Jersey lottery twice in a four-month period, the *New York Times* reported that this was a "one-in-17-trillion long shot." Indeed, the odds are one in 17 trillion that a *specific* individual who buys a *single* ticket for each of *precisely two* New Jersey lotteries will win the jackpot each time. Yet, the more appropriate question is "What is the likelihood that *somebody*, out of all the millions of people who buy lottery tickets in the United States, will win a major lottery twice?" In fact, the odds are better than fifty-fifty that there will be a double winner somewhere in the United States during a period of just seven years, and better than one in thirty that there will be a double winner during a four-month period (the time period for the New Jersey woman).[23] These odds contradict the intuition (as well as the poor statistical reasoning reported by the newspaper) that the woman's win was an exceedingly rare event.

Our intuitions about the likelihood of winning a lottery are rarely anywhere close to being accurate. Suppose a million people each buy a ticket for a lottery prize of a million dollars. While everyone recognizes that they are not likely to win, they rarely realize just how unlikely it is because of their lack of experience in dealing with large numbers. However, if a million ping-pong balls were dropped onto a football field, only one of which has one's name on it, and a small mechanical scoop like those in penny arcades were to reach down and pick up one ball at random, the unlikelihood of one's ball being chosen would be much more obvious. Indeed, with odds of one in a million, the probability of winning is the same to five decimal places whether one has a ticket (1/1,000,000, or .000001) or not (.00000)!

Consider another example: Four people sit down to play bridge and deal all the cards out, thirteen to each player. There are 223×10^{25} (223 followed by twenty-five zeroes) different ways in which the cards can be distributed. Now suppose that one player ends up with all the hearts, another with all the diamonds, another with all the clubs, and another with all the spades—a so-called "perfect" bridge deal. Would that not strike you as almost unbelievably rare?

First of all, note that this particular distribution of cards is no rarer than *any other* possible distribution. It is only because it stands out visually from all the others that we see it as extraordinary. That being said, this distribution, just like any other distribution, will not occur very often. It has been calculated that:

> Such an event having once occurred, it should not logically reoccur, even if the entire world population made up in fours and played 120 hands of bridge a day, for another 2,000,000,000,000 years![24]

Nonetheless, several "perfect" bridge hands are reported each year, which has led some statisticians to believe that such reports must be dishonest. But dishonesty is not the explanation. It is the statisticians' intuition that is at fault because it is based on the likelihood of witnessing such a deal from a *randomized* deck. But note that new decks of cards are organized in ascending order by suit.

If the dealer shuffles the new deck twice and happens to interleave all the cards perfectly each time (which magicians refer to as a *Faro shuffle* when done deliberately), then no matter how often the deck is subsequently cut, the dealing will result in a "perfect" deal.[25] Since many bridge clubs begin their games with new decks, the appropriate question then is: "What is the probability that someone will do two perfect shuffles of a new deck?" With millions of bridge games played every year, this does not seem so unlikely.

Hunches gone wild and base rates

We often fail to take base rates into account when evaluating new information, and as a result our intuition can be significantly off-base. For example, when participants in one study were informed that a significant percentage of a particular model of fighter aircraft had crashed during training flights (a fact that led pilots to nickname that aircraft the "widow-maker"), most participants concluded that the aircraft was dangerous and should be grounded.[26] They reached that conclusion without looking for information about the crash rates for *other* fighter aircraft; that is, they neglected the base rate of crashes for fighter aircraft in general. The crash rates for other aircraft were actually quite similar, and, had they sought out that information, they should have been able to conclude that this particular aircraft was not unusually dangerous.

We are even more prone to erroneous conclusions when *low* base rates are involved. The *false-positive paradox* (or *base rate fallacy* as it is sometimes called) arises when the event being examined (for example, heart disease or driver intoxication) occurs with a low frequency ("low base rate"), while at the same time the process used to detect the event has a relatively higher rate of false positives (that is, it indicates a problem when there is none). Consider the following examples: (The stated prevalence rates are those that were used by the researchers.)

> A particular heart disease has a prevalence of 1 in 1000 people. A test to detect this disease has a false positive rate of five percent. Assume that the test diagnoses correctly every person who has the disease. **What is the likelihood that a randomly selected person found to have a positive result actually has cancer?**

Figure 5-1: Base rates and heart disease.

When this question was put to sixty students and staff at Harvard Medical School, more than half responded with an answer of 95 percent, and the average of all responses was 56 percent.[27] Only eleven people responded with the correct answer, which is a little under 2 percent. Of course, that seems very counterintuitive. To understand it, suppose that everyone in a city of one million people is tested. We would expect 1/1,000 of them, that is, 1,000 people, to have the disease. But because of the 5 percent false-positive rate, 5 percent of the million, or 50,000, will receive an erroneous diagnosis. Then, of the 51,000 cases diagnosed, only 1,000 (about 2 percent) actually have the disease.

Another example: Think about this for a moment.

Suppose that one percent of women who undergo mammograms actually have breast cancer, and that the mammogram correctly detects cancer 80 percent of the time. However, there is a false-positive rate of 10 percent: that is, 10 percent of cancer-free women will have positive results on the mammogram. Now, a woman is picked at random and she undergoes a mammogram and the reading is positive. Given this information, **what is the likelihood that she has breast cancer?**

Figure 5-2: Base rates and breast cancer.

The correct answer is 7.6 percent, yet ninety-five of one hundred physicians in a research study estimated the probability to be ten times higher, about 75 percent.[28] Again, to understand this, suppose that one million women undergo mammograms. According to the above example, 1 percent of them, 10,000, actually have cancer, and 80 percent of those, or 8,000, will receive that diagnosis. On the other hand, 10 percent of the 990,000 cancer-free women, that is, 99,000, will receive the cancer diagnosis despite being cancer-free. In total, then, 8000 + 99,000 = 107,000 will receive a cancer diagnosis, but only 8,000/107,000, or 7.6 percent, will actually have the disease.

And one last example:

Suppose that five percent of the time, sober drivers are incorrectly assessed as being intoxicated, but the breathalyzer never fails to detect a truly intoxicated person. Suppose further that only one in 1000 drivers is intoxicated. Now imagine that the police stop a driver at random and carry out a breathalyzer test and it indicates intoxication. **What is the probability that the person is actually intoxicated?**

Figure 5-3: Base rates and intoxication.

Perhaps by now you are not surprised to learn that the probability is only .02.[29] (Begin with 1000 drivers, only one of whom is intoxicated. Of the 999 sober drivers, 5 percent of them, or 50, will be incorrectly assessed as intoxicated. Thus, of the 51 drivers who failed a breathalyzer test, only one of them, or 2 percent (.02 when expressed as a probability) is actually intoxicated.

Hunches gone wild when on unfamiliar turf

An experienced carpenter's estimate of how much lumber is needed to build a deck may prove quite accurate. An experienced physician's intuition about what is causing a rash may be spot on. On the other hand, intuitions about things with which we have little experience are often wildly off. Consider this example from psychologist Ray Hyman: Imagine taking a sheet of ordinary typing paper and folding it in two.[30]

Now fold it again. And once again, for a total of fifty times. (This has to be only a thought experiment, for it will very quickly become physically impossible to continue to fold the paper.) The question is this: How thick will the folded paper be after 50 folds? If you were to place it on the floor, would the top of

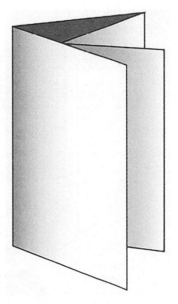

Figure 5-4: Fold a paper fifty times.

the pile reach the top of your desk? Or perhaps the ceiling? The roof of the building? What does your intuition tell you? When I ask this of my students, almost never does anyone suggest that the pile would extend even as high as the ceiling, and many students laugh at any suggestion that it would reach that high.

Here we are dealing with a question with which most people have no experience. The surprising answer is that it would stretch more than 93,000,000 miles—beyond the sun! This is so counterintuitive that, although it is relatively easy to show through calculation that this is so, many people have difficulty even then in accepting the logical conclusion.

Or consider the so-called *Monty Hall problem*: Imagine that you are a participant in a television game show and you have won the right to pick one of three doors. You have been told that behind each door is a prize that will be yours to keep. Behind one of the doors is a brand-new automobile, behind another is a new microwave oven, and behind the third is a roll of toilet paper. You choose door one, but before it is opened the television host offers you a chance to change your choice. Before you respond, he opens one of the two other doors—always the one that has the lesser of the two prizes. Suppose for example that he has opened door two, exposing the microwave oven. From a probability point of view, does it make any sense to change your choice to door three?

Figure 5-5: Monty Hall, Let's make a deal.

Intuitively, it seems to make no sense to do so, for it would seem like there is a fifty-fifty chance that the car is behind door one or door three. When this puzzle was first presented on an internet forum frequented by professional statisticians and psychologists, that was the initial, off-the-top-of-the-head conclusion from many people. It was interesting to observe the arguments that developed over the course of a week, as one after the other capitulated and agreed that one should indeed make the switch.

But why switch? Here's the thing: when you made your choice (door one), the probability was one-third that you had chosen the door with the car, and two-thirds that it was behind one of the other two doors (two or three). After the host opens one of those doors (two, for example) and it does not have the car (for he must open the door corresponding to the lesser of the two prizes), the probability is still one-third that the car is behind door one and two-thirds that the car is behind either door two or door three, but now door two is open, and you know that it is not there. That means that the probability is now two-thirds that the car is behind door three. So of course you should switch your choice. This is a striking example of how badly our intuition can mislead even those with advanced knowledge of statistics and probability.

Hunches gone wild and dread risks

Intuition can be particularly misleading where *dread risks* are involved. A dread risk involves an event that is very unlikely but that carries extremely negative consequences should it occur. The fear of the possible consequence, such as harm to your child, produces an emotional response that puts System 1 thinking into the driver's seat. As a result, our intuitions divert us from employing System 2 and making a reasoned assessment.

In our evaluation of risk, we are more readily influenced by an event that takes a number of lives all at once than by situations where larger numbers of people are killed, but individually and over a longer time period.[31] This situation is exemplified by what happened following the 9/11 attacks on New York's World Trade Center. Researchers examined the extent to which the resulting dread of flying led to decreased air travel and increased automobile travel (which in reality involves more risk than air travel). During the three months following the terrorist attack, the automobile death rate in United States increased significantly,[32] which was interpreted as reflecting efforts to minimize flying because of a greater perceived risk.

SYSTEM 2: RATIONAL PROCESSING

Intuitions employing System 1 thinking can be useful when making decisions in familiar situations. Yet, as we have seen, they can be highly misleading in novel situations despite how compelling they might seem. If we do not want to live life by the seat of our pants, we need to turn more often to System 2 rational processing, which is vital for most problem-solving. However, we have to learn how to reason. We are not born with logic but have to acquire it.

System 2 thinking is conscious, deliberative and largely verbal. While it is superior to System 1 in terms of problem-solving, understanding cause-effect relations, and planning, it is relatively slow and limited in resources. It requires our attention and it focuses on one hypothesis at a time, for it is not able to take into account all possible hypotheses at once.

In *Thinking Fast and Slow*, Kahneman offers a number of examples of System 2 thinking, the "thinking slow" of his title, including the following:

- Focus on the voice of a particular person in a crowded and noisy room.
- Look for a woman with white hair.
- Search memory to identify a surprising sound.
- Check the validity of a complex logical argument.

System 2 processing involves effort, often considerable effort, and when people tire of the effort they may fall back on the hunches or impressions provided by System 1.[33] Of course, System 2 thinking can take into account the products of the experiential System 1; you can examine your hunch to see whether it "makes sense." However, as noted earlier, intuitions are often difficult to resist or modify, and a strong "hunch" can often overwhelm the products of careful reasoning.

Yet System 2 has its own pitfalls, and even when we do our best to think critically and rationally, we are vulnerable to error. Among the traps of faulty logic are *belief bias*, *abductive reasoning*, and *enthymematic reasoning*.

Belief bias

An important source of error that interferes with logical problem-solving is what psychologist Keith Stanovich refers to as *belief bias*—basing acceptance or rejection of an argument's conclusion on its "believability" rather than on its logical validity.[34] This bias is the result of beliefs that we already hold, and thus we have difficulty evaluating conclusions that conflict with what we think we already know about the world.[35] That is, we *project* beliefs that we already have onto new information under consideration. Consider this example of how prior belief can lead us into illogic:

- Premise 1: All living things need water to survive;
- Premise 2: Roses need water to survive;
- Therefore: Roses are living things.

Is the conclusion logically valid? You may be surprised to learn that 70 percent of university students who were given this problem thought so and deemed the conclusion logically correct.[36] It is not, of course. Although it happens to be true, the conclusion is not *logically* valid. This becomes obvious when we consider this logical equivalent of the above example:

- Premise 1: All human beings need food in order to survive;
- Premise 2: Cows need food in order to survive;
- Therefore: Cows are human beings.

Of course, no one will mistake this conclusion about cows as being logically sound. But why did all those students make the mistake with the roses? They were distracted from good logic by the fact that the conclusion, that roses are living things, happens to be true. No one makes that mistake with the second example, given that the conclusion is obviously false. The lesson is that we should not judge the quality of our logic simply on the basis of the correctness of the conclusion that we have reached.

This tendency to automatically insert prior knowledge—for example, that roses are living things—biases our problem-solving and interferes with logical analysis. In everyday life, this predisposes us toward seeing connections among events that are in line with our expectations, even when the connections are not there. This can be a serious problem for researchers as well, leading them erroneously to perceive trends in their data that are in line with their expectations.

Abductive reasoning

This kind of reasoning—sometimes referred to as *inference to the best explanation*—as a source of error in logic was studied in depth by philosopher C. S. Peirce.[37] It occurs when we are confronted by some sort of surprising fact, such as "the cows have all died, and we cannot find any physical reason for their deaths." However, if Ellen, who is suspected of being a witch, had put a curse on the cattle, then we would expect them to die. Since they did die, that suggests that Ellen really did put a curse on them.

Thus, this kind of reasoning has this form:

- A surprising fact, F, is observed (e.g., all the cows have mysteriously died);
- But if P (the proposition that Ellen put a curse on the cattle) were true, F would be expected.
- Hence, in light of F, there is reason to suspect that P is true, that Ellen put a curse on the cattle.

The conclusion is not logically sound, for there is no actual evidence to support the belief that Ellen put a curse on the cattle.

Despite the risk of error, abductive reasoning can sometimes lead to correct conclusions in the absence of any other information, and for that reason it is an important component of medical diagnosis. Physicians tend to go with whatever hypothesis best explains a patient's symptoms. It also shows up in scientific thinking. For example, in the early 1800s, astronomers discovered that the orbit of Uranus, the farthest planet in the then-known solar system, departed from what was predicted by Newton's theory of gravitation. Either Newton's theory was wrong, which seemed unlikely given its success over the previous two centuries, or something else was causing the departure. If there were another as yet undiscovered planet in the solar system, this would explain the observations. This abductive reasoning led to the search for and the eventual discovery of Neptune.[38]

Enthymematic reasoning

An *enthymeme* is an argument in which an unstated premise plays an important part. Philosopher Nicholas Rescher points out that much of our problem-solving is enthymematic in form, and when the unstated premises are in error, our conclusions will be in error too.[39] For example, suppose that we conclude that our friend Ralph will be in favor of gun control because he is a liberal intellectual. Consider the implicit argument involved here:

- Ralph is a liberal intellectual.
- Therefore, Ralph will support gun control.

This conclusion is based on the unstated assumption that all liberal intellectuals support gun control. Since this is unlikely to be true, the reasoning is faulty, whether or not the conclusion is correct in Ralph's case.

Whether we rely most on intuition or on reason or a combination of the two, it is important to remember the biases that lie in wait to trip us up. As a result, even those who pride themselves on subjecting their beliefs to reason can fall into error.

TWO KINDS OF BELIEF SYSTEMS

People do not subject all information to the same degree of logical analysis. Many people may be skeptical about manufacturers' claims for their products or take politicians' pronouncements with a grain of salt, and yet not submit beliefs of a religious or supernatural nature to critical analysis. Consider two stories:

- I returned home one night late in the evening, lit the fireplace in the living room, and sat down to read the newspaper. I was alone in the house, but a few minutes later, something strange happened. I heard a clatter in another room and ran to investigate. To my amazement there was a cow in my kitchen!
- I returned home one night late in the evening, lit the fireplace in the living room, and sat down to read the newspaper. I was alone in the house, but a few minutes later, something strange happened. The room suddenly became very chilly, the fire dimmed inexplicably, and to my amazement I saw a strange glow hovering above the old wing chair in which my late grandfather used to sit while smoking his pipe.

The first of these stories reliably elicits a ripple of laughter when presented as part of a lecture. Even though there is nothing impossible about the story's content, listeners immediately consider it to be implausible. On the other hand, the second story invariably produces a hushed reaction. Ears perk up. Some listeners are eager for more details, while skeptics—always a minority, it seems—often challenge the account and suggest logical explanations. No one smirks.

These reactions reflect differences in how people treat stories that involve implausible but "normal" events and those that suggest a supernatural element. For many people, a story that touches on supernatural belief escapes logical scrutiny. This granting of a "free pass," this exception from critical analysis, is rooted in childhood. Children are encouraged to apply "common-sense" logic to information and beliefs relating to the everyday world, but in many families and many societies, supernatural and religious claims are usually exempted from such scrutiny. Psychologist Jerome Frank concluded that as a result most people acquire two separate belief systems, each with different criteria.[40] The first of these he labelled the *scientific-humanist belief system*, governed by logic and critical thinking, and the second, the *transcendental belief system*, in which logic and critical thinking are supplanted by faith and interpretation of personal experience. Many religious parents, not to mention religious leaders, promote faith over reason when it comes to religious matters, and as a consequence belief in what would otherwise appear unbelievable and illogical is considered a mark of one's devotion. In the words of St. Augustine (340–430 CE.):

> Faith is to believe what you do not yet see; the reward of this faith is to see what you believe.[41] ... Therefore, seek not to understand that thou mayest believe, but believe that thou mayest understand.[42]

Moreover, in some religious communities, the mere questioning of religious dogma is considered to be blasphemous, and any scrutiny is likely to elicit guilt, which then motivates a person to cease questioning and to reaffirm the belief. As a consequence, religious beliefs are largely impervious to disconfirming evidence.

It is difficult to escape the development of a transcendental belief system even if brought up outside religion, for childhood stories are filled with ghosts and other imaginary creatures that defy logic. As a result, even if we do not believe in ghosts, we may feel uncomfortable or even a little frightened while walking through a graveyard late at night. Consider this example: On one occasion when my son was small, he and his friends demanded a ghost story. Instead of going to look for a book of ghost stories, I made one up from whole cloth. To my surprise, as I was making it up, I experienced a strong shiver down my spine. I was scaring myself with my own fiction! This is the legacy of having been frightened by ghost stories in childhood.

SYSTEMS 1 AND 2 WORKING TOGETHER

Both intuition and reason are important in our day-to-day lives, and most of the time we fluidly switch back and forth between these two systems as needed. Yet reason often fails us, when we are frightened, disoriented, ill, sleep-deprived, or in a highly emotional state.[43] That is when our thinking typically becomes more non-analytical, concrete, and action-oriented, all of which are attributes of System 1.[44] Even though thinking that occurs in a highly emotional state may *feel* more valid, such confidence is often unjustified.

There are significant individual differences in the extent to which people rely upon System 1 (experiential) or System 2 (rational) processing of information, and these differences appear to be quite stable.[45] Because of these differences in information-processing styles, people will interpret events, especially ambiguous events, in different ways. Suppose for example that a highly "experiential" individual and a highly "rational" individual encounter a strange light while walking through a graveyard at night. To the former, this may suggest a ghost, and that individual may "see" and remember something very ghostlike; whereas, the other individual simply dismisses the odd light, although unexplained, as something that presumably has a normal explanation. In this way, the meaning that is attached to an ambiguous stimulus varies with the degree to which a person is experientially oriented.[46]

Sometimes we become aware of a strong conflict between System 1 and System 2 thinking. For example, a person who has a dread of high places may "know" logically that there is no danger in taking an elevator to the top of a high building. System 1 signals danger, while System 2 indicates that all is safe and there is really nothing to worry about.[47] Yet challenging the fear by forcing oneself into an elevator can result in such distress that the fear is significantly strengthened, even though all the while the individual recognizes intellectually that there is nothing to fear.

THINKING ABOUT UNCERTAINTY

Life is filled with uncertainties. In response, we often think in terms of probabilities. How likely is it that it will rain tomorrow? Or that the economy will tank next year? Or that our team will win the championship? Or that global warming will ruin our lives?

One way to think about probabilities is in terms of relative frequencies. If a jar contains one hundred jelly beans of which only twenty are red, then the relative frequency of red jelly beans is 20/100. If you were to close your eyes and pick one at random, we would say that the *probability* of picking a red jelly bean is 20/100, or 0.2.

That is straightforward enough, but what does that have to do with the likelihood that your team will win the championship or that the economy will tank? Such questions are not like dealing with jelly beans in a jar; in such cases, we cannot examine relative frequencies. In this case, we are dealing with *subjective* probabilities. That is, we are using numbers to communicate our confidence that something will or will not happen. If I tell you that I think the probability that Julie and Harry will marry is 0.2, I am essentially saying that it is as likely that they will marry in my opinion as it is that I would pick a red jelly bean from that jar at random.

By five or six years of age, children can predict which of two events is most likely to occur based on relative frequencies. Researchers wanted to know whether such predictions are intuitive or whether they are rational conclusions based on having been taught to understand simple arithmetic at that age. In considering that question, they assessed people from two preliterate indigenous Mayan groups in Guatemala and compared them to Mayan school children, as well as to Italian adults, in terms of the ability to make basic probabilistic evaluations.[48] The preliterate groups were important because, lacking literacy and any formal education, they had had no opportunity to have been taught about mathematical probability.

The experiment was quite straightforward. In one of the tests, two containers full of tokens were described. One container was said to have a higher proportion of red tokens, and the other a lower proportion but a higher *total* number of red tokens. They were asked from which container it would be more likely to draw a red token with your eyes closed. Other tests required modifying their predictions based on new evidence or combining probabilities in more complicated ways. What is interesting is that the preliterate groups performed just as well as the school children and the Italian adults. This points to the possibility that we are actually born with some very basic ability to make probabilistic evaluations based on relative frequencies. And it seems that we are not alone: even the great apes—chimpanzees, gorillas, and others—show some ability in this regard.[49]

Yet, despite whatever rudimentary ability we may be born with, our brains are not set up to accumulate the information required to readily assess relative frequencies and probabilities. The heart of the problem is tied to the way our brains make associations, for recall that we are predisposed to a connection between two things that occur close together in time. In the same way, we remember significant pairings of circumstances (e.g., we remember that a member of a particular ethnic group was rude to us) but do not automatically keep track of non-pairings (e.g., when a member of that same ethnic group was polite). We cannot evaluate the possible relationship between two variables (e.g., between a particular ethnic group and rudeness) without information about both pairings and non-pairings.

Perhaps this inability to keep track of non-pairings explains why the development of the mathematics of probability occurred so late in mathematical history. Sophisticated forms of mathematics, including compound-interest tables and methods for solving quadratic equations and even some cubic equations, were developed in ancient Babylon. The ancient Greeks were proficient in geometry, and, during the Middle Ages, Islamic scholars made significant advances in number theory and algebra. Yet during all that time, even though games of chance were common, it appears not to have occurred to anyone to study the probabilities that underlie such games. It was only in the sixteenth century that Italian mathematician Geralamo Cardano (1501–1576) established the basic concepts of probability that govern games of chance. Cardano's work, marking the beginning of the development of probability theory, came eons after humans were able to solve quadratic equations.

Finding patterns: What *goes with* what?

We constantly find patterns in the information received through our senses, and at times perceive patterns that are not actually there. We also readily find patterns in *temporal* events. For example, children quickly learn that the distant strains of particular music herald the arrival of the ice-cream truck. Observations of temporal patterns become part of common lore that is passed down through the generations. For example, someone notes on several occasions that a red sky at sundown is followed by a lovely day, and a red sky at sunrise is often followed by a storm. Even though no one is likely to conclude that a red sky at night *causes* the next day to be a lovely day, the adage "Red sky at night, sailors' delight; red sky in morning, sailors take warning" can be taken as a guide to forecasting the weather. The problem is that unless we keep careful records, we cannot be sure that a meaningful association actually exists between red skies and the oncoming weather. Perhaps half the time that we see a red sky at night, the weather is stormy rather than calm the next day, but we do not take note of it.

People often used to say that "it always rains after you wash your car." This did not mean anyone believed that washing a car actually *causes* it to rain. The saying likely came to mind only when someone was inconvenienced by rain just after taking the trouble to wash the car. A proper evaluation would involve keeping track not only of how many times it rained later in the day after washing the car but also of how often it rained on days when you had *not* washed the car, and how many times you washed the car and it did not rain. Suppose we collect these data, making entries daily for four hundred days in a row:

	Rain	No rain
Washed car	(20)	80
Did not wash car	60	240

Figure 5-6: Does it usually rain after washing the car?

What we will remember is that a whole lot of times (twenty), it rained soon after we had washed the car. True enough. Yet, had we recorded *all* of this data, we would have seen that most of the time (eighty of the hundred times we washed the car), it did not rain. And the frequency of rain is the same when we washed the car ($20/100 = 1/5$) and when we did not ($60/300 = 1/5$). Clearly, there is no relationship between washing the car and the onset of rain, but we are automatically influenced by the coincidence of the two events, *washing the car* and *rain*. Our brains do not take notice of when it rains and we did *not* recently wash the car, or when we wash the car and it does not rain. As a result, we come to believe in an association between washing the car and rain. This false belief is referred to as an *illusory correlation*.

Psychological research has demonstrated the difficulty that people have in judging relationships between events such as this. For example, in one study, participants were presented with a series of trials relating to cloud-seeding, the practice of dropping crystals into clouds with the goal of causing rain.[50] On each trial, it was indicated whether cloud-seeding had occurred and whether this was followed by rain soon afterward. Although there was no statistical association between seeding and rain, the participants concluded that cloud-seeding had indeed led to rain. Why would they reach this erroneous conclusion? Because, once again, it was a matter of being overly influenced by the trials when seeding and rain occurred together, and less influenced by the other pairings: seeding/no rain; no seeding/rain; no seeding/no rain.

Another example: While I was a passenger with a friend driving along an expressway in Montréal, another driver made an erratic move, cutting us off. My friend shouted in exasperation, "What an idiot! It's either a woman driver, or a man with a hat!" After pointing out the sexist nature of his comment, I asked, "But what's this about a man with a hat?" He responded that men with hats are typically bad drivers, a claim that was new to me. In any case, he then made a point of catching up with the offending driver, and to my surprise, it was indeed a man with a hat! But that is not the end of the story. For some time afterward, each time that I observed someone driving poorly, I couldn't help but look to see whether the driver was a man with a hat. And from time to time that indeed was the case. Had I not known about illusory correlations, this association would have been automatically reinforced on an intermittent basis. And, as noted earlier, intermittent reinforcement strengthens associations to the extent that they become difficult to overcome.

Figure 5-7: Reckless man behind the wheel (Shutterstock / zoff).

Finding patterns: What *causes* what?

Our mental lives are built around causal relationships: drink water and thirst is slaked; sit by a fireplace and feel warm; stroke the family cat and it purrs; step on the gas pedal and the car accelerates. Our brains have evolved to make rapid judgments of what *causes* what based on our perception of what *follows* what, and these judgments often occur before there is time for rational processing to take place. Much of the time when an event (B) follows another event (A), it is because B was caused by A. Touch a hot stove, feel pain, and we correctly come to believe that the hot stove *caused* the pain. Eat seafood and later feel sick, and we readily assume that the seafood made us ill. While our assessments of causality are accurate much of the time, they can also be wildly wrong.

The observation that one event follows another is not a sufficient basis for assuming that one caused the other, and when we make that assumption, without any evidence of an actual causal link, we are falling into the logical fallacy of *post hoc, ergo propter hoc* ("after this, therefore because of this"). For example: A new factory begins production and a number of people in the vicinity fall ill. Some may jump to the conclusion, without any other supporting evidence, that something associated with the factory is causing the illness. Or a number of refugees move to one's town, and not long after the petty-theft rate increases. Again, without any supporting evidence, some will blame the refugees for the increase in crime. (The reader will note that these are examples of abductive reasoning.)

Our motivation to find causes is so powerful that it makes it difficult to comprehend significant events for which we cannot determine the cause. For example, scientists describe the almost unfathomable complexity of the universe from the subatomic to the intergalactic level. But what nags at many people is: "How did it start? Where did it come from?" For many, the need to find causality is satisfied by belief in a god or gods, even though this should—but does not—bring up another question: How did the god or gods come into being?

Both religion and science can respond to our need for understanding: Your loved one died as a result of a streptococcus infection. Your loved one died because God called her to be at his side. Lightning bolts are sent by angry gods to punish us, or lightning bolts are discharges of electrons that have accumulated in the atmosphere. Which explanation is more satisfying depends on the individual's belief system.

***

Logic does not come to us naturally. We have to acquire it. And even when we do, logic can be trumped by intuition and emotion or sullied by the various heuristics and cognitive biases that lie as pitfalls waiting for us to tumble into them. Intuition, on the other hand, serves us well in some situations but can lead us terribly astray in others.

Perceiving, remembering, learning, thinking—these all play important roles in the shaping and maintenance of our beliefs. But just what are beliefs and what determines if and when they change? It is to these questions that we now turn.

PART III

BELIEF STABILITY AND CHANGE

Beliefs define how we see the world and act within it; without them, there would be no plots to behead soldiers, no war, no economic crises and no racism. There would also be no cathedrals, no nature reserves, no science and no art. Whatever beliefs you hold, it's hard to imagine life without them. Beliefs, more than anything else, are what make us human.

—Graham Lawton[1]

To understand why people do the things they do, we must understand the beliefs that underlie their actions. The chapters in this section focus on how beliefs are formed and cultivated, building on the processes of perception, memory, learning, thinking, and feeling; on how some beliefs resist change while others submit to contradictory information; and on how beliefs can motivate people to achieve difficult goals, even to the extent of sacrificing their own lives in the effort.

CHAPTER 6

IN THE GARDEN OF BELIEF

When people will not weed their own minds, they are apt to be overrun by nettles.
—Horace Walpole, 4th Earl of Orford (1717–1797)[1]

A belief system is somewhat like a family flower garden. Wander through it and you spot the rose bushes that have been there since you were a child; you have no idea who planted them. On the other hand, you remember that your mother planted those rhododendrons over in the corner. And look, there are the perennials that you put in when you were a teenager; you recall choosing them from the seed catalogue. A few dandelions thrive among the flowers, unwanted but so difficult to eradicate. And near the fence are some flowers that grew from seeds that blew over from the neighbor's garden.

Like the flowers in the garden, many of our beliefs were sown early in our lives, back before we can remember. Others were planted by our parents, teachers, or peers, or acquired through personal experience. And then there are the weeds—sexist beliefs, for example—that were planted long ago and, despite efforts to eradicate them, keep coming to the surface from time to time.

Virtually everyone shares many of our beliefs: Living things depend on oxygen, water, and nourishment to survive; infants need care; the sun will rise tomorrow in the east. But we all hold some beliefs that are contrary to those of many other people. Some believe that executing convicted murderers will deter others, while many believe that capital punishment is not a deterrent and view it as barbaric. Large numbers of people believe that human activity is bringing about catastrophic climate change, while others reject this out of hand.

And then there are beliefs about other possible realities. Billions of people around the world worship their god or gods daily, while only a minority are atheists. Most people believe that paranormal phenomena, such as extrasensory perception and precognition, are real, while most scientists strongly doubt that such phenomena exist. And, taught by their trusted elders, millions of children fervently believe that there is an ageless old man at the North Pole who, with the help of elves and a flying sled pulled by reindeer, flies around the world during one special night of the year delivering toys to deserving children everywhere.

Of course, we do not like to think of ourselves as foolish, irrational, or easily gulled, and yet each of us is likely to hold some beliefs that are simply wrong. The stickler is that they seem to us just as reasonable as any of our other beliefs. Even though we may roll our eyes at other people's apparent credulity when they espouse beliefs that for us defy reason, we generally remain confident about the wisdom of our own. Satirist Ambrose Bierce (1842–1914) wryly defined "absurdity" as "a statement of belief manifestly inconsistent with one's own opinion."[2] *Theirs* are absurd, *ours* are justified by reason or experience.

WHAT IS A BELIEF?

Although various influences that affect belief have already been addressed, it is time to ask about the actual meaning of the term. Just what are beliefs? They are certainly not "things." They cannot be located by a brain scan or detected by measuring neural impulses. They leave no neurological traces to be uncovered through autopsy. Indeed, a moment's reflection reveals just how vague the concept is. *Belief* can mean a variety of things depending on the context. For example:

> Trust: *I believe what you tell me.*
> Self-confidence: *Believe in yourself, or no one will believe in you.*
> Faith: *For God so loved the world that he gave his only begotten Son, that whosoever believeth in him shall not perish, but have everlasting life.*
> Confidence in one's senses: *Seeing is believing.*
> Confidence in others' abilities: *I believe that the Maple Leafs will win the Stanley Cup.*
> Optimism: *I believe that everything will work out all right.*
> Certainty: *Paris is the capital of France. I believe that.*
> Less than certainty: *You are looking for a post-box? I believe there is one just down the street.*

Belief and *believe* adapt themselves well in everyday usage. We read these various references without confusion because we understand their meanings within the context. Yet finding a precise definition has been a vexing matter, one with which philosophers have wrestled for millennia. That problem has proven so intractable that many philosophers now consider *belief* to be useless as a scientific or philosophical concept and no more helpful in understanding how our minds/brains work than were the four humors of Hippocratic medicine in understanding how our bodies function.[3] Yet, other philosophers argue that the concept of belief still has some usefulness, and although it may not be meaningful from a neuroscientific perspective, it helps us to think about and communicate about people's intentions.[4]

Notwithstanding the difficulties with definition, social psychologists consider a belief to involve both *content* and *conviction*. The content consists of mental representations of experiences that come about in various ways.[5] This can be through direct experience (e.g., lemons are sour), through reading, listening to someone, or reasoning (e.g., if you attempt a spacewalk without a space suit, you will die).[6] *Conviction* refers to one's certainty about the belief. The level of conviction (psychologists refer to this as a *subjective probability estimate*) can vary. Some beliefs are held with the fullest of confidence, while others are associated with some degree of uncertainty.[7] You may be certain that Paris is the capital of France but not completely sure that Quito is the capital of Ecuador. In the absence of at least some conviction, there is no belief.[8] For example, we have zero conviction that Santa, unicorns, or Batman exist, even though we all possess mental content that allows us to describe each of them in detail.

In other words, beliefs reflect our conviction that the information we have about something is correct or that some event or situation has actually occurred or will occur.[9] The degree of conviction can change over time; it can be influenced by emotion and can vary with the situation.[10] For example, an atheist might be surprised that a childhood belief in a deity emerges unexpectedly when in a situation of great peril. (This brings to mind a colleague who, when asked whether he believed in God, replied, "Only when I'm scared.")

It may be surprising to learn that, because of the way our brains work, it is actually easier to come to believe in something than it is to disbelieve. To understand why, it is first necessary to understand that we process new information in two stages, one involving comprehension and the other evaluation.[11] This two-stage processing was recognized in the seventeenth century by philosophers René Descartes (1596–1650) and Baruch Spinoza (1632–1677).[12]

Descartes, in distinguishing between comprehending something and believing it to be true, argued that new information is first understood and then, in a separate second step, evaluated and mentally marked (in modern neuroscience parlance, "tagged") in the brain as either true or false. His viewpoint, often referred to as the "Cartesian" viewpoint, corresponds with what would seem to be common sense: first we take in information and then we actively decide whether it is correct. You are informed that *Supersuds* is the best cleanser, but your brain does not tag the message as true or false until you evaluate it a moment later.

Figure 6-1: René Descartes (1596–1650).

Spinoza, on the other hand, maintained that information cannot be comprehended without first tentatively accepting it to be true.[13] He argued that evaluation occurs only *after* that acceptance. If that were true, then the message that *Supersuds* is the best cleanser is immediately tagged as true. Only a moment later do you consider whether that information makes sense in terms of what you already know, and then possibly tag it as false. Thus, to Spinoza, believing occurs automatically, while disbelieving is a more complex process.

Modern empirical research shows that Spinoza was correct. As counterintuitive as this may seem, there is abundant and converging evidence from different research domains that we automatically believe new information *before* we assess it in terms of its credibility or assess its consistency with beliefs that we already hold.[14] Acceptance is the brain's *default bias*,[15] an immediate and automatic reaction that occurs before we have any time to think about it. Only at the second stage is truth evaluated, resulting in confirmation or rejection.

What this means is that even though you know that Elvis is dead, were someone to announce that he is alive and sitting in a restaurant at the end of the mall, that announcement will be tagged "true" the instant it reaches your brain, even before you are consciously aware of it. But a second later, as the information comes into consciousness, the evaluation stage begins and only then—even

Figure 6-2: Baruch Spinoza
(1632–1677).

though the delay is a mere blip—are you aware of your conscious assessment that the information is false.

Note that failure to pass through the second stage would leave the unvetted information tagged as true.[16] Such a failure can occur when an individual's cognitive resources are overwhelmed by fatigue, by illness, or by physical or emotional distress. Moreover, the prefrontal cortex, where we do our "thinking," is critical for evaluating truth or falseness, and someone who has suffered damage in this region will typically experience a "doubt deficit," a decreased ability to detect false information. Such an individual is as a result more vulnerable to con artists and religious fundamentalism.[17]

The ability to evaluate the falseness of a statement is a specific skill, and it is one of the last language-processing skills to develop in a child.[18] If Descartes were correct, children should develop the ability to deny the truth of a statement at the same time that they are able to recognize it as true, but they do not. Until children are old enough to make denial assessments, they are especially suggestible and uncritical.

Thus, we are compelled to believe what we are told, initially, just as we are "compelled" to believe what we see.[19] As psychologist Daniel Gilbert eloquently states:

> Findings from a multitude of research literatures converge on a single point: People are credulous creatures who find it very easy to believe and very difficult to doubt. In fact, believing is so easy, and perhaps so inevitable, that it may be more like involuntary comprehension than it is like rational assessment.[20]

PRIMITIVE BELIEFS

Some beliefs are so basic that we hold them to be true with such confidence that we never question them. Most often, these are beliefs that are shared by everyone—for example, a belief that unsupported objects fall to the ground, or that people cannot survive without food. Psychologist Milton Rokeach referred to these as *primitive beliefs*,[21] using "primitive" in the sense of "fundamental." New information is screened for compatibility against such beliefs and, if inconsistent with them, may be ignored or even rejected. As a result, someone with a primitive belief that there is life after death is more likely to believe reports of a ghost than would someone without it. Primitive beliefs are typically difficult to modify, for they are essentially articles of faith and not usually open to question.

BELIEF, KNOWLEDGE, AND EVIDENCE

> *To learn to distinguish the possible from the implausible is to develop one part of wisdom; it leads as well as anything can to true belief. But wisdom's better part bids us remain aware that we have less than the whole truth about us, even in those matters we understand best. Such awareness can never be misplaced since "the whole truth" about anything is but a fanciful ideal.*
>
> —Philosophers W. V. Quine and J. S. Ullian[22]

An entire branch of philosophy, epistemology, is devoted to the study of belief and knowledge. To philosophers, knowledge is more than just correct belief, and until relatively recently, philosophers defined knowledge just as Plato did some 2,500 years ago.[23] In order for us to "know" something, Plato said:

- It first of all must be true;
- Not only must it be true, but we must accept (believe) that it is true;
- We must have sufficient evidence to justify accepting it to be true.

Thus, according to this Platonic approach, we cannot "know" something if it is not true. If ghosts do not exist, then people who believe in them do not have "knowledge" of their existence. Even if ghosts exist and one believes that they exist, one still does not *know* that they exist without sufficient evidence.

The Platonic requirement for sufficient evidence means that knowledge cannot be equated with belief, even if the belief turns out to be correct. Consider this example: in 1915, Alfred Wegener, a German scientist, proposed his theory of continental drift based on the then flabbergasting notion that the earth's continents float about on the surface of a liquid core. As much as he believed this to be true, Wegener could not produce sufficient evidence, and so his ideas were generally rejected or ignored by other scientists. Even though his belief in continental drift turned out to be correct, and even though he believed it to be so, Wegener did not have knowledge, in the Platonic sense, at the time. It was only many years later that accumulating evidence demonstrated the truth of his claim. Today, continental drift is part of scientific knowledge; in 1915, it was only his belief.

The Platonic tripartite approach to defining knowledge as "true justified belief" was challenged and shown to be inadequate in the mid-twentieth century by philosopher Edmund Gettier, who persuasively argued that an individual may have sufficient justification for believing in a proposition that is false, but, even though the three conditions could be satisfied—truth, belief, justification—she would not possess knowledge.[24] For example, suppose that Veronica believes that "Bob is in the garage." Now, it is true that Bob is in the garage (satisfying the first stipulation), and Veronica believes that he is there (second stipulation). Her justification for her belief is that she can see Bob through the garage window. From her point of view, she has satisfactory evidence. However, it is not Bob whom she sees, but his brother Ray, who was also in the garage, whom she mistakes for Bob. In this situation, she is correct, but Gettier would argue that she does not have sufficient justification for this to be considered knowledge.

Psychologists are not much concerned with the finer points of what constitutes knowledge, but they are particularly concerned with Plato's third point, the question of sufficient evidence. Since evidence is at the root of modern science, the question about sufficiency is at the heart of many scientific disputes. In antiquity, Greek astronomer Claudius Ptolemy (100–170 CE) declared that the sun moved around the earth, a viewpoint that jibed with everyday perception and one that was echoed in Christian dogma. Indeed, Ptolemaic, geocentric belief remained unchallenged for many centuries. Such dogma was not sufficient evidence for Nicolaus Copernicus (1473–1543), who carefully observed the movements of the planets and declared that the geocentric model of the solar system was untenable. Nevertheless, Copernicus lacked sufficient empirical evidence to support his theory. It was Galileo who subsequently produced that evidence.

Even if we extol the virtues of critical thinking and pride ourselves on being rational, many of our most important beliefs are not verifiable in any practical sense, and very often our only "evidence" is based on the pronouncements of authorities.

BELIEF AND THE IMPERCEPTIBLES

Alice laughed. "There's no use trying," she said. "One can't believe impossible things."

"I daresay you haven't had much practice," said the Queen. "When I was your age, I always did it for half-an-hour a day. Why, sometimes I've believed as many as six impossible things before breakfast."

—Lewis Carroll

Figure 6-3: Queen of Hearts (Shutterstock / Pushkin).

It is one thing to believe in the existence of things that we can directly perceive, such as trees, dogs, and airplanes. It is quite another to believe, as we all do, in the many things that we cannot perceive at all. Microbes, atoms, radiation, radio waves—even though their existence was unknown during most of recorded history, we all now believe that they are real. Who has seen the wind? We feel its pressure against our faces and we have all seen leaves swirling and napkins propelled from picnic tables. While we attribute this to the invisible wind, it was only in 1738 that physicist Daniel Bernoulli published his book *Hydrodynamica*, in which he described the air as being composed of molecules of matter bouncing against one another. When these molecules are in more or less sustained motion in a particular direction, this becomes our invisible "wind."

We come to believe in many imperceptibles in childhood. As a young child listening to my parents' large, old-fashioned radio, I believed at first that tiny people lived inside and did the talking and sang the songs. My parents explained in so many words that this was a preposterous idea and that the voices and music were actually carried through the air from hundreds of miles away by "radio waves." Their explanation seemed no less preposterous to me at the time than my own did to them, but I accepted it because "they knew a lot of things."

Figure 6-4: An old-fashioned radio.

Consider another imperceptible force: Let go of an object and it falls to the ground. Why does it do so? We say that it falls because of gravity. How do we know there is gravity? Because objects fall. This is circular reasoning. For most of us, gravity is simply a label, not an explanation. Gravity is actually an extremely complex concept and does much more than make things fall. Every object has mass, and gravity is associated with mass. Each of us exerts our own gravitational force on everything around us, including the planet beneath our feet. The reason that we fall to the ground when knocked over rather than the earth being pulled up to hit us in the head is because the earth's mass, and therefore its corresponding gravitational force, is huge compared to our own.

We only think of gravity as something that causes unsupported objects to fall *down* because that is all that we ever experience. However, imagine that you know nothing about gravity or our planet, and you observe the earth from some distance through a very powerful telescope. Suppose as well that what we earthlings consider to be north is at the top of the globe from your perspective. As you watch, you note that when a postal worker in Tuktoyaktuk on the shore of the Arctic Ocean lets go of a parcel, it quickly moves *downward* to the globe, but when a worker in Ushuaia at the tip of South America loses his grip on a screwdriver, it immediately moves *upward* until it touches the globe. You further observe that when a tour guide in the Galapagos, at the equator, lets go of her clipboard, it quickly moves *sideways to the right* until it contacts the globe, while at the equator on the other side of the world, in Libreville, Gabon, an egg rolls off a table and then immediately moves *sideways to the left* until it too is in contact with the globe. This is the reality: objects do not "fall" because they are unsupported; they are pulled toward the earth by the invisible force that we call gravity.

Throughout history, people have tried to explain this invisible attraction in various ways. Aristotle believed that objects fell to the ground because their natural place was at the center of the earth, which he also believed to be the center of the universe. Newton considered gravity to be a force that pulled objects toward each other; he was able to show that this force is proportional to the product of the masses and inversely proportional to the square of the distance between them. Einstein, on the other hand, viewed gravity not as a force but as the result of the curvature of space-time due to an uneven distribution of mass/energy.

The label "gravity" is enough for most of us, but even then we do not always apply the label correctly. For example, why do the occupants of the International Space Station float about in their cabin? Most people answer without hesitation that this is because there is no gravity in space, but they are mistaken. The earth's gravitational force at the International Space Station is actually about 90 percent of what it is here on the ground, and if there were no gravity at the space station there would be nothing to keep it from hurtling away into outer space. So why do the astronauts float? It is because they are actually falling. While that seems counterintuitive, it is because the space station moves so quickly in its orbit around the earth (17,500 mph) that despite continually falling toward the floor of the cabin, the astronauts never reach it, for it is falling just as quickly. As a result, they appear to float.

While we feel the effects of gravity on our bodies, many other imperceptible forces do not affect us directly at all. Watch as two magnets pull themselves toward each other. We cannot see or feel the force between them, but we are content to label what we observe as being due to magnetism. We also believe in atoms and molecules and germs, even though we see no direct evidence for them. And many people believe in other imperceptibles, such as mental telepathy, precognition, and invisible spirits. Why should we believe in molecules and magnetic fields but reject telepathy? Once more, it is not only a question of sufficient evidence but of evidence that is sufficiently persuasive to the authorities upon whom we rely.

BELIEF AS PROCESS

Does a belief exist when you are not thinking about it? Psychological research indicates that many beliefs are dynamic productions that come into existence just at the moment that we consider them. If asked at a different time or in different circumstances, we may access various other bits of information and come up with a different estimate of likelihood.[25]

By way of analogy, imagine listening to a musician playing a song or a raconteur telling a story. We never think of what we hear as something fixed, something that was stored inside the performer's brain waiting to spring forth fully formed and immutable on demand. Instead, we know that it is forged in the moment and, although obviously based in prior learning, it is influenced by the present situation. Thus, the rendering will vary somewhat from one situation to the next, depending in part on the reactions of the audience. Similarly, a belief can vary somewhat from situation to situation and from time to time. It is our belief of the moment. This does not mean that beliefs vary willy-nilly. Important beliefs generally show considerable stability.

We can create new beliefs spontaneously. For example, suppose that you are asked whether an octopus is able to live on land, away from the sea. It is unlikely that you have ever considered this question before, and yet you can instantly formulate a belief based on a combination of other knowledge and logic. This ability to generate new beliefs rapidly and hold them with great conviction often serves us well, but it also leaves us vulnerable to error when misperception and misinterpretation come into play.

BELIEF AS ANTICIPATION

Another way to think about beliefs is in terms of expectancy. From this perspective, when you say that you believe that the Number 9 bus stops at the Westdale Plaza, this means that if you were to ride the Number 9 bus, you would expect it to stop at that plaza. If you believe that someone has slipped poison into your wine, you will not drink it (unless you have a death wish). And if you believe that planting a bomb in a public place is the only way to help win freedom for your people, you are more likely to do so than if you lack that belief. In each case, there is an expectancy—if I do *this*, then *that* is likely to follow.

Philosopher Susan Sterrett describes beliefs in terms of anticipatory *schemas*.[26] These are schemas about what causes what, what follows what, and what will happen if I do this or that. If we see a dog and a fish both swimming in a pool of water, our beliefs, our anticipatory schemas, indicate that, taken out of the water, the fish will die but the dog will not. Violation of anticipation is disorienting. If your toaster popped toast into the air and it remained suspended without any visible means of support, you would be unlikely to go off to work content that "the law of gravity was suspended in my kitchen this morning." Instead, you would be strongly motivated to find an explanation. Was someone playing a trick? Was the toast being held up by invisible threads?

Because of their anticipatory nature, beliefs can bring about both intentional behavioral actions and involuntary physiological reactions. If you believe that wearing a seatbelt will protect you in the event of an accident (or that you may get a traffic ticket if you do not wear it), you are likely to wear it each time you drive. If you believe that you have just seen a ghost, your heart may race and your palms may sweat; in this case, the belief has triggered an unintentional physiological response.

The anticipatory nature of beliefs is also important on a social level. Sterrett points out that if a number of people believe that their bank will run out of money in the near future, this shared belief will lead to a run on the bank, turning the expectation into a self-fulfilling prophecy.

As Sterrett writes,

> beliefs can affect not only our decisions and our verbal behavior, but beliefs also affect perception (at times even literally "blind" us to some fact or other), influence where our attention becomes focused, make us weak-kneed, make us blush, or make our hearts race.[27]

BELIEF AS FEELING

> *When the intensity of emotional conviction subsides, a man who is in the habit of reasoning will search for logical grounds in favor of the belief which he finds in himself.*
> —Bertrand Russell[28]

Content and conviction: those two key features of belief can influence one's emotions and be influenced by them. Experiencing anxiety when thinking about an event often leads to overestimating the likelihood of the event. For example, if you are walking through the woods late at night with a friend, and the friend wonders aloud whether there are bears about, the anxiety that this question triggers can result in increased conviction that bears are lurking nearby. The thought that there may be bears nearby in turn increases anxiety, which then leads to more thinking about the danger posed by bears. Cognition and emotion are caught in a feedback loop.

There is sometimes a disconnect between our emotions and what we would like our beliefs to be. You may logically conclude that gay marriage should be enshrined as a legal right, and yet, because of your socialization and conditioning history, you may have a negative emotional reaction to the news that two male colleagues are about to marry. You may not like your own reaction, and you may even try to pretend it is not there. Yet some beliefs are so strongly intertwined with emotion that emotion trumps logic. For example, your sixteen-year-old son was due home at ten p.m. and it is now eleven. Your logic tells you that he has likely lost track of time and will be home soon, but, because of emotion, you come to believe that something bad has happened to him.

Philosopher Tamar Gendler coined the term *alief* to describe a sort of partial belief in which a particular situation elicits emotional and behavioral responses that are at odds with what one believes to be true. For example, if you stand on the glass platform high up on Toronto's CN Tower, or walk along the glass cliff at the Grand Canyon, you know intellectually that you are safe, but the intuition of System 1 tells you otherwise. Or you may believe that air travel is very safe and yet feel panicky as you board an aircraft.

The emotional aspect associated with many beliefs has not escaped attention. Back in the nineteenth century, William James wrote that "In its inner nature, belief or the sense of reality, is a sort of feeling more allied to the emotions than anything else."[29] And another preeminent psychologist, in the early twentieth century, William McDougall, stated, "I feel sure, then, that those are right who have classed belief as an emotion. . . . But if so, what kind of an emotion is it?"[30]

Today, psychologists do not consider belief to be an emotion, but it is clear that belief and emotion mutually influence each other.

THE FEELING OF KNOWING

Memory researchers point out that a remarkable characteristic of human memory is "knowledge of its own knowledge."[31] You *know* whether you know which city is the capital of Uzbekistan, even if you cannot think of it at the moment. You *know* whether you know the rules pertaining to offsides in hockey.

Neurologist Robert A. Burton suggests that the "feeling of knowing" is a primary emotion, like fear and anger.[32] He describes this feeling as involuntary, and not based on the possession of actual knowledge. In other words, we can have a strong feeling that we know something, even if we do not.

Devout Hindus might experience this powerful feeling of knowing with regard to their belief in the existence of Ganesh, the god with the head of an elephant, just as Christians might experience an emotional sense of certainty with regard to their belief in the reality of Jesus Christ. Of course, such a strong feeling of knowing bolsters the conviction that the belief is correct.

Burton suggests that this feeling of knowing is likely linked to a specific region of the brain and hypothesizes that:

Despite how certainty feels, it is neither a conscious choice nor even a thought process. Certainty and similar states of "knowing what we know" arise out of involuntary brain mechanisms that, like love or anger, function independently of reason.[33]

He suggests that it may eventually be possible to elicit this feeling of knowing directly through neural stimulation, just as it was demonstrated many years ago that déjà vu can be elicited by stimulating a particular region of the brain.[34] Burton, again:

the feelings of knowing, correctness, conviction, and certainty aren't deliberate conclusions and conscious choices. They are mental sensations that happen to us.[35]

Intellectual knowledge and its emotional concomitants can in certain circumstances become disconnected. Think about the many common experiences where we experience the feeling of knowing something without being aware of how we have come to know it. You have returned to the city where you grew up years ago and you cannot remember the street of your favorite delicatessen. Yet, as you drive in the vicinity, you suddenly have a strong feeling that you should turn left at the next corner, and then right. To your surprise, there it is. We often refer to this as an intuition or a hunch, and of course we realize that it depends on past learning of which we are not consciously aware.

The feeling of knowing is powerful, and at times we can be absolutely certain that we know something, such as a name, even though we cannot remember it at the moment. (Recall the discussion of the tip-of-the-tongue phenomenon in chapter 3.) At other times, the feeling of knowing is missing when it should be present. Think, for example, of an obsessive-compulsive behavior such as checking the door to see if it is locked just after having locked it. When I was a teenager, I worked in a small-town lumber yard each afternoon after school, and when work ended at six p.m., I would leave with the manager, and then wait and watch each time as he first locked the door, took two steps, walked back to check to see that the door was locked, and then walked five steps. . . . He always repeated this procedure three times, which made no sense to me at the time. Despite *knowing* at a cognitive level that the door was securely locked, the *feeling* of knowing, that sense of certainty, was lacking, and this produced a degree of anxiety that could only be reduced by checking the door again—several times.

In addition to the tip-of-the-tongue phenomenon in which one "knows" that one knows something, Burton points to *blindsight* and *Cotard's syndrome* as two other examples of a disconnect between a strong feeling of knowing and actual knowledge. Blindsight occurs in individuals in whom the visual processing region of the brain (the occipital cortex) has been destroyed by disease or injury. Thus, while the rest of the visual system remains intact, the individual is bereft of any *conscious* awareness of visual stimulation. When undergoing visual testing and asked to indicate when a light is flashed in various parts of the visual field, the individual can respond correctly even while insisting that the responses are simply guesses. This ability to respond correctly without being aware of having seen anything comes about because some nerves coming from the retina bypass the (now damaged) visual cortex and go directly to parts of the brain associated with automatic reflexes. Thus, while the conscious part of the brain is in the dark (so to speak), other parts of the brain are aware and can trigger appropriate responses that are subsequently interpreted by the conscious mind as only being guesses. And how surprising it is to the individual when told that all of the "guesses" were correct given that the feeling of knowing is absent.

Cotard's syndrome results from a particular kind of neurological damage, although it can also occur in the context of certain psychotic states. It is sometimes referred to as the "walking corpse" syndrome, for the individual is overwhelmed by the deluded belief that he is actually dead, or that part of his body is decaying. Imagine one's emotional distress: You look in the mirror and see your face, but do not recognize it. The feeling of knowing is absent. If that is not you in the mirror, who is it? And what happened to you? The disconnect between the part of the brain responsible for facial recognition and the part of the brain that produces the emotional response of recognition is a major factor in leading some individuals to the belief that they must be dead.

Another relatively rare condition, *Capgras syndrome* (sometimes referred to as the *illusion des sosies*, or illusion of doubles), also involves a disconnect between perception and belief. In this case, the individual clearly recognizes all the attributes of another person—"yes, she looks identical to my sister"—but nonetheless believes that that person is an imposter, an imposter who looks exactly like and sounds exactly like the person in question. Again, there is a disconnect between the part of the brain responsible for facial recognition and the region that produces the emotional response of recognition. On a cognitive level, everything would indicate to the individual that this is her sister, but the normal, expected emotional reaction (a strong feeling of recognition) that would occur in the presence of one's sister is absent. How can one make sense of this? The feeling of knowing is missing. "She looks and sounds and acts like my sister, but I have no feeling of actual recognition, and so she must be an imposter."

So, given that our cognitions can be disassociated from the emotions that usually accompany them, we can at times have cognitions that are correct but do not "feel" correct, while at other times we might experience the feeling of knowing in the absence of any corresponding cognitions. This may also account for mystical experiences in which the individual is overwhelmed by a powerful sense of "knowing."

BELIEFS AS SOCIAL CONSTRUCTIONS

In recent decades, what has become known as the postmodernist movement developed in reaction against the scientific belief that there are universal laws governing nature and against scientists' focus on objective evidence as the arbiter of truth. From the postmodernist perspective, groups and societies *construct* their beliefs about everyday reality, and these beliefs are then reinforced by people's interpretations of their experiences.[36] In other words, reality is whatever we perceive and imagine it to be. While postmodernism has had significant influence in literature, art, architecture, and the humanities, its implicit opposition to the notion of scientific objectivity and evidence has made it unwelcome in the halls of science.

SOCIALLY SHARED BELIEFS

Humans are naturally gregarious, and each one of us belongs to various groups that are defined to a large degree by a set of common beliefs that distinguish members from nonmembers.[37] Think of the shared beliefs of an environmental group, a political group, or a victim-support group. Perceptions and interpretations of reality are influenced by these beliefs. If everyone in the group believes in witches, we too may come to interpret strange events in terms of witchcraft.

Socially shared beliefs endure across generations, even when there are deliberate societal efforts to expunge a particular belief. For the better part of a century the Soviet Union not only discouraged but also attempted to eliminate religion, considering it to be superstition. Yet, following the breakup of the

Soviet Union, there was a strong resurgence of organized religion both in Russia and other former Soviet republics. And in Western society, belief in ghosts and other supernatural manifestations is widespread despite the fact that almost all scientists discount such beliefs. Although such beliefs are never formally taught in the school system, they are transmitted from generation to generation and remain extremely resistant to change.

Someone who deviates from central and important group beliefs risks being excluded from the group, and failure to accept important shared beliefs may be viewed as a threat to the group's well-being. The beliefs of socialists and communists in the United States during the McCarthy era, of dissidents in modern China, of atheists in Christian-dominated societies, of "infidels" in Islamic countries, and of suffragettes in the early twentieth century were considered a threat to society and were met by social pressure, retribution, ostracism, incarceration, or even death. Thus, pressure to conform deters most people from expressing ideas that go against important shared beliefs.

Shared political and religious orientations influence the acceptance or rejection of beliefs rooted in scientific evidence. Recent research carried out in the United States has found that political conservatism and religiosity both independently predict lack of confidence in or outright rejection of scientific data. However, such rejection is not across the board but varies with the subject matter.[38] Climate-change skepticism is consistently predicted by political conservatism, but, on the other hand, skepticism about the safety and value of vaccinations is consistently predicted by religiosity. And skepticism about the safety of genetically modified foods is not related either to political or religious conservatism but rather to low confidence in science in general, something which in turn is, not surprisingly, associated with religious conservatism.

BELIEFS AND CONFLICT

Among the beliefs inculcated early in a child's life are beliefs about other groups, nations, and races.[39] Indeed, much of intergroup conflict and violence is based on religious, ethnic, or national group identity and upon beliefs that have been handed down sometimes across centuries. Enduring conflicts are often rooted in shared historical beliefs that feed intergroup enmity and an "us-versus-them" perspective. As noted in chapter 1, this is a breeding ground for conflict and violence. Five types of core collective beliefs significantly influence intergroup conflicts:[40]

Superiority: The belief that members of one's group are in some way superior to members of the other group. Sometimes the belief has a theological basis, where one's own religion is viewed as the only true religion and all others are considered pagan or even diabolical. The Nazis' belief in Aryan superiority fueled their efforts to conquer the world.

Injustice: A particularly powerful motivator is the belief that one's group has been significantly wronged by another group and that this injustice needs to be avenged. There are many examples. Recall the Battle of the Boyne and the Battle of Kosovo Polje discussed earlier.

Vulnerability: The belief that one's group is vulnerable to harm from the opposing group. For example, Israelis and Palestinians feel themselves to be particularly vulnerable to harm from each other, with the result that disputes over resources and territory are viewed as issues of basic survival.

Distrust: The belief on each side that the leaders and members of the opposing group are untrustworthy and out to deceive renders conflict very difficult to resolve. This belief is often fed by beliefs in injustice and vulnerability.

Helplessness: A belief in collective helplessness can inhibit a group from defending itself against an oppressor. Black South Africans under apartheid shared such a belief, which discouraged rebellion against their white masters.

When such beliefs are deeply entrenched, resolution of intergroup conflict is unlikely to be achieved on the basis of logic and rationality alone. Negotiated settlements usually have little to offer in terms of salving collective feelings of injustice or invulnerability or distrust. Each new generation grows up being indoctrinated with the collective belief and the conflict carries on.

MIRROR-IMAGE BELIEFS

When the Cold War was at its peak in the 1960s, the world lived under the threat of nuclear Armageddon. It was during that time that American psychologist Urie Bronfenbrenner visited the Soviet Union. He found a strong similarity between the views that Soviet citizens held about the United States and the views that American citizens held about the Soviet Union. He concluded that "the Russians' distorted picture of us was curiously similar to our view of them—a mirror image."[41] Soviets and Americans alike saw the other country as the warmonger. Each saw the other's government as exploiting and deceiving its people. Each believed the mass of people on the other side was not sympathetic to its government, and each believed that the leaders of the other side could not be trusted. Each felt the other side was all too ready to risk total war. Mirror-image beliefs are self-sustaining, leading each side to act in a manner that, in Bronfenbrenner's words, "confirms and enhances the fear of the other to the point that even deliberate efforts to reverse the process are reinterpreted as evidence of confirmation."[42] Again, such beliefs render conflict resolution based solely on rational analysis unlikely to succeed.

VALUES

Beliefs typically align with an individual's values. These are abstract notions that encompass everything a group believes to be good, moral, ethically acceptable, and socially desirable,[43] and they serve as guiding principles in people's lives.[44] For example, both freedom and equality are important values for most people in democratic societies. Among other things, they influence beliefs about how wealth should be distributed. Freedom implies the right to earn as much income as you want, while equality implies that the state has a duty to tax your wealth and distribute some of it to those with less. Rokeach analyzed the writings of a number of well-known authors from across the political spectrum and found that social democrats and moderate liberals valued both freedom and equality highly, while conservatives valued freedom more highly than equality.[45] The writings of left-wing writers favored equality more than freedom, while Adolf Hitler's writings suggested that he considered neither freedom nor equality to be important. Analysis of the speeches made by British members of Parliament and United States senators revealed a similar pattern with regard to the relationship of values to a liberal or conservative worldview.[46]

Some values are of such importance and have such influence on our beliefs that they are referred to as *sacred* values. In this case, *sacred* refers not specifically to religion, even though many such values are religious in nature,[47] but rather to values that a community considers to be absolute and of such significance that they must not be compromised, watered down, or negotiated.[48] They relate to moral norms, the sanctity of human life, the right to justice, central aspects of national or ethnic identities, fundamental religious beliefs, and even the environment. For example, suppose a company has to choose between protecting the environment or increasing company profits. People for whom protection of the environment has become a sacred value will strive to prevent environmental protection from being negotiated away and will react with moral outrage at any trade-off.[49]

External threat to a group can lead to secular concerns being transformed into sacred values that trump concern for individual rewards and costs.[50] For example, Iran's insistence in recent years on developing its nuclear energy capabilities, which would also provide the ability to produce nuclear weapons, has being strongly opposed by most Western nations. This has transformed the quest to acquire nuclear energy capability into a sacred value rooted in national pride for many Iranians.[51] Once secular issues become sacralized in this way, conflicts between groups become much more difficult to resolve. High external threat to a group often enhances the power of sacred values by integrating them with religious belief, making the conflict even more difficult to manage or resolve.[52]

IDEOLOGY

An *ideology* is an integrated and coherent set of beliefs and values shared by members of a group that provides a common framework for interpreting society and the world and defines how the world *should* be.[53] Ideologies define important goals, as well as the methods that are morally appropriate for achieving those goals.[54] We often think of ideologies in terms of political worldviews such as fascism, conservatism, socialism, or liberalism.[55] For example, a conservative ideology is likely to involve advocating limited government, strengthening traditional norms relating to family values, and promoting capitalism and free enterprise. Yet, as was noted in the discussion of terrorism, *religious* ideology can also have powerful effects on the world in which we live.

FUNCTIONS OF BELIEF

Beliefs, whether idiosyncratic to an individual or shared by groups, play a vital role in helping us to survive in a complex and ever-changing environment. They serve several important functions:

Beliefs motivate and guide our actions

Without beliefs to guide us, daily life would be chaos, for rather than acting on the basis of past experience and knowledge, we would have to approach every situation as though it were a novel one. Our beliefs provide a cognitive roadmap that corresponds more or less accurately to the world in which we live. Beliefs can push us into action: a smoker who comes to believe that smoking leads to lung cancer is likely to be motivated to give up smoking. Beliefs can motivate us to persist at difficult tasks: we believe that if we practice enough, we will be able to play the trumpet; that if we study enough, we will graduate; that if we work enough, we will succeed; that if we take the medicine, our health will improve. Without such beliefs, an individual may abandon important goals and sink into feelings of helplessness.

Some beliefs help keep us safe: Don't drink river water because it might carry disease; wear your seatbelt because it will help protect you in the case of an accident; get regular exercise because it is good for your health. Other beliefs can lead us into danger: Belief that naturopathic remedies cure cancer; belief that you can drive home safely even though you are intoxicated; or belief that the risk of infection from unprotected sex is minimal.

Beliefs help us to understand our world and provide meaning and purpose

Beliefs explain the world to us and, whether rooted in reality or not, make it seem more predictable: The road is slippery because there is water on it. I am feeling tired because I did not have enough sleep. I did not get the promotion because management discriminates against my ethnic group. Harry became an alcoholic because he is weak-willed.

Beliefs also provide a framework, a structure, a sense of purpose for our lives. Why are we here? What happens when we die? What does the future hold? Is there some way to improve our lot in society? How did human beings originate—through evolution over billions of years from microorganisms living in the sea, or created out of nothing by a supreme deity? The structure provided by the belief system provides answers to such questions, and we are generally more at ease and more content when the world about us seems to make sense. (Recall the discussion of teleo-functional reasoning in chapter 4.)

Transcendental beliefs such as the belief that worthy souls go to heaven can have powerful positive effects for those searching for meaning in life, or facing death, or grieving the loss of a loved one. Because belief in transcendental reality offers us respite, comfort, and salvation, it tantalizes us with what philosopher Paul Kurtz referred to as the *transcendental temptation.*[56]

Beliefs offer relief from anxiety

While transcendental beliefs serve to reduce existential anxiety, other beliefs reduce anxiety in moments of danger and grant us peace of mind in times of uncertainty.[57] For example, "The search party will be looking for us by now and we will be rescued."

Psychological research has demonstrated a widely shared *belief in a just world*, that is, a belief that our world is basically fair and that our actions lead to appropriate and predictable outcomes.[58] Thus, if we "do the right thing"—wear the seatbelt, get the exercise, obey the law—we will minimize our risks. This can lead to partially blaming victims for their plight: "She was badly injured in a car accident, but she was not wearing a seatbelt." The unspoken subtext is, "I always wear a seatbelt, so what happened to her is not a particular threat to me."

Fallacious positive beliefs can serve people well at times. Belief in the power of a magical amulet, for example, may allow a person to calm down enough to be able to choose effective action to deal with a crisis, although the amulet will be given the credit. Of course, false beliefs can also at times rob us of peace of mind, for if we believe that there are enemies everywhere, or that we have contracted some terrible disease despite the family doctor's reassurance to the contrary, we will then suffer emotionally because of that belief.

Psychologist Shelley Taylor describes research indicating that mildly depressed people often are actually more realistic in their beliefs about the world than are happy people.[59] The latter tend to see the world through rose-colored glasses, maintaining false beliefs that help reduce anxiety and promote well-being. For example, happy people are more likely to underestimate the probability of being killed in an accident or of developing cancer, while depressed people may be more accurate in the evaluation of such risks. Patients about to undergo surgery and who deny that it involves any significant risk typically have fewer postsurgical complications and are discharged earlier than other patients.[60] On the other hand, such positive illusions have their downside. When people fail to see their own weaknesses, or underestimate the threat inherent in a particular situation because of such illusions, they may fail to achieve important objectives, or even put their health and safety at risk.[61]

Beliefs tell us who we are

Our beliefs define us personally, socially, and politically, and our self-esteem depends both on our beliefs about ourselves and our beliefs about how others regard us. How would you describe yourself? Are you a "decent" person? An honest person? A hard-working person? Your answers reflect your beliefs about yourself, and these beliefs have a powerful influence not only on whether you continue to be decent, honest, and hardworking, but on whether you are happy in life and whether you like yourself. You may think, "I am a good person and I try never to harm others," or "I am useless and I will never succeed at anything." This is such a powerful process that psychotherapists spend much of their time attempting to teach their clients to challenge and modify depression-spawning negative beliefs about themselves.

Beliefs organize social behavior

As noted earlier, we share many of our beliefs with others in our group or society, and shared belief systems help define groups and build social cohesiveness. It is because of common beliefs that groups and societies can take concerted action toward common goals. The community that is rife with conflicting beliefs will have difficulty in coordinating its actions and in defining goals that are acceptable to all.

***

Our beliefs represent the world to us. They define what is real and what is fantasy, they tell us who we are, they identify friend and foe, and they inform us of our duties and responsibilities. They motivate our actions and indicate which are morally justifiable and which are not.

Before people's actions and allegiances change, their beliefs must change. Yet, many beliefs are so entrenched that change is unlikely to occur. We shall now explore the tenacity with which people sometimes cling to their beliefs even in the face of powerful evidence that contradicts them.

CHAPTER 7

PRESERVING THE ROSES

The human understanding when it has once adopted an opinion . . . draws all things else to support and agree with it. And though there be a greater number and weight of instances to be found on the other side, yet these it either neglects and despises, or else by some distinction sets aside and rejects, in order that by this great and pernicious predetermination the authority of its former conclusions may remain inviolate.

—Francis Bacon (1561–1626)[1]

BELIEF STABILITY

To understand the garden, we need to understand the soil, for some plants thrive in one kind of soil but not in another. And so too in the Garden of Belief. Based both on circumstances and character, people vary in terms of how willing and able they are to let new beliefs take root, especially those that do not fit in with their existing beliefs. Some people tend to be relatively open-minded in this regard, while others are doggedly resistant and cling tenaciously to their existing beliefs and reject conflicting information out of hand.

We are all generally reluctant to change deeply ingrained beliefs, but that is not in itself a bad thing. Life would be difficult and confusing if important beliefs were to change each time we encountered new information that challenged them. It would not serve us well to stop vaccinating our children because of a single news report suggesting that vaccinations cause harm, or to stop wearing seatbelts because of a magazine article that claims they do more harm than good. Some degree of stability in our beliefs is important, and yet complete rigidity would deprive us of learning from new experiences and from adapting our beliefs to changing circumstances. We need to distinguish between new information that justifies belief change and that which does not.

Figure 7-1: Galileo Galilei (1564–1642).

Some of our beliefs are extremely stable and we cannot simply change them at will. Consider Galileo (1564–1642). He was prosecuted for disseminating his belief that the earth revolves around the sun, in opposition to the official geocentric "reality" of the Roman Catholic Church. Vigorously confronted by the Inquisitors-General, he had little choice but to recant to avoid condemnation as a heretic, which was punishable by death. As a result, he abjured his belief in the heliocentric solar system and publicly declared that the sun moves around a stationary earth. Yet it would have been impossible for him to truly change this belief as the authorities demanded. Legend has it that even as he was signing his recantation stating that the earth was stationary (figure 7-2), he muttered *Eppur si muove*, "nevertheless, it moves."

MAINTAINING BELIEF

We can usually find a way to maintain important beliefs even in the face of compelling contrary evidence.[2] Belief stability is promoted by a number of factors:

- *Importance:* The more important a belief is to the individual, the more it is likely to resist change. For example, the beliefs of a devoutly religious person are unlikely to change, while less important beliefs—perhaps regarding the benefits of exercise, for example—will be more responsive to new information.
- *"Primitiveness:"* Primitive, or fundamental, beliefs are very resistant to change, and they provide a foundation against which incoming information is screened for compatibility. This is true even for some people's primi-

tive beliefs that appear irrational to us, for they do not appear so to the people who hold them. Many religious beliefs, typically acquired at a young age, before critical thinking skills have had a chance to take root, acquire the status of primitive beliefs and are resistant both to logical analysis and to influence from others. Similarly, the belief that if you jump off a roof you will fall to the ground is a primitive belief that is virtually unchangeable.

- *Value-laden*: Beliefs that reflect our values are also generally very stable. Dialogue is difficult with regard to value differences, and attempts to persuade through logical analysis are usually doomed to failure. You would be unlikely to change your beliefs about incest or slavery, no matter how persuasive someone's attempts were, because these beliefs are associated with important values.
- *Interconnectedness:* Important beliefs are often highly interconnected with other beliefs, and this adds to their stability because change in one would require modifying others as well. Consideration of too much change can be wrenching. It may be easier to change nothing.
- *Self-esteem*: Beliefs that bolster self-esteem resist change. As result, unless someone is low in self-esteem to begin with, information that implies that one was in error, or reflects poorly on oneself, one's family, or one's group or nation is less likely to lead to belief change because of the threat to self-esteem.
- *Public pronouncement:* Resistance to changing an important belief is usually intensified once it has been made public, for "backing down" involves a loss of face.
- *General acceptance*: Beliefs shared by almost everyone are unlikely to be questioned and therefore unlikely to change. Just as it would be difficult to persuade most people today that the earth is not a globe, years ago when it was "common knowledge" that the earth was flat, that belief too was highly resistant to change.
- *Group influence*: We often look to others in our group as a means of judging the accuracy of our beliefs. Indeed, most of us prefer the company of others who share our important beliefs rather than that of those who challenge them. As sociologist Peter L. Berger observes,

> we obtain our notions about the world originally from other human beings and these notions continue to be plausible to us in very large measure because others continue to confirm them.[3]

Figure 7-2: Galileo's Abjuration (1633)

I, Galileo Galilei, son of the late Vincenzio Galilei of Florence, aged 70 years, tried personally by this court, and kneeling before You, the most Eminent and Reverend Lord Cardinals, Inquisitors-General throughout the Christian Republic against heretical depravity, having before my eyes the Most Holy Gospels, and laying on them my own hands; I swear that I have always believed, I believe now, and with God's help I will in future believe all which the Holy Catholic and Apostolic Church doth hold, preach, and teach.

But since I, after having been admonished by this Holy Office entirely to abandon the false opinion that the Sun was the centre of the universe and immoveable, and that the Earth was not the centre of the same and that it moved, and that I was neither to hold, defend, nor teach in any manner whatever, either orally or in writing, the said false doctrine; and after having received a notification that the said doctrine is contrary to Holy Writ, I did write and cause to be printed a book in which I treat of the said already condemned doctrine, and bring forward arguments of much efficacy in its favour, without arriving at any solution: I have been judged vehemently suspected of heresy, that is, of having held and believed that the Sun is the centre of the universe and immoveable, and that the Earth is not the centre of the same, and that it does move.

Nevertheless, wishing to remove from the minds of your Eminences and all faithful Christians this vehement suspicion reasonably conceived against me, I abjure with sincere heart and unfeigned faith, I curse and detest the said errors and heresies, and generally all and every error and sect contrary to the Holy Catholic Church. And I swear that for the future I will neither say nor assert in speaking or writing such things as may bring upon me similar suspicion; and if I know any heretic, or one suspected of heresy, I will denounce him to this Holy Office, or to the Inquisitor and Ordinary of the place in which I may be.

I also swear and promise to adopt and observe entirely all the penances which have been or may be by this Holy Office imposed on me. And if I contravene any of these said promises, protests, or oaths, (which God forbid!) I submit myself to all the pains and penalties which by the Sacred Canons and other Decrees general and particular are against such offenders imposed and promulgated. So help me God and the Holy Gospels, which I touch with my own hands.

I Galileo Galilei aforesaid have abjured, sworn, and promised, and hold myself bound as above; and in token of the truth, with my own hand have subscribed the present schedule of my abjuration, and have recited it word by word. In Rome, at the Convent della Minerva, this 22nd day of June, 1633.

I, GALILEO GALILEI, have abjured as above, with my own hand.[4]

Group support for beliefs can also involve group pressure to stick with them, and people often face considerable internal pressure to conform to the beliefs of their group. Deviation from important beliefs can result in being ostracized, and people often yield to this pressure to protect their relationships with others who are important to them. At a larger social level, beliefs that threaten a society or its leadership may bring devastating retribution, particularly in a totalitarian state.

Group influence does not need to be coercive in order to be effective. While a large majority of scientists believe that the climate is warming because of human reliance on burning hydrocarbons for energy, there are significant pockets of people who strongly disagree. One might think that this reflects a lack of scientific understanding or information, but that is an insufficient explanation. Consider research that assessed beliefs about climate change in a representative sample of 1,540 adults in the United States.[5] Two hypotheses were examined: the *science comprehension* hypothesis that it is only because of a lack of scientific knowledge that people fail to take climate change seriously, and the *cultural cognition* hypothesis that people form perceptions of societal risks that are in line with the values of the groups with which they identify.

The evidence clearly supported the cultural cognition hypothesis. Greater science literacy and numeracy were *not* associated with an increased perception of the seriousness of climate-change risks. Indeed, people with the highest degrees of science literacy showed the greatest polarization. That is, they either strongly believed that humans are causing climate change, or they strongly believed that this is not the case. Their perceptions of climate-change risks were in line with the values of the groups with which they identified. This suggests that if you live in a community where oil production is the main industry, you are much more likely to believe that human-induced climate change is not occurring, regardless of your scientific literacy.

Similar findings have been reported with regard to beliefs about the risks associated with vaccines.[6] When the United States Centers for Disease Control recommended that all adolescent girls should be vaccinated against the human papilloma virus, which is transmitted through sexual contact and causes cervical cancer, research showed that people's belief about the vaccine's benefits and dangers reflected shared group and cultural beliefs—for example, that the protection offered by vaccination would increase promiscuous and unsafe sex. Exposure to more information, whether from news reports or from advocates, resulted in greater polarization of beliefs as people moved toward one extreme or the other, again reflecting the cultural nature of the conflict over the vaccine.

BELIEF IN THE FACE OF CONTRARY EVIDENCE

> *Every man who attacks my belief, diminishes in some degree*
> *my confidence in it, and therefore makes me uneasy; and I am*
> *angry with him who makes me uneasy.*
> —Samuel Johnson (1709–1784)[7]

Even if we like to think of ourselves as open-minded and willing to consider new information carefully, there are bound to be times when that is not the case. For one thing, people are often unwilling to admit their mistakes because to do so would challenge self-esteem, and the higher one's station, the greater the risk of public humiliation and blame. As psychologists Carol Tavris and Elliot Aronson point out, when people are directly confronted by evidence that they are wrong, most do not change their point of view or course of action but instead strive to justify it even more tenaciously.[8]

As for open-mindedness, we are all usually quite selective in terms of what information we bother even to consider. The deeply rooted capitalist is unlikely to pore over books on communist theory, the devout Christian does not give serious consideration to atheist arguments, the atheist is not interested in Christian dogma, and the environmentalist is not likely to spend time considering industry arguments that downplay environmental concerns.

Furthermore, it is not all that difficult to defend a firm belief against challenges and contrary information. Indeed, research has found that beliefs can survive even when the evidence that originally supported them has been completely demolished. As psychologists Lee Ross and Craig Anderson have observed,

> beliefs can survive potent logical or empirical challenges. They can survive and even be bolstered by evidence that most uncommitted observers would agree logically demands some weakening of such beliefs. They can even survive the total destruction of their original evidential basis.[9]

Several psychological processes operate to protect and preserve cherished beliefs even in the face of compelling contradictions.

Discounting principle

Belief can be preserved by discounting the source of contrary information. One might have expected that Donald Trump's insistence that Barack Obama was not eligible for the presidency of the United States because he had been born outside the country would have ended once Obama produced his birth certificate proving that he had been born in Hawaii. Trump and his followers instead discounted the source of the evidence by questioning the authenticity of the birth certificate.

Another example: Edgar Nernberg is an amateur fossil expert with a strong belief in Creationism (the belief that God created the universe and its earthly inhabitants about six thousand years ago).[10] While operating a backhoe to excavate a basement in 2015, he uncovered the outlines of five fish embedded in sandstone. Immediately recognizing their significance, he contacted a paleontologist, who subsequently concluded that the fish had lived some 60 million years ago. If true, that would directly counter Nernberg's Creationist belief. However, according to a newspaper report, Nernberg dismissed the paleontologist's fossil-dating as erroneous and instead maintained that the fish most likely lived shortly before the Great Flood described in the Bible, some 4,300 years ago by his reckoning. By discounting the expert's assessment, he was able to maintain an important belief.

Loopholism

Instead of discounting the source of contradictory information, people can also preserve belief by downplaying the relevance of the new facts. This is what psychologist Ray Hyman refers to as *loopholism*.[11] The new information is rejected by finding a loophole, arguing that "it is not the same thing." For example, if research finds that a homeopathic remedy has no effect, the homeopathic believer may dismiss the research on the grounds that the remedy was not properly prepared, or that the circumstances under which it was administered were not appropriate.

Rationalization

People generally find inconsistency among their various beliefs, feelings, and behaviors to be uncomfortable. Psychologist Leon Festinger labeled this discomfort *cognitive dissonance*.[12] The inconsistency can often be removed through rationalization. For example, suppose that you have always believed that people should do everything they can to get a good education, but you have just abandoned your university studies in order to have more time to go traveling with your friends. This produces cognitive dissonance. You remove it by rationalizing that while you can always go back to school, if you withdraw from your friends at this time you may lose them. Therefore, you conclude, you have made a good decision.

Confirmation bias

As was noted in an earlier chapter, we all tend to seek information that supports our beliefs, although we may not be aware of doing so.[13] Often, this results in a confirmation bias, which can contribute to misinterpretation of evidence. For example, many people have made efforts to find something magical or paranormal in the shapes of the Egyptian pyramids. Some have claimed that the dimensions of the pyramid correspond to the dimensions of the earth, suggesting the builders must have had knowledge far beyond what the Egyptians of the time could have possessed. There are many aspects of the pyramids that can be measured, and focusing only on those that fit with one's belief can generate what appears to be a profound correspondence, even if it is actually meaningless.[14]

Scientists, too, can become so invested in a particular theory or hypothesis that a confirmation bias influences their interpretation of new information. Sociologist Ian Mitroff studied forty-two scientists involved in soil analyses during the moon exploration program.[15] Some were theoreticians and others were empirical researchers. Each was interviewed about their predictions concerning the composition of the moon rocks that were being collected and then interviewed again after the rocks had been brought to earth and analyzed. When faced with actual data from soil analysis that contradicted their predictions, the empiricists modified their views in line with the data, but the theoreticians tended to maintain their prior beliefs and find ways to interpret the data so that it was not incompatible with their predictions. Physicist Max Planck (1858–1947) was referring to such intransigence of scientific belief when he wrote,

> A new scientific truth does not triumph by convincing its opponents and making them see the light, but rather because its opponents eventually die and a new generation grows up that is familiar with it.[16]

More recently, two samples of researchers, those in one group who believed that playing video games leads to increased aggression and those in the other who had found no evidence to support that claim, were provided with new evidence that was actually mixed and inconclusive. Individuals in both groups interpreted the information as supporting their own position, and this resulted in them having increased confidence in their views and in a widening of the differences between them in terms of their beliefs.[17]

Confirmation bias often shows up during disputes, in which case it is sometimes referred to as the *myside bias*.[18] Because of a preference for "my side" of an issue, an individual's beliefs interfere with evaluating whatever challenges those beliefs, and, as a result, opposing arguments are often given short shrift. In this case, not backing down plays an important role, and people typically engage in debate primarily to justify their own point of view.[19] Research has found that the *myside bias* is not related to intelligence, but is influenced more by how skilled one is at logic and reasoning.[20] Odd as it may seem, people who maintain that good arguments should be based in facts are actually *more* prone to the myside bias, for they often overvalue their own "facts."[21]

Pollyanna principle

In general, we prefer pleasant beliefs over unpleasant ones.[22] It is more pleasant to believe, for example, that most people would help a stranger during an emergency than it is not to believe it. The *Pollyanna principle* leads to the application of a lower standard of evidence when assessing information that we welcome.

Compartmentalization

People are often successful in isolating incompatible beliefs from each other.[23] Religious beliefs are often isolated from secular beliefs, so that changes in the latter do not affect them.[24] Thus, a scientist may at the same time be a devout Christian, Hindu, or Muslim and espouse beliefs that are directly at odds with her scientific beliefs. The same is often true with regard to beliefs in psychic phenomena. Such compartmentalization, even by scientists, has long been recognized. In 1896, William James observed,

> At one hour scientists, at another they are Christians or common men, with the will to live burning hot in their breasts; and holding thus the two ends of the chain, they are careless of the intermediate connection.[25]

Similarly, psychologist Gordon Allport wrote in 1955,

> No paradox is more striking than that of a scientist who as citizen makes one set of psychological assumptions and in his laboratory and writings makes opposite assumptions respecting the nature of man.[26]

DISCONFIRMATION AND THE BOOMERANG EFFECT

As noted earlier, people are less likely to back down from their belief if they have declared it publicly. Indeed, falsification of an important belief that has been publicly shared with others can at times boomerang and actually strengthen the belief. A good example is that of a self-styled 1950s religious leader, Dorothy Martin (1900–1992), who became better known as "Marion Keech," the pseudonym given her by the social psychologists who infiltrated her group of believers and observed their reactions first-hand on the night she predicted the world would end.[27] Mrs. Keech claimed to have received a message from God indicating that the world was about to be destroyed by a flood. Reflecting her earlier involvement with Dianetics, the precursor to Scientology, she persuaded her followers that spaceships would be sent by an advanced extraterrestrial society to save them.

Following her instructions, her adherents prepared themselves for rescue on the appointed date. They had sold their possessions, quit their jobs, and said goodbye to their disbelieving families. They were careful to remove all bits of metal from their clothing, including metal eyes on shoes and hooks from brassiere straps, that might interfere with the spaceships' electronics. Having endured the disbelief and even ridicule of friends and family, they now gathered together at the appointed hour. Nothing happened. Hours passed but no spaceships came, and the world did not end. More hours passed before Mrs. Keech retired to her bedroom to pray. She emerged a short time later with the glorious news that, because of their show of faith, God had decided to spare the world.

While one might expect that her followers would be disillusioned and fall away from Mrs. Keech, their reaction was just the opposite. They began to proselytize, making efforts to bring others into her group. They sought interviews with newspapers and, contrary to their earlier avoidance of publicity, undertook a campaign to spread their beliefs as widely as possible. The explanation for this strange outcome lies in cognitive dissonance. Members of the group either had to admit to themselves and their friends and family that they had been foolish, or they could continue to believe that they had acted reasonably and that their faith had spared the world. They essentially doubled down, extolling the importance of Mrs. Keech's teachings in an effort to persuade others.

The psychologists who observed Mrs. Keech's group concluded that several conditions are necessary for people to become even more strongly committed to a belief after it has been proved false:[28]

1. The belief has had some influence on the believer's behavior, making it observable.
2. The individual has taken some nearly irrevocable action in light of the belief.
3. The belief must be capable of being refuted by real events.
4. The disconfirming evidence must be recognized by the believer.
5. Subsequent to the disconfirmation, there must be continuing social support for the original belief. This became apparent when others of Mrs. Keech's devotees who lived in another city and lacked the group support soon fell away from her influence and gave up their beliefs after her prophecy failed to materialize.

Mrs. Keech, of course, was not alone in predicting the end of the world, and other apocalyptic predictions come and go. For example, in 2011, evangelist Harold Camping concluded, based on his own biblical analysis, that the world was to end that year. A series of earthquakes would move around the world on May 21, striking each region at 6 p.m. local time, bringing with it the Rapture through which 200 million devout Christians would be taken up into heaven as a prelude to the second coming of Christ. The world was then to be destroyed by a fireball five months later, on October 21. His California-based religious broadcasting group, Family Radio International, spent millions of dollars advertising the May 21 Judgment Day around the world, and this included putting up five thousand billboard announcements around the United States. In anticipation, many of Camping's followers abandoned their extended families, quit their jobs, sold all their possessions, and budgeted their finances on the basis that they would not need money after May 21. The failure of the Rapture to materialize was all but incomprehensible within their belief system. They were presumably mightily relieved when two days later, on May 23, Camping announced that he had misunderstood, but now realized that May 21 had been "an invisible Judgment Day," when "Christ came and put the world under judgment." He maintained that the timetable was unchanged and that the world would end with the

Apocalypse on October 21, 2011. As we know, he was mistaken. Unlike Mrs. Keech, Camping apologized for his error, depriving his followers of the opportunity to believe that their faith had saved the world.

DOGMATISM

This chapter began with reference to open-mindedness. This is related to *openness to experience*, one of five major personality traits that have been identified by psychologists (the so-called "Big Five"[29]). The others are extroversion, agreeableness, neuroticism, and conscientiousness. Openness to experience involves intellectual curiosity, active imagination, insightfulness, preference for variety, and aesthetic sensitivity.

Dogmatism is the opposite of being open-minded and open to experience. It is characterized by a close-minded collection of beliefs that are held with rigid certainty[30] and that the individual strives to keep isolated from contradictory information and competing ideas.[31] As a result, the seeds of new, conflicting beliefs fall on stony ground. Because contradictory information can be threatening and create tension, such rigidity appeals to those who are uncomfortable with challenges to their beliefs and lack of order. In addition, too much information can be overwhelming, and it is easier to accept a simple conclusion without considering a variety of points of view. In this way, dogmatism serves to minimize stress by closing an individual off from threatening new ideas.

While the roots of dogmatism lie in childhood, it is not simply the product of a rigid ideology promoted by parents. As psychologist Judy Johnson points out, dogmatism is not actually about any *particular* belief or ideology.[32] Rather, it is a defensive strategy stemming from deep feelings of insecurity primarily associated with the individual's sense of identity. Social reasoning and social development are influenced by the child's interactions with other people, and inadequate parenting and the failure to develop nurturing social relationships can lead to distrust, and even fear, of authority figures. The child's need to be accepted by others in the group has a significant impact on belief formation, and when group members also share a dogmatic approach to reasoning, this will reinforce the child's cognitive style. In addition, pressure from peers to adhere to a homogeneous set of beliefs interferes with the development of healthy questioning, and limited exposure to competing ideas helps to maintain a rigid belief structure.

Dogmatism involves several elements.

- *Need for cognitive closure.*[33] This is the desire for definite, black-and-white answers to questions. Information involving ambiguity, shades of gray, and unpredictability is discounted or ignored.
- *Narrowing.* This refers to the deliberate and selective rejection or discrediting of information inconsistent with one's current beliefs and the dismissal of any challenges to those beliefs.[34] It often leads to the confirmation bias discussed earlier, a focus on information that supports or confirms one's beliefs.
- *Lack of personal insight.* Dogmatic individuals have a need to be "right," and their preoccupation with the rightness of their position prevents them from recognizing both their own motivation and how other people react to their dogmatic rigidity.
- *Emotionality.* Dogmatic individuals often experience anxiety, fear, and even anger, when important beliefs are challenged. Moreover, they tend to be pessimistic and generally anxious about the world at large. Such emotionality may result in glorification of people or groups who share their beliefs.[35]

Dogmatic belief often contributes to mass movements, be they political or religious, reactionary or revolutionary, and successful dogmatic leaders demand and receive strict adherence to their beliefs. The American philosopher and social commentator Eric Hoffer referred to dogmatic individuals as *true believers* who cling to their beliefs despite opposing arguments or evidence.[36] He too concluded that it is because of perpetual feelings of insecurity that they dedicate themselves to a cause that brings meaning, purpose, and self-esteem.

AUTHORITARIANISM

Authoritarianism involves dogmatism but extends beyond it. Following the Second World War, as the world tried to come to terms with the horrors of Nazism and the Holocaust, psychologists made efforts to try to identify and understand the psychological characteristics of the "potential fascist."[37] Researchers identified an authoritarian personality syndrome characterized both by rigid, dogmatic thinking and by a perception of the world in superior-versus-inferior, us-versus-them terms. Authoritarians submit to those with power over them, but wield their own power over subordinates. A modern revision of this concept, right-wing authoritarianism, gives additional attention both to the importance of the social environment and to strong adherence to conventional social values. Hostility and punitiveness are directed toward both out-groups and people who deviate from those values.[38] Such an orientation strongly influences one's interpretation of events and the credibility one gives to particular information sources.

Psychiatrist Erich Fromm viewed the attraction to authoritarian political regimes as an "escape from freedom."[39] He argued that freedom within a democratic society brings a certain degree of uncertainty and unpredictability, whereas an authoritarian system, although limiting individual freedom, provides order. Certainty and order are anxiety-reducing to the authoritarian.

BELIEF PRISON

Some belief systems are so extremely difficult to escape from that they are like a prison. For example, fundamentalist religion teaches people to believe in the literal truth of the Holy Book, and it also teaches that it is sinful to question the scriptures. Believers may experience considerable guilt even when their questioning is private, but when it is public they are likely to face significant pushback from other fundamentalists. The consequences can be severe. In some religious sects, questioning or disavowal of the faith can lead to *shunning*, in which case even family members reject those who have expressed religious doubt, to the extent that they turn away when they encounter them in the street. It is not surprising, then, that it is usually much easier to suppress one's doubts. This leaves no easy way out of the prison.

GROUPTHINK

Groupthink is the tendency for group members, especially those in tightly knit, elite groups facing an important issue, to converge upon a common set of beliefs without fully considering all the possible alternatives.[40] This is most likely to occur when decisions have to be made under time pressure and in a crisis. Personal doubts are set aside as members strive for "quick and painless" unanimity,[41] and their collective confidence in the wisdom and ability of the group promotes excessive optimism and risk-taking. Any warnings about the soundness of the beliefs upon which their decisions are based are discounted.[42]

A number of important United States political and military fiascos, including the pursuit of the defeated North Korean Army beyond the thirty-eighth parallel, the launching of the Bay of Pigs invasion of Cuba, the escalation of the American involvement in the war in Vietnam, and the Watergate cover-up have been attributed to groupthink.[43] In each case, decision makers coalesced around a set of misguided beliefs that led to unwise decisions.

CLINGING TO FALSE BELIEFS: DELUSIONS AND OVERVALUED IDEAS

Several years ago, a middle-aged man came to see me in my clinical practice. He was extremely affable, and for the first ten or fifteen minutes nothing about him struck me as unusual. He then abruptly asked whether I did surgery. Thinking that he might be confusing psychologists with psychiatrists, I explained that psychiatrists, but not psychologists, are trained first as physicians. As part of that training, they presumably participate in some surgeries, but they are not surgeons. I asked why he had raised the question, and he told me that he needed to have his fingers amputated. Why? Because he was constantly fighting the urge to stick them up his rectum, and so he wanted to have them removed. When I asked about the source of this strange urge, he replied that there was a small piano up his rectum, and that he was obsessed with the desire to play it. I asked if he had considered having the piano removed instead. He responded excitedly to the suggestion, which apparently had not occurred to him. He then asked me if I was able to remove the piano!

His belief is an example of a powerful delusion. It turned out, not surprisingly, that he had previously been diagnosed with schizophrenia and was receiving monthly injections of antipsychotic medication that controlled most of his psychotic symptoms. His rectal piano delusion, however, was deeply entrenched and unassailable.

Delusions are false beliefs held with great conviction that persist despite evidence or logic to the contrary. A delusion often begins with an unusual experience, and the person comes up with an odd explanation for it and then sticks with an explanation even when faced with evidence to the contrary.[44] It may seem that a delusion is simply a faulty belief reflecting an error in reasoning, but there is more than faulty reasoning at play. Indeed, some people diagnosed with schizophrenia are able to recognize their delusions as being different and in some way separate from their "real" beliefs.[45]

Not all false beliefs are delusions, of course. If you are convinced that rabbits are nibbling on the hostas in your garden when the damage is being caused by slugs, no one would consider this to be a delusion. When does a false belief become delusion? This depends on how reasonable or unreasonable the belief is in the context of your particular society and how tenaciously it is held in the face of contrary information. For example, if you believe that rabbits are eating your hostas even though they are on the balcony of your apartment forty stories above the ground where there are no rabbits, then your belief has become delusional.

Figure 7-3: Ganesh, the Elephant God.

Social context is very important. Belief that your life is governed by an invisible creature with a human body and the head of an elephant would be considered delusional in western society because it seems so strange and unreasonable. On the other hand, belief that your life is governed by a god with a human body and the head of an elephant would not be considered delusional by Hindus, whose god *Ganesh* has just such a form.

While all delusions are unreasonable, some are also bizarre, and these are most often associated with schizophrenia. They appear to involve a significant dysfunction in perception,[46] an inability to distinguish truth from fiction,[47] and a failure to recognize the irrationality that is involved.[48] The belief that the Martians are controlling your brain, the belief that there is a piano up your rectum, and the delusions associated with the Cotard's (the belief that you do not exist or are dead) and Capgras syndromes (the belief that a loved one is actually an imposter) described in the previous chapter are all bizarre, for they are extremely implausible or impossible, while the delusional belief that your supervisor is secretly plotting to have you fired is not.

Non-bizarre delusions fall into several types. A delusion of persecution involves the strong belief that you are being stalked, conspired against, spied upon, or even poisoned by a person or persons "out to get you." A delusion of grandeur involves the false belief that you are a genius or famous or wealthy or exceedingly powerful. Erotomania is a delusion that another person, possibly a superior at work or a teacher or someone important or famous, is seriously in love with you. A delusion of jealousy is the unfounded belief that your partner is cheating on you. A somatic delusion involves the mistaken belief that something strange is happening to your body, such as an invasion by parasites. All these beliefs are often held with great confidence and respond neither to reason nor to contrary evidence. Non-bizarre delusions usually result in a diagnosis of delusional disorder, a condition in which the individual, apart from the deluded belief, remains otherwise normal and high-functioning,[49] although delusions of persecution are also frequently associated with schizophrenia.

In diagnosing delusions, clinicians typically look for three elements: (1) falseness or impossibility; (2) unjustified feeling of certainty; and (3) incorrigibility—the delusion does not submit to reason. These are not infallible guidelines. The criterion of falseness can be problematic,[50] for delusional beliefs are sometimes impossible to prove false; one cannot prove to a deluded individual that Martians are not sending radio signals to his brain. Moreover, some delusions vary in strength over time, and so they are not held with unwavering certainty. And sometimes people who appear delusional because they insist that they are being followed actually *are* being followed.

Overvalued ideas

An overvalued idea is similar to a delusion—a sort of a "delusion light"—but in this case the individual acknowledges the possibility that the belief may not be true.[51] People with overvalued ideas hold their beliefs with as much conviction as do deluded individuals, but these beliefs tend to develop slowly over time, while delusions more typically have an abrupt onset and involve content that is more improbable. In addition, compared to those with overvalued ideas, people with delusions are relatively indifferent to the reactions and opinions of others.[52]

There are some significant problems involved in drawing a line between delusions, overvalued ideas, and simple self-deception. For example, consider the self-deception of someone diagnosed with a terminal illness who refuses to accept the diagnosis and carries on, planning for the future as though her illness does not exist.[53] This is unlikely to be treated as a delusion but would instead be recognized simply as an effort to minimize anxiety. However, delusions can sometimes help people explain abnormal, scary experiences and thereby provide some control over emotional distress.[54]

COLLECTIVE DELUSIONS

There have been many instances throughout history where large numbers of people have come to share the same delusion, and people no doubt drew increased confidence in their faulty perceptions, interpretations, and memories of an event because others reacted in the same way. Sometimes, collective delusions involve apparent physical illnesses—or even shrinking genitals! (There is more to be told about this, in chapter 12.) These are not delusions in the clinical sense discussed above. Instead, these shared, erroneous, and sometimes bizarre beliefs are the products of social influence that is typically generated in times of significant social anxiety and in the absence of either a clear understanding of the source of the anxiety or a means to deal with it. Charles Mackay's *Memoirs of Extraordinary Popular Delusions and The Madness of Crowds*,[55] published in 1841 and still in print today, documents a vast array of historical collective delusions, including, for example, the wide-spread belief in witchcraft that spread through Europe in the Middle Ages, a belief that generated countless eyewitness accounts of supposed demonic activities. We are not immune to the development of such widely shared but mistaken mass ideas, despite the remarkable advances in scientific thinking.[56]

CONSPIRACY THEORIES

Almost everybody believes that Neil Armstrong and other Americans walked on the moon, but there is a small number people who insist that the landings were faked and that there is a conspiracy to keep the public from finding out the truth. In a similar vein, conspiracy theorist Alex Jones, who has a large following, has claimed that the 2012 massacre in the Sandy Hook primary school in Newtown, Connecticut, which resulted in the deaths of twenty first-graders and six adults, was faked. He stated that the school had been closed years earlier and that an analysis of news video clearly revealed that actors were playing the roles of the grieving parents.[57]

Conspiracy theories are often held with quasi-religious conviction.[58] Distrust of authorities is at the root of these beliefs,[59] and such distrust extends to scientific authorities as well, and to the rejection of well-established scientific findings.[60] Adherents coalesce both intellectually and emotionally around such theories because they generate feelings of group belongingness and cohesion.[61]

As we have seen in earlier chapters, people seek explanations for events in their lives and are uncomfortable when none can be found. Some conspiracy theories provide clear answers to troubling concerns. For example, when people cannot understand why they cannot get ahead in life while others around them do so, a conspiracy theory that blames the problem on some target group provides an answer.[62] Such theories are based in xenophobia, fear of minorities, and the "threatening hand of the stranger."[63] The thinking is: "We cannot get ahead in our careers because the immigrants are taking over."

Once a conspiracy theory takes form, it is nourished by rumors and becomes unfalsifiable because any challenge is explained away, typically by attributing it to the conspirators. Consider again the "birther" conspiracy theory in the United States: In 2010, a Harris public opinion poll reported that 25 percent of those polled (and 45 percent of the Republicans in the sample) believed that Barack Obama's presidency was illegitimate because he was not a natural-born citizen of the United States as required by the American Constitution.[64] The birther controversy turned into a conspiracy theory when the birthers argued that the birth certificate that Obama ultimately provided was likely a forgery. After all, for Obama to fake his birth certificate and get away with it, there would have to be many other people helping him and covering up for him. A study involving university students in the United States concluded that racial prejudice was at the root of this particular conspiracy theory.[65] The researchers argued that because contemporary social norms discourage outright racism, especially in university settings, prejudiced individuals, perhaps even without awareness, manifested their racist feelings about Obama by focusing on something seemingly unrelated to race, the "conspiracy."

Conspiracy theory and disaster

Rumors thrive following a disaster. People first try to get as much information as they can in order to take any necessary action. Next, they consider who is at fault for the disaster. Rumors then tend to focus on finding a guilty party and seeking retribution or punishment. Such rumors, combined with a lack of information and distrust of authorities, sometimes grow into conspiracy. Those identified as being responsible are likely to be from a group viewed negatively, suspiciously, or with disdain in the past.[66] For example, polls reveal that a significant number of people continue to believe in a conspiracy that covered up the truth surrounding the 9/11 attacks in New York City.[67]

The "faked moon landings" and birther conspiracy theories, along with Holocaust denial—a conspiracy theory that argues that Nazi concentration camps were simply work camps—are all examples of *secular* conspiracy theories. There is another type, the *supernatural* conspiracy theory, which involves phenomena that lie beyond what we understand to be the natural world. For example, according to one such theory, shape-shifting, interdimensional reptilians have assumed human form and are taking control of the world's political and economic institutions. As strange as that claim is, it has attracted a large audience. It is championed by blogger David Icke, whose discussion forum includes 100,000 participants and whose YouTube channel has received close to three million views.[68]

Conspiracy mentality

Some people may subscribe to only one particular conspiracy theory, but for others, thinking in terms of conspiracies is their usual way of making sense of events in the world. This predilection is referred to as a *conspiracy mentality*.[69] Research has linked this way of thinking to a wide range of maladaptive social behaviors, including refusal of vaccinations, noncompliance with critical, life-saving drug prescriptions, and disregard for environmental concerns.[70]

Conspiracy thinking is related to schizotypy,[71] a personality dimension involving paranoia, unusual sensations, deficits in emotional and interpersonal functioning, and anomalies of perception.[72] These symptoms are similar to, but less severe, than those found in schizophrenia. "High-schizotypals" are much more likely to find ambiguous information anxiety-arousing, to reject conventional explanations as unreasonable, and to settle on an alternative explanation in the form of supernatural or conspiracy thinking.[73]

MORAL PANIC

Moral panics, a close relative of conspiracy theories, involve beliefs that emerge and spread throughout a group as a result of widespread, acute anxiety based on the fear that society is undergoing a rapid moral decline.[74] The problem is often blamed on some particular group or category of people and is most likely to occur in times of great social or economic upheaval. In the absence of solid evidence to support it, the panic is fed by speculation and rumor.

A satanic ritual abuse epidemic began in the United States in the 1980s and then, over the next decade, gradually spread through much of the world. It was claimed that there was a widespread conspiracy involving "people in high places" who worshipped Satan and who ritualistically tortured children, not only abusing them sexually but even at times murdering them as a means of offering human sacrifices to the devil. Many police forces received training on how to detect and assist satanic ritual abuse victims, and social workers and therapists already involved in "recovering" supposedly repressed memories of childhood sexual abuse applied their techniques to "recover" memories of satanic ritual abuse. Over time, it became clear to investigators that there was no evidence to back up the claims. The conspiracy theory gradually died away. This moral panic reflected anxiety about dramatically changing sexual norms and the possible threat that those changes posed to children.

***

In the normal course of things, the astronomer believes in black holes, the parapsychologist believes in psychic powers, and the theist believes in supernatural beings. The right-wing conservative believes that only conservative economic policies can bring greatness to the land, while someone on the left believes that only socialist policies can do so. The physician believes in the power of antibiotics to conquer disease, the homeopath believes in the healing power of "water with memory," and children believe in Santa Claus. None readily abandons these beliefs. However, while some such beliefs—such as black holes or the value of antibiotics—are amenable to modification if challenged by persuasive evidence, others—such as belief in the supernatural or water memory—are extremely resistant to change.

A step up from such committed belief is close-minded dogmatism where any information contrary to one's pet beliefs is ignored or rejected in order to minimize discomfort or distress. A further step up takes one into the realm of delusional belief where rejection of disconfirming evidence is total.

While obstinate devotion to a disparaged belief can bring many negative consequences, this is not always so. Many important innovators have had to endure ridicule before ultimately establishing the soundness of what seemed to others to be preposterous beliefs. After all, they laughed at Henry Ford's beliefs about streamlined automobile production. As psychiatrist William Sargant noted,

> The whole process of civilization depends almost entirely on a number of people being born in each new generation who have important new beliefs and ideas, and hold onto them with obsessional tenacity. . . . This means that the originators of new ideas and the founders of new systems are rarely themselves "normal" people; if they were they would drop their new notions comparatively quickly in the face of the hostility of their fellows.[75]

Yet, while people did indeed laugh at Henry Ford, we must remember conjurer James Randi's observation: They also laughed at Chuckles the Clown.[76]

CHAPTER 8

TENDING AND TILLING

Reasoning will never make a Man correct an ill Opinion, which by Reasoning he never acquired.

—Jonathan Swift, 1720[1]

CULTIVATING NEW IDEAS IN THE GARDEN OF BELIEF

Although people tend to downplay, ignore, or reinterpret information that challenges important beliefs, beliefs nevertheless do change at times and new beliefs do form, and this can occur surprisingly quickly. Yet, just as the gardener selects new flowers that fit well into the existing garden, so too do people usually add or modify beliefs in a manner that maintains consistency.

Although religious belief is well protected from change, from time to time even religion has to bend to the power of evidence. Consider, for example, the consequences of an experiment carried out by Benjamin Franklin in June 1752. He demonstrated by the rather dangerous procedure of flying a kite during a thunderstorm that lightning is simply a form of electricity.[2] Based on this knowledge, he invented the lightning rod and unintentionally set in motion a direct challenge to Christian belief.

Roman Catholic dogma of the day considered lightning to be the "finger of God," delivering divine retribution for certain sins, including impenitence, incredulity, and (ironically, as we shall see) neglecting the repair of churches. Challenging God's will by interfering with the finger was not to be tolerated—although it is not clear why theologians thought that a lightning rod would stymie an omnipotent deity. Protestant churches joined in the condemnation of the lightning rod, but nothing succeeds like success—and the lightning rod was a huge success. Secular buildings (even brothels) fitted with Franklin's rods no longer suffered damage from lightning strikes, while churches with their high steeples continued to experience the wrath of the finger of God.

Between 1750 and 1783, lightning damaged close to 400 church towers and electrocuted 120 bell-ringers in Germany alone. A mountain church in Rosenberg, Austria, was struck so frequently and with such loss of life that peasants feared attending service. Its spire was rebuilt three times. Finally, in 1778, twenty-six years after Franklin's invention, church authorities permitted a lightning rod to be attached, after which it suffered no more damage.[3]

Theology succumbed to the necessities of experience, and cognitive dissonance was resolved by a change in belief. The church came to believe that lightning is a natural phenomenon rather than a divine intervention, and rationalized that God was pleased that humans were using their intellects to understand and control nature.

EXTREME BELIEF CHANGE: CONVERSION

Change in institutional belief—witness the acceptance of the lightning rod—typically comes slowly, but there are times when an individual's belief can change rapidly. The classic story is of Saul's conversion. In 36 CE, he was traveling to Damascus with the intention of killing all the Christians in the city. Then, on the way, the story goes, he saw a blinding light, heard the voice of the Lord, and converted to Christianity on the spot.

Sudden conversions are relatively rare, for they require a profound change in fundamental, primitive beliefs. When they do occur, they are usually triggered by an emotional experience that is so overwhelming that emotion trumps reason. As a result of the conversion, the new set of beliefs becomes so deeply embedded that it is all but immune to criticism.[4] The company of others who are reacting with similar emotion (at a revival meeting, for example) may make such an experience more likely. While conversions usually involve religious belief, there are similar instances where someone who has been skeptical about supernatural phenomena suddenly, following a powerful emotional experience, becomes a believer in precognition or mental telepathy.

I once looked on as a prominent philosopher fulminated with conjurer James Randi about intelligent, educated people who believe in "psychic nonsense." How could they be so stupid, he wondered? Randi quietly took a

Gideon Bible from the hotel room bedside table and asked the philosopher to flip through it and to pick any page at random while Randi averted his eyes. He further instructed him that once he had picked a page, he should select any major word from the top line of that page. Finally, as the philosopher closed the Bible and Randi took it from him, Randi asked him to concentrate intently on the word that he had chosen. Moments later, Randi wrote something on a piece of paper, and then asked the philosopher to reveal his chosen word. Randi had written the identical word. The philosopher reacted with astonishment, to the extent that he seemed to tremble in confusion. This appeared to be like a conversion experience, for he declared that what Randi had done was impossible, beyond normal human ability, and could only be explained as a genuinely paranormal event. He went on to say that he had never believed in the paranormal, but that he had obviously been wrong. After allowing him to fluster for a few minutes, Randi then calmly announced that what he had done was done by trickery, and suggested that now perhaps the philosopher could understand how intelligent, educated people sometimes come to believe in "psychic nonsense."

Note that there are no sudden conversions from supernatural belief to skepticism.

DATA-DRIVEN OR THEORY-DRIVEN

Experience can sometimes bring about change in even a primitive belief, as almost happened with the philosopher. Now consider a more mundane challenge to a primitive belief, involving what psychologists refer to as *conservation of area*. This is a straightforward notion: the total area of a surface cannot be increased or decreased by dividing it into pieces and rearranging them. This makes logical sense, and according to the renowned Swiss psychologist Jean Piaget, everyone acquires this belief in middle childhood.[5] Thus, if you take a sheet of paper and cut it into four pieces, the total combined area does not change no matter how you move the pieces about.

Some years ago, I conducted research involving what is known as a "vanishing area" puzzle.[6] Such puzzles involve changing the arrangements of pieces of a geometrical figure with the result that the area appears to increase or decrease. The particular puzzle I used was invented by puzzle-maker Sam Lloyd in the nineteenth century.[7] Begin with a square piece of paper, eight units by eight units divided into four pieces, as shown (figure 8-1). The combined area of the four pieces is 8 × 8 = 64 units. Of course, no matter how you rearrange the parts, the total combined area cannot change.

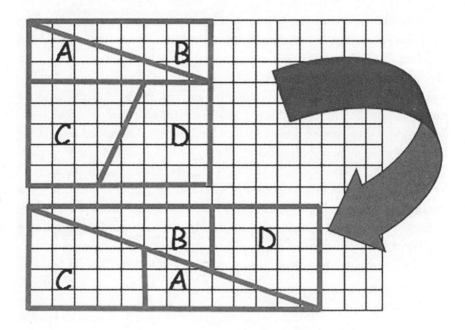

Figure 8-1: Disappearing square?

However, when the pieces are rearranged as shown in the lower figure, they fit nicely together to form a rectangle that is 5 units wide by 13 units long. The combined area is now 5 × 13 = 65 units. The area has apparently increased by one unit.

In my research, university students were first shown this demonstration and then allowed to manipulate the four pieces for themselves. Although all had initially expressed firm belief in the principle of conservation of area, one-third of them quickly flip-flopped when faced with this challenge and stated that they now believed that the area of a surface *can* be changed by rearranging its parts. One could say that they were *data-driven*. They changed their belief to be in line with the data confronting them. The remaining two-thirds of the students were *theory-driven* and stuck with their theory, their belief in area conservation. They nonetheless reported considerable frustration and confusion as they tried to make sense of the apparent increase in area.

As a footnote to the story, I subsequently presented these data to the psychology department of the University of Geneva, Piaget's university, although Piaget himself had retired by that time. I expected these psychologists to be surprised that so many students had quickly abandoned conservation of area, but instead they focused on the demonstration itself, and they too expressed frustration and puzzlement as each in turn shifted the four pieces of paper about, trying to understand the apparent change in area.

This demonstration reflects the fact that when a deeply held belief is challenged by experience, some people stick stubbornly to their belief even when puzzled by the data, and some modify their belief to fit with the data. Neither approach guarantees being correct.

By the way, if your curiosity has been aroused, the apparent change in area occurs because the slopes [angles] of the diagonal elements in the second figure are not equal. The four pieces only appear to fit together, but there is a slender, imperceptible, wedge-shaped gap between them that accounts for the additional unit of area.

PERSUASION AND BELIEF CHANGE

While personal experience encourages and sometimes impels belief change, many of our beliefs are modified as the direct result of others' efforts to change them for us. Family and friends at times try to bring our beliefs in line with their own. Environmentalists want us to believe that conservation is necessary in order to save the planet. Public health officials strive to persuade us to believe that practicing safe sex is vital to our well-being. Politicians make every effort to lead us to the belief that voting for them will bring better government. Advertisers tempt us to believe that their products will serve our needs better than those of competitors. And just as missionaries backed by the power of their European governments persuaded colonized peoples to believe in the Christian God while giving up belief in their own deities, contemporary missionaries go door to door in an effort to bring people to the faith of the Mormons or Jehovah's Witnesses.

Not only are we the targets of persuasion, but each of us at times undertakes to bring others to our own beliefs. Why do we want to change people's beliefs? There are several possible reasons:

- *Altruism or paternalism.* We believe that we are acting in the targets' best interests and that they will benefit from sharing our belief.
- *Social responsibility.* We want to build a better society. For example, by changing beliefs about the dangers of drinking and driving, we can make the roads safer for everybody.
- *Egotism.* Our egos are boosted when we persuade others to agree with us.
- *Anxiety.* We may feel threatened by ideas that challenge our own. Bringing people into agreement with us overcomes the threat.
- *Tension reduction.* Differences in important beliefs often result in relationship strain. We are more attracted to and comfortable with people who share our important beliefs.[8]
- *Control.* Dissent in a group makes management of the group more difficult.
- *Profit.* Persuading someone to buy your product or to believe in your scheme is rewarded by personal gain.

ROUTES OF PERSUASION

Persuasion can occur either by a *central* or a *peripheral route.*[9] Central-route persuasion occurs after one has given careful thought to the message. Peripheral-route persuasion, on the other hand, reflects a sort of cognitive laziness, for instead of evaluating the soundness of an argument, we rely upon peripheral factors such as the expertness, credibility, or attractiveness of the source. Central-route persuasion leads to more lasting belief change, whereas persuasion via the more rapid peripheral route is less likely to endure. We all respond at times in both ways to various attempts to influence us. Central-route elaboration is more likely when dealing with something of importance to us, when we have enough time to think about it, and when we have enough knowledge to be able to do a decent evaluation.

In addition, people vary in what psychologists refer to as *need for cognition*, a personality trait involving a strong desire to "think about things" and examine arguments.[10] Those with a high need for cognition are more likely to rely upon the central route and as result tend to be more resistant to persuasion, while people with a lower need for cognition are more susceptible to influence by peripheral factors such as the attractiveness of the source.[11]

Of course, the credibility of the source is important for either central-route or peripheral-route persuasion. If the source is considered unreliable, the message is likely to be rejected in any case.

SOCIAL CONTAGION: SEEDS BLOWING IN THE WIND

Contagion is a social psychological metaphor that describes a rapid spreading of emotion, belief, and behavior throughout a crowd or population, somewhat analogously to how disease spreads from person to person.[12] The rapid dissemination of fads, whether commercially driven, such as Pokémon, or verbal, such as *twenty-three skidoo* (1920s), the more recent *groovy* or *cool,* or saying "no problem" in place of "you're welcome," are examples of contagion.

Beliefs are often fed by rumors, and rumors are spread through contagion. The speed of their dissemination has increased enormously with the nearly instantaneous communication provided by the internet through which people around the world interact relatively anonymously, posting and reposting information often with little or no concern for accuracy. Whether fact-based or not, rumors can have very significant consequences for individuals and nations alike. For example, a rumor that a nation is about to devalue its currency can lead to huge losses on world stock markets, and a rumor that a deadly and contagious disease has broken out can be devastating for a city or country that relies heavily on tourism.[13]

There are number of important factors involved in rumor formation:[14]

- *General uncertainty.* In the absence of solid information about an important event, rumors fill the need for understanding and serve to shape collective beliefs.[15] For example, suppose that several police cars pull up in front of your office building and police officers cart a few people away with them. In the absence of any factual explanation, the situation is ripe for rumor.
- *Credibility.* The credibility of a rumor is an important determinant of whether it will thrive or die. When a rumor offers seemingly credible information about what is going on, it is likely to be treated seriously and to reduce uncertainty. As it spreads, its apparent credibility may increase with the retelling, as elements that seem difficult to believe are dropped.[16]

- *Personal relevance.* We naturally take more notice of rumors that bear on something important and relevant to our lives.
- *Personal anxiety.* Anxiety often makes it more difficult to tolerate uncertainty, and so the anxious individual welcomes any information that will reduce unease.[17] For example, general concern that a company may close down is likely to make its workers more susceptible to rumors that appear to provide relevant information.

Urban legends have many of the characteristics of rumors.[18] They are accounts of supposed events that are told and retold as true stories and whose origin is usually attributed to "a friend of a friend," and many have enjoyed wide circulation. What is interesting about them is that most people believe them to be true, initially at least, and retell them assuring their listeners of their truth. For example, you may have heard the account of the cement-truck driver who returns home unexpectedly and finds a convertible parked in front of his house and his wife in bed with a stranger. He does not say anything to either person but fills the convertible with cement before driving away.[19] And then there is the story of a man visiting a large city who wakes up naked in a bathtub filled with ice. He notices a large incision on his torso and finds a note telling him to call 911 because he has just had a kidney removed![20] These are good stories, so good that the people who retell them want them to be true. Some such stories appear to reflect generalized anxiety related to rapid technological or social change.[21]

PERSUASION: PROPAGANDA

It is one thing to persuade your friend to believe as you do about some issue, but it is quite another to persuade a group or a nation. As advertisers and politicians know all too well, the mass media provide a channel that can be used for dissemination of propaganda through which large-scale belief change can be engineered.

In modern times, *propaganda* refers to the attempt to persuade people to believe something that is not actually true. Yet the term was not always pejorative. When the Vatican established the *Sacra Congregatio de propaganda fide* on June 22, 1622, "propaganda" simply referred to the propagation of Christian beliefs that the church held to be true. There was no intention to bamboozle people with known falsehoods.

It was largely because of the nefarious but effective work of Joseph Goebbels, the Nazi Minister of Propaganda, that the word took on the sinister and aversive connotation that it carries today. Goebbels developed propaganda into a form of persuasion involving both misinformation and the withholding or selective presentation of true information in such a way that rapid, peripheral-route thinking would be most likely. Goebbels drew his inspiration from his leader, Adolf Hitler, who wrote in *Mein Kampf* that propaganda fails unless one fundamental principle is kept in mind, and that is to confine it to a few points and to repeat them over and over.[22] Hitler also advocated the use of the *große Lüge*, the "Big Lie," the notion that a truly colossal lie becomes believable because people assume that no one would dare to distort the truth to that degree.

Hitler laid out several other cardinal rules for successful propaganda: Avoid abstract ideas and appeal instead to the emotions; use stereotyped phrases and avoid objectivity; put forth only one side of the argument; constantly criticize enemies of the state, and focus on a particular enemy for special vilification. He stressed that the propagandist must understand the emotions of the masses and find the psychologically correct way to arouse those emotions.

Mass media provide propagandists with the ability to reach millions of people quickly and economically, and the ubiquity of the internet has made the reach almost universal. It is often difficult to draw a line between advertising, public-service announcements, and political declarations on the one hand and propaganda on the other. The difference depends on our perception of the honesty or dishonesty of the message. Successful propaganda is not viewed as propaganda by those who are persuaded by it.

Propaganda, white and black

In what is known as *white* propaganda, the source is out in the open and clearly identified. Because of this, a source that is not credible is usually simply ignored by the target group. This is what happened with much of the German radio propaganda directed at Allied soldiers and the British public during the Second World War, in which no attempt was made to hide the fact that the messages came from the enemy. The infamous *Lord Haw-Haw* (actually William Joyce, a Nazi sympathizer broadcasting from Germany) and *Tokyo Rose* (the name used by Allied forces in the South Pacific to refer to any one of about twenty English-speaking Japanese women who delivered propaganda messages) evoked laughter and derision rather than any belief change.

The success of white propaganda depends on listeners recognizing it as a reliable source of truth. During the Second World War, the British Broadcasting Corporation (BBC) made the specific decision to report *the truth, nothing but the truth and, as near as possible, the whole truth.*[23] Reflecting this policy, Allied losses were described with as much fidelity as were victories. As a result, the BBC gained the trust of its target audiences in Germany and elsewhere. As historian V. M. Plock has observed,

> It is fascinating to see how the BBC provided the German public with accurate information during the war and thereby began to re-educate individuals who had been living, willingly or unwillingly, with 12 years of Nazi propaganda.... To be effective in exposing Nazi propaganda as lies and teach German listeners to become responsible citizens of a peaceful, unified Europe, the BBC German Service had to first gain their trust.[24]

With *black* propaganda, on the other hand, the true source is hidden and an effort is made to make it appear that the message comes from within the target group. In principle, this should boost the appeal of the message—and frequently it does—since the source, although unidentified, is not viewed as an outsider or enemy. One way to undertake black propaganda is through rumor dissemination. Note, however, that while rumor can be an effective propaganda tool, it is not without its risks, for once set in motion it cannot be controlled and may evolve in an unpredictable way.

Consider this successful example of black propaganda used as part of a cigarette advertising strategy in the United States in 1934. According to sociologist Tamotsu Shibutani, the strategy involved two-person teams entering a crowded subway car or bus at opposite ends, and then, as they moved toward each other, engaging in conversation while other people were standing between them.[25] One person would begin by loudly recognizing his friend and then calling out something like *Hey Joe—did you*

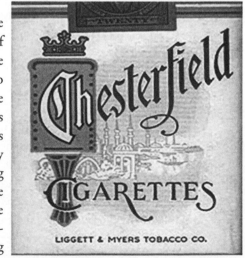

Figure 8-2: Chesterfield cigarettes of bygone days.

hear that they have found a leper working in the Chesterfield factory in Richmond, Virginia? A few such incidents were enough to start a rumor about the risks of catching leprosy by smoking Chesterfield cigarettes, and Shibutani reported that this led to a significant drop in their sales. The campaign was never officially acknowledged by the competitor who initiated it.

Propaganda is not used just to target enemies or competitors or to promote particular politicians and their ideas. It can also be effective as a means of increasing cohesiveness within a group. For example, during the Nazi era, German filmmaker Leni Riefenstahl directed, produced and co-wrote *Triumph des Willens* ("Triumph of the Will"). Released in 1935, it is considered to be one of the greatest propaganda films of all time. Its aim was to persuade the German people to believe in Nazism, and its theme was Germany's return to glory with Hitler as savior.

Figure 8-3a: Riefenstahl's *Triumph of the Will.*

Figure 8-3b: Leni Riefenstahl.

Illusory truth effect

While it has been said that familiarity breeds contempt, familiarity also breeds believability. The more often that someone has been exposed to particular information, the more likely it is that it will be judged as believable and true. This is known as the *illusory truth effect*, and it occurs automatically when an individual recognizes that she has encountered the information in the past but cannot remember whether it was presented as being true or false.[26] This can also occur even when people do not remember that they have been previously exposed to the information.[27] This effect has been demonstrated in many different contexts, including advertising and eyewitness testimony.[28]

What accounts for the illusory truth effect? If we cannot remember the source of information (source amnesia), then the only remaining influence is its familiarity,[29] which is then taken as an indication that it is true. Why should that be so? We associate quick recall and vividness of a perceptual memory with reality. Repetition of information makes it more familiar and easier to recall, and we associate this ease of processing with truth.[30] To put this into everyday terms, if you have a difficult time forming a picture in your mind of an event that occurred while you were in high school, you are less likely to be certain about its accuracy than if it comes quickly and is vivid and clear.

In a study of the illusory truth effect, participants were presented with invented but plausible statements and then, two weeks later, asked to rate those statements as well as a new set of statements in terms of their truth or falsity. The two-week-old statements were rated significantly higher in terms of truth than were the newer statements, even though none had any truth to them. Moreover, even when statements had been preceded by the phrase "Few people believe that," they were still treated as being more likely to be true than new statements not carrying such a qualifier. Thus, even when warned that information is unlikely to be true, there is a tendency to view it with increased confidence when it is subsequently recalled.

The effectiveness of repeating propaganda phrases over and over is due to the illusory truth effect; what one has heard many times begins to take on the mantle of truth. Joseph Goebbels assiduously employed repetition in his propaganda campaigns, and is frequently (but erroneously) quoted as having stated that "If you tell a lie big enough and keep repeating it, people will eventually come to believe it." (What he actually wrote was, "The English follow the principle that when one lies, one should lie big, and stick to it. They keep up their lies, even at the risk of looking ridiculous."[31] The obvious irony is that he was describing his own technique, while the British, through the BBC, actually chose to tell the truth.)

The role that familiarity plays in our assessment of recalled information is also well understood by advertisers, who often repeat simplistic messages about their products over and over, well aware that any annoyance produced by repetition will be more than compensated for by the increased familiarity of the message—"Wonder Soap washes cleaner . . ." Experimental evidence supports both Goebbels and the advertisers.[32]

PERSUASION: GASLIGHTING

In the 1938 play *Gas Light*, set in the Victorian era and later made into a 1944 film starring Ingrid Bergman, a husband undertakes to rid himself of his wife by persuading her that she is insane and then having her committed to a mental hospital. He endeavors to do this surreptitiously by leading her to believe that she cannot trust her own sense of reality. At one point, he sneaks into the empty flat above theirs to search for jewels that had been hidden by the former occupant, who had been murdered. When he turns on the gas lights in the flat above, the lights in his own flat dim slightly, and his wife both notices the dimming and hears the sounds of his footsteps upstairs. When she later mentions this to him, he convinces her that she is hearing and seeing things that are not real, that there were no footsteps and that the lights had not dimmed. (Hence, the term *gaslighting* for this kind of manipulation.)

Today, *gaslighting* refers to callous psychological manipulation intended to undermine people's confidence in their ability to know what is real and what is not by leading them to question the validity of their perceptions, memories, and beliefs. Although the term is most frequently used to describe emotional abuse in close relationships, it was also applied in 2017 to describe what many people consider to be Donald Trump's relentless attempts to undermine people's sense of truth and reality.[33] This includes his efforts to turn his opinions into fact and other people's facts into opinions, as well as his attempts to change perceptions of reality through vigorous but erroneous claims, such as those concerning the size of his inauguration crowd or the magnitude of his Electoral College victory. It has been pointed out that, with regard to some outrageous claims, he has subsequently denied that he made them. In other words, he is telling people that what they think they heard him say never actually happened.[34] His supporters, presumably through peripheral-route persuasion based on their admiration and respect for him, believe what he says, whereas his opponents, subjecting his comments to central-route vetting, do not.

PERSUASION: ALTERCASTING

Altercasting is a powerful persuasion technique that succeeds by pushing people into a particular role.[35] Taking on the role makes an individual more likely to focus selectively on information relevant to that role and to develop beliefs that go along with it. Many people use altercasting as a persuasion technique without realizing it. For example,[36]

> *You're a good carpenter. Can you make me a window?*
> *You look like a kind person. Can you sign our petition against animal cruelty?*

In each case, one is implicitly assigning a role to the other person, be it "good carpenter" or "kind person," making it more likely that the individual will take on the role when considering a response.

Con artists are often adept at using altercasting. Psychologist Anthony Pratkanis describes a very common approach, "playing the hayseed," where the con artist acts like a country bumpkin and the target is put in the role of the expert or know-it-all, increasing his confidence to make good decisions as he becomes involved—and victimized—in the scam.[37] Altercasting is not restricted to con artists, for advertisers often employ it to persuade people to purchase their products.[38] For example, automobile manufacturers may begin an advertisement by stressing that good parents naturally want to protect their children, and then going on to praise the safety features of their vehicles. Identifying with their parental role makes parents more likely to focus on the safety of their children, leaving them more likely to respond positively to the advertiser's pitch.

PERSUASION: "BRAINWASHING"

During the 1940s, *hsi nao* (Chinese for "scrub the brain," and later translated into English as *brainwashing*) was developed in China as a kind of therapy for citizens whose impure thoughts kept them from seeing the merits of communism.[39] This involved imprisonment that protected the individual from "intellectual contamination" by others, combined with a steady diet of communist teachings. Social isolation also deprived the individual of group interactions that can provide strength and resistance. Encouragement and reinforcement were provided for adopting "proper" forms of thinking and behavior, and punishment was the consequence of straying from the proper path. Eventually, freedom would be the reward when authorities were convinced that the individual had developed a genuine belief in communism. You will recognize this as essentially a form of operant conditioning in which the individual is reinforced for speaking and behaving in the desired manner.

Hsi nao, involving isolation and step-by-step reinforcement, can be remarkably effective in bringing about changes in behavior,[40] but modern attempts at indoctrination usually depart significantly from this approach. Instead, political prisoners, even in modern China, are often subjected to various forms of torture, or kept sleep-deprived, in the belief that this will increase their susceptibility to indoctrination and confession.[41] Coercion carries no magic in changing beliefs. It is simply a means of weakening an individual physically, mentally, and emotionally in order to reduce resistance, and it typically brings about compliance rather than actual belief change.

PERSUASION: "WE HAVE WAYS OF MAKING YOU TALK . . ."

Torture and deprivation have often been used with the goal of forcing prisoners to reveal information or to confess to crimes. Consider this account of Chinese physician Charles Vincent, imprisoned for three and a half years during Mao's thought reform and re-education program. Vincent was kept in chains and subjected to ongoing physical and mental abuse and humiliation while being repeatedly interrogated about supposed subversive activities:

> You are annihilated . . . exhausted . . . you can't control yourself, or remember what you said two minutes before. You feel that all is lost. . . . From that moment the judge is the real master of you. You accept anything he says. You don't pay any more attention to your life or to your handcuffed arms. . . . You just wonder when you will be shot—and begin to hope for the end of all this.[42]

He noted that he gradually began to believe his own false confession:

> You begin to believe all this, but it is a special kind of belief. You're not absolutely convinced, but you accept it—in order to avoid trouble—because every time you don't agree, trouble starts again.[43]

In recent years, there have been political discussions in Western nations about whether torture is ever justified in the attempt to gain important information from captured terrorists. However, the use of torture flies in the face of the opinions of interrogation experts who conclude that it is unsuccessful as a means of extracting information, not only because it inspires resistance, but also because it elicits false confessions, all of which renders information obtained from torture unreliable.[44]

During the Second World War, Hanns Scharff, the German Luftwaffe interrogator responsible for interrogating captured Allied fighter pilots, gained a reputation as a "master interrogator." He never used torture, considering it to be counterproductive, but instead used methods that led prisoners to perceive him as a kind of friend, someone who could help them through a difficult situation. This allowed him to obtain reliable information that would not have been produced by torture. Because his methods were so effective, many of his techniques continue to be taught to interrogators in the United States military, and are reflected to some extent in the Reid technique discussed below.

PERSUASION: INTERROGATION AND FALSE CONFESSIONS

More than four-fifths of criminal cases are resolved through confessions.[45] Judges and juries alike are overwhelmingly influenced by confessions and find it difficult to believe that anyone would ever confess to a crime that she had not committed. It seems natural to assume that people would confess only when guilty, but recent research has clearly shown that *false* confessions are not uncommon. There are many instances where innocent people have confessed to murders, rapes, violent assaults, and other crimes, of which they were subsequently proven to be innocent through DNA evidence.[46] Once the confession is on record, however, it cannot be undone. Rescinding carries little weight, for it is assumed that the guilty individual simply is trying to avoid punishment.

The Innocence Project in the United States and the Association in Defense of the Wrongly Convicted in Canada are dedicated to exonerating innocent people who have been convicted and incarcerated. According to the Innocence Project, more than one out of four who have been wrongfully convicted and later exonerated by DNA evidence had either confessed or made an incriminating statement.[47] Of course, some individuals—children, mentally handicapped

individuals, people whose memories have been affected by alcohol or drugs—
are more vulnerable to interrogations designed to elicit confessions, but normal
and otherwise well-functioning individuals are also susceptible to interrogation pressure and have confessed to terrible crimes that they did not commit.[48]
Innocent people often believe that they do not need a lawyer, or that asking for
a lawyer might suggest guilt, but without a lawyer they leave themselves open
to manipulation that they may not be able to resist.[49] And even though police
departments are required to caution those being interrogated about their right
to silence, this often does not lead the person to fully understand the risks of
continuing to be interviewed without legal representation.[50]

False confessions are usually the product of intense interrogation carried out
over many hours, with little or no opportunity for refreshment or rest. On top of
that, isolation, anxiety, and fatigue increase vulnerability to persuasion. The *Reid
technique* is a powerful interrogation procedure that is widely employed by police
departments across North America.[51] It succeeds in eliciting confessions from
individuals who have waived the right to have a lawyer present. The interrogator
plays both "good cop" and "bad cop" at once, alternating between *maximization*
and *minimization*. Maximization involves leveling direct accusations, announcing
that the investigator is certain that the suspect is guilty, and deliberately inter-
rupting the suspect when he tries to deny guilt. Often, the police officer claims
to have hard evidence of the person's guilt (even when there is no such evidence).
The maximization procedure often leads to the suspect feeling hopeless about his
situation, even when he knows himself to be innocent. Then, through minimization, the interrogator appears to become sympathetic and understanding, and
undertakes to help the suspect morally justify the criminal act, suggesting that
it is normal, that anyone might have committed the offense under the circumstances. Confession is promoted as the first step toward dealing with the problem,
implying that cooperation may lead to more lenient treatment.

Such interrogations can be lengthy and emotionally draining, and it is likely
to seem that the only way out of the aversive situation is to give the interrogator
what is wanted—a confession. Sometimes, the individual actually comes to believe
that she must be guilty in light of the incriminating information the police claim
to have. This kind of self-delusion is encouraged when the interrogator suggests
a pseudo-technical explanation such as "repressed memory" to explain how the
suspect could have committed the crime without any recollection of it.

Laboratory research has demonstrated how powerful false incriminating
evidence can be both in leading people to confess guilt for something they have

not done and in the development of false memories and beliefs in line with the presumed wrongful act.[52] In one experiment that involved the use of a computer keyboard, participants were accused of having caused the computer program to crash by hitting the wrong key.[53] In reality, they were all innocent, and indeed they all initially denied the accusation. Yet when participants heard that a witness (a confederate of the researcher) had reported having witnessed them press the key, many subsequently confessed to having caused the damage. Later, when asked in another context by someone not apparently associated with the experiment, those participants still reported that they had caused the program to crash, and invented details of their behavior consistent with having caused the problem. Of course, confessing to hitting the wrong key has quite different consequences than confessing to murder, but it is all a matter of degree. The same processes are in play.

Witnesses, interrogations, and the Reid technique

Witnesses too are subjected at times to police interrogations that push them to provide evidence beyond what they actually observed. They may be even more susceptible to coercive interrogation given that they face little or no consequence if their testimony should wrongly implicate a stranger. A study was carried out to examine the power of the Reid technique to produce misleading testimony when used to interrogate witnesses.[54] It was motivated by an actual case of an innocent man wrongly imprisoned for three and a half years following a conviction based on misleading witness evidence obtained through the technique. In that study, each participant (all were university students) sat in a laboratory room with another person, who, unbeknownst to the participant, was working with the experimenter. A researcher entered the room and distributed some logic tests for them to complete, and then, a few minutes later, the researcher returned and asked if either had seen a cell phone that had been left behind. (In fact, there was no cell phone.) Later, after the pretend participant had gone, the real participant was questioned about the missing cell phone. In half the cases, participants were questioned in a straightforward manner about whether they had seen the other person take the phone, and in this case, no one implicated the other individual. The other half of the participants were interrogated using the Reid technique. They were told that the researcher knew that the other person had stolen the phone and insisted that the participant should simply describe what had happened. Five of the thirty people subjected to the Reid technique finally indicated that they had witnessed the other person take the phone, and they went on to say that they were confident in this assertion. This interrogation lasted only thirty minutes. Police interrogations can last for many hours.

Memory retrieval and false memories of guilt

Even more worrisome is the demonstration that false memories of actually having committed a crime can be generated in a controlled experimental setting. Consider this experiment, which employed the same suggestive memory-retrieval techniques often used by therapists and others in their attempts to reveal hidden, or "repressed" memories.[55] The participants were seventy university students who had never committed any crime, and they were told only that the research concerned how well people could remember their childhoods. Information had been obtained beforehand from parents with regard to a significant incident in each of the students' lives during their adolescence. In a series of three forty-minute sessions, each student was asked to recall two events from five years earlier, both the actual event confirmed by the parents and an event invented by the experimenter (a criminal assault that led to the involvement of the police). They were told that their parents had described these events to the researchers.

When they could not remember the false event, memory-retrieval techniques were brought into play. Shockingly, by the end of the three interviews, more than 70 percent of the participants reported that they now believed that they had committed that crime five years earlier. They went further, creating the details of the crime on their own, recalling vivid sensory memories, becoming emotional, and expressing guilt. Some of the participants continued to insist that they were guilty of the crime even after they were told that it had never occurred. Such is the power of interrogation combined with memory-retrieval techniques to distort and create memories and false confessions.

PERSUASION: FAKE NEWS, ALTERNATE FACTS, AND POST-TRUTH

Many people in this modern age, especially the young, have turned away from traditional news sources where journalistic standards provide an important check on ersatz information. They rely instead on internet sites and blogs, some of which are fake-news sites that deliberately publish false news, whether for political reasons or financial gain. Fake-news sites have proliferated in recent years and became a subject of considerable concern during the 2016 United

States presidential election. For example, false accounts of a variety of criminal activities by Hillary Clinton were intended to undermine her bid for the presidency. Evidence emerged showing that Russia was involved in the deliberate attempt to mislead the American public. Similarly, the 2016 debate over the United Kingdom's referendum on membership in the European Union (Brexit) involved repeated dissemination of demonstrably false claims.

Beliefs are only as reliable as the evidence and information upon which they are based. A functioning democracy is reliant upon accurate information about world events, and citizens need accurate information in order to understand what is going on in their nation and to make reasoned choices at election time. The attack on truth, facts, and reason by exaggeration, disinformation, and outright lies led the Oxford Dictionary to choose *post-truth* as its word of the year in 2016, noting that the use of the term had increased 2,000 percent during that year. They define "post-truth" as "relating to or denoting circumstances in which objective facts are less influential in shaping public opinion than appeals to emotion and personal belief."[56] If the quest for truth loses favor in a post-truth world, beliefs shaped by wishes and emotion will put all our futures in peril.

False news can be highly effective in persuading people to change their beliefs, in part because of the illusory truth effect. In one study, one group of participants was presented initially with false news reports and again a second time five weeks later with the same false reports. These participants perceived the message as more plausible and truthful than did other participants who had not had the earlier exposure.[57] Some evidence suggested that false memories had also been created because some of the participants reported, incorrectly, that they had initially heard the news report from a source not associated with the experiment. As unsettling as it is, this again suggests that exposing people repeatedly to false information is likely to increase belief in that information. Not only that, but there is also research evidence that indicates that increased familiarity as a result of repeated exposure to information can even serve to retroactively increase one's assessment of the source's credibility.[58]

One might hope that young people, despite their reliance on the internet for their news, would be able to distinguish fake from real news. Unfortunately, the results of research carried out with almost eight thousand middle-school, high-school, and college students in the United States are not encouraging in that regard.[59] Most of the students mistook fraudulent news reports for fact and material clearly labelled as "sponsored news content" for journalism. The researchers concluded that:

at each level—middle school, high school, and college . . . young people's ability to reason about the information on the internet can be summed up in one word: bleak. . . . [W]hen it comes to evaluating information that flows through social media channels, they are easily duped.[60]

Not only must society deal with deliberately misleading news sites, some politicians in recent times have muddied things even further by labeling traditional news media that have criticized them, as being purveyors of fake news. Not long after Donald Trump's presidential inauguration in January 2017, the term "alternative facts" was used to justify falsehoods emanating from the White House. This brings to mind George Orwell's 1949 novel *1984*, in which the totalitarian government has its own alternative facts, known as *newspeak* and *doublethink*. In Orwell's words, "The past was erased, the erasure was forgotten, the lie became the truth."[61]

Correcting false information

How do we respond to new information that indicates that prior information was incorrect or even outright false? Research shows that when we have been provided with information that we initially judge to be true, it continues to influence both our memory and our reasoning to some degree, even when we later learn that it was incorrect.[62] This is known as the *continued influence effect*. Even warning people about this effect before giving them false information followed by a retraction fails to overcome it completely.[63] As the saying goes, once the bell has been rung, you cannot *unring* it.

Why would people continue to be influenced by information that they are informed is false? The explanation appears to be that people typically prefer a complete explanation for important events over an incomplete one, and if the initial information provides a complete explanation, it may be hard to let go of, even when it is later reported to be erroneous. Initial news about an airplane crash creates an immediate mystery—what happened? If this is followed by a report that a terrorist's bomb blew up the airplane, you now have an explanation that makes sense. We often construct a neat little package of events in our heads, and then if told later that part of the package is not true—that the crash was not due to a bomb—this creates a gap. If not due to a bomb, what was the cause? And so, in the absence of another explanation, it is not easy to put the original false explanation totally out of mind. In addition, people generally fail to recognize that the discredited information was the sole basis for their belief and therefore do not realize that their belief is now groundless.[64]

The continued influence effect is evident in everyday life. Think about when a person is arrested and charged with having sexually abused a child but is later found to have an alibi. Many people will continue to believe the charge was correct, unless another acceptable explanation for the crime is forthcoming—for example, that the real culprit has been apprehended. Provision of a reasonable alternative explanation makes the package whole again. Similarly, laboratory studies of jury decision-making have found that jurors more often return a not-guilty verdict when an alternative suspect is proposed than when the defense only gives reasons for why the defendant was not guilty.[65]

Formal retractions

What happens when jurors are asked to ignore information that the judge has ruled inadmissible? At least in the context of a psychological experiment, mock jurors were able to avoid relying on inadmissible information, but there were nonetheless subtle continuing effects. When asked to give their impression of the defendant and to assess his aggressiveness, the retracted information continued to affect their view of the defendant's character.[66]

And what about newspaper retractions? First of all, while an original story may have made the headlines, we all know that the retraction is often a small article somewhere on an inner page. Leaving that problem aside, can people correct what they believe when presented with a retraction of the erroneous information? A study of news media coverage during the 2003 Iraq war revealed numerous corrections and retractions of news items.[67] For example, a report that Iraqi forces were executing enemy prisoners as soon as they surrendered was retracted a day later, and the claim that weapons of mass destruction had been found was also subsequently disclaimed. The researchers examined the effects of such retractions and disconfirmations on memories and beliefs related to events during that war. The research was carried out in the United States and Australia (both of which were part of the "coalition forces") and in Germany (which had opposed the war). Participants were questioned about true events, fictional events, and events that had been first reported as fact but later retracted. The Australian and German participants discounted the retracted information after learning that it was false, but participants in the United States did not and continued to rely on the incorrect, retracted information. The researchers interpreted this difference as the result of greater suspicion on the parts of Germans and Australians about the motives underlying the war against Iraq.

In another study, in which the initial information about a fire indicated that negligence was involved, simple retraction of the claim of negligence did little to counter the effects of that initial report. Later on, when asked to consider how the insurance company might respond, participants reasoned that the claim might be rejected because of the negligence of the owners. On the other hand, when the retraction was accompanied by information providing an alternative explanation (arson materials were found at the site), then subsequent references to the retracted information (about negligence) were reduced.[68] The provision of such an alternative allows individuals to revise their beliefs about cause rather than simply negating the incorrect information.[69]

PERSUASION: RADICALIZATION AND A LICENSE TO KILL

> *Terrorists do not fall from the sky, they emerge from a set of strongly held beliefs. They are radicalized. Then they become terrorists.*
>
> —Brian Jenkins, Senior Adviser to the President of the RAND Corporation[70]

Terrorism, and in particular suicide terrorism, was addressed in chapter 1. Recall that radicalization involves identification with a particular group and the belief that violent actions against innocent people are noble and worthy rather than despicable.[71] But an important question was left unaddressed: *how* is it that people's beliefs change to the extent that they can accept that the deaths of innocent individuals are justifiable? The answer lies in the process of *radicalization*.

Psychologist Fathali Moghaddam likens Islamic radicalization to a stairway ascending five floors, with the terrorist act occurring only on the fifth.[72] At the bottom of the stairway are large numbers of people suffering from feelings of deprivation, humiliation, alienation, or anger. Some of them climb to the first floor in an effort to find a solution, where they undertake actions to achieve social justice. If this does not resolve their frustrations, some then climb to the second floor where their growing sense of injustice results in increased outrage. At this level, belief is bolstered by radical Islamic messages that insist that there are no legitimate avenues for dealing with the injustice they feel. They may encounter leaders who point to the enemy responsible for their problems and encourage them to direct their anger and frustration toward that enemy. Individuals motivated to express their anger in physical action then climb up to the third floor, where they begin to learn about terrorist groups and come to accept the morality of terrorism. Those who accept this new moral perspective climb up to the fourth floor and are now well on their way to becoming terrorists. They begin to see the world from a rigid "us-versus-them" perspective and are introduced to the secret world of the terrorist network, where violence is seen as an appropriate and justifiable action. A few will be chosen to climb to the fifth and final floor, where they now are groomed to carry out terrorist acts, some of which involve sacrificing their own lives.

Terrorism and the internet

The preponderance of terrorist activity in North America, Western Europe, and Australia in recent years has involved radicalized individuals who launched their attacks in the countries in which they were born and raised.[73] Modern terrorist groups are skilled in using the internet as an effective recruitment tool.[74] "Global Islamist terrorism" produces and disseminates large numbers of online videos aimed at spreading an ideology of religion-sanctioned violence in response to perceived atrocities committed against Muslims and Islam.[75] (In addition, detailed do-it-yourself instructional videos teach the viewer how to make improvised explosive devices and suicide vests.[76]) As noted earlier (chapter 1), those who respond to internet recruitment begin to identify with the organization and to share its goals, even if they have never had any direct contact with it. A bond is created among people in the virtual Muslim community as they dream of a world where Islamic law and justice are paramount. This is likely to have particular appeal to young immigrants and children of immigrants who feel alienated from the larger society. At the same time, viewers are helped to rationalize horrific violence.[77] Individuals attracted to such propaganda develop more and more extremist beliefs while withdrawing from people in their own community who might provide some balance for these extreme views.

Protest converts

How can we account for Western non-Muslims who *convert* to Islam and then become extremists and suicide terrorists? These "protest converts" are disaffected, angry, and rebellious youth looking for an honorable cause for which to fight.[78] They find it in radical Islam. By way of historical comparison, consider the tens of thousands of young volunteers from countries all over the world who joined the International Brigades to defeat General Franco's forces in the Spanish Civil War of 1936–1939. They put their lives on the line, even though most of them had no connection with Spain or its people and were unable even to speak the language. In modern times, those who feel that they do not fit into society and are angry but do not really know why can find solace in an internet community that provides acceptance and a sense of purpose, as well as identifying the supposed cause of the world's misery. Such converts are prized by radical groups because they are generally free to travel throughout Europe and North America without arousing suspicion.[79]

Conversion is facilitated and encouraged by extremist Islamic websites, where non-Muslims growing up in Western countries with little or no knowledge of Islam learn only the extremist interpretation of the religion. Prisons also provide an excellent training ground for inculcating radical Islamic beliefs, and a number of prison converts, including the infamous shoe-bomber, Richard Reid, have committed terrorist attacks upon their release.[80]

Consider the words of twenty-four-year-old Canadian convert to Islam John McGuire, who later was killed while fighting for Daesh/ISIS. He was shown in a propaganda video wearing a *keffiyeh* (a Palestinian scarf) and holding a Kalashnikov rifle. He called upon Muslims in Canada to launch attacks on Canadian soil:

> I was one of you: I was a typical Canadian. . . . I grew up on the hockey rink and spent my teenage years on stage playing guitar. . . . I had no criminal record. I was a bright student and maintained a strong GPA in university. So how could one of your people end up in my place? And why is it that your own people are the ones turning against you at home? The answer is we have accepted the true call of the prophets and the messengers of God.[81]

While Daesh/ISIS carries out direct suicide attacks, it has also been successful in inspiring so-called "lone-wolf" attacks in which an individual's beliefs, shaped by online propaganda, culminate in terrorist acts, even though there has been no direct contact with ISIS. In other cases, attacks are carried out by "remote control." While, again, there is no direct contact with Daesh/ISIS members, one of their agents directs the "lone-wolf" terrorist through encrypted communication over the internet. Particular targets and methodologies are provided and in some cases weapons are also provided. An example: in July 2016, a teenaged Afghan refugee armed with a knife and axe attacked a score of passengers on a train in northern Bavaria before he was killed by police. This was taken at first to be a lone-wolf attack, but subsequent analysis of the attacker's cell phone showed that he had been in direct contact with an ISIS handler until the moment he boarded the train.[82]

STATE-SPONSORED RADICALIZATION AND TERRORISM

> *Let us be terrible to prevent the people from being terrible!*
> —Georges Jacques Danton, justifying the Reign of Terror

The terms *radicalization* and *terrorism* immediately bring to mind individuals groomed by a minority to fight against the state, but sometimes states themselves undertake to radicalize their citizens.[83] The Nazis' propaganda machine radicalized much of the German nation to vilify and persecute Jews, and this led German soldiers and police to believe that normally unconscionable murderous actions were not only necessary but also morally justified.

Psychologist Herbert Kelman described the Nazi process to change beliefs and overcome normal restraints against violence.[84] First there was *authorization*. Citizens were persuaded to believe that the usual moral principles did not apply in the current situation and that they were absolved from the responsibility for making moral choices. They needed only to follow orders. Next, the target group was *dehumanized*. The Nazis set out to persuade their citizens that Jews, the Roma ("gypsies"), and other target groups were subhuman, that homosexuals were depraved, and that cognitively disabled individuals were aberrations who did not deserve to live.

In addition, the Nazis used state-directed terror to control both their own population and the people of conquered nations. They reinforced the belief that resistance would not only fail but would bring heavy consequences. The Gestapo tactic of *Nacht und Nebel* (Night and Fog) involved arrests without warning of suspected dissidents who were then either killed immediately or sent to concentration camps where death often soon followed.

Believe us! Resistance is futile

The Nazis ruthlessly discouraged terrorism directed against them by means of massive retaliation against innocents. One terrible example: On May 27, 1942, Free Czech agents, trained and organized by the British, assassinated SS Obergruppenführer Reinhard Heydrich in Prague. In retaliation, the SS and the Gestapo hunted down and executed anyone whom they thought was connected to Heydrich's death; more than 1,000 people were killed. In addition, 500 Jews were arbitrarily arrested in Berlin and 152 were immediately executed as part of the reprisal.

But it was not over yet. To ensure that the message was clear, the small Czech village of Lidice, falsely accused of complicity in the Heydrich killing, was liquidated. All 172 men and boys aged sixteen and older were shot to death, and all the women and children were sent to concentration camps—women to one, their children to another. The town was then leveled, a grain field was planted where it had once stood, and the name of the village was removed from German maps.[85]

Such monstrous retaliation is intended to instill the belief that resistance will only bring greater suffering. Terrorism, even suicide terrorism, does not succeed against powerful governments with such total disregard for humanity; the costs are simply too high. As for nonviolent resistance, it is a nonstarter. Mahatma Gandhi's hunger strikes would have been pointless against the Nazis. He would simply have been eliminated. However, while state terrorism saps enthusiasm for rebellion, it also results in growing animosity toward the state and ultimately increases support for future terrorists.[86]

The Nazis were not unique, of course. All dictators eventually resort to terrorism directed toward their own people to bring them to the belief that resistance is futile. Stalin, Mao, and many other demagogues maintained control over their citizens in this way. State-sponsored terrorism often involves secret police, arrests without warrant, and the "disappearing" of suspected dissidents. After the military coup in Chile in 1973 that brought Augusto Pinochet to power, an army death squad, the *Caravana de la Muerte* (Caravan of Death), was established to carry out the torture and execution of pacifist political dissidents. Pinochet's government "disappeared" a further three thousand opponents; they were taken away and never seen again. Large-scale "disappearances" have occurred in a number of other countries as well, among them Argentina, which is infamous for its *Desapa-*

recidos (the "disappeared"). During the Argentine military junta (1976 to 1983), thousands of suspected dissidents were picked up by the police and military and were never seen again. It was later learned that many victims had been put aboard airplanes and dropped to their deaths over the Atlantic Ocean.

WHEN BELIEFS COLLIDE

If we all held exactly the same sets of beliefs, society would stagnate. Differences in belief stimulate intellect, promote change, and drive creativity. On the other hand, we encounter beliefs at times that are so opposed to our own cherished beliefs, and that are held with such conviction, that rational dialogue is not possible. The beliefs collide.

There are times when in good conscience we want to try to change some of those beliefs. The belief that the measles-mumps-rubella (MMR) vaccine causes autism (a belief triggered by a fraudulent research paper that was subsequently withdrawn by the scientific journal that published it[87]), the belief that energy therapy can cure serious illness, and the belief that climate change is a hoax and that our planet is not warming all threaten serious consequences both for those hold these beliefs and for others as well. Those with opposing opinions might understandably want to challenge such beliefs.

What should we do when beliefs collide, and we want to try to bring someone to our belief? (It can be helpful to consider how difficult it would be for someone to persuade you to change an important belief of your own.) Presenting "facts" is not enough, for there will be disagreement on just what are the facts. Citing experts is ineffective, for there will be disagreement on who are the experts. Pointing out weaknesses in a person's thinking goes nowhere and will only turn the interaction into a battle rather than resolve which ideas are correct.

Before undertaking an effort to change someone's belief, it is important to be aware that information that strongly challenges cherished beliefs can at times have the paradoxical result of strengthening them instead. This *backfire effect* has been observed in a number of studies.[88] In one study, politically conservative participants read mock news articles that involved a misleading claim, supposedly coming from the government, that tax cuts would lead to increased federal revenue.[89] Some of the participants then read a credible refutation of the claim by a prominent economist. While about one-third of the participants believed the initial claim, that proportion increased to two-thirds when exposed to the refutation. Other research has focused on the fallacious belief that the MMR vaccine causes autism.[90] While information refuting the link between MMR and autism led to skepticism in many participants that the vaccine causes autism, a backfire effect was found among those parents who were initially most critical of vaccines. The refutation resulted in a *decrease* in their intentions to have their children vaccinated.

Keeping that concern in mind, while there is no magic bullet for persuading people to change their beliefs, the psychological literature provides a number of suggestions.

- *Plant a seed of doubt.*[91] Well-entrenched beliefs rarely succumb to argument. If such beliefs change, the change usually comes from within. Therefore, the goal should be to bring a person, in a nonconfrontational manner, to consider that re-examination of the belief is in order.
- *Find a wedge issue.*[92] In planting a seed of doubt, it is important to understand the individual's cognitive framework so as to present arguments that fall within the individual's "latitude of acceptance"[93] and will not be rejected out of hand. Suppose that you oppose capital punishment, while your friend strongly supports it. Neither direct confrontation nor arguments favoring your point of view are likely to be effective. On the other hand, if you can find a "wedge issue" on which you can both agree—for example, how some people who have been executed were later proven innocent—you may motivate your friend to think more carefully about the negatives associated with capital punishment. This may initiate movement toward belief change. As Blaise Pascal noted in the seventeenth century, "People are generally better persuaded by the reasons which they have themselves discovered than by those which have come into the mind of others."[94]
- *Counter-explanation.*[95] In some situations, such as in a classroom, belief change can be promoted by asking individuals to play the role of someone defending the position contrary to their own. In playing that role, they are more likely to become aware of the strengths of the competing arguments and of the weaknesses in their own.
- *Do not focus on what is false.*[96] Rather than focusing on what is false in the other person's beliefs, it is more generally more effective to emphasize what you believe to be true. For example, refuting myths about vaccination in an effort to change the attitudes of people who are opposed to

vaccination is ineffective, but stressing the dangers posed by communicable diseases does lead to positive change.[97]

- *Avoid creating a face-losing situation.* Conflict over beliefs can quickly change into a conflict about who is going to win. People do not like to be perceived as backing down from their beliefs. Belief change is facilitated by providing a way to save face despite the change.

We are often the targets of deliberate efforts—whether through face-to-face persuasion, advertising, propaganda, indoctrination, or radicalization—to change our beliefs in a direction desired by other people in service of their interests rather than our own. This creates a challenge for us all: to be flexible enough to modify our beliefs appropriately when new and credible information is presented, while at the same time to be steadfast enough to preserve them from manipulation by others. As is addressed in the next chapter, this challenge is amplified when people deliberately set out to befriend us and gain our trust in order to deceive and take advantage.

CHAPTER 9

CREDULITY AND DECEIT

A certain extent of credulity, or, more properly, belief, may, indeed, be considered as absolutely necessary to the well-being of social communities; for universal skepticism would be universal distrust. Nor could knowledge ever have arrived at its present amazing height, had every intermediate step in the ladder of science, from profound ignorance and slavery of intellect, been disputed with bigoted incredulity.

—R. A. Davenport (1845)[1]

We like to think of ourselves as thoughtful individuals who are not overly influenced by the beliefs and suggestions of others. Yet all of us, even those who are dogmatically unflinching with regard to key beliefs, are at times suggestible—that is, uncritically receptive to such influence. Fortune-tellers, scammers, and imposters would not be so successful if this were not so. Suggestibility can significantly influence perception, memory, thought, mood, and action.[2] Imagine, for example, tasting a sandwich after your friend has suggested that it is a bit "off," or attending a play that your favorite reviewer has savaged. Suggestibility can lead to serious consequences in some circumstances, such as the false recollections of having been abused in childhood based on a therapist's suggestion, or confessing to a crime when one is innocent in response to an interrogator's insistence that one is guilty.

It is important to distinguish *suggestibility* from *compliance*, in which there is verbal agreement without actual acceptance. Compliance can occur for a number of reasons, such as the desire to avoid disagreement or tension, an attempt to please, or an effort to end the discussion.

Suggestibility occurs in two forms, direct and indirect.[3] Direct, or *imagi-*

native, suggestibility involves reactions to *overt* suggestions, such as with hypnosis: "Your eyelids are becoming very heavy and soon they will close..." No deception is involved. Such suggestibility can also of course be tapped without hypnotic induction.[4] In this case, people are simply invited to fantasize and to experience their fantasy as though it were reality. (Hypnosis is discussed in greater detail in chapter 11.)

Indirect suggestibility is independent of imaginative suggestibility.[5] It involves yielding to subtle, covert suggestions without being aware of doing so. Deception is involved, for the attempt to influence is not obvious. As we have seen, eyewitness reports are vulnerable to contamination simply by asking slanted questions. Indirect suggestibility is also involved in the placebo response in which people report improvement in their symptoms after receiving an inert substance presented as having medicinal properties.[6] Direct and indirect suggestibility appear to involve different patterns of brain activity. The indirect suggestibility that is involved in placebo responses is associated with *increased* activity in the prefrontal cortex, while direct, imaginative suggestibility is associated with *decreased* activation in that region.[7]

Research has compared individuals who had allegedly falsely confessed to a crime ("false confessors") with individuals who proclaimed their innocence despite forensic evidence supporting their guilt ("resisters").[8] The two groups were matched in terms of age, gender, intelligence, memory ability, and the seriousness of their crimes. The false confessors scored higher in terms of both suggestibility and compliance. Intelligence was not a factor. As was discussed in greater detail in the previous chapter, it is strange but true that people of normal intelligence at times confess to serious crimes that they did not commit.[9]

SUGGESTIBILITY AND THE BARNUM EFFECT

Suppose that you have been to a palm reader or astrologer and were given this feedback:

> You have a need for other people to like and admire you, and yet you tend to be critical of yourself. While you have some personality weaknesses, you are generally able to compensate for them. You have considerable unused capacity that you have not turned to your advantage. Disciplined and self-controlled on the outside, you tend to be worrisome and insecure on the inside. At times,

you have serious doubts as to whether you have made the right decision or done the right thing. You prefer a certain amount of change and variety and become dissatisfied when hemmed in by restrictions and limitations. You also pride yourself as an independent thinker and do not accept others' statements without satisfactory proof. But you have found it unwise to be too frank in revealing yourself to others. At times you are extroverted, affable, and sociable, while at other times you are introverted, wary, and reserved. Some of your aspirations tend to be rather unrealistic.

If you are like most people, this will seem to be a pretty good description of your personality. There is a reason for that, as we shall see.

In 1948, psychologist Bertram Forer administered a personality test to his students, and then, without looking at their responses, gave each student identical feedback (the above personality description) which he had copied from a newspaper astrology column.[10] The students were then asked to rate the assessment, and most of them rated it as being an accurate description of themselves. As a result, they concluded that the personality test that they thought had generated the description was valid. It is such *personal validation*, based on one's personal reaction that reinforces belief in the abilities of astrologers, palm readers, and psychics.

Forer's demonstration has been repeated many times over the intervening years, always with similar results. The bogus description appears valid to people for two reasons. First of all, it contains generalities, most of which apply to everyone, and second, people are very adept at interpreting information in a matter consistent with how they see themselves. This interpretation of a generalized personality description as an accurate, and even specific, description of oneself is referred to as the *Barnum effect*, in reference to circus impresario P. T. Barnum's claim that his show had "something for everybody." Like Barnum's circus, Forer's generalized personality description contains something for everyone.

The seeming accuracy of some personality tests still in extensive use is actually due to the Barnum effect. For example, despite severe criticism about its lack of validity, the *Myers-Briggs Type Indicator* is used around the world by human resources departments in the selection and training of employees. Yet, the apparent accuracy of its assessments has been shown to be due to the Barnum effect.[11]

SUGGESTIBILITY AND COLD READINGS

A *cold reading* involves various techniques to persuade an individual, even a total stranger, that the "reader" has obtained information about the individual that could not possibly be acquired through normal means. In other words, it appears to involve "mind reading." Cold reading involves a number of elements, including the use of the kind of generalities found in Forer's "personality assessment." A good cold reader goes beyond generalities and adds elements to the reading based on careful observation of the individual. Physical features, manner and sophistication of speech, movements, clothing, jewelry, and so forth, all provide cues. Add to this what the reader can guess on the basis of the person's age, gender, and subculture, and one has the basis for what will seem to be a strikingly accurate assessment. The reader can make the reading even more specific by posing questions and observing feedback in terms of eye movements, bodily mannerisms, and so on, that suggest whether he is on the right track.[12]

Some cold readers have earned a reputation and a considerable fortune by pretending to use extrasensory perception. On the other hand, many neighborhood palm readers and psychics deceive themselves as well as their clients and genuinely believe that they have extraordinary "paranormal" abilities. This can occur completely without awareness, as psychologist Ray Hyman, an authority on cold reading, learned early in his life.[13] While he was a teenaged student, he earned money through palm readings, even though at the outset he did not believe that there was any validity to the practice. Over time, the readings became so automatic that he eventually came to believe that he was truly reading the lines in people's palms and revealing hidden information. The clients' positive reactions convinced him of this. However, a respected conjurer of his acquaintance gently suggested that he test his belief by deliberately telling his clients the *opposite* of whatever the lines on their palms supposedly indicated. Hyman agreed to this, and the first time he did so, his client reacted with total silence. This was no surprise to him, for he expected failure. He was thoroughly surprised, however, when after a long pause his client responded that this was the best reading she had ever had.[14] He repeated this test with other clients, who likewise responded enthusiastically. He came to realize that the success of the reading depends on the ability of the clients to find correspondence between it and events in their lives. He learned as well that clients almost always *want* the reader to succeed and will usually find a way to make sense of whatever is said to them. This point is echoed by another accomplished cold reader, Ian Rowland:

> In the course of a successful reading, the psychic may provide most of the words, but it is the client that provides most of the meaning and all of the significance.[15]

Hyman also advises that, to ensure success, it is advisable at the outset to enlist the cooperation of the individual by indicating that one's words may not always communicate exactly what is meant, but that the individual will recognize what they mean in terms of his life. This places the onus on the client to make sense of ambiguous statements. Thus, if the reader mentions "a difficult time early in your life," that may bring to mind the death of a puppy to one person, being bullied in school to another, and, to a third, the family home having been flooded. This can be very striking emotionally and is likely to increase suggestibility even further.

SUGGESTIBILITY AND THE SENSES

Our perceptions can certainly be affected by suggestion. As a classroom demonstration of suggestibility, I challenged students to identify a well-known brand of perfume by smell alone, without seeing its label. I then held up a closed vial of colorless liquid and explained that it was the concentrated essence of the perfume. To make this more believable, I described (based on personal experience) how tourists in Cairo are frequently importuned to purchase concentrated essences that are claimed to be the bases of the finest Parisian perfumes and they are told that dilution of such an essence with pure alcohol will provide a batch of expensive perfume at very low cost. I went on to say that the essence is so strong that it would be unpleasant to the nose were the students to smell it directly. I then opened the vial to allow its fragrance to waft throughout the room and asked students to raise their hands when the fragrance reached them. After a few hands had been raised, a student at the back of the room suddenly stood and somewhat aggressively announced that she was very upset at my thoughtless action. She informed me that the fragrance had just reached her, and, because she suffered from multiple chemical sensitivity, this had triggered a severe migraine headache. She left the room in a hurry, and she subsequently registered a complaint with my dean. The dean later contacted me and expressed significant concern about her migraine, her emotional distress, and my role in triggering both. He had difficulty at first in grasping what had actually occurred when I explained that the student had not stayed around long enough to learn that there was no "essence" in the vial, but only tap water. It took a little while for him to wrap his head around the fact that her migraine was not the result of a fragrance, but of suggestibility. Her imagination had led her to believe that she detected the fragrance and then, presumably because of past associations between fragrance and headache, the headache developed as a conditioned reaction.

My classroom demonstration of suggestibility was inspired by an 1899 lecture given by psychologist Edwin Slosson. During his lecture, he poured distilled water over a piece of cotton and told his students that it was a chemical with a strong odor, one that no one would have smelled before.[16] He asked them to raise their hands when the odor reached them, and within fifteen seconds, most of the front-row students had raised their hands, and within a minute, three-quarters of the audience had done so.

In the late 1970s, Professor Michael O'Mahony, a specialist in chemical-induced sensory experiences, provided a similar example of the power of suggestion on British television. During the telecast, he informed the audience that he was about to play a tone which was of the same frequency as the vibrations of molecules that produce the odor of a particular substance.[17] This is a nonsensical idea, of course, but he went on to explain that, as he sounded the tone, listeners would experience a pleasant country fragrance. Close to two hundred viewers responded with reports of having smelled grass, flowers, or manure, and some indicated that they were also experiencing allergic reactions such as sneezing. He subsequently repeated this demonstration on radio with similar results.

SUGGESTIBILITY AND SUBJECTIVE STATES

Psychologists Stanley Koren and Michael Persinger developed what has been called the *God Helmet*, a helmet-like apparatus that delivers a magnetic field to the wearer's head. Their research found that about 80 percent of participants subjected to the magnetic field while wearing the helmet reported having a mystical experience, which for some involved the presence of an invisible, sentient being.[18] While the researchers concluded that the magnetic field had affected people's brains to the extent that mystical experiences were elicited, critics soon pointed out that the magnetic field that they employed was five thousand times weaker than that of a typical fridge magnet, far too weak to penetrate the skull and have any influence on neurons.[19] Attempts by others to replicate this research failed, leading to the conclusion that the apparent effects of the God Helmet were due not to a magnetic field but to the suggestibility of the participants.[20]

Our subjective states—our emotions—are especially influenced by suggestion. While in graduate school, a fellow student and some of his friends were about to go to movie—a comedy—when he decided to bring some marijuana with him to be smoked just prior to the film. This, he thought, would make the comedy funnier. His wife told him that she had put the marijuana in a plastic bag in the refrigerator, and so he grabbed the bag and he and his friends headed for the cinema. They smoked a joint and went in to watch the film. He reported that they giggled for a good twenty minutes or so as they experienced the effects of the marijuana. However, he slowly began to realize that something did not feel quite right, that he was not actually "high." He learned later that in his haste he had grabbed a small bag of dried parsley by mistake. It was suggestibility, not the herb, that brought on twenty minutes of mirth.

FACTORS INFLUENCING SUGGESTIBILITY

Some people do seem to be generally more responsive to suggestion than others, and people also vary in suggestibility at different times or in different circumstances. Researchers have been unable to discover a clear basis for these differences.[21] Yet a number of factors are likely to play a role, including the individual's personality and emotional state, the status and expertise of the source of the influence, and the risks and rewards associated with being persuaded.

Age

Children, lacking an adult level of critical thinking and reality testing, are particularly vulnerable to various suggestive influences.[22] This has been a particular problem for the justice system whenever children have been interviewed with regard to possible sexual abuse.

Personality

There are few solid findings with regard to any role that personality might play in suggestibility. Although psychological measures have been developed to measure suggestibility, both in terms of a general tendency to yield to persuasion[23] and a vulnerability to manipulation during interrogation,[24] compelling evidence of a *trait* of general suggestibility has not been found.[25] Yet the research literature does suggest that people who are more generally acquiescent and cooperative, who are less assertive, or who harbor low self-esteem all tend to be more vulnerable to suggestion.[26]

Physical and emotional state

People tend to be more suggestible whenever their mental, emotional, and physical resources are heavily taxed. For example, sleep deprivation and the stress that it produces generally render people more suggestible, decreasing both the ability and the motivation to evaluate information critically and to note discrepancies between what one remembers and misleading information presented by an interrogator.[27] Across the centuries, jailers and interrogators have recognized that prisoners deprived of sleep, food, or water become increasingly amenable to admitting guilt. This helps explain why some people confess to crimes that they did not commit.

Anxiety and fear also generally increase suggestibility, and advertisers often deliberately stimulate people's anxieties when touting their products. For example, social anxiety is aroused by an advertisement that highlights the possibility of unknowingly having bad breath, and by adding that other people, even if offended, are unlikely to say anything. The solution to the anxiety? "Use our mouthwash and all will be well."

Loneliness also renders some people easy prey for con artists seeking to take their money but who appear sincere in offering friendship or romance. And then there is greed. When the promise of significant reward in return for little effort is involved, some people rush to join the con artist's scheme, unwittingly participating in the depletion of their own bank accounts. We shall return to the discussion of con artists later.

Characteristics of the source

We have seen in earlier chapters how characteristics of the source strongly influence the impact of the message. Consider this report from *The Compleat Mother*, published by the Canadian Women's Health Network.[28]

> Another one of nature's surprises is that men can breast-feed babies. According to endocrinologist Dr. Robert Greenblatt, who developed the sequential oral contraceptive pill, any normal male can begin to produce breastmilk by letting a baby suckle on his nipple for several weeks. There are many historical references to male lactation. For example, 19th-century German explorer Alexander Freiherr von Humboldt described a 32-year-old man who breastfed his child for five months. In more recent times, a 55-year-old Baltimore man was the wet-nurse of the children of his mistress.

Given that this information strikes most people as counterintuitive, its source becomes of particular importance. If the report were taken from the sensationalist *National Enquirer*, reasonable people would simply dismiss it with a laugh. On the other hand, the late Dr. Greenblatt really was an accomplished endocrinologist, and so long as we accept that, our prior belief about male lactation may change as a result of reading that passage.

SUGGESTIBILITY AND THE BRAIN

Recall that our brains initially accept information to be true, and only in a second stage evaluate it and then possibly deem it false (chapter 6). This process of falsification is associated with a particular region (ventromedial) of the prefrontal cortex. Research has compared the suggestibility of patients who have suffered damage in this region with that both of patients with damage in other regions of the brain and people with no brain damage.[29] That research involved presenting participants with misleading advertisements and later assessing the extent to which they thought the claims were truthful as well as their expressed intentions to purchase the advertised items. People with damage in the ventromedial prefrontal cortex were much more influenced by the misleading suggestions than were people in either of the other two groups. This finding fits with other evidence indicating that individuals with damage in that region are more vulnerable to being deceived by con artists.[30] The fact that this region gradually atrophies and loses functionality as people move into old age may help explain the greater vulnerability of the elderly to misleading information and fraud. It is as though their ability to doubt becomes compromised.

CREDULITY

Suggestibility as it becomes more pronounced magnifies into *credulity*, a tendency to be overly open to believing information that most people would consider ridiculous. While this can often lead to sorrow, it is important to note that the potential costs of believing false information are generally lower than those experienced by dogmatic individuals who reject information that turns out to be true. For example, refusing to believe that the storm troopers are coming for you and your family involves a greater potential cost, if the news is correct, then erroneously believing that they are coming when they are not. Thus, a bias toward credulity when danger is at hand has some survival value. Not surprisingly, credulity with regard to threatening information is most pronounced in people who believe that the world is generally a dangerous place.[31]

In regard to credulity, we have all heard the phrase "bullshit baffles brains." A team of researchers subjected that idea to analysis by studying receptivity to what they aptly called "pseudo-profound bullshit."[32] They presented participants with sentences that, while syntactically coherent, were devoid of any meaning, consisting only of randomly chosen, vague buzzwords such as "Wholeness quiets infinite phenomena." Some participants actually judged these sentences to be profound, at least to some degree. Those who were more credulous, higher in "bullshit receptivity," were also found to have lower levels of general cognitive ability, and they were less likely to demonstrate an analytical thinking style. It is also interesting that they were also found to be more positively disposed toward belief in religious and paranormal phenomena.

We are all likely to be credulous at times, depending on situational circumstances. We may be taken in by "snake-oil salesmen" hocking worthless remedies, used-car dealers offering remarkable bargains, attractive men and women using their beauty and charms to lighten our wallets, or financial planners who promise stellar returns on investments.

GULLIBILITY

Credulity morphs into *gullibility* when it results in action; that is, when a person is "gulled" into unwise and naïve behavior based on credulous acceptance of erroneous or misleading information.[33] Consider the old story about a man offering to sell the Brooklyn Bridge. If you believe that the man owns the bridge, you are credulous, but if you write out a check to buy it, you are gullible.[34] And there are people who, because of social anxiety and a desire to make themselves more sexually appealing, respond gullibly to advertisements that promise—indeed guarantee—larger breasts or bigger penises at little cost and with no effort (figure 9-1).

Figure 9-1: Advertisements that stretch the imagination.

Certainly, some people have a history of being duped, but just as no trait of suggestibility has been found, pronounced vulnerability to being gulled does not appear to be a personality trait either. Instead, such vulnerability rests on a combination of situational, cognitive, and personality factors. Psychologist Stephen Greenspan describes how these factors can combine, and suggests that, while any one of these factors is enough to explain gullible behavior, usually at least two such factors are involved at the same time (figure 9-2).[35]

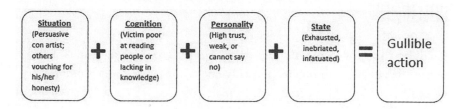

Figure 9-2: Roots of gullibility.

As the figure shows, first there are situational variables, such as the persuasiveness of the con artist or the presence of others who vouch for the con's honesty. Add to that cognitive factors, such as a lack of knowledge about what is proposed (financial investments, for example), and then compound it both with a poor ability to judge people's intentions and with personality factors such as a tendency to trust people too readily or a difficulty in saying "no."[36] Agreeableness (one of the so-called "Big Five" personality traits identified by psychologists) and indirect suggestibility are also likely to play a role.

All this adds up to an individual who is very vulnerable to persuasion and ripe for the fleecing. The susceptibility to being gulled is increased when the individual's critical-thinking ability is reduced because of infatuation, illness, inebriation, or exhaustion.

Gullibility and trust

We all can be scammed, and the only way to avoid this completely would be never to trust anyone. Still, it is not trust *per se* that is the usual problem. Being a high truster is not the same as being gullible. Rather, gullibility involves the foolish or naïve over-willingness to trust in situations where there are obvious warning signs that something is wrong.[37] Trust can be viewed as a by-product of social intelligence, the ability to gauge other people's feelings and intentions and to understand social relationships.[38] Individuals high in social intelligence are generally able to maintain a high level of trust and yet be cognizant in situations where such trust is not justified. This allows one to be free to take greater risks in pursuing opportunities than someone who is a low-truster and assumes that no one is to be trusted.[39] Thus, gullibility reflects not incautious trust but a lapse of rationality.[40]

DECEIT

Mundus vult decipi, ergo decipiatur.
(The world wants to be deceived, so let it be deceived.)
—Attributed to Petronius (27–66 CE)

For every sucker, there is someone willing to practice deceit, and, on top of that, many times we deceive ourselves. Wishful thinking often involves beliefs that are more aligned with our wants and needs than with reality, but self-deception goes a step further when we ignore or discount information that would challenge an important belief.[41] This results in persuading ourselves of something that is not really true, but which we prefer to believe.[42] Cognitive biases, such as confirmation bias and motivated cognition addressed in an earlier chapter, play an important role in self-deception and lead us to seek out information and interpret information in line with our beliefs and wishes.

Most of us manage to deceive ourselves at various times, when hope and emotion triumph over experience and reason.[43] We may dupe ourselves into believing that an acquaintance is an honest friend when all signs point to the contrary, that a chest pain is merely indigestion when it indicates something more serious, that a particular investment is wise despite its inherent risk, or that a romantic partner is ideal despite warnings from our friends.

Self-deception in science

Recall that when physicist René Blondlot along with a number of other scientists believed that they had observed N-rays, very faint beams of light that represented a new form of radiation, their expectations had fooled their perceptions, for there were no light beams (chapter 2). The history of science contains many examples of such self-deception. In modern times, we have the example of *cold fusion*. On March 23, 1989, two accomplished chemists, Stanley Pons and Martin Fleischmann, announced that they had produced nuclear fusion in a tabletop apparatus operating at room temperature. If their discovery were true, this would present the world with a low-cost source of massive amounts of renewable energy. Although a few other researchers reported being able to replicate the cold fusion findings, hundreds of others could not. Most physicists had been highly skeptical at the outset because such fusion, involving the fusing together of lighter nuclei to form a heavier nucleus while releasing enormous energy in the process, was believed possible only at temperatures of millions of degrees. Various sources of error were eventually discovered in the experimental set-up, and two months after the initial announcement, the American Physical Society declared the cold fusion claim dead. Pons and Fleischmann, excellent chemists in their own right, had deceived themselves. Ultimately, mistakes such as these are rooted out when others in the scientific community are unable to replicate the findings.

Hoaxes in science

The history of science is peppered with clever hoaxes that have fooled otherwise careful scientists. The Piltdown Man hoax, perpetrated in Sussex in 1912, is one of the best known. Amateur paleontologist Charles Dawson "discovered" the skull and jawbone of what was subsequently taken to be the "missing link" in the evolution between apes and humans. It was only decades later, in 1953, that his "discovery" was recognized as a fake, created by joining an ancient human skull to the jaw of an orangutan. It was determined that Dawson had perpetrated the hoax, but he was dead by that time. What was his motive? He had been unsuccessful in his efforts to join the Royal Society, and his faked prowess as a fossil hunter was most likely an attempt to gain scientific prestige. But how did he successfully fool professional scientists? Science writer Michael Price explains that the timing was right. British scientists were eager to produce fossils to rival those being discovered in Germany at the time, and so:

> Dawson was able to fool the experts of the day by employing the same trick used by successful con artists since time immemorial: He showed them what they wanted to see.[44]

The search for fame has not been the only motive behind scientific hoaxes. The quest for profit, revenge, or simply the desire to show the scientific community how vulnerable it is to deception have also figured largely.

Imposters

In 1951, during the Korean War, American Ferdinand "Waldo" Demara (1921–1982), later known as "The Great Imposter," presented himself at the recruiting office of the Royal Canadian Navy in Saint John, New Brunswick. He identified himself as a Canadian physician, Joseph Cyr. The Navy was at war and medical doctors were badly needed, and so "Dr. Cyr" was quickly enlisted without the usual time-consuming vetting of his credentials.

Figure 9-3: Ferdinand Waldo Demara (Associated Newspapers / Rex Features).

Demara was subsequently commissioned as Surgeon-Lieutenant on the HMCS *Cayuga*, bound for duty in Korea. He had never had any medical training, but relying on a textbook and the assistance of his Sick Berth Attendant, he performed a number of minor surgeries, including dental work on the ship commander's infected tooth. When several wounded South Korean fighters were brought aboard, he removed a bullet from one man and amputated the foot of another. Not only did the patients survive, but the ship's officers were so impressed that they wanted to recommend him for a medal.

When news of his accomplishments reached home and came to the attention of the real Dr. Cyr, the authorities were alerted and the imposter brought to ground.[45] It turns out that this was not his first impersonation, nor would it be his last. He had earlier posed variously as a monk ("Brother John"), a university professor, a cancer researcher, and a deputy sheriff.

Psychologist Maria Konnikova has described a number of famous imposters who have stolen other people's identities and managed to escape detection for considerable periods of time.[46] Some of them, like Demara, were content only to play the role of the person whose identity they had stolen, while others used the deception to con people out of large sums of money.

Con games

There is a long and fascinating history of con games perpetrated by confidence tricksters (or, more colloquially, "con artists"). They are referred to as *confidence* tricksters because their scams depend on gaining a person's confidence. They target their victim, the "mark." (The term apparently derives from the old practice of pickpockets circulating in a crowd. One member of the team would note in which pocket a man put his wallet after he paid for something. He then brushed against the man and marked that pocket with chalk, presenting a target for a partner who followed behind.)

Psychologist Loren Pankratz compares a con game to a stage play in which one of the actors, the mark, is unaware of having been scripted into a drama designed to separate him from his money.[47] The con and, often, a company of actors play their roles so cleverly that the mark willingly hands over money in expectation of a large financial return. The contextual setting is perfectly arranged to make everything appear genuine. The various actors pretend not to know one another, and they deliver their lines so sincerely that the mark remains unaware of the inevitable outcome until it is too late. It is, of course, advantageous if the mark does not report the theft, and this can be accomplished if, even while grieving the financial loss, the mark remains unaware of having been swindled, or believes that he has become involved in illegal activity.

In comparison to a con game, the *bank sneak* technique, used in days gone by, involved luring bank employees into a distracting drama while money was grabbed from their tills, all without a gun being necessary. As Pankratz points out, the bank sneak had to steal the money, whereas, in a con game, the mark voluntarily gives his cash to the swindler.[48]

The con game is an act of financial seduction. Some are parted from their money in a greedy attempt to increase their wealth, even if aware that questionable means are involved. Others fall victim because of loneliness, most often losing large sums of cash in an effort to help someone who is posing as a romantic partner.

Healthcare scams prey upon people's anxieties: the target is offered the opportunity to buy what is touted to be a remedy for a health problem, sometimes at great expense. Some healthcare scams have been so successful that they have become institutionalized. In the 1970s, news of amazing cures at the hands of the "psychic surgeons of the Philippines" began to spread, and people faced with terminal illnesses were given new hope of survival. As ridiculous as the claim sounds today, it was said that the "surgeon," often after taking a "psychic X-ray" of the patient's body, psychically "operated" by moving his hands over the body of the patient and apparently reaching in through the skin, plucking out what was said to be blood and malignant tissue. After the mess was wiped away, the skin was left intact. These "operations" were painless, and people believed (for a while) that they had been cured. Articles and books proliferated, and this encouraged many more people in the West who were suffering from terminal illnesses to spend a great deal of money, sometimes even selling their homes to raise the funds, in order to travel to the Philippines and have their lives saved. At the peak of the scam, in the early 1970s, approximately eight thousand foreigners were going to the psychic surgeons each month, some even before they had undergone conventional medical treatment. Travel agencies set up tour packages to accommodate the demand. Sadly for these miracle seekers, there were no cures, for there had been no treatment but only sleight of hand.[49] These many thousands of desperate people had been scammed.

Ponzi schemes

Some scams are so subtle that even the most critically minded and financially astute can fall victim. A good example of this is the Ponzi scheme. It takes its name from fraudster Charles Ponzi who, back in 1920, began what is now more generally referred to as a *pyramid scheme*. In this scheme, investors are offered very attractive rates of return and early investors actually receive them, unaware that their earnings are actually taken from investments made by later targets. Ultimately, the scheme collapses when there are no longer sufficient new investors to cover everyone's expected payments. By that time, however, the fraudster will have attempted to skip town with a great deal of money. It was just such a Ponzi scheme operated by New York financier Bernie Madoff that led to his being sentenced in 2009 to 150 years in prison after pleading guilty to defrauding many thousands of investors of billions of dollars.[50]

Ponzi schemes have been a popular form of fraud for a very long time. Such a scheme, in this case involving fraudulent insurance, is described in Charles Dickens's 1843 novel, *The Life and Adventures of Martin Chuzzlewit*. The unscrupulous Tigg Montague persuades people to invest in life insurance, although he has no intention of honoring the policies.[51] When a few people die prematurely, their policies are paid out from funds gathered by persuading other people to buy coverage.

The Spanish Prisoner and Nigerian email scams

The Spanish Prisoner scam began in the late 1500s. This scam emphasizes the need for secrecy, and the target is led to believe that he has been chosen carefully as someone who can be trusted to maintain confidentiality. The target is informed by the con artist that a close friend, a wealthy person of high status, is being held prisoner under a pseudonym in a Spanish prison. The true identity of the prisoner cannot be revealed, the mark is told, without risking very serious consequences, and so the prisoner is relying upon his friend (the con artist) to raise money for his escape. He offers to reward any benefactor handsomely once he is free. Once the target has bitten, various problems ostensibly arise that require more money in order to free the prisoner, and on it goes until the mark either runs out of money or refuses to give more.

A remarkably similar and widespread modern scam surfaced in the 1980s and continues to the present day, despite massive efforts by authorities to warn people away from it. It involves email solicitations and is known variously as the *Nigerian scam* or the *419 scam* (referring to Section 419 of the Criminal Code of Nigeria, which outlaws such fraudulent practices). Just as with the Spanish Prisoner scam, these scam letters typically begin with appeals to secrecy, trust, and confidentiality.[52] The target is advised that someone of high station in Nigeria wants to transfer a large amount of money out of the country but cannot legally do so. If the target assists in this transfer, significant financial reward will be forthcoming. Once the target shows interest, then there are requests for ever-larger remittances of money to facilitate the transfer, which hints at being illegal, or at least not quite legal. The target's greed is stoked and fuels the scam.

It is estimated that there are more than 800,000 perpetrators of this scam around the world, and, in 2013 alone, they raked in $12.7 billion.[53] Many of these scammers are not actually from Nigeria, but use a Nigerian address because Nigeria's reputation for corruption makes the possibility of stranded fortunes more believable.[54]

DETECTING DECEIT

We may like to think that we can tell when someone is deceiving us, but the signs that we rely upon to detect dishonesty, such as nervousness, fidgeting, or averting one's gaze, are not reliable indicators. Empirical research clearly demonstrates that people, be they judges, psychologists, job interviewers, police officers, or members of the general public, are generally no more accurate in identifying a dishonest person than they would be if they simply flipped a coin.[55] Mistaken confidence in detecting deceit makes us putty in the hands of the con artist.[56]

One might think that people such as customs officers, whose job involves detecting deceit, should by virtue of training and experience be able to catch liars, but they are no more successful than the rest of us. In one study, passengers waiting in an airport were recruited, and after being reassured that they were not risking getting themselves into trouble, half of them were asked to "smuggle" contraband through customs, including miniature cameras, pouches of white powder, and so on, while the other half were not.[57] They were offered monetary prizes for successfully fooling the customs agent. Their inspections by a United States customs officer were videotaped.

These videos were shown to other US customs inspectors and to a sample of lay people, all of whom were informed that half the travelers were carrying contraband. Both groups were in general agreement about which travelers were likely to be guilty, and they focused on people who displayed poor eye contact, nervous mannerisms, and hesitations in speech. However, neither the customs inspectors nor the lay people did any better than chance at spotting the actual "culprits," and, in fact, people in both groups were more likely to pick the honest folks as being the smugglers. Nonetheless, customs officers generally believe that they can detect deceit. This is not surprising, for even though they depend upon unreliable cues in choosing who should be searched, by chance alone some of those people they choose to inspect are likely to be found to be guilty, reinforcing their belief in their detection skills.

Yet another study assessed the lie-detection abilities of people from a number of different walks of life—including police officers, psychiatrists, college students, business people, municipal and superior court judges, CIA and FBI polygraph administrators, and US Secret Service agents.[58] They watched videotaped interviews of ten student nurses, five who were lying and five who were telling the truth. The only participants who succeeded beyond the chance level were the Secret Service agents who, as a group, were correct on average 64 percent of the time. None of them scored below chance; and almost a third of them achieved an accuracy rate of 80 percent or more. The researchers suggested that the success of the Secret Service agents reflected the fact that they are trained to look for different cues than those other people use. Because Secret Service agents must constantly scan crowds to protect government leaders from attack, they are likely to become particularly sensitive to nonverbal cues, while police officers, judges, and others rely more on verbal cues.

Assessing the truthfulness of strangers is one thing, but what about people we know well? People in relationships typically trust each other's honesty and also feel fairly sure that they would be able to tell if the other person was lying. Unfortunately, research shows that we are not generally any more accurate in detecting deceit in our partners than in other people.[59]

Just as troubling, clinicians also lack detection skill in judging the credibility of their patients.[60] Psychologists and psychiatrists need to be wary of deceit, particularly when doing formal assessments, and especially when assessments are for forensic purposes. Yet, they do no better than lay people in detecting lies, even when employing clinical and personality tests that attempt to detect responses that reflect lying or exaggerating. Such tests result in many false positives, and, in any case, whether people lie or exaggerate on a test gives little basis for evaluating the truthfulness of their personal accounts. In one study, six actors feigned the symptoms of post-traumatic stress disorder (PTSD) while being assessed at a clinic that specializes in assessing and treating that problem. All six were taken to be genuinely suffering from PTSD.[61]

Such findings led law and psychiatry professor Ralph Slovenko to comment,

> A good poker player probably knows better than a mental health professional whether or not a person is lying. A psychiatrist is a doctor, not a lie-detector.[62]

TECHNOLOGY AND LIE DETECTION

There have been many efforts over the years to find technical means to detect deception. At one time, it was believed that the administration of certain drugs, "truth serums" such as scopolamine, sodium amytal, and sodium pentothal, would overcome an individual's efforts to dissemble and deceive. Yet, the promise of these drugs was not fulfilled, and statements made under their influence are just as likely to be false as they are to be true.

The famous "lie detector," or polygraph, which involves measuring physiological correlates of anxiety, such as increased galvanic skin response (the extent to which the skin conducts electricity, which is related to perspiration), continues to be used in the effort to separate falsehood from fact. We cannot control autonomic reactions, and so the polygrapher compares responses to neutral questions ("Did you eat asparagus last week?") with those to critical questions ("Did you murder your husband?"). A more pronounced autonomic reaction to the second type of question suggests anxiety and possible guilt. This is problematic, however, for a heightened reaction to the second question might also reflect anger at being asked such a question, fear of being falsely accused of murder, shame at being suspected by the police, or grief stimulated by being reminded about the murder.[63]

A more sophisticated approach involves asking about details that only the police and the actual perpetrator would know. For example, if the victim was wearing brown corduroy pants, the polygrapher might ask the suspect a series of "yes" or "no" questions, such as whether the victim was wearing blue jeans, running shorts, black trousers, or brown corduroys. If the accused responds "I don't know" to all the questions but reacts physiologically only to the brown corduroys, that would suggest some "guilty knowledge" that only the perpetrator would have.

Debate continues about the polygraph's usefulness, and skepticism about its validity has grown among qualified researchers and professionals. Most now believe that lie detection using the polygraph lacks a sound theoretical basis, that its claims of high validity cannot be supported, and that people can easily fool it.[64] The polygrapher's expectation of a stronger physiological response when a person lies compared to when telling the truth can be thrown into disarray by people who mentally distract themselves during critical questions in order to avoid a physiological reaction or bite their tongues during neutral questions in order to produce a strong response. In this way, the lies of the guilty can go undetected.[65]

More sophisticated physiological measures such as functional magnetic resonance imagery (fMRI) and electrical evoked potentials have also been explored as a means of detecting deception and show some promise, but more research is required before these measures can be considered reliable and valid.[66]

Psychological research has struggled to find other ways to increase the ability to detect deceit.[67] Research initially suggested that interrogators can improve their ability to detect lies during an interview by having individuals relate their accounts of an event backward in time. It was believed that a person who is telling the truth can do so in reverse without difficulty, while a liar needs to take more time to reverse the temporal flow of the lie. Yet recent research shows that this approach is also an unreliable guide in detecting lies.[68]

The search for a reliable lie detection technique continues, yielding promising results from time to time. For example, differences in response times when responding to items on a personnel test appear to distinguish between participants who have been instructed to lie and those who have been told to tell the truth.[69] That is, those who are faking take relatively longer to answer questions about themselves. The quest goes on.

No matter how intelligent we are or how educated we might be, we can all be fooled, although perhaps some more readily than others We are all vulnerable to the development of faulty beliefs based on deceptions perpetrated by others and on our own self-deceptions. Yet we are poor at detecting deceit in others, just as we often fail to recognize that we have deceived ourselves. Learning to apply critical thinking both to our own perceptions, memories, and contemplations and to the attempts of others to influence us is our best, and perhaps only, defense. More study is needed to identify cues that might reliably indicate deceit, but even if they can be found, such indicators may prove to be of little value when confronted by the persuasive charms of seasoned liars who are skilled at inducing trust and leading people to believe them.

PART IV

KNOWING OURSELVES

While we may accept that our perceptions and memories of the outside world might suffer from distortion and even wishful thinking at times, and while we may acknowledge that our beliefs can at times be skewed by the cognitive biases that affect us all, we all like to think that we know ourselves with some accuracy. We assume that our beliefs about our bodies, although possibly distorted at times by self-esteem issues, are fairly accurate. We know if we are good at sports, or are afraid of the dark, or have a missing limb. We know when we are healthy or feeling ill. And we know when we are dreaming and we know when we're awake.

Or do we? The chapters in this section examine the extent to which our beliefs about our bodies, our minds, and our well-being sometimes stray significantly from reality.

CHAPTER 10

BELIEFS ABOUT OURSELVES

γνῶθι σεαυτόν.
(Know thyself.)

K now thyself. These words, inscribed in the forecourt of the Temple of Apollo in ancient Delphi, possibly borrowed from an even more ancient temple in Luxor, Egypt, exhort us to try to understand ourselves. As Plato expressed in *Phaedrus*:

> I must first know myself, as the Delphian inscription says: to be curious about that which is not my concern, while I am still in ignorance of my own self, would be ridiculous.[1]

Of course, we all hold many *beliefs* about ourselves. We believe that we are tall or short, compassionate or tough-minded, bright or not so bright, healthy or sickly, well-liked or unpopular. But can we ever really *know* ourselves? Some beliefs, especially those relating to our bodies, might seem unchallengeable, but even those can be wrong. Think of the anorexic teenager who sees a fat person reflected in the mirror, or a physically attractive woman with low self-esteem who wishes she were not so plain. Self-knowledge is even more a challenge when it comes to understanding our "minds." Experimental psychologists in the late nineteenth century, such as Wilhelm Wundt and Edward Titchener, attempted to improve understanding of internal mental states through *introspection*, which involved training people in a systematic method for exploring their thoughts and feelings. This was not an entirely new idea. Again, Plato:

> [W]hy should we not calmly and patiently review our own thoughts, and thoroughly examine and see what these appearances in us really are?[2]

This effort to find a reliable procedure for exploring consciousness ultimately failed both because it is impossible to be unbiased in self-examination and because we can never be aware of the many nonconscious processes that influence our thoughts and feelings.

We have seen in earlier chapters that many of our beliefs are shaped by our perceptions, but what we perceive is only a constructed representation of reality. Given that our perceptions are constructions, one might wonder whether there really *is* a world "out there," or whether it is simply the product of our imagination. How can we even be sure that our bodies are real, or that we exist at all? This question troubled seventeenth-century philosopher René Descartes. In his *Second Meditations*, he wrote,

> I have convinced myself that there is absolutely nothing in the world, no sky, no earth, no minds, no bodies. Does it now follow that I too do not exist? No: if I convinced myself of something then I certainly existed.... So after considering everything very thoroughly, I must finally conclude that this proposition, I am, I exist, is necessarily true whenever it is put forward by me or conceived in my mind.[3]

This contemplation led to his famous conclusion, *Cogito ergo sum*, "I think, therefore I am."

THE BODY AS MACHINE

Descartes considered the body to be a sort of mechanical apparatus, and this is not far off the truth, for our bodies operate much of the time like machines on automatic pilot. Sit in the hot sun and perspiration automatically cools us to maintain proper body temperature. Decide to push a button on your phone, and somehow your brain sends the appropriate signals to the muscles to make this happen simply in response to your thought. Bite into a sandwich, and there is no need to worry about keeping your tongue out of harm's way, for during the countless times that you chew during your lifetime it is only rarely bitten. We remain blissfully ignorant about how all this happens inside us. We have no awareness of how the foods we eat are separated into nutrients and roughage and the good parts delivered to the billions of cells throughout our body, just as we remain unaware of the multitude of bacteria in our guts that play a vital role in keeping us alive. (Indeed, there are as many or more microbes within each of us as there are human cells,[4] rendering each of us a kind of "united nations" of independent organisms working together.)

We have no direct knowledge about our internal anatomy. Surgeons aside, whatever we believe about our pancreas or intestines has been taught to us in the same way that we have come to believe that the earth is a globe and that the pharaohs built the pyramids. Indeed, the internal workings of the human body were almost a complete mystery for most of recorded history. Before William Harvey described the circulation of the blood in the seventeenth century and identified the heart as the pump that drives it, most physicians believed that the lungs pushed blood around the body.[5] Our understanding of human anatomy and physiology has increased enormously since then, but even now much remains to be learned.

Our physiology determines many of our behaviors and our likes and dislikes. Sugar is yummy, alcohol promotes relaxation, and recreational drugs produce "highs" all because of it. Smoking cannabis produces pleasant feelings (for most people), while smoking parsley does not. This is because, unlike parsley, particular molecules from the cannabis plant fit like lock and key into specific receptors in the brain, receptors that normally respond to cannabinoids that are produced in limited quantities by the body itself. Cannabis molecules flood those receptors, producing the sought-after euphoric effects. Similarly, sniffing gasoline has a rapid effect on other receptors, resulting in feelings of euphoria, disorientation, increased libido, slowed reflexes, and even hallucinations. Without these receptors, there would be no "high," and desire for cannabis or sniffing gasoline would not exist.

You may be familiar with the paintings of American artist Cassius Marcellus Coolidge that portray dogs engaged in human activities such as playing poker (figure 10-1). Imagine for a moment a group of human poker players in the midst of a game when some weird cataclysmic event suddenly turns them all into Coolidge's dogs. Unaware of their sudden transformation, they continue to enjoy the game. When the bulldog gets up to get another drink, the collie to its left experiences a powerful compulsion to sniff its rear. The players, not yet accustomed to their new canine identity, soon turn to contemplation about the source of this compulsion but get nowhere in trying to understand what makes rear-end sniffing so compelling.[6]

Whether dogs "sniffing ass" or teenagers "sniffing gas," the answer lies in physiology. Dogs have specialized scent-detectors that respond to *pheromones*, chemical substances released by the *apocrine gland*, a special kind of sweat gland found in all mammals, including humans.[7] Pheromones provide them with important social information about another dog's sex, reproductive readiness, age, and health. Human apocrine glands are concentrated in the armpits and groin, which explains the embarrassing situation that can arise when being greeted by someone's dog. Dogs sniff at the pheromones in our groins, and they are especially inquisitive when encountering someone for the first time.

Figure 10-1: Canine poker (*A Friend in Need*, by Cassius Marcellus Coolidge).

Although physiology plays an important role in determining our motivations, likes, and dislikes, which in turn influence the beliefs we construct about ourselves, its effects are strongly moderated by experience. A teenager whose first taste of beer is sour and unappealing may nonetheless continue to imbibe in deference to social pressures and gradually come to enjoy its flavor. Conversely, someone whose early experience with alcohol is followed by severe vomiting may forever find the taste and smell of liquor aversive.

While many beliefs about our bodies are generally formed in ignorance of what is really going on inside us, one would think that some beliefs are not in doubt. For example, we should surely have no confusion about which body parts belong to us or where our bodies are located in space, for we can both *see* and *feel* the movements of our limbs. As we shall see, things are more complicated than they seem.

The body maps

Our brains are generally good at monitoring our physical movements and tracking where our bodies are located in space. Close your eyes and you will have no difficulty raising your left forefinger to touch the tip of your nose. This is because your brain computes the specific locations of both your nose and finger. Feedback from sensors (*proprioceptors*) in the muscles and joints combined with information from the visual system and the vestibular system (in the inner ears), is matched up with detailed maps of body regions situated in the brain's cortex. These maps provide us with a dynamic image of ourselves, a *kinesthetic awareness* of the position and movement of all parts of our body and how they are moving through space.

The sense of our body and its location in space is, like perception and memory, a construction that normally enables us to interact appropriately with the environment. Yet this construction process can be thrown off, and our beliefs about where we are or what belongs to our body can fall into error. Everyone from time to time experiences the sensation of a leg that has "gone to sleep." This experience, known as *paresthesia*, occurs when pressure on a nerve blocks signals from the leg (*proprioceptive feedback*) from reaching the brain. As a result of this lost communication, the leg is left devoid of feeling and its muscles beyond one's control, although we can still see it and know that it is there. Imagine what would happen if *all* the body's proprioceptive feedback were blocked and we were at the same time unable to see ourselves. This is likely what occurs when people report leaving their bodies and floating above them, the so-called out-of-body experience. More about that in the next chapter.

A brain confused

Losing feeling in a leg is a temporary and minor aberration in our tracking of our bodies and their locations in space. More significant is the phenomenon of *phantom limb* in which sensations, often painful, seem to occur in a limb that no longer exists. An individual whose hand has been amputated may feel pain that seems to come from the missing hand. The nerves that once connected the hand to the brain, although now truncated, continue to stimulate the part of the brain's body map that corresponds to the hand, and the brain then treats those messages as though they are coming from the nonexistent hand itself.[8] The individual *knows* that the hand is not there, *sees* that it is not there, and yet *feels* it.

A contrary experience is that of *anosognosia*, the inability to recognize that one has an obvious physical defect. We would expect that someone suffering from hemiplegia (paralysis on one side) as a result of a stroke or traumatic brain injury would certainly be aware of this dysfunction. After all, if your left arm is paralyzed, you cannot move it. Yet, someone suffering from *anosognosia for hemiplegia* remains blissfully unaware of that paralysis. In this case, accompanying damage to another part of the brain interferes with the process of proprioceptive feedback that would normally indicate whether the limb has moved, leaving the individual to believe that it moves without difficulty. But how could one fail to *see* that the limb has not moved? This failure comes about because the neurological damage also produces an inability to process specific visual information, in this case from the left visual field, and so there is a complete lack of feedback information that would indicate that an intended movement of the arm has not taken place.[9]

Another fascinating but rare neurological condition, *alien hand syndrome*, involves a limb that moves in the absence of any deliberate effort, as though it has a mind of its own and is beyond the individual's control. In one such case, a woman developed the syndrome after awaking from coronary bypass surgery.[10] To her shock and amazement, her left hand had become autonomous to the extent that it would try to choke her while she was sleeping, and it would unbutton her blouse when she wanted to stay covered. Just like Dr. Strangelove (in the eponymous movie), she had to use her right hand to keep the left hand from acting against her wishes. A brain lesion was subsequently discovered that was responsible for this condition.

Even more unusual, in recent years a small number of people have reported unbearable emotional agony because of an "alien" limb—an arm or leg that feels as though it does not belong to them. This condition is referred to as *Body Integrity Identity Disorder*. Although some such cases may reflect complex brain dysregulation, researchers suspect that most such reports result from the "alien" limb having been for some reason excluded from body maps, with the result that it feels as though it does not belong. This condition typically develops in early childhood, and some sufferers have sought and received amputation to relieve their misery. Amputation of the undesired (but healthy) body part typically results in a very significant improvement in the individual's quality of life.[11]

Body transfer illusion

While damage to the brain underlies conditions such as anosognosia and alien hand syndrome, even the normal brain can at times become confused about what is and what is not part of the body. In other words, its body maps can be thrown off kilter. It was believed until recently that body maps were inborn, "hard-wired" into our brains. That belief was challenged by research published in 1998.[12] In an experiment, a participant sat with one arm resting on a table and with a screen positioned beside the arm to hide it from the participant's view. A life-sized rubber model of an arm and hand was placed directly in front of the participant, and then the researcher, using two small brushes, simultaneously stroked both the participant's hidden hand and the rubber hand. After several minutes of watching the stroking of the rubber hand while feeling the stroking of the real hand, participants reported *feeling* the touch of the brush *on the rubber hand*. This was such a powerful illusion that many participants indicated that the dummy hand felt as if it were their own. In other similar studies, participants have flinched when the researcher appeared about to smash his fist on the rubber hand, reported being surprised when they could not lift a rubber finger when asked to do so, and pointed to the rubber hand when asked to point to their real hand.[13]

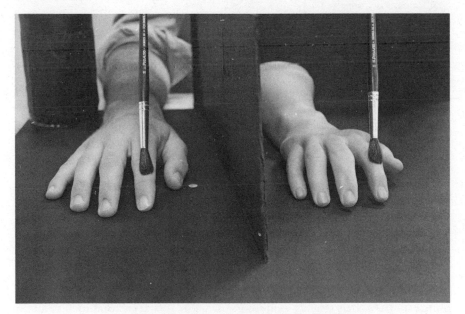

Figure 10-2: Real hand, false hand (Kings College, London).

Feedback from the senses determines body ownership, and when such feedback is deliberately manipulated, it is the fake rubber model that wins.[14] The rubber-hand illusion occurs because the brain, in its efforts to maintain an image of the body and its position in space, relies more on vision than it does on touch. When there is a conflict between the senses, visual input dominates. One *feels* the stroking of the real hand but *sees* only the rubber hand being stroked. The brain temporarily adjusts its body maps and treats the visible rubber hand as the real hand. Because it "looks like my hand" and "feels like my hand," the brain concludes that "this is my hand!"[15]

Psychologist Henrik Ehrsson used functional magnetic resonance imaging (fMRI) to monitor participants' brain activity while they were experiencing this illusion.[16] On average, they reported feeling as though the rubber hand was part of their own body after only eleven seconds, and the stronger the reported feeling, the greater the activity in a particular region of the brain (the premotor cortex).

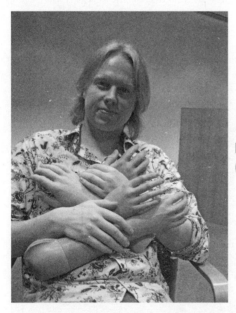

Figure 10-3: The many hands of Dr. Ehrsson (photo by Jenny Gimpel, © Henrik Ehrsson).

Virtual-reality experiments have demonstrated that the rubber-hand illusion can extend to the entire body. In one such study, male participants were fitted with both a head-mounted virtual-reality apparatus and stereo headphones.[17] They then visually explored a virtual-reality scene that included two virtual figures, a young girl and a woman. The viewing point (as seen through the head-mounted display) was then shifted so that the participant observed the scene "through the eyes" of the virtual girl, whose head movements were synchronized with the participant's. In addition, the participant's shoulder was occasionally stroked at exactly the same moment that the virtual woman was observed to stroke the virtual girl's shoulder. Participants reported a strong illusion of a transfer of body ownership, as though the virtual girl's body were in some way their own, and when the woman suddenly slapped the girl's face, they reacted with a significant physiological response. This effect was not found in other participants who did not view the scene from the virtual girl's perspective, or when the girl's head movements were not synchronous with their own, or when their shoulders were not stroked simultaneously with the girl's.

THE GHOST IN THE MACHINE

Descartes considered the body to interact with the mind through the brain's pineal gland, which he believed to be the seat of the soul and the spot where all thinking takes place.[18] Of course, we now know that the pineal gland has no such function. Yet Descartes's insistence that the mind is separate from the body (*mind-body dualism*) continues to resonate with large numbers of people. After all, we all *feel* as though we are conscious beings housed in bodies that generally do the mind's bidding. British philosopher Gilbert Ryle (1900–1976), in rejecting dualism, referred to this notion of an immaterial mind in a physical body as a belief in the "ghost in the machine."[19]

Modern psychology and neuroscience consider mind and brain to be a single integrated phenomenon. The brain is the organ, and the mind is the brain in action. Consciousness is tied directly to neuronal activity and does not exist independent of the flesh. This *psychoneural identity* hypothesis—mind (psycho) and brain (neural) are one—is supported by overwhelming and converging evidence:[20]

- *Phylogenetic evidence*: When one compares the brains of various organisms, the greater the complexity of the brain, the greater the evidence of cognitive abilities.
- *Developmental evidence*: Cognitive abilities emerge as the child's brain matures. If for some reason the brain does not mature, the result is arrested intellectual development, leaving individuals with various cog-

nitive difficulties, such as with planning, anticipating, and connecting behavior with consequences.

- *Experimental evidence*: Electrical or chemical stimulation of groups of cells in the brain during surgery elicits perceptions, memories, and desires that are like those produced by those same cells during normal functioning.

- *Experiential evidence*: As discussed earlier, a variety of natural substances, such as hallucinogenic drugs, interact with specific cells in the brain, resulting in predictable changes in consciousness.

- *Clinical evidence*: The effects of brain damage on consciousness are also predictable, depending on the site affected, and such changes are largely irreversible. It does not take much injury to the brain to produce significant changes in the "mind." Further, when brain function is impaired to the extent that dementia results, the individual's ability to recognize people or to remember the past, or even the very recent present, inexorably declines, and striking personality and behavior changes follow. Thus, it is a triumph of hope over reason when people take comfort in the belief that their own personalities, memories, and intelligence and those of their loved ones will in some magical way survive or be restored once the entire brain has died away.

CONSCIOUSNESS

Consciousness involves awareness of oneself as distinct from rest of the world. It contains all the sensory, perceptual, and memory structures necessary to be cognizant in the present moment. It is an *emergent phenomenon*. That is, it is the end product of a number of converging neurological processes that cannot be broken down into a number of smaller and simpler parts.[21] *Primary phenomenal consciousness* refers to the actual content of consciousness—the sensations, perceptions, and emotions that make up our subjective experience at a given moment.[22] *Reflective consciousness* (sometimes referred to as *meta-consciousness*[23]) involves thinking about and evaluating the content of primary consciousness. For example, when you hear a siren while driving, that perception is part of primary phenomenal consciousness. Reflective consciousness occurs as you evaluate the perception, realize that an emergency vehicle is approaching, and pull your vehicle to the side of the road.

The existence of consciousness implies that it confers some evolutionary advantage over organisms that are not conscious. Perhaps such advantage rests in the important functions that it serves.[24] While nonconscious processes (System 1) appear to involve limited activation in one part of the brain at a time, consciousness combines information from across a range of brain regions. (However, many cognitive neuroscientists believe that the nonconscious processes nonetheless remain the major players, feeding information into the higher conscious processes.[25]) Consciousness allows us to control the processing of information, to select the information that we need while ignoring the rest, to pause while obtaining further information when needed, and to shift information around in novel ways in order to find solutions to problems. Still, conscious processing has its limits. We can process only a limited amount of information at a time, and we need to do so in a serial manner.[26] When faced with the need for many decisions at once, a processing bottleneck can occur, making it a challenge to reach an effective decision.

The mystery of consciousness

The notion of consciousness is wrapped up in mystery, for it is not clear how collections of atoms, molecules, and neurons can produce *experience*. And because consciousness is an experience, we cannot measure it directly. We can only infer that people around us are likewise conscious (*theory of mind* again). Pet owners often confidently extend theory of mind to their pets, and much of this is simple anthropomorphism because they interpret their pets' behaviors and facial expressions through their knowledge of human expression of emotions. Yet, since no consciousness-producing structure or process has been found that is unique to human brains, it is possible that the inventiveness shown by some animals in responding to novel challenges may reflect some degree of conscious processing.[27]

Even if some animals do possess a degree of consciousness, that does not necessarily mean that they are aware that they exist as separate beings. Self-awareness is an important part of human consciousness, but research suggests that only a few animals are likely to possess it at anything resembling the human level. The standard method for evaluating self-awareness is to test for self-recognition in a mirror. Put a mark on a chimpanzee's forehead, and it will soon put a finger on the mark when it sees itself in a mirror. Such ability has been demonstrated in orangutans as well, and there is suggestive evidence that Asian elephants, dolphins, and magpies may also have this ability.[28] This does not necessarily mean that they possess anything akin to human consciousness, which includes self-concept, theory of mind, and so forth.[29]

"Artificial" consciousness

Since collections of atoms and molecules can produce the *experience* of consciousness for us, could that experience occur elsewhere, in computer circuitry for example? We will probably never know for sure, but as psychologist Susan Blackmore has pointed out, none of the arguments advanced against the possibility of a conscious machine have succeeded in proving it impossible.[30] If an intelligent robot were to act as though it were conscious and told us that it was conscious, how could we disprove it? Experts in artificial intelligence (AI) predict that within a few short decades AI will be equal to human intelligence by every conceivable measure and that, once that occurs, machines designed by other intelligent machines will quickly become *super-intelligent*, exceeding human intelligence by leaps and bounds in certain ways. Concern is growing about how to limit the development of super-intelligence so that humans do not risk being harmed, and in 2014 renowned physicist Stephen Hawking and several of his colleagues issued a warning:

> One can imagine such technology outsmarting financial markets, out-inventing human researchers, out-manipulating human leaders, and developing weapons we cannot even understand. Whereas the short-term impact of AI depends on who controls it, the long-term impact depends on whether it can be controlled at all.[31]

This warning was echoed in 2017 by Elon Musk, chief executive officer of SpaceX and Tesla, who warned that artificial intelligence poses a fundamental risk to civilization and called for proactive legislation in order to ensure the survival of the human race.[32] Only time will tell whether these warnings are alarmist or prescient.

THE UNCONSCIOUS

The concept of the unconscious mind is deeply rooted in human history. Reference to it is found in many ancient texts, including the Hindu Vedas, written thousands of years ago, and the *Kabbalah*, an ancient body of Jewish mystical teachings. Paracelsus (1493–1541), a German-Swiss physician who based his medical knowledge on astrology (which was not unusual during that era), wrote that unconscious thinking about certain diseases can bring them on, and because of this he is often given credit for the first mention of the unconscious as a clinical concept.[33]

In 1869, Eduard von Hartmann summarized the work of several German philosophers in his *Philosophie des Unbewussten* (Philosophy of the Unconscious).[34] This book had considerable influence on how others, including psychiatrists Sigmund Freud and Carl Jung, came to view the "unconscious mind." The unconscious gained greater attention with the discovery of hypnotic phenomena,[35] since actions carried out under hypnosis appeared to be completely unintentional and the individual seemed to have no awareness of why the actions had been performed. This suggested to Sigmund Freud that unconscious processes and motivations might underlie normal behavior as well.

The Freudian unconscious is a swirling cauldron of unacceptable impulses and aggressive and sexual conflicts that are supposedly "repressed," prevented from reaching consciousness because they would be too upsetting for the individual to bear. Freud believed that such repression was at the root of all mental disorders. His ideas dominated psychiatry and clinical psychology for the better part of the twentieth century.

The modern psychological view of the unconscious, or "nonconscious," is very different from that of Freud. It refers not to hidden conflicts and unacceptable urges, but to the many mental activities that occur without being available to the explicit processes of consciousness.[36] Nonconscious factors strongly influence many of our decisions to act; implicit guidance systems guide our actions, whether picking up a cup of coffee or making a comment during a conversation.[37] Because of this, social psychologists generally equate "unconscious" with "unintentional."[38]

Nonconscious activity is important for our survival and well-being. As psychologists Michael Graziano and Dylan Cooke explain,

> Protective mechanisms are essential in extreme, life-threatening situations; but they are also essential in everyday life. They allow us to walk through a room without hitting the furniture, keep a healthy distance from a cliff edge, run through a twiggy forest without poking out an eye, brush away an insect, reach safely around a prickly object, or sit at a desk without bruising our elbows and arms as we work. Our lives would be impossible without these mechanisms in place and working in the background.[39]

Of course, when we undertake a novel task, conscious attention is essential. Yet, as we practice and eventually master the task, it becomes automatized and we can then perform it without having to think about it. Automatic processing and control is generally preferable, particularly with regard to routine, well-learned activities, for this frees up consciousness to deal with other things such as problem-solving or making plans. (Once again, recall the discussion of System 1.) Indeed, as psychologist Barry Beyerstein pointed out, the "job" of consciousness is to make the control of as many activities as possible nonconscious.[40] A pianist who has mastered a piece would be in difficulty if automatic processes were not governing the movement of her fingers. You can ride your bicycle without any need to think about steering or remaining upright while at the same time carrying on a conversation with a fellow rider, and yet if you suddenly encounter a section of the bicycle path that involves rough pavement, you will automatically switch back to conscious control for as long as necessary.

Attempting to re-impose conscious control over a well-learned task often interferes with performance. British humorist Stephen Potter advised his readers, tongue-in-cheek, to use this fact to improve their chances of besting their competitors in a game.[41] For example, as your opponent is getting ready to take a shot in a billiard game, you ask, "Which do you look at just before you take your shot, the shooter ball, or the target ball?" The question pushes the player to switch from nonconscious to conscious control of the cue in contemplation of a response, which may well result in a missed shot.

People's conscious beliefs about their own behavior are often at odds with actual causes.[42] Well-entrenched routines can automatically trigger thoughts and feelings, leaving us ignorant of why those thoughts and feelings occurred.[43] (Recall the earlier discussion of intuition and blindsight,

Figure 10-4: Gamesmanship
(published January 1, 2010, by Moyer Bell
[first published 1947]).

which showed that perceptions do not need to enter fully into consciousness for them to affect behavior.)[44] Even when we believe that we have freely formed a thought or made a choice, the thought or choice has likely been strongly influenced by nonconscious processes. Consider this example:

- Write down the first *color* that comes to mind.
- Now write down the first *flower* that comes to mind.
- And finally, write down the first *piece of furniture* that comes to mind.

Did you write *red* or *rose* or *chair*? Most will have written at least one of these words, and some may have written all three. This demonstration can elicit a powerful emotional response, especially when cast in the framework of something psychic, but there is no mental telepathy involved here. You may think that you have freely chosen your answers, but thoughts do not come into our head at random. People who share the same language and culture are more likely to come up with the same colors or flowers or pieces of furniture. These commonalities, products of our collective experience, are referred to as *population stereotypes*.[45] Yet it feels as though we have made a free choice.

I recall a conversation with someone who held a strong belief in mental telepathy, and, with the goal of showing how easy it is to mistake population stereotypes for telepathy, I told her that I was going to "read her mind." I then asked her to think, but not say aloud, her answers to the above questions. She silently chose *red, rose, and chair*, and was obviously shocked when I then named all three. Unfortunately, my demonstration backfired, for she took it as strong evidence of my telepathic powers.

On the other hand, there are situations in which we *are* aware of the conflict between what is conscious and what is nonconscious. We "know" one thing on an intellectual level and yet our feelings, produced by nonconscious processes, stand in opposition to our belief. Consider phobias, for example. An individual with a strong fear of spiders may recognize intellectually that the fear is unjustified and yet be unable to overcome the fear reaction.[46] Or recall those times when you have had thoughts or reactions that you did not want. For example, you may at a conscious level sincerely want your colleague to succeed but nonetheless experience envy or jealousy when he does. My friend Steve Mackay describes this metaphorically as a contest between "small mind" and "big mind": Your small mind (the products of System 1) reacts with envy and jealousy, while your big mind (System 2) attempts to overcome the small-mindedness with a rational, mature response.

AHA!

We have probably all experienced situations in which a sudden insight presents the solution to a problem with which we have been wrestling. According to legend, this is what occurred when Archimedes observed the water level rise as he got into his bath. He suddenly understood that the volume of water he had displaced had to equal the volume of the submerged part of his body. The realization so startled him that he is said to have run naked through the streets shouting "Eureka! Eureka!" ("I have found it!"). This captures the essence of the "Aha" phenomenon. It is a sudden flash of insight, accompanied by a feeling of excitement, that occurs without conscious effort and provides a solution to a problem that one had not been able to solve.

Figure 10-5: Problem-solving with insight.

It has been suggested that the Aha! experience occurs when the brain finds relevant information, or even a solution, at a nonconscious level, and then suddenly becomes conscious of it.[47] Research shows that solutions resulting from such insight involve activity in parts of the brain different than those involved in non-insightful problem-solving.[48] A distinct pattern of unconscious neural activity has been found to precede the "aha" experience by up to eight seconds,[49] and then, approximately a third of a second prior to the solution, a sudden burst of high-frequency neural activity occurs in a region of the right hemisphere associated with making connections across various areas the brain.[50]

A study conducted many years ago, although not well-controlled by today's research standards, suggests how insight can be triggered by cues that escape our awareness.[51] Each participant entered a gymnasium where two ropes were suspended from the ceiling, and the task was to tie them together, although the cords were too far apart for a person to reach both at the same time (figure 10-5). A few tools lay in the corner of the room, and the solution was to tie a tool to the end of one rope, set it swinging, and then while grasping the other rope, grab it as it swings by. Only 40 percent of the participants came up with this solution on their own. For the remaining participants, the researcher then provided a cue. For some of them, he casually twirled one of the ropes as he spoke to the participant. This did not lead to solving the problem. For others, he gently set one of the ropes swinging by a touch of his finger while he was chatting. Most of those participants then solved the problem within forty-five seconds, even though none of them subsequently reported having noticed the cue. Their Aha! insight was triggered by a cue of which they were not aware.

TO THINK OR TO BLINK . . .

According to author Malcolm Gladwell's influential book *Blink: The Power of Thinking Without Thinking*, we often make better and more accurate decisions in "the blink of an eye" than when we engage in conscious deliberation. By way of example, he described a man who was able in an instant to spot fake antiquities that had fooled several experts. He suggested that, instead of pondering over choices, we should just "go with our gut." However, following Mr. Gladwell's advice might be a big mistake. Although some early research did conclude that nonconscious decisions are superior,[52] attempts to replicate that counterintuitive finding have not succeeded.[53] Yet this does not mean that conscious decision-making is invariably better, for we can sometimes overthink things to the extent that we end up with a faulty decision based on unimportant criteria—or with no decision at all.[54]

IDEOMOTOR ACTION

The gap between conscious and nonconscious mental activity is further demonstrated by the phenomenon of *ideomotor action*, which refers to purposeful movements that people sometimes make without any awareness that they are doing so. Indeed, most behaviors have an ideomotor component. For example, when you talk silently to yourself, tiny muscular movements, sub-vocalizations, corresponding to the pronunciation of each word occur in the larynx. These movements occur completely without awareness and are undetectable except by measuring devices.

The term *ideomotor action* was first used in a medical lecture delivered by physician William Carpenter in 1852.[55] Carpenter described how tiny muscular movements corresponding to expectation or desire occur without deliberate willing or emotion, and he went on to explain how this is reflected in certain supposed "psychic" phenomena in which objects move apparently without human intervention, movements that are then attributed to invisible external forces.

Ideomotor action has long been of interest to psychologists.[56] Psychologist Ray Hyman has described how two prominent nineteenth-century physical scientists discovered that ideomotor action accounted for some celebrated "psychic" phenomena.[57] French chemist Michel-Eugène Chevreul (1786–1889) studied the *pendule explorateur* ("exploring pendulum").[58] This involved an object suspended by a thin thread held by the hand of a "diviner." The object's movements were taken to represent information from some mysterious, psychic source. When held above a board bearing the letters of the alphabet, the pendulum's movements would spell out answers to questions posed by those seeking guidance. (Something similar occurs with the Ouija board, discussed in a later chapter.)

Chevreul's interest was piqued when a few chemists began using the *pendule explorateur* to analyze the composition of various chemical compounds. His first experiences with the pendulum astonished him, for when it was held over a dish of mercury, it moved as he had been told that it would. To eliminate the possibility that some unrecognized normal physical force was at play, he placed a plate of glass between the pendulum and the mercury. The pendulum's movements then stopped, suggesting that he had interfered with some sort of force. He then blindfolded himself and had his assistant either insert or remove the glass plate without his knowledge. When he was wearing the blindfold, the pendulum did not move, and he realized that it was he himself who was unknowingly responsible for its earlier movements. After he understood this, he could no longer reproduce the effect even without the blindfold. This demonstration taught him how easy it is to "mistake illusions for realities, whenever we are confronted by phenomena in which the human sense organs are involved under conditions imperfectly analyzed."[59]

Further study of the pendulum illusion in modern times has found that visual feedback is not always needed to obtain the basic pendulum effect.[60] This can easily be demonstrated. Make a small pendulum and acquaint a friend with the old saying that the pendulum will move in a circle over the hand of a female and in a straight line over the hand of a male. Then, ask your friend to hold the pendulum, with eyes closed, above the hand of either a male or female. You are likely to observe the predicted movement because your friend knows what to expect. Through tiny, unintended, imperceptible movements of the hand, what is expected is produced.

It was also in the mid-nineteenth century that British physicist Michael Faraday (1791–1867) became interested in table-turning, a then-popular "spiritual" phenomenon that involved a number of people placing their fingers lightly on a table, following which the table began to shake and move, sometimes moving for some distance with all the fingers still in contact with it. He conducted a table-turning experiment in 1853 with individuals he considered trustworthy and honorable. Without their knowledge, he attached several sheets of slippery, waxed cardboard to the top of the table using rubber bands to hold them in place. He reasoned that if a person were unknowingly applying pressure to the table and pushing it, this would cause the top sheets to shift in one direction, but if the table were somehow moving on its own and pulling the individual along with it, the sheets would then be displaced in the opposite direction. By examining the sheets after the table had been observed to move about, it was obvious to Faraday that the participants were the unwitting cause of the movement—they were pushing the table.

Our tiny, unintended movements that are imperceptible to humans can serve as cues to some animals. Consider, for example an "amazing" nineteenth-century horse, *Kluge* ("wise") *Hans*, that became famous in English-speaking countries as *Clever Hans* when his owner, Wilhelm von Osten, demonstrated the animal's apparent mathematical ability to enthusiastic crowds. When von Osten asked Hans to add five and three, for example, Hans responded by tapping his hoof eight times. He developed even more astonishing abilities and over time appeared able to name people by tapping out the letters of their name on an alphabet board. He could also tell the time, it seemed. Accounts of the horse's skills spread throughout Europe, leading a dozen scientists to carry out an investigation. They found no evidence of signaling by von Osten or any other trickery. It seemed that Hans was indeed clever.

But how could Hans give answers to personal questions to which even his trainer did not know the answer? When unable to come up with a normal explanation, people often conclude that something paranormal must be going on, and so it was with Clever Hans. Some people speculated that he was receiving information from spectators via extrasensory perception.

Figure 10-6: Clever Hans with Mr. von Osten.

Psychologist Oskar Pfungst undertook a careful study of Hans's abilities. He confirmed that the trainer was not signaling the horse, for even when von Osten was sent from the room, the horse's abilities were not diminished. Pfungst ultimately discovered that Hans was actually responding to unintentional and almost imperceptible movements on the part of the human questioner. A small change in posture once the question was asked was Hans's cue to begin tapping, and a small and unconscious movement of the person's head when he arrived at the correct number of taps led him to stop. Since these movements were unintended by the questioner and imperceptible to other spectators, the answers were attributed to the horse. Yet Hans responded only mechanically, and if the questioner did not know the answer to a question, Hans could not provide it either. As Hyman noted,

> The horse was simply a channel through which the information the questioner unwittingly put into the situation was fed back to the questioner. The fallacy involved treating the horse as the source of the message rather than as a channel through which the questioner's own message was reflected back.[61]

Clever Hans was only one of a number of seemingly amazing and sensitive animals that gained popularity in that era. One of them, *Lady Wonder*, an American horse in Virginia, apparently spelled her answers to questions by pushing over alphabet blocks. All that was required for Lady Wonder to succeed was that questions be written down and given to the horse's trainer. Like Clever Hans, Lady Wonder could also do simple arithmetic. The trainer attributed the horse's ability to a combination of high intelligence and mental telepathy. Lady Wonder was profitable; more than 150,000 people paid to consult her at three questions per dollar. In 1927, pre-eminent parapsychologist J. B. Rhine carried out six days of investigation and concluded that mental telepathy was indeed involved:

> There is left only the telepathic explanation, the transference of mental influence by an unknown process. Nothing was discovered that failed to accord with it, and no other hypothesis seems tenable in view of the results.[62]

Conjurer Milbourne Christopher also examined Lady Wonder's abilities and discovered that she was responding to cues intentionally provided by the trainer.[63] The horse moved its head across the series of letters until a subtle movement of the trainer's stick cued it to choose a particular letter. As it turns out, then, Lady Wonder was not nearly so clever as Clever Hans, who could detect subtle and unintended movements by any questioner, not just from his trainer.

Ideomotor action and mind reading

Hyman describes how some clever conjurers learned from Clever Hans.[64] They found that they were able to start, stop, and turn in response to subtle, nonconscious cues provided by other people. A typical demonstration involved having an audience member hide an object (sometimes the conjurer's paycheck) somewhere in the hall while the conjurer was out of the room, and then, upon his return, he would take the hand of any audience member who knew where the object was hidden and move about the auditorium, pulling the person here and there until the item was found. While these conjurers misleadingly described their skill as mind reading, skeptics referred to it as "muscle reading," as the conjurers were responding to subtle changes in resistance unconsciously produced by the audience member who unknowingly guided them to the hidden item.

Others improved on this act. Hyman points to Eugene de Rubini from Moravia who amazed American audiences in the 1920s with his apparent demonstrations of telepathy as he found the hidden object without any direct contact with the audience member who had unwittingly served as guide. Rubini agreed to be tested, and it was determined that in order to succeed he had to be able to see the audience member, at least out of the corner of his eye, even though that person generally walked behind him. Again, the audience member was unconsciously providing cues that led Rubini to the hidden object. Hyman believes that Rubini himself was unaware of the actual cues that he was picking up to guide him.

Ideomotor action and dowsing

Ideomotor action is also the basis for dowsing (see figure 10-7). The dowser, sometimes known as water-diviner or water-witcher, traditionally uses a Y-shaped willow stick (although in modern times this is often replaced by two L-shaped metal rods, one held in each hand) in the search for water and sometimes for minerals. The dowser walks back and forth over an area of land with the two arms of the Y held one in each hand so that the shaft of the Y points forward. Then, seemingly without the dowser's influence, the shaft suddenly flips downward (or, in the case of metal rods, the two rods suddenly cross one another), and the dowser announces that water has been detected. And, oftentimes, this assertion is reinforced when digging on the spot does lead to water.

Some dowsers, rather than walking over the area of interest, work with a map of the region instead. In place of using a dowsing rod, which would be rather difficult to wield over a map, they use a pendulum suspended from the fingers and believe that when the pendulum is held over the spot where water can be found it will begin to move.

Figure 10-7: Dowser at work (Shutterstock / Grandpa).

Hyman, along with anthropologist Evon Vogt carried out an extensive study of dowsing as practiced across the United States.[65] Their research found no evidence that dowsing "works," nor any psychic ability on the part of the dowsers. They concluded that the practice is an instance of "magical divination," where the movement of the dowsing rod is actually only the product of ideomotor action. Hyman notes that some modern dowsers accept that ideomotor action plays an important role in causing the movement of the dowsing rod or pendulum, but they insist that the unconscious ideomotor action is initiated by occult forces.[66]

How can we account for belief in the usefulness of dowsing if it does not work? Belief in the efficacy of dowsing is sustained primarily as a result of suggestibility and occasional reinforcement, even if the reinforcement occurs by chance alone. For one thing, if you dig deep enough, you will probably find some ground water just about anywhere, but whether it is enough water to justify putting in a well is another matter. It is interesting to note that in a careful test of dowsing conducted in Germany, which was ultimately deemed a decisive failure to find any evidence that dowsing "works," the researchers themselves, before analyzing their data, had the impression that successful dowsing ability had been "unquestionably demonstrated."[67] When even researchers can be fooled by their initial impressions, it is not surprising that dowsers deceive themselves.

Ideomotor action also underlies a modern intervention for autism known as *facilitated communication*. It was trumpeted as allowing severely autistic children to communicate their thoughts, thoughts that appeared to be surprisingly sophisticated and complex. The technique involves a "facilitator" who holds the autistic child's hand above a keyboard with the goal of steadying the hand to permit the child to press the keys. These children, who had been essentially cut off from the world, now seemed able to express remarkable knowledge about a wide array of subjects. Parents and therapists were thrilled.

Closer investigation revealed that it was the facilitator's knowledge, not the child's, that was being expressed, even though the facilitator remained completely unaware of it. In studies in which one picture was shown to the child while the facilitator was shown another but led to believe that it was the same picture as the child had seen, the facilitated response described only what the facilitator had seen. Small ideomotor movements on the part of facilitator while guiding the child's hand were responsible for the words that were typed out. In subsequent research, a confederate of the experimenter posing as an autistic individual made only random movements in response to questions. Nonetheless, with the facilitator's guidance of the hand, meaningful answers were produced, and facilitators expressed the firm belief that the answers were from the supposedly autistic person.[68]

Facilitated communication has had significant and unfortunate consequences. On a number of occasions, "facilitated" messages have referred to alleged sexual abuse of the child by the parents (abuse that had never occurred), resulting in the parents' arrest and prosecution. Although now totally discredited by scientists, this technique is still being promoted in some quarters, and is all too frequently still being used in both educational and clinical settings.[69]

MENTAL CAUSATION

In May 1643, Princess Elizabeth of Bohemia wrote to René Descartes seeking an explanation for "how the mind of a human being, being only a thinking substance, can determine the bodily spirits in producing bodily actions."[70] That is, how can the immaterial mind cause the physical body to move? Descartes's response was rather evasive, and her question remained unanswered for almost five centuries until, in 2008, psychologist Daniel Wegner commented,

> Imagine a magician who can make things happen merely by thinking of them. The magician thinks "I'd like the lights on," and before you know it . . . There is light! Right there and then, a hand has reached out and turned on a lamp. . . . Human action is a kind of magic, an astonishing ability to think of something and thereby make it happen. Although a lamp will seldom light on its own merely if we want it to, we find that our fingers leap to the switch and light that lamp when the idea comes to mind.[71]

Wegner is describing a *sense of agency*, the feeling that we are controlling our own actions. Think back for a moment to ideomotor action. In that case, a sense of agency was absent, and even though an individual caused something to happen, there was no intention to do so, and it seemed that the action occurred independently of the person.

Wegner, along with other researchers (e.g., Michael Gazzaniga,[72] Benjamin Libet[73]), argue that impulses to act are initiated *nonconsciously*, triggered by

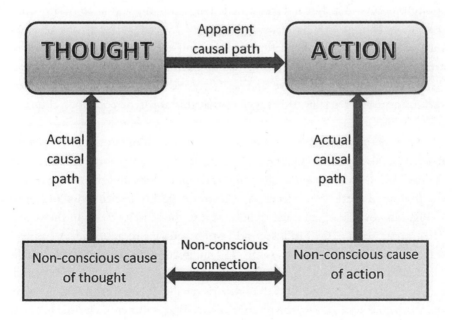

Figure 10-8: The illusion of willing.

various preferences, norms, and previous experiences in similar situations, and that our sense of agency occurs when we consciously make sense of the action after the fact.[74] When we intend to do something, such as turn on the radio, our hand then reaches out to do so. Since the thought precedes the action and is consistent with the action, and there is no other plausible cause for the action, it naturally seems that the thought was responsible for the action. Wegner refers to this sense of agency as an *illusion of willing*,[75] (figure 10-8) which is deeply embedded in all of us, given our lifelong histories of having had thoughts that were followed by corresponding actions.

This illusion of willing can be experienced even when thought and action occur one after the other simply by coincidence. Suppose you concentrate on trying to stop a clock and it suddenly stops. It may be difficult to resist the feeling that your thought caused it to stop. This has been observed in experiments where participants have been asked to concentrate on causing an event, and then, just at that moment, the event occurs because of surreptitious intervention by the experimenter.

Wegner argues that an unconscious event triggers *both* the thought and the action, and this view is well-documented within cognitive neuroscience. The thought occurs first, but it takes a little longer for the action to occur; thus, it seems as though one has caused the other.[76] Indeed, accumulating research suggests that nonconscious mental processes initiate our actions long before we are even aware that we intend to act, by as much as ten seconds in some cases. Although we all like to believe that we freely and consciously choose between various courses of action, this suggests that this apparent conscious choice is only an illusion.[77]

Consider a major-league batter at the plate as he looks at the pitcher. Neuroscientists know how long it takes, on average, for information from the retina to reach and be recognized in the inferior temporal lobe and then be passed to the prefrontal cortex for a decision to be made, in this case to swing or not to swing. Moreover, a signal must then be sent to the muscles to begin the swing. This takes a total of 250 milliseconds, or one-quarter of a second. A baseball traveling at about 90 mph takes only 350 milliseconds to travel from the pitcher's hand to home plate. That leaves only 100 milliseconds, a tenth of a second, to aim and swing at the ball if the batter is relying only on information at the point where the ball leaves the pitcher's hand. That is not enough time to react. Similarly, a professional cricket batsman has to hit a ball traveling at close to 100 mph, reaching the batsman in less than half a second after leaving the bowler's hand.[78] Tennis players face a similar situation when returning a 150 mph serve. So how do baseball batters, batsman, and tennis players manage to hit the ball? At one time, it was assumed that this was because top athletes had faster reaction times than the rest of us, but researchers have discovered that this is not the case. Their reaction times were no different than those of people in general.

Figure 10-9: Too fast for conscious control.

Top athletes are distinguished from those of lesser talent by their ability to anticipate the play. While unaware that they are doing so, they gather information from the opponent even *before* the ball is thrown. In baseball, for example, clues coming from the pitcher's wrist and elbow position during the windup provide important information about what kind of pitch is likely forthcoming, even though the batter does not have time to be consciously aware of the cues. Of course, such information is an imperfect guide, and this explains why even highly skilled batters connect with the ball only about one-third of the time Baseball writer Jonah Lehrer summarized in everyday language what scientists have determined:

As soon as the pitcher begins his wind-up, the batter will automatically start to pick up on "anticipatory clues" that help him winnow down the list of possibilities. A torqued wrist suggests a curveball, while an elbow fixed in a right angle means that a fastball is coming, straight over the plate. . . . The batters, of course, aren't consciously studying these signs: they can't tell you why they decided to swing at a certain pitch. And yet, they are able to act based upon this information.[79]

Consistent with this, research has demonstrated that expert cricket batters can accurately predict the location and speed of a ball based only on a one-second video of the bowler's windup.[80]

The reader may find it difficult to accept that professional baseball players do not have time to react to the pitch *after* the ball has left the pitcher's hand. After all, they may point out that batters are able to duck if the ball is coming directly toward them, but this avoidance behavior relies on a different process, the *looming* response. This occurs when the image of an object on the retina rapidly expands, indicating that the object is coming directly toward one. As psychologists Michael Graziano and Dylan Cooke observe,

Whether the object is moving to you, or you are moving toward it, a defensive mechanism must react to this relative motion. The motor output involves an elaborate set of components, including squinting, blinking, ducking, veering, shrugging, raising the arm to block a threat, withdrawing the arm or other body parts from a threat, and even a defense-related retraction of the eye into the orbit.[81]

Such information takes a shortcut to the amygdala, which is associated with the fight or flight response, triggering rapid avoidance behavior.[82]

While it is natural for us to assume that we consciously choose to behave as we do, it is troubling to many people to learn that nonconscious processes are in the driver's seat. Yet, we should not be troubled. After all, it is still our brains, it is still *us* "making the choices."

***

Consciousness, which is the basis for self-awareness, occurs late in the chain of processing in the brain. One might almost say that our conscious activities are afterthoughts. Nonetheless, such afterthoughts come in very handy for survival, for slower, deliberative conscious activity is an important component of the phenomenally complex and well-integrated process of brain functioning. Because of the many nonconscious influences that underlie our thoughts and actions and beliefs, these "afterthoughts" leave us ignorant of much about ourselves, and as a result we never *really* know ourselves. As a result, it is likely that our beliefs about ourselves and about why we do the things we do are sometimes somewhat wide of the mark and at other times just plain wrong.

CHAPTER 11

NOT QUITE IN OUR RIGHT MINDS

*I can't reveal the mystery to either saint or sinner; I can't state
at length what I've said curtly; I achieve an altered state that I
can't explain; I have a secret that I cannot share.*
— Omar Khayyám (1048–1131)

L'*Estasi di Santa Teresa*, Bernini's magnificent sculpture in Rome's Santa Maria della Vittoria church, captures in marble a remarkable experience reported by a sixteenth-century nun (now Saint), Teresa of Ávila. Born Teresa Sánchez de Cepeda y Ahumada in Spain in 1515, she entered a convent when she was twenty years old and dedicated her life to serving her God. Later, in her forties, she began to experience powerful visions that she interpreted as involving direct contact with the divine. Here is her description of one such experience in 1562:

> I saw an angel close by me, on my left side, in bodily form. This I am not accustomed to see, unless very rarely. . . . He was not large, but small of stature, and most beautiful—his face burning, as if he were one of the highest angels, who seem to be all of fire: they must be those whom we call cherubim. . . . I saw in his hand a long spear of gold, and at the iron's point there seemed to be a little fire. He appeared to me to be thrusting it at times into my heart, and to pierce my very entrails; when he drew it out, he seemed to draw them out also, and to leave me all on fire with a great love of God. The pain was so great, that it made me moan; and yet so surpassing was the sweetness of this excessive pain, that I could not wish to be rid of it. The soul is satisfied now with nothing less than God. The pain is not bodily, but spiritual; though the body has its share in it, even a large one. It is a caressing of love so sweet which now takes place between the soul and God, that I pray God of His goodness to make him experience it who may think that I am lying.[1]

Figure 11-1: Bernini's Ecstasy of Saint Teresa (1652, photo by author).

Teresa was profoundly moved by this apparent encounter with an angel, although one cannot fail to note the sexual overtones of her account. Orgasm is sometimes associated with mystical experiences,[2] and her report suggests a sexual reverie that she interpreted, in the context of her presumed sexual naïveté, in religious terms.

As we have seen in earlier chapters, nonconscious processes are fundamental to our experience of consciousness and the beliefs associated with it. There is more than one form of consciousness, however, and alternate versions of consciousness, generally rare and unexpected, can lead us to believe that we have encountered angels, demons, or aliens, or have risen out of our bodies and journeyed to heaven's door. Such experiences are often overwhelming and so realistic that they are taken to be genuine even though in all likelihood they are the dramatic theatrical productions of our own brains.

TRANSCENDENTAL EXPERIENCE

Throughout history, there have been many accounts of people who have reacted with awe or alarm to strange, unexpected, and overwhelmingly "wonderful" experiences that have seemed to transcend reality.[3] Although relatively infrequent, such experiences are not uncommon either, and in surveys carried out in the United States and Great Britain, approximately one-third of people report having had at least one such occurrence.[4]

Such *transcendental experiences* have been of interest to psychologists almost since the beginning of the discipline. William James discussed the topic at length in his 1902 classic, *The Varieties of Religious Experience*,[5] and he focused on four characteristics: *ineffability* (incapable of being expressed in words), *noetic quality* (one has the sense of having gained knowledge not available through normal experience), *passivity* (the experience occurs without any effort by the individual), and *transience* (of short duration).

James's description does not include either the ecstasy or the vividness that Saint Teresa reported, but other psychologists have focused more on those particular aspects, applying various labels, including *ecstatic*, *mystical*, or *numinous* (mysterious, inspiring, arousing spiritual emotion) to capture the strong and positive emotions that are reported. German theologian Rudolf Otto (1869–1937) coined the term *mysterium tremendum et fascinans* to describe such an awe-inspiring experience that is beyond one's ability to understand (*mysterium*), is associated with fear and trembling (*tremendum*), and leads one to believe that one is in the presence of a deity. He viewed such experiences as intensely positive and endowed with fascination and attraction (*fascinans*).

Psychologist Abraham Maslow preferred the term *peak experience*, which he described as involving a disorientation of time and space combined with powerful feelings of awe, humility, and such profound joy that people sometimes describe it as a "sweet death."[6] He wrote,

> The peak experience is felt as a self-validating, self-justifying moment which carries its own intrinsic value with it. . . . It is felt to be so valuable an experience, so great a revelation, that even an attempt to justify it takes away from its dignity and worth.[7]

THE ROOTS OF TRANSCENDENCE

Someone who has a transcendent experience is likely never to forget it. Of course, the interpretation of the experience depends on the individual's belief system. While religious people are likely to interpret it as involving union with the divine, nonreligious people are more likely to use terms such as "profound enlightenment," "cosmic consciousness," or "being at one with the universe."[8] Transcendental experiences triggered by psychedelic drugs do not appear to differ from similar experiences that occur spontaneously, but when people have taken psychedelic drugs, they, not surprisingly, typically attribute the experience to the drug, whereas it is more likely to be viewed as mystical and meaningful when it occurs out of the blue.

Thus, the importance of the experience varies with the context in which it occurs and with the explanation the individual applies. The effects of context and attribution were evident in a study carried out on Good Friday in 1962. Volunteer students at Harvard Divinity School were divided at random into two groups. One group was administered psilocybin, a hallucinogen, while the other group received niacin, a vitamin that produces noticeable physiological changes but has no hallucinogenic effects.[9] None of the participants knew which substance they had received.

The divinity students then attended a worship service in the school's Marsh Chapel. Nine of the ten students who had received psilocybin, compared with only one of the ten who had received niacin, reported having had a powerful mystical experience during the service. They misinterpreted the effects of the psilocybin as something akin to Otto's *mysterium tremendum et fascinans*. Even though they knew that there was a fifty-fifty chance that they had received the psychoactive drug, this religious setting tipped the balance so strongly that they believed their experience to be profoundly spiritual.

Their descriptions of their experiences appeared indistinguishable from those described by various mystics across the ages. When interviewed twenty-five years later, they reported that those experiences had been the high point of their spiritual lives.[10] In 2002, similar results were obtained in a better-controlled version of the Marsh Chapel study.[11] When these participants were followed up two months later, they too rated their experiences as having had substantial spiritual significance and meaning for them.

The nature of such experiences makes it difficult at times to distinguish them from psychotic or dissociative disorders. Some clinicians have gone so far as to suggest that the historical accounts of transcendental experiences described by such major religious figures as Moses, Abraham, St. Paul, and Jesus reflect psychosis. If that were so, then,

> persons with primary and mood disorder-associated psychotic symptoms have had a monumental influence on the shaping of Western civilization.[12]

Yet even if the transcendental experiences associated with people like Moses and Jesus resemble those of psychotic individuals, other characteristics important for the diagnosis of psychosis are lacking. Just as context is important to an individual's interpretation of a transcendental experience, so, too, does context serve the clinician in distinguishing between a spiritual, transcendental experience and one that is psychotic or dissociative. When there is no pre-existing impairment, when the experience is relatively short-lived, and when the individual recognizes that the content of the experience was not reality, it is unlikely to be considered psychopathological.[13]

ALTERED STATES OF CONSCIOUSNESS

A transcendental experience is a specific case of an *altered state of consciousness*, a short-term conscious state that differs significantly from the usual, "normal" state of conscious awareness. Altered states range from common experiences, such as dreaming, to more infrequent events such as the transcendental experiences discussed above, to psychedelic drug "trips."[14] Normal consciousness involves subjective experiences that correspond more or less accurately to the world outside: When you see a cow, there is a cow out there; when you taste salt, there is something salty on your tongue. That is, what we perceive is *representative* of the real world that we are perceiving. An altered state of consciousness, on the other hand, involves changes in neurocognitive functioning that result in dramatic distortions of incoming perceptual data, leading to a temporary but significant *global* misrepresentation of the world.[15] *Partially* distorted representations, such as perceptual illusions or auditory hallucinations, are not considered to be altered states because the individual continues to track reality to a significant degree.

Altered states of consciousness attracted scientific interest in the middle of the nineteenth century, as medical researchers and others subjected reports of visions, ecstatic experiences, apparitions and the like to the emerging scientific skepticism about such matters.[16] Psychological and physical explanations were considered, while notions of the paranormal and supernatural were rejected.

As understanding of the neurological foundations of consciousness increases, transcendental experiences begin to make sense as natural consequences of how our brains work.[17] Normal consciousness relies on the proper functioning of many interrelated brain systems. As we go through each day thinking, perceiving, and remembering, those systems work smoothly together, creating a subjective experience of stable reality that is based both on memory and on sensory information from the outside world. The content of the subjective experience varies considerably from one person to another, even for people in the same situation, and the relative contributions of external sensory information and memory shift from one moment to another. Our very sophisticated imaging capability allows us to create a realistic model of the world "in the mind's eye," to analyze problems with it, and to run through possible actions to solve them.[18] Disruption of these systems can occur spontaneously at times in reaction to various physiological and psychological triggers, such as those brought on by stress or disease, resulting in altered states in which the perception of reality is distorted and artificial.[19]

PSYCHOLOGICAL PERSPECTIVES ON ALTERED STATES

Although many people interpret some altered states in religious terms, psychologists view them as manifestations of unusual brain functioning that result in depersonalization, derealization, and hallucinations.[20]

Depersonalization refers to the feeling of being detached from oneself, as though one is living in a dream. It begins with a feeling of unreality. The individual senses that he is altered in some way, and gradually feels as if he is observing himself, and experiencing his thoughts, feelings, sensations, and actions, from somewhere outside the body. This often involves distortions in both perception and the sense of time, as well as feelings of emotional and physical numbing. It may even seem as though parts of the body are growing or disappearing.

Derealization involves distortions in the perceptions of objects and people to the extent that they may appear unreal. It may even seem as though the external world is in a fog, or that everything in it has become lifeless, while the individual continues to feel normal and unchanged.

The distorted perceptions of depersonalization and derealization can seem more real and meaningful than normal perceptions because of the strong emotion that usually accompanies them. As a result, they are taken as revealing eternal truths, "transcendent reality," or supernatural knowledge. Needless to say, this then has a significant impact on the individual's beliefs.

Hallucinations are perceptions that appear to be accurate representations of the world outside, but originate within the brain. To be considered altered states of consciousness, hallucinations must involve a complete misrepresentation of reality.[21] Hallucinations that are only partial, for example a vivid and involuntary perceptual "hallucinatory" experience superimposed on normal perception and recognized by the individual as not being real, do not constitute an altered state. And while many psychotic individuals experience hallucinations, not all hallucinations are indicative of psychosis.

Hallucinatory perceptions are produced by the same brain mechanisms that process sensory information from the outside world.[22] Electroencephalogram recordings show that the areas of the brain involved in processing external sounds are also activated during auditory hallucinations,[23] and visual images too, whether from the external world or generated internally, involve a common set of cerebral mechanisms.[24] The hallucination takes form when neural systems that process information from the external world are flooded by neural discharges from memory, resulting in an experience that seems as real as if it had been brought about by external events.[25] As a result, hallucinations are indistinguishable from perceptions of actual events, and, because they possess the detail and emotional accompaniment that we associate with reality, they are mistaken for reality.[26]

Many transcendental experiences involve hallucinations, but most hallucinations would not be considered to be transcendental, for they lack key transcendental attributes such as ecstasy or a feeling of oneness with the divine or universe.

Hallucinations can be visual, auditory, olfactory (smell), visceral (involving distorted perceptions about one's body and feelings of being touched), or gustatory (taste). Auditory hallucinations are commonly associated with schizophrenia, and people who experience them may report hearing voices talking to them or about them, or they may "hear" their own thoughts as though they have been said aloud despite their efforts to prevent this from happening. Visual hallucinations appear three-dimensional and solid and may even throw shadows.[27] They often, but not always, reflect schizophrenia but are less common than auditory hallucinations in that disorder. Olfactory hallucinations typically result from head injuries, temporal-lobe seizures, brain tumors, or Parkinson's disease. Visceral hallucinations, unpleasant sensations that seem to come from one's internal organs, occur with schizophrenia, but may also result from an organic brain condition like delirium or from cocaine or amphetamine abuse. Gustatory hallucinations occur both with schizophrenia and with some types of epilepsy.

The apparent reality of a psychotic hallucination sometimes results in horrific acts that appear to the individual to be rational in the apparent circumstances. For example, in 2008, a young man, Vince Li, traveling on a bus near Winnipeg, heard what he took to be the voice of God. The voice told him that the man sitting beside him was an alien, and it ordered him to kill him to save the world. He was warned that if he did not follow this order, he himself would die immediately. Now, suppose that this were reality and not a hallucination. Suppose that there really were an alien sitting beside you and that a Supreme Being were ordering you to destroy it before it could harm humanity. In such a case, it would be rational to follow the order, and in so doing you might become a hero to your people. That was Mr. Li's belief at the time. Unfortunately, it was a belief to kill for, and so he attacked the young stranger with a knife, stabbed him repeatedly and ultimately decapitated him. Mr. Li was subsequently diagnosed with paranoid schizophrenia.

NEUROPSYCHOLOGY, HALLUCINATIONS, AND ALTERED STATES

Electrical or magnetic brain stimulation, especially of the temporal lobes, can bring about transcendental states involving feelings of mystical enlightenment and out-of-body experiences.[28] (Out-of-body experiences are discussed in more detail in a later chapter.) For example, a patient who was electrically stimulated in the right angular gyrus of the brain while undergoing evaluation for epilepsy treatment reported feeling that she was outside of her body and viewing it from a bird's-eye view.[29] (Creating a bird's-eye view is a normal function of this part of the brain.) Such a complete distortion of reality constitutes an altered state of consciousness.

Some epileptic seizures (such as complex partial seizures in temporal-lobe epilepsy) produce experiences that meet the criteria for an altered state, including a dreamy state with extremely realistic hallucinations and delusions, along with complicated automatic behaviors that seem to others to be voluntary and deliberate.[30] Intense feelings of meaningfulness are often involved and at times there is also a feeling of a loss of agency—of being under the control of some unseen entity. When your behavior appears to occur without you having initiated it, it is natural to surmise that someone else must be in control. In times past, such behavior often led to the assumption that an individual was possessed.[31]

Various important historical figures have described visions that were consistent with what can occur with temporal lobe epilepsy.[32] Joan of Arc's visions are the first to come to mind. They endowed her with a special sense of purpose that led her to rise from her lowly status as an uneducated farmer's daughter to become a religious military leader who inspired thousands of followers.

Migraines also involve hallucinations at times. About one-third of migraine-sufferers experience a visual disturbance, an "aura," as the headache develops. The aura typically involves only zig-zag lines, but some people experience very detailed and complex hallucinations that can be superimposed on external perceptual experience. To complicate the matter further, some migraine-sufferers occasionally experience the hallucinations and other aspects of the migraine aura in the absence of a headache.[33]

CONDITIONS CONDUCIVE TO HALLUCINATIONS AND ALTERED STATES

Anything that pushes the brain's representational system away from reliance upon incoming sensory information and toward internal memory images makes hallucinations and altered states more likely. While various brain disorders can be the cause, there are a number of transient conditions that can be involved as well.[34]

Physical influences include dehydration, oxygen-deprivation, hyperventilation, hypoglycemia, extended fasting, extreme pain, exhaustion, sexual activity, alcohol, and psychoactive drugs. The celebrated writer Aldous Huxley suggested that seekers of the mystical have throughout history employed such methods to alter their body chemistry.[35] The physical rituals and meditative manipulations that have evolved in some religious traditions influence brain chemistry in a way that may trigger and intensify altered states.[36] Consider that many of the great mystics of history have endured self-inflicted pain, withdrawn from society, and fasted to the point of hypoglycemia and near starvation, all of which might contribute to the triggering of their experiences. Some have also engaged in self-flagellation, which may bring about an altered state triggered by adrenaline and histamine secretion.

In 1799, Humphry Davy, a giant in the history of chemistry, experimented with nitrous oxide ("laughing gas"). Putting his life at risk at times, he inhaled the gas in order to study its effects and discovered that it led to "sublime emotion connected with highly vivid ideas."[37] His experiences were so pleasant that he began to use the gas recreationally and encouraged friends and colleagues to do the same. As a result, nitrous-oxide inhalation became popular with philosophers and literary people of the day. Following somewhat in Davy's footsteps a century and a half later, Huxley reported that he experienced a dramatic altered state of consciousness while breathing air that was 30 percent carbon dioxide.[38] The experience was so powerful and so redolent of the kinds of experiences often described as having occurred in a religious context that it led him to suggest that the long periods of chanting by medicine men, shamans, Christian and Buddhist monks, and the hours-long singing and screaming by religious revivalists are likely to elevate carbon dioxide levels, possibly resulting in altered states.

Increased stimulation brought about by new and demanding environments such as the arousal that accompanies mountain climbing or the sensory overload resulting from intense and repetitive rhythmic music can trigger an altered state. Bereavement also leads to heightened emotions, and there have been frequent accounts of people seeing the living figures of their deceased loved ones.

Anything that *decreases* the arousal system of the brain, such as meditation, severe fatigue, or extreme social isolation, can also make hallucinations more likely. Long-distance seafarers, such as Joshua Slocum and Frances Chichester, who made solo circumnavigations of the globe, have reported vivid hallucinations.[39]

Hallucinations can also occur when the brain is deprived of normal visual stimulation. For example, when people are blindfolded for a prolonged period, they begin to report visual hallucinations.[40] And then there is *Charles Bonnet syndrome*, a condition brought on by failing eyesight. It is a somewhat common neurological disorder in which visual hallucinations occur in the absence of psychiatric symptoms. These hallucinations are limited and quite predictable in their content, and the individual does not react like a psychotic person but gradually learns to interpret them as hallucinatory.

Hallucinatory imagery also can result from aberrations in the sleep-wake cycle and be manifested through *hypnagogic* and *hypnopompic* imagery and *sleep paralysis*, phenomena that are discussed later in this chapter.

Meditation

While meditation can at times lead to an altered state of consciousness involving visual hallucinations and profound mystical feelings, this is not typically the case. Instead, the conscious state during meditation is characterized by disconnection from external stimuli and from sensations originating within the body, resulting in deep relaxation and the *relaxation response*.[41] This response is essentially the opposite of the "fight or flight" response, and is associated with slow and shallow breathing, slowing of heart rate, reduction of oxygen consumption, and changes in electrical activity in the brain, which can be measured by an electroencephalogram.[42] It is accompanied by feelings of tranquility and, at times, feelings of transcendence or even ecstasy may follow.

Medical researcher Herbert Benson first identified the relaxation response. He suggested that the methods used by mystics and monks to bring about transcendence are the same as those that trigger the relaxation response. He described four necessary conditions: 1) being in a quiet environment without distractions; 2) assuming a comfortable position to limit muscular tension; 3) avoidance of distracting thoughts either by repeating a phrase over and over, by staring at an object, or by focusing on one's breathing; and 4) a passive attitude in order to allow the response to develop. Many different meditative methods incorporate these components, and Benson concluded that:

> The Relaxation Response is a universal human capacity, and even though it has been the focus of the religion of both East and West for most of recorded history, you don't have to engage in any eccentric practices to bring it forth.[43]

All meditative techniques involve conditions similar to those outlined by Benson: focusing attention on a simple stimulus for an extended period of time, avoidance of analytic thinking, and a willingness to go along with unusual experiences.[44] This is all reflected in "Transcendental Meditation," introduced to the West in the 1960s by the Maharishi Mahesh Yogi, in which the individual silently repeats a "mantra"—a meaningless syllable—over and over again.

In sum, altered states of consciousness can be understood as part of the wide range of human experience tied to healthy physical mechanisms including the brain. Such experiences are rare because most people do not seek them or desire to bring them about, but when they occur spontaneously, they can be overwhelming, especially in a context that promotes a supernatural explanation. British psychiatrist William Sargant, after studying mysticism in a number of different cultures, concluded that

> the same, physiological processes underlie experiences of "possession" by gods or spirits or demons, the mystical experience of union with God, the gift of tongues and other phenomena of "enthusiastic" religious experience, the inspired utterances of oracles and mediums, faith-healing, and some aspects of witch-doctoring, and the behavior of people under hypnosis, under certain drugs, or in states of sexual excitement.[45]

HYPNOSIS

Hypnotic procedures appear to have been used since ancient times, but the modern notion of hypnosis began to take form when physician Franz Mesmer introduced the concept of "animal magnetism" in the eighteenth century. He believed that every individual is surrounded by a magnetic field and that this field can be manipulated to promote healing. Étienne Félix d'Hénin de Cuvillers (1755–1841) was influenced by Mesmer's work, but rejected the notion of animal magnetism. Instead, he viewed Mesmer's effects as a result of the clients' beliefs and suggestibility. He coined the word *hypnotisme* based on the Greek root for sleep, "hypnos."[46]

In 1842, James Baird (1796–1860), a Scottish surgeon who is sometimes referred to as the "Father of Hypnosis," pioneered its use as a means of anesthesia in surgery. This was prior to the introduction of ether and chloroform in the mid-1840s. He thought that the hypnotic procedure led to fatigue in various parts the brain, producing a "nervous sleep."

After hypnosis was replaced by anesthesia in the operating room, it became the tool of entertainers and charlatans, and to this day most people are exposed to hypnosis through entertainment. Hypnotists in literature and film typically put people into a "trance," ostensibly taking control of their bodies and minds. As we shall see, modern research suggests that this notion of a trance-like transfer of control to the hypnotist is a myth.

The stage hypnotist "hypnotizes" members of the audience and has them perform all sorts of silly stunts.[47] These demonstrations fit with the common belief that the hypnotized individual has surrendered control of her thoughts and actions to the hypnotist. Often, such phrases as "you are going to sleep . . ." are part of the procedure, and this promotes the erroneous belief that the person is indeed asleep and only aware of what the hypnotist allows into her consciousness. Electroencephalographic research clearly demonstrates that hypnotized individuals are actually fully awake rather than being in a sleep-like state.[48]

The historical belief that hypnosis provides a pathway to the unconscious and to "repressed" memories has been responsible for efforts in modern times to use hypnosis to uncover supposedly hidden memories of trauma. As noted in an earlier chapter (chapter 3), there is convincing evidence that memory produced under hypnosis is unreliable because fictional memories produced with hypnosis may subsequently be recalled as genuine.[49]

A major difficulty in studying hypnosis is that it is only an experiential phenomenon. There is no physiological measure that can indicate when a person is hypnotized. We have to rely instead upon what the hypnotized person tells us. Nor is the observed behavior of the "hypnotized" individual a reliable indicator because it could simply be the result of compliance with suggestion.[50]

There is now general agreement among researchers that being hypnotized does not constitute being in an altered state of consciousness,[51] although there are occasional cases in which hypnotized people have experienced hallucinatory or delusional content and memory.[52] Most researchers agree with Hénin de Cuvillers that hypnotic behavior primarily reflects responsiveness to suggestion.[53]

In light of this, it would be appropriate to replace the term *hypnotizability* by *imaginative suggestibility*. "Hypnotized" people behave in the way that they think they are expected to behave. In other words, "hypnosis" is a response to suggestion and to the influence of the situation.[54] Nonetheless, participants may attribute their actions to hypnosis, and because of such an attribution, the behavior can feel to them as though it is involuntary. It is important not to underestimate the power of suggestion in influencing behavior. Suggestibility has particular importance in the treatment of somatoform disorders (disorders that appear to be physical in nature but are actually of psychological origin). Even when specific hypnotic procedures are not involved, the success of psychological treatment of such disorders is correlated with receptiveness to suggestion.[55]

People vary from being highly responsive to completely resistant to hypnotic suggestion. About 15 percent of people are easily hypnotized, while 10 percent are very difficult to hypnotize. These differences reflect both how suggestible individuals are in general and also their beliefs about what hypnosis entails, such as whether it involves giving up control to the hypnotist.[56]

There has been considerable curiosity about whether hypnotized individuals will perform dangerous or anti-social acts if instructed by the hypnotist. In a study that examined this question, hypnotized people were at one point asked to put their hands into a box that contained a venomous, red-bellied black snake, and at another point instructed to throw what they were informed was nitric acid into the face of a research assistant.[57] Five of the six hypnotized participants complied with these instructions, which might seem to support the power of hypnosis to overwhelm personal autonomy. On the other hand, all of another six participants, who had not been hypnotized but had been instructed to try to fool a professional hypnotist into thinking that they were, also complied with both instructions. Thus, demonstrations or experiments that appear to show compliance with dangerous or antisocial instructions may simply show that the participants do what they think is required of them while being confident that the hypnotist or researcher will not allow any harm to ensue.

Fantasy proneness

Fantasy-prone individuals are typically very responsive to hypnotic induction.[58] Such people spend a great deal of time fantasizing, sometimes to the extent that their fantasies become indistinguishable from reality and are so all-encompassing that the individual becomes virtually lost in them. This results in temporarily losing recognition of time and place and even their own personal identities. Some are even able to reach orgasm without any physical stimulation simply by fantasizing a sexual encounter. The resulting confusion between fantasy and reality often feeds various paranormal and supernatural beliefs. Indeed, people who identify themselves as mediums and psychic healers are often fantasy-prone.[59]

SLEEP, DREAMS, AND ALTERED STATES

We spend about one-third of our lives unconscious, fast asleep. Sleep is vital for our well-being, indeed for our very survival.[60] Although most of us need seven or eight hours' sleep each night, some people seem to function well on much less. Resting the body does not take the place of sleep, for sleep-deprivation eventually leads to both physical and mental deterioration.

But what is so important about sleep that we need to spend so much of each day unaware of what is going on around us? As one sleep researcher observed,

> If sleep does not serve an absolutely vital function, then it is the biggest mistake the evolutionary process has ever made.[61]

The function of sleep continues to be a matter of debate. Many explanations have been offered, but there is no scientific consensus about its purpose. It has been suggested that it evolved because it forced early peoples to hide themselves away at night, thereby escaping the dangers of unseen nocturnal predators and increasing their chances of survival and reproduction. This is unlikely, for people are even more vulnerable to attack when unconscious, and it does not explain why nocturnal animals also need sleep. Another suggestion has been that sleep allows us to save energy during those hours when we cannot do much anyway because of darkness.[62] If that were the prime advantage, what a waste all those sleep-filled hours would be for us now in a world where electricity lights up the night.

Modern research points to more specific functions of sleep, although its full importance is still not completely understood. Researchers generally agree that sleep is physically restorative.[63] It allows necessary tissue-maintenance to occur without interference from the normal physical demands of daytime activity.[64] This restorative process involves, among other things, the secretion of growth hormone, which not only promotes physical growth in children, but also contributes to tissue repair in adults. In addition, sleep provides the opportunity for "garbage pickup" in the brain. When neurons are busy doing their brain-work while we are awake, they metabolize glucose to fuel their activities, and that process produces waste chemicals.[65] Researchers have discovered that the abundant glial cells surrounding neurons shrink a little during sleep, providing physical gaps among them that allow cerebrospinal fluid to flush the waste products away.[66]

Sleep involves much more than rest and physical restoration. It may seem as though our brains are relatively inactive during a good night's sleep. After all, conscious thinking has stopped and there is very little incoming sensory information. Researchers shared this view until the invention of the electroencephalograph at the end of 1920s, which allowed the measurement and recording of electrical activity in the brain. Their electroencephalograms (EEGs) revealed that, rather than being in deep repose, our brains become very active at regular intervals throughout the night. The nature and purpose of this activity was a complete mystery at first.

It was only in the early 1950s that sleep researchers discovered a surprising phenomenon while observing individuals sleeping in the laboratory. Several times each night, coincident with periods of intense electrical activity in the brain, an individual's eyes move about rapidly under the lids.[67] Those phases of sleep are now referred to as rapid eye movement (REM) sleep, or *paradoxical sleep*. (The "paradox" is that the brain seems to be at the same time both asleep and highly activated.[68])

There were more surprises. It was soon discovered that, when awakened during REM sleep, people—usually about 80 percent of the time—report that they are dreaming.[69] These dreams are typically elaborate, vivid, and tinged with emotion.

REM sleep occurs not only in humans but also in all mammals, birds, and even in lizards.[70] This long evolutionary history suggests that it has an important function, but there is much speculation about what that function might be. Research has found that when people are deprived of REM sleep as a result of being awakened each time they enter that part of the sleep cycle, they compensate by having more REM sleep as soon as possible.[71] This automatic compensation again suggests that REM sleep is important. Other research indicates that sleep, and REM sleep in particular, is necessary for normal mental functioning. Compromised sleep leads to deterioration in attention, memory, and decision-making ability. Maintaining a healthy quality of sleep appears to promote cognitive functioning and possibly mitigate against age-related declines in cognitive ability.[72]

THE SLEEP CYCLE

We cycle through periods of REM and non-REM sleep several times a night, with the first cycle taking somewhere between 75 and 100 minutes. The REM/non-REM cycles become longer over the course of the night, and later cycles can be as long as 120 minutes.[73] The function of these repeated cycles of sleep remains a mystery.

About one-quarter of an adult's typical night's sleep is spent in REM sleep, while babies and young children spend even more. Electrical activity in the brain varies greatly throughout the night as we pass back and forth between non-REM and REM sleep. If you were to examine an EEG record of electrical brain activity as a person nods off to sleep, the changes would be readily observable. When awake, the EEG reveals rapid, irregular, low-voltage electrical waves known as *beta waves*, which result from large numbers of neurons firing at different times in an unsynchronized manner. This reflects the fact that the cortex, where we do our thinking, is highly active and attentive to the world outside. Then as the individual relaxes, brain activity slows down and beta waves give way to slower *alpha waves*. These waves are reliable markers of relaxation and are due to irregular firing of neurons across large areas of the brain.

Gradually, as the individual drifts off to sleep, brain activity slows further and the alpha waves are replaced by even slower but stronger *theta waves*. This is known as *Stage I* sleep. The individual becomes more and more drowsy, gradually drifting into unconsciousness. Only about five percent of a night's sleep is in Stage I. Five or ten minutes later, the person moves into *Stage II*, where theta waves continue to dominate but are punctuated by sudden, short, pronounced bursts of electrical activity. This lasts for fifteen minutes or so, before transition into *Stage III*. At this point, heart rate and respiration slow down, muscles relax, and brain activity slows even more. Slow, large, strong *delta waves* make their appearance, reflecting synchronized activity in the brain because of extensive patterns of neurons firing at approximately the same time. Growth hormone begins to be secreted.

Another thirty minutes or so go by, and the individual drifts into *Stage IV*. Brainwave activity is now completely delta wave, and now the individual is deeply asleep and would be difficult to awaken. (Someone awakened at this point would be likely to move lethargically, feel confused, and take several minutes to become fully awake.) The secretion of growth hormone that began in Stage III continues during this stage, and because of this Stages III and IV are often referred to as "restorative sleep."

And then the excitement begins. After having been asleep for between seventy and ninety minutes, the individual enters *Stage IV REM*. The first episode lasts for only few minutes, but these REM periods become longer and longer as the sleep cycles recur, and the last one may be as long as one hour. Not only do the eyeballs move rapidly under the lids, but other dramatic changes occur as well. The body is essentially paralyzed; males experience erections and females produce vaginal secretions (unrelated to any sexual dreams); blood flow to the brain increases; and, as noted earlier, an individual awakened at this time is likely to be in the middle of a dream.

As the night wears on, Stage III and the non-REM portion of Stage IV all but disappear, especially in the elderly, and most of our sleep for the rest of the night now involves cycling between Stage II non-REM and Stage IV REM.[74]

DREAMS

We have seen how our perceptions, thoughts, and memories are heavily influenced by nonconscious processes of which we are not aware. Given how difficult it is to "know ourselves" during our waking hours, how much more of a challenge it is when we try to make sense of active, conscious-like experiences that occur while we are sleeping. Dreams have always fascinated, puzzled, inspired, and frightened us, and they have been an important focus in art, literature, psychiatry, psychology, and folk mythology. In some societies, dreams are believed to involve communication with other people, or to be divinely inspired, to be portents of future events, or to reflect an alternate reality similar to waking life. Some societies view them with such importance that anthropologists refer to them as *dream cultures*.[75]

Freud viewed dreams as the "royal road to the unconscious," while Jung considered them a vehicle for the expression of a collective unconscious that supposedly embodies knowledge accumulated across generations. Most bookstores carry a variety of books about dream analysis, and throughout much of the twentieth century many psychotherapists used dream analysis in an effort to understand their clients' problems. Modern clinical psychology, on the other hand, gives little value to the content of dreams, except to the extent that they may reflect our worries and anxieties.

A dream is an altered state of consciousness.[76] As we go to sleep, we lose awareness, but when we begin to dream, we become aware once again, albeit in a manner quite different from that of waking consciousness.[77] We have lost contact with reflective thought, for we do not recognize that we are asleep. Dreams seem real at the time and we remember them post hoc as having a narrative structure like an unfolding story. The events can range from realistic (e.g., a situation in one's workplace) to fantastical (e.g., swimming with a polka-dotted dolphin in a purple sea). Dreams can be banal or brilliant, depressing or inspiring, pleasant or frightening, fantastical or familiar, erotic or unstimulating. In the dream, we participate in an elaborate and sometimes bizarre piece of theater in which we maintain our identity while all the other characters, even though they are the creations of our own brain, seem to have a life of their own. Neuropsychologist Antti Revonsuo eloquently describes this nighttime drama:

> But we are not alone in this alternative reality—there are other apparently living, intelligent beings present, who seem to share this reality with us. We see and interact with realistic human characters in our dreams. Their behavior and their very existence in the dream world seem to be autonomous. The dream people who I encounter within the dream seem to go about their own business: I cannot predict or control what they will say or do. Yet, they, too, are somehow produced by my own dreaming brain.[78]

As discussed earlier, dreaming can occur in any sleep stage, although it is primarily associated with REM sleep.[79] And just as dreaming can occur without REM, REM sleep can occur without dreaming. Some dreams also occur during non-REM sleep, but they are typically more thought-like and less vivid or emotional than REM dreams,[80] although a small percentage of non-REM dream reports are indistinguishable from those associated with REM.[81] Because dreaming is not completely correlated with REM sleep, it seems likely that dreaming and REM are generated by different mechanisms in the brain and that, whether in REM or non-REM, dreaming involves a degree of activation of parts of the brain associated with waking consciousness.[82]

THE FUNCTION OF DREAMS

The function of dreaming has puzzled researchers past and present, and some researchers suggest that it does not have any function but is a meaningless by-product of other important activities that occur during sleep.[83] Most researchers, however, disagree with that view. It has been suggested that dreams provide a useful simulation of social interactions in the waking world, a "virtual-reality model" that brings together unrelated themes and ideas unencumbered by the logical restrictions that can inhibit conscious thought.[84]

The consensus is that dreaming reflects REM activity associated with breaking down our daily autobiographical experiences into their components and then recombining the memory elements to make them more salient and easier to retrieve.[85] In this view, events of the day are transformed into long-term memories through biochemical processes during REM sleep that physically alter the neurons associated with memory. This *memory consolidation* process takes time, and it is advantageous for this to occur while no resources are required for sensory processing of incoming information.[86] Recent research has now identified the particular neural activity that occurs specifically during REM sleep that appears essential for normal memory consolidation.[87]

It appears, then, that REM sleep and dreaming enable the building of numerous cross-connections between new material and existing elements of memory that will aid creativity when one is awake regardless of whether the dream is remembered.[88] This might explain the insight that sometimes occurs during sleep. For example, in his research that led to the discovery of insulin, medical scientist and Nobel laureate Frederick Banting (1891–1941) was confronted by a perplexing problem that he could not solve. The problem seemed insurmountable, but he awoke suddenly one night, jotted down what had come to him in a dream, and went back to sleep. The next morning, he was startled to find what he had written during the night provided the solution to the problem.[89]

HYPNAGOGIC STATES

A *hypnagogic state* is a state between wakefulness and sleep characterized by short episodes of hallucinatory experience.[90] (When experienced while moving from sleep to wakefulness, the experience is referred to as a *hypnopompic* state.)

When in such a state, the individual usually is not aware of being partially asleep and experiences a blend of perceptual information from the external world and information from memory itself. This may involve faces or landscapes or social situations, and the imagery is usually vivid and relatively brief. The experience is relatively common. For example, in a survey carried out in the United Kingdom, 37 percent of respondents reported experiencing hypnagogic hallucinations and 12.5 percent reported hypnopompic hallucinations.[91]

People sometimes wake during the night and mistake a hypnopompic state for being wide awake. Hypnopompic imagery is often vivid, realistic, and sometimes bizarre, and the most commonly reported image is that of a "face in the dark." Both hypnagogic sleep and hypnopompic sleep are likely to be the sources of many reports of apparitions,[92] and are also symptomatic of some neurological disorders.

NIGHTMARES

Nightmares typically occur during REM sleep and involve frightening situations that may reflect the dreamer's fears and worries, or a frightening theme from a recent book or television program. Young children awaking from nightmares are particularly frightened because of poor or absent reality-testing ability, but their parents assure them that the nightmares are only fantasy, and so they gradually grow to view such dreams as fiction.

NIGHT TERRORS

Night terrors are extremely frightening experiences that, unlike nightmares, occur while in very deep Stage IV non-REM sleep. They typically occur within two to three hours after falling asleep. A night terror is not simply a nightmare. It is essentially a panic attack that occurs while sleeping. It involves extreme autonomic nervous-system arousal, with greatly increased heart rate, respiration, and other physiological changes associated with the fight-or-flight response. The dreamer appears to an observer to be terrified, and if she awakens, feelings of terror will be paramount and may continue for some time.

SLEEP PARALYSIS

From nightmare to night terror, can it get any worse? Indeed, it can. Consider this report from the celebrated nineteenth-century author Guy de Maupassant (1850–1893):

> I sleep—for a while—two or three hours—then a dream—no—a nightmare seizes me in its grip, I know full well that I am lying down and that I am asleep. . . . I sense it and I know it . . . and I am also aware that somebody is coming up to me, looking at me, running his fingers over me, climbing onto my bed, kneeling on my chest, taking me by the throat and squeezing . . . squeezing . . . with all its might, trying to strangle me. I struggle, but I am tied down by that dreadful feeling of helplessness that paralyzes us in our dreams. I want to cry out—but I can't. I want to move—I can't do it. I try, making terrible, strenuous efforts, gasping for breath, to turn on my side, to throw off this creature who is crushing me and choking me—but I can't! Then, suddenly, I wake up, panic-stricken, covered in sweat. I light a candle. I am alone.[93]

Maupassant provides a description of a personal, vivid, and terrifying experience known as *sleep paralysis*. It occurs when the paralysis associated with REM sleep persists while the individual moves from REM sleep into a hypnopompic state. Thus, it is a combination of REM sleep and semi-waking consciousness in which the sleeper becomes aware of the generalized state of paralysis while believing herself to be wide awake. Not only does the individual feel paralyzed and unable to talk but also senses a heavy weight on the chest, becoming unable to breathe. Sleep paralysis also frequently involves hearing voices and having hallucinatory visions, such as a demon sitting on one's chest or a frightening sense of an evil presence nearby. Out-of-body experiences are also sometimes reported. All the while, the individual appears to an observer to be deeply asleep and possibly dreaming. An episode can last anywhere from one to several minutes and ends either spontaneously or when someone touches the individual.

Psychologist James Allen Cheyne reports that the various experiences associated with sleep paralysis can be categorized into three clusters:[94]

(1) The *vestibular-motor* type of sleep paralysis involves unusual bodily experiences such as a feeling of floating outside one's body, flying through space, or falling or spinning. Unlike other types of sleep paral-

ysis, these experiences are often accompanied by feelings of happiness and contentment.

(2) The *incubus* type of sleep paralysis involves the illusory feelings of breathing difficulty and intense pressure on the chest described above by Maupassant. The dreamer fears suffocation and death. At times, there are also accompanying vestibular-motor sensations such as a feeling of being thrown about or even being sexually penetrated. These experiences have often been interpreted as sexual attacks.

(3) The *intruder* type primarily involves a *feeling of presence*, a sense that someone is nearby in the room, watching, waiting, and planning some sort of horrible act. This is typically accompanied by sensory experiences that may include demon-like figures, loud noises, footsteps, whispering, and even touching and grabbing the sleeper. The brain's threat center, the amygdala, is activated, triggering a sense of impending doom associated with the feeling of a presence and a massive fear response.

Cheyne points out that, throughout history, accounts of what has surely been sleep paralysis have been interpreted through the dominant belief system of the day.[95] When belief in Satan and witchcraft was strong, it was generally accepted that the sleeper had been attacked by demons. This almost certainly accounts for the numerous reports in the Middle Ages of *incubi* and *succubi*, supposed demons that came to people's beds at night and forced sexual intercourse upon them (incubi attacking women, succubi attacking men). The incubus was believed to impregnate its victims with "demon seed," while the succubus impregnated itself through sexual intercourse. It was also believed that these demons would sometimes steal their victims' souls during sleep. The belief in these visitations was so strong in the 1300s that the creatures were actually defined in law. In addition, the *Malleus Maleficarum*, the Inquisitor's guidebook, dealt at length with methods for getting rid of the demons, but supposed victims ran the risk that their reports might lead to them being considered to be witches, the terrible consequences of which were even more horrific.

Sleep paralysis is undoubtedly at the root of many other folk beliefs involving horrifying visitors that come in the night and sit on a sleeper's chest. The *Old Hag* of Newfoundland folklore involves waking in terror in the night with difficulty breathing because of an apparent but invisible heavy weight on one's chest. Equivalents of the Old Hag are part of the mythology of many other cultures.[96] Because belief in demons is relatively rare in modern times, particularly in Western cultures, such experiences are now understood differently. Similar experiences, for example, have been attributed in current times to abductions by aliens. More about this in a later chapter.

Estimates of the frequency of sleep paralysis vary. A study of medical students at Duke University carried out in the early 1960s reported an incidence rate of 6.1 percent, whereas the rate among college students in Newfoundland in the mid-1980s was estimated to be between 15 to 23 percent.[97] A systematic review of thirty-five studies reported that 7.6 percent of the general population, 28.3 percent of students, and 31.9 percent of psychiatric patients reported having experienced at least one episode,[98] and it suggested that the similarly high rates among students and psychiatric patients may reflect regular sleep disturbances that make sleep paralysis more likely.

LUCID DREAMING

A lucid dream is one in which the dreamer is both aware of being in a dream and able to some extent to manipulate the course and content of the dream. Such dreams, which occur during REM sleep, provoked fascination even in ancient times, and were described by Aristotle and St. Augustine, among many others.[99] Research suggests that brain areas associated with dreaming and those associated with waking consciousness are both activated during a lucid dream, making it somewhat like hypnagogic sleep in that regard.[100]

SOMNAMBULISM

Sleepwalking (*somnambulism*) is not uncommon, and about 15 percent of the population has experienced it at one time or another. Sleepwalking usually occurs during deep Stage IV non-REM sleep. Contrary to popular belief, there is no danger in awakening the sleepwalker (although this is usually quite difficult to do because of the depth of the sleep). Sleepwalkers have been known to carry out activities that we normally associate with being wide awake. For example, someone may get up in the night, go to the kitchen, make a sandwich, pour a glass of milk, and return to bed after finishing the snack, all the while having been fast asleep.

A more dramatic example: Kenneth Parks, a Toronto man in his early twenties, who was married with an infant daughter, suffered from severe insomnia related to worry over being unemployed and having outstanding gambling debts. Early in the morning of May 23, 1987, he left his bed and drove twenty-three kilometers to his in-laws' home and stabbed his mother-in-law to death and assaulted his father-in-law, who survived. He then drove himself to the police station and told the police "I think I have killed some people . . . my hands"—apparently only realizing at that moment that his hands were severely lacerated. No apparent motive for the murder and assault were ever established. He claimed to have loved his parents-in-law and maintained that he could not remember anything about the event.

Because of his history of sleepwalking, a group of specialists, including psychiatrists, psychologists, a sleep expert, and a neurologist, concluded that he actually had been asleep and unaware of his actions when he committed the crime. They found no evidence of psychosis or other mental pathology. Since they concluded that the crime had been triggered by a collection of factors that would be unlikely to recur, they argued that the likelihood of committing such a crime again was small.[101] In 1988, a jury accepted the sleepwalking defense and declared Parks not guilty. When the verdict was appealed, the Supreme Court of Canada upheld the acquittal.

Aggression during sleepwalking is extremely rare and the Parks case was an anomaly. Yet he is not the only sleepwalker to have driven a car.

***

At times, our brains produce remarkable experiences that, although generated internally, are indistinguishable from actual perceptions of the outside world. Because of their apparent reality and the emotion that accompanies them, it is not surprising that people interpret these experiences literally and believe that they have been in the presence of the divine, or have been sat upon by the Old Hag, or have been visited by a ghost in the night. The unusually strong emotions that often accompany these experiences can have long-lasting effects, not just with regard to the experiences themselves but on a person's beliefs about the very nature of reality and the world in which we live.

CHAPTER 12

BELIEF AND WELL-BEING

Believe that life is worth living and your belief will help create the fact.

—William James

We all recognize that our thoughts directly influence our bodies: ruminate about an insult and your body tenses up; become angry about that insult and your face flushes; entertain an erotic thought and a more pleasurable physical reaction follows; and being informed that you have just eaten roasted rat brings feelings of nausea. (And if this simple mention of roasted rat makes you squirm, your reaction echoes the point.) The connection between the brain and body is bidirectional: pain or hunger triggers impatience and testiness, and genital stimulation triggers erotic thoughts.

The influence of belief upon the body is tied to the nervous system, that river of fibers that connects body to brain. To better understand this influence, a brief primer about the organization of the nervous system will be helpful. It consists of two major divisions, the *central nervous system* (CNS), comprising the brain and spinal cord, and the *peripheral nervous system* (PNS), which connects the CNS to all of the various organs, glands, muscles, and blood vessels.

The peripheral nervous system is itself divided into two parts, the *somatic* and the *autonomic* systems. The somatic nervous system is the "voluntary" system that allows us to control our movements; we use it each time we choose to walk, talk, or chew gum. The autonomic nervous system, on the other hand, is not under our direct control. It regulates the internal workings of the body, including heart rate, respiration, movement of food through the alimentary canal, the saline level in the blood, pupillary dilation and contraction, and many other processes vital to survival. Its activities coordinate with the *endocrine system*, which comprises various glands such as the pituitary, thyroid, hypothalamus, ovaries, and testes. These two systems work so closely together that they are collectively referred to as the *neuroendocrine system*.

The autonomic system is again divided into two divisions, the *parasympathetic* and the *sympathetic*, which work largely in opposition to one another. Activation of the parasympathetic system is associated with general relaxation, whereas activation of the sympathetic system (combined with hormone secretion through the endocrine system) readies the body for action. Pronounced sympathetic arousal constitutes the *fight-or-flight response* (whereby the body prepares itself for extreme muscular action in response to threat). In some animals—lions and tigers, for example—such activation typically leads to "fight," while in others—say, rabbits and mice—it results in "flight."

This reaction involves a number of significant changes in the body. Stress hormones, including adrenaline, noradrenaline, and cortisol (a steroid that promotes the breakdown of fats into sugars, which provides energy) surge into the bloodstream energizing the body. Heart rate and respiration increase, providing more oxygen to the muscles. Constriction of some blood vessels, such as those in the hands and feet, makes more blood available to the large muscles in the arms and legs. (This explains the cold hands and feet associated with fear and anxiety.) Tears and saliva are inhibited, and hence the dry mouth associated with fear. Other changes include dilation of the pupils, relaxation of the bladder, cessation of digestion, and inhibition of phallic erection (which accounts for the association between performance anxiety and impotence).

It is important for our survival that this fight-or-flight system works without need for conscious intervention. There is no time for contemplation when a bus careens toward you, and as soon as the danger is recognized, the autonomic nervous system automatically prepares your body for extraordinary exertion to get out of harm's way. On the other hand, if you saw movement out of the corner of your eye and thought that a bus was racing toward you when it was not, then this stressful physiological arousal is unnecessary, for your body is now energized and you are ready to run as fast as you can, even though there is no reason to do so. You try to calm yourself, but extra glucose and adrenaline continue to circulate in your bloodstream. Your body is now like an automobile in neutral with the accelerator pressed to the floor: The motor is racing, but the car is going nowhere. This is not good for the car, nor for your body.

At times, we experience fight-or-flight arousal even without awareness of the trigger. This is because part of our brain is always on the alert, scanning the environment for potential danger. On the other hand, since for the most part we *learn* about what is dangerous and what is not, fight-or-flight arousal often occurs *after* our evaluation of the situation. For example, you hear a strange noise and, based on past threats, you conclude that there is someone outside your door who intends to do you harm. This interpretation elicits the fight-or-flight response.

STRESS

Pioneering research carried out by Hans Selye during the 1950s led to the commonly accepted belief that health and well-being are adversely affected by stress. Thus, it has been argued, stress causes arousal of the sympathetic nervous system leading to the release of stress hormones such as adrenaline that have negative effects on the immune system and render the person more vulnerable to disease. Yet, while it may make intuitive sense that stress is harmful for health, research now shows that it may not be stress *per se* that poses a risk to one's health but the *belief* that stress is bad for you. Psychologist Tom Witkowski describes a number of studies that support this conclusion.[1] For example, one study estimated that over an eight-year period, 182,000 Americans suffered early deaths not because of the stress that they were under, but because of their *belief* that the stress was harmful to their health.[2] Another large study in Britain followed some seven thousand men and women over a period of eighteen years to see whether people who believed stress is harmful to their health were at increased risk of cardiac problems.[3] The rate of myocardial infarction was more than twice as high in those who indicated at the outset that they believed stress to be harmful compared to those who believed that their health was not affected by stress. We see once again the power of belief.

It may seem difficult at first to understand how the *belief* that stress is bad for us can be deleterious to our health. This comes about because the way we interpret a situation is critical to our physiological response.[4] If we believe that stress poses a risk to health, then experiencing stress can produce anxiety and chronic sympathetic nervous system arousal and its associated injurious effects. This does not occur when stress is viewed not as a threat but as a challenge.[5] A study of middle-level executives who were experiencing high levels of work-related stress found that those who interpreted the stress as a challenge rather than as a threat experienced few if any negative consequences.[6] They were resilient. In metallurgy, *resilience* refers to a material's ability to bend but not break under physical stress, and resilient people are people who "bend but do not break" when under psychological stress. In line with this, research shows that resilient people react with a lower increase in diastolic blood pressure while attempting a difficult task, reflecting lower physical responsiveness to stress.[7] They also recover more quickly from injuries[8] and cope better with pain.[9]

WHEN EMOTIONS TURN DEADLY

Circumstances can trigger a wide range of emotional reactions, including elation, surprise, fear, anger, anxiety, sorrow, or despair. Those emotions are accompanied by varying degrees of activation in the autonomic nervous system. Excessive autonomic activation can bring deleterious, possibly even fatal, consequences.

Scared to death

Have you ever been "scared out of your wits?" Perhaps a friend unexpectedly jumped out from behind a tree and gave you a fright, or you came suddenly face–to–face with a snarling dog. If so, you will remember just how quickly and violently your heart began to pound, and it no doubt took a few minutes before it slowed down once you felt safe.

Sherlock Holmes, in Arthur Conan Doyle's *The Hound of the Baskervilles*, investigated the death of Sir Charles Baskerville, who was found lying dead in his driveway with his face contorted by fear. He had had a chronic heart condition, and his death was apparently caused by a heart attack brought on by intense fear at the sight of a ghostly hound, a hound he believed to be the Hound of Hell (see figure 12-1).

Death from cardiac arrest triggered by terror is not just fiction, and Sir Charles's name lives on in real life, for the *Baskerville effect* refers to sudden death brought on by intense emotion. Extreme sympathetic nervous system arousal can result in so much adrenaline reaching the heart that it triggers a particular kind of arrhythmia, *ventricular fibrillation*. This in turn leads to a sudden drop in blood pressure and vascular collapse, which can be lethal.[10] There is medical speculation that ventricular fibrillation brought on by high arousal of the sympathetic nervous system might be a major contributor to death in at least some cases of sub-arachnoid hemorrhages, prolonged seizures, head injuries, asthma attacks, cocaine and amphetamine reactions, and alcohol withdrawal.[11] People with a pre-existing cardiac disorder are presumably at greater risk.

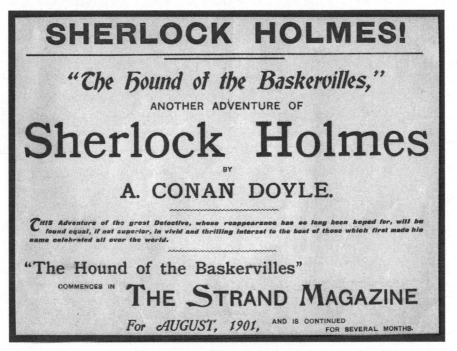

Figure 12-1: Hound of the Baskervilles.

A 1980 study reviewed thirty years of homicidal assaults in Cleveland, Ohio, in which victims unexpectedly died as a direct result of assault despite not having sustained any internal injuries.[12] Medical records, including autopsy reports, revealed that these victims had suffered cardiac damage similar to that observed in the hearts of laboratory animals that had been subjected to extreme stress. These deaths were deemed the likely result of overwhelming cardiac stress brought about by adrenaline and other hormones associated with intense fear.

Severe stress, extreme fear, and accompanying autonomic arousal often occur during natural disasters such as tornados, tsunamis, and earthquakes. There is accumulating evidence that shows that such autonomic arousal is also associated with increased risk of sudden cardiac death in these circumstances.[13] For example, while all the residents of four counties of Washington State survived a powerful earthquake in 2001, the incidence of sudden cardiac death increased significantly in the forty-eight hours following the quake. Those already suffering from coronary artery disease were most likely to succumb.[14] The powerful Northridge earthquake that struck Los Angeles in 1994 also resulted in a steep increase in sudden deaths of people suffering from cardiac disease (twenty-four compared to a typical daily average of about five), leading investigators to conclude that the deaths were not due to physical exertion but to the emotional distress. In another study, acute psychological stress was considered the most significant factor in the sudden and unexpected deaths of one hundred British men who had been suffering from heart disease.[15] A quarter were clearly stressed within thirty minutes of their deaths. (Stressors included being attacked by a dog, being in a traffic accident, and participating in an automobile race for the very first time.)

Conan Doyle's fictional Sir Charles not only suffered from a heart condition but also had a powerful superstitious anxiety regarding a curse that had been put on his family name, a curse that threatened vengeance in the form of a Hound from Hell. Beliefs and expectations may be just as powerful in real life. Consider, for example, culturally shared superstitions about death. In Japanese and Chinese cultures, the number four is considered extremely unlucky because of its association with death. (In Mandarin, Cantonese, and Japanese, the words "four" and "death" are pronounced almost identically.) Researchers wondered whether sudden deaths would be more frequent among Chinese and Japanese Americans on the fourth day of each month, given the possible stressful implications associated with that "unlucky" day.[16] They examined computerized death certificates for more than 200,000 Chinese and Japanese Americans and compared them with those of more than 47 million white Americans. They found that Chinese and Japanese American cardiac mortality peaked on the fourth day of each month, and this peak was particularly large for deaths resulting from chronic heart disease. This is consistent with the Baskerville effect. Yet, while the study is suggestive, it was not possible to ascertain from death certificates whether these particular individuals held a strong superstitious fear of the number four.

Other research has found that Chinese Americans die significantly earlier than would be expected when they happen to have an ill-fated combination of disease and birth year as defined by Chinese astrology and traditional Chinese medicine (TCM).[17] A study of more than three thousand Chinese Americans who died from lymphatic cancer found that those who had been born in the "earth years," which, according to TCM, makes people particularly susceptible to diseases involving tumors and lumps, died on average at 59.7 years. Those born in other years lived almost four years longer, to 63.6 years.[18] Similar differences were found for a number of other disease-date combinations, and the strength of the effect was correlated with strength of commitment to traditional Chinese culture. No such difference was found for white Americans who died from similar causes in the same period.

Now consider the *sudden unexpected nocturnal death syndrome* (SUNDS). The term was coined to refer to the unknown cause of the deaths of 117 Hmong men who had immigrated to the United States from Laos (all but one of whom were apparently in good general health), all of whom died unexpectedly in their sleep. This large number of sudden and unexpected deaths presented a mystery, because these men did not live in close geographical proximity of each other nor had any of them been physically ill prior to their deaths. This piqued the interest of a psychologist who was researching sleep paralysis.[19] She discovered that these men had shared a strong cultural belief about the danger of attack by spirits during the night. As we have seen, reports of demonic attacks are relatively common during sleep paralysis, and this led the researcher to attribute these men's deaths to extreme autonomic arousal brought on during sleep paralysis by the apparent fulfilment of their deepest fear, visitation by an evil spirit. Again, it is important to keep in mind that this is only speculation, for there was no way of ascertaining whether these men actually had experienced sleep paralysis just before they died. The researcher concluded,

> in the context of severe and ongoing stress related to cultural disruption and national resettlement (exacerbated by intense feelings of powerlessness about existence in the United States) and from the perspective of a belief system in which evil spirits have the power to kill men who do not fulfil their religious obligations, the solitary Hmong man confronted by the numinous terror of the nightmare (and aware of its murderous intent) can die of SUNDS.[20]

These several studies do not establish cause and effect but point to the possibility that significant emotional distress related to superstitious belief may bring deleterious physical consequences.

Broken Heart Syndrome

Many popular songs have referred to suffering from a broken heart as a result of a lost love—for example, Brooke Valentine's "Dying from a Broken Heart." Such "hurtin' music" communicates the torment of unrequited love through reference to metaphorical death. As we shall see, there sometimes may be more than metaphor involved.

Actor Carrie Fisher died suddenly from cardiac arrest in December 2016, and her grief-stricken mother, Debbie Reynolds, suffered a stroke and died the following day. Many newspaper accounts suggested that Reynolds had died from a broken heart. Although most physicians would give little credence to such a claim, evidence has been accumulating in recent years that suggests they may be wrong. For example, a 2005 report in the *New England Journal of Medicine* described nineteen patients, none of whom had had pre-existing coronary problems, who developed *stress-induced cardiomyopathy* during a period of severe emotional distress.[21] This is a temporary condition involving a profound and life-threatening dysfunction of the heart brought on by exaggerated sympathetic autonomic nervous system resulting in a flood of stress hormones that disrupts normal pumping activity in one part of the heart while the rest of the heart pumps normally. In about half the cases, this distress was triggered by news of the sudden and unanticipated death of a loved one. The reaction is now referred to as *broken-heart syndrome* and is being reported in medical literature around the world. It is not yet known whether genetic factors put some people at greater risk of developing the syndrome.

Death by hex

As European colonizers spread out across the world in the late nineteenth and early twentieth centuries, accounts of strange religious and magical practices of aboriginal peoples garnered considerable attention back home. Among these accounts were numerous reports of individuals who had apparently died soon after being "hexed" by a priest or shaman. For example, in 1906, Major Arthur G. Leonard, a British soldier in the colonial administration in southeastern Nigeria, described what he had witnessed along the Lower Niger:

> I have seen more than one hardened old Haussa soldier dying steadily and by inches because he believed himself to be bewitched; no nourishment or medicines that were given to him had the slightest effect either to check the mischief or to improve his condition in any way, and nothing was able to divert him from a fate which he considered inevitable.[22]

There are many similar historical anecdotes:

In Australia...aborigine sorcerers carry bones extracted from the flesh of giant lizards, and when these slivers are pointed at a person while a death spell is recited, the individual invariably sickens and almost always dies . . . only the nangarri, or medicine man, may save him by initiating a complex ritual. But should the nangarri refuse to cooperate, the victim will almost certainly die.[23]

And a more recent account from 2004:

In East Timor, the main type of magic that purportedly results in sudden death is fekit . . . and the power is wielded by a buang . . . a "witch" or person with supernatural powers who can supposedly kill a person indirectly.... Fekit is usually transmitted by a simple act involving an inanimate object, such as tossing a small pebble or kernel of corn at the victim. The victim is said to die shortly thereafter with a rapidly progressive febrile illness, or suddenly while sleeping.[24]

There have also been many Caribbean reports of deaths brought about by the sticking of needles into "voodoo dolls" made to resemble an intended victim. *Voodoo* refers to a religious belief system that is widespread in some Caribbean countries, as well in as some regions of the southern United States. It is a blend of ritualistic elements of Roman Catholicism with the religion and magic brought to the Americas by enslaved Africans. Voodoo priests are believed to heal or harm by harnessing the power of the unseen world. The term *voodoo death* has since been generalized in popular usage to refer to all putative deaths brought about by curses and hexes.

Physiologist Walter Cannon (1871–1945), the same man who coined the term "fight-or-flight response," reviewed a number of reports of such deaths among indigenous peoples in Africa, Australia, New Zealand, South America, and Haiti. Despite his uncertainty about the reliability of the accounts, he concluded that "voodoo death" results from overwhelming emotional stress caused by terror. Consistent with what is now called the Baskerville effect, he argued that fear produced by a voodoo hex leads to over-stimulation of the autonomic nervous system, which then may bring life-threatening consequences. Cannon concluded that this can result in death, sometimes because of a cerebral hemorrhage.[25]

Cannon's speculations about the consequences of overstimulation of the autonomic nervous system were supported by the work of Emilio Mira, an army psychiatrist during the Spanish Civil War who detailed many cases of soldiers suffering from extreme anxiety.[26] For the most part, they were able to return to active duty following treatment, but he described more than 120 cases of what he called "malignant anxiety." These soldiers appeared overwhelmed by anguish and bewilderment to the extent that they could barely respond to questions. Moreover, their pulse rates stayed permanently at or above 120, their respiration was rapid, their urine was concentrated and acidic, and their temperatures rose quickly over the course of several days. Some of these soldiers ultimately died. Few autopsies were possible under wartime conditions, but those that were conducted often revealed that death was due to cerebral hemorrhage. Mira suggested that those who died must have had overly reactive autonomic nervous systems that could not bear the heightened arousal brought on by sudden and powerful emotional shock when they were already physically exhausted because of lack of food and sleep.

Cannon also pointed out that that not all supposed voodoo deaths result from sudden and extreme physiological reactions. Sometimes these deaths come about more gradually, and in this case, he felt that belief was the key factor. He suggested that when an entire community shares the victim's belief about the lethality of the hex, the victim then becomes an outcast and bereft of social support. The resulting social isolation leads to feeling even more vulnerable to the supposed powers of the spirit world, and the victim becomes too terrified to eat or drink. As a result, death finally claims another victim.

Cannon's description fits with many accounts of voodoo hexes that refer to symptoms of depression, such as lethargy, extreme feelings of guilt, decreased appetite and libido, and social withdrawal.[27] Physician Harry Eastwell, who studied voodoo-like practices among the indigenous people of east Australia, similarly attributed voodoo death to an extreme sense of helplessness and despair brought on by belief in the power of the hex.[28] He suggested that this leads to a "given-up" complex, which, combined with starvation and dehydration that increase vulnerability to infectious disease, is then the ultimate cause of death.

Thus, these researchers suggest two routes for voodoo death—the quick and the gradual. The quick occurs because of hyperarousal in the autonomic nervous system, leading to death through heart attack or cerebral hemorrhage. The gradual involves terror-induced depression, starvation, and dehydration.

Are the reports reliable?

It is important to remember that these conjectures about the causes of voodoo death are simply that—conjectures. They are conclusions based primarily on anecdotes. Recall the discussion in earlier chapters of the biases and weaknesses in perception and memory: anecdotes can be highly unreliable. Consider the example of the famous *Indian rope trick*. Accounts of having witnessed it first-hand began circulating a century ago. It was reported that thousands of people had on many different occasions watched a *fakir* throw the end of a rope into the air, where it remained fixed as though it were a pole. A small boy then climbed up the rope and disappeared into nothingness. Angry words were exchanged between the *fakir* and the boy, and then the *fakir*, with a knife held in his teeth, climbed up the rope only to disappear as well. Screams were heard, and after this apparent commotion in the sky, the *fakir* returned down the rope. To the horror of spectators, he then took a large basket and caught the boy's body parts as they fell from the sky. He covered the basket with a cloth, uttered an incantation, and the boy emerged from the basket, apparently unscathed.

No one believed that the boy had actually been cut up into pieces, but the feat of climbing the rope and disappearing into the sky and then reappearing later presented an intriguing mystery. Some investigators suggested that the spectators were victims of their own extreme suggestibility, while others believed that mass hypnosis of the audience was involved.

While the Indian rope trick seems to cry out for a rational explanation, we should heed the advice given by physician Horatio Prater in 1851 during his investigation of Mesmerism: First, be sure that there is a phenomenon to investigate.[29]

Figure 12-2: Indian Rope Trick.

Psychologist/magician Ray Hyman has repeatedly recommended something similar, with what I like to call the *Hyman Imperative*: "Before seeking an explanation, first be sure that there is something to explain." And as it turns out, in this case there is nothing to explain, for the account of the Indian Rope Trick is a complete fiction.

A century after the accounts began to circulate, Peter Lamont, a noted magician and a researcher at the University of Edinburgh, discovered that the Indian Rope Trick was a hoax perpetrated by the *Chicago Tribune* in 1890 in an attempt to increase the paper's circulation.[30] The newspaper confessed to the hoax some months after it first appeared, but that admission did nothing to stem the popularity of the story as it spread far beyond its Chicago roots. The world was left with many reports of supposed direct observations of something that never occurred. This is an early example of an urban legend.

And so, with respect to voodoo deaths, we should also apply the Hyman Imperative and ask, "Have people *really* died after having been cursed by a voodoo witch doctor?" We must be careful not to confuse anecdote with fact, or "what seems to be" with what really is. Remember, the *only* evidence for voodoo death is anecdotal. In underdeveloped countries, medical histories are often inadequate or nonexistent, and there is usually no formal, legislated process requiring inquiry into such deaths. As a result, information is not available about the exact circumstances surrounding a reported voodoo death or about other possible causes. Instead, these deaths are interpreted through the framework of traditional belief systems that often suggest magical and superstitious causes.

Anthropologists Janice Reid and Nancy Williams go further and argue that there is no such thing as voodoo/hex death and that belief in its occurrence is the result of cross-cultural misunderstanding whereby Western observers have projected a superstitious explanation onto the actions of natives.[31] They accuse many researchers of uncritical acceptance of accounts of hex deaths and of misunderstanding the behaviors and rituals that surround illness in other cultures. For instance, the wailings of relatives when a loved one has been hexed has been interpreted as a sign of their despair brought on by the belief that their loved one is dying and that nothing can be done. On the contrary, according to Reid and Williams, wailing and communal chanting do *not* reflect despair but instead are intended to be comforting and reassuring. In their own research, they found that rather than attributing their illnesses to the power of a hex, sick individuals and their families alike were hesitant to speculate about the cause or the course of the illness, for they had often seen very ill people recover fully.

This perspective is echoed by an investigation of deaths that were supposedly the result of *fekit*, described earlier, which is popular in the culture of East Timor. It was concluded that the majority were likely due to undiagnosed diseases, but some were suspected of having been caused by poisoning![32]

This leaves the picture a confusing one in which claims and speculations about hex deaths are countered by accusations of misunderstanding and cultural insensitivity. Yet, whatever the final judgment will be about the reality of hex deaths, one thing is certain: belief wields a substantial influence over feelings of illness, as we shall see below.

ILLNESS WITHOUT DISEASE

There is an important distinction between *illness* and *disease*. *Feeling* ill is not the same as being sick. Whereas *disease* (sickness) refers to biological dysfunction ("pathophysiology"), *illness* refers to the *experience* of bodily symptoms, which may or may not reflect disease.[33] Illness is influenced by our beliefs about disease, our cultural interpretation of symptoms, our biases and emotional needs, and even by self-delusion. We sense the signs of physical dysfunction in our bodies and we *interpret* those signs, which determines how we respond emotionally. As has been suggested with regard to voodoo death, it is now widely recognized that a patient's beliefs and emotions play an important role both in the perception of being ill and in recovery from illness.

We all recognize that disease can occur without feeling ill (e.g., undetected, early-stage cancer). We can also feel ill without having a disease. We typically assume that physical symptoms reflect underlying physical pathology, and so someone who reports frequent dizziness and fainting spells needs to be examined for neurological compromise, and, similarly, reports of severe chest pain require examination for a possible cardiac condition. And yet there may be nothing physically wrong in such cases. The symptoms might be a manifestation of anxiety, which often can be accompanied by a variety of physical symptoms, including fainting, sweating, weakness in the limbs, chest pains, rapid heart rate and headaches. Because of the distinction between disease and illness, treatments for disease are often inappropriate for illness, and successful treatments for illness sometimes have nothing to do with disease. There are a variety of conditions that mimic physical disorders but are emotionally based. Consider the example of hysteria.

HYSTERIA

There are indeed many people whose "illnesses" reflect only worry and anxiety rather than any physical disorder. Such *somatoform* illnesses typically "make sense" in terms of what is expected and acceptable within the individual's contemporary society. Thus, in the Victorian era, it was considered normal for women to faint at times, either from fear or from an "attack of the vapors." Physicians of the day classified such behavior as "hysteria" in reference to physical symptoms brought about by emotion rather than physical pathology.

The term *hysteria* originated in ancient Greece, deriving from the Greek word for uterus. Greek physicians of those times had only rudimentary knowledge of human physiology. They considered hysteria to be a female disorder resulting from a lack of sexual satisfaction that caused the uterus to move upward until it squeezed the heart, lungs, and liver, producing feelings of suffocation, extreme fear, loss of emotional control, and symptoms of physical distress. Here is Plato's description in *Timaeus*:

> when remaining unfruitful long beyond its proper time, [the womb] gets discontented and angry, and wandering in every direction through the body, closes up the passages of the breath, and, by obstructing respiration, drives them to extremity, causing all variety of disease.[34]

The wandering-uterus theory lost its appeal over time once physicians began dissecting human bodies, but the view that hysteria is a female physical disorder brought on by lack of sexual satisfaction continued even into Victorian times. Medical treatment during that era often involved extensive vaginal massage by a physician or midwife that continued until the patient reached the curative state of "hysterical paroxysm" (i.e., orgasm).[35] Mechanical vibrators were developed to lessen the physician's exhausting masturbatory burden. As anthropologist Wade Davis observed,

> Part of what was going on in Victorian England was related to a phenomenon that Western anthropologists had noted in "primitive" societies but overlooked in their own culture. For just as an individual's sickness may have a psychosomatic basis, it is possible for a society to generate physical ailments and conditions that have meaning only in the minds of its people.[36]

Sigmund Freud brought about a sea change in opinion with regard to hysteria. Although he, too, considered it to be primarily a female disorder, he viewed it as a manifestation of underlying *psychic* conflict. Treatment shifted from massage of the clitoris to massage of the psyche.

Women do not faint from attacks of the vapors anymore, and "hysteria" is no longer a formal psychiatric term, but people still do develop physical symptoms based in emotional difficulties rather than in an actual physical disease, as with the somatoform disorder, in which an emotional problem is "converted" into what seems to be a physical one. Thus, individuals, even though they have nothing physically wrong, may experience apparent paralysis in a limb, or apparent blindness, non-epileptic seizures, sweating, palpitations, fainting, headaches, or nausea. They unhesitatingly believe that the symptoms are due to physical pathology. And yet those suffering from a somatoform disorder are often quite calm and surprisingly philosophical in their acceptance of the paralysis, blindness, or other symptoms.

However, the diagnosis of hysteria in times past or somatoform disorder in times present is based on ruling out a physical basis for symptoms, and that is not always easy to do with confidence. Yet it is tempting to physicians, when medical investigations fail to turn up a physical basis for a patient's complaints, to conclude that the symptoms are hysterical and then make a referral to a psychologist. I personally have had several people referred to me on that basis who actually presented as psychologically normal, and whose symptoms were subsequently determined to have a physical basis after all. And it turns out that most of the "attacks of the vapors" so frequently observed in Victorian times were likely not "hysterical" but instead resulted from severely restricted movement of the diaphragm caused by the very tight corsets that were fashionable. When excited or alarmed or engaged in vigorous physical activity such as dancing, the wearer was unable to take in enough oxygen and then fainted as a result.[37] (Although considered to reflect hysteria by many physicians of the day, some medical specialists attributed the symptoms to a physical cause, and in the mid-1860s warnings appeared in the medical journal *Lancet* pointing, for example, to "the evil effects of the fashionable custom of compressing the female thorax: Tight lacing seriously limits, and almost annihilates, the respiratory movement of the diaphragm."[38]

Yet "hysterical" reactions—somatoform disorders—do occur. A personal example: As a psychological consultant in a large rehabilitation hospital for injured workers, I was asked to provide treatment for Mr. A, a man who had injured his back in a slip-and-fall accident in the factory where he worked. Although physicians could find nothing physically wrong with him, he was confined to a wheelchair, having reported that he had lost all sensation in his legs and could not stand or walk. The combination of a failure to find any physical basis for his complaints and his stoic attitude suggested a somatoform disorder.

He was responsive to psychological intervention and before long was walking the corridors of the hospital, pushing his wheelchair. Everything was progressing well until a weekend visit home. When he returned to the hospital, he was once again in a wheelchair, reportedly unable to walk, and he now passively resisted further psychological intervention.

What had happened? A visit to his home by a social worker revealed that several of Mr. A.'s family members were employed in the same factory, but he was the first to have been promoted to supervisor, filling a vacancy left by the previous supervisor, who had developed serious psychological problems following the workplace death of a man working under his supervision. Mr. A. had been hesitant about the promotion, fearing the responsibility, but was swept up on the wave of excitement expressed by his family, and so he reluctantly took the position. This left him feeling trapped. He experienced considerable anxiety about his responsibilities and yet could not share these feelings with his family. The slip-and-fall accident and the resulting "paralysis" provided an honorable escape from the trap, allowing him to avoid the workplace without having to admit to his family that he was not "up to the job."

While he had appeared to be genuinely pleased at walking again in the safety of the hospital, everything changed after his wife remarked during his weekend visit home that he was doing so well that he would soon be back at work. This was no doubt the trigger for increased anxiety, and he reported that when he awoke the next morning, he had again lost sensation in his legs and was "paralyzed." The "solution" to his emotional conflict was back in full force, even though it appeared that he was unaware that he was not actually paralyzed.

One might ask whether he was malingering, that is, consciously pretending to be paralyzed in order to avoid a return to work. While one can never assess the presence or absence of malingering with certainty, that explanation seemed unlikely in his case. Had he been malingering, it is unlikely that he would have risen out of his wheelchair and demonstrated significant recovery for all to see while at the hospital. In addition, instead of quietly accepting his plight, he probably would have protested loudly and persistently about the failure of medical practitioners to successfully treat his paralysis, and may have complained of extreme pain as well.

Mass hysteria

Hysteria can affect entire groups of people faced with a common source of anxiety. A shared belief in a threat (for example, that a new wind farm nearby may cause physical disorders) leads to stress that influences physical reactions. The anticipation that people will be made ill results sooner or later in some individual experiencing symptoms and attributing them to the situation (e.g., the noise of the windmills, or the electrical fields surrounding them). This reaction intensifies the anxiety for others, some of whom then "succumb" to similar symptoms. The symptoms soon spread throughout the community, adding more and more to collective anxiety and distorting perceptions even further. This is typically referred to as *mass psychogenic illness*, although *collective anxiety attack* is a more appropriate term, for it correctly directs attention to anxiety and away from illness.[39] The symptoms range across an enormous spectrum and can mimic a wide array of organic disorders.

History provides many examples of collective anxiety. During the fifteenth and sixteenth centuries, there were outbreaks of manic behavior in European nunneries in which nuns, believing themselves to be possessed by the devil, ran about barking like dogs, clawed their way up trees as cats do, and then jumped out of the trees in imitation of birds.[40] It is widely reported as well that dancing manias spread like wildfire in fourteenth-century, plague-ravaged Europe. Large numbers of people took to the streets frenetically dancing to nonexistent music, sometimes for days at a time until they were no longer able to stand. The dancing was generally attributed to demonic possession, except in Italy, where it was believed to be caused by the bite of a tarantula. (This is claimed to be the origin of the term *tarantella*, a type of fast-paced Italian folk dance.)

Yet, just as with accounts of voodoo deaths, we must remain cautious when making judgments about such outbreaks of mania based on historical accounts.[41] While many reports were well-documented, some others reflect the erroneous interpretation of the observers of the time. For example, recent translations of first-hand medieval European descriptions of some dancing manias provide a prosaic explanation: The dances were highly structured rather than spontaneous, and they involved members of unfamiliar religious sects who were engaging in strange or foreign ritualized activities that were misinterpreted by locals as evidence of some sort of madness.[42]

There is plenty of modern evidence of collective anxiety attacks, however, and the "contagion" of symptoms can take many forms.[43] In 1983, nine hundred people in the Israeli-occupied West Bank reported a variety of physical symptoms, including headache, stomach upset, discoloration of the limbs, and even blindness. Initially, most of the sufferers were Arab schoolgirls, and Arab leaders quickly assumed that the illnesses were caused by chemical toxins being spread by Israeli agents. The Israeli government, meanwhile, accused the Arabs of deliberately faking the symptoms for political purposes. The epidemic spread, and soon some Israeli soldiers and police fell ill as well. Yet, ten days after the outbreak began, medical investigators concluded that there was no toxin and there was no physical illness. The symptoms were attributed to a collective anxiety attack, and they soon disappeared with medical reassurance that nothing was wrong.

In 2012, a dozen students in a western New York high school began to grunt and shout as they apparently experienced involuntary tics and twitches. Sometimes their limbs or facial muscles would suddenly spasm, but no underlying physical cause could be found for their behavior. As is so often the case in such circumstances, physicians were initially baffled and parents and teachers were worried, suspecting environmental contaminants might be the cause. No such contaminants were found, and the disorder was confined almost completely to young girls. Ultimately, it was recognized that this too was an instance of collective anxiety.[44]

Even more bizarre, in 1984–85 and then again in 1987, epidemics of a strange disorder spread rapidly through the Guangdong region in China. Thousands of men reported that their penises were shrinking, and they believed they were about to die. This particular hysterical disorder is rare, but not so rare that it does not have a name. It is known as *koro*, and it has been part of recorded history for thousands of years. The 2,300-year-old Chinese tome *The Yellow Emperor's Classic of Internal Medicine* refers to it as *suo-yang*.[45] The more modern term is genital retraction syndrome, and it can afflict women as well, who report suffering from perceived retraction of genitalia and breasts. It has occurred in many different parts of the world but most often in Southeast Asia and parts of Africa. Of course, it is the *perception* of shrinkage, rather than any actual physical manifestation, that is involved.

THE WORRIED WELL

Radiologist Peter Hicken has described to me his recurring exchange with a pathologist colleague whenever they encountered one another in a hospital corridor:

Dr. Hicken: "How are you doing, Moe?"

Pathologist: "Fine, I think. But you never quite know whether anything's growing inside you."

How true. We never quite know whether anything is growing inside us. Fortunately, most of us do not give it a thought so long as we have no symptoms. However, some people worry about their health even in the absence of symptoms, and they misinterpret normal physical reactions as symptomatic of something more serious.[46] The historical gallery of *hypochondriacs* includes famous figures such as Charles Darwin, Adolf Hitler, Marcel Proust, Florence Nightingale, Glenn Gould, and Howard Hughes.

Hypochondria derives from the Greek words *hypo* (under) and *khondros* (breastbone cartilage). The ancient Greeks used it as a label for "melancholy without any real cause," based in the belief that organs below the breastbone, including the gallbladder, liver, and spleen, were the source of melancholy.[47] In the late eighteenth century, Scottish physician William Cullen shifted the meaning of the word to refer to an unfounded belief that one is ill. He described people suffering from hypochondriasis as:

> particularly attentive to the state of their own health, to even the smallest change of feeling in their bodies; and from any unusual feeling, perhaps of the slightest kind, they apprehend great danger, and even death itself. In respect to all these feelings and apprehensions, there is commonly the most obstinate belief and persuasion.[48]

Hypochondriacs suffer from irrational anxiety about their health, sometimes to the point of delusion. An upset stomach may be interpreted as a sign of stomach cancer, or a bad headache as a sign of a brain tumor. When examination and testing by a physician finds nothing, the hypochondriac may conclude that the tests were inadequate. Even when people become intellectually aware that they are hypochondriacs, it is difficult to break out of the pattern of excessive worry and anxiety related to their physical condition.

Media coverage of health risks and disorders promotes inappropriate worry about health. Not only does such coverage raise anxiety about possible medical problems, but information provided through the media is often inaccurate. For example, much of what is communicated by televised medical talk shows under the guise of expert advice has been found either to have no evidence behind it or to be contradicted by the best available evidence.[49]

The resulting anxiety that such media discussions generate leads to super-fluous medical consultations, and this in turn is frustrating to the doctor. In the words of one physician,

> One of my least favorite types of patient is the worried well. Treating them seems to me like a bottomless pit of meaningless medicine, with little progress or reward. They convince themselves they're acutely moribund, and it's our job to prove that they're perfectly healthy. It's a Sisyphean task and it's excruciat-ingly frustrating.[50]

Frustrated physicians ultimately produce frustrated and disappointed patients who are upset that their physicians appear uninterested. Hypochon-driacs, discouraged by the dwindling interest that their physician shows in their complaints, often turn to "doctor-shopping," searching out a new physician who strives to get to the root of the problem, orders a wide range of tests, and then ultimately concludes that there is nothing physically wrong. This prompts a search for yet another physician, and the diagnostic revolving door spins again. The internet further fuels the problem by providing a gold mine of informa-tion to feed anxieties with suggestions of new diseases that might account for apparent symptoms. "Alternative medicine" practitioners (see chapter 14) are unlikely to experience the frustration that physicians do because they do not base their diagnoses on physiological evidence. As result, they are more likely to be viewed as responding with interest and compassion to whatever complaints are brought to them.

Hypochondriasis is often the basis for new, "modern" disorders. Psycholo-gist Loren Pankratz explains that people interpret symptoms of illness in terms that fit with the contemporary beliefs, expectations, and values of their soci-eties.[51] For example, *multiple-sensitivity syndrome* is a modern "disorder" that supposedly involves allergic reactions to a wide variety of chemical products, despite the absence of evidence that chemical products are causing the reaction. It is a modern example of collective anxiety, in this case regarding the prolifera-tion of food additives and manufactured chemical substances.

Another similar modern example is *electromagnetic hypersensitivity*, now often referred to with the awkward moniker of *idiopathic environmental intol-erance attributed to electromagnetic fields (IEI-EMF)*. This "disorder" involves unexplained headaches, dizziness, and skin irritation, which sufferers believe is caused by electromagnetic radiation from cellular telephones, Wi-Fi stations, and computer screens. Once again, there is no demonstrable physical basis for the symptoms, and careful research demonstrates that IEI-EMF sufferers who claim that they can feel the effects of an electromagnetic field are actually unable to tell whether they are in the presence of an electromagnetic signal or not. Acute symptoms are triggered not when actually in an electromagnetic field, but when these individuals are misled into *believing* that they are in an electromagnetic field.[52] While IEI-EMF sufferers interpret their symptoms as severe and even disabling, the actual cause of their distress lies in their beliefs, not in the environment.

THE POWER OF POSITIVE THINKING

Just as there are beliefs to die for, there are also beliefs to live for, beliefs that sustain and energize people in the face of adversity, motivating them to fight on, often to endure and survive. There are countless examples of people surviving overwhelming threats to their lives, motivated only by the almost unreasonable belief that they can indeed survive. Consider one remarkable example: On January 8, 1912, six British explorers, the secondary team accompanying Scott on his fateful Antarctic mission, left their ship with enough supplies to last six weeks. The weather turned, and they were forced to spend the entire winter in a small snow hut virtually bereft of supplies. They had no way of knowing that Scott and his team had already perished, but, although faced with constant privation and almost certain death, they survived and later made their way to an Antarctic port, reaching it only that November.[53] Their remarkable survival was in considerable measure attributable to the belief that they *could* make it, which motivated their efforts despite the overwhelming odds against them.[54]

While our thoughts can trigger sympathetic nervous system arousal that energizes us, so too can they lead to apathy or inertia or depression that saps our energies. Imagine that a boat has overturned a mile from shore, and as the boater begins to swim he tells himself that he is not going to be able to make it to shore, that he is going to die. Such thoughts are self-defeating, and a person who thinks in this way is less likely to muster the energy to swim the distance. On the other hand, if he were to believe that he could make it to shore as long as he keeps swimming, his chances of survival would be much greater.

Few of us will end up having to swim for shore, but a pattern of negative thinking throughout one's life brings its own negative consequences. Longitudinal research, in which people are assessed repeatedly over several years, indicates that pessimists are at greater risk of developing poor health and even of dying earlier than average.[55] On the other hand, as psychologist Martin Seligman's research[56] has found, people who are optimistic and satisfied with their lives tend both to have better health and to live longer than average. Seligman explains this difference in terms of how beliefs influence actions. Because pessimists have little confidence that their actions will be effective, they are less likely to take preventative health measures or to comply with medical advice. Optimistic individuals, on the other hand, feel more capable of managing difficult circumstances, and this leads to considering novel ways of handling their difficulties.[57]

In other words, optimists have a sense of personal control over their circumstances that pessimists lack. In fact, they typically *overestimate* how much control they actually have over the kind of random, destructive events that pose a risk to us all.[58] For example, they tend to underestimate the risk of being in a serious automobile accident (because they think of themselves as careful drivers), or of developing a crippling disease (because they keep themselves in good physical shape). Psychologists refer to this as an *illusion of control*.[59] Eat properly, exercise well, avoid dangerous pastimes, minimize stress, and one will live a long life. (Recall the *just world* belief, chapter 6.) This sense of personal control, even when illusory, enhances mental health and promotes more effective coping when physical health is threatened.[60] Of course, while modest positive illusions can be helpful, they become maladaptive if excessive.[61]

Once again, we have seen the power of belief, and how what we believe can directly influence our bodies through the autonomic nervous system. When we believe that we are safe, we relax. When we believe that we are in danger, the autonomic nervous system prepares us to fight or run, and such activation can at times be so extreme that it proves fatal. Beliefs about our state of health do not always reflect the actual state of our health but do, to some degree, contribute to it. Our beliefs also influence recovery from disease and injury, as is discussed in the next chapter.

CHAPTER 13

BELIEF AND HEALING

It is far more important to know what person the disease has
than what disease the person has.

—Hippocrates

There are three kinds of healing: natural, technological, and interpersonal.[1]
Natural healing occurs when the body heals itself without intervention. You
cut yourself and the wound heals on its own, or you have a cold and your immune
system destroys the pathogens responsible for it. *Technological healing* involves
external intervention through pharmaceuticals, surgery, or other medical procedures. It has a very long history, from trephination (the attempts of early peoples
to cure illness by cutting holes in the skulls of disturbed individuals to allow
demons to escape) to the many techniques of modern, science-based medicine.

Interpersonal healing leads to improvements in illness (but not in disease,
for remember, feeling ill is not the same as actually being sick) as a result of
the *context* in which the treatment is given. Various aspects of social interaction, including the clinician's professionalism, empathy, reassurance, and demonstrated interest in the patient's well-being, are critical to the context within
which interpersonal healing occurs. The treatment setting itself, whether the
doctor's office, a hospital, the acupuncturist's clinic, or the shaman's quarters,
often plays an important role as well because, through personal experience, it is
the place where healing begins. While both natural and technological healing
occur whether a patient is conscious or not (wounds heal and medications work
even on unconscious patients), interpersonal healing depends upon the patient
being alert and attentive.[2]

Memories of past social interactions in which treatment was received, as
well as beliefs (expectations) about the effectiveness of the treatment, also con-

tribute to the context, as do the therapeutic rituals that are almost universal in dealing with the sick.[3] For example, healers of the Haudenosaunee (Iroquois) *False Face Society* wore wooden masks and employed chants, rattles, and dancing to scare away the evil spirits believed to be causing illness.[4] Quite apart from their practical purposes, modern physicians' white coats, stethoscopes, and routine procedures ("rituals") such as measuring blood pressure or temperature have an influence not dissimilar to the masks and rattles of healers in pre-technological societies. All of these rituals, shamanic or modern, provide assurance that one is in good hands, that the healer has arrived.

Figure 13-1: A mask of the Haudenosaunee (Iroquois) False Face Society (Wikimedia Creative Commons, Wellcome Images, CC CY-SA 4.0 International).

As neuroscientist Fabrizio Benedetti notes, prehistoric shamanism, which relied upon a good relationship between the sick and the shaman, provided the first example of real medical care:

> The sick trusts the shaman and has strong beliefs in his therapeutic capabilities, thus he refers to him for any kind of psychological, spiritual, or physical discomfort. In this way, the shaman became a central figure in any social group and acquired more and more prestige and a higher social status over the centuries and across different cultures.[5]

FEELING BETTER

Feeling better after taking a nostrum or following treatment by a physician or shaman does not necessarily mean that one *is* better. When we are hopeful about the effects of a medicine, most of us are likely to want to believe that our condition has improved, even when it has not. We typically rely on ambiguous signals when we ask ourselves if we are feeling better:[6] "Is my pain now less or greater than it was yesterday?" "Is my nose running less?" "Am I more energetic than I was last week?" "Am I less depressed now than three weeks ago?" But answers to these questions provide only subjective evidence. Without some objective measure, one cannot be sure that there has been actual improvement.

The power of suggestion

Recall Franz Anton Mesmer (1734–1815). He was a Viennese physician at a time when physicians' treatments offered little medical benefit and often caused harm. He qualified as a physician in 1766 after writing a dissertation describing the influence of the planets on human health.[7] He concluded that just as the movements of the planets were controlled by a mysterious force (gravity), so too were human bodies influenced by another mysterious force, *animal gravity*. He described animal gravity as a mysterious "subtle fluid" that moved throughout the body through a system of channels[8] that had been earlier described by physician George Cheyne (1671–1743). Cheyne considered the body to be:

> a Machine of an infinite Number and Variety of different Channels and Pipes, filled with various and different Liquors and Fluids, perpetually running, glideing [*sic*] or returning backward, in a constant circle.[9]

Mesmer believed sickness occurred when there were blockages in these channels and pipes that interfered with the flow of the "subtle fluid." The physician's task was to manipulate this animal gravity, bringing it back to a harmonious state, just as most contemporary "alternative" and "complementary" treatment approaches are based on regulating the flow of "energy" throughout the body.

Mesmer subsequently replaced his concept of animal gravity with *animal magnetism*. He had come to believe that the "subtle fluid" had magnetic properties in light of his apparently successful treatment of twenty-eight-year-old Franziska Österlin through the use of magnets. She suffered from intermittent paralysis, among other complaints. Mesmer described her problems in this way:

> since her childhood, [she] seemed to have a very weak nervous manner, had undergone terrible convulsive attacks since the age of two . . . [and] had an hysterical fever to which was joined periodically, persistent vomiting, inflammation of various visceral organs, retention of urine, excessive toothaches, earaches, melancholic deliriums, . . . blindness, suffocation, and several days of paralysis and other irregularities.[10]

He attempted to treat her by applying various remedies available to physicians at that time, including bleeding, blistering, and various medicinal nostrums, but to no avail. He sought out better treatment methods, and in 1774 met Father Maximillian Hell, a Jesuit priest and the Austrian Astronomer Royal. Father Hell described how he had cured a baroness who suffered from chronic and severe abdominal pain by having her wear a heart-shaped magnet for only four days.

Mesmer was so impressed by this report that he borrowed Father Hell's magnets to treat Franziska Österlin. He attached one magnet to her feet and another to her chest, and she soon reported severe burning pains that began at the site of each magnet and moved throughout her body. To Mesmer's amazement, her symptoms diminished over the course of a night and then finally disappeared. Mesmer pronounced her cured. Occasional relapses were quickly resolved by a repeat of this magnet therapy, and he ultimately advised her always to wear several magnets as a prophylactic.[11]

Following this apparent success, Mesmer considered the manipulation of animal magnetism to be the key to all healing. He also reported that while magnets had a strong physical influence upon people whose harmony has been "disturbed," they had no effect on healthy individuals.[12]

Physicians in Vienna were hostile to Mesmer's views and treatments, and so he moved to Paris, where news of his new treatment spread rapidly. He was soon overwhelmed with people seeking his cure, and in the name of efficiency he began to treat a number of people at the same time. To do so, he designed a *baquet*, a large wooden tub with many protruding metal rods (figure 13-2). The tub was filled with water and iron filings that had been "magnetized" through the supposed application of his own animal magnetism. His clients moved around the outside of the tub, pressing against the metal rods with those parts of their bodies that needed healing.

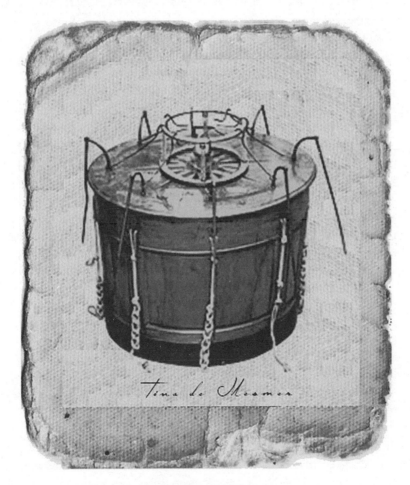

Figure 13-2: Mesmer's baquet.

Musicians provided ethereal background music, which added to the emotional impact of the hocus-pocus.[13] Mesmer, dressed in gold slippers and a lilac silk robe, wandered among his clients, sometimes passing his hands over their bodies to directly deliver his magnetic influence and at other times touching them with an iron wand. While some of his patients remained calm and apparently felt little or nothing during the treatment, others perspired, vomited, laughed hysterically, or experienced violent convulsions.

The treatment met with great acceptance from the general populace, and Mesmer's claims of amazing cures were supported by enthusiastic testimonials, some from prominent individuals. These reports elicited strong skepticism from other members of the medical profession, who persuaded King Louis XVI to set up a Royal Commission. Its members included several important scientists and physicians, as well as Benjamin Franklin, who was at that time the United States Minister Plenipotentiary to France.

Franklin was skeptical at the outset. Just prior to his appointment to the King's Royal Commission, he wrote on March 19, 1784:[14]

> As to the Animal Magnetism, so much talk'd of, I am totally unacquainted with it, and must doubt its Existence till I can see or feel some Effect of it. None of the Cures said to be perform'd by it have fallen under my Observation; and there being so many Disorders which cure themselves and such a Disposition in Mankind to deceive themselves and one another on these Occasions, and living long having given me frequent Opportunities of seeing certain Remedies cry'd up as curing everything, and yet soon after totally laid aside as useless, I cannot but fear that the Expectation of great Advantage from the new method of treating Diseases will prove a Delusion. That Delusion may however in some cases be of use while it lasts. There are in every great rich City a Number of Persons, who are never in health, because they are fond of Medicines, and always taking them, whereby they derange the natural Functions, and hurt their Constitutions. If these People can be persuaded to forbear their Drugs in Expectation of being cured by only the Physician's finger or an Iron Rod pointing at them, they may possibly find good Effects, tho' they mistake the Cause.[15]

The Commission carried out a detailed examination of Mesmer's procedures and claims, and conducted a number of experiments comparing the effects of his treatment with those of "sham" procedures. For example, in one case women wearing blindfolds were asked to indicate where the magnetic energy was being applied. Sham mesmerism worked just as well as the "real thing," and so the Commission concluded that there was no such thing as Mesmer's animal magnetism and that any results of this treatment were due to imagination and expectation.[16]

As a result, despite the fact that he seemed to be curing a wide variety of ailments that no one else could successfully treat (and which in later years were considered hysterical, without any underlying physical basis), Mesmer was deemed a charlatan and soon became an object of public ridicule. His methods quickly fell into disrepute, and no one was curing hysterics anymore. The Royal Commission, and Mesmer himself for that matter, had failed to recognize the significance of what in the fullness of time provided the foundation for modern hypnosis. The Commission could not abide his theory, and Mesmer could not see beyond it. As neurologist Douglas Lanska explains,

> In retrospect, it is clear that traditional physicians in the late-eighteenth century had little to offer their patients therapeutically . . . whereas Mesmer could demonstrate cases "cured" by his treatment that had previously failed all conventional approaches. While one might be tempted to dismiss his thera-peutic successes as only applicable to hysterical or imagined illness, some of his patients went on to lead quite functional lives when before they were deemed hopeless invalids, a point that even his detractors acknowledged.[17]

Mesmer's successes foreshadowed the modern-day notion of placebo treatments.

PLACEBOS

As noted in the discussion of interpersonal healing at the beginning of this chapter, the belief that one's illness is being effectively treated can in and of itself have salutary consequences for one's physical and emotional well-being.[18] Even though Mesmer's treatment did not have any direct physical effect, his patients reported significant benefits in terms of overcoming their symptoms. Such improvement, whether following procedures such as Mesmer's or after the administration of a "sugar pill," is generally referred to as a *placebo effect*, although it would be more appropriate to refer to it as a placebo *response*, since the placebo itself does not have any *direct* effect.[19] While often used as a means of pleasing patients who repeatedly demand but do not actually need medication, placebos have also at times been administered to avoid demoralizing patients who suffer from disorders for which there is no effective treatment, although this raises prickly ethical issues.

Placebos have long been employed by physicians, and their use is relatively common at present. A survey of Canadian physicians and psychiatrists published in 2011 reported that one in four have employed placebos in their practice.[20] A similar survey of internists and rheumatologists in the United States in 2007 found that more than half of the respondents had used placebo treatments in the previous year.[21]

The term *placebo* derives from Psalm 114:9 of the Latin Bible: *Placebo Domino in regione vivorum* ("I will please the Lord in the land of the living"). The term was first applied in a medical context in 1785, when it was described as a medicine given more to please than to benefit the patient,[22] but the actual concept dates to ancient times. For example, in *Charmides*, Plato essentially refers to a placebo response when his character replies to a question about a cure for headache:

> So I told him that the thing itself was a certain leaf, but there was a charm to go with the remedy; and if one uttered the charm at the moment of its application, the remedy made one perfectly well; but without the charm there was no efficacy in the leaf.[23]

Prior to the development of scientific medicine, the benefits of most therapies (bleeding, purging, sweating, and a host of nostrums such as "crystallized tears from the eye of a deer that had been bitten by a snake" and "moss that had grown on the skull of someone who had died a violent death") were undoubtedly due to the placebo effect.[24] Yet, no matter how bizarre or how ineffectual the treatments actually were, belief in their power to cure was widespread. Of course, physicians using those remedies also considered them to be potent cures, and their confidence probably added to the apparent efficacy. Indeed, until the development of objective methods to assess treatment outcomes, the success of *most* medical treatments was unknowingly the result of the placebo response.[25]

Although treatments involving bleeding, purging, and the administration of tears from the eye of a deer have been abandoned, contemporary society is no stranger to bizarre and magical treatments. Practitioners of homeopathy, aromatherapy, Qigong, and many other "complementary/alternative" treatments (addressed in the next chapter) unwittingly rely upon placebo responses for any apparent improvement in symptoms.[26]

Nonetheless, the placebo response is likely to play some role in *all* treatment, science-based or otherwise, and the apparent success of at least a few modern treatments is largely because of it. For example, in 2008, an exhaustive analysis of research into the effectiveness of antidepressants found none of the four leading antidepressant medications to be any more effective than placebos in reducing depression.[27] (Not surprisingly, this report elicited considerable controversy among psychiatrists who regularly prescribe antidepressants.)

Of course, one might argue, if patients improve why should we care whether it is because of a placebo response? One concern is that the patients will then attribute their recovery to the medication, reinforcing the belief that they have a *biological* vulnerability, which might leave them more vulnerable to experiencing depression again in the future.[28]

As noted earlier, just because you feel better does not necessarily mean you are better. Reported symptomatic relief does not necessarily reflect actual physical improvement. Because of the placebo response, researchers have learned not to rely solely upon the reports of patients when judging treatment effectiveness. For example, in a study of prostate-cancer sufferers, over half of the men who had received only placebo medication believed that they had experienced significant improvement of their symptoms, including faster urine flow.[29] Unfortunately, there was no improvement in terms of the objective measure of prostate size, which had gradually increased across the course of the study. Similarly, a study of the effects of a placebo on Parkinson's disease concluded that a placebo produced an immediate subjective sensation of improvement without significant objective improvement.[30]

Performance-enhancing drugs

Given that medication provided by a physician can produce placebo responses, researchers wondered whether there might also be a placebo response associated with banned performance-enhancing drugs that some athletes use in the attempt to increase their performance. To examine this question, athletes' performances in a series of 1,000-meter, timed trials were compared before and after the administration of either a placebo or a performance-enhancing drug.[31] Those who received the placebo achieved times almost as fast as those produced by the athletes who had received the actual drug. When another group of athletes was administered the active drug *without knowing that they had received it*, they showed no significant increase in performance. Clearly, expectation was key to a positive outcome. In another study, national-level powerlifters in the United States were given a placebo but were told that it was a fast-acting anabolic steroid.[32] It produced immediate improvements in performances on the bench press, in squats, and in dead lifts. Moreover, its "effects" were still evident a week later. Half of the participants were then informed that they had received only a placebo, and their performance improvements generally quickly disappeared.

Sham surgery

One might be confident that the effects of surgical interventions do not involve a placebo response. Well, at least not if the intervention involves removal of a diseased appendix or a cancerous tumor (although, even then, side effects such as pain and nausea certainly can be influenced by placebos). However, placebo responses *have* been reported in some types of surgery. The results of the first placebo surgery study were reported in the *New England Journal of Medicine* in 1959. Surgeon Leonard Cobb operated on seventeen patients who were suffering from angina pectoris, a painful condition caused by lack of sufficient blood flow to the heart muscle. In those days, the standard surgical treatment for this condition, pioneered by Italian surgeon Davide Fieschi in 1939, involved making tiny incisions in the chest wall and then tying knots in two of the mammary arteries, thereby increasing blood flow to the heart muscle, resulting in a reduction or elimination of pain. Cobb carried out the Fieschi procedure on eight patients, but for the nine others in the study he merely made incisions in the chest wall without tying off any arteries; hence, the term *sham* surgery. For those nine, then, there could be no change in symptoms due to increased blood flow to the heart muscle. Yet, the patients who had received the sham surgery reported the same degree of symptom improvement as did those who had undergone the real surgery. Because of Cobb's work, the Fieschi procedure was soon abandoned.

Arthroscopic surgery on the knee is often highly effective when carried out to repair specific damage to ligaments and cartilage, but its effectiveness in the treatment of arthritis was not clear until a study in 2002 compared its effects with sham surgery.[33] The surgeon carried out the usual procedure on some patients, but for others an incision was made on the knee and then stitched closed. Six months later, the arthritic patients who received the sham surgery were just as satisfied with the relief that they had obtained as the patients who had received the real thing, leading the surgeon to abandon the procedure. A subsequent Finnish study found no differences in outcomes for actual and sham arthroscopic knee surgery for a torn meniscus.[34] And yet another study found no significant benefit from arthroscopic surgery for degenerative knee conditions in middle-aged or older patients with knee pain, whether signs of osteoarthritis were present or not.[35]

Controversy about placebos

Modern medical interest in placebos was greatly stimulated by the first scientific review of placebo effects, published by Henry Beecher in 1955. He analyzed fifteen studies in which inert substances had been administered to more than a thousand patients afflicted by a number of different diseases, and he reported that a third of the patients recovered as a result of the placebo alone.[36] Since that time, many other studies have similarly reported apparent medical recoveries based on placebo treatment.

Beecher's findings engendered considerable controversy about whether he had really demonstrated the effectiveness of placebos. One important issue concerns how he defined "placebo." Some researchers compare the outcomes of patients receiving genuine treatment to those of patients receiving sham treatment and then consider *any* improvement in the sham treatment group to be a placebo response. Yet, even when the placebo treatment appears to have been as effective as the medical treatment, factors other than the placebo may be responsible. Such factors include natural healing, cyclicity, and regression toward the mean.

If natural healing occurs over the course of the study, both placebo and treatment will be given credit for the recovery unless comparisons are made with a group that receives no intervention (either placebo or actual treatment). This would lead to the mistaken conclusion that both placebo and treatment were equally effective, even though neither had any effect and it was natural healing that led to recovery in each case.[37]

Cyclicity refers to the repeated waxing and waning of symptoms. If a treatment or placebo is applied when pain is at its worst, the pain is likely to soon improve spontaneously as part of its cycle, producing a false sense that the treatment or placebo was responsible for the change. My late aunt provides a good example. She suffered from severe arthritis and intermittently wore a copper bracelet that she said provided pain relief. She would put on the bracelet when the pain became severe and then, over the next few days, the pain would lessen. When I asked her why she removed the bracelet at that point, she responded that its effects were so powerful that it might be harmful to wear it all the time. Her belief in its effectiveness was reinforced by putting on the bracelet when the pain was at or near the top of its cycle of severity, and she unknowingly avoided disconfirmation of its effectiveness by removing it when the pain began to subside.

Statistical regression toward the mean can also fool researchers into concluding that changes have occurred, when in fact nothing has changed.[38] Even for conditions that are not cyclical in nature, there is always some random variation in the measure of the severity of symptoms. If researchers begin by choosing patients who present with the most severe symptoms on some measure, the next measurement is likely to be less pronounced simply because of the random variation. This can mistakenly be interpreted as an improvement even when there has been none.[39]

When researchers reanalyzed Beecher's data and took these and other potential contaminating factors into account, they found no evidence of a placebo effect in any of the studies that he had analyzed.[40] Similarly, another systematic review of all published studies reporting placebos to be as effective as genuine treatment was published in the *New England Journal of Medicine* in 2001.[41] Again, after eliminating contaminating factors, no evidence was found to suggest that placebo treatment led to any *objective* clinical improvement. However, significant placebo effects were found for *subjective* measures, including reported pain. A follow-up analysis with additional data produced similar results.[42]

Thus, while placebos do not in and of themselves provide effective treatment of *disease*, they can lead to improvements in subjective *illness*. And, as it turns out, they can have a significant effect on the experience of pain, which of course is also subjective.[43]

Placebos and pain

People typically view pain purely as a physical problem and consider its treatment to be the province of the physician and the pharmacist. Research clearly shows, however, that cognitive and sociocultural factors play a major role in the actual pain experience.[44] Because of this, placebos can produce significant pain decreases in many patients. Indeed, placebo analgesia is the most studied and best understood type of placebo response.

Pain has puzzled and intrigued humans since the dawn of history. Its presence was blamed on gods and demons long before infections, cancers, and other medical causes were discovered. Its absence has also puzzled and intrigued. For example, consider the frequent accounts of soldiers wounded in battle who, despite grievous injuries, have reported that they felt no pain. In some cases, seriously wounded soldiers have continued to fight on, seemingly unaware of their wounds. The Roman philosopher Titus Lucretius Carus (95–55 BCE) drew attention to this phenomenon:

> scythed chariots reeking with indiscriminate slaughter often lop off limbs so instantaneously that that which is fallen down lopped off from the frame is seen to quiver on the ground, while yet the mind and faculty of the man from the suddenness of the mischief cannot feel the pain; and because his mind once for all is wholly given to the business of fighting, with what remains of his body he mingles in the fray and carnage.[45]

Similarly, in his *Practical Observations in Surgery* (1816), military surgeon Alexander C. Hutchison wrote that

> Every officer, seaman, soldier, or marine, who had undergone amputation from gun-shot wounds, and had fallen under my observation and management, have all uniformly acknowledged, that at the time of their being wounded, they were scarcely sensible of the circumstance, till informed of the extent of their misfortune by the inability of moving their limb; although, sometimes, previously aware of having received a smart blow on the injured part.[46]

And during the First World War, another military surgeon reported that

> between half and 70 percent of serious war wounds . . . were attended with comparatively little serious or agonizing pain.[47]

These accounts suggest that these soldiers' pain was somehow being switched off. Attention certainly plays a role. A person who focuses on the pain and ruminates about it is likely to experience more pain than a person whose attention is drawn to other matters. Think about such a simple thing as a paper cut. It stings, but when your attention is drawn to something else, such as a telephone conversation, you are likely to forget all about it. Once the conversation is over, the sting grabs your attention again. Of course, there is a big difference between a paper cut and a battle wound, but both involve pain.

The effort to understand how the pain experience can sometimes be greatly reduced or even completely suppressed led to the finding that the pathways used to carry pain signals to the brain can be partially or even fully blocked in some circumstances. It is as though there are gates that can be closed to prevent pain signals from generating conscious experience.[48] A body of research has elaborated on this gate theory, which has held up well over time.[49]

Given that neural mechanisms can reduce the pain experience or even prevent it from reaching consciousness, it should not be surprising that placebo treatments can have a significant effect on the experience of pain. Yet the placebo response varies greatly from one person to another, from having no effect to complete pain relief. Psychosocial variables such as optimism, general anxiety, coping ability, and hypnotic suggestibility are important factors underlying this variability.[50]

Behaviors associated with pain, such as winces, groans, slow and careful movements, and withdrawal from social interactions, are often reinforced by the attention of others.[51] These behaviors communicate suffering where, without them, a person may appear healthy. Because of the conditioning process, such behaviors often continue even when physical healing has occurred and serve not only to persuade others but also the individuals themselves that they remain disabled by pain.

Placebos and learning

The placebo response is a *learned* response; it is shaped by experience.[52] In other words, we are likely to experience a placebo response if we have learned an association between symptom improvement and specific environmental cues, including treatment procedures. This learning can involve beliefs (expectancy effects), observation of others (social learning), and conditioning.

Expectancy effects

When you take an aspirin in response to a headache, you expect—believe—that it will alleviate pain. This expectation is based on past experience that associates the tablet with pain relief. Apart from the actual pharmacological benefit, your belief that your headache will go away is likely to lead you to relax a bit more, and this may itself provide significant relief if the headache is tension-based. Even with ailments more serious than a headache, the belief that one has received effective treatment is likely to elicit calming emotional responses (reduction of sympathetic nervous system arousal) and counter distress about one's symptoms. As a result, you may sleep better, eat better, socialize more, experience improved mood, and take on a more positive outlook, all of which can have positive effects on your physical health.[53]

The placebo response can be triggered not only by pills and potions but by the same factors that are important in interpersonal healing discussed at the beginning of this chapter. The words, attitudes, and actions of medical professionals, the treatment setting with its stethoscopes, X-ray machines, syringes, and various procedures,[54] the quality of the doctor-patient relationship[55] (which plays an important role in terms of how confident the patient will be that pain relief will follow treatment[56]), and the cultural context all influence expectations about the efficacy of various treatments. Because of this, it has been suggested that the placebo response might better be referred to as a *context effect*.[57] As physician Harriet Hall explains,

> What's effective is not the placebo, but the meaning of the treatment. We enter into a human relationship with a caring person who offers to help us. We may be given a token of that caring in the form of a prescription. We may have a conditioned response to expect improvement because we have been helped in the past. We get a story, a narrative that explains why we feel sick and what we can do to get better. We get hope, support, human warmth, touch. All these factors might lead to an actual physiological response in which our pulse rate drops, we relax, our stress hormones decrease, and other changes facilitate healing, or at least comfort.[58]

Expectation is so influential that *different* expectations of the same placebo treatment can lead to contrary effects. For example, individuals falsely informed that they had been given a stimulant responded with increased heart rate and blood pressure, while the same placebo, when described as a tranquilizer, resulted in decreased heart rate and blood pressure in other patients.[59] Even the color of a pill can influence the placebo response.[60] In one study, medical students were told that they were to receive a drug that would have either sedative or stimulant effects, but they were not informed of which.[61] Each student was then given either one or two placebo capsules, and the capsules were either pink or blue. About a third of the students reported drug effects, and two capsules produced reports of a stronger effect than just one. The color of the capsule influenced its effects. In the absence of information about whether they were stimulants or depressives, the blue placebo pills were reported to have depressant effects, while the pink placebos were described as having acted as stimulants. Other placebo studies have similarly found that the color of a pill makes a difference. For example, in one study, patients reported falling asleep significantly more quickly and sleeping longer after having taken a blue (placebo) capsule than after an orange one.[62] In other research, red placebos were found to be more effective at relieving pain than either blue, green, or white placebos.[63]

Given that simple expectancy leads to reported medicinal effects following placebo treatment, then it is to be expected that similar effects occur with genuine treatment. Treatments that are known to be useful show a significant *reduction* in effectiveness when expectancy is eliminated by administering the treatment without the patient's knowledge.[64] For example, in a study of post-operative pain following the extraction of a molar, patients who received six to eight milligrams of morphine intravenously *without* their knowledge (medication without expectancy) reported only the same level of pain relief as patients who observed themselves being injected with what they thought to be pain medication but was actually only a placebo (expectancy without medication).[65] That is, the analgesia based on expectancy alone was equal to that of the actual drug stripped of expectancy.

Another study of five commonly used analgesics yielded similar findings. Patients unaware of having received pain medication rated their pain as being much more severe compared to when they knew that they had been given a drug, and a much higher dosage of the medication was needed to reduce their pain to the same level as that produced by an informed administration.[66]

Newer treatments are typically associated with stronger placebo effects because people have higher expectations for something new. Over time, the initial high expectations of the treatment wane, and the placebo response wanes along with it.[67]

Social learning

Our expectations (beliefs) about the effectiveness of a treatment most often come through direct experience, or through reading or watching television. We also can build up strong expectations through social learning, that is, through the observation of other people's reactions. Observing someone responding positively to a placebo increases the expectation that the treatment will be effective, and this socially learned expectancy augments the likelihood that one will experience a placebo response. This was clearly demonstrated in a study in which participants agreed to be subjected to painful stimuli.[68] Before receiving the pain-causing stimulus, participants in one group observed another person (a confederate of the researcher) apparently experiencing an analgesic effect when a green light was illuminated. This simple observation led to a substantial placebo response in those participants when in the presence of the green light.

Conditioning effects

We have seen that neutral stimuli, such as the doctor's office, injections, pill bottles, capsules, white coats, and stethoscopes can serve as conditioned stimuli capable of eliciting responses such as relaxation associated with symptom improvement.[69] Conditioning plays a significant role in symptom-production as well, especially in vaguely defined conditions with symptoms that cannot be medically explained, such as fibromyalgia, chronic fatigue syndrome, and multiple chemical sensitivity. People can be quickly conditioned to experience both physical and psychological symptoms. The conditioning is assumed to act directly on the autonomic and endocrine systems, resulting in conditioned changes in autonomic arousal, muscle tension, and respiration.[70] For example, participants in one study inhaled air containing more than the normal proportion of carbon dioxide for a short time.[71] Carbon dioxide has no taste or smell, but within about two minutes, it produces significant physiological effects including a racing heart, sweating, and feelings of suffocation (all associated with sympathetic nervous system arousal). For some of the participants, a foul-smelling odor was added to the air, while for others, either a neutral or pleasant odor was mixed in. Subsequently, as much as a week later, exposure to the foul-smelling odor alone was still enough to produce an elevated level of those same physiological responses. It is interesting to note that this association formed only for foul-smelling odors and not when neutral or pleasant odors were used.

The same researchers then introduced an interesting twist: Other participants were put through this same experimental procedure, but no odors were involved. While experiencing the symptoms brought on by the carbon dioxide, the participants were simply asked to *imagine* themselves in a stressful situation, such as being stuck in an elevator. Later, eliciting those thoughts was enough on its own to bring on the symptoms. And just as it was only foul-smelling odors that led to conditioning in the earlier study, in this case conditioning occurred only with negative, stressful thoughts and not for neutral or positive thoughts.

This suggests that such conditioned reactions involve the brain's threat-response system. It is also of interest that such conditioning was greatest in people who measured high in terms of "negative emotionality," that is, prone-ness to reacting to negative experiences with anxiety, guilt, depression, or anger. Researchers suggest this may be because such people are more likely to rumi-nate about the effects of their symptoms, which leads to stronger autonomic responses that in turn may amplify the perception of threat.

Recall (chapter 9) the student in my class who developed a migraine to what she thought was a vial of perfume but which in fact was only water. Many migraines are the result of vascular constriction triggered by autonomic nervous system arousal. It is likely that through past associations between fragrance and headache, her migraine resulted from a conditioned reaction to her belief that perfume was being wafted about the room.

Conditioned secretions

Evidence is accumulating that points to the important role of conditioned secre-tion of neurochemicals in placebo pain reduction.[72] Cues that have been associ-ated with pain relief in the past, such as taking medication, or even the soothing words of the therapist or the medical setting itself, can become conditioned stimuli that lead to the release of endorphins ("endogenous morphine," an opioid produced by the body itself). Endorphins dull pain and produce feelings of well-being similar to the "runner's high," the exhilaration that long-distance runners sometimes experience as they come close to overwhelming their bodies' resources.[73] Higher levels of endorphin release have also been found to occur in people who are higher in measures of optimism and resilience. It is also sus-pected that there may be genetic differences in regard to endorphin secretion.[74]

The influence of endorphins in reducing pain by placebo has been dem-onstrated by the administration of Naloxone, a drug that blocks endorphins, following the administration of the placebo. In this case, no placebo response occurs.[75] In one such study, patients who had undergone an extraction of an impacted molar reported decreased pain following administration of a placebo, but this reduction in pain disappeared once these patients were given Nal-oxone.[76] Other research has demonstrated that the classically conditioned release of endocannabinoids (a kind of bodily produced marijuana) also plays a role in placebo analgesia.[77]

It has become apparent there is more than one kind of placebo response and more than one mechanism for eliciting a placebo response. Some placebo responses involve reward mechanisms in the brain, while others operate on anxiety mechanisms.[78] As a demonstration of this, consider a study of placebo effects on headaches associated with being at high altitude.[79] Placebo oxygen (that is, participants falsely believed that they were inhaling pure oxygen through a mask) led to pain relief accompanied by a set of specific physiological changes. While placebo aspirin was also effective in reducing the pain, it was accompanied by a different set of physiological changes.

Placebos and neuroscience

Placebo effects show up in neural activity. Particular neurotransmitter pathways are involved in the experience of pain, and it has been suggested that genetic variations in these pathways can influence the extent to which an individual is likely to respond to a placebo.[80] Brain scanning through functional magnetic resonance imaging (fMRI) has demonstrated that pain relief following placebo administration is associated with a decrease in brain activity in regions of the brain associated with the pain experience.[81] Researchers have also reported that patients suffering from irritable bowel syndrome, a disorder known to involve a strong psychological component, responded to placebo treatment not only with subjective reports of decreased pain, but also with a significant reduction in neural activity in parts of the brain.[82]

The ability to evaluate information and generate expectancies is tied to the prefrontal lobes of the brain, and, as a result, that region of the brain is of special importance for placebo effects. Indeed, the role of the prefrontal region is so central that when this area is damaged, placebo responses no longer occur.[83] Thus, as prefrontal functioning deteriorates in Alzheimer's patients, medications become less effective as well, presumably because of the reduction of the placebo effect that accompanies all medications.[84]

Placebos and hypnosis

Hypnosis has often been used effectively in the management of pain,[85] for example, in reducing pain during childbirth, dental extractions, and even surgery. This is explained in large part by the placebo response.[86] As discussed in an earlier chapter, hypnosis does not involve a special state of consciousness, and the key to hypnotic success is expectation. Believing that hypnosis will effectively reduce pain both reduces anxiety and diminishes the focus on pain that would otherwise be accentuated by fear.[87] The resulting placebo response has been observed in a study in which volunteers suffering from chronic headaches were administered either hypnotic treatment, a placebo treatment, or no treatment. They then recorded their headache activity over a period of eight weeks. While the no-treatment group reported no significant change in headache activity or severity, both the hypnotic and the placebo subjects reported significant and equivalent decreases in pain.[88]

POINTING THE BONE

Recall the reports from Australian aboriginal societies indicating that after a shaman applies a hex by pointing a bone at someone, the individual typically dies within a few days.[89] Whether that actually occurs is disputable, but it brings us to the discussion of the converse of a placebo response, the *nocebo* response (from the Latin *nocebo*, meaning *I shall harm*). Rather than the physical relief brought by a placebo, the inert nocebo elicits negative consequences, such as increased pain. This response involves a mixture of pessimistic expectations and the reinterpretation of symptoms in a negative light, along with possible conditioned internal responses.[90] Expectancy in this case is a stressor,[91] and the individual comes to believe that he or she has suffered negative side effects following what is actually an inert treatment.

Such a nocebo effect was demonstrated in a study in which pain patients were given a non-opioid analgesic for two days in a row.[92] On the third day, all received a placebo instead of the analgesic, but half of them were told that it would reduce their pain and, sure enough, they reported a strong reduction in pain. The rest of the patients were told that the placebo was a *hyper*-algesic agent that would increase pain, and indeed most of those patients reported increased pain. Placebo and nocebo are two sides of the same coin. Expectancy can bring either positive or negative effects to the subjective experience of illness and pain.

THEOLOGICAL PLACEBOS

> *The blind receive their sight, and the lame walk, the lepers are cleansed, and the deaf hear, the dead are raised up and the poor have the gospel preached to them.*
>
> —Matthew 11:5

The power of the placebo response makes it easy to persuade many people to believe that supernatural intervention has cured their ills. Faith healers and the reputations of holy shrines such as Lourdes, Fatima, and St. Joseph's Oratory attest to the persuasive power of such attributions. Psychologist Jonathan Smith notes that:

> The invocation of supernatural cures is a part of Christianity. . . . For millennia Christians have celebrated miraculous cures brought about by saints. Healing shrines, including the famous shrine of Lourdes in France, attract millions every year. In the 19th century, Mary Baker Eddy founded Christian Science, a denomination that stresses that illness is the result of erroneous beliefs and that faith in the healing power of God largely eliminates the need for physicians.[93]

Unfortunately, the power of the placebo also opens wide the doorway to the charlatans and frauds who throughout history have taken advantage of the suffering and the desperate. Investigations into faith-healing carried out by surgeon William Nolen,[94] conjurer James Randi[95] and others bear witness both to the outrageous lengths to which religious charlatans have gone to separate the desperate from their money, and to the ease with which people of faith can be deceived in the name of religion.

We can believe that we have a disease when we have not, and we can believe that we have recovered from a disease when we have not. Inert substances, so long as we believe them to be effective treatments, can lead to significant subjective improvement. Such is the power of belief, and, because of it, claimed remedies can seem effective when they are not, as we shall see next.

CHAPTER 14

FOLK REMEDIES AND ALTERNATIVE MEDICINE

Plus ça change, plus c'est la même chose.
—Jean-Baptiste Alphonse Karr (1808–1890)

T hese are remarkable times. Heart, lung, and kidney transplants are common-place; sophisticated MRI and CT scanners peer through flesh and bone; laser scalpels and microsurgery repair damaged nerves and tissue; artificial hips and knees serve in place of timeworn joints; sight dimmed by cataracts is restored through artificial lenses. Smallpox, once an agent of unrelenting devastation and death, has been banished. Polio is easily prevented by a vaccine. Some cancers are virtually curable. AIDS, not long ago virtually a death sentence, is now controllable as a chronic illness.

And yet, as we have seen, until relatively recently in human history, medicine has been a mixture of folk remedies, magical incantations, and erroneous belief. And although we should perhaps not be surprised at the foolhardiness of people centuries ago, gullibility has not seemed to diminish even as the world moved into the scientific era. Consider how the philosophical commentary of physician Rufus Blakeman, written in 1849, applies widely even today:

> It is a fact, difficult of explanation, that individuals who in all cases exercise a sagacity and caution in their selection of skillful artisans for the structure or repair of their most ordinary mechanisms for domestic use, should make an exception to their customary rule when the vital fabric on which their health and life are dependent, is concerned. In this case, it is most surprising that those should be discarded who possess a scientific knowledge of its structure

and economy; and that confidence should be reposed in pretenders who are not only wanting, to a lamentable degree, in moral and mental endowments, but are totally devoid of a knowledge of the intricate mechanism for which they profess to [offer treatment].[1]

What accounts for belief in folk remedies that either lack evidence of being effective or have been shown to be ineffective?

HEALING THE SICK

Although healers have played a central role in every society throughout the ages, it is only relatively recently that effective treatments have been available for a wide variety of ailments. In ages past, magic and religion commingled to provide a framework for understanding and treating disease. In Ancient Greece in about 800 BCE, around the time that Homer wrote the *Iliad* and the *Odyssey*, disease was viewed as divine retribution for offences against the gods. Gradually, that idea lost favor and more emphasis was put on "rational" explanation. Pre-Socratic philosophers influenced Greek physicians, who came to accept that humans are a part of the natural world and are subject to the same laws. Physicians such as Hippocrates began the systemic observation of medical ailments and tried to use logic in choosing treatment. This led toward the accumulation of evidence-based knowledge and away from supernatural explanations.

Time marches on. Eventually, the Greek empire declined and was supplanted by the Romans, although remnants of Greek rationality persisted for a time. Galen (129–198 CE), a Greek physician living in Rome, promoted Hippocrates's teaching, but with Galen's death several centuries of enlightened Greek ideas about health and illness ended. After the fall of Rome in 476 CE, Greek rationalism and Greek medicine were forgotten, and, as Europe sank into the Dark Ages, superstition reigned once more and the spirits were back with a vengeance. The practice of medicine took on many forms as physicians relied on magical charms, astrology, and various herbal preparations. Meanwhile, the Christian church, like the ancient pre-Hippocratic Greeks, taught that illness was retribution from God and viewed sickness as a punishment of sinners.

Fortunately, Greek ideas about medicine survived in Arabia and Persia. Medicine was of great importance to Islamic leaders, and rational inquiry was encouraged. Galen's logical approach was embraced and his careful (although erroneous) anatomical studies were valued. Greek knowledge was translated into Arabic and became the predominant Islamic approach to healing. And just as Hippocrates had viewed mental illness as rooted in the physical brain, so too did Islamic physicians, who constructed the world's first mental asylum in Baghdad in 792. Medical centers were subsequently built across the Islamic world. By 931, physicians were required to pass examinations of their medical knowledge and skill before being allowed to practice.

Avicenna (965–1040), an outstanding Islamic physician, philosopher, mathematician, and astronomer, summarized all available medical knowledge in his million-word encyclopedia of medicine, *Al-Qanun fi al-Tibb* (*Canon of Medicine*). He recognized the contagious nature of tuberculosis, described meningitis for the first time, identified the soil and water transport of diseases, and stressed a psychological approach to dealing with mental illness. Later, during the Renaissance, when the progressive ideas of the Ancient Greeks began to be rediscovered in Europe, it was Avicenna's *Canon of Medicine* that became the standard medical textbook across Europe. And when modern science eventually took root, with its emphasis on testing theory against data, medicine finally began to make long strides toward understanding and conquering many illnesses.

At the end of the nineteenth century, all Canadian medical training was provided in universities, but while some physicians in the United States were trained in universities the majority obtained their training either through apprenticeships not dissimilar to those in the skilled trades[2] or from private, profit-oriented medical schools where they studied under the physician who owned the school.[3] Many competing medical practices were taught in these private schools, some of which were rooted in pseudoscience and superstition, such as homeopathy, osteopathy, and chiropractic. It has been noted that, at that time,

> Traditionally, clinical medicine was, at best, an art of healing, with minimal scientific foundation. Whatever genuine therapeutic success physicians achieved was likely due to placebo effects or natural healing, rather than benefit produced by the active ingredients of treatment agents.[4]

Out of consternation about the plethora of competing and non-science-based medical programs, the Carnegie Foundation commissioned a non-physician, Abraham Flexner, to examine medical education in detail and to make recommendations for improving it. His report, *Medical Education in the United States and Canada*, was published in 1910, and in it he recommended that medical education follow the German model, which focused both on scientific research and clinical training. This report is considered by many to be the most important event in the history of American and Canadian medical education. It set the course for modern training and led to the establishment of high standards. As a result, 80 percent of the medical schools that were in operation in the United States were closed down. Scientific, evidence-based medicine was put on a solid footing, for the time being, at least.

Unfortunately, an unintended consequence of the Flexner Report was that medical students subsequently received little guidance in terms of empathic interaction, how to comfort the sick and how to understand the patient's perspective. Some physicians even rejected the notion that this should be part of their role.[5] Over time, this turn of events contributed to the appeal of alternative therapies.

Despite the remarkable successes of science-based medicine, our modern era is witnessing a resurgence of magical rituals, potions, and practices that have offered treatment to the afflicted and hope to the despairing since ancient times. This is reflected in what people choose to read. When next in your favorite bookstore, stroll over to the Health section. If the shelf space dedicated to "natural healing," "self-healing," "intuitive healing," and other do-it-yourself-forget-about-medical-science healing methods were any guide, one might wonder why hospitals and medical schools still exist. Wander a little farther to the Occult section, where titles proclaim the wonders of psychic healing and the beneficial health effects offered by the judicious placement of crystals. Now, go around the corner into Religion for books that extol the healing power of prayer. The market for such information is large and growing.

Similarly, alternative practitioners, including homeopaths, naturopaths, acupuncturists, aromatherapists, and many others have attracted a wide following. Their persuasive messages, despite the lack of any reasonable scientific evidence to support them, resonate with many people, and public demand has been so strong that alternative/complementary medicine has tiptoed into some medical-school programs.[6]

These non-science-based, often fantastical, theories and treatments hold attraction to those who fear the possible risks and side effects of modern medicine. They also appeal to the "worried well," people who fear that they have health problems even though physicians can find nothing wrong with them. Others suffer from chronic pain and their physicians have told them that they will just have to live with it. And then there are those who have diseases deemed incurable by modern medicine.

For people who do not understand the difference between magical and science-based remedies, how tempting it is to believe that disease can be cured, microbes destroyed, cancer cells stopped, and pain relieved simply by eating the right nutrients, harnessing one's "inner energy," lining up crystals in the pre-scribed fashion, applying "psychic powers," or soliciting divine intervention.

Those who rely on alternative medicine may believe that they are choosing a risk-free treatment regimen, but they often fail to recognize the potential costs of eschewing lifesaving science-based medicine. Consider this sad example from Alberta in 2016. Collet and David Stephan were convicted of "failing to provide the necessaries of life" to their nineteen-month-old son Ezekiel.[7] Fearing that the boy was suffering from viral meningitis, they nonetheless ignored the advice of a nurse friend who told them that the child needed to be seen by a physi-cian. Instead they went to a naturopath who treated their child with tincture of Echinacea. Not long after, Ezekiel died. They no doubt cared deeply for their child, and they provided what they thought to be appropriate treatment. Their mistaken beliefs and poor judgment cost their child's life and ruined their own.

Just what is *alternative* medicine anyway? (Note that many contemporary practitioners now use the term *complementary* medicine, which sounds less oppositional and projects an image more in league with scientific medicine.) Well, for one thing, the "medicine" part of it is a misnomer. As writer and film-maker Tim Minchin has observed:

> . . . alternative medicine . . . has either not been proved to work or been proved not to work. Do you know what they call alternative medicine that's been proved to work? Medicine.[8]

This is an important point, for if good research were to demonstrate that a particular alternative treatment is effective with regard to some ailment, it would soon become part of mainstream medicine.

Central to most alternative therapies is *vitalism*, the notion that an energy field, a *vital force* (variously known as *élan vital* or *prana*) flows within each individual. Of course, there is no objective evidence that such a force or energy exists, and the whole idea makes no sense in terms of modern biology and physics. Nonetheless, vitalism has a long history in traditional healing practices, and most of the modern "alternative" therapies claim that all disease is the result of some sort of imbalance or disturbance of the vital force.

Before exploring some of the reasons that alternative medicine has such strong appeal in modern times, first consider some of the most popular kinds of alternative treatment.

A POTPOURRI OF ALTERNATIVE TREATMENTS

Traditional Chinese Medicine and Qigong

Traditional Chinese medicine (TCM) grew out of an ancient Chinese philosophical and cosmological belief system that eventually came to be known as Taoism. *Tao* (pronounced "dow") refers neither to a deity nor to nature itself, but literally means "the way of the world." It supposedly keeps the world running through the constant release of its energy.[9] Treatment through TCM includes herbal remedies, acupuncture, dietary advice, and *Qigong*.

Around 600 BCE, the great moral philosopher Lao-Tzu taught that it is the unimpeded flow of *Qi* (pronounced "chee," meaning "vital breath") throughout the body that maintains the essential harmony between the two basic energies of life, *yin* and *yang*, and keeps a person alive.[10] Sickness follows when the flow of Qi, which is distributed through a network of invisible meridians, is disturbed in some way. Lao-Tzu developed *Qigong* (meaning "manipulation of Qi") as an art for both attaining martial fitness (*Tai chi* is its modern form) and as a therapeutic technique to keep Qi flowing properly.

Over time, Qigong came to be associated with paranormal powers and some modern Qigong masters still claim to be able to start fires with their thoughts, to deform the paths of laser beams, and to see through opaque objects such as walls. Others are said to be able to diagnose illness simply by "seeing with their ears," and some even claim they can cure cancer and AIDS and heal broken bones.

Fascination with Qigong can interfere with critical thinking and provide opportunities for charlatans. In 1994, a Qigong master gave a presentation to a large audience at the National Institutes of Health in Bethesda, Maryland. He demonstrated the power of Qigong by asking a volunteer to tightly hold a wooden pencil horizontally between his hands. The master then took a folded dollar bill and cleanly broke the pencil in two with one quick chop of the bill. A few weeks later, conjurer James Randi and I were invited to speak about that performance in the same auditorium. Some of those present indicated that the pencil-breaking demonstration had impressed them with the paranormal power of Qigong, but after having watched a video of the master's presentation, it was obvious to me that he had simply performed one of the first simple magic tricks that I learned as a child—"how to break a pencil with a dollar bill."

In modern times, a revival of popularity of Qigong across China was accompanied by a revival of traditional mystical, spiritual, and moral beliefs. The Chinese government considered this a threat to state control and imposed strict limits on Qigong practice, closed down many Qigong hospitals and clinics, and permitted Qigong, stripped of its mystical and spiritual aspects, to be used only in the context of traditional Chinese medicine.[11] Then, in the mid-1990s, Qigong was proclaimed a pseudoscience and its promoters deemed to be charlatans. Groups that continued to espouse its spiritual mystical values—such as the *Falun gong*—were categorized as "evil cults" and were suppressed.[12] Nonetheless, its popular appeal continued, and so, since 2000, the Chinese Health Qigong Association has been responsible for assuring that the practice of Qigong is restricted to state-approved forms.[13] Of course, there is no such governance of Qigong outside of China, and millions of people around the world now practice it.

In 1988, I traveled to China with five other members of the Committee for the Scientific Investigation of Claims of the Paranormal (since renamed the Committee for Skeptical Inquiry). We had been invited to examine the abilities of several children who had become famous for, so it was claimed, being able to read written notes with their armpits or buttocks. (Seriously!) As part of our visit, we also observed a Qigong master at work. He stood several feet away from the feet of a middle-aged woman who was lying face down on a gurney. We were told that she suffered from severe back pain that had not responded to Western medicine. She could not see the Qigong master, but, as he moved his hands in the air, she began to move and writhe about in dramatic fashion, no small feat for a person with a serious back condition. It seemed at first that her movements followed the movements of his hands, but closer observation showed this not to be the case. Changes in her movements *preceded* changes in his. While the master appeared to sincerely believe that he was the leader in this odd therapeutic dance, he was unwittingly being led. As far as we could tell, both believed that it was the invisible Qi transmitted from the master's hands that caused her to move about.

Acupuncture

Acupuncture has a direct relationship with Qigong and the teachings of traditional Chinese medicine. Based on the reported symptoms, the acupuncturist diagnoses where the flow of Qi has been compromised, and then inserts needles at key points along the meridians to return the flow to normal, thereby restoring health.

Many patients in Western societies swear by the effectiveness of this treatment, especially with regard to chronic pain. Some physicians have themselves undergone acupuncture training and use it in their practice. And yet there is no persuasive evidence that acupuncture really works, and this has led many scientists to argue that it has been afforded an undeserved respectability in Western medicine. For one thing, *sham* acupuncture (treatment that appears to be acupuncture but is not) produces the same benefits as actual acupuncture. It does not matter where one sticks the needles, whether along the prescribed meridians as acupuncturists believe is necessary, or not, and it does not matter whether one sticks them in deeply, as acupuncturists would do, or just twirls them on the surface.

However, the controversy over acupuncture never seems to die away. In 2012, Dr. Andrew Vickers and colleagues at the Memorial Sloan-Kettering Cancer Center carried out a large meta-analysis of all published research involving randomized controlled trials of acupuncture. Nearly 18,000 European chronic-pain patients were included in this analysis. The researchers concluded that:

> Although the data indicate that acupuncture is more than a placebo, the differences between true and sham acupuncture are relatively modest, suggesting that factors in addition to the specific effects of needling are important contributors to therapeutic effects.[14]

This suggests at least modest effects of acupuncture, but Edzard Ernst, professor emeritus of Complementary Medicine at the University of Exeter, disagrees. He originally began his research into acupuncture with a strong belief in its effectiveness but was persuaded by accumulating evidence that it does not work. Regarding the Vickers study, he wrote,

> The differences between the results obtained with real and sham acupuncture are small and not clinically relevant. Crucially, they are probably due to residual bias in these studies. Several investigations have shown that the verbal or non-verbal communication between the patient and the therapist is more

important than the actual needling. If such factors would be accounted for, the effect of acupuncture on chronic pain might disappear completely. . . . Moreover, we should be clear about the fact that, in all of these trials, the therapist knew whether he was administering real or sham acupuncture. Arguably, it is next to impossible to completely keep this information from the patient.[15]

In line with Ernst's finding, another review of all acupuncture research conducted around the world since 2000 also concluded that there was very little evidence to support the claim that acupuncture is effective in reducing pain.[16]

Acupuncture has also been touted as an effective treatment for a host of other maladies, including fibromyalgia, rheumatoid arthritis, chronic asthma, high blood pressure, insomnia, and depression. However, in yet another study of acupuncture efficacy, which examined all acupuncture research published since 1900, it was concluded that:

Taken as a group, reviews of clinical studies published since 1900 on the clinical efficacy of acupuncture do not support the notion that acupuncture is effective for any variety of conditions and cast doubt on efficacy for some specific conditions for which acupuncture has been reported as effective.[17]

And while alternative medicine in general is assumed to be a risk-free alternative to science-based medicine, acupuncture carries some serious risks. Although relatively rare, serious adverse effects (including five fatalities) were found in that review. Infections and collapsed lungs were the most common cause.

Homeopathy

It is hard to imagine anything more clearly pseudoscientific than homeopathy. Nonetheless, it has established itself in the minds of many millions of people as a reliable and appropriate treatment for almost any kind of illness. Many pharmacies in North America and Europe sell homeopathic remedies.

In 2010, the British Medical Association denounced alternative medicine in general as being pseudoscience. Its Junior Doctors Committee was even more outspoken and likened homeopathy to witchcraft,[18] even as Dr. Peter Fisher, the Queen's Physician, continued to advocate the use of homeopathic medications. He advised that:

Doctors should put aside bias based on the alleged implausibility of home-opathy. When integrated with standard care homeopathy is safe, popular with patients, improves clinical outcomes without increasing costs, and reduces the use of potentially hazardous drugs, including antimicrobials.[19]

So, what exactly is homeopathy? It is a "therapeutic method" developed by German physician Samuel Hahnemann in 1796. Like Qigong and acupuncture, it involves a supposed energy, a vital force within the body that, if disrupted, results in disease. Homeopaths believe that, to cure disease, one must restore the vital force to harmonious balance.

Homeopathy involves strange concepts that are clearly incompatible with modern science, not to mention common sense. Consider two of its basic tenets: According to the *Law of Similars* ("like cures like"), a substance that produces particular symptoms in healthy people will, when administered in tiny doses, cure those same symptoms in sick people. If some substance brings on headaches when ingested, then a minute dose of that same substance is said to cure head-aches. The *Law of Infinitesimals* informs us that the lower the dosage of the med-ication, the *greater* its effectiveness. In other words, less is more. Because of this, homeopaths administer infinitesimally small doses of the original substance.

Because of the Law of Infinitesimals, dilution is basic to homeopathy, but it is not simply a matter of mixing the medication with water. One also must *succuss* (shake) the substance as it is being diluted; this supposedly leads to *poten-tization*, which is claimed to transmit some form of information or energy from the original substance to the final diluted remedy.

Here is how the dilution works: First, one chooses either X potency (one in ten) or C potency (one in one hundred). X potency involves taking one part of the original substance and diluting it with nine parts of water. The mixture is shaken vigorously (succussion), and this results in 1X potency. This is only the beginning. One part of this new dilution is now added to nine parts of water and succussed again, resulting in 2X potency. This process is repeated many times. The resultant remedy can be delivered to the patient either as a liquid or through powders or tablets infused with the liquid.

Similarly, C (one in one hundred) potency involves taking one part of the original substance and diluting it with ninety-nine parts of water. Again, the mixture is shaken vigorously and the result is referred to as 1C potency. Then one part of this new dilution is mixed with ninety-nine parts of water and suc-cussed again, many times.

And, as astounding as it may seem, some homeopathic remedies are diluted to 200C. In such a case, the active substance has been diluted in the ratio of one part substance to ninety-nine parts of water and then this is repeated with succussion two hundred times in a row. The resulting probability that there remains even one molecule of the active substance is incredibly small, one over 10^{400} (one followed by four hundred zeroes). Put this in perspective: the total number of atoms *in the entire universe* is estimated to be very much smaller, only about 10^{100}, that is, one followed by a "mere" one hundred zeroes.[20] Clearly, homeopathic remedies have virtually nothing of the original substance left. But homeopaths argue that because of "water memory," the "essence" of the original substance remains and stimulates the body to heal itself.

What about testing? Homeopaths claim to test their remedies, but their method of testing is unconventional, to say the least. They do it through what they refer to as *provings*. Provings do not involve what we might think of as research to establish "proof" of effectiveness. A proving simply involves having one or more healthy people take the undiluted remedy and record whatever symptoms, physical or emotional, that they then experience. Then—think back to the *Law of Similars*—the homeopath infers that when the substance is heavily diluted it will cure those same symptoms.

There are some wondrous examples of recently developed homeopathic treatments. Consider a remedy made from taking a little bit of stone from the Berlin wall, crushing it, and then diluting, succussing, and diluting it repeatedly. (The dilution of the homeopathic preparation that I have in my possession, shown in figure 14-1, is 200C.) What does Berlin Wall treat? Remember the *Law of Similars*. What did the Berlin Wall do at a *macro* level? It *blocked* people. So, at a micro level . . . it *unblocks,* either physically or emotionally.

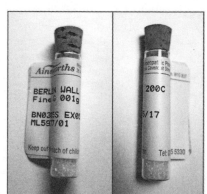

Figure 14-1: Berlin Wall homeopathic preparation (photo by the author).

Consider these excerpts from a "proving" of Berlin wall.[21] (Remember, these are the words of healthy people after consuming a bit of the undiluted powder from the Berlin wall as they supposedly experience symptoms that the corresponding homeopathic remedy will cure):

- Sensation as if there is a wall, an incredible distance between the people I really love and me. I cannot go to the people I really want to be with. It is a big suffering.
- Holding the remedy for a while gives a tremendous rise of grief and sadness, so huge you would drown in it.

Proof indeed! But if the Berlin Wall remedy strains credibility far beyond the breaking point, there are other homeopathic remedies that surpass it in weirdness. Consider *Light of Saturn*. It is produced by exposing powdered milk sugar to the light coming through the eyepiece of a telescope focused on Saturn. *Venus Stella Errans* is produced similarly, using a telescope focused on Venus. In each case, "provings" were carried out to affirm the usefulness of these remedies with regard to whatever they are claiming to cure.

As for infectious diseases, homeopaths apply the same two principles, the Law of Similars and the Law of Infinitesimals. They begin with mucus, feces, or saliva taken from a person infected with a particular disease and go through a long series of dilutions and succussions to produce what they refer to as a *nosode*, which is then added to a sugar pill. There are nosodes for influenza, measles, rubella, hepatitis, meningitis, diphtheria, polio, and other infections. Homeopaths tout nosodes as being as effective, or even more effective, than regular vaccines, and they claim them to be safer, without side effects, and free of any of the chemicals or preservatives that are added in minuscule amounts to some vaccines.

A homeopathic remedy is nothing but a placebo, for it has no active ingredients.

Naturopathy

Naturopathy is also rooted in vitalism and presumes a vital force that guides metabolism, reproduction, growth, and other bodily processes. When its flow is disturbed in some way, disease is the result. Naturopaths use herbal remedies, as well as applying traditional Chinese medicine and homeopathy to restore the flow, with the goal of restoring and maintaining good health. They combine their treatment with dietary and lifestyle counselling. They typically discourage recourse to scientific medicine and generally reject vaccinations.

Chiropractic

The origins of chiropractic, too, are tied up in vitalism. Daniel David Palmer was born in Port Perry, Ontario, in 1885. At age twenty, he moved with his family to the United States, where he became a grocer and a "magnetic healer" with a keen interest in Spiritualism. He came to believe that altered "nerve flow" (a non-detectable energy, essentially the vital force again) was the basis of all disease. And how does nerve flow become altered in the first place? According to Palmer, it is because vertebrae in the spinal column become misaligned:

> A subluxated vertebra . . . is the cause of 95 percent of all diseases. . . . The other five percent is caused by displaced joints other than those of the vertebral column.[22]

Palmer believed that subluxations interfere with the vital energy conveying information from brain to various parts of body. By restoring the spine to its proper form through spinal adjustments, illnesses are cured. By maintaining the spine and proper alignment through regular adjustments, optimal health and wellness follow. And thus, chiropractic was born.

Physician Harriet Hall, a leading critic of alternative medicine, has written,

> Most chiropractors are still telling patients their spine is out of alignment and they are going to fix it. Early chiropractors believed that 100 percent of disease was caused by subluxation. Today most chiropractors still claim that subluxations cause interference with the nervous system, leading to suboptimal health and causing disease.[23]

No scientific evidence has ever been forthcoming to support the existence of the spinal subluxations that chiropractors routinely diagnose. None has ever been observed by orthopedic surgeons, neurosurgeons, or radiologists. And yet, chiropractors, who take their own X-rays, claim to be able to reliably detect them.

Some modern chiropractors do not accept the notion of subluxations and limit themselves only to manual therapy that is consistent with scientific medicine. Yet, as Hall points out, the great majority of chiropractors and chiropractic organizations consider subluxation to be central to their practice.[24] In a survey conducted in the early 2000s involving a random sample of chiropractors from across North America, 90 percent indicated that spinal adjustments should not be limited just to treatment of musculoskeletal conditions, and more than 75 percent considered subluxations to play a significant role in about 60 percent of visceral conditions.[25] A majority believed that chiropractic adjustments lead to improvement in migraine headaches (90 percent), dysmenorrhea (84 percent), middle-ear inflammation (77 percent), and asthma (76 percent), and, in addition, 80 percent considered homeopathy to be an appropriate treatment within chiropractic practice.

Some chiropractors use even more questionable methods, such as comparing the lengths of the patient's legs to determine the position of spinal subluxations, or applied kinesiology, a system based on testing a patient's arm strength to diagnose organ dysfunctions throughout the body. A small number employ other dubious methods, including "live blood-cell analysis," hair analysis, and ear candling.

There are signs that the core belief in subluxation is beginning to be challenged within chiropractic itself. Sam Homola, a retired chiropractor who practiced for forty years, is a knowledgeable critic of his own profession. He is bluntly critical in his assessment of some of chiropractic's basic claims.[26] Similarly, a research study carried out by three chiropractors and a physical education specialist concluded that:

> No supportive evidence is found for the chiropractic subluxation being associated with any disease process or of creating suboptimal health conditions requiring intervention. Regardless of popular appeal this leaves the subluxation construct in the realm of unsupported speculation. This lack of supportive evidence suggests the subluxation construct has no valid clinical applicability.[27]

Based on such evidence, Hall argues that:

> the subluxation construct must go. And without the subluxation, the whole rationale for chiropractic collapses, leaving chiropractors no justifiable place in modern medical care except as competitors of physical therapists in providing treatment of certain musculoskeletal conditions.[28]

Aromatherapy

Although "essential oils" (*non*-oily aromatic liquids taken from various plants, herbs, woods, and spices[29]) have been used to promote emotional and physical well-being since ancient times, the "Father of Aromatherapy" is considered to be a French chemist, René-Maurice Gattefossé, who coined the term *aromathérapie* in the early part of the twentieth century. While working in the development of perfumes in 1910, Gattefossé severely burned his hand during an experiment and reacted by plunging it into the nearest container of liquid, which happened to be a vat of lavender essential oil. He was apparently astonished by how rapidly his hand healed, with little scarring. This led to his focus on research with essential oils. He applied some of his *aromathérapie* treatment to wounded soldiers in the First World War.[30]

Aromatherapy, through its use of essential oils, is claimed to be able to alter cognitive functioning, mood, and physical health. According to the webpage of the Canadian Association of Aromatherapists, "essential oils"

> contain the life force of the plant and have the ability to strengthen our immune system and to stimulate our body's natural healing abilities.[31]

Aromatherapists further claim that their essential oils influence the limbic system through the olfactory nerve, and that the limbic system in turn stimulates immunity to diseases and brings "balance" to the body. It is also claimed that aromas stimulate the secretion of hormones that influence motivation, moods, creativity, stress levels, sex drive, metabolism, temperature, and even insulin production.[32]

Different oils, of course, are said to bring about different effects. For example, it is claimed that basil eases mental fatigue, bergamot opens the heart to life and love, cyprus provides peace, comfort, and strength, juniper promotes well-being and inner strength, and that vetiver, referred to as the "oil of tranquility," promotes stability and security.

Therapeutic Touch

Therapeutic Touch is yet another "energy therapy." It was developed in the early 1970s in New York by nursing instructor Doris Krieger and psychic healer Dora Kunz. Practitioners place their hands near a patient's body (no actual touching is required) in order to detect and manipulate the "energy field." The therapist then transfers energy from her own hands to the patient. This technique has in recent years been taught alongside conventional medicine in a number of nursing schools across North America.

Reiki

This is yet another "energy" therapy. It, too, supposedly involves manipulation of the "universal life energy" to stimulate the integration of mind/body/spirit and enhance the "natural healing mechanism."[33] The therapist employs a sequence of twelve different hand positions to manipulate the energy, with the hands moving close to, but not actually touching, the person's body.

Thought-Field Therapy

This is a North American proprietary treatment (with some details of the therapy not publicly revealed for "commercial reasons") that is similar in some respects to Qigong and acupuncture.[34] Using the meridian system associated with acupuncture, the therapist taps the region of the skin supposedly associated with the individual's psychological and emotional problems. The number of taps is chosen to correspond to psychological symptoms, and energy is supposedly transferred with therapeutic benefit by tapping at the right place and at the right rate.[35]

Cranial-Sacral Stimulation

This is another alternative approach that is said to relieve pain and tension through gentle, barely detectable manipulations of the skull in order to "harmonize with a natural rhythm in the central nervous system."[36] It is claimed that these manipulations influence the circulation of cerebrospinal fluid and as a result bring about powerful therapeutic effects on a number of maladies, even cancer. There is no evidence to support the notion that such manipulations have any influence on cerebrospinal fluid.

This is only a sampling of some of the better known "alternative" approaches to medicine. There is no good evidence that any of them result in anything other than placebo responses at best. The list of alternative therapies continues to grow, and nothing seems too bizarre to attract willing patients, provided that it is packaged well. The use of terms such as "energy," "holistic," and "natural" should be a warning signal to those considering using them.

ALTERNATIVE MEDICINE AND ANTI-VACCINATION

If you truly believed that illness is the result of a disturbance in Qi or some other variation of the *vital force*, then you would never need or want vaccination. What's more, your opposition to vaccination would have been strengthened in 1993 when Andrew Wakefield, a British surgeon and medical researcher, suggested that the measles virus might cause Crohn's disease, a serious inflammatory bowel disorder.[37] Two years later, he published further research, this time claiming that he had firmly linked the combined MMR (measles/mumps/rubella) vaccine to Crohn's.[38] Other researchers failed to find evidence that either the measles virus or the vaccine had any relationship with the disease.

Subsequently, Wakefield was contacted by a woman whose child was suffering both from bowel problems and from autism. He then directed his interest to possible connections between vaccines and autism, and in 1998 published a paper in one of the world's most prestigious medical journals, the *Lancet*, claiming to have established a link between the MMR vaccine and autism.[39] Misleading reports that the MMR vaccine was dangerous spread like wildfire.

The *Lancet* retracted Wakefield's paper in 2010 after determining that it was fraudulent,[40] but the damage had been done, and vaccination rates in many countries dropped significantly, well below the 95 percent level recommended by the World Health Organization for "herd immunity."[41] In 2017, media headlines began to appear, bearing messages like this: "Deadly measles outbreak spreads in Europe as vaccinations fall."[42]

To this day, many people continue to erroneously believe that the MMR vaccine can trigger autism, and so the "anti-vax" movement continues to be popular, putting untold numbers of children at risk from diseases that they otherwise would not contract. While it is true that a small number of children who are vaccinated against diphtheria, measles, mumps, tetanus, whooping cough, and other serious infections do experience adverse effects, those effects are generally minor, and are certainly trivial compared to the major benefits gained from the immunity conferred by these shots against these diseases.

Many alternative practitioners were heartened by Wakefield's supposed "evidence," which they took to support their opposition to vaccination in general. For example, a 2004 study of students of the Canadian College of Naturopathic Medicine found that only a minority, 13 percent, would recommend a full series of vaccinations for children.[43] A 2002 survey of students of the Canadian Memorial Chiropractic College found that, while most of the incoming students had a positive attitude toward vaccination, anti-vaccination attitudes became *more* prevalent as the students progressed through the program.[44] This was almost exclusively due to students relying on informal sources of vaccine information rather than something they were taught in their formal lectures. A large, 2010 Washington State study[45] reported that young children whose primary health care was provided by chiropractors or naturopaths were significantly less likely than other children of similar age to be up to date in terms of vaccinations. A 2011 Canadian study surveyed parents of children receiving their primary healthcare from naturopaths and found that only half of the children had received all the recommended pediatric vaccines.[46]

REASONS FOR BELIEF IN ALTERNATIVE MEDICINE

Given that medical science has made spectacular advances overcoming smallpox, diphtheria, polio, diabetes, childhood leukemia, some forms of cancer in adults, tuberculosis, several venereal diseases, and many others, one might well wonder then why so many people turn away from scientific medicine and rely instead on magical treatments of no proven value.

There is a real problem here with ignorance and wrong-headedness. People living today have not experienced the terrible effects of the diseases that they are now protected against, and so perhaps suffer from a degree of naïveté. Yet, their motives are not wrong. Just as people have always protected their families, they want help for themselves and for loved ones. No one deliberately self-deludes and opts for what they know to be phony treatment. No one wants paramedics to provide Therapeutic Touch at the scene of an accident, and no one goes to a chiropractor to fix a broken leg. Much of the time when modern medicine offers safe and reliable treatments, most people opt for them. People look for alternatives when they misunderstand or fear conventional treatments and when they are led to believe that supernatural/magical/pseudoscientific therapies are not only effective, but safe and free from side-effects. Science-based medicine obviously does not respond to *all* their needs, but it is important to recognize that many of those needs are not medical in nature. The dissatisfaction that some people have with modern medicine stems from a number of factors.

Cold technology versus bedside manner

We all appreciate the importance of a physician's bedside manner. A clinician who seems genuinely interested in our well-being and offers encouragement and reassurance will leave us in quite a different mood than a clinician who is "all business" and lacking in interpersonal skills. Unlike interactions with the family doctor of a half-century ago, a visit to a modern physician is typically a very brief one, and most often terminates either with a prescription for pharmaceuticals, a referral for tests, or a referral to a specialist. In addition, the traditional relationship between physician and patient has always involved a pronounced imbalance of power, which has often resulted in restricted communication, leaving many feeling that they have not obtained all the information that was desired from the doctor.

Alternative practitioners, on the other hand, typically strive to be socially engaging, and they provide a much more positive social interaction and spend more time with you. They appear to understand your problem and to be interested in you and your life. They are generalists who, unlike family physicians, rarely refer you on to someone else. A patient is likely to leave the alternative practitioner's office with a sense that the practitioner has listened, and understood, cares, and knows what to do. Follow-up appointments are usually made to monitor progress.

Note that many of these attributes were those of the traditional family doctor of old. The change in approach began with the unintended consequences of the Flexner Report discussed earlier. While "using its head" in its focus on science, medicine lost its heart to some extent. As some researchers have pointed out:

> Traditionally, clinical medicine was, at best, an art of healing, with minimal scientific foundation. Whatever genuine therapeutic success physicians achieved was likely due to placebo effects or natural healing, rather than benefit produced by the active ingredients of treatment agents.... As the 20th century progressed, concerns were raised that the art of healing, based on intuitive clinical judgment of the physician-patient relationship, was being eclipsed by the science and technology of medicine.[47]

Thus, the change came about, according to medical professor Angus Rae, in reaction to the Flexner approach to medicine that emphasized the importance of science:

> Many now see physicians as more interested in the science of medicine than in patients themselves, one reason why millions seek satisfaction in alternative care.[48]

The proliferation of pharmaceuticals in the 1960s and 1970s, which pushed simpler, older remedies into disuse, also played an important role. For example, as physician James Le Fanu has noted, after anti-inflammatory drugs became available, the skills of rheumatologists "revolved around juggling various toxic regimes of drugs in the hope that the benefits might outweigh the sometimes grievous side effects."[49] All other therapies, such as massage, manipulation, and dietary advice, were discarded, only to be "rediscovered" by alternative practitioners in the 1980s.

Fear of modern medicine

Often, the appeal of alternative medicine is bolstered by the fear that the technological cure may be worse than the disease. Some people fear surgery, chemotherapy, and radiation. Many people have become worried about the long-term effects of medication, and indeed some widely used drugs have turned out to have lethal effects on some people, while other medications have resulted in addiction. Alternative therapies, on the other hand, are always touted as being completely safe, as well as effective.

Steve Jobs, the marketing genius who headed Apple Corporation, developed a rare slow-growing form of pancreatic cancer, but put off for many months the recommended surgical removal of the tumor while he instead relied on alternative treatments, including acupuncture and dietary supplements. Before he died, he explained why he had not immediately undergone the potentially lifesaving surgery: "I didn't want my body to be opened . . . I didn't want to be violated in that way."[50]

Alternative therapies offer hope

Modern medicine is not only very good at curing a wide variety of ailments that invariably used to kill, it is also very good at predicting when it cannot cure.

Being told that there is nothing that medicine can do to cure your fatal illness or to take away your chronic pain is dispiriting, to say the least. Alternative therapists offer hope and do not make predictions about death or perpetual pain and suffering. (Recall from chapter 9 the flood of desperate people who went to the Philippines for "psychic surgery.")

Steve McQueen was one of the best-known actors of the 1960s and 1970s and often played "anti-hero" roles that led him to be known as the "King of Cool." He developed a persistent cough in 1978, and the following year was diagnosed with mesothelioma, a form of lung cancer. The prospect for recovery was poor. Out of desperation, he sought alternative treatment in Mexico, where he was treated with prayer sessions and Laetrile, a concoction made from apricot pits that is banned in the United States and Canada because of its total lack of therapeutic value. At first, McQueen believed that he was recovering from his cancer, but by November 1980, his condition had worsened. At that point, he turned again to conventional medicine and underwent surgery to remove the cancerous tissue from his neck and abdomen. He survived the surgery but died the next day. His diagnosis had been a virtual death sentence, and he had turned to alternative therapies in a last-ditch, but fruitless, attempt to survive.

Authority and trust

We all regularly rely on authorities for important information, but often the boundary is blurred between genuine experts and those who promote pseudoscience. It is often difficult for laypeople to distinguish between them. This difficulty is increased by the usage of the title "doctor" by naturopaths, chiropractors, and others, whose therapies also often qualify for insurance coverage. Terms such as "alternative medicine" and "complementary medicine" add to the confusion because people infer that they are part of medicine. In addition, some practitioner organizations, such as those set up by chiropractors and naturopaths, are well-organized and market their therapies in such a way as to misleadingly suggest that their treatments are supported by good science.

Information overload and confusion

The explosion in medical and health-related information available through the media has increased the ranks of the "worried well," discussed earlier. Media coverage of health risks and disorders leads people to worry inappropriately about their health, and this results in superfluous trips to doctors. This in turn leads to a frustrated and disappointed patient when the physician seems to lose interest. In contrast, alternative practitioners typically respond with interest and compassion.

There are some conditions that physicians can do little about

Some medical problems, such as chronic aches and pains, cannot be eliminated completely. Once again, repeated visits to a physician are likely to be frustrating both for physician and patient, but the encouragement and hope provided by an alternative therapist is rewarding. Some physicians are undoubtedly relieved to have such patients take their woes to others.

Testimonials

Personal testimonies from others, even from anonymous strangers, can give some people confidence with regard to even the wildest of claims. For example, when people report that they have "beaten cancer" by using some alternative remedy or by learning to harness their inner energies, this provides a very powerful temptation for others who are suffering from similar ailments. Consider the so-called Hallelujah Diet, developed by Reverend George Malkmus and based on nutritional advice apparently concocted from the book of Genesis.[51] Reverend Malkmus's mother died from colon cancer, a cancer that he falsely claimed was caused by the biopsy she had undergone. When he later developed colon cancer himself, another pastor suggested that he focus on better nutrition, and the result was the Hallelujah diet, which he says cured him of the cancer, for he is alive and reportedly healthy thirty years later. His website has also provided many other testimonials of remarkable cures due to this diet. However, people were never informed that his colon cancer was self-diagnosed, and that he had never consulted a medical doctor about it but instead relied on chiropractors and nutritionists for diagnosis. Although he offers himself as living proof of a cure, he has not produced reasonable evidence that there was any disease in the first place.

This highlights a major problem with testimonials: when people make claims of having been cured, an accurate initial diagnosis is usually not available, and so we cannot really assess whether there was anything that needed curing. Moreover, follow-up is just as important, for some people who offer compelling testimonies of recovery may only think that they have recovered. This is also a major failing of many televised "faith healings," where we have no way of knowing if the supplicant's diagnosis is accurate, or if there is any actual evidence of recovery after the "healing." When skeptics have sought such evidence, they have found either that there was no objective evidence of disease to begin with, or that there was no objective evidence that the individual had recovered as a result of the "healing."[52]

Consider the tragic testimonial provided by one of my students in her defense of alternative medicine. She announced to the class that her mother had been diagnosed with breast cancer a year earlier but had declined surgery, radiation, and chemotherapy. She had instead treated herself through "self-focused energy therapy" that she had learned somewhere. Although the student admitted that her mother still had a large lump in her breast, they both somehow knew that the tissue was no longer malignant. Sadly, even before the course was over, the student's mother died from the very cancer that she was so certain had been cured, leaving the student overwhelmed with grief and with her belief in the efficacy of alternative therapy shattered.

Alternative therapies seem to work

Many people are satisfied with their alternative practitioners. This should not be surprising when it is illness without disease that the person brings to the practitioner's office. Positive experiences produced by placebo treatments will be attributed to the effectiveness of the alternative therapy.[53] The contextual cues provided by the therapy, including the jargon, the paraphernalia, and the warmth and confidence exuded by the practitioner, provide a fertile field for the placebo response. And don't forget that somatoform illnesses, lacking any physical pathology, respond well to placebo treatment.

In addition, in the case of a genuine ailment, recovery that occurs through natural healing will be attributed to the alternative therapy. Of course, we can make this misinterpretation with regard to conventional treatment, for we have no means on an individual basis to assess the role that natural healing plays in our recovery. I have experienced this first-hand. During that same trip to China that involved the visit with the Qigong master, and after spending a week in a highly polluted Beijing, I developed laryngitis so badly that I could barely speak. I was taken to the outpatient clinic at the main Beijing Hospital, where I was given two medications, each labelled in Chinese and English. The first was an antibiotic, *Erythromycin*, and the second was *Shedan Chuanbeiye*, which the label described as "Snake Bile and Tendril-leaved Fritillary Bulb Solution" (figure 14-2). My interpreter strongly advised the latter, for she always used it when her children suffered from sore throats. I opted for the antibiotic. Within a few days, I had fully recovered, thanks to the antibiotic. Or so I believed.

Figure 14-2: Chinese medicine (photos by the author).

This episode was included as part of the published account of our investigations in China, prompting a physician to write a letter to the editor pointing out that the description of my symptoms indicated that I was suffering from a virus, something that antibiotics do not touch.[54] He concluded that I had spontaneously recovered and would have done so whether I had taken the Erythromycin or the snake-bile preparation, or nothing at all. In other words, he suggested, I had chosen my magic, just as the interpreter would have chosen hers.

I had fallen victim to the *post hoc ergo propter hoc* fallacy ("after the fact, therefore because of the fact"), just as many people do when they take remedies that in reality have no effect. For example, Echinacea, or purple coneflower as it is also known, is a herb considered by some people to be an effective remedy for a number of ailments, including the common cold. It is widely sold in health food stores and in some pharmacies as well. A definitive study conducted in 2005 found that Echinacea has no effect at all on the common cold.[55]

The dice are loaded in favor of belief in alternative therapies

If a patient improves for whatever reason and to whatever degree following treatment, the alternative therapy gets the credit. If there is no improvement or if there is deterioration, the alternative therapy can be excused on various grounds—for example, that it was not started soon enough or that conventional medicine had already "poisoned" the patient. Sadly, a few years ago, a former school chum was diagnosed with cancer. She sought treatment through naturopathy and believed that it was working. As time went by, it became clear the cancer was growing, and so she finally opted for chemotherapy while continuing with the naturopathic treatment. After she succumbed to the cancer, some of her friends defended naturopathy, claiming that she had died because "the chemo poisoned her."

THROWING STONES IN A GLASS HOUSE: PSYCHIATRY, PSYCHOLOGY, AND PSEUDOSCIENCE

Although pseudoscientific "alternative medicine" continues to stand as a beacon to credulous and sometimes desperate people seeking physical recovery or improvement, many pseudoscientific psychiatric and psychological diagnoses and treatments have also been promoted in the name of science over the years by some psychologists and psychiatrists.[56] For example, fifty years ago, "refriger-ator" mothers, described as treating their children in a cold, withdrawn manner, were considered to be the cause of autism. After all, it was noted, they were observed to interact with their child in a distant manner. But the experts did not realize that this was the result, rather than the cause, of the impoverished social interaction. These mothers had become cold as result of the complete lack of positive emotional feedback from their children. Similarly, schizophrenia was attributed at one time to the inadequate and inconsistent child-rearing pro-vided by "schizophrenogenic" mothers. Of course, all of this is now recognized as nonsense.

Recovered memories

The recovered memory craze was discussed in detail in an earlier chapter. Many psychiatrists and clinical psychologists, social workers, and psychotherapists of other stripes, climbed onto the recovered-memories bandwagon in the 1980s as it began to roll across North America, and they applied techniques that they believed could wrestle traumatic memories from patients who presented with a variety of complaints but were unaware of any childhood abuse. These therapists were unknowingly creating false memories and triggering serious emotional responses to those memories, which led to criminal charges against innocent people.

Following on the heels of the recovered memory fad was the multiple personality disorder craze. This disorder had until that time been considered extremely rare, but suddenly it was being diagnosed widely. People who sought help for a variety of problems, some as mundane as a desire to lose weight or stop smoking, were led to believe that they had many personalities living inside them, personalities that had formed as a reaction to childhood sexual abuse, the memories of which had supposedly been repressed. The same dubious memory-recovery techniques were used to "confirm" the presence of these many per-sonalities. Another flavor of this recovered-memory frenzy involved so-called satanic ritual abuse, also discussed earlier. No babies were ever reported missing. No bodies were ever found, and the only so-called "evidence" was produced by the memory-recovery techniques.

Munchausen by proxy

Psychologist Loren Pankratz has addressed the problems associated with diagnoses of Munchausen syndrome by proxy (now also variously referred to as *Factitious disorder by proxy* or *Pediatric condition falsification*).[57] The term refers to a parent's (typically a mother's) fabricated reports of a child's medical symptoms (and sometimes even the actual induction of such symptoms) in order to bring about unnecessary and potentially harmful medical care such as surgery. Why would any parent do this? Supposedly to garner the attention associated with the sick role, but in this case, the attention brought by the child's sickness.

Of course, what is key to this diagnosis is the parent's intent, and that can only ever be inferred. As a result, when a mother's presentation of her child's problems is unusual or problematic, the assumption is too easily made that she is intentionally seeking unnecessary medical intervention, sometimes resulting in criminal charges of child abuse. Pankratz discusses his own professional experience:

> Yet, intentions are often presumed. I am repeatedly amazed when experts who have not interviewed the mother conclude that she is receiving secondary gain by caring for her sick child.[58]

The "diagnosis" brands these mothers with a destructive label from which it is very difficult to ever escape. As a result, even while struggling to manage the medical care of their children, parents become entangled in legal battles and criminal charges. The situation usually could have been resolved clinically without involving the police or courts.

EMDR

While walking through the woods sometime in 1987, psychology graduate student Francine Shapiro was deep in contemplation about difficulties she was experiencing when she was surprised to note that as she moved hers eyes about quickly from side to side, the intrusive and upsetting thoughts disappeared.[59]

Out of this experience, so she informed the therapeutic world, *Eye Movement Desensitization and Reprocessing* (*EMDR*) was born.[60] The technique involves instructing the client to focus on an upsetting memory while moving the eyes rapidly back and forth following the motion of the therapist's waving finger. The client is told to continue to focus on the negative thoughts and memories, all the while moving the eyes, until able to connect positive thoughts to them. It is claimed that this provides the most effective treatment for post-traumatic stress disorder, and it is said to be equally effective for a wide range of psychological disorders, from bedwetting, phobias, eating disorders, and gener-alized anxiety, to paranoid schizophrenia, learning disabilities, substance abuse, and even pathological jealousy.[61]

EMDR is now widely used in the treatment of a variety of psychological conditions, and its use has been endorsed by a number of professional thera-peutic bodies. Thousands of therapists have been trained and licensed by Fran-cine Shapiro and her associates to employ EMDR, and they are reinforced in their beliefs in the efficacy of the approach by the feedback from their clients, who sometimes consider it to have brought on a miracle cure of their problems.

There are two important issues concerning EMDR, one to do with theory and the other with practice. First, the theory behind this therapy does not make sense in terms of everything we know about the brain and about psycholog-ical disorders. Indeed, EMDR meets the criteria for pseudoscience.[62] Secondly, research by impartial scientists indicates that whatever benefits are derived from the therapy, they have nothing to do with eye movements.[63] Instead, they are the result of imaginal exposure; that is, the individual is being gradually desensitized to the troubling thoughts and memories through repeatedly being encouraged to think about them in a relaxed setting.[64] Imaginal exposure has for many years been part of the standard treatment for anxiety disorders. Psychologist Scott Lilienfeld examined the evidence for EMDR and wrote,

> The most reasonable conclusion to be drawn from the extant literature is that EMDR is no more effective than standard treatments that rely on exposure to anxiety-provoking stimuli and is almost certainly effective because it happens to incorporate such exposure.[65]

Seasonal Affective Disorder (SAD)

This refers to the development of depression during the seasons when there is little sunlight. Treatment involves exposure to special ultraviolet lamps. Yet doubt has been raised about whether the disorder actually exists. In 2016, a large study involving a cross-section of more than 34,000 American adults was carried out to examine the relationship between depression and exposure to sunlight.[66] No relationship was found between reported depression and either the seasons or latitude of residence or the amount of sunlight exposure on the day of the interview. Based on their data as well as other reports in the literature that examined the relationship of depression to actual exposure to sunlight, the authors concluded that:

> The idea that depression occurs along with seasonal changes or worsens in winter appears to be a well-entrenched folk theory.[67]

While their research could not definitively rule out the existence of SAD, they conclude that if it does exist it is with a much lower base rate than is claimed at present.

And many more therapies

Psychologist Tomasz Witkowski has documented the many therapeutic techniques employed in treating psychological and psychiatric problems that have been presented as being scientific but whose roots are deeply embedded in pseudoscience.[68] There are more than five hundred varieties of psychotherapy, with new ones being added on a regular basis.[69] However misguided or foolish many of these techniques may be, and despite lacking valid evidence of effectiveness, they continue to be employed in the mistaken belief that they work. This has led psychologist Lilienfeld and his colleagues to warn that many health professionals are "insufficiently cognizant of the manifold reasons why ineffective or even harmful treatments can appear effective to the unaided eye."[70]

Misjudgment, misunderstanding, and pseudoscience have all played prominent roles in the age-old quest to find treatment for what ails us. Our beliefs play a significant role in how we respond to treatment and, whether there is any objective effect or not, the placebo response provides a platform for the positive evaluation of even the most ridiculous of therapies. This history should teach all of us, practitioners and patients alike, to be cautious and to await careful evaluation when new treatments are introduced.

However, the appeal of pseudoscience is strong, and it sometimes leaches into conventional psychological and medical practice, where it dons the mantle of scientific respectability. This makes it an even greater danger than the snake-oil treatments that typify alternative/complementary medicine. Let careful scientific research rather than hyperbole, gushing testimonials, or "ancient wisdom" be the foundation for our beliefs about what is or is not effective treatment.

PART V

BELIEF IN A WORLD BEYOND

The preceding chapters have explored the many vulnerabilities of perception, memory, contemplation, and reality testing. At times, our beliefs fall into error because we cannot tell the difference between what is occurring only inside our heads and what is happening in the world around us. At other times, our experiences are shaped by our beliefs and desires, leading us to experience what we expect or hope to experience rather than what is real.

The chapters in this next section explore beliefs associated with magic, superstition, religion, and the paranormal through examination of how they reflect our constructed representations of reality.

CHAPTER 15

MAGIC AND SUPERSTITION

Any sufficiently advanced technology is indistinguishable from magic.

—Arthur C. Clarke

A young woman is handcuffed before lowering herself into a large canvas postal bag that sits inside an open trunk. The postal bag is closed over her head and tied shut, and then the trunk closed and locked. The conjurer climbs atop the trunk and lifts a curtain to conceal himself. A moment later, the curtain drops to reveal the young woman standing in his place. She quickly unlocks the trunk, opens the postal bag, and—to the astonishment of onlookers—out steps the handcuffed conjurer (see figure 15-1). Spectators have witnessed a magical metamorphosis.

This is the magic of modern times. Doves, rabbits, and playing cards appear out of nowhere. Coins pass through tables. A card buried in the deck rises magically to the top. An audience member is levitated on stage with no visible means of support. People are thrilled by such apparent violations of the laws of nature, even though they do not believe that anything other than clever trickery is involved.

"Real" magic, as opposed to the stage kind, is assumed to involve *super*natural, or "paranormal," influence. In pre-technological societies, belief in "real" magic is expressed through the rituals and the incantations of shamans, witchdoctors, and soothsayers, whereas in more technologically sophisticated societies such belief is focused on the supposed psychic powers of some "gifted" individuals. "Real" magic lies on a continuum with religion, with miraculous events at the religious end being attributed to omnipotent, discarnate deities. (Some anthropologists argue that *all* belief involving supernatural agency, whether deemed to be magical or otherwise, is a form of religion.[1])

Figure 15-1: Houdini's metamorphosis.

Modern-day conjuring has a long history that is commingled in its origins with "real" magic. Its magic wands and incantations date back to ancient rituals of shamans and wizards who believed that they were defying the laws of nature and performing miracles. If the "magicians" of centuries past could supposedly bend nature to their wills, then in the words of Jean Eugène Robert-Houdin (1805–1871), considered to be the father of modern conjuring, the modern-day conjuror is but *an actor playing the part of a magician.*[2]

Conjuring can be traced at least as far back as ancient Egypt, where famous practitioners of the "dark arts" performed amazing feats, such as cutting off and then restoring the head of an animal without having caused it any apparent harm. (This conjuring effect is echoed today in the misogynistic demonstration of "sawing a woman in half.") The skills of Egyptian conjurers made their mark in the biblical book of Exodus. It is recorded that, in a meeting that Moses and Aaron had with the Pharaoh,

> Aaron cast down his rod before Pharaoh and before his servants, and it became a serpent. But Pharaoh also called the wise men and the sorcerers; so the magicians of Egypt, they also did in like manner with their enchantments.[3]

It turns out that one needs neither deity nor devil to turn a rod into a snake. A particular kind of serpent, the Egyptian cobra, becomes motionless and "rod-like" when pressure is applied just below its head. By presenting it with the appearance of a rod and then flinging the "rod" to the ground, it appears to be transformed into a snake that wriggles across the floor.[4] Even some modern-day Christian fundamentalists accept that the Pharaoh's magicians relied on such deception, but they maintain that it was God who turned Aaron's rod into a serpent, one so powerful that it consumed the others:

> Their feeble attempts to mimic the miracle performed by Moses and Aaron was thwarted when God manifested His power by causing the rod of Moses and Aaron to consume all the other rods of the magicians.[5]

Throughout its history, Christianity has wrestled with the distinction between conjuring and dabbling with the devil. In its early days, Christianity itself was considered to be a supernatural cult by the Romans, and it was stigmatized with the label *superstitio.*[6] After gaining ascendancy, however, Christianity in turn deemed the beliefs and practices of pagan groups to be superstitio, and pagan deities were declared to be demons. As for conjurers, known as "jugglers" in those days, they posed a problem since it was believed that only God does miracles and yet they were performing what appeared to be miracles. This led to the suspicion that their marvels might involve the assistance of Satan.[7] As historian of magic Michael Mangan points out:

> From its earliest days, then, Christian orthodoxy has tended to identify "juggling" with evil and with the Devil. The kind of magic which involves invoking spirits, and the kind which involves trickery are both regarded with suspicion: both are the domain of the Father of Lies.[8]

Suspicion of being in league with Satan and practicing the devil's "black arts" posed danger to conjurers throughout the medieval period when witchcraft was part of common belief. With the arrival of the Inquisition, initiated by the Roman Catholic Church in the thirteenth century to combat heresy, the risk increased, and as the Inquisition morphed into the infamous witch-burning epidemic that spread across Europe, accusations of diabolism generally resulted in execution.[9] Fortunately, the historical evidence suggests that few conjurers actually suffered that fate.[10]

THE APPEAL OF CONJURING

Conjuring has survived across the millennia despite the risk of confusion with satanic forces and notwithstanding the rise of modern science and universal education. This suggests that its apparent distortion of reality touches something important in humankind. We know that the rabbit did not materialize out of the air, but we are thrilled when it appears to do so. And yet, the thrill quickly disappears if we are shown how the trick was done.

As Rufus Blakeman wrote in 1849,

> it is a trait of the human mind, to contemplate with interest whatever is presented to it as deviating from ordinary natural events. Hence, whatever is noble or strange, or whatever affects the senses through an obscure mechanism, arouses the passions, and if incapable of being represented by distinct sensations, such exaggerated coloring is presented by the imagination, that the mind becomes excited to a sense of wonder or marvelousness.[11]

It is not simply the apparent distortion of reality that grabs people's attention when watching the conjuror, for no one is similarly astonished by the distortions of reality that are so common in modern filmmaking. We casually dismiss them as "special effects." Conjuring, on the other hand, involves a tension between the disturbing yet exciting suggestion that the laws of nature are really being violated, and the awareness that all is done through deception.[12] As psychologists Ronald Rensink and Gustav Kuhn explain,

> The more convinced the spectator is that the event cannot happen, the more powerful the effect, and the stronger the sense of wonder. Even if the observer does not believe in magic, there is still a split second in which reality is suspended, and wonder exists.[13]

As we shall see, the line that separates magical and rational thinking is sometimes a very thin one, and even the most rational individual can be tempted at times, at least for a moment, by supernatural or paranormal explanations. We are all vulnerable whether we recognize it or not, and those who remain unaware of this are perhaps the most vulnerable of all.

CONJURING AND SKEPTICISM

The account of a spooky image above the chair of my dead grandfather (as discussed in chapter 5) draws more attention and fascination than one about a cow in my kitchen, as surprising as the latter situation might be. Similarly with conjuring. Even when people do not really believe that anything psychic is involved, they are more entranced by something that has an air of transcendental mystery than by something that is "just a trick." Of course, this poses a problem for the ethical conjuror and there is no easy solution, as I found out when a professional conjuror consulted me. He was seeking advice about how to present his mind-reading act in a manner that did not encourage belief in psychic phenomena but at the same time did not take away the fascination and entertainment value associated with supposed psychic powers.

In Professor Michael Mangan's words, the conjuror offers

> ... tantalizing glimpses of wonder which suggest that, perhaps, after all, there are possibilities that lie beyond the everyday realities of "common sense." It is

a double-game which magicians have played through the ages. The conjuror's act is made out of sleights of hand, trick equipment, lies and misdirections. We know that. And yet its effectiveness depends on its ability to make suckers of us nonetheless. At its most effective, it leaves us in two minds and in an imaginative space somewhere in-between wonder and skepticism.[14]

Some performers, either from the conjuror's stage or evangelist's platform, exploit the appetite for wonder and, to their considerable profit, present themselves as gifted psychics who can read minds, communicate with the dead, and heal the sick. This has led notable conjurers such as Harry Houdini and James Randi to devote themselves to exposing those who make such false claims.

SYMPATHETIC MAGIC

To anthropologists, *sympathetic magic* (using "sympathetic" in its sense of "having a special affinity") refers to the belief common in pre-technological societies that unseen forces link everything in nature together, and that objects that are similar to each other or have been in contact maintain a mutual influence on each other. These forces are assumed to obey natural laws, so by coming to understand those laws, one can gain control over nature.

Anthropologist Sir James Frazer (1854–1941) categorized sympathetic magic into two types, *homeopathic* and *contagious*.[15]

Homeopathic magic is based on "like causes like." Similar objects are assumed to share similar properties. What happens to one of the objects will affect the other. The voodoo doll is a good example. It is believed that whatever harm is inflicted on a doll representing a particular human target will be inflicted on the target as well. Stick a pin in the doll and the target feels the pain.

Contagious magic is based in the belief that objects that have been in contact continue to influence one another even after being separated. As a result, magic performed on anything that has been in contact with a person can be used to cast a curse or spell on that person. Because of such belief, kings and emperors in bygone days carefully disposed of their nail clippings and discarded hair to prevent their enemies from employing them to do them harm.

Anthropologist Bronislaw Malinowski described a third kind of magic, *word magic*. Words and sounds, through their "sympathetic" associations with objects and events, are believed to have a direct influence on the world.[16] Word magic is reflected to some degree even in modern times whenever people avoid certain discussions, such as the possibility of failing an exam, having a car accident, or performing poorly in a job interview, because of the uneasy feeling that speaking about the dreaded outcome might somehow serve to bring it about.

MAGICAL THINKING

Magical thinking refers to the attribution of a cause-and-effect relationship between two actions or events in the absence of knowledge or concern about how, or even if, they actually influence each other. The magician or shaman delivers an incantation or performs a ritual action in order to bring about some outcome, such as rain to end the drought, protection of the village from an enemy, or the cure of an illness. If the desired outcome follows, whether by sheer coincidence or for other reasons, the magic is given the credit.

Such magical thinking is not confined to pre-technological peoples, however. Anthropologist Richard Shweder emphasizes that magical thinking does not distinguish among cultures, regardless of how technologically advanced they may be.[17] Blowing on dice "for good luck" before throwing them, or belief that one can put a thought in another's mind via extrasensory perception are common modern examples. However, even more mundane actions such as taking a megadose of vitamin C in the belief that it will head off a cold without any knowledge of how it does so (in fact, vitamin C has been shown to have no effect on the common cold), and using a television remote control with no idea of how pushing a button on the remote turns on the television also fit the definition of magical thinking.

Yet it is hardly satisfying to equate taking a megadose of vitamin C or using a television remote with sticking pins into a voodoo doll. After all, one assumes that somebody somewhere understands how vitamin C and the remote work.

Because of this, psychologists typically restrict the term "magical thinking" to situations where an individual believes that the supposed causal link between two objects or events actually involves some kind of special ("magical") process that goes beyond the natural physical laws governing the world.[18] From this perspective, putting pins in a voodoo doll reflects magical thinking, but taking a megadose of vitamin C or using a television remote does not.

Yet this does not really resolve the problem because it is not always easy to identify when someone actually considers a causal link to be magical. Consider these scenarios:

- Let's begin again with the voodoo doll. A man goes to a voodoo priest and asks for a ritual to be performed over a voodoo doll resembling a specific individual. When that person falls ill, the illness is attributed to the voodoo ritual. When we ask the man for an explanation, we are advised to talk to the voodoo priest, "who knows about such things."
- A man consults a homeopath about an ailment and is provided with a homeopathic remedy with a funny name, *Lycopodium*. He knows nothing about it or how it works, but when the ailment goes away, he attributes the apparent cure to the remedy. When we ask him for an explanation, we are advised to talk to the homeopath, "who knows about such things."
- A woman consults her physician about ongoing pain and is prescribed a medication with a funny name, *cyclobenzaprine*. She knows nothing about it or how it works, but when the pain subsides, she attributes this relief to the remedy. When we ask her for an explanation, we are advised to talk to the physician, "who knows about such things."
- A woman of the Zande people of north-central Africa suffers her first epileptic seizure. Epilepsy is treated in that society by burning and then eating the skull of a red bush monkey.[19] After she takes the treatment, she has no further seizures. She attributes this to the power of the remedy. When we ask her for an explanation, she tells us to talk to the folk doctor, "who knows about such things."

Which of these reflects magical thinking? While the anthropologist might say that they all do, the psychologist would want more information. While we might take for granted that the woman treated by cyclobenzaprine does not believe that anything magical is involved, we cannot tell, based only on the information provided, whether the man who goes to the voodoo priest or the man who takes the homeopathic preparation or the Zande woman who consumes the burnt bush monkey believes that something magical is implicated, or whether they simply see themselves as lacking knowledge about the workings of a natural, normal process that is understood by their respective "experts." That is, we cannot tell simply on the basis of behavior whether magical thinking is involved. It is the belief about the presumed causal link and not the practice itself that is key.

MAGICAL THINKING IN CHILDREN

An appreciation for basic causality takes root early in an infant's life. Touch fire, feel pain, and one learns that the fire "caused" the pain. Feel hungry, eat food, the hunger subsides, and one learns that food made the hunger go away. The newborn's brain comes equipped to seek out such relationships between events, and infants begin to show interest in cause and effect at as early as eight months of age.[20] Generally, such associations provide a good guide to causality because when one event occurs after another, very often the first did indeed cause the second. Bang a drum and hear noise; pull the cat's tail and the cat squeals; hit a ball and the ball moves. These automatic associations make it difficult *not* to perceive causal relationships when events occur together, even if only by happenstance.

Pioneering work into children's appreciation of causality and their tendency toward magical thinking was carried out by Swiss psychologist Jean Piaget, who studied how infants come to interpret cause and effect in situations when two unrelated events occur one after the other. For instance, a baby laughs just before the mobile above her head is moved by a gust of air, and now the baby is likely to laugh again and again while staring at the mobile, as though the laughing had caused the movement. Piaget referred to this as *magico-phenomenalistic causality*, "magico" because there is no appreciation or concern about the link between the presumed cause (laughing) and the observed effect (movement of the mobile), and "phenomenalistic" because the *personal* perception of the coincidental occurrence of the two events leads the infant to react as though they are causally related.[21] The child's *belief* that she is *causing* the event to occur is fundamental.[22]

Piaget concluded that this form of thinking characterizes the thoughts of children between the ages of about two to seven because they have not yet developed the capacity for logical analysis. As result, they are inclined to interpret some of the events happening around them as being caused by their own thoughts—for example, if daddy trips and hurts himself not long after the child was angry at him for not letting her watch more television, she may conclude that her bad thoughts caused his injury. It is only after repeated experience and explicit teaching that the child gradually acquires a more realistic view of causal relationships in the physical world. Yet, logical training or not, the brain by its very nature remains forever vulnerable to magical thinking.

While magical thinking permeates the mental life of young children, it does not simply reflect a confusion between fantasy and reality.[23] Even children as young as three or four years old are generally able to distinguish between reality and nonreality, and they are aware of the magical nature of some of their beliefs. For instance, they know that simply *thinking* about something is not enough to make it happen, but they also believe that *wishing* can make things occur.[24] Before blowing out the birthday candles, they "make a wish" for something and recognize the wish as potentially more effective than simply thinking about the desired outcome.

MAGICAL THINKING IN ADULTS

Magical thinking is common among young children, but there is no sharp division between the way children think magically and the way that adults think at times,[25] and psychological research demonstrates that in certain circumstances children and adults behave alike as though they believe that magic is real.[26] For example, many adults express strong belief that they can feel when someone is staring at them, even if they cannot see the person.[27] (More about this in a later chapter.) Further, the child's distinction between thinking and wishing is not really all that dissimilar from adults who on the one hand know that thinking about something is not enough to make it happen, but on the other hand believe that "scientifically impossible" events can occur through psychic powers or prayer.

Do you sometimes think "magically?" Almost certainly you do, for magical thinking comes automatically at times to everyone and generally is not under conscious control.[28] Although there is considerable variability among people in terms of their susceptibility, even many well-educated adults behave as if they believe in sympathetic magic in some situations.[29] For example, in circumstances involving high stress, such as serious illness, or in situations where there is a lack of control such as in games of chance and important sporting events, we become more vulnerable to magical thinking, presumably in the attempt to restore some sense of control in our lives.[30]

Magical thinking and tempting fate

Imagine that you are nearing graduation from high school and have just applied to a prestigious university for a competitive scholarship. Many people, even while recognizing the irrationality, would try to avoid thinking that they will win the scholarship for fear of "jinxing" themselves. This was demonstrated in a study in which participants were asked to rate the likelihood that a student applying to attend graduate school at Stanford University would be accepted.[31] They were informed that the applicant's mother had sent him a Stanford T-shirt even before he was accepted, and some participants were told that he immediately wore the T-shirt, while others were told that he put it in a drawer while awaiting a decision. The participants were then asked to assess the likelihood that he would receive an offer from the desired program. Those who had been informed that he had worn the T-shirt prior to acceptance rated his chances as being lower than did those in the other group. He was apparently guilty of having tempted fate. Similarly, many people feel uncomfortable in thinking about bad things because of a nagging irrational fear that this might bring about the events, even though logic tells them that there is no link between their thoughts and what the future may bring.

Magical thinking and agency detection

Recall the discussion of teleological reasoning. Children at the age of about one year begin to consider events and situations as having been caused by an agent, by someone or something with a particular goal in mind.[32] A ball does not roll into the room on its own; someone must have tossed it. A loud thump in the next room must have been caused by someone. As the child matures and eventually becomes an adult, encountering an organized pattern leads to the automatic thought that someone must have created the pattern,[33] that it was deliberately designed and is not the result of happenstance. This reflects a spontaneous and naïve notion of the second law of thermodynamics, which states that the amount of disorder, technically known as "entropy," in an isolated system never decreases but will always stay the same or increase. That is, the universe moves inexorably from order to disorder, from distinct patterns to randomness. A whole egg can turn into a broken egg, but a broken egg cannot become whole again. Thus, an organized pattern suggests agency, that it was organized on purpose.

Agency detection is related to what philosopher Daniel Dennett refers to as *intentional stance*: our brains have developed in such a way that we automatically look for intention, for agency, when reacting to the world around us.[34] Present children or adults with geometrical forms moving about on a computer screen, and they will automatically react as though purposeful activity is involved— for example, "the square is chasing the rectangle."[35] This cognitive bias, this tendency to look for agency, underlies the quest to find hidden messages in unusual natural events, and we are puzzled or anxious when we cannot find them. If it appears that no human agent could have produced a significant event, the child may come to suspect that an *invisible* superior being is responsible. This notion that "things happen for a reason," whether in reference to a door flying open or someone dying unexpectedly, is basic to religion.[36]

Hyperactive agency detection

Just as a rabbit dashes to safety when it sees a sudden movement in the tall grass, so too do humans automatically react to cues associated with danger, often even before we can determine whether the danger is real. Information from the senses normally is directed to the sensory cortex for processing, but when danger is detected it takes a shortcut directly to the amygdala, the part of the brain that triggers the fight-or-flight response, and emergency action is initiated (see chapter 12). This shortcut is sometimes referred to as the *amygdala hijack*, an automatic reaction to threat that occurs before we have time to consciously consider the information (see figure 15-2).

This *hyperactive agency detection*, this automatic tendency of our brains to be keenly attuned to signs of danger while attributing agency to apparently threatening events, is vital for survival.[37] Even if there is no actual danger, it is better to be prepared to fight or run if the danger turns out to be real.[38] Yet failure to identify the actual cause of fear and the feeling of being in danger can again lead to the conclusion that the cause is present but cannot be seen, fostering belief in undetectable agencies such as spirits, ghosts, or gods.[39]

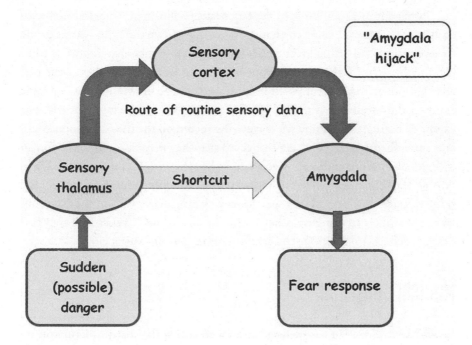

Figure 15-2: Amygdala hijack.

Apparent mental causation

Apparent mental causation—which occurs when an event that you were thinking about subsequently takes place—is an important factor in magical thinking. For example, when people's thoughts occur immediately before a particular event and other plausible causes are absent, they tend to draw the inference that their thoughts caused the action.[40] (This is related to the *illusion of willing* discussed in an earlier chapter.) You may not like to admit thinking in this matter, but while watching a hockey game or football game on television, have you never yelled at a particular player to pass the puck or run with the ball, as though your exhortations would somehow have an effect? People often do this, even while fully aware that the player cannot hear them. Although we know *intellectually* that we can have no effect, at the level of System 1 thinking it is as though our verbal intervention will spur the player on. (And what about watching a video of a game that you missed when it was broadcast live? You probably do not cheer in the same way, given that the game has long been over. It is too late to have any influence.)

Psychologist Emily Pronin suggests that this illusion of magical influence comes about because, being constantly aware of our own thoughts, we are prone to overestimate their connection to the external events that follow them.[41] Again, this reflects the brain's propensity to associate events that occur one after the other. Some clever psychological studies have shown how easily people can be led to assume that their thoughts have power in the external world. For example, participants in one study were instructed on the use of a voodoo doll, and subsequently many of them suspected that they may have put a curse on an individual who pretended to have a headache. They were all the more likely to do so if they had first been led to have negative thoughts about the person.[42] The same researchers observed that spectators watching players shooting basketballs were more likely to think that they had influenced a player's success if they had first generated visualizations consistent with successful scoring.

MAGICAL CONTAGION

Would you be able to throw darts at a dartboard with a baby's picture on it? Although one knows that it is just a picture and that throwing darts at it will have no effect on the baby, research shows that many people would find it difficult to do so.[43] Why the hesitation? Perhaps it is simply because of a sense of propriety; one just does not do such things.[44] Or perhaps, without realizing it, the hesitation is a subtle reflection of sympathetic magic and its law of similarity—what happens to the picture of the baby might affect the baby. Of course, none of us would for a moment consciously consider that this might occur. Now, imagine this: someone gives you a sweater that was once worn by Adolf Hitler. It has been carefully cleaned, and it is a nice sweater, and its style and color would suit you. Will you wear it? Again, research finds that many people would not, almost as though the sweater had been magically contaminated by Hitler's crimes.[45]

Similarly, people are reluctant to wear sweaters that have previously been worn by a convicted killer or by someone who has suffered some misfortune, such as an amputation.[46] Many adults are even unwilling to wear a thoroughly washed sweater that had previously been worn by a homeless person, even though there is no risk of physical contamination.[47] And even when they know that hepatitis or HIV cannot be transmitted merely through bodily contact, people still are averse to wearing clothes or touching objects that belong to people who have those diseases. All this reflects the magical law of contact.[48] It is as though the object's contact with its previous owner has imbued it with some of the undesirable characteristics of that person. This brings to mind a friend's report that, while she was looking to buy a home a few years ago, her real estate agent described a particular house that was for sale as having a "stigma" because it had been the scene of a murder. According to the agent, many people refused to buy the house for that reason. It was as though it were contaminated.

The law of contact also seems to be reflected in research in which adults reacted with considerable reluctance to the prospect of drinking a glass of juice that had been touched by a sterilized cockroach.[49] While they knew rationally that they were safe from contamination, their intuitive reaction was as though contact with the cockroach had somehow affected the juice. In another study, a participant watched as sugar was poured from a commercial package into each of two bottles.[50] The participant then personally attached the label *sugar* to one bottle and the label *cyanide* to the other. Even though participants "knew" that the cyanide-labelled bottle contained only sugar, for they had labelled it themselves, they were nonetheless reluctant to taste the sugar from the "cyanide" bottle. It was as though the label itself affected the contents.

These examples seem to involve thinking based on contagious magic. People react to Hitler's sweater as though it has been altered in some nefarious way by his having worn it. However, recall that to psychologists it is the *belief* about the presumed causal link that is important, the belief that there is something involved that goes beyond the normal limitations of the natural world. In the cases described above, it is unlikely that anyone actually believed that magical contamination had occurred. More likely, they were faced with a conflict between strong negative emotional reactions associated with System 1 thinking and the logic of System 2. Those emotional reactions, whether to the invitation to throw darts at a baby's picture, to wear Hitler's sweater, to drink juice that had been in contact with a sterilized cockroach, or to consume sugar from a bottle labeled "cyanide," were products of their learning histories in which anxiety or disgust developed as conditioned emotional responses. As psychologists Laura Kim and Nancy Kim suggest:

> adults' intuitions seem to globally match the intuitions of young children, perhaps because of deeply engrained, visceral, and automatic reactions to aversive sources such as vomit and blood, or perhaps an intuitive hyper-avoidance strategy adopted in childhood that is never fully overridden by learned, science-based information in adulthood, but rather may be retained throughout.[51]

Yet, that being said, there seems to be something in addition to System 1-System 2 conflict involved; perhaps there is a little magical thinking as well. Take Hitler's sweater, for example. The mention of Hitler or the sight of his belongings may well trigger negative emotions, but, as psychologist Paul Rozin asks:

> why would many individuals become more upset by wearing an innocent-looking sweater that was once worn by Adolf Hitler than by holding a book written about him, with his name and picture on the cover and the story of his life inside?[52]

Napoléon's Candle and King Henry's Sword

In the Musée Napoléon near Cendrieux, France, one can gaze upon the very candle that was burning on Napoléon's bedside table on that night in 1821 when he died in exile on the island of Saint Helena. The candle, so the guide explains, was extinguished at his death and has never been lit since. It is not difficult to experience a sense of awe about that particular stick of wax, as though it somehow provides a connection to the great man himself—perhaps reflecting the law of contact again. But what if we were to be informed that this was not the actual candle but an exact copy? That feeling of awe would disappear.

Or another example. You learn that your elderly English aunt has died and has willed you something quite spectacular: Henry VIII's sword and scabbard. This is surely a valuable piece, and in deference to you aunt's kindness, you decide not to sell it, but to keep it as a treasured memento. How does it feel when you grip it in your hand? Does not the realization that Henry himself once held this very sword give you goose bumps? And yet, why should this piece of metal, despite how finely shaped and tempered it is, bring forth such emotion? Is it because the sword, having been in contact with Henry's hand, somehow draws you closer to Henry? You would surely react quite differently if this same sword had been the possession of only a lowly foot soldier. Sadly, when you subsequently have the sword evaluated for insurance purposes, you discover that it is ersatz, a recent reproduction. It is still the same sword that had earlier thrilled you, but now something has changed. Those exquisite emotions have disappeared. It is as though the magic has gone.

Similar examples are legion. People might pay a fortune for a common teaspoon that once belonged to Galileo, but would pay nothing for an identical spoon lacking such illustrious provenance. Quite apart from the oppressive resale value, Galileo's spoon produces emotion in you. Your father's watch has value to you because it was *your* father's watch; its importance is drawn from the person with whom it had been in contact. And whether it is the "miraculously preserved" organs of saints found in the reliquaries of European churches, or the particular hockey pucks, baseballs, or jerseys from celebrated sports events that are sought after by collectors, it is as though people intuitively attribute invisible properties to these unique objects that seem to link them with important people and events of the past. That piece of wood is more than a piece of wood; it is part of the True Cross. This baseball is not any ordinary baseball; it is the ball that Babe Ruth hit on his first home run. That piece of human bone is no ordinary human bone; it was once part of a saint.

Even little children are subject to such influence. In one study, children between the ages of three and six were shown a "copying machine" that supposedly could make copies of objects.[53] Each child was then presented with either a metal spoon "that once belonged to Queen Elizabeth" or a silver goblet that had no identified ownership. The object was then put into the ostensible "copying machine" and the child was shown both the original and the copy. While the children considered a copy of the silver goblet to be just as valuable as the original, they were not interested in the duplicate of the metal spoon. Why? Because it had not belonged to the Queen.

These reactions occur in just about everyone, but just as a negative emotional reaction to Hitler's sweater likely reflects a conditioned emotional response acquired earlier in life, so too can these positive responses be the result of one's learning history. Whatever emotional reaction is associated with famous people or famous historical events, be it veneration or thrall, is also likely to be triggered to some degree by anything associated with the individual. The feeling elicited by holding King Henry's sword is derived from the emotion one felt when reading about King Henry and his exploits, and the feelings associated with holding your father's watch—be they positive or negative—likely reflect a conditioned emotional reaction that produces feelings similar those experienced when in your father's presence.

Yet, as with Hitler's sweater, it often feels as though there is more involved than simply the elicitation of emotions experienced in the past, as though the magical law of contact has some influence after all.

SUPERSTITION

> *A visitor to Niels Bohr's country cottage, noticing a horseshoe hanging on the wall, teased the eminent physicist about this ancient superstition: "Can it be true that you, of all people, believe it will bring you luck?" "Of course not," replied Bohr, "but I understand it brings you luck whether you believe it or not."*[54]

Are you superstitious? Do you have a "lucky number?" Have you ever "knocked on wood" for good luck? Do you flinch when a black cat crosses your trail? Do you worry about bad luck coming your way if you break a mirror? Even in these modern times, such superstitions, remain strong among adults,[55] to the extent that they are part of the daily routine for many people.[56] A survey carried out in the United States in 2014 reported that about 20 percent of respondents believed that knocking on wood prevents bad luck and that it is unlucky to walk under a ladder. About 14 percent indicated that they believed that opening an umbrella indoors brings bad luck, that Friday the thirteenth is an unlucky day, and that breaking a mirror brings seven years of bad luck.[57] In the United Kingdom, a 2003 survey reported a surprisingly high level of superstitious behavior even among people with a scientific background.[58] Approximately 77 percent of respondents indicated that they were at least a little superstitious, and 42 percent indicated they were somewhat or very superstitious. The survey also found that superstitious belief was associated with a tendency to worry about life, a strong need for control, and a low tolerance for ambiguity. Women reported significantly more superstition than did men. Even among people who are not superstitious, vestiges of cultural superstitions persist in such phrases as *good luck* to encourage someone who is about to sit an examination, or *knock on wood* to express the hope that all will go well in future.

Superstitions are beliefs or practices that are both groundless in themselves and inconsistent with the scientific knowledge in the community to which one belongs.[59] They reflect a particular kind of magical thinking in which a specific object or situation is treated as though it has magical powers. The behaviors associated with superstitions—for example, throwing a pinch of salt over your left shoulder after having accidentally spilled some salt—serve to reduce anxiety by supposedly warding off bad luck. Of course, what we consider to be superstitious is dependent upon our understanding of how the world actually works. It is likely that people who knock on wood for good luck know intellectually that what they are doing is irrational but nonetheless feel somewhat compelled to carry out the ritual.

Whether we consider a behavior to be superstitious depends on how reasonable the belief associated with it appears to be. For example, consider the *Sauce-Béarnaise syndrome*.[60] Psychologist Martin Seligman coined this term with reference to having become violently ill one evening after eating steak covered with béarnaise sauce. For the next ten years, béarnaise sauce was so aversive that he could not even think about it without feeling queasy. He later learned that all his coworkers had suffered from stomach flu at around the same time that he became ill, and even though he then realized that he had probably been sick because of stomach flu, he could not break the link with béarnaise sauce. Note that although he learned this aversion in the same manner that the pigeons learned their superstitious behaviors (chapter 4), no one would think of avoidance of that particular sauce as superstitious. His belief was in error, but it never involved notions of magical causality.

Human beings are not much different from Skinner's "superstitious" pigeons insofar as we too can acquire superstitious behaviors through random reinforcement. This was demonstrated in a Japanese study in which each participant was seated in front of three large levers but given no particular instructions to perform any specific task.[61] Each was told that "if you do something, you may get points on the counter. . . . Try to get as many points as possible." Points were delivered randomly, but just as with Skinner's pigeons, the participants tended to repeat actions that happened to be produced just prior to a point being scored, even though those actions had no effect on the production of points. Three of the participants developed superstitious behaviors such as a series of long pulls after a few shorter pulls, or touching a number of things in the experimental booth. Another study involved children who interacted with a large Bobo doll that dispensed marbles completely independent of the child's behavior.[62] The children were told that when they obtained enough marbles, they would be given a toy. Again, just as with Skinner's pigeons, three-quarters of the children demonstrated distinctive superstitious behaviors, such as repeatedly touching Bobo's face or grimacing at him, as though these behaviors were responsible for producing marbles.

Of course, since the participants in these studies did not know that the rewards were being awarded only at random, it would make sense to try to find a pattern. But the "patterns" that they found did not actually exist. The researcher concluded that we regularly experience circumstances in which we do not know the contingencies between what we do and what happens to us, and a single "reinforcement" may be enough to lead us to repeat an action, as though it had caused the desired event. The behavior may continue despite many instances of no reinforcement.

Superstition does not simply equate with ignorance, nor, as psychologist Stuart Vyse, points out, is it related to low intelligence or to mental or emotional problems, although superstitious people tend to be somewhat more anxious.[63]

Psychologists Jan Beck and Wolfgang Forstmeier describe how our brains have evolved to automatically interpret the world around us in terms of causality and intention, which gives our species superior competitive ability. And because we are often unable to observe cause-and-effect relationships directly, we have to make assumptions about the causal arrow that leads from cause to effect. These assumptions may often be magical, but they provide powerful explanations for phenomena that would otherwise seem inexplicable.[64]

Superstitious athletes

Anyone who watches professional sports has no doubt observed superstitious behaviors by some players. A top hockey player insists on being the last person to leave the ice following the opening warm-up; a football player always touches the grass just before the game begins; a professional golfer always wears his lucky socks for an important game. If the superstitious behavior is not performed, the player is left feeling somewhat less self-assured about his or her ability.

Why so much superstition among athletes? It is because competitive athletic events are the perfect setting for superstitions to develop, for they involve discrete actions and discrete outcomes, and chance plays a large role in the outcomes. The baseball player who wears a particular wristband for the first time and hits a home run is in a position similar to Skinner's pigeon. And keep in mind that intermittent reinforcement leads to the most resistant effects, so a superstitious action does not have to "work" each time. Superstitious behavior is greatest both among members of the *better* teams, and among the *best* players within a team,[65] perhaps because individuals and teams that frequently lose will experience much less reinforcement.

Superstitions such as crossing one's fingers or always wearing a particular piece of clothing during an important game have been found to enhance subsequent performance.[66] This has also been observed in the laboratory. One study found that superstitions involving lucky charms or keeping fingers crossed led to increased feelings of confidence and self-efficacy among participants, which was followed by improved performance.[67]

The most superstitious athletes are also more prone to tension prior to a game than non-superstitious athletes, and their superstitious rituals are most evident when more is at stake, such as when facing a crucial game. Superstition is also more prominent among professional players whose self-identity is most dependent on their success as an athlete and who report feeling that they have little control over what life serves up to them.[68] Superstitious rituals, then, serve the important function of regulating tension, reducing anxiety, and promoting a sense of control, and therefore contribute to better performance in circumstances filled with uncertainty.[69] In addition, superstitions also help distract from thoughts that might increase anxiety.[70] This is why most athletes practice their superstitious rituals prior to a game or during a break and not during the game itself.

Superstitious behaviors also involve little cost or effort. On the other hand, ignoring the superstition because one knows it to be irrational can result in increased anxiety. If an action makes you feel better and little effort or cost is involved, why not carry it out? This is similar to the cost-benefit analysis known as *Pascal's wager*: Blaise Pascal, an outstanding seventeenth-century mathematician and philosopher, reasoned that people actually bet with their own lives on whether or not God exists. He argued that if there is even a small probability that God exists, the costs of not believing will be monumental; whereas, if God does not exist, the costs associated with worshipping him are relatively small by comparison. He advised, therefore, that the rational person should live as though God exists and should make efforts to be viewed positively in God's eyes:

> Let us weigh the gain and the loss in wagering that God is. Let us consider the two possibilities. If you gain, you gain all; if you lose, you lose nothing. Hesitate not, then, to wager that He is.[71]

Of course, one might wonder why an all-seeing God would not see through this gambit.

SHARED SUPERSTITIONS

People who have been taught superstition in childhood, even if they consciously reject the beliefs, may still find themselves feeling anxious when walking under a ladder or confronted by a black cat in their path. This anxiety can be relieved by walking around the ladder and avoiding the cat. Even though they may think their superstitions silly, they may still take such evasive actions to relieve their anxiety. But in doing so, they also inadvertently strengthen the superstition because the avoidance is reinforced by anxiety reduction. On the other hand, if they try to ignore the superstition, they may unconsciously be on the lookout for negative occurrences and interpret any untoward event as a consequence, thereby again reinforcing the belief.

Many superstitions with origins far back in time are culturally shared. As psychologist Stuart Vyse informs us,

> for the detective who wants to predict whether an individual is superstitious or not, the best single piece of information is whether he or she is a member of one of the traditionally superstitious social or occupational subgroups.[72]

For example, superstition about the number thirteen is common in Western society. Some people are so concerned about avoiding anything numbered thirteen that they have been described as suffering from *triskaidekaphobia*, a fancy way of saying that they have a phobia associated with thirteen. Many modern high-rise buildings do not have a thirteenth floor—that is, there is no floor numbered thirteen. Only 10 percent of condominiums in Manhattan that have thirteen or more stories actually label the thirteenth floor as "thirteen."[73] Instead, the floor may be numbered "fourteen" (although superstitious people often see around this and avoid the fourteenth floor because they know that it is really the thirteenth), or in some cases it may be used only as a utility floor.

Similarly, in Chinese culture, the number four is considered unlucky, while the number eight is supposed to be extremely lucky. And then there is *Feng Shui*, an ancient Chinese belief system based on the notion of invisible forces that link humans, architecture, the earth, and the universe. Its dictates require orienting buildings, including homes, in a particular, favorable direction determined by reference to compass points, nearby bodies of water, and so forth. North American real estate agents are aware that potential buyers of Chinese descent may insist on buying houses with particular orientations and avoiding others.

SOME SUPERSTITIONS NEVER DIE

Consider the superstition about bad luck if a black cat crosses your trail. This can be traced back to ancient Egypt, where the goddess *Bast*, daughter of the sun god *Ra*, was the protector goddess and defender of the Pharaoh. Originally considered to have the head of a lion, she became identified over time with the domesticated cat and was worshipped by Egyptians for millennia. Cats were considered to be sacred to Bast, and some believed that she herself sometimes took the form of a black cat. Black cats were citizens' favorite pets, for it was believed that caring for such a cat would win favor with Bast. In fact, black cats were so honored that they were often mummified after they died. Harming a black cat—or any cat for that matter—was an offence punishable by death. As a result, you might well have become anxious when you encountered a black cat in your path while riding in your chariot.

In the religious turmoil of the Middle Ages, black cats were considered to be the otherworldly assistants—or "familiars"—of witches, doing everything at the witch's command.[74] Anyone found with a black cat was accused of being a witch, a condemnation that often resulted in torture and death. A modern derivative of this belief is relatively widespread, even though people do not think of it as a superstition—the notion that one should not leave a baby alone with a cat in the room for fear that the cat will curl up and go to sleep on the baby's face, resulting in suffocation. A moment's reflection shows how nonsensical this is. A baby having trouble breathing because a cat is lying upon it would move and squirm so much that any cat would run away. The precaution traces back to the Middle Ages, when it was "known" that a baby's soul was not yet tightly bound to the body and that the bond between body and soul was also more vulnerable to being severed when one was asleep. Imagine then the risk if a black cat, a witch's *familiar*, were left alone with a sleeping baby. The cat would take the soul of the infant, the parents would be left bereft, and the devil would be the richer.

The fear of a weakly tethered soul shows up in other ways as well. Saying *Gesundheit!* (German for "good health") or *Bless you!* after someone sneezes derives from the superstition that one's soul momentarily leaves the body during a sneeze, leaving it vulnerable to capture by the devil. The blessing was originally meant to ward off such peril.

Consider a related superstition that refused to die, but over time underwent transformation into seemingly rational form: Many hospitals, even into the latter decades of the twentieth century, had a policy of removing plants and flowers from patients' rooms at night. This was done, it was claimed, because although living plants produce oxygen (via photosynthesis) during the day, they consume oxygen at night, and a decrease in oxygen in a patient's room could be detrimental. Of course, after a moment's thought, the absurdity of this is obvious. After all, a living plant consumes only a miniscule amount of oxygen at night, and since when are hospital rooms hermetically sealed? The practice once again traces back to the medieval belief that the bond between body and soul is weakened during sleep and becomes even more tenuous during illness. A sleeping sick person, then, would be particularly vulnerable to efforts to wrest away the soul. This is where the plants come in. Satan's little minions (not cats this time) were believed to hide themselves in the foliage of plants, and the practice of removing plants at night was to remove those minions from the room. The practice continued over the centuries, while the explanation for it evolved from worry about devilry and witchcraft to something that seemed to make more sense, concern about depleted oxygen levels.

As logical and rational as we like to think ourselves to be, we are born magical thinkers and, to a degree, magical thinkers we remain. Vestiges of sympathetic magic manifest themselves from time to time in our emotional reactions and behaviors, even though we often do not recognize the connection. This leaves us vulnerable to error, especially when making attributions of cause and effect in times of enhanced emotion or troubling uncertainty. When logic fails, magical thinking lies in wait, ready to step in to fill the void with erroneous beliefs that seem to offer explanation.

CHAPTER 16

THE GOD ENGINE

If God did not exist, it would be necessary to invent him.

—Voltaire

f you think it bizarre to abandon the bodies of deceased loved ones atop tall towers to be devoured by birds, then you probably were not reared as one of the world's 2.6 million Zoroastrians.

If you think it absurd to believe that diseases are caused, not by germs, bacilli, or viruses, but by lapses of faith, then you probably were not reared as one of the world's 150,000 Christian Scientists.

If you think it strange to believe that humans are the descendants of *Thetans*, a group of omnipotent gods, and that our emotional problems are due to "engrams" in the brain created by traumas in prior lives on another planet, then you probably were not reared as one of the world's 500,000 Scientologists.

If you think it weird to worship a god with the head of an elephant, or in the worship of another god, Shiva, to rub clarified butter on a temple *lingam* that is considered by some scholars to be a stylized phallus, then you probably were not reared as one of the world's one billion Hindus.

If you think it curious to wave silk or paper streamers ("ōnusa") over someone in a rite of purification, or for new-car owners to take their cars to a shrine to be prayed over and purified, then you probably were not reared as one of the world's 2,700,000 Shintos.

If you think it peculiar to snip away the foreskins of baby boys in the service of religious faith, then you probably were not reared as one of the world's 14 million Jews or 1.6 billion Muslims.

Figure 16-1: One world, many religions.

If you think it odd for priests to wear masks over their mouths to avoid breathing in and killing microorganisms, then you probably were not reared as one of the world's 4.2 million Jains.

If you think it inconceivable that "ancient Hebrews of America" buried golden tablets written in Egyptian in a hillside in the United States, and that these were later recovered and translated with the help of an angel, then you probably were not reared as one of the world's 15 million Mormons.

If you think it horrifying that parents, in the name of religion, deny life-saving blood transfusions to their dying children, then you probably were not reared as one of the world's 7.1 million Jehovah's Witnesses.

If you think it shocking to celebrate one's faith by eating the flesh and blood of one's heavenly savior through a spiritual transformation of bread and wine (symbolical or literal depending on your sect), then you probably were not reared as one of the world's 2.2 billion Christians.

Religion obviously takes many forms. There are more than 10,000 different religions in the world today,[1] and while most of these involve relatively small numbers of devotees, the major religions each encompass hundreds of millions of followers. Almost nothing seems too bizarre to be incorporated into religious belief, but what may appear strange to the outsider does not seem so to the faithful. Being reared in a particular religion desensitizes one to its absurdities and irrationalities to the extent that even those who later abandon it often cannot fully appreciate the strangeness of some of their former beliefs and practices.

LESLIE AND GOPAL

Consider four-year-old Leslie, who is busy learning about the world. Her young mind takes in enormous amounts of information on a daily basis, and she automatically finds patterns, establishes cause-effect relationships, and integrates her experience with knowledge provided by her parents, television, and prekindergarten. She learns that things are not always as they appear: Sweets, although they taste good, are not good for you in large quantities, and some animals, even though they look cuddly, are dangerous. She has complete trust in what her parents tell her and has no reason to doubt their word. They are Christians, and her mother spends considerable time reading Bible stories to her. She attends Sunday School, where she learns more about God and Jesus. At bedtime, she recites a prayer, "Now I lay me down sleep, I pray the Lord my soul to keep; if I should die before I wake, I pray the Lord my soul to take." She does not yet understand the full significance of those words, but the prayer, along with putting on her pajamas and brushing her teeth, is part of her nightly ritual. As she grows and learns more about the world, Leslie wonders about some of the miracles she encounters in her religious teachings. She is told not to question and to accept such mysteries as being beyond human comprehension: "God works his wonders in mysterious ways."

Leslie's friends attend Sunday School as well, and they also believe in God. She hears political leaders refer to God and to prayer, and when she is frightened she says a silent prayer and then feels relieved knowing that God is watching over her. As time goes on, Leslie learns through experience that prayer "works"—for example, when her puppy was sick, she prayed for its recovery and now it is healthy again. When her grandfather died, she was comforted by the knowledge that she would see him again one day in heaven.

And then there is four-year-old Gopal, who is also busy learning about the world. Like Leslie, he is learning all manner of things and his brain is developing rapidly. He too recognizes that things are not always as they seem—for example, that the world is a globe even though it looks to be flat. He accepts that fact without evidence, for he trusts his parents' and grandparents' teachings. He is also learning through direct experience. He attends the temple once a week with his family, and he watches as the priest rubs ghee (clarified butter) over the Shiva lingam, although he is too young to consider the lingam as a phallic symbol. His mother bakes bread on a weekly basis and insists the first loaf be given to a passing sacred cow. When Gopal raises questions about reincarnation and about Ganesh, the god with the head of an elephant, he is taught that logic does not apply in such matters. As Gopal grows, he feels at peace in the temple whenever he is troubled, and he finds that his prayers are often answered. Everyone around him shares his religious beliefs. And when his grandfather dies, he is comforted by his belief in reincarnation and his expectation that his grandfather will live again, many times.

Leslie's and Gopal's experiences are very similar, even though their religious beliefs are quite different. They find plenty of apparent support for their beliefs, for they have been taught them by trusted elders and are shared by just about everyone they know. Their beliefs offer comfort when in sorrow or distress, and direct experience seems to confirm the power of prayer. Why would either of them have any reason to doubt? If Gopal is correct in his beliefs, he is fortunate to have been born into a Hindu family rather than a Christian one. And so too Leslie, given her confidence in the truth of her Christian faith, is equally fortunate in that she was reared a Christian and not a Hindu.

Of course, Leslie and Gopal cannot both be right, for their beliefs are incompatible. Leslie believes in one god and eternal life in heaven for the faithful, while Gopal worships many gods and believes in reincarnation. When they are adults, Leslie may well wonder how someone like Gopal can believe in such fantasies, while Gopal may be equally puzzled by Leslie's faith in her religious illusions.

RELIGION IS POWERFUL

Religion in its many forms has been a dominant, perhaps *the* dominant, belief system throughout human history. Virtually every society in every era, from the most ancient to the most modern, has borne witness to its power to motivate, inspire, comfort, inflame, unite, divide, or destroy. Magnificent talents and extraordinary labors have been devoted to religious expression through music, literature, and art. The pyramids of Egypt, the temples of Greece, Rome, India, and Angor Wat, and the rich and splendid cathedrals of Europe were erected in worship of the gods, often at huge human cost. Entire adult lives have been devoted to helping the poor, the sick, and the downtrodden in service of an invisible deity. Other devotees have withdrawn into ashrams, monasteries, or temples, maintaining isolation from the ordinary world to seek union with the divine.

Whether pathway to heaven or, as Marx argued, opiate of the masses, religion continues to exert extraordinary power over individuals, families, communities, and nations. There is no one—politician, scientist, revolutionary, entertainer, emperor, demagogue—who has had as much influence on both human history and individual lives across the centuries as such towering religious figures as Christ, Mohammed, and Buddha. Even in this era of nuclear medicine, cellular telephones, space exploration, and the internet, billions of people daily supplicate their deities, seeking guidance, forgiveness, or divine intervention.

And, on its flip side, the dark side, religion has fueled hatred, racism, inquisitions, crusades, jihads, massacres, martyrdom, and going off to war with "God on our side." Guided by ancient texts and oral traditions, the faithful carry out acts that are noble or loving, destructive or vengeful, all in the service of a divine imperative that they believe mere humans can never hope to understand fully.

RELIGION IS PERVASIVE

Although scholars of the Enlightenment predicted the demise of religion with the rise of universal education, they greatly underestimated its deep-rootedness. Even in these modern times, a large majority of the world's population has been brought up in one or another religion; more than 80 percent of the world's people identify with a religious denomination.[2] Not surprisingly, there are significant cross-cultural differences. Globally, the world's most religious nation is Thailand (94 percent of its population identifies as being religious), with Armenia, Bangladesh, Georgia, and Morocco following very closely behind, all at 93 percent.[3] Yet, while overall only 11 percent of the world's people identify themselves as atheists,[4] 61 percent of Chinese,[5] 31 percent of Japanese,[6] and a quarter of the people in the former East Germany[7] do so. In the United States, the world's most powerful and technologically advanced nation, only about 3 percent of the population describe themselves as atheists.[8] In Canada, while approximately one-third of respondents to a national survey considered their religion to be highly important to them, just more than one quarter self-identified as having "no religion," a category that has been growing in number in recent decades.[9] (Referring to oneself as an atheist implies a conviction that there is no god, whereas indicating that one has no religion is more ambiguous.)

Religious conviction, however, is changing even in the United States. The number of Americans who report being "absolutely certain" that God exists has dropped from 71 percent in 2007 to 63 percent in 2014.[10] On the other hand, evangelical churches continue to gain membership in the United States, with a growth of more than two million new members between 2007 and 2014.[11]

What about scientists? Do they believe in God? Psychologist James Leuba conducted a survey of a random sample of a thousand scientists in the United States in 1914 and reported that close to 40 percent of respondents expressed a personal belief in the existence of God.[12] He then separated out the four hundred "elite" scientists in the sample and considered their responses separately, and now the percentage of believers fell to 27.7 percent. He carried out a similar survey in 1933, and this time the percentage of elite scientists holding a belief in God had dropped almost by half, to 15 percent.[13]

Leuba's 1914 survey was repeated in 1996.[14] Responses from a random sample of scientists at large were little changed from those in 1914. However, another survey, in 1998, involving only elite scientists, members of the National Academy of Sciences, found that only a small minority, about 7 percent, expressed a belief in God or a higher power.[15] Similar results were reported in a British survey of elite scientists from the Royal Society of London.[16] Simply put, belief in God among preeminent scientists has been dropping over the last century to the extent that it is now relatively rare.

RELIGION IS PERSISTENT

Religious belief systems have deep roots, and efforts by autocratic governments to eradicate them have foundered. Seventy-five years of deliberate suppression of religion in the former Soviet Union failed to eliminate it, and formal religion is now burgeoning in the nations that once comprised the Soviet bloc. Even in China, where religion is still officially discouraged, and where, as noted earlier, almost two-thirds self-identify as atheists, there has been an upsurge in both Buddhism and Christianity in recent years. It may come as a surprise that China is predicted to have before long more Christians than any other country in the world.[17]

| Zeus | Marduk | Bast | Jupiter |

Figure 16-2: Gods that are no more.

Sic Transit Gloria

Religion in general is persistent, but the glory associated with some deities has faded over time. Even though major religions such as Islam, Christianity, Hinduism, and Buddhism have endured for many centuries or millennia, others have enjoyed great appeal for extended periods of time, only to disappear into the history books. No longer does anyone worship Zeus, the supreme god of the ancient Greeks. Marduk, the Babylonian god of creation has been long forgotten. And no one prays to Bast, the Egyptian goddess of protection, or to Jupiter, the supreme god of the Romans (see figure 16-2). Likewise, there are no modern worshippers of the Norse God Odin, the Incan Apocatequil, or the Aztec Huehueteotl. Those bygone gods were central figures in highly developed theocracies, and belief in their reality wielded power over countless generations of people who spent much of their lives seeking their guidance and protection. Their influence guided both people's daily lives and decisions of state, and they were as real to their devotees as are today's deities to contemporary worshippers. And, yet, they are no more. They did not disappear because their adherents became atheists. Rather, they gave way to other gods and other religions.

Odin   Apocatequil   Huehueteotl

Figure 16-3: More gods that are no more.

RELIGION IS IMPORTANT

Despite its apparent conflict with modern scientific beliefs, religion continues to resonate with billions of people around the world, educated and uneducated alike, and worshipers consider it to be of vital importance. Add to the list of strange beliefs described at the beginning of this chapter: Large numbers of people believe that humans are discarnate souls trapped in "meat bodies" (Scientology); that a compassionate god sent his only son to earth so that he could be killed in atonement for the sins of the faithful (Christianity); that cows are sacred (Hinduism); that meat and milk must not be consumed together (Judaism); that one must wear only sacred underwear (Mormonism); or that exactly 144,000 anointed souls will rule with Christ in paradise (Jehovah's Witnesses). The fact that such strange, yet powerful, beliefs survive and flourish in our present modern and highly technological society suggests that they serve an important need.[18] We shall return to this need later in the chapter.

RELIGION IS EMOTIONAL

Believers not only *know* that their faith is grounded in truth, they *feel* its power. This feeling ranges from quiet contentment, to exuberance, to agitated excitement (as in Pentecostal rallies), and even to ecstasy. Religion not only can directly arouse emotion, attacks against it can elicit emotional responses so powerful as to rouse violence against those deemed to be blasphemers. Religion not only generates emotion, but it also provides for many people the unrivalled capacity to deal both with emotional crises and with existential anxieties involving the meaning of life, fear of death, and control of one's own destiny.[19]

RELIGION IS SOCIAL

Religion serves an important role in defining group identity. This is often a useful and good thing, but group identity can lead to sectarian violence, which more often reflects intergroup conflict over economic or territorial matters than an actual fight over religious dogma.[20] For example, Hindus, Muslims, and Sikhs historically lived in relative harmony in India until the British left in 1947, at which time political leaders of the Muslim minority opted for the establishment of a nation of their own, Pakistan. This triggered a massive ethnic cleansing, resulting in the mass migration of 14 million Hindus, Sikhs, and Muslims, the deaths of upward of a million people, and the brutal torture and rape of countless women. The battle was not over religious truth; it was a clash of social groups that were defined by religion. Similarly, in Northern Ireland, the long internecine battle between Protestants and Catholics was not actually a dispute over which version of Christianity was the "correct" one, but a clash of social groups again defined by religion.

THE ESSENCE OF RELIGION

As we have seen, religions vary widely in terms of core beliefs, but they all share a similar form in that they relate not to something of this world but to a domain unconfined by constraints of matter and energy, flesh and blood, time and space. No wonder, then, that, *religion* is a fuzzy concept that defies precise definition.[21] It is multilayered and people approach religious concepts and express their religious devotions in varying ways. Yet there are three key aspects that characterize religion.[22] First, religion involves a belief in supernatural agents or processes that contrasts with what is believed to be true about the natural world. Second, it involves some form of public commitment to supernatural agents or processes through investment of time, sacrifice of property, or even the sacrifice of one's life. Third, the belief in supernatural agents or processes serves to mitigate existential anxieties around such concerns as loneliness, injustice, death, and the meaning of life.

ORIGINS OF RELIGION

Religious belief systems are highly complex, and the world's major religions are guided and directed by historical texts that are generally considered by the devout to be divinely inspired—for example, the Jewish Torah, the Christian Bible, the Muslim Koran, the Hindu Vedas, and the Buddhist Tripitaka. But religion existed long before there were such texts. Of course, no one can say for sure when it began, any more than one can ascertain when art or music began. However, as the nineteenth century turned to the twentieth, anthropologists roamed the world making attempts to understand and explain the specific roots of the many indigenous religions that were being discovered.

Making sense of nature

Nineteenth-century anthropologists posited that religion arose from the efforts of the ancients to make sense of the world around them through the development of supernatural explanations for important events that they could not otherwise understand. Natural events, such as hurricanes and thunder, may have elicited both fear and awe, supporting the belief that these phenomena were caused by invisible beings. In earlier times, the nighttime sky was much more visible than it is today for most people, and early peoples found what they thought to be important patterns in the stars. Every society up to and including the Romans interpreted particular patterns of stars as representing various divine beings. Note that Christianity, too, places God in the heavens, and according to Christian belief it was the appearance of a star that signaled the birth of the Messiah.

Making sense of death

Anthropologist Edward Tylor (1832–1917) considered that early peoples must have found death puzzling.[23] A person who is alive and animated suddenly stops moving, and her body gradually grows cold. This may well have seemed as though some animating force had left her body. And, Tylor speculated, if that person later appeared in a dream, it might be natural to assume that her animating force, her personality, continued to live beyond the body. This, he suggests, led to the concept of the soul, and it is not a large step from belief in a soul to belief in powerful, discarnate spirits who control the world. Tylor's explanation of the development of religion is overly simplistic, but considerable cross-cultural and historical evidence suggests that dreams play a significant role in promoting the development of concepts of the divine and in reinforcing belief in supernatural beings and life after death.[24]

Divine law and order

Sociologist Emile Durkheim (1858–1917) suggested that religion developed as early peoples tried to make sense of social forces, including conflict and war, by attributing them to some supernatural agent.[25] This belief made it important to avoid offending that agent, and fed into the development of a religion that gradually became the compendium of the society's most important laws. This served to preserve social order, for one ignored such laws at one's peril because of the potential wrath of the all-seeing, all-knowing gods. Further, in deference to their gods, people gathered in groups to honor and worship, and this social interaction served to unite people into groups.

Thus, from this perspective, the establishment of religion occurred spontaneously as a means of explaining social forces and preserving order and social unity. People's expectations about what was moral and about how society should function shaped the particular supernatural concepts and religious beliefs that developed within the society.[26]

Serving dependency needs

Sigmund Freud (1856–1939) viewed the concept of a deity as an outgrowth of the child's dependency needs.[27] In the traditional family, the father was all-powerful, both providing for and defending the family, but children grow up and fathers grow old. The gradual recognition that the father was no longer (and perhaps was never) able to defend and protect created great anxiety, Freud argued, and in order to manage that anxiety, people came to believe in a substitute, an omniscient and omnipotent Heavenly Father. Freud's explanation was in accord with the Christian Lord's Prayer, which begins, "Our Father, who art in heaven."

Providing meaning and certainty

Psychologist Albert Ellis (1913–2007) argued that people have invented gods and devils in order to provide some meaning and certainty to their lives,[28] and other scholars have also emphasized that religion offers meaning to life and provides answers to questions about our place in the world.[29] Most religions promise a continuation of life after death, along with comforting rationalizations in times of threat or loss. Think of such common sayings as: *The good die young*; *This must have happened for a reason*; *God's in his heaven, All's right with the world*; and *God is on our side.*

While such speculations about the origins and functions of religion are interesting and may seem to make some sense, one must remember that they are only speculations. Efforts to move beyond speculation have led contemporary researchers to two major theoretical orientations about the genesis of religion: adaptation theory and cognitive theory.

ADAPTATION THEORY AND SOCIAL ORDER

Adaptation theory views the development of religion in functional terms. That is, it considers religion to have become culturally important because it promotes social solidarity and enhances cooperation and bonding within groups (as earlier suggested by Durkheim), which in turn increase the likelihood of survival and reproduction of individuals and the long-term survival of the groups themselves.[30] According to this approach, *believing* in religion and *belonging* to religious groups developed hand-in-hand.[31]

Researchers have linked belief in a God or gods to the rise of cooperation in large groups.[32] As human social organizations developed, cooperation was vital for group success, but as we all know, social loafers in every group attempt to share the benefits, while minimizing their own efforts. Even if the chieftain, the king, the Emperor, the government, the dictator, or the police were to attempt to eliminate social loafing and enforce cooperation, they could not be everywhere at once, nor could they see into people's minds to monitor intentions that may precede forbidden behaviors.

Gods, however, do not have such limitations. According to adaptation theory, the belief in surveillance by an invisible, all-powerful being promoted conformity to social norms and deterred individuals from becoming freeloaders and cheats.[33] (This *supernatural punishment hypothesis* is also consistent with Durkheim's view of religion as a means of social control.) When a deity is considered to be all-knowing and able to "see into the heart and soul" of the individual, no sin goes unnoted.[34] As a result, in the succinct words of one researcher, "Watched people are nice people."[35] (Perhaps this notion of supernatural surveillance explains why an image of an eye is a central feature in the representation of the divinity in some religions.[36]) Napoléon Bonaparte (figure 16-4) captured this notion of religion as social control in his statement to his Conseil d'État, on March 4, 1806:

> Quant à moi, je n'y vois pas le mystère de l'incarnation, mais le mystère de l'ordre social; la religion rattache au ciel une idée d'égalité qui empêche le riche d'être massacré par le pauvre.[37]

> As for me, I do not see the mystery in the incarnation [Christ as both God and human], but the mystery of the social order: religion attaches to Heaven an idea of equality that keeps the rich from being massacred by the poor.

Important behaviors were either mandated or declared taboo by religion, and believers had little choice but to accept that a powerful supernatural being deemed them so.[38] Fear of one's god or gods promoted cooperation, trust, and self-sacrifice, which served group needs. It was also likely to promote greater trust of other group members, for they too would be divinely punished should they transgress.[39] As religion became deeply established within a group, the religious beliefs and rituals taught to young people became an important part of their social identities, and their corresponding roles and duties further contributed to the functioning and cohesiveness of the group.[40] Ritual religious activity such as chanting and dancing contributed to the establishment of emotional bonds and a sense of community, serving to increase group cohesiveness. In addition, religious rituals and taboos made it easier to identify by their nonparticipation those nonbelievers who might otherwise undermine group solidarity.[41]

Figure 16-4: Napoleon Bonaparte.

According to adaptation theory, the resulting adherence to a common set of rules and values led to a society that could out-compete, out-survive, and out-reproduce groups that were less prosocially oriented.[42] This prosocial orientation is reflected in the Golden Rule, which promotes cooperation among the faithful, and which is found in one form or another in all major religions:

- Zoroastrianism: *Whatever is disagreeable to yourself do not do unto others* (Shayast-na-Shayast 13:29).
- Islam: *Do to all men as you would wish to have done unto you; and reject for others what you would reject for yourselves* (Hadith 2, 75).
- Taoism: *Regard your neighbor's gain as your own gain, and your neighbor's loss as your own loss* (T'ai Shang Kan Ying P'ien).
- Confucianism: *Surely it is the maxim of loving kindness: Do not unto others that you would not have them do unto you* (Analects 15, 23).

- Buddhism: *Hurt not others in ways you yourself would find hurtful* (Udana-Varga 5:18).
- Hinduism: *This is the sum of duty: Do naught unto others which would cause you pain if done unto you* (Mahabharata 5.1517).
- Judaism: *What is hateful to you, do not to your fellow men* (Talmud Shabbat 31a).
- Christianity: *All things whatsoever ye would that men should do to you, do you even onto them* (Matthew 7:12).

Once a belief in supernatural beings has taken root in a group, beliefs about how one should relate to the divinity then develop. Such beliefs are likely to bear on social attachment (for example, *God the Father, walking hand-in-hand with Jesus*), the importance of kinship (for example, ancestor worship), social exchange (the gods provide what humans need, in exchange for particular rituals or sacrifices), and status hierarchies (the gods exact submission from humans).[43]

Intergenerational transmission of religion

The *gene-culture co-evolution theory* proposes that as beliefs and practices are passed down from generation to generation, they are subject to a kind of natural selection similar to the natural selection process for genes.[44] Those aspects of cultural heritage that are most conducive to the survival of the group will be passed on to the next generation, enhancing its prospects for survival, and that generation in turn will pass the beliefs and practices onto a subsequent generation. To the extent that religious beliefs succeed in promoting social solidarity and bonding within groups, they will be favored for transmission from generation to generation.

The theory also speculates that individuals who best serve the welfare of the group may become the preferred mating partners and as a result be most successful at reproduction. Consequently, whatever genetic characteristics that might have contributed to such behavior—perhaps those affecting aspects of personality such as anxiety-proneness or the propensity to experience emotions such as guilt and shame—would be more likely to make it into the next generation's gene pool. In this way, it is suggested, genes and cultural variables interact to favor cross-generational promotion of prosocial behavior, and to the extent that religion is associated with prosocial behavior, religious belief will be socially transmitted along with it.[45]

COGNITIVE THEORY: THE GOD ENGINE

While adaptation theory views belief in the supernatural as an adaptive response to social needs, promoting cooperation and obedience to social norms, it is the cognitive theory of religion that is by far the dominant one at present.[46] It considers religious belief to have developed not as a solution to personal and social needs but rather as the automatic by-product of the systems that evolved for everyday cognition.[47] Religion, according to this perspective, developed by default. Belief in the supernatural is a natural consequence of the way our brains work, and, just as beliefs in general are products of the *Belief Engine*, religious beliefs in particular can be thought of as the products of a metaphorical *God Engine* that endows them with significant power over people's lives and strong resistance to change. The content, of course, varies significantly from religion to religion.

Readers who accept the validity of their own religious beliefs without question and view their religion as the one true faith may be unwilling to consider them to be the automatic products of a God Engine. Be that as it may, they should still have some curiosity about the source of the fervor and commitment that billions of other people around the world show for their own, quite different, religious beliefs. This cannot be explained by the ecumenical argument sometimes put forth that everyone "worships the same god in different ways," for many religions are completely incompatible with one another. For example, Hinduism's pantheon of gods and its many cycles of reincarnation cannot be reconciled with Christianity's monotheism, personal redemption, and a single everlasting life.

Predisposed to Believe

Our brains propel us to believe in the supernatural. A number of automatic processes and cognitive biases combine to make supernatural belief the automatic default. The effect is so powerful that children, as we have seen earlier, spontaneously develop the idea of a deity based on their interpretation of their own experiences, and any religious teaching that they may receive then fits well with what they have already come to believe.

Because of the God Engine, almost anything can become the subject of religious devotion. Almost anything? The eminent nineteenth-century polymath Sir Francis Galton (1822–1911), cousin of Charles Darwin, was fascinated by the impact of religion. He traveled widely and examined diverse religious beliefs and was one of the first scientists to try to investigate its power and appeal. As part of his inquiry, he put up a picture of Punch (of the traditional Punch and Judy show) on his wall and made a point of praying to it morning and night.[48] After doing so for several weeks, he found that he was automatically making mental supplications to Punch during moments of difficulty or stress, even though he was aware that he was "making the whole thing up." While expressing his now unacceptable contempt for pre-technological cultures, he wrote:

> I addressed it with as much quasi-reverence as possessing a mighty power to reward or punish the behavior of men toward it, and found little difficulty in ignoring the impossibilities of what I professed. The experiment gradually succeeded. I began to feel and long retained for the picture a large share of the feelings that a barbarian entertains toward his idol, and learnt to appreciate the enormous potency they might have over him.[49]

Figure 16-5: Punch.

Galton's "experiment" offers anecdotal evidence of the ease with which religious notions can take root.

A number of factors, including some of the developmental processes introduced in earlier chapters—magical thinking, agency detection, theory of mind, teleological reasoning, and reality testing—render children very vulnerable to supernatural interpretations of events and are particularly important in the development of religious belief. Because of this, they warrant further examination.

We are born magical thinkers

Magical thinking plays such a significant role in religion that some researchers consider it to be the very foundation of religious belief.[50] Suppose that the sky darkens with the approach of a frightening thunderstorm. Someone importunes Zeus to send the storm away, and, by coincidence, the storm abates. Fear is reduced, the action of praying has been reinforced, and Zeus is credited with having quieted the storm. A conditioned emotional response may also develop so that praying to Zeus in future will reduce anxiety. Similarly, when various religious rituals including prayer have been repeatedly paired with positive feelings in childhood, those rituals and prayer are likely to elicit those same feelings in adulthood.

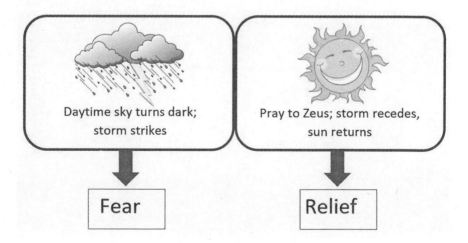

Figure 16-6: End of the storm.

We are born agency detectors

From a very early age, we look for reasons and intentions behind events. Recall hyperactive agency detection, our automatic tendency to react with a fight-or-flight response to danger while looking for the cause and intention behind the threatening event. Failure to find a cause for the feeling that one is in danger can lead to the conclusion that the cause, the agent, is present but invisible, fostering belief in undetectable agencies. Virtually all religions involve extraordinary, awe-inspiring phenomena. And because people everywhere have similar experiences, beliefs in supernatural beings—gods, ghosts, angels, and demons—have developed in every culture and society.[51] In the words of cultural anthropologist Scott Atran,

> All supernatural agent concepts trigger our naturally selected agency-detection system, which is trip-wired to respond to fragmentary information, inciting perception of figures lurking in the shadows and emotions of dread or awe.[52]

Interpreting events as divine interventions, messages, warnings, or punishments serves as further confirmation of the existence of the divine being. Indeed, in every society that anthropologists have examined, uncontrollable tragedies have been viewed by many people as having been deliberately caused by some supernatural agent. An unexpected and violent storm may be interpreted as an expression of God's wrath in response to some transgression. The epidemic of HIV-AIDS was taken by some fundamentalist Christians in the United States to be God's punishment for homosexuality.[53] But God, in the beliefs of many, does not only punish. When fifty miners are killed in the collapse of a mine shaft and only one survives, many Christians will fault humans for the deaths of the fifty, but give God the credit for the "miracle" survival of one. (That God apparently allowed the other fifty to die is rarely considered or is somehow explained away.)

There are only a limited number of attributes that can be reasonably associated with a hypothetical supernatural agent, and as a result it is not surprising that many similarities are apparent among the supernatural beings envisioned by peoples around the planet. For example, we might attribute to a supernatural being counterintuitive physical properties such as being a ghost, or counterintuitive biological properties such as never aging or dying, or counterintuitive psychological properties such as prescience or extraordinary perception. However, not all possible combinations of such abilities are likely to persist in the belief system or be passed on to subsequent generations. The representations of supernatural beings that persist are recognizable, easily remembered, easily communicated, and useful in dealing with problems.[54] Examination of a wide variety of mythologies, anecdotes, cartoons, religious writings, and science fiction bears testament to this.[55]

We develop theory of mind

Recall that infants become able to distinguish animate objects from inanimate by five months of age. This is followed by the development of theory of mind sometime before the third year as children come to understand that humans and animals have internal mental processes similar to their own. This leads directly to *dualism*, the notion that mind is separate from matter,[56] and this in turn paves the way for belief in disembodied spirits and intelligent deities whose minds function in a similar manner to our own.[57] As a result, it should not be surprising that about half of all four-year-olds have an imaginary friend.[58]

Some cleverly designed experiments have shown that children's concepts of a god are not simply extensions of their concepts of what people are like.[59] In one such experiment,[60] children aged three to six from practicing Christian families were given a closed, unmarked paper bag and a closed cracker box bearing a picture of crackers on the label. When asked what was inside the cracker box, the children not surprisingly responded "crackers." The researcher then opened the box to reveal only a collection of small rocks, and then showed the children that the crackers were actually in the paper bag. The children were then asked where their mothers would look first if they came looking for crackers, and where God would point if he wanted to show you where the crackers were.[61] While the children recognized that their mothers would be guided to the cracker box by a false belief based on the label, a large majority of them responded that God would know where the crackers were and would not be subject to a false belief. Similar findings have been found in other cultures, for example with Mayan children.[62] Being godlike involves powers that go beyond being people-like.

We develop promiscuous teleological intuition

As they reason about the world around them, children appear innately prone to consider objects and events as serving an intentional purpose, and this teleological bias to perceive that things happen for a reason operates promiscuously (in that it is applied to just about everything).[63] Of course, such reasoning eventually leads to contemplation about some sort of extraordinary intelligence that guides the world, and this paves the way for belief in supernatural beings responsible for creation.

Reality testing

As has been discussed earlier, children have to learn to distinguish fantasy from reality. They learn that nightmares are not real, that the tooth fairy and Easter bunny are fictions, and that Santa Claus does not exist. Yet, where religious beliefs are concerned, religious parents not only do not teach their children to reality test, they typically teach them *not* to reality test. Religious beliefs are justified by faith alone and are not to be subjected to reason. In the more fundamentalist religions, children are further taught that it is not only inappropriate but sinful to question religious teachings, and the resultant guilt aroused by any doubts about their religion is a powerful deterrent to future intellectual challenges. In consequence, these beliefs may remain forever insulated from reality testing, and therefore be very unlikely to change.

	Santa Claus	Deity
Taught to young children at an age when critical faculties are undeveloped	✓	✓
Involves physically impossible feats	1. Climbs down chimneys 2. Flying reindeer 3. Delivers gifts around the world in a single night	1. Hears all prayers simultaneously 2. Visits earth as human or animal 3. Transcends space, time, and physical laws
Makes no logical sense	Child is too young to question	It is a matter of faith; logic is inappropriate
Belief is shared by peers, providing social support	✓	✓
Outgrowing the belief is a sign of maturity	✓	✗

Figure 16-7: Santa and the deity.

Compare belief in Santa Claus with belief in a deity. (See figure 16-7.) Both beliefs are communicated to children at a time when their ability to reason is undeveloped. Both beliefs involve physically impossible feats and make no logical sense. Both beliefs are typically shared by the child's peers, but while all adults look askance at any twelve-year-old who still believes in Santa Claus, religious parents look askance at the twelve-year-old who no longer believes in the deity.

As children strive to make distinctions between reality and fantasy, making wishes comes easily to them. Note that praying and making a wish are very similar, for each involves a mental process intended to bring about some desired outcome without any physical effort on one's own part.[64] While praying is part of a system of *institutionalized* magical beliefs (religion) taught by adults and shared with family, wish-making is something that one does independently of others; it is *non-institutionalized.*[65] When family and cultural influences support and encourage religious beliefs while discouraging and disparaging other magical beliefs, children, at some time between ages four and eight years, come to view praying and wish-making quite differently.[66] They typically show both increasing belief in the power of prayer and decreasing confidence in the effectiveness of personal idiosyncratic magical beliefs, including wish-making.[67]

We are taught religion

Children do not become Christians, Muslims, Buddhists, or Jews on their own. They learn religion, which is intertwined with a group's history and culture. Recall the stories of Leslie and Gopal. Children typically grow up believing in and practicing the religion in which they were reared, and are often taught as well that other religions are unworthy of serious consideration.[68]

The development of language ability not only gives the growing child a powerful tool for the symbolic analysis of events, it also makes possible the acquisition of massive amounts of information from others. Children learn much about the world through their own experiences but when it comes to things they cannot observe directly—for example, their internal organs, the shape of the earth, or the revolution of the earth around the sun—they uncritically accept the teachings of adults.[69] It is therefore not surprising that they uncritically accept religious teaching about invisible entities that they cannot observe directly. By the time they are five or six, children brought up in a religious milieu attribute to their deity special cognitive abilities to see and hear things that ordinary mortals cannot.[70]

We are more likely to remember "ontological" violations

Children develop an intuitive ontology—an understanding about what exists, about what is real—early in life.[71] An *ontological violation* is something that it is considered impossible in the normal world, such as waving one's arms in order to fly. Of course, many religious beliefs involve ontological violations—such as an omniscient deity who can hear people's prayers wherever they may be in the world.

Violations of ontological expectations are better remembered than beliefs that intuitively make sense.[72] For example, "a man who walked through a wall" is an ontological violation, while "a man with six fingers," although unusual, does not violate our beliefs about what is possible and what is not. Research has found that reference to a man who walked through a wall is recalled more readily over a period of months than reference to a six-fingered man. This effect has been found not only in the West, but also in Tibet and with the Fang people, one of the main Bantu tribes in Gabon.[73]

Religious beliefs involving violations of our intuitive (ontological) understanding of the world are both more attention-grabbing and memorable. Because they are more memorable, they are also more likely to be communicated to others.[74] The advantage that a memorable idea has in terms of being transmitted from generation to generation may be small, but over many generations its influence is amplified as it becomes an inherent part of the culture.[75]

Psychologist Patrick Boyer points out that although individuals and groups can be credulous at times, there are limits to what people will believe in the name of religion, and so only certain religious beliefs, those that provide solace or offer explanations for strange events, are likely to be transmitted over extended periods of time. While something too counterintuitive (e.g., a species of super-intelligent beetles that control television networks) may not take hold, the notion of a God who possesses some human qualities but also has omniscience and prescience may be just counterintuitive enough and not too much. Boyer writes,

> I do not think that people have religion because they relax their usually strict criteria for evidence and accept extraordinary claims; I think they are led to relax these criteria because some extraordinary claims have become quite plausible to them.[76]

Boyer also points out that it does not take much effort to maintain religious beliefs, and that people do not have to work very hard to persuade themselves that these beliefs are true.

To sleep, perhaps to dream . . .

Recall anthropologist Edward Tylor's speculation that early humans most likely interpreted dreams of dead loved ones as an indication that they live on after their physical deaths. There is considerable evidence, both cross-cultural and historical, that dreams do provide people with what seems to be verification of their beliefs in supernatural beings and life after death, and contribute to the development of religious rituals, beliefs, and concepts of the divine.[77]

Emotional experience

While each religion has its own set of beliefs and practices, and while the major religions are guided by holy texts supposedly divinely dictated or inspired eons ago, religion is much more than a set of dictates and beliefs, for strong emotional experience is often involved. It is one thing to debate the appeal of various religious beliefs and it is quite another to "experience" the divine. Many religious people have reported having felt the power of a divine presence, often during prayer. (Recall the *mysterium tremendum* experience of people who believe that they are in the presence of the divinity, chapter 11.) Some religions deliberately encourage such experiences, and the resurgence of charismatic and Pentecostal Christianity, sometimes involving speaking in tongues and laying on of hands, attests to the appeal of a mixture of emotion and spirituality.

Religion answers existential questions

Why are we here and what happens when we die? Where did the world come from, and when did it begin? Religion provides answers to many questions that otherwise would go unanswered: Consider these creation stories:

Creation story #1 (King James Bible, Book of Genesis):

> In the beginning, God created the heaven and the earth. And the earth was without form, and void; and darkness was upon the face of the deep. And the Spirit of God moved upon the face of the waters. And God said, Let there be light: and there was light. And God saw the light, that it was good: and God divided the light from the darkness. And God called the light Day, and the darkness he called Night. And the evening and the morning were the first day.

Creation story #2: (Native North American, *Achomawi*):

> In the beginning, all was water. Then a cloud formed in the clear sky, became lumpy and turned into Coyote. Then a fog developed and became lumpy and Silver Fox was formed, and then Coyote and Silver Fox both became people. And they began to think. And they thought a canoe, and it became real and they floated in it for many years. One time while Coyote was sleeping, Silver Fox combed his hair and then took the combings, flattened them and spread them out on the water until they covered the surface of the water. Then he thought, "There should be a tree," and now there was a tree. And then he did the same with shrubs and rocks and people and birds and fish.[78]

Creation story #3: (The Big Bang, Modern science)

> About 13.8 billion years ago, a singularity, an infinitesimally small point of infinite density, suddenly exploded and began to expand rapidly to form the universe as we now know it, with a diameter at present of some 93 billion light years at present and still expanding. (That is, light emanating from one edge of the universe would take 93 billion years to reach the other edge.) The universe is estimated to contain between 100 and 200 billion galaxies, with each galaxy comprising hundreds of billions of stars.

All three stories may seem fantastical in their own way, and all three are accepted on faith by those who believe them. While the first involves trust in the validity of the Book of Genesis and the second in the oral traditions of North American First Nations peoples, the third requires trust in the conclusions of modern science. While scientists understand the logic and the data that support the Big Bang explanation, it is beyond the layperson's ability to do so.

Such explanations provide a feeling of understanding to people puzzled about how the world began, even though they leave other mysteries in their wake. Those who attribute the origins of the universe to their god or gods conveniently ignore the question about where their god or gods came from. On the other hand, the Big Bang explanation also leads to another mystery, the origin of that singularity.

Reinforcement of religious belief

Religious beliefs and actions are reinforced in a number of different ways.

Coincidence

Recall the discussion of superstitious conditioning: An action is followed by a desired outcome purely by happenstance, leading the individual to believe incorrectly that the action brought about the outcome. Now, consider prayer: No matter to which god one prays, subsequent events that would have occurred whether one prayed or not can often be interpreted as the desired answers to one's prayers. After all, even without divine intervention, people sometimes unexpectedly recover from severe illness; rains do come to end droughts; lost loved ones are often found safe; and people do get promotions at work. However, when preceded by prayer, these events may appear to be miraculous. Even if prayer is "reinforced" only intermittently, recall that intermittent reinforcement results in learning that is the most resistant to decay. And the gods cannot lose, for any apparent failure of prayer is generally explained away: "Sometimes, God says no."

Peace, comfort, and anxiety reduction

Research has found that religious belief increases when people are reminded of human mortality.[79] Religion provides a bulwark against existential anxiety and fear of annihilation. It offers comfort in times of threat and can help one to deal with the loss of loved ones, especially if one believes that our personalities survive death.

Religious belief and prayer also offer an important shift in focus when faced with anxiety and uncertainty.[80] When under stress, people with strong religious conviction show less reactivity in the part of the brain associated with anxiety (the "anterior cingulate cortex").[81] The framework that religion provides can help an individual to remain calm and to deal with difficult circumstances.[82] Of course, an emotionally balanced atheist with a good sense of purpose might react similarly.

Increased sense of control

Feeling a lack of control makes people more vulnerable to a decrease in critical thinking and an increase in magical thinking. In a series of experiments, participants who were led to feel a lack of control showed an increased tendency to see images where there were none, to form illusory correlations when shown stock market data, to be vulnerable to conspiracy theories, and to develop superstitious behavior.[83]

Religion not only serves to reduce anxiety but also increases a sense of order and control in an otherwise seemingly uncontrollable world. Belief in a benevolent god who watches over the world and answers prayers provides a sense of control when all around us is chaos and calamity.[84] "God is in His heaven— All's right with the world."[85] As a result, belief in God increases when people are under extreme levels of stress. Reflecting this, researchers have found that both in Western and non-Western contexts, pronounced government instability promotes increased religious belief.[86]

Companionship and attachment

Many religious people form strong emotional attachments to their deity. Such attachment may either mirror strong feelings of childhood closeness to parents or compensate for unsatisfactory relationships with them.[87] Further, if one believes in a god who listens and watches over us, this belief provides a sense of never being alone. This is very important in a world where loneliness is a significant problem for many. (However, when one observes a lineup of students at a campus coffee shop, every one of them using a smart phone to text or make a phone call, it seems that one need never really be alone these days. Of course, loneliness involves more than simply being alone.)

Self-enhancement

Religion is often a source of significant self-enhancement.[88] "God sees the little sparrow fall ... I know he loves me too."[89] Perhaps you feel unimportant or ignored or rejected, but if you know that your God loves you, this gives you a reason to feel good about yourself.

Group solidarity

With rare exceptions, religion does not occur in a social vacuum. Religious beliefs and practices are shared and reinforced by family, friends, and neighbors, and provide an important basis for social identification. Adherents feel themselves to be part of a moral community with its sacred values, norms, and ethical expectations.[90] Religious identity provides something that no other social identity can offer: a sense of eternal belongingness and a set of sacred beliefs that provide certainty about the world and one's place in it. These unique characteristics, combined with powerful emotional experiences and strong bonds with other members, imbue it with more importance to many people than any other form of social identity.[91]

RELIGION: THE DARK SIDE

While religion can inspire creativity and noble goals, it can also bring distress and harm.[92]

Sin, guilt, and low self-esteem

The notion of sin is essential to many religions, and as a result, devout individuals may experience very significant guilt when questioning scripture or departing from what is considered to be "proper" behavior. Such guilt keeps many from straying from the faith, and the propensity for guilt can extend to the point that a serious accident or personal tragedy may be interpreted as God's punishment for insufficient piety. Some religions also contribute to low self-esteem and feelings of worthlessness through teaching that all flesh is corrupt and that we are born in sin.

Conformity pressure

There is implicit pressure to think and behave appropriately arising both from the desire to please the deity and to avoid supernatural displeasure or punishment. Deviation from fundamental beliefs can be seen as threatening to the group, and in some religions, failures to adhere to what is deemed appropriate are severely punished. Such punishment can be physical, theological (e.g. *disfellowshipping* by Jehovah's Witnesses; excommunication by the Roman Catholic Church), or social (e.g., shunning by Mormons). And, as touched on earlier, divine regulation fosters self-regulation, which can be carried to the extreme.[93]

Human sacrifice

In bygone times, religious belief in many cultures led to ritual sacrifice of humans to please the gods. For example, in order to promote the continuing existence and prosperity of their society, Aztecs offered human sacrifices to honor the gods by nourishing them with human flesh and blood. Thousands of people— some estimates are as high as 20,000—were sacrificed every year.[94]

Another example: Carthage at its peak was a powerful society; it dominated the Mediterranean for centuries before being crushed by the Romans in 146 BCE. The Carthaginians also practiced human sacrifice, ritually giving up their own children to their gods. The Greek historian Plutarch (c. 45–120 CE) described their sacrifice:

> With full knowledge and understanding they themselves offered up their own children, and those who had no children would buy little ones from poor people and cut their throats as if they were so many lambs or young birds.[95]

Prejudice, discrimination, and violence

Rigid, orthodox beliefs are usually accompanied by intolerance, and some religions openly justify and promote prejudice and even violence toward others who do not share their beliefs.[96] There are many historical examples. In 1066, Christian crusaders on their way across Europe to the Holy Land murdered countless numbers of defenseless Jews. In 1099, crusaders took control of Jerusalem and slaughtered not just Jews, but Muslims and Eastern Orthodox Christians as well. In the late twelfth century, the Medieval Inquisition began, and in the middle of the thirteenth century Pope Innocent IV issued a papal bull authorizing the Inquisitors to use torture to extract confessions from suspected heretics and witches brought before them. And in modern times, members of some religions have called for the extermination of nonbelievers.

While the practice of Christianity has often failed to reflect the love, compassion, and forgiveness that is central to the Christian message, it is not alone. Almost all religions have provided their share of intolerance, resulting in abuse, suffering, and death, all in the name of their deities.

WOULD THE WORLD BE BETTER OFF WITHOUT RELIGION?

Well-known critics of religion such as biologist Richard Dawkins, psychologist Sam Harris, and philosopher Daniel Dennett are adamant that religion is harmful to individuals and society alike. They argue that it discourages the pursuit of intellectual solutions for serious social issues and fosters intergroup animosity and conflict that all too often result in lethal aggression. Get rid of religion and the world will be a better place, they tell us. Indeed, many individuals do very well without any religion at all, and for others the secular humanist movement provides the individual and group functions of religion without the supernatural component.

Nonetheless, we must not overlook the fact that some very intelligent and well-educated people, great leaders among them, are devoutly religious, and many of them have worked for peace, tolerance, and respect for individual and human rights. Conversely, some atheists have been genocidal tyrants. Expunging religion will not by itself rid the world of intolerance, injustice, war, and genocide.

Regardless of whether the god to whom one prays is real, belief in a deity has positive consequences for many people. Psychologist Scott Lilienfeld points out that empirical data consistently suggest both a positive relationship between religious belief and prosocial behavior and a negative relationship between religious belief and criminal behavior.[97] That is, the greater the extent of their religious belief, the more likely it is that people will be helpful and cooperative and the less likely that they will engage in criminal acts. Although these associations are modest and the causal link is ambiguous, Lilienfeld argues that the empirical data do not support the notion that the world would necessarily be better off without religion. Indeed, there is accumulating evidence that religious belief is related to better mental and physical health,[98] and there are several reasons for this:

1. Religious beliefs provide coping mechanisms for dealing with stress and deprivation, thereby lessening the likelihood that the individual will suffer from anxiety or depression. Religious beliefs can inspire positive

thinking, resulting in cognitive reappraisal of stressful events in a way that makes them more bearable.

2. Religions in general embody important rules about how to live one's life and how to interact with others. By following the rules (for example, not taking advantage of others, being faithful to one's partner), the individual may encounter less stress in life than would otherwise be the case.

3. Most religions encourage communal activities, which provide important social support. In addition, religions in general encourage positive virtues such as integrity, reliability, and forgiveness that are likely to promote positive social relationships, and in turn have a positive effect on self-esteem and mental health.

Yet, while religion plays a central role in the lives of many people, a secular belief system that addresses these important human needs can do the same, without need of supposed supernatural governance.

The architecture of our brains predisposes us to the development of supernatural and religious beliefs, and transmission of these beliefs to children at an age when critical thinking acumen is lacking assures their continuation across generations. For many people, religious beliefs serve important functions, both personal and social, and provide answers to existential questions that are rarely amenable to reason and scientific inquiry.

When we attempt to persuade believers that religion is but a human creation, we may undermine an important coping mechanism without offering a viable alternative in its place. Yet, when religion transfers the responsibility for finding solutions to our problems to a deity, when dogmatic belief wins over critical thinking, when authoritarian religious leaders seek to rule behavior by scriptural fiat, when believers are led into guilt and feelings of unworthiness or intolerance of others, then religion is both inimical to individual and societal well-being and destructive of rationality itself. Fundamentalist religious dogma—and blind, fanatical adherence to any system of belief, religious or otherwise—is a formidable enemy of reason.

CHAPTER 17

THINGS THAT GO BUMP
IN THE NIGHT

From ghoulies and ghosties and long-leggedy beasties
And things that go bump in the night,
Good Lord, deliver us!

— Traditional Scottish prayer[1]

Things *that go bump in the night* . . . You are all alone, spending the night in an old house, trying to fall asleep. And as you lie there, you hear a noise in the next room. Anxiety. What is it—an intruder? An errant raccoon, a squirrel? You get up, put on the lights, and investigate. That's odd; now everything seems normal. The doors are locked and the windows secured. You go back to bed, and then, as you are dozing off again, you hear another sound, as though something is being dragged across the floor. You recall someone having mentioned that this house is haunted. As you think about that, your heart begins to race . . .

Things that go bump. This expression captures metaphorically those things that sometimes bump up against the materialistic view of the world, events that do not respond to reason and instead appeal directly to the magical thinker in each of us. Apparitions, precognition, alien visitors, extrasensory perception, walking barefoot over fire, the Bermuda Triangle . . . the list is lengthy.

Remember the *Wizard of Oz*? "Pay no attention to the man behind the curtain," the Wizard intones into his microphone after being discovered by Toto, the dog. He endeavors to conceal from Dorothy and her friends that he is not a wizard at all, but just an ordinary man using machines to generate his "magic." The world inside our brains is somewhat like the Wizard's kingdom. We are ignorant of the machinery "behind the curtain," the myriad neural processes constantly at work outside of conscious awareness, and as a result we can be at times puzzled, frightened, or entranced when information from those hidden processes seeps into consciousness as if by magic.

Figure 17-1: The Wizard.

And the machinery of our brains is both immense and complex. There are about 86 billion neurons in the human brain, each with multiple connections through its synapses to other neurons.[2] As physiologist Stephen Smith explains,

> One synapse, by itself, is more like a microprocessor—with both memory-storage and information-processing elements—than a mere on/off switch. In fact, one synapse may contain on the order of 1,000 molecular-scale switches. A single human brain has more switches than all the computers and routers and Internet connections on Earth.[3]

Synapse

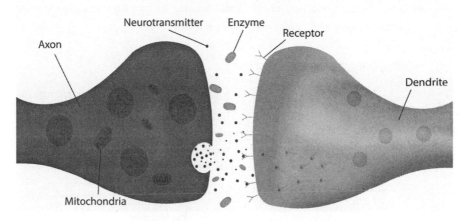

Figure 17-2: Synapse (Shutterstock / joshya).

That is what is behind our curtain. Because so much brain activity is non-conscious, everyone is likely on occasion to be struck by remarkable experiences imbued with great emotional significance and that seem to defy rational explanation. You dream of Uncle Harry's death and he dies the following day. You are in conversation with a close friend, and just as you are about to bring up an event from long ago, your friend practically steals the words out of your mouth. Like the ghosts and goblins of childhood stories, such experiences "go bump in the night." Being unable to see behind the curtain, people are stymied for rational explanations and are then tempted to conclude that something *paranormal* has occurred.

ANOMALOUS EXPERIENCE

Supposed paranormal, or psychic, experiences are said to involve mental abilities that go beyond the natural limits of nature as modern science understands it. Such experiences imply that the "mind" is not subject to the physical limits that constrain the brain. They include among others:

- *mental telepathy*, communication between two brains without the use of the normal sensory channels,
- *precognition*, the perception of future events before they occur,

- *psychokinesis*, the influence of one's thoughts and wishes on the movement of physical objects, and
- *out-of-body experiences* (OBE), the feeling of having risen out of one's physical body and perceiving it from above.

Extrasensory Perception	Numerology
Poltergeists	Spontaneous Human Combustion
Energy Fields	Therapeutic Touch
Out-of-Body Experiences	Qigong
Psychic Sleuths	Psychokinesis
Alien Abductions	Faith Healing
Precognitive Dreams	Near-Death Experiences
Astrology	Past-Life Regression
Apparitions	Bermuda Triangle

Figure 17-3: The many faces of pseudoscience.

There is no persuasive evidence that such phenomena actually exist, and much good reason to believe that they do not. Yet parapsychologists, those researchers who devote their efforts to the study of these supposed phenomena, insist that they are real. While they might attribute your dream of Uncle Harry's death to precognition and your friend's theft of your words to mental telepathy, these terms explain nothing. They are only labels and have no independent meaning. This brings to mind a radio interview from many years ago in which the celebrated author and biochemist Isaac Asimov recalled that when he was a boy, his father took him into the woods one day and taught him how to identify a maple, an oak, a willow, a birch, and so on. That evening, he asked Isaac what he had learned in the woods, and Isaac replied that he had learned about trees, about maples and oaks and willows and birches. His father responded that he had learned nothing about trees; he had learned only their names.

Mistaking a label for an explanation not only gives a false sense of understanding but diverts people from looking for an actual explanation for their experiences. Believing that you have communicated through mental telepathy is not the same as actually having communicated through mental telepathy. Believing that your dream of Uncle Harry's death was precognitive is not the same as it actually having been precognitive.

The psychological approach explores such experiences through the lens of psychology and neuroscience. In this context, these events are referred to as *anomalous experiences*, a term coined by my late colleague, psychologist Graham Reed.[4] These experiences do not seem to fit with our knowledge of how things work in the brain in the physical world, which makes them anomalous and deserving of investigation, but that does not necessarily mean that they *do not* fit. Psychologist Christopher French, who heads the Anomalistic Psychology Research Unit in the psychology department at Goldsmiths, University of London, defines *anomalistic psychology* as a sub-discipline of psychology focused on explaining

> paranormal and related beliefs and ostensibly paranormal experiences in terms of known (or knowable) psychological and physical factors. It is directed at understanding bizarre experiences that many people have, without assuming that there is anything paranormal involved.[5]

Parapsychology, on the other hand, involves a search for evidence to prove that normal explanations for anomalous phenomena are insufficient, in the belief that they reflect another reality, involving nonphysical aspects of our minds and personalities not bound by the laws of the material world.

PARAPSYCHOLOGY

> *He who believes in it [the paranormal] carries out experiments in sorcery, and he who does not believe in it as a rule does not. But since man is known to have a great tendency to find confirmed what he believes in, and to this end might even apply a great ingenuity to deceive himself, to me the success of such experiments only proves that those conducting them believe in them to begin with.[6]*
>
> —Psychologist Wilhelm Wundt (1832–1920)[6]

In the late nineteenth and early twentieth centuries, science was on a roll. Stunning discoveries of new forms of energy such as X-rays and radiation, emerging evidence of the complex geological history of the earth, exciting new discoveries in chemistry, astronomy, and biology, and major advances in medicine all spoke to the power of the scientific method. Not all of those developments in scientific thinking jibed well with religious dogma. An outstanding example of this was Darwin's theory of evolution and natural selection, which challenged belief in the divine creation of the universe and humanity's special place in it. Being religious, many scientists found it difficult to reconcile the theory with the static, immutable dictates of their faith. Even some whose religious faith was already in decline worried about the implications for morality were there no prospect of reward and punishment in an afterlife. Cambridge philosopher Henry Sidgwick was one of those. Historian J. J. Cerullo noted that:

> For his ethical system to achieve coherence, Sidgwick found himself required to postulate that the human personality survives bodily death, so that the sacrifice of personal gratification necessitated by social duty could eventually be compensated. Demonstration of survival, for Sidgwick, became something of an obsession.[7]

At this same time, Spiritualism was all the rage in Europe and North America. Large numbers of people believed that they were able to communicate with deceased loved ones through the assistance of a spirit medium. The Spiritualists for the most part saw themselves on the side of science, investigating what they considered objectively observable phenomena. As historian Lawrence Moore wrote,

> For most of the 19th century, leading Spiritualists had a childlike faith in empirical science as the only approach to knowledge. They tried to emulate the scientific method . . . they copied and helped popularize scientific language.[8]

In an age when new scientific discoveries were rapidly changing the understanding of how nature worked, it made sense for scientists to show interest in what was being reported from the séance parlors. It was possible that, just as with X-rays, radio waves, and radiation that had been hidden from human knowledge until science uncovered them, there might be a psychic dimension of nature awaiting discovery.

Such ideas generated so much fascination that in 1882 an elite group of British scholars joined with some leading Spiritualists to establish the Society for Psychical Research (SPR), with the goal of subjecting spiritualistic phenomena to formal scientific investigation.[9] Henry Sidgwick was its first president. The membership included eight fellows of the world's pre-eminent scientific body of the day, the Royal Society, along with past British prime minister W. E. Gladstone, future prime minister Arthur Balfour, poet Alfred Lord Tennyson, and author Lewis Carroll (Charles Dodgson).[10] Psychologist William James also became an early supporter of their work.

For some of these people, Spiritualism and its phenomena reasonably accommodated both their appreciation of science and their wish to believe in postmortem survival.[11] Historian Lawrence Moore notes that most of these early psychical researchers and their supporters had experienced a personal religious crisis earlier in their lives. Typically, they had been reared by strongly religious parents, and the impressive scientific developments that were taking place brought their faith into conflict with their logic. Dedicated to science, but unable to accept fully the emerging scientific materialistic view of humanity, they sought to establish the soul and postmortem survival on a solid scientific basis. Moore wrote that,

> most parapsychologists, from the very time that they lapsed into agnosticism, began searching for evidence to sustain the view that individual life held meaning.[12]

Although the SPR made conscientious efforts to investigate the spiritualist phenomena that apparently were occurring regularly in séance parlors, their studies of spirit mediums and other "gifted" psychics failed to produce the persuasive evidence that the researchers were seeking, and, over the course of time, the mediums and psychics were either caught in outright fraud or strongly suspected of it.

The SPR also undertook a "census of waking hallucinations," in which more than four hundred interviewers investigated the reports of 17,000 non-institutionalized people who had reported having had a hallucination. Of special interest were *phantasms of the living*, the apparent ghostly appearances of people who died within a period of twelve hours before or twelve hours after the hallucination.[13] The analysis of these anecdotes led investigators to conclude that, although there were only a few "fairly conclusive cases," there did appear to be some connection between the deaths and the apparitions that was not due to chance alone.[14] Still, their only data were anecdotal reports, and over and over again whenever an anecdote's details could be checked against recorded fact, memories were found to be so distorted that they were too unreliable to serve as scientific evidence. Research along these lines continued for quite some time, but the lack of progress eventually prompted a move toward studying psychic phenomena in the laboratory.

Joseph Banks Rhine (1895–1980), a botanist who was later acknowledged as the "father" of American parapsychology, was reared in a religious home and had originally intended to become a minister. After being drawn to the study of supposed psychic phenomena, he established the first laboratory for experimental research into parapsychology in the 1930s at Duke University. He applied the methods of experimental psychology to the study of telepathy, clairvoyance, precognition, and psychokinesis, while expressly stating that these studies were for him a stepping stone to the scientific study of the soul. His "directing motive" was to find evidence of postmortem survival.[15]

While one cannot study *spontaneous* "paranormal" experiences in the laboratory, Rhine believed that paranormal abilities should be observable in carefully planned experiments. There was a major problem, however. In mainstream psychology, the concept of the control group is essential to most empirical research. Beginning with two similar groups of participants, the effects of a variable can be assessed by applying it to one group and not the other, and then comparing the two. For example, if interested in the effects of a study technique on success in examinations, one could use the technique with one group and compare the results with those of another similar group where the technique was not used. Such control groups are not possible in parapsychology, for parapsychologists believe that there is no way to turn psychic ability on or off. One cannot have one group "use" ESP and the other not, because even those who are instructed not to use their psychic powers may unwittingly do so. In addition, since parapsychologists believe that paranormal phenomena can neither be blocked by any kind of barrier, nor affected by distance, it is impossible to compare participants in "blocked" and "unblocked" conditions.

Rhine's solution to this problem, and this is now basic to almost all parapsychological research, was to rely on a statistical comparison with what one should expect in a chance situation if nothing paranormal is occurring. For example, if one participant is given a list of words or numbers with the goal of transmitting them telepathically to another participant, does the number of correct responses "received" by the latter exceed what would be expected by chance alone? Or, in a psychokinesis experiment in which dice are rolled by a mechanical apparatus, can the participant by the power of willing "cause" a particular number to come up with a frequency that departs significantly from what would be expected by chance?

While this kind of comparison might seem reasonable, it is actually falla-cious to equate departures from chance with paranormal influence. Statistical analysis can only confirm that there has been a departure from chance expecta-tion, which means that such an outcome is unlikely (but not impossibly so) to occur by chance alone. It cannot identify the cause, which could among other things be a flaw in the experimental procedure. Imagine as well if a devoutly reli-gious researcher were to run the same experiment that produced above-chance results for the parapsychologist, but after having prayed for a statistical depar-ture from chance. The observed departure from chance could just as well, and just as erroneously, be taken as evidence for the existence of God.

Although Rhine claimed during the 1930s to have produced evidence that put parapsychology's claims on a sound scientific footing, subsequent analyses revealed flaws and biases in his experimentation to the extent that parapsycholo-gists today do not refer to his data when arguing for the reality of the para-normal. Since his time, parapsychologists have developed a number of more sophisticated research strategies. For example, remote viewing studies involve one participant, the "sender," visiting a series of geographical locations and con-centrating on their features while another, the "receiver," reports his thoughts and impressions, and then a number of judges evaluate how much correspon-dence there is between the two. Other studies involve isolation of participants from distracting sensory stimulation in the hope that this will allow their brains a better opportunity to detect telepathic messages. Randomization has been improved through the use of random number generators that are based on the pure randomness of radioactive decay, which according to quantum theory is completely unpredictable However, despite creative research paradigms, sophis-ticated technology, and advanced statistical analyses, this modern research, like Rhine's, has failed to demonstrate the existence of paranormal phenomena, and the parapsychologists' dream of reaching the holy grail of scientific acceptance is no closer to fruition now than it was in 1882 when the Society for Psychical Research was founded in London.

PARAPSYCHOLOGY AND MODERN SCIENCE

It is not surprising that there is a conflict between parapsychology and mainstream science, given that, by its definition, paranormal phenomena are incompatible with the scientific worldview.[16] While it is true that parapsychology has not been welcomed to the halls of science, it is not for lack of consideration of its claims. As parapsychology took formal shape in the late-nineteenth century, a number of distinguished European psychologists rose to the challenge of investigating claims of telepathy, clairvoyance, and spiritualistic communication.[17] At the Fourth International Congress of Psychology, held in Paris in 1900, an entire section of the program was given over to psychical research and spiritualism. It was the failure to find substantial evidence that led psychologists to turn away from the pursuit of these putative phenomena.

Similarly, when the American Society for Psychical Research was established in 1885, several prominent psychologists were among its officers, and again it was the absence of evidence that led to their loss of interest. In 1938, the American Psychological Association, in an effort to bring parapsychological research into the mainstream, organized a round-table discussion of parapsychology and invited parapsychologists to provide their best case. The initiative did not go anywhere beyond the round-table due to a lack of persuasive evidence. There have been other opportunities as well, and although some parapsychologists continue to claim that their exclusion from the mainstream halls of science is because of the ignorance, bias, and even fear on the part of mainstream scientists, that criticism is baseless.

Scientists' unwillingness to accept the reality of paranormal phenomena reflects neither ignorance nor fear. It must be remembered that scientists are no strangers to the bizarre and do not shy away from the strange or the unexpected. Indeed, scientists recognize the existence of many phenomena that might seem even more unlikely to a layperson than extrasensory perception. For example, physicists believe, on the basis of solid evidence, that a single electron can be in two different places at the same time, that space and time are not fixed but are relative to the motion of the person observing them, and that empty space is actually curved in the vicinity of large objects.

There are a number of reasons why one should remain skeptical about parapsychological claims and why parapsychology has not been accepted as a part of modern science:[18]

1. The *failure to produce compelling evidence* is the central problem. Despite a near 140-year history of formal investigation, there has never been a single demonstration of a supposed psychic phenomenon that has been "strongly replicable," meaning that any competent, neutral scientist following the specified methodology can produce the same effect. Replication is a key safeguard against methodological error, self-delusion, and fraud. There is no other area of scientific research that lacks a single replicable demonstration of its subject matter. If there were truly any reliable evidence of paranormal influences, parapsychologists would be knocked over by the stampede of mainstream scientists eager to understand and explore the phenomena.

   Parapsychologists react to this problem in different ways. Some have even suggested that paranormal phenomena are elusive and do not obey the laws of physics as we know them, and therefore the usual methods of science need to be modified, even to the extent that the demand for replicability should be abandoned. To suggest that the very criteria developed over centuries to help protect from error and wishful thinking should be softened to accommodate parapsychological claims will never find sympathy with the mainstream scientific community.

2. *Modern science has no need for paranormal explanations.* Nothing in the normal conduct of scientific research points to strange anomalies that suggest the influence of mind over matter.[19] Take, for example, psychokinesis. Even though physicists work with almost unimaginably small forces and tiny bits of matter, they have never observed anything that suggests that the outcomes of their experiments vary depending on the thoughts, wishes, and theoretical expectations of the individual who runs the experiment.

3. *Negative definition of subject matter*: Unlike any discipline in mainstream science, the subject matter of parapsychology is defined exclusively in negative terms. That is, the supposed detection of a paranormal influence depends on ruling out all normal explanations. The problem, of course, is that no one can ever be sure that all normal explanations have been excluded. For example, both a psychic whose cheating goes undetected or a "successful" parapsychological experiment where unrecognized methodological problems accounted for success would mistakenly be taken as evidence of the paranormal because no normal cause is apparent.

4. *Unfalsifiability:* Falsifiability is an important characteristic of most scientific hypotheses. Parapsychologists' hypotheses are unfalsifiable because of the employment of various "effects" that can explain away failures. One such "effect" is the *experimenter effect*. If two researchers carry out identical experiments and one finds evidence of a supposed psychic effect while the other finds nothing, that difference will be attributed to the (assumed) difference in the psychic abilities of the two experimenters themselves. Thus, even a failure to replicate is not considered as a failure, but is taken as something that reflects the quirkiness of the paranormal.

5. *Lack of progress:* Psychic phenomena, if they exist, are no better understood now than they were a century ago. There has been no accumulation of knowledge, and no well-articulated theory supported by data has been developed. Every other area of scientific research has shown a gradual accumulation of knowledge and an evolution of increasingly more sensitive and sophisticated methodology. Instead, the history of parapsychological research is a series of different research strategies, each promising a breakthrough before ultimately being discarded.

6. *Methodological weaknesses:* Over and over again, careful examination of parapsychological experiments by a variety of experts has found serious errors in methodology and analysis. I have personally reviewed a large selection of parapsychological research studies and in every case found significant flaws that rendered the conclusions untenable.[20] I have found no evidence that suggests that paranormal phenomena actually exist.

7. *Reliance on statistical decision-making:* As noted earlier, statistical decisions do not point to specific explanations for departures from chance. Parapsychologists automatically assume these departures to be due to psychic influences, by there is no justification for making such inferences.

8. *Failure to fit with other areas of science:* Geology, medicine, biology, chemistry, neuroscience, physics—these widely diverse areas of scientific research all contribute to a unified understanding of how the world works. Findings in biology do not counter what is known in physics, nor do geologists produce evidence that makes no sense to chemists. However, if parapsychologists' claims are correct, then there is something fundamentally wrong with the knowledge accumulated in virtually all other areas of science.

Paranormal forces, unlike any other force or energy known to physics, apparently know no bounds. Mental telepathy and psychokinesis are said not to be affected by physical barriers and to work just as well and just as strongly whether over a distance of a few feet or thousands of miles, or even forward or backward in time. Donald Hebb, one of the founders of modern neuroscience, pointed out that:

> The external reasons for doubt in ESP lie in the fact that it would mean a revolution of natural science. The evidence is not that good. If it doesn't matter how far apart the two heads are when one brain radiates to the other (in telepathy), then there is something fundamentally wrong with physics; and if the second brain can sort out and make sense of such broadcast waves, there is something equally wrong with neurophysiology. Mistakes have been made in those fields before, maybe they're wrong again. But their practical successes make that unlikely.[21]

In fact, parapsychologists show virtually no interest in the contradictions between parapsychology and neuroscience.[22] Yet, as neuropsychologist Barry Beyerstein pointed out, there are profound implications if psychic forces are genuine.[23] Perception, memory, and emotion involve extremely complex neurochemical interactions resulting from the integration of the activities of millions of widely distributed neurons. The "perception" associated with ESP would occur without the requisite activity of specialized peripheral receptors and nerves, and the hypothetical psychic signal would somehow influence the internal chemical processes of millions of neurons, doing so in the correct sequence and following the appropriate anatomical pathways in order to produce an effect in consciousness. Neuroscientists view this as being highly unlikely.

9. *The specter of fraud*: Fraud raises its ugly head from time to time in every research discipline, but sooner or later it is uncovered when other researchers are unable to replicate the research. Because of the replication problem in parapsychology—the inability of neutral scientists to obtain the same results when repeating parapsychological experiments—fraud is more likely to escape detection. Even so, a number of important frauds in parapsychological research, some conducted by esteemed researchers considered beyond reproach,[24] have been uncovered by people within the field. This, too, contributes to the reasons for caution in the evaluation of parapsychological claims.

10. *Lack of interest in competing hypotheses:* While the focus should be on understanding anomalous experiences whatever their explanation might turn out to be, parapsychologists rarely show interest in what are likely to be "normal" explanations.

For all these reasons, parapsychology continues to lie outside mainstream science. It is primarily an exercise of belief in search of data rather than a genuine effort to understand anomalous experience.

BELIEF IN THE PARANORMAL

People in virtually every society exist in a state of contradiction, valuing and promoting reason while at the same time harboring strong transcendental beliefs that defy it. Despite the views of scientists, a majority of laypeople believe in paranormal phenomena, even though most have little knowledge or interest in the laboratory research of parapsychologists. A 2005 Gallup poll carried out in the United States reported that about three of every four Americans indicated belief in at least one form of paranormal phenomena, with ESP, endorsed by 41 percent, at the top of that list. A quarter of the respondents expressed belief in astrological influences on people's lives, while 26 percent believed in precognition and 32 percent believed that spirits of the dead can return.[25] Similarly, a survey of more than a thousand university students in New Zealand found that better than half expressed belief in telepathy, precognition, and life after death, while almost a third also expressed belief in astrology, astral projection, psychic healing, ghosts, and flying saucers.[26]

In my own research into belief in the paranormal among university students, members of the public, and university professors,[27] I found that approximately 80 percent of university students and members of the general public expressed belief in one or more paranormal phenomena, while only about 20 percent of university professors did so. With regard to the latter, paranormal belief was significantly higher among professors in the humanities than those in the social and natural sciences. Psychology professors were the most skeptical of all. This is consistent with research involving more than a thousand university professors in the United States that found social and natural scientists, and psychologists in particular, to be significantly more skeptical than humanities, education, and arts professors. The pronounced skepticism of psychologists reflects both their knowledge of psychological and neurological processes that can account for supposedly psychic experiences and their awareness of methodological and other problems in the parapsychological research literature.

WHY DO PEOPLE BELIEVE IN THE PARANORMAL?

We should not be surprised by the widespread belief in paranormal phenomena. After all, we have seen in earlier chapters that we are all born magical thinkers, and just about everyone is exposed to a transcendental belief system in childhood. There are many social and cultural influences that support belief in the paranormal, and most religions promote belief in an afterlife and, therefore, a belief in mind-body dualism. In addition, as is discussed in the next chapter, personal experience of seemingly inexplicable events is a major source of paranormal belief. Nowhere are children given any formal instruction about how anomalous, seemingly paranormal experiences can be produced by their own brains.

In addition, it has been observed both in pre-technological societies[28] and modern industrial states that superstition and belief in the paranormal increase during periods of social stress.[29] There were substantial increases in such belief, for example, in France toward the end of the *ancien régime*, which was brought to a halt by the French Revolution; in 1930s Germany; and in Russia and its satellites during the breakdown of the Soviet Union.

In modern times, ongoing political and rapid social, technological, and economic changes are producing pronounced uncertainty for many people. Some of the values acquired in childhood no longer seem to apply, and social rules that were once sacrosanct have been upended. Jobs that were once plentiful in some industries no longer exist. At the same time, rapid dissemination of competing ideas, beliefs, and values, no matter how weird, fallacious, or antisocial, has become simple and instantaneous thanks to the internet and social media.

This is not to suggest that such rapid social change leads directly to belief in the paranormal. Yet disordered times reflect a breakdown in the established social fabric, throwing many long-accepted ideas and authorities into question. Challenges to the old order abound, and science, which has been a dominant "authority" over the past century, is now confronted with suspicion and even rejection in some quarters. The erosion of confidence in science provides many opportunities for the development of irrational beliefs.

In addition to social upheaval, the past half-century has witnessed increasing levels of narcissistic individualism in western societies.[30] This promotes the belief that each individual is as competent as the next in evaluating reality and truth, regardless of training, experience, or knowledge, and suggests that intuition and personal experience are as important, or even more important, than rational inquiry. Add to this that even in the halls of academe, there are some who teach that all knowledge claims are of equal value—a scientist's, yours, mine—and that scientific knowledge is but one set of arbitrary beliefs. This encourages uncritical acceptance of paranormal and supernatural claims.

Yet believers and nonbelievers often grow up in similar environments, which raises the question of why some are drawn to belief in the paranormal while others are not. The single most common reason that people give for belief in the paranormal is their own personal experience.[31] This is no surprise. If you are startled by something that you take to be a ghost, it would not be surprising if you henceforth believe in ghosts. But what led you to assume that it was a ghost in the first place? It is the *interpretation* of experience that is important, for what is a phantom to one observer may be only a flash of diffuse light to another. A number of factors influence this interpretation.

Thinking style

People of similar intelligence, education, age, gender, and political ideology often end up with very different beliefs about the world, and this includes beliefs about the paranormal. Such belief is not related to intelligence or logic *per se*, but to the extent that a person is inclined to think intuitively rather than analytically.[32] Recall the discussion of the dual-process model of thinking involving intuitive (System 1) and intellectual (System 2) processing. Those who are more "intuitive" put more stock in their intuitions, while those who are more "analytical" rely on intellectual inquiry to vet them.[33] Belief in paranormal phenomena tends to be associated with an intuitive thinking style. Evidence for this association was found in a large study of university and vocational school students in Finland.[34]

Thinking style does not affect the likelihood of actually having an anomalous experience, but it does affect how that experience is interpreted.[35] Intuitive and analytic thinkers alike are struck by the strangeness of an uncanny event, but intuitive thinkers are more likely to consider a paranormal explanation, while analytic thinkers typically seek more mundane causes.[36] In addition, intuition-based paranormal beliefs are unlikely to respond to logical challenges, rendering them resistant to change.[37]

Distrust of science

Believers in the paranormal are rarely bothered that their intuitive faith in the reality of the paranormal is incompatible with modern scientific knowledge. For a significant segment of the population in the United States, this reflects the belief that the views of scientists cannot be relied upon, even to the extent that scientists' integrity is thrown into question. A US poll carried out in 2014 reported that only about 30 percent of respondents indicated that they trusted scientists to tell the truth "completely" or "a lot," and nearly a third trusted scientists "only a little" or "not at all."[38] It is supremely ironic that in an age when the products of science and technology are highly valued, and when the public wants scientists to hurry to find cures for cancer and Alzheimer's disease, science itself is devalued by many of the very people it serves.

Personal traits

In addition to differences in thinking style, personality factors also account for some of the differences between those who express belief in paranormal phenomena and those who do not. Some of these have been discussed in detail in earlier chapters:

1. *Fantasy proneness*: Those who believe in paranormal phenomena tend to be higher in measures of fantasy proneness.[39] People who present themselves as mediums or psychics are often fantasy-prone individuals,[40] and research has demonstrated an association between fantasy proneness and reports of out-of-body experiences.[41]
2. *Magical thinking:* People who report having had paranormal experiences tend to score higher in measures of magical thinking and are more likely to automatically attribute causality when two events occur one after the other.[42]
3. *Openness to experience* and *sensation seeking*: Those who believe in the paranormal score higher in terms these characteristics.[43] Openness to experience involves an active imagination, attentiveness to one's inner feelings, aesthetic sensitivity, and curiosity. Sensation-seeking promotes a search for experiences that are novel, complex, and stimulating.
4. *The search for meaning:* People vary in terms of how important it is to

find meaning in life. Whether based in reality or not, paranormal experiences and beliefs can provide meaningfulness and a sense of purpose in life.[44]

5. *Weakness in understanding probabilities*: When faced with ambiguity and uncertainty, we often fall back on cognitive heuristics, or "rules of thumb," in assessing the probability of events. Most people are demonstrably poor at estimating probability, but believers in the paranormal have been found to be particularly prone to errors and biases in probabilistic reasoning.[45] Other research suggests that those who believe in the paranormal tend to have a specific weakness with regard to the perception of randomness, making it difficult for them to appreciate the likelihood of chance events.[46]

6. *Memory distortion:* Our memories are all vulnerable to distortion, but some research suggests that believers in the paranormal may be more susceptible than non-believers to forming false memories surrounding events that they have interpreted as being paranormal.[47]

7. *Brain damage:* While there is no reason to think that believers and non-believers in the paranormal differ in terms of brain health, there is some evidence that brain dysfunction may play a role in the perception that one *personally* has psychic powers. For example, a study compared seventeen "sensitives" from the College of Psychic Studies in England with a matched set of seventeen controls.[48] It was found that the sensitives had more frequent histories of head injuries and serious illnesses, and two-thirds of them showed evidence of right temporal lobe dysfunction.

WE ARE ALL VULNERABLE

It is also important to remember that skeptics of paranormal phenomena who pride themselves on being rational and logical are nonetheless likely, like everyone else, to have pockets of irrationality. That is the human condition. Someone might be a skeptic with regard to paranormal claims and yet make irrational financial investments or enter confidently into marriage despite warnings from friends that the union is a bad idea. Ironically, someone else might believe in the paranormal and yet be more cautious and critical with regard to financial or romantic affairs. In other words, while people who believe in the paranormal may on average and in some respects differ from nonbelievers in terms of the factors discussed above, that does not mean that they are necessarily weaker in terms of general rational ability. A more appropriate judgment is that they give more weight to intuitive, nonanalytic interpretations of experience.

***

Despite the complete failure to provide persuasive scientific evidence for the existence of their subject matter, well-meaning parapsychologists continue in their quixotic quest to demonstrate the reality of paranormal phenomena that defy the materialistic model of the world described by modern science. This is belief in search of anomalous data rather than anomalous data in search of explanation.

Skeptical scientists continue to find fault with parapsychologists' methodology and data. Yet most of mainstream science actually pays little attention to parapsychology, both because its claimed phenomena make no sense in terms of what is known about how the world and the brain work, and because there is nothing in the data of science itself that calls out for a paranormal explanation. Meanwhile, largely on the basis of personal experience and intuition, much of the public maintains a deep-seated belief that paranormal phenomena are real, a belief that rarely succumbs to challenge.

CHAPTER 18

ILLUSORY EXPERIENCE

Thought, as a subtle juggler, makes us deem things supernatural
which have cause common as sickness.

—John Webster (1580–1634)[1]

Parapsychologists strive to demonstrate that psychic phenomena are genuine. "Ufologists" try to persuade us that we are being visited by unidentified flying objects (UFOs) piloted by intelligent beings from outer space. Astrologers argue that their horoscopes are based on the natural influence of the stars and planets on our bodies. Numerologists insist that numbers, including those corresponding to the letters in our names, define our futures. Alternative practitioners offer cures based on manipulations of energy fields.

And as we have seen, many people believe them. This has created a huge market for books, movies, and television programs that reflect and promote belief in the paranormal. The media and the public show scant interest in the fact that mainstream science finds no evidence to back up such beliefs.

Earlier chapters have examined the many vulnerabilities of the Belief Engine, and this knowledge alone should make us hesitate when tempted by a paranormal explanation for an anomalous experience. Just as when we wrongly convict someone of a crime, we make two errors when we erroneously attribute an experience to something paranormal. In the case of the crime, the wrong person is punished and then no one looks further for the real culprit, who goes free. Similarly, when a paranormal explanation is applied to a puzzling event, not only is the explanation almost certain to be wrong, but the search for the correct, natural explanation is abandoned.

Personal experience is a major source of belief in the paranormal. Although there is neither persuasive scientific evidence nor any good theoretical basis upon which to base belief in extrasensory perception, the *experience* of what *seems* to be ESP is a common one. Who among us has not encountered some sort of amazing coincidence that appears to defy normal explanation? Perhaps just as you were about to telephone someone with whom you have not spoken for ages, that person calls you first. Or perhaps you have had a strong feeling or dream that something unexpected was about to happen, and then to your surprise it soon occurs. However, remember the analogy with the Man behind the Curtain in the Wizard of Oz: such seemingly telepathic or precognitive experiences can be expected to occur from time to time simply as products of the way our brains work.[2] The various influences that contribute to these and other strange experiences such as déjà vu, the feeling that you are outside your body, or the sense that someone is staring at you are explored in this chapter.

EXTRASENSORY PERCEPTION

Recall that the term "extrasensory perception" (ESP) is applied to experiences that appear to involve direct knowledge either of what someone else is thinking (mental telepathy), of objects or events that one cannot perceive directly (clairvoyance), or of future events (precognition), all without need for the normal physical channels upon which perception normally relies. When people apply this label to strange experiences that they cannot explain, they are oblivious to the various normal influences that can give rise to what they take to be ESP experiences. These include the following.

Nonconscious cues

We are never conscious of all the information that our brains receive from the outside world, and when nonconscious information spills into consciousness, we have no ready explanation for its appearance—the Man behind the Curtain again. This can lead us to attribute it to ESP. For example, suppose that while visiting your elderly Aunt Jane, you did not *consciously* register that she was breathing with a little more difficulty than usual, that her color was off, and that she did not smile as much as in the past. Yet your brain picked up these cues at a nonconscious level, which triggered some slight anxiety that you interpreted as a feeling, a "hunch," that something might be wrong. Her death the following day turns the "feeling" into what seems to have been a powerful precognitive experience. Because of traditional child-rearing practices that have differentially encouraged girls to be attentive to other people's needs, women are often better than men at picking up such cues, albeit without awareness, and are generally superior in integrating various sources of information with regard to another person's emotional state.[3] This likely accounts for the popular belief in women's intuition, for, even though not conscious of these cues, women are more likely to interpret them as a "feeling." In other cases, we may fail to consciously attend to sensory information although it continues to have an influence at a non-conscious level. A personal example: Some years ago, while standing in a ticket queue at a cinema, I idly began thinking about someone from out of town whom I had met on only one occasion a few weeks earlier. A few minutes later, ticket in hand, I rounded a corner of the cinema and, to my astonishment, there he was! It seemed to be a startling coincidence. Out of curiosity, I returned to the ticket line, where it became immediately apparent that I could clearly hear his rather distinctive voice above the din. I had obviously heard him without being aware of it, and that had triggered my thoughts.

Common history

Being unaware of the triggers for our thoughts likely accounts for another common experience that strikes many people as paranormal, and that is when two people suddenly think at the same time of something or someone without any obvious reason for doing so. For example, suppose that a decade ago you and your partner holidayed in Jamaica for a week, and on the final evening you attended a beach party. There you met Harry, a portly, red-headed man from San Francisco. Harry had imbibed a little too much rum, which perhaps explains why he attempted to perform the limbo. Moving somewhat clumsily to the beat of loud reggae, he tipped over backward as he tried to dance his way under the limbo pole. Then, as he lay on his back like a large, beached turtle, people gathered round and joined him in laughter.

Now, ten years later, you and your partner are strolling down a city street. During a short pause in the conversation, Harry for some reason comes to your mind, and, just as you are about to mention him, your partner exclaims, "Do you remember that red-headed guy from San Francisco who we met in Jamaica?" You react with great surprise. Surely, this must be mental telepathy? What other explanation could there be?

It turns out that as you strolled down the street, you both failed to notice that the reggae music that Harry had danced to in Jamaica could be heard in the background, coming from a record store as you passed by. Although neither of you consciously took note of the music, your brains did, and because of your common history, the music triggered similar chains of thought in each of you that led directly to Harry. No need for telepathy here.

Narrowing of the timeframe

Sometimes, an event that seems to be a very unlikely coincidence is not nearly so unlikely as it appears. Consider this example: A friend recounted an astonishing coincidence that she suggested might have involved ESP. She was about to telephone a friend in another city, someone with whom she had not spoken for several weeks, and just as she was reaching for the telephone, it rang—and it was her friend! ESP? Or remarkable coincidence? Or was there more to the story? With a little prompting, she reported that her friend was to leave the following day on an extended trip to Europe, and that when they had last spoken, they had agreed to be in touch before her departure. Further information: On past occasions when either telephoned, it was usually just before suppertime, in order to catch the other at home but not yet at dinner. And when did this remarkable coincidence occur? Just before suppertime. So, rather than a "temporal space" of several weeks when either might have called, the call occurred just before suppertime on the last day before the friend's trip. This of course reduces the "coincidence" from something remarkable to something not surprising at all.

Anxiety

Anxiety often promotes contemplation of negative events or even catastrophe. We may not always be aware of the cause of the anxiety, but it is not surprising that at times it corresponds to subsequent events. Consider a mother whose son has embarked on a months-long hitchhiking trip in South America. He texts her every so often, typically once every three to five days, although she does not keep track of the frequency. Now, six days have gone by, and although she reminds herself that there is nothing to worry about because it has often been quite some time between messages in the past, she has difficulty suppressing the strong feeling, the hunch, that he has come to harm. A day or two later, he texts to inform her that he had been attacked, and, although he was not injured, his phone had been stolen leaving him unable to contact her before now. She makes an immediate connection between the attack and her hunch and assumes that telepathy was involved. A more likely explanation is that as time wore on without hearing from him, she was becoming more and more anxious despite reassuring herself that there was nothing to worry about, and that this anxiety was the basis for her "hunch." The passage of time since his last call was both responsible for her anxiety and the result of the problem that her son had encountered. Despite appearances, again there is nothing paranormal here.

PRECOGNITIVE DREAMS

Subtle influences can also feed into our dreams, making them at times appear to be precognitive. Such dreams hold a particular fascination for many people. For example, in early April 1865, Abraham Lincoln told his friend and biographer Ward Lamon about a powerful dream in which he experienced a "death-like stillness" in his body and heard crying and sobbing outside his room. He got up to see what was going on and found people dressed in funeral garments gathered around a corpse. When he asked who had died, he was informed that this was the body of the president, who had been assassinated. Two weeks later, he was shot dead by John Wilkes Booth. Coincidence? Precognition? Or simply an unverified anecdote?

Lincoln had much to be anxious about at that time, for he had received many death threats while in office, and an assassination plot had been uncovered just prior to his inauguration. In addition, on one occasion an assassin shot at him and missed, leaving a hole in his top hat. Given this context, a dream relating to his own death is perhaps not particularly surprising.

There are a number of other factors that can also play a particular role in reports of precognitive dreams.

Selective memory

Suppose that you dream of being in a serious car accident. Unless you actually have a car accident in the days that follow, the dream will almost certainly be forgotten, for we usually remember only the "hits."[4] Suppose as well that you have had a number of similar dreams over the course of a few years, again none of which were followed by car accidents. All have been forgotten. Finally, you have a dream of a car accident and a day later someone runs into your vehicle. This dream stands out as extraordinary given that you do not recall any of the previous similar dreams. It therefore appears to have been precognitive, and you may remember it all your life. Had you been able to remember the earlier dreams, this one would probably not have seemed so special, and you may have attributed it to simple coincidence.

Going back to Lincoln's dream, one wonders whether he had had similar dreams of assassination that were subsequently forgotten when they did not connect with subsequent events.

Memory distortion

Research shows that we often misremember dreams (as we do other events as well) in ways that make them seem to correspond more closely to what we have recently experienced.[6] Consider my experience over the years with several students who reported frequent precognitive dreams. In each case, I asked the student to begin making notes of each dream immediately upon awakening, and also to make notes about the details of any subsequent events that seemed to match the dream. In all cases, the students subsequently informed me that their precognitive dreaming had stopped. My assumption is that prior to keeping records, the students were either misremembering their dreams in such a way that they seemed to correspond to subsequent experiences, or they were interpreting their subsequent experiences in such a way as to make them match their dreams, just as people do with the cold readings, discussed earlier. Keeping records eliminated the misremembering.

Did Ward Lamon remember correctly what President Lincoln had said? Had he made notes of it at the time? Or did the telling of the dream come to mind only in the aftermath of Lincoln's assassination, at which time he unwittingly reconstructed it in his memory in a way that made it seem more prescient than it actually was? Of course, we shall never know.

Hypnopompic imagery

Hypnopompic imagery, which is a blend of imagery and perception that occurs at times as a person is waking up, is another source of what can seem to be precognitive dreams. Such imagery often relates to anticipations about the day to come, and these anticipations occasionally coincide with subsequent events.[5]

Multiple endpoints

If you dream about a fire truck smashing into a pizza parlor, *multiple endpoints* (a term used by conjurers to describe how a given trick can be ended success-fully in various ways) can provide spurious fulfilment of the dream. A driver who loses control of his vehicle and runs into a house, a fire truck involved in a road accident, a pizza parlor that catches fire, a truck that runs into your parked car . . . there are so many possibilities that could correspond to some extent to the dream. If one looks for it, one can usually find a way of linking a dream to some subsequent event, and it is interesting to note that people who frequently report supposedly precognitive dreams are also more prone to find linkages between unrelated events in general.[7]

Confusing the timeline

Sometimes, as people reconstruct memories of their experiences, a dream that occurred *after* an event is subsequently remembered as having occurred *before* it, leaving the impression that the dream was "precognitive." Similarly, a person may dream twice about an event, first before and then again after, and later mix up the order of the two dreams so that the latter dream is remembered as having predicted the event. For example, a day or so after receiving an email from friend Veronica who is holidaying in Vietnam, she shows up in a rather ordinary dream. A few days later, news is received that she was killed in a traffic accident, and this triggers another dream, this time involving Veronica's death. Weeks or months or years later, the dream about her death is erroneously recalled as having pre-ceded rather than followed the sad news of her demise.

Dreams and emotion

Particularly vivid dreams or nightmares can overwhelm a person with the feeling that the dream must portend something important. A graduate-school friend of mine, who was strongly skeptical about claims of paranormal phenomena such as precognitive dreams, came to the university one morning shaken by what he described as having been a powerfully vivid dream the night before. In the dream, his favorite uncle had died, and he told me that even though he did not believe that precognition is a real phenomenon, he would have great dif-ficulty in maintaining this disbelief were his uncle to die anytime soon. Each time his telephone rang over the next few days, he half expected to hear that his uncle had passed away. However, his uncle lived on for many more years, fortunate both for the uncle and for my friend's skepticism. There is an important moral to this story: Even the beliefs of ardent skeptics can dissolve into magical thinking when confronted by emotion-laden events that seem to defy normal explanation.

Dreams and meaningfulness

Sometimes the content of dreams can be so emotionally striking that it seems powerfully meaningful, even though the actual meaning may be unclear. Consider this example provided by psychologist Loren Pankratz regarding the experience of a family member.

During a dark period of her life, a woman dreamed that she was drifting on a small boat without means of control. A dock came into view with the strange word *Caritas* painted on its side, and people on the dock then reached out and brought her safely to shore. When she awoke from the dream, she was puzzled by *Caritas*, for she had no memory of ever having encountered it before, and did not even know if it was a real word. Her efforts to find an explanation for it yielded nothing (this was in the days before the internet). Curiosity about *Caritas* stayed in her thoughts until several years later, after taking employment with a Catholic health service, she was startled to encounter it again, this time on the masthead of a religious newsletter. The Sisters with whom she worked explained that it is part of *Caritas Cristi Urget Nos*—"The love of Christ impels us"—and they took its appearance in her dream to be a divine sign. This added even more meaning and mystery: How did this Latin word associated with the love of Christ show up on the side of the rescue dock in her dream many years earlier? It seemed inexplicable, but she decided to treat it as some sort of strange coincidence. Yet it is quite a stretch to imagine that a Latin word, correctly spelled, would show up in someone's dream by chance alone.

She is certain that her memory of the dream is accurate and, despite the earlier discussion about the vagaries of memory, let us assume that that is so and not attribute the mystery to a misremembered dream. While it is not possible to say just how this event, now long in the past, occurred, there is a possible, and even likely, explanation.

Most dream content relates to experiences and thoughts and worries of the preceding day, and given that she was going through a very difficult time, the rescue theme of her dream is no surprise. It is quite possible that she had recently encountered the word *Caritas* prior to the dream without being aware of having done so, perhaps while flipping through a magazine or newspaper. If that were so, then dreaming about it would not be unusual. And this is not a far-fetched suggestion, for the word is actually rather widely used. A quick internet search turns up many listings of *Caritas* in association with a wide variety of organizations. For example, *Caritas Cristi Urget Nos* is the motto of a Roman Catholic religious order that operates the Alexian Brothers Health System, now part of Ascension Health, which is the largest Catholic nonprofit health system in United States. And while one obviously cannot say with certainty that this is the explanation, we can be sure that many people will experience dream content reflecting information taken in without awareness, and, depending on that content, it too may leave the dreamer with a mysterious and meaningful experience.

Self-fulfilling prophecy

Dreams that seem to be precognitive may at times bring about their own fulfilment. For example, if you dream about being in a car accident, this may make you a bit more nervous the next time you drive, which might leave you more vulnerable to making an error and having an accident.

Hidden causes

Some correspondences between dreams and subsequent events may have hidden causes of which the individual will never be aware,[8] similar to the influence of the reggae music on the couple that holidayed in Jamaica, or the dream of *Caritas*. For example, suppose that your neighbor in the next apartment is watching a television news report of an airplane crash while you are sleeping. The walls are thin, and enough information about the air crash seeps into your brain to trigger a dream about an airplane crash. You wake in the morning with the dream on your mind, only to be shocked by your "precognition" when you turn on the news.

Coincidence

And, of course, "amazing" coincidences do happen and are just coincidences. Considering the huge number of discrete events in anyone's lifetime, it is highly likely that seemingly important coincidences, including those that present as apparent precognitive dreams, will occur from time to time by pure chance. It is not unlikely that with all the billions of people in the world, a number of them will dream about a disaster such as an airplane accident on any given night. Sooner or later an airplane will crash, and those people who happened to have had that dream that night may be overwhelmed emotionally by what seems to them to have been something paranormal.

STARING

Have you ever had the feeling that someone is staring at you from behind? This is a common experience, and researchers have found that *most* adults believe that they can sense the unseen stare of another person.[9] This would not have been a surprise to ancient philosophers such as Empedocles (493–433 BCE) and Plato (427–347 BCE), both of whom considered the eyes to be like a lantern, emitting rays that interact with external objects, thereby allowing them to be seen. This belief was shared centuries later even by such intellectual giants as the mathematician Euclid (ca. 300 BCE) and the astronomer and mathematician Ptolemy (100–170 CE). If rays leave the eyes, it stands to reason that people should be able, at least at times, to detect when someone is staring at them.

While ancient philosophers such as Democritus (ca. 420 BCE) and Aristotle (384–322 BCE) rejected this *extramission* explanation and instead stressed *intromission*, the notion that something comes *into* the eyes during visual perception, it was only in the Middle Ages that Alhazen (965–1040 CE), an Arab natural philosopher, finally demolished the arguments for extramission. He constructed a new theory suggesting that an optical image is formed when light enters the eye, similar to the image produced by a pinhole camera. This theory ultimately culminated in modern visual science.[10]

One might think that would be the end of it, that no modern person would give any credence to extramission, but that is not the case. Surprisingly, a series of contemporary studies in the United States has also found evidence of strong belief in extramission among both children and adults.[11] In one study, researchers simply asked whether anything leaves the eyes during vision, and 49 percent of first graders, 70 percent of third graders, 51 percent of fifth graders, and 33 percent of college students replied in the affirmative.[12]

Belief in the evil eye, the notion that something leaves the eyes of certain people that can cause disease or death to those upon whom the gaze falls, is another manifestation of belief in extramission still commonly held in some cultures. A Pew Research study in 2012 reported that such belief remains high in many Muslim communities in the Middle East and North Africa. For example, more than 90 percent of Tunisian Muslims and 80 percent of Moroccan Muslims expressed belief in the evil eye.[13]

The best-known modern Western proponent of a kind of extramission theory is British biologist/parapsychologist Rupert Sheldrake. He proposes a radical "new" theory of perception, according to which the visual images that we perceive are not located in our brains, but are "out there." That is, while vision is triggered by light entering the eyes, actual perception involves the projection *outward* of a mental image of the object. Because this mental image normally coincides with the object being seen, we do not see a double image, but, during hallucinations, only the projected image is observed. It is the projection of these images, Sheldrake argues, that results in people being able to feel when they are being stared at. His own extensive empirical research leads him to conclude that people can, more often than expected by chance, identify when someone is staring at them.[14] However, because of failures by others to replicate his findings, combined with the contradiction between his theory and modern understanding of vision, his research has had no impact on visual science.[15]

SENSE OF PRESENCE

Just as many people think that they can tell when someone behind their backs is staring at them, people also sometimes experience a strong feeling of being watched even when there is no one else around. This most often happens when in vulnerable circumstances, such as when alone at night in strange surroundings. The failure to identify a reason for the feeling increases the anxiety, and in some cases leads a person to think that there must be a ghost in the vicinity. And, of course, being in a specific locale associated with legends of ghostly hauntings often increases such anxiety and facilitates feelings of a sensed presence. Imagine walking through a graveyard on a dark night, where echoes or gusts of wind may intensify one's unease.

A more infrequent sense of presence is that of the *doppelgänger* (German for "double-goer"). This is a hallucinatory experience that involves a sense of presence of *oneself*. The doppelgänger is typically life-sized and semi-transparent, although the individual most often perceives only the head and trunk, and it mirrors the person's expressions and movements. It is typically observed only at dawn or late at night and then only for a few seconds. There have been references to such phantom doubles in mythology and occult literature going far back into antiquity. In German folklore, being "visited" by one's doppelgänger is taken to be a harbinger of imminent death.

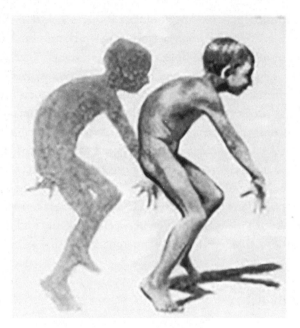

Figure 18-1: Doppelgänger.

An even more sensational version of the sensed presence experience is the *Third Man*. The term is taken from a biblical story in which two disciples, while walking on the road to Emmaus, come to believe that they are being accompanied by a resurrected Jesus.[16] Third Man experiences typically occur in times of significant stress or danger, and at such a time, an inexplicable presence is described as suddenly appearing and taking charge of the situation, rescuing the individual from impending doom.

Joshua Slocum, the first man to sail solo around the world, reported that while he was incapacitated by food poisoning, such a "presence" took the tiller and sailed his ship to safety through a forty-eight-hour gale.[17] Sir Ernest Shackleton, the famed Antarctic explorer, made a similar report. He and two crew members had set off on foot from their icebound ship with the hope of reaching a whaling station. Their quest seemed doomed to failure and they faced almost certain death, but thirty-six hours later they had reached their goal. Shackleton subsequently revealed that he had felt that there was a "fourth man" accompanying them, a person whose presence offered a sense of relief, comfort, and hope.[18] There have been many other such accounts from people of extraordinary courage—mountaineers, explorers, and astronauts—who were faced with overwhelming fear for their survival.

As powerful as these doppelgänger and Third Man experiences are, there is no reason to think that they are anything other than hallucinatory products of brains under stress. Indeed, we know that the brain has the capacity to generate such experiences, for they can be elicited by electrically stimulating particular cerebral areas.[19] In one study, the stimulation of a region of the left hemisphere (left temporoparietal junction) of a woman undergoing evaluation for surgical treatment of epilepsy led to her report of a "creepy" feeling that a shadowy person was nearby.[20] The stranger neither spoke nor moved, and was described as being young, of indeterminate sex, and like a "shadow." With further electrical stimulation, she identified the shadow as a man. At one point, she felt that he was clasping her in his arms, which she found unpleasant, and at another time she said that he was trying to prevent her from looking at a card that one of the attendants had given her to read. The movements of this illusory shadow mimicked her own movements (just as doppelgängers do), and although she could recognize that correspondence of movements, she did not recognize that the shadow was actually an illusion of her own body.

Not only are our brains capable of creating the feeling of being stared at, the appearance of a doppelgänger, and the feeling of relief and comfort of a "Third Man," they can also create another sensational experience, that of being outside one's body altogether.

OUT-OF-BODY EXPERIENCE

In some circumstances, people report feeling as if they have left their bodies and are looking down on themselves from above. This is the *out-of-body experience* (OBE). It is as though mind and brain are separate, and the mind, without need for any of the complex machinery of the brain and nervous system, is able to perceive, remember, think, and even travel about. To psychologists and neuroscientists, such experiences are clearly illusory, but most parapsychologists consider such experiences to be genuine paranormal events. However, not all do. For example, John Palmer, a leading parapsychologist, in agreement with neuroscientists and psychologists, states that:

> The OBE is neither potentially nor actually a psychic phenomenon. It is an experience or mental state like a dream or any other altered state of consciousness.[21]

How does the experience come about? In order to make sense of it, we should begin with another question: How is it that you feel that you are *in* your body? As psychologist Susan Blackmore has described, our brains are constantly constructing and maintaining a stable image of the world around us and of our place in it.[22] Our physical bodies and our consciously experienced selves usually overlap very nicely, thanks to our body maps. This alignment can be disrupted in some situations, such as when one is under pronounced stress or under the effects of certain drugs, or suffering from oxygen deprivation. Maintaining a stable model is not easy in such circumstances. (Recall, as well, that sleep paralysis involves hallucinatory experiences that also can lead to a feeling of being outside one's body and floating above it.)[23]

Imagine yourself lying on a hospital gurney following a serious automobile accident. Your eyes are closed, but you can still hear what is going on around you. You might be undergoing surgery, and it should be noted that people sometimes recall what was said around them even while under anesthesia, particularly when anesthetics are used that do not prevent sensory information from reaching the brain. Your confused brain does its best to figure out what is going on and where you are. Your eyes are closed and you cannot feel your body, and so it needs to rely on hearing and on its memory of hospital settings. It then constructs an image of you lying on the gurney and, as in many memory images, you "see" the scene from a bird's-eye view. As a result, it seems as if you are above your body looking down at it. This is not reality, but it is the best *model* of reality that your brain can construct under the circumstances.

The same kind of experience can be produced by stimulation of particular regions of the brain. In one case, electrical stimulation of a specific brain region (the right angular gyrus) of a patient being evaluated for epilepsy treatment led to the patient's report of an out-of-body experience in which she viewed her body from above.[24]

The sense of disembodiment that is central to the OBE involves a breakdown of normal activity in the temporoparietal junction, where visual, tactile, proprioceptive (positional), and vestibular (balance) information are combined to form our body image.[25] In line with this, it was discovered that a number of patients who had reported out-of-body experiences were determined to have suffered damage in this region.[26]

The illusion of being outside one's body has been created experimentally by having a seated participant wear a head-mounted video display.[27] Two video cameras were placed side by side behind the participant's chair, and the picture from the left camera was projected to the participant's left eye via the head-mounted device, and that from the right camera went to the right eye. As a result, the participant was presented with two slightly different images, providing depth perception. What the participant observed was what he would see if seated two meters behind himself. The researcher, Henrik Ehrsson, stood beside the cameras, so that, in the participant's view, he appeared to be standing beside him, and then used a plastic rod to touch the participant's chest (which the participant could not see because of the head-mounted video display). Using a second plastic rod which he moved just below the cameras, he simultaneously touched the chest of the "illusory body."

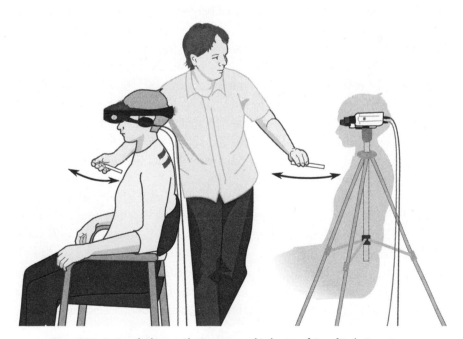

Figure 18-2: H. Henrik Ehrsson, The Experimental Induction of Out-of-Body Experiences (illustration by Annika Röhl, © Henrik Ehrsson).

Suppose you are the participant. What you see in your video headset is someone sitting two meters ahead of you, and that person appears to be you! Yet, at the same time, because of what you see, you feel as though you are sitting two meters farther back (where the cameras are). Now, you see the researcher move a rod toward a location beneath the cameras (actually, empty space) to what would be your chest if your eyes were actually where they seem to be, and at that moment you feel the touch of the rod against your chest (figure 18-2).

Participants reported that they felt as though they actually had been outside of their bodies, sitting behind themselves and observing themselves. They reacted physiologically (as measured by skin-conductance response, reflecting emotional arousal) when the illusory body (the empty space beneath the camera) was struck with a hammer.

There are two key components to this illusion of being outside one's body and observing it from a distance. First, visual information (from the video headset) provides information about where one is located in the environment, and second, the correlated visual and tactile perceptions of the illusory body (seeing the rod approach the illusory body and then feeling its touch) reinforce the perception that one is actually located behind one's body. This demonstrates the relative ease with which the usual sense of being in one's body, which is the basis for being conscious of oneself, can be derailed.

Body-swap illusion: In another study using similar procedures, participants came to view a mannequin's body as if it were their own. The effect was achieved as they watched the mannequin being touched at the same time that they felt corresponding tactile stimulation applied to their own bodies.[28] Follow-up studies using this technique also led participants to report feeling physically separated from their bodies and to state that their bodies no longer felt as though they were part of themselves.[29]

The out-of-body illusion and the body-swap illusion, along with the *rubber-hand illusion* (discussed in chapter 10), remind us that our brains compute where we are in space by combining visual, proprioceptive, and tactile information. Through the contrivance of these experiments, the participants' brains were tricked into the impression that they were outside their bodies. Given that our brains are capable of producing such experiences through these simple procedures, we should not be surprised that they occur spontaneously at times.

NEAR-DEATH EXPERIENCES

The out-of-body experience is a central component of the so-called *near-death experience* (NDE) in which resuscitated individuals report that while they were dying they had remained conscious and had experienced a transition toward an afterlife in which, among other things, they were briefly reunited with deceased relatives. Although not frequent, neither are these reports uncommon, and they have been described in literature across the centuries going back to that of the ancient Greeks.[30] In the United States, approximately three percent of the population reports having had such an experience,[31] and in Holland 18 percent of several hundred successfully resuscitated cardiac-arrest patients reported that they too had experienced an NDE.[32] It is not surprising that such reports especially appeal to people who have abandoned their religious beliefs yet yearn for the promise of living on after death.

It was with the 1975 publication of psychiatrist Raymond Moody's bestseller *Life after Life* that the near-death experience became part of common culture.[33] Moody described several elements that he said make up the prototypical near-death experience. According to Moody's description, the dying person hears an unpleasant, loud ringing or buzzing sound and then floats outside her body and views it from above, observing family members and medical personnel gathered round the deathbed. Next, the individual is drawn quickly down a long tunnel toward a bright light, which turns out to be a "Being of Light." Waiting at the end of the tunnel are friends and relatives who have predeceased the individual. The Being of Light helps the person to quickly review the events of the life just passed ("panoramic review"), and this is accompanied by overwhelming feelings of peace, joy, and infinite knowledge. Then some sort of barrier is encountered, and the individual is reluctantly pulled back to her physical body. The experience is powerful, even transformational, and survivors often report that they no longer fear death, for they now "know what it is like."[34]

However, other NDE researchers have reported NDEs that vary considerably from the popular portrayal provided by Moody. Psychologist Kenneth Ring, who believes in the supernatural nature of NDEs, has pointed out that these experiences are not as homogeneous as Moody has claimed, and that important elements such as hearing a loud buzzing or ringing, being drawn down a tunnel, approaching a Being of Light, or approaching a boundary were infrequent or absent in the accounts that he studied. Indeed, *none* of Ring's respondents reported encountering a Being of Light.[35] Other researchers have also pointed to the varying content of NDE reports, which does not mesh with the generality of Moody's description. For example, children who report near-death experiences sometimes recall having met their living schoolmates and teachers, or even cartoon characters.[36] And not all such reported experiences are pleasant ones, for according to cardiologist Maurice Rawlings, a Fundamentalist Christian, many near-death experiences involve what seem to be visits to hell.[37]

However, most psychologists and neuroscientists reject the notion that consciousness lives on after death and instead view these reports as the inventions of a disordered brain. Just as our brains can generate strange sensations of being outside our body, or emotionally overwhelming mystical experiences, or powerful, realistic nightmares and hallucinations, so too, it is reasoned, can they produce these "near-death" reveries that upon resuscitation are interpreted as visits to the door of an afterlife.[38] They also point out that, from a medical point of view, these resuscitated individuals had never actually died.

These two interpretations of the experience—quasi-religious, postmortem survival and reverie in a disordered brain—are captured in the contrasting reports of two neurologists' personal NDEs. First, consider the account of neurosurgeon Dr. Eben Alexander, who states that prior to his own powerful NDE experience he had viewed near-death experiences as nothing other than the manifestation of biochemical processes within a disturbed brain.[39] He describes how his belief changed dramatically when he contracted bacterial meningitis in 2008 and went into a deep coma for seven days. When he emerged from the coma, he reported that although his brain had been nearly dead, his mind had remained alive and alert and he had experienced wondrous things. Abandoning all scientific rigor, he took his experience at face value, and in an article in *Newsweek* entitled "Proof of Heaven: A Doctor's Experience with the Afterlife," he wrote:

> There is no scientific explanation for the fact that while my body lay in a coma, my mind—my conscious, inner self—was alive and well. While the neurons of my cortex were stunned to complete inactivity by the bacteria that had attacked them, my brain-free consciousness journeyed to another, larger dimension of the universe: a dimension I'd never dreamed existed and which the old, pre-coma me would have been more than happy to explain was a simple impossibility.[40]

After this powerful epiphany, he went on to write that his experience had taught him about "the unconditional love that I now know God and the universe have toward us."[41]

Although Alexander's account has been well-publicized and carries considerable influence because of his profession, there appears to be more to the story than his jettisoning of scientific objectivity. An investigative journalist challenged his account of what actually occurred, stating that although he claimed to have been in a coma with no higher brain activity, a doctor who cared for him indicated that he had actually been conscious, though hallucinating.[42] Whatever the case, Alexander has cavalierly dismissed neuroscience and concluded that he had been in the presence of God.

Neurologist Ernst Rodin described his own experience that occurred while undergoing exploratory cancer surgery.[43] He reported being overwhelmed by one of the most intense and happy experiences of his entire life, and added that he was absolutely certain at the time that he had died and was free of his body. When he awoke and found himself in the recovery room, he expressed strong resentment at having been brought back from his blissful state of apparent death. Yet his subsequent professional interpretation of this experience is quite different from that of Dr. Alexander. He considered it to have been a powerful delusion triggered by anesthesia combined with his anxiety about the possibility of dying from cancer.

Rodin went on to explain that unless death is instantaneous, such as from a bullet to the brainstem, the final pathway to death involves anoxia—a loss of oxygen supply. As the oxygen supply diminishes, this produces an increased feeling of well-being and sense of power, while at the same time triggering a loss of critical judgment. Fantasy is mistaken for reality, and, ultimately, delusions and hallucinations rule the experience until the individual is completely unconscious. He went on to say that were he to have such an experience again while actually dying, he would almost certainly again mistake the hallucinatory experience for reality because of the inability to critically evaluate his situation due to the gradual shutting down of his brain.

Research problems

Although a few dedicated researchers have made efforts to find scientific support for the supernatural explanation of the NDE, this quest is fraught with methodological difficulties. First of all, one is dealing only with subjective reports of people's experiences; there is no objective way to assess their accuracy. As Dr. Rodin points out, fantasy can easily be mistaken for reality, especially when higher cognitive functions are impaired because of physical compromise. And then there is the problem of memory. Every such report is only a memory of what was apparently experienced—and we have already explored the vulnerabilities of memory. Even more problematic, most of the reports and books written about near-death experiences rely on accounts that are many years old, throwing the reliability of the memories even more into question. Oftentimes, such accounts have been gathered in response to newspaper advertisements seeking people who have had such experiences, and so their memories may be distorted not only by the passage of time but also by the descriptions of NDEs presented by books and movies. Through imagination inflation, simply imagining an event, even though it never happened, can result in what seem to be actual memories of the event. Perhaps this accounts for psychologist Christopher French's finding that a significant number of people who had not reported having had an NDE immediately after resuscitation from cardiac arrest inexplicably "remembered" having had one when asked two years later.[44]

Reverie in a disordered brain

There is simply no reasonable evidence that NDEs are anything other than products of a distressed brain.[45] Although proponents of the supernatural explanation for NDEs vigorously disagree, such experiences are best understood in terms of misleading models of reality constructed by a brain when its normal functioning has gone awry. Furthermore, in light of the overwhelming evidence that our experience of mind results from the neuronal activity of the brain, the notion that we have a mind that can leave our brain behind and yet maintain all the functions that the brain serves, including vision, hearing, touch, and so on, makes no sense to begin with. This is a contradiction that those who believe in postmortem survival cannot explain away.[46]

There are a number of physical influences that can contribute to NDEs, including the effects of lack of oxygen (anoxia), heightened levels of carbon dioxide (hypercarbia), secretion of endorphins, and abnormal temporal-lobe activity.[47] For example, carbon dioxide inhalation can trigger hallucinations and, because of impaired circulation and respiration, people suffering from cardiac arrest are subject to increases in carbon dioxide levels in the bloodstream. A study carried out in Slovenia compared carbon dioxide levels in resuscitated cardiac-arrest patients who had reported NDEs with those who had not.[48] The levels in patients who had reported NDEs were significantly higher.

Other researchers have described how some features of the NDE might come about. For example, the experience of being drawn down a tunnel into the light fits with what is known about the physiology of the visual system.[49] The retina is packed with receptor cells at the center, but the density of cells drops off significantly toward the periphery. If these cells begin firing at random, as can occur when extreme physical compromise results in decreased oxygen supply to the eyes, the great number of cells firing at the center will produce the perception of a bright light, a light that appears to fade toward the edges of the retinal circle, and this will produce a tunnel effect.[50] (This kind of visual tunnel can also result from extreme fear itself, and both anoxia and fear are common when near death.) In addition, studies of cannabis, mescaline, and LSD intoxication have reported frequent accounts of the perception of a bright light that creates a tunnel-like perspective.[51] It is clear, then, that the brain is fully capable of experiencing such a light and tunnel without need of anything supernatural.

Reports of blissful feelings may simply arise from activation of dopamine and opioid brain systems, which come into play under situations of trauma and fear.[52] As for reported encounters with the dead, many scientific studies have demonstrated that brain pathology—in Parkinson's disease, for example—also can lead to such visions.[53]

Drug-induced hallucinations

Psychologist Ronald Siegel reports great similarity between NDEs and drug-induced hallucinations. Religious images are very common in the latter, as are, as noted above, reports of a bright light in the center of the visual field creating a tunnel-like perspective.[54] Such hallucinations also commonly involve seeing oneself from above as well as vivid recollections of childhood experiences in what seems to be a panoramic review. (Panoramic review of one's life history can also be elicited by stimulation of a certain part of the brain during surgery.)[55] The strong similarity between these reports and Moody's description of near-death experiences again points to underlying mechanisms in the central nervous system as the source of what Siegel describes as "a universal phenomenology of hallucinations."[56]

Psychiatrist Karl Jansen has described how all of the classic features of the near-death experience can be produced by injecting a normal, healthy person with between fifty and one hundred milligrams of the anesthetic ketamine. The ketamine molecule binds to receptors in parts of the cerebral cortex associated with memory, cognition, and perception, sites that also play a role in psychosis and epilepsy.[57] This suggests that ketamine is stimulating those same parts of the brain that are activated when someone is spontaneously experiencing an NDE.

Other substances in the brain, such as glutamate, also bind to the same receptor sites as ketamine. It is interesting to note that some of the conditions that can trigger a near-death experience, such as anoxia, temporal-lobe epilepsy, and hyperglycemia, are associated with the flood of glutamate that overwhelms those receptor sites. Jansen suggests that the conditions that lead to a flood of glutamate may, just as with ketamine, result in an altered state of consciousness that mimics a near-death experience.[58]

Such processes may occur naturally, and similar responses are evoked in situations of extreme danger. For example, dopamine and opioid systems become active when an animal is under predatory attack. Thus, these endogenous systems come into play during highly traumatic events and have likely evolved to aid in the survival of the organism.[59]

Jansen's suggestion that highly traumatic or dangerous events might lead to NDE-type experiences is borne out in the psychological literature. There are many reports of NDEs experienced by patients suffering from serious medical complications but who were not near death.[60] In one study, well over half the patients who reported near-death experiences had not been near death, even though most of them considered later on that they had been.[61] It was the *belief* that they were close to death that appeared to be the primary catalyst for the experience. To make sense of their seeming encounter with the afterlife, some came to believe that they had actually died.

Over a century ago, Albert Heim collected reports of more than thirty people who had survived serious falls in the mountains.[62] He reported that they recalled having experienced a total absence of anxiety or pain, a rapid review of their entire lives, and a feeling of being immersed in beautiful music and tumbling into a blue heaven studded with rosy cloudlets. In another study, of 104 people who had survived extreme danger, a number of elements similar to those in the NDE were also reported: a sense of detachment from the physical body, the panoramic review of one's life, a sense of harmony, feelings of joy, an apparent slowing of time, and speeding up of mental activity. It was only those people who had experienced some degree of cerebral dysfunction as a result of near-drowning or serious illness to whom mystical aspects of the experience occurred; such aspects were not found in the case of falls or automobile accidents not involving head injuries.[63]

It is not surprising that people who experience a near-death experience are emotionally moved by it. When we awaken from a vivid dream or nightmare, we immediately reassure ourselves that it is "only a dream." This reflects our child-hood training in which our parents quickly reassured us when we woke up in fear from a nightmare that it was only our imaginations at play. We have had no such training with regard to NDEs, and this reflects the lack of a cultural history with regard to such experiences. It was not until recently, with the advent of medical lifesaving measures that often bring people back from the brink of death, that NDEs became relatively common.

For many, the scientific description that views death as the demise of tissue and the extinction of consciousness cannot compete with the soothing belief in a joyous afterlife in which the spirit, endowed with all the capacities of the living physical brain, triumphs over the decay of the flesh.[64]

DÉJÀ VU

Imagine that you are on your first trip to England. After flying to London, you have rented a car and driven down to Canterbury Cathedral. It is early morning and the church is all but empty. As you wander over the time-worn stone floor, you are struck by the beauty of the colored shadows cast before your feet by the sunlight streaming through the glorious stained-glass windows. Somewhere, a children's choir is at practice, and their ethereal voices add to the solemnity of the place. You come upon the plaque that marks the spot where Thomas Becket was assassinated on December 29, 1170, and it is at this point that you are sud-denly overcome by a powerful feeling of recognition, of familiarity, as though you have been here before.

This is *déjà vu* ("already seen"). What is so bewildering is the obvious con-trast between feeling ("I've been here before") and cognition ("I know that I have not"). The emotional impact often pushes people to seek an explanation and, for some, the answer lies in precognition. They assume that their brains had precognitively acquired information that now makes the spot seem so familiar. Others take the experience to suggest reincarnation and "memory" based on the experience of an earlier lifetime.

Déjà vu was a subject of deliberation even in antiquity. Plato, Aristotle, and

Pythagoras all attributed it to reincarnation, but with the ascendancy of Christian theology in Europe, reincarnation became theologically and philosophically unacceptable. Consistent with the belief that mental disorders were the result of satanic possession, St. Augustine concluded that déjà vu was caused by malignant spirits.[65]

Figure 18-3: Thomas Becket, Archbishop of Canterbury was murdered on this spot by four knights of King Henry II on December 29, 1170.

Déjà vu first attracted scientific interest in nineteenth-century France, where hypnosis, hysteria, and dissociative phenomena had become important topics of medical investigation. It was French philosopher and psychical researcher Émile Boirac who gave the phenomenon its name, which was subsequently carried over into English.

Déjà vu experiences are relatively common: surveys find that at least two-thirds of individuals report having experienced it, and most have had a number of episodes.[66] The experience occurs everywhere in the world. For example, in a South African sample comprised mostly of adult, middle-class, university graduates, 96 percent reported having had at least one such experience.[67]

There are a number of variations of the déjà vu experience, including among them *déjà entendu* ("already heard"), the strong feeling that you have heard what is currently being said at some earlier time, even when this is highly unlikely; *déjà pensé* ("already thought"), the strong feeling that you have earlier had the identical thought that you are having at the moment when this is highly improbable; *déjà gôuté*, the strong feeling of inexplicable familiarity evoked by a particular taste; and *pseudo-presentiment*, the strong feeling that you were aware just an instant in advance that something—such as the ring of your telephone—was about to happen.[68]

The opposite of déjà vu is *jamais vu* ("never seen"). In this case, there is a failure to recognize something that one has experienced in the past and should indeed recognize. This is a rare occurrence for normal individuals, but is not uncommon with some types of epilepsy.

Déjà vu as memory error

Some instances of déjà vu may be based on the similarity between a current situation and some earlier situation that does not immediately come to mind. For example, perhaps years before your visit to Canterbury, you were exposed to photographs of the cathedral. Memory is involved in another way as well, for we remember that we have never actually been in the situation before.[69]

Déjà vu as recognition error

Pierre Janet, a giant of nineteenth-century psychiatry, insisted that déjà vu should be viewed as an error of perception, not of memory. Psychologist Graham Reed echoed this point, explaining that people ask the wrong question when experiencing déjà vu.[70] Instead of asking "How is it that I *remember* this place even though I've never been here before?" they should ask "How is it that I feel as though I *recognize* this place even though I've never been here before?"

Recall the automatic way in which our brains take in information from the outside world and match it against stored experience before deciding whether it is novel or familiar. Throughout each day, each time we walk into a room, listen to a song on the radio, or speak to someone by telephone, our brains go through such a recognition process. Think, for example, of when you unexpectedly encounter a friend on the street. Even if the individual has done her hair very differently, is wearing a new outfit quite different from what she has worn in the past, and has her arm in a cast as a result of a fall, you will likely have no difficulty in recognizing her.

But then, from time to time, there are instances of *fausse reconnaissance*, false recognition. For example, you "recognize" your friend some distance away in a crowd, but then as you approach you realize that this is a case of mistaken identity; this is not your friend. No one invokes a paranormal explanation for this kind of recognition failure, and you might even be able to identify the cues that led to the error. With déjà vu, however, we are unaware of the possible cues that led our recognition process astray.

Odors (and tastes as well) can be particularly potent stimuli in the elicitation of déjà vu. Although odors do not have the same ability that other sensations have to stimulate the cortex (where we do our thinking), they do stimulate cells in the brain's limbic system, which is involved with arousal and emotion. As a result, they are sometimes particularly effective in bringing about emotional reactions.[71]

Déjà vu as brain anomaly

Déjà vu may involve more than just errors of recognition. Some scientists have speculated that the experience is produced by a conflict between two sources of information in the brain. As far back as the late nineteenth century, it was suggested that the phenomenon arises when information reaches two parts of the brain at different times.[72] Because the two hemispheres of our brain do not always work in synchrony, the processing of information in the dominant hemisphere may give rise to a feeling of familiarity and recognition if the other side of the brain already "knew" about this same information moments earlier. This may possibly account for the unusual case of a man who regularly experienced déjà vu while shaving, though shaving was obviously something that he had experienced many times before.[73] It was the inappropriate feeling of novelty that was so strange. His brain somehow recognized the situation not just as familiar, but as novel at the same time.

Déjà vu is often experienced as part of the aura that precedes a loss of consciousness during a temporal-lobe epilepsy episode. During the 1950s, neurosurgeon Wilder Penfield elicited reports of feelings of déjà vu by electrically stimulating the temporal lobes of conscious, locally anesthetized, temporal-lobe epilepsy patients.

In sum, although déjà vu is not considered by parapsychologists to be a paranormal phenomenon, it is yet another seemingly inexplicable experience that pushes some people to explain it in terms of precognition or reincarnation.

PSYCHOKINESIS

Psychokinesis refers to the supposed power to influence physical objects in some way by "the power of the mind" alone. We all know that we cannot just by thinking about it turn on the coffee pot or move the garbage can to the curb; we have to use our muscles and physically carry out the tasks. Yet every one of us has probably at some time tried to influence the movement of people or things through thinking alone. Most people have rolled dice and "wished" for a certain number to come up. Many others have stared at someone's back and tried to make the person turn around. Recall the illusion of willing.

There is no persuasive scientific evidence to suggest that psychokinesis actually exists. If it were to exist, then much extensively tested contemporary scientific knowledge is just plain wrong. Yet parapsychologists believe that it is indeed real, and that it can be used to influence objects and events, not only in the present but also in the past. Were such an ability actually to exist, then—and this is no joke to parapsychologists—if you have done poorly on an examination you could do more studying and then psychokinetically reach into the past and redo the exam armed with this extra knowledge, or, more simply, skip the studying and use this retro-psychokinesis to modify the original grade that was registered by the teacher. She will never notice the change because you have changed the stream of time itself.

While parapsychologists make attempts to demonstrate psychokinesis in the laboratory, there have been a number of self-proclaimed psychics who claim to demonstrate it on a regular basis. Conjurers often make objects appear or disappear, but we know that they are using tricks. In contrast, Israeli magician Uri Geller came to the United States claiming to be a psychic who could, among other things, psychokinetically bend spoons. For years, he successfully persuaded many people of his supposed psychic powers. It was thanks chiefly to the efforts of conjurer James Randi that he was exposed as a trickster.[74]

I once observed firsthand the emotional impact on spectators of an apparent psychokinesis demonstration. In this case, conjurer Henry Gordon was explaining to reporters that Geller was not a psychic but only a conjuror using tricks to fool people. A reporter then informed Gordon that he had personally observed Geller bend a key by the power of his mind. He challenged Gordon to do the same and then handed him a key. Gordon concentrated on the key, but after a few minutes said that his powers were not working for some reason (an excuse often used by Geller in difficult moments) and handed back the key. Then, at the end of interview, he asked the reporter if he could have another try with the key. The reporter pulled the key from his pocket and reacted with shock as he announced to everyone that the key had bent while it was in his pocket!

What he had not been aware of—and Gordon did not enlighten him—was that Gordon had surreptitiously bent the key while handling it, and then, hiding the bend with his thumb, looked the man straight in the eye (to minimize the likelihood that he would look down at the key) and placed the key into his outstretched palm, pressing down slightly so that the hand closed almost automatically. The reporter had put the *bent* key into his pocket, believing it to be unchanged. Therefore, he could only ascribe its bend to a psychokinetic miracle that had occurred after the key was in his pocket.

✱✱✱

Our brains have the capacity to produce wondrous, puzzling, overwhelming, and sometimes frightening experiences that can seem to be beyond normal explanation. Both because of lack of knowledge about the workings of the brain and its ability to produce such experiences and because such experiences are usually accompanied by strong emotion, reason often fails, and people turn instead to the paranormal, supernatural realm in their search for understanding. The beliefs that flow from this offer not only appealing (albeit erroneous) explanations but comfort as well.

CHAPTER 19

A CABOODLE OF STRANGE BELIEFS

Throughout history, every mystery ever solved has turned out to be . . . not magic.

—Tim Minchin[1]

Nature abounds with the strange. The weirdness of quantum entanglement, curved space, time dilation, gravitational waves, the very beginnings of the universe in a Big Bang—these are all strange indeed, even though scientists have every reason to believe that they are real. Human experience also abounds with the strange, but, in this case, much of it is fantasy.

SHADES OF THE PAST

As we have seen, some of the most prominent figures in the history of parapsychology were motivated by the desire to find scientific evidence of survival after death. Although most contemporary parapsychologists do not openly express such a motivation, fascination with the question of survival continues to be reflected in the work of a few researchers who study reincarnation, past-life regression, and various forms of supposed communication with the dead.

Reincarnation

Although it is an integral part of Hinduism, belief in reincarnation is not widespread in most of the world, and most parapsychologists have shown no interest in the subject, with the notable exception of the late psychiatrist Ian Stevenson of the University of Virginia. Stevenson studied thousands of young Asian children who had demonstrated what he considered to be signs of having been rein-carnated. These signs were manifested either through comments made by the children that suggested knowledge from a previous life or birthmarks and phys-ical deformities corresponding in location or shape to scars from bullet or knife wounds of people who had died before these children were born and of whom they were the supposed reincarnations.[2] Stevenson also believed that fears and preferences from an earlier life could be carried over to the present one. For example, if a child has a phobia of water in the absence of any experience that might have produced such a reaction, she may be the reincarnation of someone who had drowned. Similarly, he argued that reincarnation might be involved when children possess skills that they have not been taught but were known to have been mastered by the "remembered" individual.

Although Stevenson recognized that he had been unable to provide suf-ficient evidence of reincarnation to persuade other scientists, a few researchers have continued his reincarnation research, focusing on "experimental birth-marks."[3] The term refers to a custom in some Asian countries to mark the body of a person who has just died with a "death mark," usually made with soot. This is done so that a baby born with a corresponding birthmark will be recognized as a reincarnation of the deceased. Stevenson reported a score of such cases in Thailand and Myanmar,[4] and those who are now continuing his research have reported another eighteen cases in those two countries.[5]

Not surprisingly, such research is plagued by methodological problems. First of all, when relatives put a death mark on a loved one, there will naturally be a subsequent effort to find a child with a corresponding birthmark. Of course, any correspondence is going to be a subjective matter, resulting in a likely confir-mation bias as people search to find their reincarnated loved one. The reincarna-tion researchers are themselves vulnerable to a confirmation bias in their search for evidence, which may result in a failure to explore other possible explanations when they do find correspondences that appear interesting.

Secondly, with regard to memories, mannerisms, and behavior, by the time that a child is old enough that these attributes can be assessed, she has already been exposed for several years to the stories and expectations of those looking for a new version of their departed loved one. This is likely to result in an unwit-ting shaping of the child's utterances, memories, and mannerisms, so that they become more and more similar to what the adults are seeking.

These methodological problems, combined with the obvious incompat-ibility of reincarnation with everything that scientists have learned about the human brain and the world in which we live, essentially doom such research to irrelevance.

Past-life regression

Belief in reincarnation has led to the use of hypnosis in the effort to produce "age regression" that takes people back to "past lives." Of course, as we have seen earlier, hypnosis is tied to suggestibility, and the products of hypnosis are often based in imagination.

Past-life regression became famous following the publication of the best-selling book *The Search for Bridey Murphy* (still in print), which described how a Colorado woman, Virginia Tighe (referred to as Ruth Simmons in the book), was "regressed" through hypnosis and then began to speak in a strong Irish brogue as she described in detail her "previous" life as Bridey Murphy living in Cork, Ireland. Both the brogue and her apparent knowledge of life in Ireland at that earlier time persuaded psychiatrist Stevenson that this was evidence of reincarnation.[6]

Skeptical investigators could find no evidence of a Bridey Murphy who had ever lived in Cork, and experts in Ireland assessed her accounts of Irish life as contrived and unrealistic. In 1956, a newspaper reporter for the *Chicago American* visited Tighe's hometown and met a woman who had lived across the street from her for many years. The woman was Irish, and she informed him that she had on many occasions related accounts of Irish life to young Virginia. In addition, it turned out that Tighe had participated in a high school drama program during which she had mastered a strong Irish brogue. To top the story off, that Irish neighbor who lived across the street—her maiden name was Bridey Murphy.

Of whether Ms. Tighe was only deceiving others or was also fooling herself, one cannot be sure. In any case, her story was instrumental in triggering a craze of past-life regression seminars, retreats, and books that continues to the present. "Past-life regression therapists" offer treatment for current emotional problems by dealing with supposedly unresolved emotional challenges from earlier lives.

In 1978, I took part in a television debate with Helen Wambach, a California psychologist whose book *Reliving Past Lives* was garnering considerable media attention at the time.[7] When she described having hypnotized many hundreds of people and taken them back to past lives, I asked if she had ever carried out a study in which half the participants were hypnotized and, as a control condition, half were not, and then all were asked to describe the details of an earlier life. She replied that she had done so. The result? She said that there were no differences between the accounts produced by those who had been hypnotized and those who had not. When I responded that this clearly pointed to imagination as the source of the supposed past-life memories, she disagreed. She told me, with what I recall as having been a suspicious twinkle in her eye, that the comparison showed just the opposite, that one does not need to be hypnotized to access a past life!

It is no surprise that the suggestibility associated with hypnosis leads to stories of apparent past lives when individuals with a belief in reincarnation are encouraged to fantasize in that direction. Consistent with the temptations of fantasy, most report having lived an earlier life as a person of some standing or importance, while few ever seem to have been mere "ordinary" folk. And such fantasy can take people to strange places. Following a public lecture, I was not surprised when a woman in the audience challenged my skepticism about reincarnation, nor was I surprised when she told me that she had learned through past-life regression that she had once lived as an officer in Napoleon's army and had died from a bullet to the chest. I *was* surprised, however, when she volunteered that in her very first incarnation she had been a dinosaur!

Automatic writing

"Automatic" writing is purported to involve a direct communication from the spirit world manifested through the movement of a pen on paper without any conscious effort on the part of the writer (the *automatist*). There have been many celebrated automatists over the years, some of whom turned their apparent talents into bestselling books. For example, Jane Roberts (1929–1984) published a number of bestsellers that she claimed were written through automatic writing by a spirit named *Seth*.

Those who defend the phenomenon as genuine communication from the dead rely on characteristics such as:

(1) The content exceeds what the writer could have known through any normal means.
(2) The handwriting is significantly unlike that of the writer and may be similar to that of the deceased individual to whom the writing is accredited.
(3) The pen writes while balanced against the fingers in a manner that would make normal writing impossible.

While most automatic writings are purported to be messages from the spirit world, some have had even more bizarre origins. For example, the automatic writings of a famous nineteenth-century Swiss medium Catherine Élise Müller, better known in England by her pseudonym Hélène Smith, were supposedly authored by an intelligent being on Mars and written in the Martian language. When psychologist Théodore Flournoy investigated her abilities, however, he concluded that her productions reflected a blend of imagination with knowledge obtained from books that she had read in childhood.[8] It was as a result of this investigation and the assumption that she had forgotten about her childhood readings that he coined the term *cryptomnesia* to refer to the retrieval of a forgotten memory that is then mistaken for something new and original.

One of the best-known automatists was Grace Rosher (1889–1980), a British portrait artist. On an afternoon in 1954, Rosher had just finished writing a letter to a friend when her pen reportedly continued to move on its own as it lay against her fingers. She said that as she watched, and without any effort on her part, the pen wrote her a letter in the handwriting of her recently deceased fiancé. This was the beginning of a series of automatic writings from her fiancé, from deceased relatives, and from the famous physicist Sir William Crookes. Rosher published several successful books about her experiences and explained her initial "revelation" in this way:

> We had first met in our youth and the affectionate friendship continued unbroken through the years. His sudden passing… was a severe blow…. [When I started to receive messages] I passed through agonizing periods of doubt, fearing lest I might be the victim of unconscious self-deception. Now, four years since those messages appeared, I have had many proofs of the authenticity of the communications … that doubt is no longer possible.[9]

Figure 19-1: Grace Rosher.

British psychical researcher Simeon Edmunds, skeptical about the paranormal attribution of Rosher's writings, had the opportunity to observe her directly. He reported that she began to write with her pen held in a normal manner but then relaxed her grip and made a fist, leaving the pen resting loosely between thumb and forefinger. Next, she raised her forefinger so that the pen was balanced against it. He noted that at the end of each word, the pen rocked a little and the nib lifted from the paper without any obvious movement on her part. As impressive as this was, he remained unconvinced. He subsequently presented his students with a photograph of Rosher doing her automatic writing and challenged them to try to reproduce the effect. Some of them were actually able to do so. He concluded:

> Whatever the explanation of the content of Miss Rosher's scripts and her ability to produce handwriting resembling that of deceased persons, there is clearly nothing paranormal in her ability to write with a pen balanced across her finger.[10]

Automatic writing is a form of ideomotor action where the writer is unaware of the subtle movements responsible for the script. It is likely as well, as psychologist Terrence Hines concludes, that it involves a mild form of dissociation.[11] Suggestion plays a strong role and can produce a dissociation between thought and writing movements, as well as reduced awareness of writing, leading to the feeling that there is no control over the movements of the pen.[12] It is also interesting to note that automatic writing has been observed in several people who have suffered stroke damage in the right hemisphere, suggesting a breakdown with regard to a sense of agency.[13]

Electronic Voice Phenomena

People have long attempted to communicate with loved ones whom they believe have a continued existence in a spirit world. In their efforts, some assume that the spirits will seek to take advantage of modern technology to communicate with the living. In the late 1870s, Thomas Edison (1847–1931) attempted to develop a "telephone to the dead" by amplifying the sounds from his phonograph and listening for voices. Convinced that we survive death, he also made a pact with his engineer, William Dinwiddie, that whoever died first would try to communicate from beyond the grave. Edison's account of his work with his spirit phone was described in the final chapter of his *Diary and Sundry Observations*, published posthumously in 1948, but that chapter was omitted from later English-language editions. Fortunately, a 1949 French translation of the book, which includes that chapter, has recently been discovered and republished.[14] Of course, we must remember that Edison was pursuing this work at a time when spiritualistic belief was widespread, and when séances appeared to establish the reality of survival after death.

Although there is no indication of a connection with Edison's efforts, the attempt to use modern electronic devices to hear the voices of the dead continues through the study of what are now referred to as *electronic voice phenomena* (EVP): Take an ordinary tape recorder, turn it on, and let it run without saying a word. Later, play back the tape and listen to the static, and if you hear voices, this is either a tribute to your imagination, or, as EVP proponents claim, evidence of spirit communication.

In 1959, Friedrich Jürgenson (1903–1987), a philosopher, recording artist, and the court painter to Pope Pius XII, was listening to recordings of birdsong that he had made in his garden, when, to his surprise, he detected human voices amidst the sounds of birds, including the voice of his late mother. This triggered an interest in using modern technology to receive communications from the dead. (It is worth noting that Jürgenson also reported sometimes hearing voices that he took to be telepathic messages even when not listening to his tape recorder.)

Subsequently, Latvian psychologist Konstantin Raudive (1909–1974) devoted many years of study to EVP and made more than 100,000 audiotapes, reportedly under strict control conditions, leading to the publication of his book *Breakthrough* in 1971. He reported having heard the voices of a wide range of dead people in his audiotapes, including such notables as Hitler, Lenin, and Stalin. Later, he began to investigate a parakeet called Putzi, claimed by its owner to be communicating messages from her recently deceased teenage daughter. He came to the conclusion that the bird was serving as an "energy field" for the transmission of spirit voices.[15]

Although there is still fascination with EVP in some quarters, it draws no interest either from psychologists or from mainstream parapsychology. Research by neutral scientists, such as that of psychologist Imants Barušs, who attempted to replicate Raudive's work, has not produced any evidence of EVP.[16]

If not spirit voices, what were Raudive and others hearing? EVP researchers had first considered and then rejected the possibility that the voices were due to *cross-modulation*, whereby signals from radio stations are picked up by the electronics of a tape recorder and translated into weak sounds. Apophenia, through which we can spontaneously perceive patterns of words and meaning from random noise, provides explanation enough for the experiences of those motivated to find such patterns. Recall the claims of backward messages in "Stairway to Heaven." This explanation, however, does nothing to dampen the enthusiasm of those who continue to believe that EVP provides a channel of communication with the dead.

Ouija boards

Ouija boards have been used by many people in their attempts to contact the spirits of the dead. (The name comes from a combination of the French and German words for "yes," *oui* and *ja* respectively.) The Ouija board was patented by the Kennard Novelty Company in the United States in 1891. Developed during the Spiritualism craze, it provided a convenient and direct way of apparent communication with the spirit world. It involves a board containing the letters of the alphabet as well as the words *yes* and *no* and a *planchette* (French for *small board*), a small heart-shaped piece of wood that moves easily across the board. Two or more people place their fingers on the planchette, ask a question, and then watch as the planchette apparently moves on its own, pointing to suc-

Figure 19-2: Ouija Board.

cessive letters that spell out answers. The participants typically are astonished at the results, although only a little experimentation would show them that the planchette can offer correct answers only when one of the participants *knows* the answer. Because of its original association with Spiritualism, some people to this day worry that they might be indulging in the "black arts" or risking diabolical possession by playing with the Ouija board.

The combination of the ideomotor actions of the participants further masks the individual responses, and it is this combination of actions rather than influences from the spirit world that moves the planchette. Recall that ideomotor action involves unconscious and involuntary motor movements reflecting suggestion, expectation, or preconception. Because these motor movements are not consciously made, the maneuvering of the planchette is attributed to external, invisible forces.

Hauntings

From the ghost of Hamlet's father walking the battlements of Elsinore Castle to Dickens's ghosts of Christmas past, present, and future to Casper the friendly ghost, our literature is filled with apparitions. Around the world, a substantial proportion of people believe that ghosts are real. A 2013 Harris poll reported that 42 percent of Americans indicated they believe in ghosts,[17] and a poll carried out in Britain in 2014 found that 34 percent expressed the same belief.[18] In other research, about 15 percent report having seen a ghost with their own eyes.[19]

If there are no ghosts, why do so many people report having seen one? The answer lies in how our perceptions are affected by expectation and suggestibility. Researchers James Houran and Rense Lange examined the role that expectancy plays in the perception of ghostly phenomena. One study involved an old disused theater that had no reputation for being haunted. They told one group of participants that the building was known to be haunted, while those in a second group were told only that the building was undergoing renovations. Each participant was asked to wander around the building and to report back any feelings that were aroused. As Houran and Lange expected, those who had been informed that the building was haunted reported having experienced various strange sensations, such as a sense of presence, while those in the second group had nothing to report.[20]

In another study, a couple was asked to spend a month in a house that they were falsely told had a reputation for being haunted and asked to keep a diary of anything strange that occurred.[21] At the end of the month, the couple submitted a diary that included more than twenty strange happenings, including objects that had been moved, a strange malfunctioning of the telephone, and hearing their names whispered by a ghostly presence. The researchers pointed out that people who expect ghostly phenomena will take note of any small noise or movement, such as a creak in the floorboards or a curtain swaying, which then makes them more anxious and even more hypervigilant. As result, they become increasingly sensitive to small environmental effects that lead them to experience more and more physical sensations or even hallucinations.[22]

In related research, psychologist Christopher French and colleagues investigated the role that low-frequency sound and electromagnetic fields might play in ghostly experiences. They constructed a "haunted" room where those physical factors could be manipulated. Instead of them finding any influence of sound or electromagnetism, they too came to the conclusion that the best explanation for those ghostly experiences lies with suggestibility.[23]

Hampton Court Palace in London has a reputation as one of the most haunted places in England. In 2000, psychologist Richard Wiseman and his colleagues carried out a study in the palace involving more than six hundred members of the public, each of whom were asked to wander around one of two supposedly "haunted" locations—the Haunted Gallery and the Georgian Rooms—and to note down the location whenever they experienced any strange feeling or encountered any unusual phenomena. People with a prior belief in ghosts reported more strange experiences than did nonbelievers.[24] Some specific locations in those two rooms triggered unusual sensations, some of which were found to be related to natural phenomena such as changes in air temperature or subtle drafts. This research led Wiseman to conclude, just as Christopher French had done earlier, that:

> Hauntings do not require genuine ghosts, underground streams, low frequency sound waves, or weak magnetic fields. Instead, all it takes is the power of suggestion.[25]

SHADOWS OF THE FUTURE

No one in this modern age would pay heed to a daily newspaper column claiming to offer advice based on the "reading" of a chicken's intestines. Yet most newspapers continue to carry astrology columns, and they receive barrages of complaints from readers if they attempt to discontinue them. (The "entrails" reading in figure 19-3 is based on an actual newspaper horoscope composed by a famous astrologer.[26])

The desire for knowledge about what the future holds, whether for the day to come or for the long term, has no doubt been an important preoccupation ever since humans first began to contemplate the world around them. There has been no shortage of methods for divining what lies ahead. Some prognostications involved seeking the guidance of the gods, while others relied on the portents supposedly offered by nature and natural magic.

Your daily entrails . . .

Today's weather, cloudy with a chance

of rain; high   near 22°C, low tonight

15°C; sunny tomorrow

Today's entrails (from a freshly killed

free-range chicken): Business

overhead or inventory may be inflated.

Ask probing questions before

authorizing new expenditures. Strike a

healthy balance between work and

play.

Figure 19-3: If horoscopes were replaced by entrails reading.

Over a period of several centuries, the ancient Grecian oracles of the Temple of Apollo at Delphi provided glimpses of the future for rulers and common people alike. The priestess Pythia in the eighth century BCE achieved international fame for prophecies delivered as she sat on a tripod above a chasm in the temple floor and inhaled the gases that rose up from the earth below. It is said that she went into a trance and then delivered words that were incomprehensible to anyone other than her priests, who interpreted them for those who sought her advice. Her predictions were held in such high esteem that no one wanted to make a major decision without consulting her. Yet her pronouncements were often so vague and open to opposing interpretations that she was not wrong whatever happened.[27]

Cleromancy

Cleromancy, the casting of pebbles or dice, or the drawing of lots, is a method for obtaining divine guidance that traces back to ancient times. It is assumed that the fall of the pebbles or dice, or the choice of the lot (a word that gave rise to our modern *lottery*) is guided by a divine hand. The romantic ruminations of John Wesley (1703–1791), the founder of Methodism, provide a famous anecdote about the drawing of lots. Wesley wondered whether he should marry a young woman of whom he had grown extremely fond, and, in seeking God's opinion, he prepared three lots, marking the first one "Marry," the second, "Think of it not this year," and the third, "Think of it no more." He prayed for an answer, and then drew the lot marked "Think of it no more." Obedient to this divine advisory, he did not propose marriage.

Many other forms of divination, including astrology, palmistry, the *I Ching*, tarot cards, tea-leaf readings, and numerology, are presumed to provide supernatural information about the future without the assistance of any god or gods.

Astrology

The belief that the heavenly bodies influence our personalities and our destinies is an ancient one that has taken root in many cultures. In ancient Greece, Pythagoras discovered that the pitch of the sound made by a vibrating string is inversely proportional to the string's length—that is, the shorter the string, the higher the pitch. He then went on to suggest that the sun and moon and planets all produce their own humming sounds based on their revolutions in orbit—

the Music of the Spheres. According to Pythagoras, "There is geometry in the humming of the strings, there is music in the spacing of the spheres."[28] Although these sounds are imperceptible to the human ear, he believed that they have a significant effect on life on earth.

Astrology was born conjoined with astronomy and survived its separation from its illustrious twin during the scientific revolution. It has flourished as a method of divination, while the reading of entrails has not. About 25 percent of respondents to a Harris Poll conducted in the United States, Canada, and the United Kingdom in 2009 agreed that "astrology, or the position of the stars and planets, can affect people's lives."[29] Indeed, astrology is so well-established that most people, even those who give no credence to astrology itself, know their astrological sign.

Figure 19-4: The zodiac.

How is it that astrology continues to have appeal despite its pseudoscientific foundations? There are a number of factors.

Historical and social support

The survival of a belief system depends on its inculcation in each new generation. We all learn about astrology somewhere along the way while growing up, even if not explicitly encouraged to take it seriously. On the other hand, we are not exposed to entrails reading.

Expectation

It is easy to find meaning in one's horoscope even if there is none. This was clearly demonstrated in research in which people were asked to evaluate each of twelve personality descriptions taken from an astrology book, one description for each sign of the zodiac, in terms of how well they corresponded to their own personalities.[30] Half of the participants were informed that these were horoscopes, and the corresponding sign of the zodiac was attached to each description. For the rest of the participants, no zodiac signs were provided, and they were instead informed that the personality descriptions had been drawn from a book entitled, "Twelve Ways of Life." Those in the first group ranked the description that corresponded to their own zodiac sign at or near the top. This is likely due to the expectation that a particular description *should* apply because it corresponds to one's zodiac sign, and people are likely to find a way to interpret the description to make it fit their view of themselves. On the other hand, one might argue that these findings reflect the accuracy of the horoscopes. That explanation fails when one considers the rankings of those in the second group. They were unaware of any relationship between the descriptions and their zodiac signs, but if the horoscopes were accurate, they should nonetheless choose the description corresponding to their sign. Their rankings were totally unrelated to their zodiac signs, a clear indication that it was suggestion, and not the validity of the horoscope, that led to the rankings in the first group.

Pseudo-compatibility with natural science

Reading the entrails of a chicken or the pattern of tea leaves at the bottom of a cup makes little sense in this scientific age, but astrology's claim that the gravitational forces of the planets affect our brains can appear vaguely "logical" to those who believe in it.

Complexity

Complicated systems for prognostication (and personality assessment) endure in part because their complexity both suggests that the system has merit and makes the system more difficult to evaluate. Astrological analysis is convoluted, and it is not easy for the layperson to assess it directly.

Illusory personal validation

This, more than anything, accounts for the popularity of astrology. Horoscopes often *seem* to be accurate, and believers will find ways to interpret subsequent events so that they fit the prediction. This jibes with the Barnum effect and with Bertram Forer's generalized "personality description," copied from a newspaper horoscope, as discussed earlier.

It is also interesting that researchers find that people generally perceive a horoscope reading as being more accurate when it is based on *specific* birth information, such as time of birth, as well as date and location.[31] Favorableness is also an important factor. People are rarely objective about their personalities and tend to be reluctant to accept unflattering descriptions of themselves. The more favorable the overall description, the greater the likelihood that the reading will be taken to be accurate. Indeed, in one study, subjects who were initially skeptical about astrology wavered in their skepticism when given flattering horoscopes.[32]

Selective memory

Of course, once a reading has been accepted, the passage of time may enhance its apparent accuracy in one's memory. In a description containing many elements, it is easy to ignore and subsequently forget those descriptors that seem not to apply at all and focus on and remember only those that seem closer to the mark.

Self-fulfilling prophecy

An astrological reading can trigger a self-fulfilling prophecy. If your horoscope tells you that you will make a new friend today, you may deliberately take steps that lead to meeting new people, or at least be on the lookout for those who might suit the prediction.

Freedom from obligations

Many belief systems are costly to the individual in that they demand considerable effort or oblige the individual to avoid various pleasures. For example, belief in a divine being and in the power of prayer involve the necessity to adhere to certain rules and values. Astrology operates in a value-free context, without any obligations.

Astrology fills needs. Even though it makes no sense from the scientific point of view, it helps satisfy both the desire to reduce uncertainty about the future and the quest for self-understanding.

Numerology

Like astrology, numerology involves a belief in a natural order in the universe that provides insight into people's characters, talents, and motivations, information about their future, and guidance in making important decisions. According to numerology, the numbers of both a person's birthdate and those corresponding to the letters in the person's name have occult significance.

Numerology's history is entwined with both mathematics and the occult. As one example, the analysis of pertinent numbers to foretell the future was an important part of the Kabbalah, an ancient Jewish mystical tradition. Because students of the occult manipulated numbers in making their prognostications, mathematics itself was suspected by many of being a tool of the occult in sixteenth-century Europe. Even Copernicus's *De Revolutionibus* (1543) aroused suspicions of magic-dabbling because Copernicus had used mathematics to reason about things that he could not directly observe.[33] As a result of such suspicion, mathematics books were burned in public bonfires in England. In 1651, Francis Bacon's biographer, John Rawley, was accused of using magic simply because he had calculated a steeple's height by using geometry.

Around that same time, John Dee (1527–1609), an English mathematician/alchemist/astrologist (who spent time seeking secret codes that would allow him to communicate with angels), had one foot firmly in science and the other in the occult, at a time when the two were beginning to diverge.[34] Despite his occult predilections (he became the court astrologer to Mary, Queen of England, and was later imprisoned for a short while, accused of using magic), he strongly defended mathematics against accusations that it involved witchcraft and the occult. Over time, suspicions about mathematics died away, and its separation from numerology was complete.

Modern numerology, although not enjoying the popularity of astrology, continues to appeal to many people. The occult section of any major bookstore and the plethora of numerological web pages attest to its continuing impact. Many of the same factors discussed earlier with regard to astrology contribute to its longevity.

Palmistry and psychic readings

In all likelihood, you have encountered a storefront psychic's place of business, announced by a neon sign in the window of a small shop or home. And you may have watched psychics on television offer what appeared to be remarkable displays of their apparent paranormal abilities. Yet, as discussed in earlier chapters, there is no persuasive evidence of anyone ever having demonstrated genuine psychic powers. Deception and self-deception through cold readings are the basis for seemingly successful palm readings and psychic readings in general. The factors discussed earlier that support belief in other forms of divination, such as astrology and numerology, are also important in understanding their continuing appeal.

OTHER STRANGE BELIEFS

Energy fields

Energy has a very specific meaning in physics. It is objectively measurable. It is quantifiable. It can take very particular forms, for example electrical energy or nuclear energy. It can change back and forth to matter. Now, think about *energy* or *bioenergy* or *bioenergetic field* as these terms are bandied about by psychics and alternative healers.[35] They offer no precise meaning. The notion that each of us is surrounded by an energy field is an attractive one to many people, but it is totally contrary to what physicists and biologists know about energy and living organisms.

As we have seen earlier, many alternative healing methods—for example, Qigong, traditional chiropractic, and therapeutic touch—are based on manipulating a supposed energy that flows through the body. The belief in such an energy field also feeds the belief in *auras*, luminous "fields" sometimes consisting of various colored layers, which supposedly surround our bodies and reflect our state of physical health and emotional well-being. While there is no persuasive evidence that such auras exist,[36] Hindu and Buddhist traditions include aura concepts, and some supposedly "gifted" people claim to have the power to see them.

In testing the claim that gifted people can see auras, one study involved a group of "aura seers" and a control group of non-seers. Each participant was taken into a room containing four large screens, with a man standing behind one of them, his head an inch or two below the top of the screen. The task was simple: given that the seers had indicated that auras extend a few inches beyond the body, the auras should be visible above the screen. The task was to indicate behind which of the four screens the man was standing. Close to 1,500 trials were conducted, but neither the seers nor the non-seers scored above the chance level.[37] The seers had failed in this simple but elegant test.

Firewalking

Walking barefoot over hot coals has been a practice in various parts of the world since ancient times. It has served variously as an initiation rite, a test of religious faith, and a demonstration of one's courage. The practice continues to this day in various regions of Southeast Asia.

We learn to respect fire as we grow up, and probably everyone has experienced being burned at some point or another. Our intuition tells us that firewalking is impossible without incurring serious burns. Naturally, then, when people demonstrate that they can walk barefoot across hot coals without harming themselves, many invoke a paranormal explanation for what seems otherwise impossible. And so, today, firewalking seminars and retreats are available to help people harness their supposed inner paranormal abilities and put them to the test by traversing a bed of hot coals. Yet neither paranormal powers nor religious faith is required. Our intuition is wrong, for in the right circumstances anyone can firewalk without being hurt. Those circumstances are the key.

In 1935, the Council for Psychical Research at the University of London organized a public firewalk in which two British scientists, along with Kuda Box, a celebrated Indian magician, walked across a twelve-foot-long path of wood embers measured to be at a temperature of 800°F. None of the three received any burns. The council informed the public that firewalking requires neither supernatural powers nor religious faith, and that the explanation for the apparent miracle lies with the low thermal conductivity of the wood embers and the fact that the contact of the embers with the soles of the feet is brief.

Figure 19 5: Firowalking
(Wikimedia Creative Commons, Aidan Jones from Oxford, UK, CC BY-CA 2.0).

In 1957, chemist M. R. Coe went further and demonstrated to the editors of a psychology journal that he could not only walk barefoot across a bed of hot coals, but could also plunge his fingers into molten lead and pop hot coals into his mouth, all without being harmed and without any need for "paranormal" talent or a trance state.[38] There is an important point here. If we mistakenly assume something to be impossible, then its occurrence mistakenly appears miraculous.

Physicist Bernard Leikand also walked barefoot across a bed of hot coals and did so without any special preparation, training, or trance.[39] He explained that our intuition about the risks misleads us because we confuse temperature with heat, and, to clarify, he used the example of baking a cake. If a cake is being baked at 350°F, then the cake, the pan, and the air in the oven are all at that same temperature, but no one would fear being burned either by briefly sticking one's hand into the oven or by touching the cake. On the other hand, touching the cake pan would cause a burn. This is because, unlike either the air or the cake, the metal pan is good at conducting heat. When your finger touches the pan, it absorbs some thermal energy (heat) from the pan, but more thermal energy quickly rushes in from other parts of the pan. In firewalking, the coals have a high temperature but they are, like the cake, poor at conducting heat. Were you to walk over metal pie plates that had been placed on the hot coals, you would certainly suffer severe burns.

And the temperatures are impressive. In 1997, physicist David Willey led twenty-three people across a twelve-foot stretch of hot coals that ranged in temperature from 1,600 to 1,800 degrees Fahrenheit (a world-record temperature in the firewalking world), and then in 1998, led another group across a bed of coals 165 feet long (another world record, this time in length).[40] No one suffered any burns.

Of course, lingering long while walking across the fire pit increases the risk of being burned. That is the lesson learned by some participants at a June 2016 Dallas workshop led by self-help motivational guru Tony Robbins, who encourages audience participation in firewalking demonstrations as a supposed means of achieving a "peak state" and accomplishing feats they never thought possible. After being encouraged to walk barefoot across a fifteen-foot stretch of hot coals, several people sustained burns to their feet, five of them severely enough to require a trip to the hospital. One of Mr. Robbins's staff told the media that those who suffered burns may have been moving too slowly because they were taking selfies.[41] Whoops!

Psychic sleuths

The original meaning of the word *sleuth*, according to the Oxford English Dictionary, was the trail left by a person or animal, and *sleuthhounds* were specially trained to follow a fugitive's trail. It is from this that the word *sleuth* came to describe a person whom we now call a detective.[42] A *psychic sleuth* professes the ability to find missing people or solve crimes using paranormal information not available through the normal senses. A number of people have become celebrated as psychic sleuths, including Dorothy Allison, Sylvia Brown, Noreen Renier, Greta Alexander, and Bill Ward in the United States, and Gerard Croiset and Peter Hurkos in Europe. They have maintained that they can use their powers to see things in the past, present, and future, and through contact with an object owned by a missing or dead individual, they can gain an impression of where the person is or the circumstances in which a crime was committed, allowing them to solve crimes that baffle the police. (Note that this claim involves the magical law of contact.)

Facts, however, show quite a different story. Careful examination shows that these "sleuths" have been successful all right, but only in fooling the public (and in some cases, perhaps themselves as well).[43] They have demonstrated an excellent ability to take advantage of information available through normal channels and to speak in generalities using some of the techniques of the cold reader. Predictions are generally vague. For example, a prediction that "the body will be found near water" could be considered correct were the body to be found near or in a lake or river, in a bathroom, near a fire hydrant, by a water fountain, or in many other places. Such "multiple endpoints" give the exaggerated appearance of success. Often, the psychic makes several conflicting claims, and, after the crime is solved by the police, the incorrect predictions are dropped and those that are closer to what the police have determined to have occurred—and sometimes even "predictions" that had not been made at all—are trumpeted as evidence of psychic ability.[44]

The Los Angeles Police Department carried out a test of the ability of twelve "professional" psychic sleuths. The study involved four crimes, two solved and two unsolved. The psychics were provided and allowed to handle physical evidence from each of the crimes. They did not produce any evidence of psychic ability.[45] A follow-up study compared the inferences of psychic sleuths with those of both students and homicide detectives.[46] Again, two solved and two unsolved crimes were involved and again physical evidence was provided to each individual. And again, there was no evidence of any psychic ability. The information provided by students and the detectives was just as accurate as that provided by the psychics.

In a similar study, psychologist Richard Wiseman and colleagues tested the performance of three "psychic detectives" compared with that of three students who did not claim any psychic skill. Each person was presented with three objects associated with three serious crimes and asked to report any thoughts, images, or ideas that were elicited by them. There was no evidence of any ability in psychic detection.[47] It is interesting to note that while none of the students felt that they had performed well, all the psychics thought that they had been successful.

Visitors from beyond the earth

The term UFO (unidentified flying object) sounds neutral enough. If you look up and catch a glimpse of a Frisbee that has been thrown past your window but you do not see enough to identify it, then that is certainly a flying object, and unidentified. When people refer to UFOs, however, there is almost always a subtext, that these objects that resist identification are likely to be alien spacecraft.

Modern interest in UFOs began on June 24, 1947, when pilot Kenneth Arnold, while flying a small airplane over the western United States, reported seeing a formation of nine "saucer-shaped" objects moving at incredible speed. After he landed, a news conference was organized to report his sighting to the public. It was then that the term "flying saucer" was coined.

Some weeks later, there was a strange crash of an airborne vehicle near a missile-testing facility in Roswell, New Mexico. To this day, there are people who believe that the vehicle was an alien spacecraft, that the United States military recovered the bodies of the aliens, and that the whole event, which came to be popularly known as the "Roswell incident," was covered up in order to avoid mass panic. This belief—this myth—lives on, without any objective evidence ever having been produced to support it.[48] And it lives on despite the report published by the Office of the Secretary of the United States Air Force in July 1994 following an exhaustive document search with regard to the event. That report indicated that the United States military had been conducting high-altitude, research-balloon launch-and-recovery operations involving humanlike dummies in that area at that time. Air Force personnel did indeed arrive shortly after the crash of a balloon to retrieve the "saucer and crew," the dummies. Through the rumor mill, the dummies were turned into alien bodies, and, through conspiracy theory, the 1994 report continues to be viewed by many as a cover-up.

In early twentieth-century England, Sir Arthur Conan Doyle (creator of the hyperrational Sherlock Holmes) documented a number of firsthand sightings of fairies around the world, along with photographs of fairies playing in the forest taken by a sixteen-year-old girl and her ten-year-old cousin. He reported all of this in his book *The Coming of the Fairies*. Researcher Robert Schaeffer noted the similarity between belief in UFOs and Doyle's belief in fairies:

> Multiple independent witnesses. A series of photographs. Worldwide sightings. Close-encounter cases. Certainly Conan Doyle did not exaggerate when

he described the evidence for fairies as "overwhelming." As he observed, "These numerous testimonies come from people who are very solid and successful in the affairs of life. . . . To wave aside the evidence of such people on the grounds that it does not correspond with our experience is an act of mental arrogance that no wise man will admit."[49]

UFOs and Venus

Nothing except the moon is brighter than Venus in the nighttime sky, and there have been many reported instances of people mistaking that planet for a fast-moving aircraft or spaceship of some sort.[50] Indeed, astronomer Philip Plait considers Venus to be responsible for the majority of UFO reports.[51] Instances of misperception of the planet as a fast-moving aircraft or a "flying saucer" are legion. For example, veteran police officers in Georgia once pursued a mysterious shining object moving at high speed, describing it as being about five hundred feet above the ground. It turned out to be Venus.[52]

Misperception of other natural phenomena have also given rise to UFO reports, leading even the National UFO Reporting Center, an organization in the United States devoted to the belief that alien spacecraft do visit our planet, to post the following statement on its website on August 30, 2009:

> We are receiving hundreds of reports every month of normal, terrestrial events, e.g. over-flights of the International Space Station, the Space Shuttle, or satellites; "flares" of light from "Iridium" satellites; the appearance of typical meteors; and observations of normal, "twinkling" stars, planets, contrails, clusters of balloons. . . . In fact, the overwhelming majority of reports that we receive now are of these normal objects and events. . . . I believe the majority of time I spend on the Hotline is devoted to trying to convince people who have been staring for hours at a star or planet that the object of interest is not a UFO![53]

How can a brightly shining planet be mistaken for a spacecraft? First of all, the *autokinetic effect* is involved. This effect was discovered during the Second World War when pilots flying one behind the other on a dark night guided themselves by the small light at the rear of the aircraft in front. Officers on the ground were puzzled by pilots' reports that these tail lights often seemed to move around wildly, leading them to view the airplane ahead as moving about erratically. This led to the discovery that when we observe a point of light against a dark background with no frame of reference, the constant and automatic movement of our retinas leads our brains to conclude that it is the point of light, rather than our eyes, that is moving. (This is why aircraft now carry blinking lights. The blinking eliminates the autokinetic effect because the visual system reestablishes the position of the light in space with each new blink.)[54]

Thus, a pinpoint of light such as the planet Venus, against a dark background over a period of time, will appear as though it is moving around, often very quickly and over substantial distances, even though there is no actual movement. Now add in streams of wispy clouds in the nighttime sky that are not visible to the eye but which, as they move in front of Venus, produce the appearance of a diffuse object first disappearing and then reappearing at what seems to be some distance (again thanks to the autokinetic effect). This suggests great speed. The effect is a powerful one, and even professional pilots have been fooled into mistaking Venus for a fast-moving object in their vicinity as they pilot their airplanes through the night.

For the record, just as in the case of the Roswell incident, no objective evidence has ever been produced to support the belief that alien spacecraft have visited our planet. Efforts to find such evidence have not borne fruit. For example, the British Ministry of Defense investigated more than 11,000 reports of UFO sightings over a period of half a century but closed its public reporting hotline in 2009, having failed to find any evidence of alien visitations.[55]

Aliens doing weird things to plants

In the late 1970s, strange circular patterns, later referred to as *crop circles*, began to appear in cornfields not far from Stonehenge, England. Each pattern seemed to be carefully drawn, and the cornstalks were bent but unbroken. Over time, the patterns became more and more complex, some of them involving a series of concentric circles, or chains of circles connected by bars. No footprints, tire tracks, or other signs of human involvement were found. Subsequently, crop circles begin to show up in Canada, the United States, Japan, and Australia, but the epicenter remained in southern England. Some investigations concluded that the patterns were produced by aliens.

Fourteen years or so later, two British pensioners, Doug Bower and Dave Chorley, confessed that they had created the earliest crop circles.[56] They had carefully planned their designs and then, following tractor tracks, had walked more than a kilometer from their vehicle to the position they had chosen. Using wooden planks and string, they were able to complete a hundred-meter-wide design in forty-five minutes. Over time, enthused by the public's excited reaction to their work, they developed more complicated and larger designs and produced about thirty circles each year over a number of years. They were amazed as "crop-circle" investigation teams began using high-tech equipment, including radar and infrared cameras, in the attempt to capture evidence of aliens at work. It was flattering when their hoaxes began to be imitated by other hoaxers. And there were many imitators. For example, in Salisbury, England, in September 2015, a father and son team confessed to having made crop circles across Wiltshire over a period of fifteen years. With the help of a team of fellow hoaxers, they had carefully designed their patterns on paper, and then spent hours under cover of darkness turning them into intricate crop circles and other more complicated figures.[57]

These confessions notwithstanding, crop circles continue to appear, and crop-circle enthusiasts continue to seek evidence proving that aliens are responsible.

Aliens doing weird things to animals

In the early 1980s, an epidemic of cattle mutilations spread across Western Canada and the United States. One news report stated:

> The Alberta RCMP has investigated about 75 suspicious animal deaths this year and has confirmed four mutilations. In the past two years in the US, mutilators have carved out the genitals, tongues, ears and/or tails of as many as 10,000 cattle. While cattle are the usual victims, horse, buffalo and goat mutilations have also been reported.[58]

Investigators stated that organs had been removed with surgical precision, that no blood was left in the carcass, and that the liver was usually found to be pulpy and yellow, as though it had been subjected to microwave radiation. No signs of human involvement, such as footprints or tire tracks, were found anywhere near the carcasses. Some investigators attributed the mutilations to satanic cults, while others argued that the mutilations often occurred in conjunction with UFO reports, and suggested that the only reasonable explanation was that aliens were responsible and were doing research on our planet's life forms.

Finally, a careful investigation was carried out by former FBI agent Ken Rommel, who concluded that the so-called "surgical" removal of organs was actually the work of animal predators and birds of prey.[59] The soft body parts, including eyes, tongues, anuses, and sex organs are the easiest parts of the body for natural predators to eat, and close examination showed teeth marks around the wounds. He noted that the animals that he had examined had died from eating poisonous vegetation such as larkspur.

Still, many people refused to accept Rommel's conclusions. Then, in the early 1990s, there were more reports of cattle mutilations in the state of Washington. Five cattle were found dead, and one laboratory analysis reported that the animals' wounds were consistent with "electrosurgical excision" and "heat-induced injury," possibly from a laser.[60] Mutilations were also reported in Alabama, and some of those reports indicated that there had been UFO sightings at around the same time. Others had seen mysterious helicopters in the vicinity. Two theories evolved in this case, the first that aliens were carrying out research and the second that government agents were flying in by helicopter at night and killing animals living near high-power lines to test them for cancer.[61]

Mystery is a powerful catalyst for belief in extraterrestrials or covert government activities. Reason—and Rommel's analysis—suggest that the answer to this mystery lies squarely in the animal world itself.

Aliens doing weird things to humans

About one percent of the population of the United States has reported having been in contact with aliens. Many of these accounts involve supposedly being taken aboard alien spacecraft and subjected to surgical examination, and then returned home with all memory of the experience erased.[62]

Several popular books written by or about claimed alien "abductees," such as John Fuller's *The Interrupted Journey* (1966),[63] Budd Hopkins's *Missing Time* (1981)[64] and *Intruders* (1987),[65] and Whitley Strieber's *Communion: A True Story* (1987),[66] were huge successes and fanned the flames of interest in alien abductions. Perhaps because of these books, a common pattern of experiences is reported in typical accounts of abductions.[67]

The putative abduction usually occurs when the person is in bed at night (although occasionally it takes place outdoors or from a vehicle). He wakes up feeling paralyzed and is overwhelmed by an intense light, a loud buzzing sound, and the feeling of some unexplained presence. Next, there is a sense of flying through the air and being somehow transported onto the alien spacecraft where he observes aliens, who are typically described as about four feet tall, gray in color, with large heads and almond-shaped eyes. Then, while restrained or paralyzed, he is subjected to a medical examination and sometimes a small object is implanted in his body. Before being returned home, the abductee's memory is erased. Symptoms of supposed abduction are said to include unexplained nosebleeds, periods of missing time, clicking in the ears, unexplained bruises or scars, unexplained phobias, and even a metallic taste in the mouth.

Given that their memories had supposedly been erased, how were the "abductees" able to make their reports? Approximately 70 percent of those who recalled having been abducted did so through hypnosis.[68] As we know, hypnosis contaminates memory through turning fantasy into what seems to be reality. Because of the supposed efficacy of hypnosis, it is no surprise that "abductees" develop a high degree of confidence in their memories of the supposed abduction experience.[69] The detail and the richness of such "recovered" accounts can be extremely impressive, and this tends to persuade people of their credibility.[70] The late Harvard psychiatrist John Mack took abduction accounts seriously.[71] He wrote,

> The experiential data, which, in the absence of more robust physical evidence, is the most important information that we have, suggests that abduction experiencers have been visited by some sort of "alien" intelligence which has impacted them physically and psychologically. Indeed, this conclusion fits so tightly with the data that I and other abduction researchers have collected, that it is doubtful to me that this possibility would be so vigorously resisted if the phenomenon did not violate our scientific world view and the implied control of our living environment that accompanies it.[72]

Mack was not alone. A substantial number of therapists began to work with "abductees," helping them to "recover" their elusive memories, in much the same way that therapists in other contexts helped people "recover" memories of childhood sexual abuse that had never actually occurred. Because it seemed that abductions were so widespread, support groups for abductees were formed in the United States beginning in the 1980s.

There has never been any physical evidence produced to support the presence of aliens or of abductions. It is interesting, too, that there have been so many abduction accounts in the United States while they have been quite rare in Canada. Perhaps Canadians are simply not so interesting to the aliens!

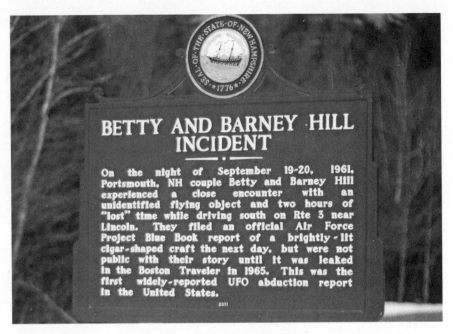

Figure 19-6: Monument to alien abduction.

Studies have shown that the "abductees," compared to control participants, show higher levels of dissociativity, paranormal belief, self-reported psychic ability, and the tendency to hallucinate.[73] The reported intensity of the experiences has also been found to correlate significantly with measures of fantasy proneness.[74] Other research indicates that "abductees" typically believed that aliens were visiting from space even prior to their experience.[75] People who both are fantasy-prone and hold such beliefs will be more vulnerable to interpreting their experiences in terms of alien abduction.[76]

There is another important consideration. Because most of these reports begin with being abducted from bed, sleep paralysis may be the basis for the experience.[77] Indeed, "abductees" often report that they suffered from sleep difficulties and sleep paralysis prior to their abductions.[78] A combination of sleep paralysis, fantasy proneness, and prior belief in alien visitations is a powerful cocktail for an experience for which abduction by aliens provides an attractive interpretation.[79] As Carl Sagan wrote,

> The culture contaminates. Movies, television programs, books, haunting pages of aliens, and television interviews with passionate "abductees"—all communicate to the widest possible community the alien abduction paradigm. So, it's

not as if each abductee has been hermetically sealed from the outside world and has no input about what others are saying. It's all cross-contaminated, and it has been for decades. I think that's the clearest evidence for it not being good evidence—that many people tell the same story.[80]

And the advice from memory researchers:

If you do not want to be abducted by aliens, you need only to make sure that you do not believe in extraterrestrial creatures.[81]

In recent years, China appears to have become the premiere destination for UFOs, surpassing the perennial favorite, the United States. One-fifth of all UFO reports now occur in China, and belief in alien visitations is widespread. China now has the largest number of UFO research organizations in the world, and its UFO magazine sells more than 400,000 copies each month. Sun Shi Li, a former diplomat, is the president of the Beijing UFO Research Society, which has 40,000 members and is the world's largest UFO organization.[82] He believes that aliens are losing interest in the United States and are being drawn to China because of its burgeoning industrialization and transformation toward becoming a world leader. He also believes that some aliens ("waixingren") are living in China at this time, disguised as humans.

Spontaneous human combustion

In Charles Dickens's *Bleak House* (1852), an odor like that of someone frying rancid meat wafted from behind the shop door of rag-and-bottle merchant Krook, an eccentric alcoholic. When neighbors investigated the source of the smell,

the odor choked them. Grease stained the walls and ceiling as if it were painted on. Krook's coat and cap lay on a chair; a bottle of gin sat on the table.... The men swung their lantern round, looking for Krook, who was nowhere to be seen. Then they saw the pile of ash on the floor. They stared for a moment, before turning and running. They burst into the street, shouting for help. But it was too late: Old Krook was gone, a victim of spontaneous combustion.[83]

Although reports of such deaths have been recorded as far back as the 1700s, it is Dickens's *Bleak House* that brought widespread attention to the idea that bodies can spontaneously ignite and burn up. However, the likelihood of a spontaneous chemical reaction in a human body leading to ignition is virtually zero. Apart from fat tissue and some methane gas, there is not much that burns readily in a human. Cremation requires a temperature of 1,600 degrees Fahrenheit for about two hours.

Researcher Joe Nickell investigated thirty historical cases of deaths that had been attributed to spontaneous human combustion.[84] These cases often involved elderly or incapacitated persons, and it was easy to demonstrate or infer how the fire had begun, and it was not in their bodies. He concluded these deaths were due to accidental fires, and that the extensive destruction of the bodies was due to factors such as the wick effect: In some cases, the heat of an external fire close to the body causes body fat to liquefy and be absorbed by clothing, which then acts like the wick of a candle. Because of this, a fire that does little damage to surroundings can result in much of a body being destroyed over an extended period of time.[85]

The Bermuda Triangle

Most people have heard about the mysterious Bermuda Triangle, where it is reported that ships and planes have frequently disappeared without a trace. Every year, new books are published, sometimes directed at children, in which the "mystery" is rehashed and elaborated. Some books claim that the mystery was first recognized centuries ago by sailors traversing the region, but the reality is somewhat different.

The "mystery" is not a mariner's tale from ages past, but one that began only in 1952 when writer George X. Sands wrote a piece in *Fate* magazine about an unusual number of boating and aviation accidents off Bermuda. Then, in 1964, freelance writer Vincent Gaddis wrote in *Argosy* magazine that a number of ships and planes had disappeared without explanation in that same area, which he named the "Bermuda Triangle." The "mystery" was expanded upon by other articles in the popular press, and then books began to appear. In 1969, the cover of John Spencer's *Limbo of the Lost* carried these words:

> More than a thousand people ... over a hundred ships and planes ... swallowed up into the sea without a trace!

In 1974, Charles Berlitz's *The Bermuda Triangle* fleshed out the account of the mystery even further. Other books followed.

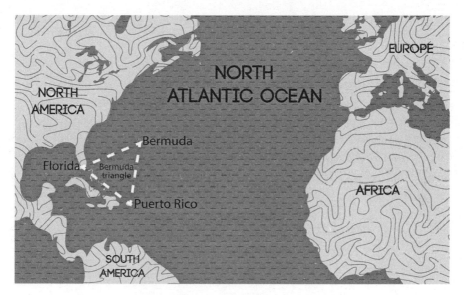

Figure 19-7: The Bermuda Triangle (Shutterstock / WindVector).

Then, in 1975, librarian Lawrence Kusche, who had begun his research into the Bermuda Triangle in the belief that the stories were genuine, published the *Bermuda Triangle Mystery: Solved*.[86] He had discovered through a thorough investigation, involving, among other sources, both naval records and the insurance records of Lloyd's of London, that there was no mystery. He deemed the Bermuda Triangle a *manufactured* myth that succeeds in selling large numbers of books. Every single case of a plane or ship that went down had a reasonable, normal explanation. In some cases, ships that various authors had described as having disappeared in "calm seas" had actually foundered in raging storms. In other cases, the wrecks of ships that had been described as having mysteriously disappeared never to be seen again had been found and the reasons for their sinkings were clear and understandable. In one case, a ship described as sinking in the Bermuda Triangle had actually disappeared thousands of miles away in the Pacific Ocean.

Although the accident records of both Lloyd's and the US Coast Guard clearly show that the so-called Bermuda Triangle region is no more dangerous than any other part of the ocean, new books extolling its "disturbing" and "destructive" character continue to be published. The "mystery" is too good, and too profitable, to be derailed by fact.

***

This is but a sampling of the many strange and diverse beliefs that continue to command large followings, despite the defiance of logic and the lack of any objective evidence. That they continue to resonate is testament to the power of creative imagination, self-deception, and strong emotion unconstrained by critical thinking. It also speaks to the appeal of the seemingly mysterious and otherworldly to a wide audience throughout history. Borrowing the words of nineteenth-century French writer Jean-Baptiste Karr: *Plus ça change, plus c'est la même chose.*

PART VI

VETTING BELIEF

Knowing a great deal is not the same as being smart; intelligence is not information alone but also judgment, the manner in which information is collected and used.

—Carl Sagan

Previous chapters have detailed how vulnerable is our thinking to distortion and error and how at times our beliefs are based only in fantasy. Yet imagination also has an important role to play in our lives, and we would be much the poorer were we to suppress it. What is vital is the ability to distinguish imagination from reality, and, in order to do so reliably, we need to be able to think critically.

CHAPTER 20

A FIREWALL TO FOLLY

The beginning of thought is in disagreement—not only with others but also with ourselves.

—Eric Hoffer[1]

In Tom Stoppard's play *Rosencrantz and Guildenstern Are Dead*, the two title characters engage in a coin-flipping game. Guildenstern is bewildered as Rosencrantz repeatedly calls "heads" and wins more than ninety times in succession. He does not understand that they are both only fictional characters in a fictional world where anything can happen and the only limits are the boundaries of imagination. Later in the play, Guildenstern refers to "reality" as "the name we give to common experience," and observes how "thin" reality is compared to the richness of human imagination. Writer Gary Bauslaugh relates this to our everyday lives:

> Reality is thin, in a way, because a rigorous look at facts does not allow for God or many other things we can think of. But it is thin in the way that truth is thin. It is not the whole world of humans, but it is a very important part of that world—not to be sought to the exclusion of all else, but not to be minimized. Scientists pursue truth like a dog does a bone, and so they should, but Stoppard points out the limitations of this. Fiction, when pursued artfully, can defy the laws of probability in a way that is insightful and edifying.[2]

And so it is that we live our lives in two partially overlapping realms, imagination and reality. Imagination is "thick" in that it has no bounds. It includes mermaids and flying horses and can expand to take in *Star Trek*'s holodeck and the many incarnations of *Doctor Who*. Reality, on the other hand, is "thin"; it is bounded, constrained by the laws of nature, by what is actually possible. It is reality that abruptly pulls us to the ground when we lose our footing, and it is reality that produces pangs of hunger when we go without food. But it is imagination that allows us to be moved by Hamlet's soliloquy and to travel down the rabbit hole with Alice.

Figure 20-1: Flying horse (Shutterstock / Antracit).

And it is imagination that has propelled humans to achieve feats once considered impossible. Flying is but one example. Humans have probably always yearned to fly, and thirteenth-century English philosopher Roger Bacon (1220–1292) predicted that one day,

> an instrument may be made to fly withal if one sits in the midst of the instrument, and do turn an engine, by which the wings, being artificially composed, may beat the air after the manner of a flying bird.[3]

Long before the invention of the airplane, attempts to fly were made by flapping artificial wings attached to the arms in imitation of birds. It soon became apparent that human arms are not up to the task, and so assistive devices, "ornithopters," were built to do the flapping. Leonardo da Vinci designed a number of ornithopters, although he never succeeded in enabling human flight (see figure 20-2). Despite his failure, imagination led him to dream:

> There shall be wings! If the accomplishment be not for me, 'tis for some other. The spirit cannot die; and man, who shall know all and shall have wings.[4]

When humans finally took to the air, pioneer aviator Wilbur Wright captured the essence of Leonardo's dream in his address to members of the Aero-Club de France in 1908:

> The desire to fly is an idea handed down to us by our ancestors who, in their grueling travels across trackless lands in prehistoric times, looked enviously on the birds soaring freely through space, at full speed, above all obstacles, on the infinite highway of the air.[5]

Other spectacular accomplishments—sending people to the moon, transplanting living hearts, linking billions of people together through the internet, and building automobiles that drive themselves—would not have come about if imagination, guided by logic and grounded in empirical evidence, had not led the way.

CONFUSING FANTASY WITH REALITY

Yet, while imagination can lead, it can also often mislead, and when allowed to roam unfettered by reason, it brings belief in ghosts, goblins, gods, and devils, the "water memory" of homeopathy, and supernatural manifestations of our own intellects, such as mental telepathy, precognition, and psychokinesis. And when the line between imagination and reality becomes indistinct, madness reigns.

It is all too easy to confuse fantasy with reality given that we have only our constructed views of reality to work with and given the myriad ways in which those constructions are subject to distortion. As we have seen in the preceding chapters, our perceptions can mislead us, and this is especially a risk when in strange situations or during times of heightened emotion. The vagaries of memory can mislead us as well, even to the extent that we can sometimes "remember" events that never occurred. Further, because our brains are programmed to look for agency and to make rapid associations between events that occur closely together in time, we are vulnerable to assuming cause-effect relationships even when events occur together only by coincidence. When logic fails, especially in times of great despair or when faced with important events that we cannot explain, magical thinking is ready in the background, offering up supernatural explanations to fill the void. Mental processes of which we are not conscious are constantly at work and can insert information into

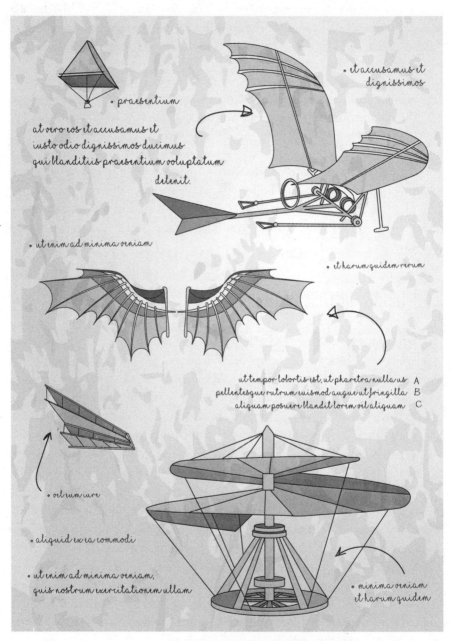

Figure 20-2: Leonardo da Vinci's Ornithopter (Shutterstock / Kwirry).

consciousness that leaves us puzzled about its source and leads some to find supernatural explanations. Our experiences and beliefs are further influenced by expectancy and suggestibility and by the various cognitive biases that undermine rational thought.

We have also seen how we can make subtle, goal-directed movements without being aware of doing so (recall the Ouija board), and then come to believe that the events that we ourselves have initiated were caused by some invisible, external force. Nor are we always consciously aware even of where our bodies are located in space, and this can give rise to the sensation of phantom or alien limbs, body-transfer illusions, and out-of-body experiences. Altered states of consciousness can produce strange and compelling experiences that instill beliefs about alternate realities.

Despite all this, our beliefs do a remarkably good job of helping us to survive and to navigate a complex world. Yet, no matter how smart we are, no matter how well-educated, and no matter how confident we may be in our ability to think critically, we are all vulnerable to developing fallacious beliefs and to mistaking the products of imagination for reality.

Earlier chapters have stressed the importance of the development of reality testing as children gradually become able to distinguish between what is real and what is fantasy. Just as children have to learn to abandon magic and to rely more and more upon reason, so too has civilization trudged along the path from magic to reason, even if history shows that it has sometimes been a matter of two steps forward and one step back. And science has been the standard-bearer of reality testing. Scientific methodology provides by far the best approach that humanity has ever developed across the centuries for separating fact from fiction and wishes from reality. It is not infallible, of course, but it is self-correcting over time.

SCIENCE, IMAGINATION, AND CRITICAL THINKING

Many people are ignorant of the important role that imagination plays in science, while some others give imagination too much credit and want to attribute great advances in science, such as Einstein's $E = mc^2$, to intuition alone. Modern science requires *both* imagination and empiricism. As economist-philosopher Kenneth Boulding explained with regard to the rise of modern science,

A high value [was] placed on a curiously uneasy combination of logic and imagination in forming theories...with testing as the selective factor. Without fantasy, science would have nothing to test; without testing, fantasy would be unchallenged.[6]

It took a very long time for humans to build a model of intellectual inquiry based on the formal testing of imagination against reality, with imagination reined in by logic and reason. Four centuries ago, in 1620, Francis Bacon made the novel argument that science (which in his day was part of philosophy) needed reform.[7] He called for a new way of thinking:

Those who have handled sciences have been either men of experiment or men of dogmas. The men of experiment are like the ant, they only collect and use; the reasoners resemble spiders, who make cobwebs out of their own substance. But the bee takes a middle course: it gathers its material from the flowers of the garden and of the field, but transforms and digests it by a power of its own. Not unlike this is the true business of philosophy; for it neither relies solely or chiefly on the powers of the mind, nor does it take the matter which it gathers from natural history and mechanical experiments and lay it up in the memory whole, as it finds it, but lays it up in the understanding altered and digested. Therefore, from a closer and purer league between these two faculties, the experimental and the rational (such as has never yet been made), much may be hoped.[8]

Bacon's goal, notwithstanding his questionable use of mindless insects to make his point, was that scientific inquiry must involve both observations about the world and the use of reason and logic to make sense of those observations.

In Bacon's time, the world was a magical one in which superstition reigned, and this was slow to change. In 1687, a half century after Bacon's declaration, Isaac Newton, who pursued alchemy on the side, established one of the most important milestones on the path to modern scientific reason with the publication of *Philosophiae Naturalis Principia Mathematica*. This work not only presented a mathematical description of gravitational force and the laws of motion but forcefully demonstrated that there is a logical order to the world that can be understood through rational analysis. For the first time, someone had worked out in precise detail, in the language of mathematics, a complex description of the workings of nature that corresponded with observation. The success of his theory in describing the effects of gravity both on earth and in the heavens pointed to a new way of studying nature in which any systematic discrepancy between theory and observation, no matter how small, is taken to indicate something important.[9]

Nonetheless, in the sixteenth and seventeenth centuries, many intelligent and educated people still believed in witchcraft, divination, ghosts, and fairies, and we have seen earlier how resistant such beliefs are to disconfirmation. If the magic or the prayer does not work, the failure is explained away and does not weaken the belief. We might wonder then how it was that such a predominantly magical belief system was gradually abandoned in favor of science and reason. British historian Keith Thomas suggests that the pursuit of magical knowledge was actually conducive to empirical research and inductive thought.[10] Whereas religion in the medieval period was "passive," promoting contemplative resignation, the pursuit of magic was "active." Interest in astrology promoted careful observation of the heavens. The alchemist's search to turn base metals into gold resulted in greater understanding of chemical processes. The pursuit of numerology, based in the belief that numbers are the key to all the mysteries of the universe, stimulated mathematical thinking. Gradually, Thomas argues, the mechanistic philosophy of emerging science triumphed over magic because of its relative superiority as a guide to understanding and controlling nature.

Yet the abandonment of magic required more than the knowledge that was accumulating as the scientific-industrial revolution took root, and Thomas concludes that the changes that occurred in the late seventeenth century were more attitudinal than technological. That is, a new faith in human initiative and the ability to solve problems without need of magic gradually developed, although it is not clear why this new confidence developed at that time. This changing attitude was reflected in the Protestant Reformation and its teaching that people should seek solutions themselves before turning to God, for "God helps those who help themselves."

Until the nineteenth century, science and philosophy continued as one, with those who pursued *scientific* inquiry being referred to as *natural* philosophers. Critical thinking at that time relied on the checks and balances offered by logical analysis, but the importance of examining actual empirical evidence, as suggested by both Bacon and Newton, had not yet been formalized. As empirical exploration began to flourish, it became clear that this had to change.

Historian Laura Snyder describes how at a meeting of the British Association for the Advancement of Science on June 24, 1833, poet and philosopher Samuel Coleridge (1772–1834) insisted that members of the Association who "worked with their hands" performing experiments or digging out fossils must no longer refer to themselves as "natural philosophers."[11] This was because, he argued, they were no longer doing philosophy. William Whewell (1794–1866), whose research spanned the fields of mathematics, physics, geology, astronomy, and economics, responded that if "philosopher" were not an appropriate label for empirical researchers, then, analogous to the word *artist*, they should henceforth refer to themselves as *scientists*. And thus the "scientist" came into being.

Whewell and his colleagues dedicated themselves to promoting Bacon's imperative that theory must be vetted against data, and they ultimately shepherded the practice of science into its modern form.[12]

THE COMPELLING NATURE OF BELIEFS AND THE IMPORTANCE OF CRITICAL THINKING

Beliefs that are held with great conviction are compelling because they provide understanding of the world and predict the consequences of our actions. They define reality for us. The belief that intense pain will follow after reaching into the fireplace with bare hands to adjust the logs and the belief that death will follow after stepping off the roof of a five-story building compel you to control your actions. The psychotic belief that God is ordering you to kill the "alien" seated beside you on the bus may compel you to murder. The belief that members of a particular visible minority are "all thieves" may compel you to avoid "those people." And the belief that blowing yourself up in a crowd of innocents is a brave and honorable way to help your people and serve your god may compel you to become a suicide terrorist.

While we may wish to challenge ill-founded beliefs, it is important to remember that people who hold them do not recognize their beliefs as fallacious, just as we do not recognize errors in our own beliefs. So, what to do in times such as these, when the dogmatic forces of political and religious fundamentalism have become so powerful in some countries? What do we do when the planet is heating up and heading for disaster and the most powerful political leader in the world brands climate change a hoax? What do we do when religious fundamentalists of all stripes turn their backs on science and reason and instead take their guidance from ancient tomes that they consider to provide "living truth," the received wisdom of their god? What do we do when the unfiltered, unverified gossip of social media competes with and even supplants professional journalism, when politicians denigrate the latter as "fake news," and when large segments of the public lose trust in reliable news institutions? (A 2017 Pew Research poll carried out in the United States reported that 85 percent of Republicans and Republican leaners, compared to 46 percent of Democrats, believe that the reports of the traditional news media are having a negative effect on their country.[13])

The core beliefs of dogmatic political or religious fundamentalists are unlikely to change no matter what we do, for those beliefs are well entrenched. The facts of life, as Marcel Proust observed, "do not penetrate to the sphere in which our beliefs are cherished; they did not engender those beliefs, and they are powerless to destroy them."[14] Yet we can work to change the outlooks of people whose beliefs are not so dogmatically anchored that they are beyond influence. And the best way to do this, in addition to correcting false information, is to teach people, especially young people, not *what* to think, but *how* to think critically. This should be the goal of progressive people everywhere, and with this rests the future of our collective welfare, and indeed our planet.

Critical thinking offers the best tool for minimizing error in our beliefs, but no human being can, over the course of a lifetime, independently develop the requisite skills that took the scientific community centuries to develop. Instead, we need to benefit from humanity's intellectual history and *learn* to think critically. As I have written elsewhere,

> Just as speech develops automatically, and yet we have to study grammar and composition in order to become good speakers and writers, so too does thinking develop automatically, but we have to study logic and critical analysis if we are to become good thinkers. Yet, while the need for years of language instruction is well recognized by society, the need for thinking instruction—that is, in the ability to think critically—generally is not.[15]

Courses in critical thinking are now widely offered, but while they can be extremely helpful in teaching critical thinking skills, their completion is no guarantee that the graduate will always apply those skills when they are most needed. This is in part because such analysis takes effort, and in part because the analysis can be distorted by our biases, wishes, and emotional needs, and by the implicit pressures from the important groups to which we belong. It is often easier to find reasons to bolster beliefs that we *want* to be true—such as, "my country is fair and compassionate toward refugees," or, "I am unselfish and always try to consider others' feelings"—than it is to deal rationally with challenges to them.

A number of university courses that encourage critical thinking to help students distinguish science from pseudoscience have had mixed results. For example, psychologist Tom Gray assessed the effects of a one-semester university course that both emphasized critical thinking in the evaluation of evidence and offered natural explanations for various supposed paranormal phenomena. He reported that, while belief in ESP, alien spacecraft, and reincarnation fell from 85 percent of the students to 50 percent over the course of the term, many students simply did not change their beliefs at all. In other research, he found that university-level research methods and statistics courses, which might be expected to stimulate critical acumen, do not on their own enhance general critical thinking ability.[16]

Psychologist Scott Lilienfeld reminds us that psychology students are bombarded by pseudoscientific claims through both the media and pop psychology books, and that pseudoscientific ideas have crept into some psychology programs themselves. As a result, many psychology students graduate from university with little ability to identify and evaluate pseudoscientific claims.[17] He also points out that teaching science on its own is insufficient as a means of helping students to distinguish science from pseudoscience, a difficult task in any case, given that there is no clear and obvious dividing line between the two. Unless specific efforts are made to address the misconceptions that surround pseudoscience in its various forms, he argues, those misconceptions are likely to persist.[18]

It is discouraging to find that more and more people in the United States consider higher education to be a negative force, although this varies considerably with political party affiliation. The 2017 Pew Research poll cited above also reported that, while 72 percent of Democrats in their sample consider colleges and universities to be an "overwhelmingly positive force," only 36 percent of Republicans share that belief, and more than half of Republicans view colleges and universities as having a *negative* effect on the nation.[19]

Depressing as that is, there is encouraging news coming out of Uganda about the positive impact of critical thinking training on children and their parents. In one study, 120 primary schools were randomly divided into two groups, and the children in one set of schools received a critical thinking intervention while the others did not.[20] This involved textbooks, exercise books, and nine eighty-minute lessons focused on how to assess treatment claims and make informed health choices. The intervention resulted in a large improvement in children's ability to assess claims about the effectiveness of various treatments. These researchers then conducted another study that involved providing critical thinking education, through podcasts, to the parents of primary school children.[21] These podcasts, too, led to a large improvement in the parents' ability to assess health and treatment claims.

BUILDING A FIREWALL AGAINST FOLLY

Systematic application of critical thinking is our best defense against the appeal of false beliefs, the temptations offered by propaganda and con artists, and our own tendencies toward self-deception promoted by intuition and emotion. Short of undertaking formal training in critical thinking skills, we can help ourselves think more critically by keeping the following points in mind. They are not enough on their own to turn us into great critical thinkers; they can, however, help us all to become *better* critical thinkers.

1. *Beware*: *We can all be fooled*. Possibly the most common pitfall with regard to critical thinking is the belief that one is already a good critical thinker. The first step toward building a firewall against folly is to recognize that we *can* be deceived and that we can frequently deceive ourselves. No matter how good we are at critical analysis, every one of us is likely at times to depart significantly from rationality, especially in situations when emotion or intuition confronts reason. The corollary to this is that we all probably have pockets of irrationality where erroneous beliefs take shelter.

2. *Be wary of your intuitions*: *Pay attention to them, but do not trust them*. As the products of nonconscious information processing, intuitions can offer important guidance to decision-making when based on considerable past experience. On the other hand, they can also gravely mislead, especially when there has been little experience to back them up. To ignore intuition completely is unwise, but to accept it uncritically is even more so.

3. *Be wary of the Fundamental Attribution Error*, the tendency that we all have to attribute people's behaviors to their characters and intentions while overlooking or minimizing the power of the situation, which often plays the greater role in determining people's actions. It is easy to assume that suicide terrorists are deranged and merciless while ignoring the situational factors that render their actions altruistic in the eyes of their

communities, just as it is easy to believe that all homeless people are lazy, or that a student who does poorly in school lacks intelligence.

4. *Be wary of personal validation.* While personal experience can be a great teacher, personal validation—judging a claim based only on personal experience—is often a poor guide to its validity. You may have had a powerful dream that seemed precognitive, or the psychic's palm reading may have been impressive, or the yellow pill may seem to have cured your laryngitis, or your interaction with a member of a minority group may have been less than pleasant, but this in no way demonstrates the reality of precognition, the psychic powers of the palm reader, the remedial qualities of the yellow pill, or that "those people" are difficult.

5. *Beware of reliance on a single source of information.* This should be obvious, but it is all too easy to ignore this caveat, especially with regard to the news. We naturally gravitate toward sources that are in line with our beliefs, and this risks sheltering us from information that might challenge what we erroneously take to be fact.

5. *Beware of mistaking coincidence for causation.* As we have seen, we are born magical thinkers, and magical thinking continues to lurk beneath the surface in wait for reason to falter. It is often difficult to resist the idea of causation when two meaningful events occur one after the other. Challenging automatic assumptions about causality is a key aspect of critical thinking.[22]

6. *Be wary of over-interpreting correlations.* Just as with coincidence, we can all too readily mistake correlations for cause and effect. Observing that there seems to be more and more petty crime, while at the same time noting that the immigrant population is increasing, does not mean that there is a connection between the two.

Moreover, some of the "correlations" that we observe may not actually be correlations at all. They may be illusory. For example, many emergency ward physicians and nurses are convinced that admissions jump whenever there is a full moon. Forty percent of medical staff surveyed in a 2011 study expressed that belief,[23] while 80 percent of the nurses and 60 percent of the physicians who responded to another survey were convinced that there are more mental health admissions during a full moon than at any other time.[24] Such beliefs are in error, for many investigations have all found no evidence of increased admissions, for either physical or psychiatric reasons, during the full moon.[25] Again, experience can be a poor guide to reality.

7. *Compared to what?* The question of "compared to what?" is vital to critical thinking. A sort of parable: Before the carcinogenic properties of
asbestos were understood, some winemakers removed impurities by fil-
tering their wines through asbestos. A 1977 test found asbestos fibers
in every one of the fifteen wines tested,[26] and a particular Hungarian
wine was withdrawn from liquor store shelves after being measured as
having almost two million asbestos fibers per liter. Not long after, a psychologist friend came to dinner bearing a bottle of that very wine. When
I informed him of its high asbestos content, he replied—as any good
experimental psychologist might—"compared to what?" and jokingly
suggested that the city's water supply might have an even higher asbestos
count. The irony was that a newspaper reported a week later that city
water at that time was also being filtered through asbestos, and its fiber
count did indeed exceed that of the wine. Avoid the water too!

  Asking "compared to what?" is also an essential component of scientific inquiry, where it is typically addressed through the use of control
groups, a practice that took root only in the early twentieth century
but has ultimately become a mainstay of medical and psychological
research.[27] Though individuals can hardly be expected to set up control
groups, we should all endeavor, as my friend was doing, albeit in humor,
to engage in a control-group style of thinking.[28] This comes naturally in
some situations but rarely occurs in others.

8. *Keep the Scottish verdict in mind and suspend judgment.* Juries in criminal
trials in Scotland are not forced to choose between *guilty* or *innocent*;
they can also opt for *not proven*. It is often tempting to jump to conclusions: "They didn't invite us because they don't like us"; "That country
developed new weapons because they want to attack us"; "Last night's
dream about today's fire must have been paranormal." Such quick conjectures are often wrong. If more information is to be had, then by all means
we should seek it out, but in the meantime, rather than rely on whatever explanation comes readily to mind, the wiser strategy is to adopt
the equivalent of the Scots' "not proven"; suspend judgment about how
or why something happened and conclude simply that "I don't know."

***

Whether products of imagination or rooted in reality, our beliefs define the world for us. They motivate our actions, influence our emotions, feed our creativity, govern our relationships, and tell us who we are. They push us to struggle against overwhelming adversity or surrender to despair; they allow us to trust others, yet make us vulnerable to exploitation; they lead us to science-based medicine or quackery; and they promote harmony among peoples or else hostility and violence. And some grow to such powerful dominance that they become beliefs to die for.

A wise person revels in the wide expanse of imagination, anchors belief in thin reality, and does the utmost to distinguish between the two. As the Belief Engine toils away, creating, maintaining, and modifying beliefs, we must strive to subject its products to the quality control offered by critical thinking. In so doing, we need to regularly ask ourselves what has been called the most important question in science, "How do we know what we claim to know?"[29] This may lead to the realization that some of our important beliefs are based on insufficient evidence or none at all. In playing devil's advocate and contemplating possible challenges to our beliefs, we should heed the words of Eric Hoffer that began this chapter. Critical thought requires being prepared to disagree with ourselves. This is never easy, but it is the challenge for us all.

NOTES

PART I: THE POWER OF BELIEF

1. Bertrand Russell, *Analysis of Mind* (London: Allen & Unwin, 1921), p. 231.

Chapter 1: Belief to Die For

1. Voltaire, *Questions sur les Miracles, à M. Claparede, Professeur de Theologie a Geneve, par un Proposant: ou extrait de diverses lettres de M. de Voltaire, avec les réponses par M. Needham* (Andover, Hampshire, UK: Gale Ecco, 1769/2010).

2. "International Suicide Statistics," Suicide.org, http://www.suicide.org/international-suicide-statistics.html (accessed June 25, 2017).

3. "Suicide," Canada.com, 2017, http://bodyandhealth.canada.com/channel_condition_info_details.asp?disease_id=206&channel_id=1053&relation_id=28250#Facts (accessed June 25, 2017).

4. Silvia Sara Canetto and David Lester, "Gender and the Primary Prevention of Suicide Mortality," *Suicide and Life-Threatening Behavior* 25, no. 1 (Spring 1995): 58–69.

5. Michael Biggs, "Dying without Killing: Self-Immolations, 1963–2002," in *Making Sense of Suicide Missions*, ed. Diego Gambetta (Oxford: Oxford University Press, 2005), pp. 173–208.

6. William E. Phipps, "Christian Perspectives on Suicide," *Christian Century*, October 30, 1985, pp. 970–72.

7. A1B2C3 Drug Information, http://www.a1b2c3.com/suilodge/fachis1.htm (accessed June 25, 2017).

8. Baruch A. Brody, ed., *Suicide and Euthanasia: Historical and Contemporary Themes* (Dordrecht, Netherlands: Kluwer, 1989).

9. Gary Bauslaugh, *The Right to Die: The Courageous Canadians Who Gave Us the Right to a Dignified Death* (Toronto, ON: Latimer, 2016).

10. Pam Belluck, "Switzerland: More Foreigners Drawn by Assisted Suicide Law, Study Shows," *New York Times*, August 21, 2014, p. A6.

11. James R. Lewis, ed., *The Order of the Solar Temple: The Temple of Death* (Aldershot, UK: Ashgate, 2006).

12. Robert W. Balch and David Taylor, "Making Sense of the Heaven's Gate Suicides," in

Cults, Religion, and Violence, ed. David G. Bromley and J. Gordon Melton (Cambridge, UK: Cambridge University Press, 2002), pp. 170–88.

13. Rebecca Moore, *Understanding Jonestown and Peoples Temple* (Westport, CT: Praeger, 2009).

14. Charles A. Joiner, "South Vietnam's Buddhist Crisis: Organization for Charity, Dissidence, and Unity," *Asian Survey* 4, no. 7 (July 1964): 915–28, 918.

15. Jason Manning, "Suicide as Social Control," *Sociological Forum* 27, no. 1 (March 2012): 207–27.

16. Costica Bradatan, "The Political Psychology of Self-Immolation," *New Statesman*, September 17, 2012, https://www.newstatesman.com/blogs/politics/2012/09/political-psychology-self-immolation (accessed June 30, 2017).

17. David Lester, "The Role of Shame in Suicide," *Suicide and Life-Threatening Behavior* 27, no. 4 (Winter 1997): 352–61.

18. Ivan I. Morris, *Nationalism and the Right Wing in Japan* (London: Oxford University Press, 1960).

19. Michael J. Casimir and Susanne Jung, "'Honor and Dishonor': Connotations of a Socio-Symbolic Category in Cross-Cultural Perspective," in *Emotions as Bio-Cultural Processes*, ed. Birgitt Röttger-Rössler and Hans Markowitsch (New York: Springer, 2009), pp. 229–80.

20. Nori Takei and Kazuhiko Nakamura, "Is Inseki-Jisatsu, Responsibility-Driven Suicide, Culture-Bound?" *Lancet* 363, no. 9418 (April 24, 2004): 1400.

21. "Ibaraki Principal Commits Suicide," *Japan Times*, November 7, 2006, https://www.japantimes.co.jp/news/2006/11/07/national/ibaraki-principal-commits-suicide/ (accessed November 30, 2017).

22. Marshall B. Clinard and Robert F. Meier, *Sociology of Deviant Behavior*, 14th ed. (Belmont, CA: Wadsworth Cengage Learning, 2011).

23. Ibid.

24. Media Line, "Anatomy of an 'Honour' Killing: Why a Palestinian Community Demanded a Father Murder His Divorced Daughter," *National Post*, December 19, 2013, http://nationalpost.com/g00/news/anatomy-of-an-honour-killing-why-a-palestinian-community-demanded-a-father-murder-his-divorced-daughter (accessed July 15, 2017).

25. Casimir and Jung, "Honor and Dishonor," p. 243.

26. Juliet Perry and Sophia Saifi, "Brother of Pakistan's Qandeel Baloch: I'm 'Proud' of Strangling My Sister," CNN, July 18, 2016, http://www.cnn.com/2016/07/18/asia/pakistan-qandeel-baloch-brother-confession/index.html (accessed July 15, 2017).

27. Amnesty International, 1999, cited by Casimir and Jung, "Honor And Dishonor," p. 248.

28. Adrian Humphreys, "Hamed Shafia's Promise to His Sister on Her Wedding Night: If You Leave Your Husband, I'll Kill Everyone Here," *National Post*, October 26, 2012, http://nationalpost.com/news/canada/hamed-shafias-promise-to-his-sister-on-her-wedding-night-if-you-leave-with-your-husband-ill-kill-everyone-here (accessed July 15, 2017).

29. Ariel A. Roth, "The Dishonor of Duelling," *Origins* 16, no. 1 (1989): 3–7.

30. Ross Drake, "Duel!" *Smithsonian*, March 2004, https://www.smithsonianmag.com/history/duel-104161025 (accessed July 15, 2017).

31. Ibid.

32. Ashfaq Yusufzai, "Health-Pakistan: 'War on Terror' Cripples Border Hospitals," Inter Press Service News Agency, June 5, 2007, http://www.ipsnews.net/2007/06/health-pakistan -war-on-terror-cripples-border-hospitals/ (accessed July 3, 2017).

33. Fred Attewill, "Jehovah's Witness Mother Dies after Refusing Blood Transfusion," *Guardian*, November 5, 2007, https://www.theguardian.com/uk/2007/nov/05/health.religion (accessed July 2, 2017).

34. Mia Bloom, *Dying to Kill: The Allure of Suicide Terror* (New York: Columbia University Press, 2007).

35. Ariel Merari, *Driven to Death: Psychological and Social Aspects of Suicide Terrorism* (Oxford: Oxford University Press, 2010).

36. Jeremy Ginges et al., "Psychology out of the Laboratory: The Challenge of Violent Extremism," *American Psychologist* 66, no. 6 (2011): 507–19.

37. David C. Earhart, "Kamikazefication and Japan's Wartime Ideology," *Critical Asian Studies* 37, no. 4 (December 2005): 569–96.

38. Yuki Tanaka, "Japan's Kamikaze Pilots and Contemporary Suicide Bombers: War and Terror," *Asia–Pacific Journal: Japan Focus* 3, no. 7 (July 6, 2005), http://apjjf.org/ Yuki -Tanaka/1606/article.html (accessed June 23, 2017).

39. Jeff Victoroff, "The Mind of the Terrorist: A Review and Critique of Psychological Approaches," *Journal of Conflict Resolution* 49, no. 1 (February 2005): 3–42.

40. Scott Atran, "Genesis of Suicide Terrorism," *Science* 299, no. 5612 (March 7, 2003): 1534–39.

41. Martha Crenshaw, "The Causes of Terrorism," *Comparative Politics* 13, no. 4 (July 1981): 379–400.

42. Robert Nalbandov, "Irrational Rationality of Terrorism," *Journal of Strategic Security* 6, no. 4 (Winter 2013): 92–102.

43. Ginges et al., "Psychology out of the Laboratory."

44. Bill Weir and Melinda Arons, "Spending Some 'Real Time' with Bill Maher," ABC News, November 15, 2006, http://abcnews.go.com/Nightline/story?id=2654307&page=1 (accessed July 5, 2017).

45. Gustave Le Bon, *The Psychology of The Great War*, trans. E. Andrews (London: Unwin, 1916).

46. Nalbandov, "Irrational Rationality of Terrorism."

47. Robert A. Pape, "The Strategic Logic of Suicide Terrorism," *American Political Science Review* 97, no. 3 (August 2003): 343–61.

48. Nalbandov, "Irrational Rationality of Terrorism."

49. Mia Bloom, "Dying to Kill: Motivations for Suicide Terrorism," in *Root Causes of Suicide Terrorism: The Globalization of Martyrdom*, ed. Ami Pedahzur (New York: Routledge, 2006), pp. 25–53.

50. Nalbandov, "Irrational Rationality of Terrorism."

51. Ami Pedahzur, preface to *Root Causes of Suicide Terrorism*, pp. xv–xviii.

52. Rick O'Gorman, "The Evolutionary Logic of Terrorism: Understanding Why Terrorism Is an Inevitable Human Strategy in Conflict," in *The Psychology of Counter-Terrorism*, ed. Andrew Silke (Oxford: Routledge, 2012).

53. Scott Atran, "The Moral Logic and Growth of Suicide Terrorism," *Washington Quarterly* 29 (2006): 127–47.

54. Ibid.

55. National Consortium for the Study of Terrorism and Responses to Terrorism: Annex of Statistical Information, *Country Reports on Terrorism 2012* (Washington, DC: Department of Defense, May 20, 2013), https://www.state.gov/j/ct/rls/crt/2012/210017.htm (accessed May 30, 2017).

56. Spencer Ackerman, "Global Terrorism Rose 43% in 2013 Despite Al-Qaida Splintering, US Reports," *Guardian*, April 30, 2014, https://www.theguardian.com/world/2014/apr/30/global-terrorism-rose-despite-al-qaida-splintering (accessed April 30, 2017).

57. Benjamin Acosta, "Dying for Survival: Why Militant Organizations Continue to Conduct Suicide Attacks," *Journal of Peace Research* 53, no. 2 (March 2016): 180–96.

58. Atran, "Moral Logic and Growth of Suicide Terrorism."

59. Tanaka, "Japan's Kamikaze Pilots."

60. Ibid., pp. 36–41.

61. Nasra Hassan, "An Arsenal of Believers: Talking to the Human Bombs," *New Yorker*, November 19, 2001, pp. 36–41.

62. Pedahzur, preface, to *Root Causes of Suicide Terrorism.*

63. Pape, "Strategic Logic of Suicide Terrorism."

64. Robert Pape, *Dying to Win: The Strategic Logic of Suicide Terrorism* (New York: Random House, 2005).

65. Atran, "Moral Logic and Growth of Suicide Terrorism," p. 134.

66. Acosta, "Dying for Survival," pp. 180–96

67. Pape, *Dying to Win.*

68. Hassan, "Arsenal of Believers."

69. Emily Comer and Paul Gill, "A False Dichotomy? Mental Illness and Lone-Actor Terrorism," *Law and Human Behavior* 39, no. 1 (2015): 23–34.

70. Merari, *Driven to Death.*

71. Audrey Kurth Cronin, *Terrorists and Suicide Attacks* (Washington, DC: CRS Report for Congress, 2003).

72. Hassan, "Arsenal of Believers."

73. Pape, *Dying to Win.*

74. Corinne Graff and Rebecca Winthrop, "Beyond Madrasas: Assessing the Links between Education and Militancy in Pakistan" (working paper 2; Washington, DC: Brookings Institute Center for Universal Education, 2010). https://www.brookings.edu/research/beyond-madrasas-assessing-the-links-between-education-and-militancy-in-pakistan/ (accessed June 15, 2017).

75. Ibid.

76. Jeremy Ginges, Ian Hansen, and Ara Norenzayan, "Religious Belief, Coalitional Commitment, and Support for Suicide Attacks," *Evolutionary Psychology* 8, no. 3 (July 2010): 346–49.

77. Florent Gathérias, "Psychologie Succincte des Auteurs d'Attentat Suicide [Brief

Psychological Analysis of Suicide Bombers]," *Revue Francophone du Stress et du Trauma* 6 (2006): 47

78. Pape, *Dying to Win*, p. 216.

79. James Alcock and Stan Sadava, *An Introduction to Social Psychology* (London: Sage, 2014).

80. Ibid.

81. Arie W. Kruglanski and Shira Fishman, "Terrorism between 'Syndrome' and 'Tool,'" *Current Directions in Psychological Science* 15, no. 1 (February 2006): 45–48.

82. Atran, "Moral Logic and Growth of Suicide Terrorism."

83. Michael E. McCullough, *Beyond Revenge: The Evolution of the Forgiveness Instinct* (San Francisco: Jossey-Bass, 2008).

84. Ginges et al., "Psychology out of the Laboratory," pp. 507–19.

85. O'Gorman, "Evolutionary Logic of Terrorism," pp. 62–75.

86. Ian McGregor et al., "Anxious Uncertainty and Reactive Approach Motivation (RAM)," *Journal of Personality and Social Psychology* 99, no. 1 (July 2010): 133–47.

87. Arie W. Kruglanski and Edward Orehek, "The Role of the Quest for Personal Significance in Motivating Terrorism," in *The Psychology of Social Conflict and Aggression*, ed. Joseph P. Forgas, Arie W. Kruglanski, and Kipling D. Williams (New York: Psychology Press, 2011), pp. 153–66.

88. Alcock and Sadava, *Introduction To Social Psychology*.

89. William B. Swann Jr. et al., "When Group Membership Gets Personal: A Theory of Identity Fusion," *Psychological Review* 119, no. 3 (July 2012): 441–56.

90. William B. Swann Jr. and Michael D. Buhrmester, "Identity Fusion," *Current Directions in Psychological Science* 24, no. 1 (February 2015): 52–57.

91. Merari, *Driven to Death*.

92. Bloom, *Dying to Kill*.

93. Merari, *Driven to Death*.

94. Peter Bernholz, "Supreme Values as the Basis for Terror," *European Journal of Political Economy* 20, no. 2 (June 2004): 317–33.

95. Ginges et al., "Psychology out of the Laboratory.'"

96. Ángel Gómez, Lucía López-Rodríguez, Hammad Sheikh, Jeremy Ginges, Lydia Wilson, Hoshang Waziri, Alexandra Vázquez, Richard Davis, and Scott Atran, "The Devoted Actor's Will to Fight and the Spiritual Dimension of Human Conflict," *Nature Human Behaviour*, September 7, 2017, doi:10.1038/s41562-017-0193-3.

97. Jocelyn J. Bélanger et al., "The Psychology of Martyrdom: Making the Ultimate Sacrifice in the Name of a Cause," *Journal of Personality and Social Psychology* 107, no. 3 (September 2014): 494–513.

98. Arie W. Kruglanski et al., "Terrorism: A (Self) Love Story: Redirecting the Significance Quest Can End Violence," *American Psychologist* 68, no. 7 (2013): 559–75.

99. Ibid.

100. Ginges, Hansen, and Norenzayan, "Religious Belief, Coalitional Commitment, and Support for Suicide Attacks."

101. Bloom, *Dying to Kill*.

102. Clark R. McCauley, "The Psychology of Terrorism," *After September 11*, Social Science Research Council, p. 3, http://essays.ssrc.org/sept11/essays/mccauley.htm (accessed July 3, 2017).

103. Merari, *Driven to Death*, p.145.

104. Bloom, *Dying To Kill*.

105. R. W. Kurz and C. K. Bartles, "Chechen Suicide Bombers," *Journal of Slavic Military Studies* 20 (2007): 529–47, p. 537.

106. Acosta, "Dying for Survival."

107. Ibid., p. 194.

108. Ibid.

109. Fathali M. Moghaddam, *How Globalization Spurs Terrorism: The Lopsided Benefits of "One World" and Why That Fuels Violence* (New York: Praeger, 2008).

110. Jessica Stern, *Terror in the Name of God: Why Religious Militants Kill* (New York: Harper Collins, 2003), p. 283.

111. Angel Rabasa and Cheryl Benard, *Eurojihad: Patterns of Islamist Radicalization and Terrorism in Europe* (Cambridge: Cambridge University Press, 2015).

112. Duncan Gardham, "Glasgow Bomb Plot: NHS Doctor Found Guilty of Terror Attack on Airport," *Telegraph*, December 16, 2008, http://www.telegraph.co.uk/news/uknews/3688837/Glasgow-bomb-plot-NHS-doctor-found-guilty-of-terror-attack-on-airport.html (accessed June 15, 2017).

113. Emmanuel Karagiannis, "European Converts to Islam: An Evolving Threat?" National Consortium for the Study of Terrorism and Responses to Terrorism, June 2009–May 2011, http://www.start.umd.edu/research-projects/european-converts-islam-evolving-threat (accessed June 15, 2017).

114. Stern, *Terror in the Name of God*, pp. 281–82.

115. Atran, "Moral Logic and Growth of Suicide Terrorism," p. 128.

116. Herbert G. Kelman, "Violence without Moral Restraint: Reflections on the Dehumanization of Victims and Victimizers," *Journal of Social Issues* 29, no. 4 (Fall 1973): 25–61.

117. Sandra Baez, Eduar Herrera, Adolfo M. Garcia, Facundo Manes, Liane Young, and Agustin Ibáñez, "Outcome-Oriented Moral Evaluation in Terrorists," *Nature Human Behaviour* 1, article number: 0118 (2017), doi:10.1038/s41562-017-0118.

118. Atran, "Moral Logic and Growth of Suicide Terrorism," p. 139.

119. Hassan, "Arsenal of Believers."

PART II: THE BELIEF ENGINE

1. Stephen P. Stich, *From Folk Psychology to Cognitive Science: The Case against Belief* (Cambridge, MA: MIT Press, 1983).

2. Patrick Boyer, *Religion Explained: The Evolutionary Origins of Religious Thought* (New York: Basic Books, 2001), p. 299.

3. William James. *The Will to Believe and Other Essays in Popular Philosophy and Human Immortality* (1897; New York: Digireads, 2010), p. 10.

4. James E. Alcock. "The Belief Engine," *Skeptical Inquirer* 19, no. 3 (1995): 14–18.

5. Charles Babbage. *The Works of Charles Babbage: The Analytical Engine and Mechanical Notation*, ed. Martin Campbell-Kelly, vol. 3 (New York: New York University Press, 1989).

Chapter 2: When Seeing Is Believing

1. Camille Flammarion, *The Unknown* (New York: Harper Brothers, 1909), p. 11.

2. Carl J. Wenning, "New Thoughts on Understanding the Moon Illusion," *Planetarian* 14, no. 4 (1985): 10–13.

3. Gerald A. Winer et al., "Fundamentally Misunderstanding Visual Perception: Adults Belief in Visual Emissions," *American Psychologist* 57, no. 6-7 (June-July 2002): 417–24

4. Danielle R. Reed, Toshiko Tanaka, and Amanda H. McDaniel, "Diverse Tastes: Genetics of Sweet and Bitter Perception," *Physiology and Behavior* 88, no. 3 (June 2006): 215–26.

5. Ewen Callaway, "Soapy Taste of Coriander Linked to Genetic Variants," *Nature News*, September 12, 2012, https://www.nature.com/news/soapy-taste-of-coriander-linked-to-genetic -variants-1.11398 (accessed July 3, 2017).

6. Daphne Maurer and Charles Maurer, *The World of the Newborn* (New York: Basic Books, 1988).

7. William James, *Principles of Psychology* (New York: Henry Holt, 1890), p. 488.

8. Philip J. Kellman and Martha E. Arterberry, *The Cradle of Knowledge: Development of Perception in Infancy* (Cambridge, MA: MIT Press, 1998).

9. Katie Wagner and Karen R. Dobkins, "Synaesthetic Associations Decrease During Infancy," *Psychological Science* 22, no. 8 (2011): 1067–72.

10. Simon Baron-Cohen, Lucy Burt, Fiona Smith-Laittan, John Harrison, and Patrick Bolton, "Synaesthesia: Prevalence and Familiality," *Perception* 25, no. 9 (September 1996): 1073–79.

11. Julia Simner, Catherine Mulvenna, Noam Sagiv, Elias Tsakanikos, Sarah A. Witherby, Christine Fraser, Kirsten Scott, and Jamie Ward, "Synaesthesia: The Prevalence of Atypical Cross-Modal Experiences," *Perception* 35 no. 8 (August 2006): 1024–33.

12. Lutz Jancke, "Music Drives Brain Plasticity," *F1000 Biology Reports* 1, no. 78 (2009), https://f1000.com/prime/reports/b/1/78/ (accessed November 13, 2017).

13. Bryan Kolb, Robbin Gibb, and Terry Robinson, "Brain Plasticity and Behavior," *Current Directions in Psychological Science* 12, no. 1 (2003): 1–5.

14. Alan Slater and Victoria Morison, "Shape Constancy and Slant Perception at Birth," *Perception* 14, no. 3 (June 1985): 337–44.

15. Alan Slater, Anne Mattock, and Elizabeth Brown, "Size Constancy at Birth: Newborn Infants Responses to Retinal and Real Size," *Journal of Experimental Child Psychology* 49, no. 2 (1990): 314–22.

16. Leslie B. Cohen and Cara H. Cashon, "Infant Perception and Cognition," in

Developmental Psychology, vol. 6, *Handbook of Psychology*, ed. Richard M. Lerner, A. Ann Easterbrooks, Jayanthi Mistry (New Jersey: John Wiley & Sons, 2003).

17. John Locke, *An Essay Concerning Human Understanding* (London: William Tegg, 1860), p. 94.

18. Ibid.

19. Yuri Ostrovsky et al., "Visual Parsing after Recovery from Blindness," *Psychological Science* 20, no. 12 (2009): 1484–91.

20. Richard L. Gregory and J. G. Wallace, "Recovery from Early Blindness: A Case Study," *Experimental Psychology Society Monograph*, no. 2 (1963).

21. Olivier Collignon, Giulia Dormal, Adelaide de Heering, Franco Lepore, Terri L. Lewis, and Daphne Maurer, "Long-Lasting Crossmodal Cortical Reorganization Triggered by Brief Postnatal Visual Deprivation," *Current Biology* 25, no. 18 (September 21, 2015): 2379–83.

22. Rachel Keen and Kristin Shutts, "Object and Event Recognition in Toddlers," *Progress in Brain Research* 164 (2007): 227–35.

23. Cohen and Cashon, "Infant Perception and Cognition."

24. Graham F. Reed, *The Psychology of Anomalous Experience: A Cognitive Approach* (Amherst, NY: Prometheus Books, 1988).

25. Jerome S. Bruner, "Going Beyond the Information Given," in *Contemporary Approaches to Cognition: A Symposium Held at the University of Colorado*, ed. University of Colorado Psychology Department (Cambridge, MA: Harvard University Press, 1957).

26. Christopher M. Massad, Michael Hubbard, and Darren Newtson, "Selective Perception of Events," *Journal of Experimental Social Psychology* 15, no. 6 (1979): 513–32.

27. David Cohen, "Founding Fathers of the Psyche," *New Scientist*, December 17, 1994, https://www.newscientist.com/article/mg14419564-600-founding-fathers-of-the-psyche/ (accessed June 15, 2017).

28. David Morrison, "MGS Photographs' Face on Mars," *Skeptical Inquirer* 25, no. 3 (1998): 65

29. Kevin Larson, "The Science of Word Recognition," Advance Reading Technology, Microsoft Corporation, July 2004, http://www.microsoft.com/typography/ctfonts/Word Recognition.aspx (accessed July 11, 2017).

30. Sneh Duggal, "The Cougar Is out There," *Ottawa Citizen*, June 21, 2010, http://www.ottawacitizen.com/cougar there/3179785/story.html (accessed June 2, 2017).

31. Associated Press, "Wild Cat Roaming Near Disneyland Paris Isn't a Tiger," *New York Post*, November 14, 2014, http://nypost.com/2014/11/14/wild-cat-roaming-near-disneyland -paris-isnt-a-tiger/ (accessed July 3, 2017).

32. "Mountain Lion Mistaken for Large Cat," *UPI*, October 1, 2008, https://www.upi .com/Odd_News/2008/10/01/Mountain-lion-mistaken-for-large-cat/UPI-27941222908184/ ?st_rec=5101467352000 (accessed July 3, 2017).

33. Lister Sinclair, personal communication with the author, September 1985.

34. Daniel J. Simons and Michael S. Ambinder, "Change Blindness," *Current Directions in Psychological Science* 14, no. 1 (2005): 44–48.

35. Daniel J. Simons and Daniel T. Levin, "Failure to Detect Changes to People during a Real-World Interaction," *Psychonomic Bulletin & Review* 5, no. 4 (1998): 644–49.

36. Daniel J. Simons and Christopher F. Chabris, "Gorillas in Our Midst: Sustained Inattentional Blindness for Dynamic Events," *Perception* 28, no. 9 (1999): 1059–74.

37. Joseph E. Ledoux, "Emotion, Memory, and the Brain," *Scientific American* 270, no. 6 (1994): 50–57.

38. Wilson Bryan Key, *Subliminal Seduction* (Englewood Cliffs, NJ: Signet, 1973).

39. Timothy E. Moore, "Scientific Consensus and Expert Testimony: Lessons from the Judas Priest Trial," *Skeptical Inquirer* 20 (1996): 32–38.

40. Philip M. Merikle, "Subliminal Perception," in *Encyclopedia of Psychology*, 8 vols., ed. Alan E. Kazdin (New York: Oxford University Press, 2000), 7: 497–99.

41. Timothy E. Moore, "Subliminal Perception: Facts and Fallacies," *Skeptical Inquirer* 16 (1992): 273–81.

42. John R. Vokey and J. Don Read, "Subliminal Messages: Between the Devil and the Media," *American Psychologist* 40, no. 11 (1985): 1231–39.

43. Timothy E. Moore, "Scientific Consensus & Expert Testimony."

44. Roger N. Shepard, "The Mental Image," *American Psychologist* 33, no. 2 (1978): 125–37

45. Graham F. Reed, *The Psychology of Anomalous Experience*, rev. ed. (Amherst, NY: Prometheus Books, 1988).

46. Erol F. Giray et al., "The Incidence of Eidetic Imagery as a Function of Age," *Child Development* 47, no. 4 (1976): 1207–10

47. Marvin Lee Minsky, *Society of Mind* (New York: Simon & Schuster Paperbacks, 1998).

48. David Estes, Henry M. Welman, and Jacqueline Wooley, "Children's Understanding of Mental Phenomena," in *Advances in Child Development and Behavior*, ed. Hayne Reese (New York: Academic Press, 1989), pp. 41–86

49. Jacqueline D. Woolley and Henry M. Wellman, "Origin and Truth: Young Children's Understanding of Imaginary Mental Representations," *Child Development* 64, no. 1 (1993). 1–17.

50. Anaïs Nin, *Seduction of the Minotaur* (Athens, OH: Swallow Press, 1961), p. 124.

Chapter 3: Believing What We Remember

1. Tennessee Williams, *The Milk Train Doesn't Stop Here Anymore* (New York: Two Rivers Enterprises, 1963), p. 36.

2. Endel Tulving, "Episodic and Semantic Memory," in *Organization of Memory*, ed. Endel Tulving and Wayne Donaldson (New York: Academic Press, 1972), pp. 381–403.

3. Endel Tulving, "Episodic Memory: From Mind to Brain," *Annual Review of Psychology* 53 (2002): 1–25.

4. Ricki Ladowsky-Brooks and James Alcock, "Semantic-Episodic Interactions in the Neuropsychology of Disbelief," *Cognitive Neuropsychiatry* 12, no. 2 (2007): 97–111.

5. Anna-Lynne Adlam, Karalyn Patterson, and John R. Hodges, "'I Remember It as If It Were Yesterday': Memory for Recent Events in Patients with Semantic Dementia," *Neuropsychologia* 47, no. 5 (April 2010): 1344–51.

6. Daniel L. Greenberg and Mieke Verfaellie, "Interdependence of Episodic and Semantic Memory: Evidence from Neuropsychology," *Journal of the International Neuropsychological Society* 16, no. 5 (September 2010): 748–53.

7. For a discussion of autobiographical memory, see Martin A. Conway and Christopher W. Pleydell-Pearce, "The Construction of Autobiographical Memories in the Self-Memory System," *Psychological Review* 107, no. 2 (April 2000): 261–88.

8. Asaf Gilboa, "Autobiographical and Episodic Memory—One and the Same? Evidence from Prefrontal Activation in Neuroimaging Studies," *Neuropsychologia* 42, no. 10 (2004): 1336–49.

9. Mark L. Howe and Mary L. Courage, "The Emergence and Early Development of Autobiographical Memory," *Psychological Review* 104, no. 3 (1997): 499–523

10. Elizabeth J. Marsh and Henry L. Roediger III, "Episodic and Autobiographical Memory," in *Experimental Psychology* vol. 4 of *Handbook of Psychology*, ed. Alice F. Healy and Robert W. Proctor (New York: Wiley, 2012), pp. 472–94.

11. Conway and Pleydell-Pearce, "Construction of Autobiographical Memories."

12. Stanley Milgram, "The Image-Freezing Machine," *Society* 14, no. 1 (November/December 1976): 77.

13. Ibid., p. 12.

14. Ibid.

15. Errol Morris, *Believing Is Seeing: Observations on the Mystery of Photography* (New York: Penguin, 2011).

16. Deryn Strange et al., "Photographs Cause False Memories for the News," *Acta Psychologica* 136, no. 1 (January 2011): 587–603.

17. Lauren French, Maryanne Garry, and Elizabeth Loftus, "False Memories: A Kind of Confabulation and Non-Clinical Subjects," in *Confabulation: Views from Neuroscience, Psychiatry, Psychology, and Philosophy*, ed. William Hirstein (Oxford: Oxford University Press, 2009), pp. 33–66.

18. Ibid.

19. Ibid.

20. Elizabeth F. Loftus, "Planting Misinformation in the Human Mind: A 30-Year Investigation of the Malleability of Memory," *Learning and Memory* 12, no. 4 (July 2005): 361–66.

21. Craig E. L. Stark, Yoko Okado, and Elizabeth F. Loftus, "Imaging the Reconstruction of True and False Memories Using Sensory Reactivation and the Misinformation Paradigms," *Learning and Memory* 17, no. 10 (October 2010): 485–88.

22. Elizabeth F. Loftus and John C. Palmer, "Reconstruction of Automobile Destruction: An Example of the Interaction between Language and Memory," *Journal of Verbal Learning and Verbal Behavior* 13, no. 5 (October 1974): 585–89.

23. Elizabeth F. Loftus and Guido Zanni, "Eyewitness Testimony: The Influence of the Wording of a Question," *Bulletin of the Psychonomic Society* 5, no. 1 (January 1975): 86–88.

24. Stephen J. Ceci, Mary Lyndia Crotteau Huffman, Elliott Smith, and Elizabeth F. Loftus, "Repeatedly Thinking about a Non-Event: Source Misattributions among Preschoolers," *Consciousness and Cognition* 3, no. 3-4 (September 1994): 388–407.

25. Kim Hongkeun and Roberto Cabeza, "Differential Contributions of Prefrontal, Medial Temporal, and Sensory-Perceptual Regions to True and False Memory Formation," *Cerebral Cortex* 17, no. 9 (September 2007): 2143–50.

26. Maryanne Garry, Charles G. Manning, Elizabeth F. Loftus, and Steven J. Sherman, "Imagination Inflation: Imagining a Childhood Event Inflates Confidence That It Occurred," *Psychonomic Bulletin & Review* 3, no. 2 (June 1996): 208–14.

27. Eryn J. Newman and Maryanne Garry, "False Memory," in *The SAGE Handbook of Applied Memory*, ed. Timothy J. Perfect and D. Stephen Lindsay (London: SAGE, 2014), pp. 120–21.

28. D. Stephen Lindsay, "Misleading Suggestions Can Impair Eyewitnesses' Ability to Remember Event Details," *Journal of Experimental Psychology: Learning, Memory, and Cognition* 16, no. 6 (November 1990): 1077–83.

29. G. Tarcan Kumkale and Dolores Albarracín, "The Sleeper Effect in Persuasion: A Meta-Analytic Review," *Psychological Bulletin* 130, no. 1 (January 2004): 143–72.

30. Linda J. Levine and Robin S. Edelstein, "Emotion and Memory Narrowing: A Review and Goal-Relevance Approach," *Cognition and Emotion* 23, no. 5 (2009): 833–75.

31. Elizabeth A. Kensinger, "Negative Emotion Enhances Memory Accuracy: Behavioral and Neuroimaging Evidence," *Current Directions in Psychological Science* 16, no. 4 (August 2007): 213–18.

32. Daniel Reisberg, *The Science of Perception and Memory: A Pragmatic Guide for the Justice System* (New York: Oxford University Press, 2014).

33. Elizabeth F. Loftus, "Creating False Memories," *Scientific American* 277, no. 3 (1997): 70–75.

34. Elizabeth F. Loftus, James A. Coan, and Jacqueline E. Pickrell, "Manufacturing False Memories Using Bits of Reality," in *Implicit Memory and Metacognition*, ed. Lynne M. Reder (Hillsdale, NJ: Erlbaum, 1996) pp. 195–220.

35. Elizabeth F. Loftus and Katherine Ketcham, *The Myth of Repressed Memory: False Memories and Allegations of Sexual Abuse* (New York: St. Martin's Press, 1994).

36. Nicholas P. Spanos et al., "Creating False Memories of Infancy with Hypnotic and Non-Hypnotic Procedures," *Applied Cognitive Psychology* 13, no. 3 (June 1999): 201–18.

37. Elizabeth. F. Loftus and Deborah Davis, "Recovered Memories," *Annual Review of Clinical Psychology* 2 (2006): 469–98.

38. Loftus and Ketcham., *Myth of Repressed Memory*.

39. Cynthia Wesley-Esquimaux, "Residential School Survivors and Their Descendants Share Their Stories," *Globe and Mail*, May 31, 2015, https://www.theglobeandmail.com/news/politics/residential–school–survivors–and–their–descendants–share–their–stories/article24717419/ (accessed July 11, 2017).

40. Maria Buda et al., "A Specific Brain Structural Basis for Individual Differences in Reality Monitoring" *Journal of Neuroscience* 31, no. 40 (October 5, 2011): 14308–313

41. Ellen Bass and Laura Davis, *The Courage to Heal: A Guide for Women Survivors of Child Sexual Abuse* (New York: Harper & Row, 1988).

42. Ibid., p. 22.

43. Ibid., p. 58.

44. Henry Otgarr, Alan Scorbaria, and Giuliana Mazzoni, "On the Existence and Implications of Nonbelieved Memories," *Current Directions in Psychological Science* 23, no. 5 (2014): 349–54.

45. Charles J. Brainerd, "Murder Must Memorise," *Memory* 21, no. 5 (2013): 547.

46. R. v. Trochym, Judgment of the Supreme Court of Canada, February 1, 2007, https://scc-csc.lexum.com/scc-csc/scc-csc/en/item/2341/index.do (accessed June 1, 2017).

47. Brent A. Paterline, "Forensic Hypnosis and the Courts," *Journal of Law and Criminal Justice* 4, no. 2 (December 2016): 6.

48. Robert Bland, *Proverbs, Chiefly Taken from the Adagia of Erasmus*, vol. 2 (London: T. Edgerton Military Library, 1814), p. 37.

49. Gary L. Wells, Amina Memon, and Steven D. Penrod, "Eyewitness Evidence: Improving Its Probative Value," *Psychological Science in the Public Interest* 7, no. 2 (November 2006): 45–75.

50. Sven-Ake Christianson and Elizabeth F. Lotus, "Remembering Emotional Events: The Fate of Detailed Information," *Cognition and Emotion* 5, no. 2 (1991): 81–108; Gary L. Wells and Elizabeth A. Olson, "Eyewitness Identification: Information Gain from Incriminating and Exonerating Behaviors," *Journal of Experimental Psychology: Applied* 8, no. 3 (September 2002): 155–67.

51. Stephen J. Ceci and Maggie Bruck, *Jeopardy in the Courtroom: A Scientific Analysis of Children's Testimony* (Washington, DC: American Psychological Association, 2000).

52. Brandon L. Garrett, *Convicting the Innocent: Where Criminal Prosecutions Go Wrong* (Cambridge, MA: Harvard University Press, 2011).

53. Wells and Olson, "Eyewitness Identification."

54. Roger Brown and James Kulik, "Flashbulb Memories," *Cognition* 5, no. 1 (1977): 73–99.

55. Ulric Neisser and Nicole Harsch, "Phantom Flashbulbs: False Recollections of Hearing the News about *Challenger*," in *Affect and Accuracy in Recall: Studies of "Flashbulb" Memories*, ed. Eugene. Winograd and Ulric Neisser (New York: Cambridge University Press, 1992), pp. 9–31.

56. William Hirst, Elizabeth Phelps, et al., "A Ten-Year Follow-Up of a Study of Memory for the Attack of September 11, 2001: Flashbulb Memories and Memories for Flashbulb Events," *Journal of Experimental Psychology: General* 144, no. 3 (June 2015): 604–23.

57. French, Garry, and Loftus, "False Memories."

58. Steven M. Southwick et al., "Consistency of Memory for Combat-Related Traumatic Events in Veterans of Operation Desert Storm," *American Journal of Psychiatry* 154, no. 2 (1997): 173–77

59. William Hirst and Elizabeth Phelps, "Flashbulb Memories," *Current Directions in Psychological Science* 25, no. 1 (2016): 36–41.

60. William Hirst, Alin Coman, and Dora Coman, "Putting the Social Back into Human Memory," in *SAGE Handbook of Applied Memory*, pp. 273–91.

61. William Hirst and Gerald Echterhoff, "Remembering in Conversations: The Social Sharing and Reshaping of Memories," *Annual Review of Psychology* 63 (2012): 55–79.

62. James V. Wertsch and Henry L. Roediger III, "Collective Memory: Conceptual Foundations and Theoretical Approaches," *Memory* 16, no. 3 (2008): 324.

63. Henry Roediger and J. Wertz, "Past Imperfect," *New Scientist* 3043, October 17, 2015, pp. 30–31.

64. Angus Calder, *The Myth of The Blitz* (London: Pimlico, 1991).

Chapter 4: Believing What We Learn and Feel

1. Vimal Kishor, *Inspiring Thoughts of Great Educational Thinkers* (Pune, India: Amitesh Publishers, 2015), p. 161.

2. W. Scott Terry, *Learning and Memory: Basic Principles, Processes, and Procedures*, 4th ed. (New York: Routledge, 2016).

3. Leon J. Kamin, "Attention-Like Processes in Classical Conditioning," in *Miami Symposium on the Prediction of Behavior: Aversive Stimuli*, ed. Marshall R. Jones (Coral Gables, FL: University of Miami Press, 1968), pp. 9–31.

4. Robert A. Rescorla, "Pavlovian Conditioning: It's Not What You Think It Is," *American Psychologist* 43, no. 3 (1988): 160.

5. Ibid.

6. Shepard Siegel et al., "Pavlovian Psychopharmacology: The Associative Basis of Tolerance," *Experimental and Clinical Psychopharmacology* 8, no. 3 (2000): 276–93.

7. Shepard Siegel, "Conditioning of Insulin-Induced Glycemia," *Journal of Comparative and Physiological Psychology* 78, no. 2 (1972): 233–41.

8. Petra K. Staiger and Jason M. White, "Conditioned Alcohol-Like and Alcohol-Opposite Responses in Humans," *Psychopharmacology* 95, no. 1 (1988): 87–91.

9. Shepard Siegel, "Nonpharmacological Contributions to Drug Effects," in *Psychoactive Drugs*, ed. Andrew J. Goudie and Michael W. Emmet-Oglesby (New York: Springer Science, 1989), pp. 115–180.

10. Shepard Siegel, "The Heroin Overdose Mystery," *Current Directions in Psychological Science* 25, no. 6 (2016): 375–79.

11. Shepard Siegel, "Pavlovian Conditioning and Drug Overdose: When Tolerance Fails," *Addiction Research & Theory* 9, no. 5 (2001): 510.

12. Lee N. Robins et al., "Vietnam Veterans Three Years after Vietnam: How Our Study Changed Our View of Heroin," *American Journal on Addictions* 19, no. 3 (2010): 203–11.

13. Lee N. Robins, Darlene H. Davis, and Donald W. Goodwin, "Drug Use by US Army Enlisted Men in Vietnam: A Follow-Up on Their Return Home," *American Journal of Epidemiology* 99, no. 4 (1974): 235–49.

14. Ivan Petrovich Pavlov, *Essential Works of Pavlov*, ed. Michael Kaplan (1936; New York: Bantam, 1966).

15. Persi Diaconis and Frederick Mosteller, "Methods for Studying Coincidences," *Journal of the American Statistical Association* 84, no. 408 (1989): 853–61.

16. Carl G. Jung, *Synchronicity: An Acausal Connecting Principle* (Princeton, NJ: Princeton University Press, 1973), p. 8.

17. Ruma Falk, "Judgment of Coincidences: Mine versus Yours," *American Journal of Psychology* 102, no. 4 (1989): 477–93.

18. Diaconis and Mosteller, "Methods for Studying Coincidences."

19. Burrhus Frederic Skinner, "'Superstition' in the Pigeon," *Journal of Experimental Psychology* 38, no. 2 (April 1948): 168–72.

20. Ibid.

21. Karl S. Rosengren and Jason A. French, "Magical Thinking," in *The Oxford Handbook of the Development of Imagination*, ed. Marjorie Taylor (Oxford, England: Oxford University Press, 2013), pp. 42–60.

22. Jung Chang and Jon Halliday, *Mao: The Unknown Story* (New York: Random House, 2005).

23. William James, *The Will to Believe and Other Essays in Popular Philosophy* (London: Longmans, Green, 1912), p. 9.

24. D. Elton Trueblood, *Human Understanding* (Oxford: Clarendon, 1942), p. 72

25. Aristotle, *Rhetoric*, I, II, 5.

26. Nico H. Frijda, S. R. Manstead, and Sandra Bem, "The Influence of Emotions on Beliefs," in *Emotions and Beliefs: How Feelings Influence Thoughts*, ed. Nico H. Frijda, S. R. Manstead, and Sandra Bem (Cambridge: Cambridge University Press., 2000), pp. 1–9.

27. Seymour Epstein, "Integration of the Cognitive and the Psychodynamic Unconscious," *American Psychologist* 49, no. 8 (1994): 709–24.

28. Gerald L. Clore and Karen Gasper, "Feeling Is Believing: Some Affective Influences on Belief," in *Emotions and Beliefs: How Feelings Influence Thoughts*, ed. Nico H. Frijda, S. R. Manstead and Sandra Bem (Cambridge: Cambridge University Press, 2000), pp. 10–44.

29. Ibid., p. 33

30. Nico H. Frijda, Antony S. R. Manstead, and Sacha Bem, "The Influence of Emotions on Beliefs," in *Emotions and Beliefs: How Feelings Influence Thoughts*, ed. Nico H. Frijda, Antony S. R. Manstead and Sacha Bem (Cambridge: Cambridge University Press, 2000), p. 3.

Chapter 5: Thinking and Believing

1. Valerie A. Kuhlmeier, Paul Bloom, and Karen Wynn, "Do 5-Month-Old Infants See Humans as Material Objects?" *Cognition* 94, no. 1 (2004): 95–103.

2. H. Clark Barrett et al., "Early False-Belief Understanding in Traditional Non-Western Societies," *Proceedings of the Royal Society B: Biological Sciences* 280, no. 1755 (March 22, 2013): 1–6.

3. Atsushi Senju et al., "Do 18-Month-Olds Really Attribute Mental States to Others?" *Psychological Science* 22, no. 7 (2011): 878–80

4. Diane Poulin-Dubois, Ivy Brooker, and Virginia Chow, "The Developmental Origins of Naïve Psychology in Infancy," *Advances in Child Development and Behavior* 37 (2009): 55–104.

5. Alison Gopnik and Henry M. Wellman, "Reconstructing Constructivism: Causal Models, Bayesian Learning Mechanisms, and the Theory Theory," *Psychological Bulletin* 138, no. 6 (2012): 1085–108.

6. Jesse Bering, *The Belief Instinct: The Psychology of Souls, Destiny, and the Meaning of Life* (New York: W. W. Norton, 2011).

7. Deborah Kelemen, "Are Children 'Intuitive Theists'? Reasoning about Purpose and Design in Nature," *Psychological Science* 15, no. 5 (2004): 295–301.

8. Deborah Kelemen et al., "Teleo-Functional Constraints on Preschool Children's Reasoning about Living Things," *Developmental Science* 6, no. 3 (2003): 329–45.

9. Deborah Kelemen, Joshua Rottman, and Rebecca Seston, "Professional Physical Scientists Display Tenacious Teleological Tendencies: Purpose-Based Reasoning as a Cognitive Default," *Journal of Experimental Psychology: General* 142, no. 4 (November 2013): 1074–83.

10. Tania Lombrozo, Deborah Kelemen, and Deborah Zaitchik, "Inferring Design: Evidence of a Preference for Teleological Explanations in Patients with Alzheimer's Disease," *Psychological Science* 18, no. 11 (2007): 999–1006.

11. Birgitt Röttger-Rössler and Hans J. Markowitsch, introduction to *Emotions as Bio-Cultural Processes*, ed. Birgitt Röttger-Rössler and Hans J. Markowitsch (New York: Springer Science, 2009), p. 3.

12. Daniel Kahneman, *Thinking, Fast and Slow* (New York: Farrar, Straus, and Giroux, 2011).

13. Ibid.

14. Laura A. King et al., "Ghosts, UFOs, and Magic: Positive Affect and the Experiential System," *Journal of Personality and Social Psychology* 92, no. 5 (2007): 905–19.

15. Seymour Epstein, "Cognitive-Experiential Self-Theory of Personality," in *Personality and Social Psychology*, vol. 5 of *Handbook of Psychology*, ed. Theodore Millon and Melvin J. Lerner (Hoboken, NJ: Wiley, 2003), pp. 159–84.

16. King et al., "Ghosts, UFOs, and Magic."

17. Daniel Kahneman, Paul Slovic, and Amos Tversky, eds., *Judgment under Uncertainty: Heuristics and Biases* (New York: Cambridge University Press, 1982).

18. Emily Pronin, "The Introspection Illusion," in *Advances in Experimental Social Psychology*, ed., Mark P. Zanna, vol. 41 (New York: Psychology Press, 2009), pp. 1–67.

19. Timothy D. Wilson, *Strangers to Ourselves: Discovering the Adaptive Unconscious* (Cambridge, MA: Belknap, 2002).

20. Sarah Harland-Logan, "Guy Paul Morin," Innocence Canada, https://www.aidwyc.org/cases/historical/guy-paul-morin/ (accessed July 12, 2017).

21. Willem A. Wagenaar, *Paradoxes of Gambling Behavior* (London: Lawrence Erlbaum, 1988).

22. Thomas Gilovich, Robert Vallone, and Amos Tversky, "The Hot Hand in Basketball: On the Misperception of Random Sequences," *Cognitive Psychology* 17, no. 3 (1985): 295–314.

23. Stephen M. Samuels and George P. McCabe Jr., "More Lottery Repeaters Are on the Way," *New York Times*, February 27, 1986, p. C1.

24. Norris McWhirter and Ross McWhirter, *Dunlop Illustrated Encyclopedia of Facts* (New York: Bantam, 1969), p. 492.

25. Richard A. Epstein, *The Theory of Gambling and Statistical Logic* (New York: Academic Press, 1967).

26. Thomas Gray and Davina Mill, "Critical Abilities, Graduate Education (Biology vs. English), and Belief in Unsubstantiated Phenomena," *Canadian Journal of Behavioral Science* 22, no. 2 (1990): 162–72.

27. Kahneman, Slovic, and Tversky, *Judgement under Uncertainty*.

28. David M. Eddy, "Probabilistic Reasoning in Clinical Medicine: Problems and Opportunities," in *Judgement under Uncertainty*, pp. 249–67.

29. Maya Bar-Hillel, "The Base-Rate Fallacy in Probability Judgements," *Acta Psychologica* 44, no. 3 (May 1980): 211–33.

30. Ray Hyman, personal communication with the author, August 1982.

31. Gerd Gigerenzer, "Dread Risk, September 11, and Fatal Traffic Accidents," *Psychological Science* 15, no. 4 (April 2004): 286–87.

32. Ibid.

33. Robert Hogan, "The Superstitions of Everyday Life," *Behavioral and Brain Sciences* 27, no. 6 (December 2004): 738–39.

34. Keith E. Stanovich, "The Fundamental Computational Biases of Human Cognition: Heuristics That (Sometimes) Impair Decision Making and Problem Solving," in *The Psychology of Problem Solving*, ed. Janet E. Davidson and Robert J. Sternberg (Cambridge: Cambridge University Press, 2003), pp. 291–342.

35. Robyn Macpherson and Keith E. Stanovich, "Cognitive Ability, Thinking Dispositions, and Instructional Set as Predictors of Critical Thinking," *Learning and Individual Differences* 17, no. 2 (2007): 115–27.

36. Walter C. Sa, Richard F. West, and Keith E. Stanovich, "The Domain Specificity and Generality of Belief Bias: Searching for a Generalizable Critical Thinking Skill," *Journal of Educational Psychology* 91, no. 3 (September 1999): 497–510.

37. Charles Sanders Peirce, *Reasoning and the Logic of Things*, ed. Kenneth Laine Ketner (Cambridge: Harvard University Press, 1992).

38. Igor Douven, "Abduction," in *Stanford Encyclopedia of Philosophy*, last revised April 28, 2017, https://plato.stanford.edu/entries/abduction/ (accessed November 13, 2017).

39. Nicholas Rescher, *Rationality: A Philosophical Inquiry into the Nature and the Rationale of Reason* (Oxford: Clarendon, 1988).

40. Jerome D. Frank, "Nature and Functions of Belief Systems: Humanism and Transcendental Religion," *American Psychologist* 32, no. 7 (July 1977): 555–59.

41. Augustine of Hippo, *Sermons on Selected Lessons of the New Testament*, 43, cited by Dewey J. Hoitenga, *Faith and Reason from Plato to Plantinga: An Introduction to Reformed Epistemology* (Albany, NY: State University of New York Press, 1992), p. 59.

42. Augustine of Hippo, *Tractates on the Gospel of John*, Tractate 29.

43. Giora Keinan, "The Effects of Stress and Desire for Control on Superstitious Behavior," *Personality and Social Psychology Bulletin* 28, no. 1 (January 2002): 102–108.

44. Seymour Epstein, "An Integration of the Cognitive and Psychodynamic Unconscious," *American Psychologist* 49, no. 8 (August 1994): 709–24.

45. Seymour Epstein et al., "Individual Differences in Intuitive-Experiential and Analytical-Rational Thinking Styles," *Journal of Personality and Social Psychology* 71, no. 2 (August 1996), pp. 390–405.

46. King et al., "Ghosts, UFOs, and Magic."

47. Epstein, "Integration of the Cognitive and Psychodynamic Unconscious," pp. 709–24.

48. Laura Fontanari et al., "Probabilistic Cognition in Two Indigenous Mayan Groups,"

Proceedings of the National Academy of Sciences of the United States of America 111, no. 48 (December 2, 2014): 17075–80.

49. Hannes Rakoczy et al., "Apes Are Intuitive Statisticians," *Cognition* 131, no. 1 (April 2014): 60–68.

50. Herbert. M. Jenkins and William C. Ward, "Judgement of Contingency between Responses and Outcomes," *Psychological Monographs: General and Applied* 79 (1965): 1–17.

PART III: BELIEF STABILITY AND CHANGE

1. G. Lawton, "I Believe: Your Personal Guidebook to Reality," *New Scientist* 3015 (April 4, 2015): 28.

Chapter 6: In the Garden of Belief

1. Horace Walpole and Peter Cunningham, *The Letters of Horace Walpole, Earl of Orford*, 9 vols. (London: Richard Bentley, 1858), 7: 225.

2. Ambrose Bierce, *The Devil's Dictionary* (1911; New York: Doubleday, 2008), p. 12.

3. Paul M. Churchland and Patricia S. Churchland, *On the Contrary: Critical Essays 1987–1997* (Cambridge, MA: MIT Press, 1998).

4. Lynne Rudder Baker, *Saving Belief: A Critique of Physicalism* (Princeton, NJ: Princeton University Press, 1988). See also Daniel C. Dennett, "Do Animals Have Beliefs?" in *Comparative Approaches to Cognitive Sciences*, ed. Herbert L. Roitblat and Jean-Arcady Meyer (Boston: MIT Press, 1995), pp. 111–18.

5. Daniel T. Gilbert, "How Mental Systems Believe," *American Psychologist* 46, no. 2 (February 1991): 107–19.

6. Matthew Tyler Boden and Howard Berenbaum, "The Bidirectional Relations between Affect and Belief," *Review of General Psychology* 14, no. 3 (September 2010): 227–39.

7. Biology Online: Dictionary, s.v. "Belief," last modified October 3, 2005, http://www .biology-online.org/dictionary/Belief (accessed November 14, 2017).

8. Boden and Berenbaum, "Bidirectional Relations between Affect and Belief."

9. Robert S. Wyer Jr. and Dolores Albarracín, "Belief Formation, Organization, and Change: Cognitive and Motivational Influences," in *The Handbook of Attitudes*, ed. Dolores Albarracín, Blair T. Johnson, and Mark P. Zanna (Mahwah, NJ: Erlbaum, 2005), pp. 273–322.

10. Helen M. Sharp, Christopher F. Fear, J. Mark G. Williams, et al., "Delusional Phenomenology—Dimensions of Change," *Behavior Research and Therapy* 34, no. 2 (February 1996): 123–42.

11. Ricki Ladowsky-Brooks and James Alcock, "Semantic-Episodic Interactions in the Neuropsychology of Disbelief," *Cognitive Neuropsychiatry* 12, no. 2 (2007): 97–111.

12. Gilbert, "How Mental Systems Believe."

13. Ibid.

14. Ladowsky-Brooks and Alcock, "Semantic-Episodic Interactions."

15. Richard E. Petty, Duane T. Wegener and Paul H. White, "Flexible Correction Processes in Social Judgment: Implications for Persuasion," *Social Cognition* 16, no. 1 (1998): 93–113.

16. Daniel T. Gilbert, Douglas S. Krull, and Patrick S. Malone, "Unbelieving the Unbelievable: Some Problems in the Rejection of False Information," *Journal of Personality and Social Psychology* 59, no. 4 (October 1990): 601–13.

17. Erik Asp, Kanchna Ramchandran, and Daniel Tranel, "Authoritarianism, Religious Fundamentalism, and the Human Prefrontal Cortex," *Neuropsychology* 26, no. 4 (July 2012): 414–21.

18. Kyung Kim, "Development of the Concept of Truth-Functional Negation," *Developmental Psychology* 21, no. 3 (May 1985): 462–72.

19. Gilbert, "How Mental Systems Believe."

20. Ibid., p. 117.

21. Milton Rokeach, *The Open and Closed Mind* (New York: Basic Books, 1960).

22. W. V. Quine and J. S. Ullian, *The Web of Belief* (New York: McGraw-Hill, 1970), p. 90.

23. Edmund L. Gettier, "Is Justified True Belief Knowledge?" *Analysis* 23, no. 6 (June 1963): 121–23.

24. Ibid.

25. Wyer and Albarracín, "Belief Formation, Organization and Change."

26. Susan G. Sterrett, "How Beliefs Make a Difference" (PhD Dissertation; Pittsburgh: Department of Philosophy, University of Pittsburgh, 1999).

27. Ibid., p. 22.

28. Bertrand Russell, "Mysticism and Logic," in *Contemplation and Action, 1902–1914*, ed. Richard A. Rempel, Andrew Brink, and Margaret Moran (London: Routledge, 1993), pp. 155–77, 169.

29. William James, *Principles of Psychology* (1890), *Classics in the History of Psychology*, http://psychclassics.yorku.ca/James/Principles/prin21.htm (accessed December 19, 2017).

30. William McDougall, "Belief as a Derived Emotion," *Psychological Review* 28, no. 5 (1921): 316.

31. Endel Tulving, "Memory and Verbal Learning," *Annual Review of Psychology* 21 (1970): 437–84.

32. Robert A. Burton, "*On Being Certain: Believing You Are Right Even When You're Not*" (New York: St. Martin's Griffin, 2008).

33. Ibid.

34. Wilder Penfield, *The Excitable Cortex in Conscious Man* (Liverpool: Liverpool University Press, 1958).

35. Burton, *On Being Certain*, p. 218.

36. Peter L. Berger and Thomas Luckman, *The Social Construction of Reality: A Treaties in the Sociology of Knowledge* (New York: Anchor, 1966).

37. Daniel Bar-Tal, *Group Beliefs: A Conception for Analyzing Group Structure, Processes, and Behavior* (New York: Springer, 1989).

38. Bastiaan T. Rutjens, Robbie M. Sutton, and Romy van der Lee, "Not All Skepticism Is Equal: Exploring the Ideological Antecedents of Science Acceptance and Rejection," *Personality and Social Psychology Bulletin*, preprint, December 1, 2017, pp. 1–22.

39. James Alcock and Stan Sadava, *An Introduction to Social Psychology: Global Perspectives* (London: Sage, 2014).

40. Roy J. Eidelson and Judy I. Eidelson, "Dangerous Ideas: Five Beliefs That Propel Groups toward Conflict," *American Psychologist* 58 (2003): 182–92.

41. Urie Bronfenbrenner, "The Mirror Image in Soviet-American Relations: A Social Psychologist's Report," *Journal of Social Issues* 17, no. 3 (Summer 1961): 46.

42. Ibid., p. 53.

43. Daphna Oyserman, "Values: Psychological Perspectives," in *International Encyclopedia of the Social & Behavioral Sciences*, ed. Neil J. Smelser and Paul B. Baltes (Atlanta, GA: Elsevier, 2001), pp. 16150–53.

44. Shalom H. Schwartz, "Value Priorities and Behavior: Applying of Theory of Integrated Value Systems," in *The Psychology of Values: The Ontario Symposium*, ed. Clive Seligman, James M. Olson, and Mark P. Zanna (Hillsdale, NJ: Erlbaum, 1996), pp. 1–24.

45. Milton Rokeach, *Beliefs, Attitudes, and Values: A Theory of Organization and Change* (San Francisco, CA: Jossey-Bass, 1968).

46. Philip E. Tetlock, David Armor, and Randall Peterson, "The Slavery Debate in Antebellum America: Cognitive Style, Value Conflict, and the Limits of Compromise," *Journal of Personality and Social Psychology* 66, no. 1 (January 1994): 115–26.

47. Hammad Sheikh et al., "Religion, Group Threat, and Sacred Values," *Judgment and Decision Making* 7, no. 2 (March 2012): 110–18.

48. Philip E. Tetlock, "Thinking the Unthinkable: Sacred Values and Taboo Cognitions," *Trends in Cognitive Sciences* 7, no. 7 (July 2003): 320–24.

49. Martin Hanselmann and Carmen Tanner, "Taboos and Conflicts in Decision Making: Sacred Values, Decision Difficulty, and Emotions," *Judgement and Decision Making* 3, no. 1 (January 2008): 51–63.

50. Scott Atran and Jeremy Ginges, "Religious and Sacred Imperatives in Human Conflict," *Science* 336, no. 6083 (May 18, 2012): 855–57.

51. Morteza Dehghani et al., "Sacred Values and Conflict over Iran's Nuclear Program," *Judgment and Decision Making* 5, no. 7 (December 2010): 540–46.

52. Sheikh et al., "Religion, Group Threat, and Sacred Values."

53. Alcock and Sadava, *Introduction to Social Psychology*.

54. John T. Jost, Aaron C. Kay, and Hulda Thorisdottir, eds., *Social and Psychological Bases of Ideology and System Justification* (New York: Oxford University Press, 2009).

55. John T. Jost, Christopher M. Federico, and Jaime L. Napier, "Political Ideology: Its Structure, Functions, and Elective Affinities," *Annual Review of Psychology* 60 (2009): 307–37.

56. Paul Kurtz, *The Transcendental Temptation* (Amherst, NY: Prometheus Books, 1986).

57. Andrew Ortony, Gerald L. Clore, and Allan Collins, *The Cognitive Structure of Emotions* (Cambridge: Cambridge University Press, 1988).

58. Melvin J. Lerner and Leo Montada, "An Overview: Advances in Belief in a Just World Theory and Methods," in *Responses to Victimizations and Belief in a Just World*, ed. Leo Montada and Melvin J. Lerner (New York: Plenum, 1998), pp. 1–7.

59. Shelley E. Taylor, *Positive Illusions: Creative Self-Deception and the Healthy Mind* (New York: Basic Books, 1991).

60. Ryan T. McKay and Daniel C. Dennett, "The Evolution of Misbelief," *Behavioral and Brain Sciences* 32, no. 6 (December 2009): 493–510.

61. Carol S. Dweck, "Why We Don't Need Built-In Misbeliefs," *Behavioral and Brain Sciences* 32, no. 6 (December 2009): 518–19.

Chapter 7: Preserving the Roses

1. Francis Bacon, *Novum Organum* (1620), in *The English Philosophers from Bacon to Mill*, ed. Edwin A. Burtt (New York: Random House, 1939), p. 36.

2. Lee Ross, Mark R. Lepper, and Michael Hubbard, "Perseverance in Self-Perception and Social Perception: Biased Attributional Processes in the Debriefing Paradigm," *Journal of Personality and Social Psychology* 32, no. 5 (November 1975): 880–92.

3. Peter L. Berger, *A Rumour of Angels: Modern Society and the Rediscovery of the Supernatural* (Harmondsworth, UK: Penguin, 1970), p. 50.

4. *The Private Life of Galileo: Compiled Principally from His Correspondence and That of His Eldest Daughter, Sister Maria Celeste* (London: Macmillan, 1870), pp. 306–307.

5. Dan M. Kahan et al., "The Polarizing Impact of Science Literacy and Numeracy on Perceived Climate Change Risk," *Nature Climate Change*, May 27, 2012.

6. Dan M. Kahan, "A Risky Science Communication Environment for Vaccines," *Science* 342, no. 6154 (October 4, 2013): 53–54.

7. James Boswell, *The Life of Samuel Johnson, LL. D.*, 4 vols. (London: G. Cowie, 1824), 3: 9.

8. Carol Tavris and Elliot Aronson, *Mistakes Were Made (But Not by Me)* (Orlando: Harcourt, 2007).

9. Lee Ross and Craig A. Anderson, "Shortcomings in the Attribution Process: On the Origins and Maintenance of Erroneous Social Assessments," in *Judgment under Uncertainty: Heuristics and Biases*, ed. Daniel Kahneman, Paul Slovic, and Amos Tversky (Cambridge, UK: Cambridge University Press, 1982), p. 149.

10. Chris Purdy, "Alberta Creationist Finds Fossils while Digging Calgary Basement," CTV News, May 28, 2015, http://www.ctvnews.ca/sci-tech/alberta-creationist-finds-fossils -while-digging-calgary-basement-1.2396080 (accessed May 31, 2017).

11. Ray Hyman, "The Mischief-Making of Ideomotor Action," *Scientific Review of Alternative Medicine* 3, no. 2 (Fall/Winter 1999): 34–43.

12. Leon Festinger, *A Theory of Cognitive Dissonance* (Stanford, CA: Stanford University Press, 1957).

13. Serena Chen, Kimberly Duckworth, and Shelly Chaiken, "Motivated Heuristic and Systematic Processing," *Psychological Inquiry* 10, no. 1 (1999): 44–49.

14. Raymond S. Nickerson, "Confirmation Bias: A Ubiquitous Phenomenon in Many Guises," *Review of General Psychology* 2, no. 2 (June 1998): 175–220.

15. Ian I. Mitroff, "Norms and Counter-Norms in a Select Group of the Apollo Moon Scientists: A Case Study of the Ambivalence of Scientists," *American Sociological Review* 39, no. 4 (August 1974): 579–95.

16. Max K. Planck, *Scientific Autobiography and Other Papers* (New York: Philosophical Library, 1950), p. 33.

17. Tobias Greitemeyer, "I Am Right, You Are Wrong: How Biased Assimilation Increases. The Perceived Gap between Believers and Skeptics of Violent Video Game Effects," *PLoS ONE* 9, no. 4 (2014): E93440.

18. Jonathan Baron, *Thinking and Deciding*, 3rd ed. (New York: Cambridge University Press, 2000).

19. Jennifer S. Lerner and Philip E. Tetlock, "Bridging Individual, Interpersonal, and Institutional Approaches to Judgment and Decision Making: The Impact of Accountability on Cognitive Bias," in *Emerging Perspectives on Judgment and Decision Research*, ed. Sandra L. Schneider and James Shanteau (Cambridge, UK: Cambridge University Press, 2003), pp. 431–57.

20. Keith E. Stanovich, Richard F. West, and Maggie E. Toplak, "Myside Bias, Rational Thinking, and Intelligence," *Current Directions in Psychological Science* 22, no. 4 (August 2013): 258 64.

21. Christopher Wolfe and M. Anne Britt, "The Locus of the Myside Bias in Written Argumentation," *Thinking and Reasoning* 14, no. 1 (2008): 1–27.

22. Margaret W. Matlin, "Pollyanna Principle," in *Cognitive Illusions: A Handbook on Fallacies and Biases in Thinking, Judgement and Memory*, ed. Rüdiger F. Pohl (New York: Taylor and Francis, 2004), pp. 235–72.

23. Ricki Ladowsky-Brooks and James E. Alcock, "Semantic-Episodic Interactions in the Neuropsychology of Disbelief," *Cognitive Neuropsychiatry* 12, no. 2 (2007): 97–111.

24. Susan Budd, *Sociologists and Religion* (London: Collier-Macmillan, 1973).

25. William James, *The Will to Believe* (1896; New York: Dover, 1956), p. 11.

26. Gordon W. Allport, *Becoming: Basic Considerations for a Psychology of Personality* (New Haven: Yale University Press, 1955), p. 100.

27. Leon Festinger, Henry W. Riecken, and Stanley Schachter, *When Prophecy Fails: A Social and Psychological Study of a Modern Group that Predicted the Destruction of the World* (Minneapolis, MN: Lund Press, 1956).

28. Ibid.

29. Jerry S. Wiggins and Paul D. Trapnell, "Personality Structure: The Return of the Big Five," in *Handbook of Personality Psychology*, ed. Robert Hogan, John A. Johnson, and Stephen R. Briggs (San Diego, CA: Academic Press, 1997), pp. 737–65.

30. Judy J. Johnson, *What's So Wrong with Being Absolutely Right? The Dangerous Nature of Dogmatic Belief* (Amherst, NY: Prometheus Books, 2009).

31. Milton Rokeach, *The Open and Closed Mind: Investigations into the Nature of Belief Systems and Personality Systems* (Oxford, England: Basic Books, 1960).

32. Johnson, *What's So Wrong with Being Absolutely Right?*

33. Arie W. Kruglanski and Shira Fishman, "The Need for Cognitive Closure," in *Handbook of Individual Differences in Social Behavior*, ed. Mark R. Leary and Rick H. Hoyle (New York: Guilford, 2009), pp. 343–53.

34. Milton Rokeach, "The Nature and Meaning of Dogmatism," *Psychological Review* 61, no. 3 (May 1954): 194–204.

35. Johnson, *What's So Wrong with Being Absolutely Right?*

36. Eric Hoffer, *The True Believer: Thoughts on the Nature of Mass Movements* (1951; New York: Harper, 2002).

37. Theodor W. Adorno et al., *The Authoritarian Personality* (New York: Harper and Row, 1950).

38. Robert A. Altemeyer, *Right-Wing Authoritarianism* (Winnipeg: University of Manitoba Press, 1981).

39. Erich Fromm, *Escape from Freedom* (1941; New York: Holt, 1994).

40. Irving L. Janis, *Groupthink: Psychological Studies of Policy Decisions and Fiascoes*, 2nd ed. (New York: Houghton Mifflin, 1982).

41. Paul 't Hart, "Irving L. Janis' Victims of Groupthink," *Political Psychology* 12, no. 2 (June 1991): 247–78.

42. Philip E. Tetlock et al., "Assessing Political Group Dynamics: A Test of the Group-think Model," *Journal of Personality and Social Psychology* 63, no. 3 (September 1992): 403–25.

43. Janis, *Groupthink.*

44. Max Coltheart, Robyn Langdon, and Ryan McKay, "Delusional Belief," *Annual Review of Psychology* 62 (2011): 271–98. See also Max Coltheart, "The Neuropsychology of Delusions," *Annals of the New York Academy of Sciences* 1191 (March 2010): 16–26.

45. Andy Hamilton, "Against the Belief Model of Delusion," in *Reconceiving Schizophrenia*, ed. Man Cheung Chung, K. W. M. Fulford, and George Graham (Oxford: Oxford University Press, 2006), pp. 217–34.

46. Robyn Langdon and Max Coltheart, "The Cognitive Neuropsychology of Delusions," in *Pathologies of Belief*, ed. Max Coltheart and Martin Davies (Oxford, England: Blackwell, 2000), pp. 183–216.

47. Mahzarin R. Banaji and Nilanjana Dasgupta, "The Consciousness of Social Beliefs: A Program of Research on Stereotyping and Prejudice," in *Metacognition: Cognitive and Social Dimensions*, ed. Vincent Y. Yzerbyt, Guy Lories, and Benoit Dardenne (Thousand Oaks, CA: Sage, 1998), pp. 157–70.

48. Ladowsky-Brooks and Alcock, "Semantic-Episodic Interactions'."

49. Laura A. King et al., "Ghosts, UFOs, and Magic: Positive Affect and the Experiential System," *Journal of Personality and Social Psychology* 92, no. 5 (May 2007): 905–19.

50. Coltheart, Langdon, and McKay, "Delusional Belief."

51. American Psychiatric Association, *Diagnostic and Statistical Manual of the American Psychiatric Association*, 5th ed. (Washington, DC: American Psychiatric Publishing, 2013).

52. Richard Mullen and Richard J. Linscott, "A Comparison of Delusions and Overvalued Ideas," *Journal of Nervous and Mental Disease* 198, no. 1 (January 2010): 35–38.

53. Tim Bayne and Jordi Fernandez, "Delusion and Self-Deception: Mapping the Terrain," in *Delusion and Self Perception*, ed. Tim Bayne and Jordi Fernandez (New York: Psychology Press, 2009), pp. 1–21.

54. Matthew Tyler Boden and Howard Berenbaum, "The Bidirectional Relations between Affect and Belief," *Review of General Psychology* 14, no. 3 (September 2010): 227–39.

55. Charles Mackay, *Memoirs of Extraordinary Popular Delusions and the Madness of Crowds* (London: Richard Bentley, 1841).

56. Robert E. Bartholomew and M. Chandra Sekaran Muniratnam, "How Should Mental Health Professionals Respond to Outbreaks of Mass Psychogenic Illness?" *Journal of Cognitive Psychotherapy* 25, no. 4 (2011): 235–39. See also Robert E. Bartholomew and Hilary Evans, *Panic Attacks: Media Manipulation and Mass Delusion* (Stroud, UK: Sutton, 2004).

57. Dylan Baddour and W. Gardner Selby, "Hillary Clinton Correct That Austin's Alex Jones Said No One Died at Sandy Hook Elementary," *PolitiFact*, September 1, 2016, http://www.politifact.com/texas/statements/2016/sep/01/hillary-clinton/hillary-clinton-correct-austins-alex-jones-said-no/ (accessed July 15, 2017).

58. Bradley Franks, Adrian Bangerter, and Martin W. Bauer, "Conspiracy Theories as Quasi-Religious Mentality: An Integrated Account from Cognitive Science, Social Representations Theory, and Frame Theory," *Frontiers in Psychology* 4, no. 424 (2013): 1–12; published online July 16, 2013, https://doi.org/10.3389/fpsyg.2013.00424.

59. Carl F. Graumann, and Serge Moscovici, eds., *Changing Conceptions of Conspiracy* (New York: Springer-Verlag, 1987).

60. Stephan Lewandowsky, Gilles E. Gignac, and Klaus Oberauer, "The Robust Relationship between Conspiracism and Denial of (Climate) Science," *Psychological Science* 26 no. 5 (May 2015): 667–70.

61. Véronique Campion-Vincent, "From Evil Others to Evil Elites: A Dominant Pattern in Conspiracy Theories Today," in *Rumor Mills: The Social Impact of Rumor and Legend*, ed. Gary Alan Fine, Véronique Campion-Vincent, and Chip Heath (New Brunswick, NJ: Aldine Transaction, 2005), pp. 103–22.

62. Ronald Inglehart, "Extremist Political Positions and Perceptions of Conspiracy: Even Paranoids Have Real Enemies," in *Changing Conceptions of Conspiracy*, pp. 231–44.

63. Serge Moscovici, "The Conspiracy Mentality," in *Changing Conceptions of Conspiracy*, pp. 151–69.

64. Humphry Taylor, "'Wingnuts' and President Obama," Harris Interactive, March 24, 2010.

65. Eric Hehman, Samuel L. Gaertner, and John F. Dovidio, "Evaluations of Presidential Performance: Race, Prejudice, and Perceptions of Americanism," *Journal of Experimental Social Psychology* 47, no. 2 (March 2011): 430–35.

66. Gary Alan Fine and Bill Ellis, *The Global Grapevine: Why Rumors of Terrorism, Immigration, and Trade Matter* (New York: Oxford University Press, 2010).

67. Tia Ghose, "Half of Americans Believe in 9/11 Conspiracy Theories," *LiveScience*, October 13, 2016, https://www.livescience.com/56479-americans-believe-conspiracy-theories.html (accessed December 19, 2017).

68. Jan van der Temple and James E. Alcock, "Relationships between Conspiracy Mentality, Hyperactive Agency Detection, and Schizotypy: Supernatural Forces at Work?" *Personality and Individual Differences* 82 (August 2015): 136–41.

69. Martin Bruder, Peter Haffke, Nick Neave, Nina Nouripanah, and Roland Imhoff, "Measuring Individual Differences in Generic Beliefs in Conspiracy Theories across Cultures: Conspiracy Mentality Questionnaire," *Frontiers in Psychology* 4 (2013): 1–15.

70. Van der Temple and Alcock, "Relationships between Conspiracy Mentality, Hyperactive Agency Detection, and Schizotypy."

71. David Barron, Kevin Morgan, Tony Towell, Boris Altemeyer, and Viren Swami, "Associations between Schizotypy and Belief in Conspiracist Ideation," *Personality and Individual Differences*, 70 (November 2014): 156–59.

72. Mark F. Lenzenweger, *Schizotypy and Schizophrenia: The View from Experimental Psychopathology* (New York: Guilford, 2010).

73. Van der Temple and Alcock, "Relationships between Conspiracy Mentality, Hyperactive Agency Detection, and Schizotypy."

74. Erich Goode, and Nachman Ben-Yehuda, *Moral Panics: The Social Construction of Deviance*, 2nd ed. (Chichester, West Sussex: Wiley-Blackwell, 2009).

75. William Sargant, *Battle for the Mind* (London: Heinemann, 1957), p. 199.

76. James Randi, personal communication with author, October 2015.

Chapter 8: Tending and Tilling

1. Thomas Roscoe, *The Works of Jonathan Swift*, 2 vols. (London: Henry G. Bohn, 1843), 2: 205.

2. Andrew D. White, *History of the Warfare of Science with Theology in Christendom* (1898; Amherst, NY: Prometheus Books, 1993).

3. Ibid.

4. William Sargant, *The Mind Possessed: A Physiology of Possession, Mysticism, and Faith Healing* (London: Heinemann, 1973).

5. Jean Piaget and Bärbel Inhelder, *The Psychology of the Child* (1969; New York: Basic Books, 2000).

6. James E. Alcock and Timothy E. Moore, "The Vulnerability of Belief in the Conservation of Area," *Canadian Journal of Behavioural Science* 17, no. 3 (July 1985): 276–83.

7. Martin Gardner, *Mathematics, Magic, and Mystery* (New York: Dover, 1956).

8. See James Alcock and Stan Sadava, *An Introduction to Social Psychology: Global Perspectives* (London: Sage, 2014).

9. Richard E. Petty and John T. Cacioppo, "The Elaboration Likelihood Model of Persuasion," *Advances in Social Psychology* 19 (1986): 181–205.

10. John T. Cacioppo et al., "Central and Peripheral Routes to Persuasion: An Individual Difference Perspective," *Journal of Personality and Social Psychology* 51, no. 5 (November 1986): 1032–43.

11. Donna Shetowsky, Duane T. Wegener, and Leandre. R. Fabrigar, "Need for Cognition and Interpersonal Influence: Individual Differences in Dyadic Decisions," *Journal of Personality and Social Psychology* 74, no. 5 (May 1998): 1317–28.

12. Alcock and Sadava, *Introduction to Social Psychology*.

13. Gary Alan Fine and Bill Ellis *The Global Grapevine: Why Rumors of Terrorism, Immigration, and Trade Matter* (New York: Oxford University Press, 2010).

14. Ralph L. Rosnow, "Inside Rumor: A Personal Journey," *American Psychologist* 46, no. 5 (May 1991): 484–96.

15. Gordon W. Allport and Leo Postman, *The Psychology of Rumor* (Oxford: Henry Holt, 1947), p. ix.

16. Ralph L. Rosnow, John H. Yost, and James L. Esposito, "Belief in Rumor and Likelihood of Rumor Transmission," *Language and Communication* 6, no. 3 (1986): 189–94.

17. Ralph L. Rosnow and Gary Alan Fine, *Rumor and Gossip: The Social Psychology of Hearsay* (New York: Elsevier, 1976).

18. David Cornwell and Sandy Hobbs, "Rumour and Legend: Interactions between Social Psychology and Folkloristics," *Canadian Psychology* 33, no. 3 (July 1992): 609–13.

19. Jan Harold Brunvand, *The Vanishing Hitchhiker: American Urban Legends and Their Meanings* (New York: W. W. Norton, 1981).

20. Jan Harold Brunvand, *Encyclopedia of Urban Legends* (Santa Barbara, CA: ABC-CLIO, 2001).

21. Brunvand, *Vanishing Hitchhiker*.

22. Adolf Hitler, *Mein Kampf*, trans. Ralph Mannheim (1924; Boston: Houghton-Mifflin, 1943).

23. David Welch, *Persuading the People: British Propaganda in World War II* (London: British Library, 2016).

24. Vike Martina Plock, quoted in Jamie Doward, "How the BBC's Truth Offensive Beat Hitler's Propaganda Machine," *Guardian*, April 15, 2017, https://www.theguardian.com/world/2017/apr/15/bbc-truth-offensive-beat-hitler-propaganda-machine (accessed November 15, 2017).

25. Tamotsu Shibutani, *Improvised News: A Sociological Study of Rumor* (Indianapolis: Bobbs-Merrill, 1966).

26. Jason P. Mitchell, Mahzarin Banaji, and C. Neil Macrae, "The Link between Social Cognition and Self-Referential Thought in the Medial Prefrontal Cortex," *Journal of Cognitive Neuroscience* 17, no. 8 (August 2005): 1306–15.

27. Ian Maynard Begg, Ann Anas, and Suzanne Farinacci, "Dissociation of Processes in Belief: Source Recollection, Statement Familiarity, and the Illusion of Truth," *Journal of Experimental Psychology: General* 121, no. 4 (December 1992): 446–58.

28. Linda A. Henkel and Mark E. Mattson, "Reading Is Believing: The Truth Effect and Source Credibility," *Consciousness and Cognition* 20, no. 4 (December 2011): 1705–21.

29. Begg, Anas, and Farinacci, "Dissociation of Processes in Belief."

30. Henkel and Mattson, "Reading Is Believing."

31. Joseph Goebbels, "Aus Churchills Lügenfabrik (January 12, 1941)," *Die Zeit ohne Beispiel* (Munich: Zentralverlag der NSDAP, 1941), p. 364.

32. Begg, Anas, and Farinacci, "Dissociation of Processes in Belief."

33. Caitlin Gibson, "What We Talk about When We Talk about Donald Trump and 'Gaslighting,'" *Washington Post*, January 27, 2017.

34. Ibid.

35. Eugene A. Weinstein and Paul Deutschberger, "Some Dimensions of Altercasting," *Sociometry* 26, no. 4 (December 1963): 454–66.

36. "Altercasting," ChangingMinds.org, 2016, http://changingminds.org/techniques/general/more_methods/altercasting.htm (accessed November 15, 2017).

37. Anthony Pratkanis, "Pratkanis on Altercasting and CSICon—An Interview with Susan Gerbic," CSI (Committee for Skeptical Inquiry), March 14, 2017, http://www.csicop

.org/specialarticles/show/pratkanis_on_altercasting_and_csiconmdashan_interview_with
_susan_gerbic (accessed November 15, 2017).

38. Anthony R. Pratkanis, "Altercasting as an Influence Tactic," in *Attitudes, Behavior, and Social Context: The Role of Norms and Group Membership*, ed. Deborah J. Terry and Michael A. Hogg (Mahwah, NJ: Lawrence Erlbaum, 2000), pp. 201–26.

39. Edward Hunter, *Brainwashing in Red China: The Calculated Destruction of Men's Minds* (New York: Vanguard, 1953).

40. Russell A. Dewey, *Introduction to Psychology* (New York: Wadsworth, 2004).

41. Daniel T. Gilbert, "How Mental Systems Believe," *American Psychologist* 46, no. 2 (February 1991): 107–19.

42. Robert Jay Lifton, *Thought Reform and the Psychology of Totalism: A Study of 'Brainwashing' in China* (1961; Chapel Hill, NC: University of North Carolina Press, 1989), p. 23.

43. Ibid., p. 32.

44. Shane O'Mara, *Why Torture Doesn't Work: The Neuroscience of Interrogation* (Cambridge, MA: Harvard University Press, 2015).

45. Richard P. Conti, "The Psychology of False Confessions," *Journal of Credibility Assessment and Witness Psychology* 2, no. 1 (1999): 14–36.

46. Timothy E. Moore and C. Lindsay Fitzsimmons, "Justice Imperiled: False Confessions and the Reid Technique," *Criminal Law Quarterly* 57, no. 4 (2011): 509–42.

47. "False Confessions or Admissions," Innocence Project, https://www.innocenceproject .org/causes/false-confessions-admissions/ (accessed November 15, 2017).

48. Saul M. Kassin, "False Confessions: Causes, Consequences, and Implications for Reform," *Policy Insights from the Behavioral and Brain Sciences* 1, no. 1 (October 2014): 112–21.

49. Saul M. Kassin, "On the Psychology of Confessions: Does Innocence Put Innocents at Risk?" *American Psychologist* 60, no. 3 (April 2005): 215–28.

50. Brian L. Cutler, Keith A. Findley, and Timothy E. Moore, "Interrogations and False Confessions: A Psychological Perspective," *Canadian Criminal Law Review* 18, no. 2 (2014): 153–70.

51. Fred E. Inbau et al., *Criminal Interrogation and Confessions*, 5th ed. (Burlington, MA: Jones & Bartlett Learning, 2013).

52. Melissa B. Russano et al., "Investigating True and False Confessions within a Novel Experimental Paradigm," *Psychological Science* 16, no. 6 (June 2005): 481–48.

53. Saul M. Kassin and Katherine L. Kiechel, "The Social Psychology of False Confessions: Compliance, Internalization, and Confabulation," *Psychological Science* 7, no. 3 (1996): 125–28.

54. Danielle M. Loney and Brian L. Cutler, "Coercive Interrogation of Eyewitnesses Can Produce False Accusations," *Journal of Police and Criminal Psychology* (2015), published online DOI 10.1007/s11896-015-9165-6.

55. Julia Shaw and Stephen Porter, "Constructing Rich False Memories of Committing Crime," *Psychological Science* 26, no. 3 (March 2015): 291–301.

56. Alison Flood, "'Post-Truth' Named Word of the Year by Oxford Dictionaries," *Guardian*, November 15, 2016.

57. Danielle C. Polage, "Making Up History: False Memories of Fake News Stories," *Europe's Journal of Psychology* 8, no. 2 (May 2012): 245–50.

58. Alison R. Fragale and Chip Heath, "Evolving Informational Credentials: The (Mis) Attribution of Believable Facts to Credible Sources," *Personality and Social Psychology Bulletin* 30, no. 2 (February 2004): 225.

59. Sam Wineburg, Sarah McGrew, Joel Breakstone, and Teresa Ortega, *Evaluating Information: The Cornerstone of Civic Online Reasoning* (Executive Summary; Stanford, CA: Stanford History Education Group, November 22, 2016), https://sheg.stanford.edu/upload/V3LessonPlans/Executive%20Summary%2011.21.16.pdf (accessed November 15, 2017).

60. Ibid., p. 4.

61. George Orwell, *1984* (London: Penguin, 1949), p. 78.

62. Ullrich K. H. Ecker et al., "Correcting False Information in Memory: Manipulating the Strength of Misinformation Encoding and Its Retraction," *Psychonomic Bulletin & Review* 18, no. 3 (June 2011): 570–78.

63. Ullrich K. H. Ecker, Stephan Lewandowsky, and David T. W. Tang, "Explicit Warnings Reduce but Do Not Eliminate the Continued Influence of Misinformation," *Memory & Cognition* 38, no. 8 (December 2010): 1087–100.

64. Gilbert Harman, *Change in View: Principles of Reasoning* (Cambridge, MA: Bradford Books, MIT Press, 1986), p. 38.

65. Elizabeth. R. Tenney, Hayley M. D. Cleary, and Barbara A. Spellman, "Unpacking the Doubt in 'Beyond a Reasonable Doubt': Plausible Alternative Stories Increase Not Guilty Verdicts," *Basic and Applied Social Psychology* 31, no. 1 (2009): 1–8.

66. Yaacov Schul and Frieda Manzury, "The Effects of Type of Encoding and Strength of Discounting Appeal on the Success of Ignoring an Invalid Testimony," *European Journal of Social Psychology* 20, no. 4 (July/August 1990): 337–49.

67. Stephan Lewandowsky, Werner G. K. Stritzke, Klaus Oberauer, and Michael Morales, "Memory for Fact, Fiction, and Misinformation: The Iraq War 2003," *Psychological Science* 16, no. 3 (March 2005): 190–95.

68. Ullrich K. H. Ecker et al., "The Effects of Subtle Misinformation in News Headlines," *Journal of Experimental Psychology: Applied* 20, no. 4 (December 2014): 323–35.

69. Ecker et al., "Explicit Warnings Reduce but Do Not Eliminate."

70. Brian Michael Jenkins, introduction to *Homegrown Terrorists in the US and UK: An Empirical Examination of the Radicalization Process*, by Daveed Gartenstein-Ross and Laura Grossman (Washington, DC: FDD Press, 2009), p. 7.

71. Clark McCauley and Sophia Moskalenko, "Mechanisms of Political Radicalization: Pathways toward Terrorism," *Terrorism and Political Violence* 20, no. 3 (2008): 415–33.

72. Fathali M. Moghaddam, "The Staircase to Terrorism: A Psychological Exploration," *American Psychologist* 60, no. 2 (February/March 2005): 161–69.

73. Alex S. Wilner and Claire-Jehanne Dubouloz, "Homegrown Terrorism and Transformative Learning: An Interdisciplinary Approach to Understanding Radicalization," *Global Change, Peace & Security* 22, no. 1 (2010): 33–51.

74. Angela Gendron, "Militant Jihadism: Radicalization, Conversion, Recruitment," *ITAC Presents: Trends in Terrorism Series* 4 (2006): 1–18.

75. Edna Reid, "Analysis of Jihadi Extremist Groups' Videos," *Forensic Science Communications* 11, no. 3 (July 2009).

76. Lisa Myers, "Web Video Teaches Terrorists to Make Bomb Vest," NBC News, December 22, 2004, http://www.nbcnews.com/id/6746756/ns/nbc_nightly_news_with _brian_williams/t/web-video-teaches-terrorists-make-bomb-vest/ (accessed November 15, 2017).

77. Maura Conway and Lisa McInerney, "Jihadi Video and Auto-Radicalisation: Evidence from an Exploratory YouTube Study," in *Intelligence and Security Informatics: First European Conference, EuroISI 2008, Esbjerg, Denmark, December 2008 Proceedings*, ed. Daniel Ortiz-Arroyo et al. (Berlin: Springer-Verlag, 2008), pp. 108–18.

78. Angel Rabasa et al., *Beyond Al-Qaeda: Part 1, The Global Jihadist Movement* (Santa Monica, CA: RAND Corporation, 2006).

79. Ibid.

80. Ibid.

81. Andrew Duffy and Meghan Hurley, "From JMag to Jihad John: The radicalization of John Maguire," *Ottawa Citizen*, February 7, 2015, http://ottawacitizen.com/news/local-news/ from-jmag-to-jihad-john-the-radicalization-of-john-maguire (accessed November 15, 2017).

82. Rukmini Callimachi, "Not 'Lone Wolves' after All: How ISIS Guides World's Terror Plots from Afar," *New York Times*, February 4, 2017, https://www.nytimes.com/2017/02/04/ world/asia/isis-messaging-app-terror-plot.html (accessed November 15, 2017).

83. McCauley and Moskalenko, "Mechanisms of Political Radicalization."

84. Herbert G. Kelman, "Violence without Moral Restraint: Reflections on the Dehumanization of Victims and Victimizers," *Journal of Social Issues* 29, no. 4 (Fall 1973): 25–61.

85. "Holocaust Timeline: The Liquidation of Lidice," The History Place, 1997, http:// www.historyplace.com/worldwar2/holocaust/h-lidice.htm (accessed November 15, 2017).

86. Scott Atran, "Genesis of Suicide Terrorism," *Science* 299, no. 5612 (March 7, 2003): 1534–39.

87. Laura Eggertson, "Lancet Retracts 12-Year-Old Article Linking Autism to MMR Vaccines," *Canadian Medical Association Journal* 182, no. 4 (March 9, 2010): E199–E200.

88. Brendan Nyhan and Jason Reifler, "When Corrections Fail: The Persistence of Political Misperceptions," *Political Behavior* 32, no. 2 (June 2010): 303–30.

89. Ibid.

90. Brendan Nyhan et al., "Effective Messages in Vaccine Promotion: A Randomized Trial," *Pediatrics* 133, no. 4 (April 2014): E835–42.

91. Elie A. Shneour, "Planting a Seed of Doubt," *Skeptical Inquirer* 22, no. 4 (July/August 1998): 40–42.

92. George Lakoff, *Don't Think of an Elephant! Know Your Values and Frame the Debate* (White River Junction, VT: Chelsea Green, 2004).

93. Muzafer Sherif and Carl I. Hovland, *Social Judgment: Assimilation and Contrast Effects in Communication and Attitude Change* (New Haven, CT: Yale University Press, 1961).

94. Blaise Pascal, *Thoughts*, trans. W. F. Trotter (1670; New York: Cosimo Classics, 2007), p. 11.

95. Craig A. Anderson, "Belief Perseverance," in *Encyclopedia of Social Knowledge*, ed. Roy F. Baumeister and Kathleen D. Vohs, vol. 1 (Thousand Oaks, CA: Sage, 2007), pp. 109–10.

96. Stephan Lewandowsky et al., "Misinformation and Its Correction: Continued Influence and Successful of Debiasing," *Psychological Science in the Public Interest* 13, no. 3 (December 2012): 106–31.

97. Zachary Horne, Derek Powell, John E. Hummel, and Keith J. Holyoak, "Countering Antivaccination Attitudes," *Proceedings of the National Academy of Sciences of the United States of America* 112, no. 33 (August 18, 2015): 10321–24.

Chapter 9: Credulity and Deceit

1. Richard Alfred Davenport, *Sketches of Imposture, Deception, and Credulity* (Philadelphia: G. B. Zieber, 1845), p. 14.

2. Peter W. Halligan and David A. Oakley, "Hypnosis and Beyond: Exploring the Broader Domain of Suggestion," *Psychology of Consciousness: Theory, Research, and Practice* 1, no. 2 (2014): 105–22.

3. Romuald Polczyk, "Factor Structure of Suggestibility Revisited: New Evidence for Direct and Indirect Suggestibility," *Current Issues in Personality Psychology* 4, no. 2 (2016): 87–96.

4. Irving Kirsch and Wayne Braffman, "Imaginative Suggestibility and Hypnotizability," *Current Directions in Psychological Science* 10, no. 2 (April 2001): 57–61.

5. John F. Kihlstrom, "The Domain of Hypnosis, Revisited," in *The Oxford Handbook of Hypnosis: Theory, Research, and Practice*, ed. Michael R. Nash and Amanda J. Barnier (Oxford: Oxford University Press, 2008), pp. 19–52.

6. Michael Lifshitz, Catherine Howells, and Amir Raz "Can Expectation Enhance Response to Suggestion? De-Automatization Illuminates a Conundrum," *Consciousness and Cognition* 21, no. 2 (June 2012): 1001–1008.

7. Dienes Zoltan and Sam Hutton, "Understanding Hypnosis Metacognitively: rTMS Applied to Left DLPFC Increases Hypnotic Suggestibility," *Cortex* 49, no. 2 (February 2013): 386–92.

8. Gisli H. Gudjonsson, "Suggestibility and Compliance among Alleged False Confessors and Resisters in Criminal Trials," *Medicine, Science, and the Law* 31, no. 2 (April 1991): 147–51.

9. Gisli H. Gudjonsson and James A. C. MacKeith, "A Proven Case of False Confession: Psychological Aspects of the Coerced-Compliant Type," *Medicine, Science, and the Law* 30, no. 4 (October 1990): 329–35.

10. Bertram R. Forer, "The Fallacy of Personal Validation: A Classroom Demonstration of Gullibility," *Journal of Abnormal Psychology* 44, no. 1 (January 1949): 118–21.

11. Daniel Druckman and Robert A. Bjork, eds., *In the Mind's Eye: Enhancing Human Performance* (Washington, DC: National Academy Press, 1991).

12. Ray Hyman, "'Cold Reading': How to Convince Strangers That You Know All about Them," *Zetetic* 1 no. 2 (Spring/Summer 1977): 18–37.

13. Ibid.

14. Ray Hyman, personal communication to the author, June 1985.

15. Ian Rowland, *The Full Facts Book of Cold Reading: A Comprehensive Guide to the Most Persuasive Psychological Manipulation Technique in the World*, 3rd ed. (Ian Rowland Limited, 2000), p. 60.

16. E. E. Slosson "Shorter Communications and Discussions: A Lecture Experiment in Hallucinations," *Psychological Review* 6, no. 4 (July 1899): 407–408.

17. Michael O'Mahony, "Smell Illusions and Suggestion: Reports of Smells Contingent on Tones Played on Television and Radio," *Chemical Senses*, 3 no. 2 (July 1978): 183–89.

18. Michael A. Persinger et al., "The Electromagnetic Induction of Mystical and Altered States within the Laboratory," *Journal of Consciousness Exploration & Research* 1, no. 7 (2010): 808–30.

19. Craig Aaen-Stockdale, "Neuroscience for the Soul," *Psychologist* 25, no. 7 (July 2012): 520–23.

20. Pehr Granqvist et al., "Sensed Presence and Mystical Experiences Are Predicted by Suggestibility, Not by the Application of Transcranial Weak Complex Magnetic Fields," *Neuroscience Letters* 379, no. 1 (April 29, 2005): 1–6.

21. Lauren French, Maryanne Garry, and Elizabeth Loftus, "False Memories: A Kind of Confabulation and Non-Clinical Subjects," in *Confabulation: Views from Neuroscience, Psychiatry, Psychology, and Philosophy*, ed. William Hirstein (Oxford: Oxford University Press, 2009), pp. 33–66.

22. Maggie Bruck and Stephen J. Ceci, "The Suggestibility of Children's Memory," *Annual Review of Psychology* 50 (1999): 419–39.

23. Roman I. Kotov, S. B. Bellman, and D. B. Watson, *Multidimensional Iowa Suggestibility Scale (MISS): Brief Manual*, 2004, https://medicine.stonybrookmedicine.edu/system/files/MISSBriefManual.pdf (accessed December 1, 2017).

24. Gisli H. Gudjonsson, "A New Scale of Interrogative Suggestibility," *Personality and Individual Differences* 5, no. 3 (1984): 303–14.

25. R. M. Lundy, "The Internal Confirmation of Personal Constructs: Why Suggestions Are Not Accepted," in *Suggestion and Suggestibility: Theory and Research*, ed. Vladimir A. Gheorghiu, Petra Netter, Hans J. Eysenck, and Robert Rosenthal (New York: Springer-Verlag, 1999), pp. 79–90.

26. Rute Pires, Danilo R. Silva, and Ana Sousa Ferreira, "Personality Styles and Suggestibility: A Differential Approach," *Personality and Individual Differences* 55, no. 4 (August 2013): 381–86.

27. Mark Blagrove, "Effects of Length of Sleep Deprivation on Interrogative Suggestibility," *Journal of Experimental Psychology: Applied* 2, no. 1 (March 1996): 48–59.

28. Patty Stuart Macadam, "Male Lactation," *Compleat Mother* 43 (Fall 1996), cited by Laura Shanley, "Milkmen: Fathers Who Breastfeed," http://www.unassistedchildbirth.com/inspiration/milkmen-fathers-who-breastfeed/ (accessed November 15, 2017).

29. Erik Asp et al., "A Neuropsychological Test of Belief and Doubt: Damage to Ventromedial Prefrontal Cortex Increases Credulity for Misleading Advertising," *Frontiers in Neuroscience* 6, no. 100 (2012).

30. Anthony R. Damasio, *Descartes' Error: Emotion, Rationality, and the Human Brain* (New York, NY: Putnam, 1994).

31. Daniel M. T. Fessler, Anne C. Pisor, and Carlos David Navarrete, "Negatively-Biased Credulity and the Cultural Evolution of Beliefs," *PLoS ONE* 9, no. 4 (2014): 1–8, e95167.

32. Gordon Pennycook et al., "On the Reception and Detection of Pseudo-Profound Bullshit," *Judgment and Decision Making* 10 (2015): 549–63.

33. Stephen Greenspan, *Annals of Gullibility: Why We Get Duped and How to Avoid It* (Westport, CT: Praeger, 2011).

34. Ibid.

35. Ibid.

36. Ibid.

37. Julian B. Rotter, "Interpersonal Trust, Trustworthiness, and Gullibility," *American Psychologist* 35, no. 1 (January 1980): 1–7.

38. Toshio Yamagishi, Masuko Kikuchi, and Motoko Kosugi, "Trust, Gullibility, and Social Intelligence," *Asian Journal of Social Psychology* 2, no. 1 (April 1999): 145–61.

39. Ibid.

40. Keith E. Stanovich, *Who Is Rational? Studies of Individual Differences in Reasoning* (Mahwah, NJ: Erlbaum, 1999).

41. Lars Hertzberg, "Is Religion the Product of Wishful Thinking?" in *Can Religion Be Explained Away?* ed. D. Z. Phillips (Houndmills, UK: Macmillan, 1996), pp. 49–65.

42. Roy F. Baumeister, Todd F. Heatherton, and Dianne M. Tice, *Losing Control: How and Why People Fail at Self-Regulation* (San Diego: Academic Press, 1994), p. 94.

43. Greenspan, *Annals of Gullibility.*

44. Michael Price. "Study Reveals Culprit behind Piltdown Man, One of Science's Most Famous Hoaxes," *Science*, August 9, 2016, http://www.sciencemag.org/news/2016/08/study-reveals-culprit-behind-piltdown-man-one-science-s-most-famous-hoaxes (accessed November 15, 2017).

45. Clare Sharpe, "Remembering a Rascal" CFB Esquimalt: Naval & Military Museum, 2016, http://www.navalandmilitarymuseum.org/archives/articles/characters/ferdinand-waldo-demara (accessed November 16, 2017).

46. Maria Konnikova, *The Confidence Game: Why We Fall for It . . . Every Time* (New York: Penguin Random House, 2016).

47. Loren Pankratz, personal communication to the author, March 15, 2017.

48. Ibid.

49. James Randi, *Flim-Flam! Psychics, ESP, Unicorns, and Other Delusions* (Amherst, NY: Prometheus Books, 1982).

50. Harry Markopolos, *No One Would Listen: A True Financial Thriller* (New York: Wiley, 2010).

51. Charles Dickens, *The Life and Adventures of Martin Chuzzlewit* (London: Chapman & Hall, 1843).

52. Daniel Jordan Smith, *A Culture of Corruption: Everyday Deception and Popular Discontent in Nigeria* (Princeton, NJ: Princeton University Press, 2007).

53. Aviva Gat, "Millions of Victims Lost $12.7B Last Year Falling for Nigerian Scams," *Geektime*, July 21, 2014, https://www.geektime.com/2014/07/21/millions-of-victims-lost-12-7b-last-year-falling-for-nigerian-scams/ (accessed May 15, 2017).

54. Cormac Herley, "Why Do Nigerian Scammers Say They Are from Nigeria?" *WEIS*, June 1, 2012, http://research.microsoft.com/pubs/167719/WhyFromNigeria.pdf (accessed May 15, 2017).

55. Charles F. Bond and Bella M. DePaulo, "Accuracy of Deception Judgments," *Personality and Social Psychology Review* 10, no. 3 (August 2006): 214–34.

56. Konnikova, *Confidence Game*.

57. Robert E. Kraut and Donald B. Poe, "Behavioral Roots of Person Perception: The Deception Judgments of Customs Inspectors and Laymen," *Journal of Personality and Social Psychology* 39, no. 5 (November 1980): 784–98.

58. Paul Ekman and Maureen O'Sullivan, "Who Can Catch a Liar?" *American Psychologist* 46, no. 9 (September 1991): 913–20.

59. Steven A. McCornack and Timothy R. Levine, "When Lovers Become Leery: The Relationship between Suspiciousness and Accuracy in Detecting Deception," *Communication Monographs* 57, no. 3 (1990): 219–30.

60. Gerald M. Rosen and William R. Phillips, "A Cautionary Tale from Simulated Patients," *Journal of the American Academy of Psychiatry and the Law* 32, no. 2 (June 2004): 132–33.

61. Edward J. Hickling et al., "Detection of Malingered MVA-Related Posttraumatic Stress Disorder: An Investigation of the Ability to Detect Professional Actors by Experienced Clinicians, Psychological Tests, and Psychophysiological Assessment," *Journal of Forensic Psychology and Practice* 2, no. 1 (2002): 33–54.

62. Ralph Slovenko, *Psychiatry in Law/Law in Psychiatry* (New York: Brunner-Routledge, 2002), p. 122.

63. James Alcock and Stan Sadava, *Social Psychology: Global Perspectives* (London: Sage, 2014).

64. W. G. Iacono and D. T. Lykken, "The Validity of the Lie Detector: Two Surveys of Scientific Opinion," *Journal of Applied Psychology* 82, no. 3 (June 1997): 426–33.

65. Charles R. Honts, Robert L. Hodes, and David C. Raskin, "Effects of Physical Countermeasures on the Physiological Detection of Deception," *Journal of Applied Psychology* 70 (1985): 177–87.

66. C. D. Lefebvre et al., "Use of Event–Related Brain Potentials (ERPs) to Assess Eyewitness Accuracy and Deception," *International Journal of Psychophysiology* 73, no. 3 (September 2009): 218–25.

67. Bella M. DePaulo, "Spotting Lies: Can Humans Learn to Do Better?" *Current Directions in Psychological Science* 3, no. 3 (June 1994): 83–86.

68. Elise Fenn et al., "A Reverse Order Interview Does Not Aid Deception Detection Regarding Intentions," *Frontiers in Psychology* 6, no. 1298 (2015).

69. Ronald R. Holden, "Response Latency Detection of Fakers on Personnel Tests," *Canadian Journal of Behavioral Science* 27, no. 3 (July 1995): 343–55.

Chapter 10: Beliefs about Ourselves

1. Plato, *Writings of Plato: Theaetus, Ion, Apology*, trans. Benjamin Jowett (Woodstock, ON: Devoted, 2016).

2. Ibid., p. 49.

3. Lex Newman, Stanford Encyclopedia of Philosophy, s.v. "Descartes' Epistemology," December 3, 1997, last modified October 6, 2014, https://plato.stanford.edu/entries/descartes -epistemology/ (accessed November 16, 2017).

4. Ron Sender, Shai Fuchs, and Ron Milo, "Revised Estimates for the Number of Human and Bacteria Cells in the Body," *PLoS Biology* 14, no.8 (August 19, 2016), published online, https://doi.org/10.1371/journal.pbio.1002533 (accessed November 16, 2017).

5. Domenico Ribatti, "William Harvey and the Discovery of the Circulation of the Blood," *Journal of Angiogenesis Research* 1 (September 21, 2009): 3.

6. After having written this description about the poker-playing dogs, my attention was brought to *Fifteen Dogs* by André Alexis, a novel that deliciously amplifies on the theme of dogs acquiring human intelligence.

7. Stanley Coren, "Why Do Dogs Like to Sniff Crotches?" *Psychology Today*, August 7, 2014, https://www.psychologytoday.com/blog/canine-corner/201408/why-do-dogs-sniff -crotches (accessed April 15, 2017).

8. Ronald Melzack, "Phantom Limbs, the Self, and the Brain: The D. O. Hebb Memorial Lecture," *Canadian Psychology* 30, no. 1 (January 1989): 1–16.

9. Chris Frith, "The Psychology of Volition," *Experimental Brain Research* 229, no. 3 (September 2013): 289–99.

10. D. H. Geschwind et al., "Alien Hand Syndrome: Interhemispheric Motor Disconnection Due to a Lesion in the Midbody of the Corpus Callosum," *Neurology* 45, no. 4 (April 1995): 802–808.

11. Rianne M. Blom, Raoul C. Hennekam, and Damiaan. Denys, "Body Integrity Identity Disorder," *PLoS ONE* 7, no. 4 (2012): e34702.

12. Matthew Botvinick and Jonathan Cohen, "Rubber Hands 'Feel' Touch That Eyes See," *Nature* 391, no. 6669 (February 19, 1998): 756.

13. H. Henrik Ehrsson, Charles Spence, and Richard E. Passingham, "That's My Hand! Activity in Premotor Cortex Reflects Feeling of Ownership of a Limb," *Science* 305, no. 5685 (August 6, 2004): 875–77.

14. Matthew R. Longo and Patrick Haggard, "What Is It Like to Have a Body?" *Current Directions in Psychological Science* 21, no. 2 (April 2012): 140–45.

15. Ehrsson, Spence, and Passingham, "That's My Hand!"

16. Ibid.

17. Mel Slater et al., "First Person Experience of Body Transfer in Virtual Reality," *PLoS ONE* 5, no. 5 (2010): e10564.

18. Gert-Jan C. Lokhorst and Timo T. Kaitaro, "The Originality of Descartes' Theory about the Pineal Gland," *Journal for the History of the Neurosciences* 10, no. 1 (2001): 6–18.

19. Gilbert Ryle, *The Concept of Mind* (London: Hutchinson, 1949).

20. Barry Beyerstein "The Brain and Consciousness: Implications for Psi Phenomena," *Skeptical Inquirer* 12, no. 2 (1987): 163–71.

21. Piotr Winkielman and Jonathan W. Schooler, "Consciousness, Metacognition, and the Unconscious," in *The SAGE Handbook of Social Cognition*, ed. Susan T. Fiske and C. Neil Macrae (London: Sage, 2012), pp. 54–74.

22. Antti Revonsuo, Sakari Kallio, and Pilleriin Sikka, "What Is an Altered State of Consciousness?" *Philosophical Psychology* 22, no. 2 (2009): 187–204.

23. Winkielman and Schooler, "Consciousness, Metacognition, and the Unconscious."

24. Ibid.

25. Dr. Guy Proulx, personal communication to the author, May 15, 2017.

26. Winkielman and Schooler, "Consciousness, Metacognition, and the Unconscious."

27. Donald R. Griffin and Gayle B. Speck, "New Evidence of Animal Consciousness," *Animal Cognition* 7, no. 1 (January 2004): 5–18.

28. David B. Edelman and Anil K. Seth, "Animal Consciousness: A Synthetic Approach," *Trends in Neuroscience* 32, no. 9 (September 2009): 476–84.

29. Susan Blackmore, *Consciousness: An Introduction* (London: Hodder and Stoughton, 2003).

30. Ibid.

31. Annie Jacobsen, "Inside the Pentagon's Effort to Build a Killer Robot," *Time*, October 27, 2015, http://time.com/4078877/darpa-the-pentagons-brain/ (accessed November 16, 2017).

32. Samuel Gibbs, "Elon Musk: Regulate AI to Combat 'Existential Threat' before It's Too Late," *Guardian*, July 17, 2017, https://www.theguardian.com/technology/2017/jul/17/elon -musk-regulation-ai-combat-existential-threat-tesla-spacex-ceo (accessed July 17, 2017).

33. Robin Robertson, *C. G. Jung and the Archetypes of the Collective Unconscious* (New York: Peter Lang, 1987).

34. Eduard von Hartmann, *Philosophie des Unbewussten* (Leipzig: Duncker, 1869).

35. John A. Bargh and Ezequiel Morsella, "The Unconscious Mind," *Perspectives on Psychological Science* 3, no. 1 (January 2008): 73–79.

36. Max Velmans, *Understanding Consciousness* (London: Routledge, 2000).

37. John A. Bargh and Ezequiel Morsella, "Unconscious Behavioral Guidance Systems," in *Then a Miracle Occurs: Focusing on Behavior in Social Psychological Theory and Research*, ed. Christopher R. Agnew, Donal E. Carlston, William G. Graziano, and Janice R. Kelly (New York: Oxford University Press, 2009), pp. 89–118.

38. Bargh and Morsella, "Unconscious Mind."

39. Michael S. A. Graziano and Dylan F. Cooke, "Parieto-Frontal Interactions, Personal Space, and Defensive Behavior," *Neuropsychologia* 44 (2006): 845–59.

40. Barry L. Beyerstein, "Anomalous Perceptual Experiences: Believing Is Seeing Is Believing," *Scientific Review of Alternative Medicine* 6, no. 2 (2002): 73–82.

41. Stephen Potter, *The Theory & Practice of Gamesmanship* (London: Rupert Hart-Davis, 1947), p. 56.

42. Richard E. Nisbett and Timothy D. Wilson, "Telling More than We Can Know: Verbal Reports on Mental Processes," *Psychological Review* 84, no. 3 (March 1977): 231–59.

43. Winkielman and Schooler, "Consciousness, Metacognition, and the Unconscious."

44. Gastone G. Celesia, "Visual Perception and Awareness: A Modular System," *Journal of Psychophysiology* 24, no. 2 (April 2010): 62–67.

45. David F. Marks and Richard Kammann, *The Psychology of the Psychic* (Amherst, NY: Prometheus Books, 1980).

46. Winkielman and Schooler, "Consciousness, Metacognition, and the Unconscious."

47. Edward M. Bowden and Mark Jung-Beeman, "Aha! Insight Experience Correlates with Solution Activation in the Right Hemisphere," *Psychonomic Bulletin & Review* 10, no. 3 (September 2003): 730–37.

48. Jonathan W. Schooler and Joseph Melcher, "The Ineffability of Insight," in *The Creative Cognition Approach*, ed. Steven M. Smith, Thomas B. Ward, and Ronald A. Finke (Cambridge, MA: MIT Press, 1995), pp. 97–133.

49. Bhavin R. Sheth, Simone Sandkühler, and Joydeep Bhattacharya, "Posterior Beta and Anterior Gamma Oscillations Predict Cognitive Insight," *Journal of Cognitive Neuroscience* 21, no. 7 (July 2009): 1269–79.

50. Mark Jung-Beeman et al., "Neural Activity When People Solve Verbal Problems with Insight," *PLoS Biology* 2, no. 4 (April 2004): e97.

51. N. R. F. Maier, "Reasoning in Humans: II. The Solution of a Problem and Its Appearance in Consciousness," *Journal of Comparative Psychology* 12, no. 2 (1931): 181–94.

52. Ap Dijksterhuis, "Think Different: The Merits of Unconscious Thought in Preference Development and Decision Making," *Journal of Personality and Social Psychology* 87, no. 5 (2004): 586–98.

53. Todd D. Thorsteinson and Scott Withrow, "Does Unconscious Thought Outperform Conscious Thought on Complex Decisions? A Further Examination," *Judgment and Decision Making* 4, no. 3 (April 2009): 235–47.

54. Timothy D. Wilson and Jonathan W. Schooler, "Thinking Too Much: Introspection Can Reduce the Quality of Preferences and Decisions," *Journal of Personality and Social Psychology* 60, no. 2 (February 1991): 181–92.

55. William B. Carpenter, "On the Influence of Suggestion in Modifying and Directing Muscular Movement, Independently of Volition," *Proceedings of the Royal Institution of Great Britain* 1 (1852): 147–53.

56. Armin Stock and Claudia Stock, "A Short History of Ideo-Motor Action," *Psychological Research* 68, no. 2-3 (April 2004): 176–88.

57. Ray Hyman, "The Mischief-Making of Ideomotor Action," *Scientific Review of Alternative Medicine* 3, no. 2 (1999): 34–43.

58. M. E. Chevreul, *De la Baguette Divinatoire, du Pendule Dit Explorateur et des Tables Tournantes, au Point de Vue de l'Histoire, de la Critique et de la Méthode Expérimentale* (Paris: Mallet-Bachelier, 1854), cited by Randolph D. Easton and Ronald E. Shor, "Information Processing Analysis of the Chevreul Pendulum Illusion," *Journal of Experimental Psychology: Human Perception and Performance* 1, no. 3 (August 1975): 231–36.

59. Ray Hyman, "How People Are Fooled by Ideomotor action," Quackwatch, August 26, 2003, http://www.quackwatch.com/01QuackeryRelatedTopics/ideomotor.html (accessed November 16, 2017).

60. Easton and Shor, "Information Processing Analysis of the Chevreul Pendulum Illusion."

61. Ray Hyman, *The Elusive Quarry: A Scientific Appraisal of Psychical Research* (Amherst, NY: Prometheus Books, 1989), p. 425.

62. J. B. Rhine and L. E. Rhine, "An Investigation of a Mind-Reading Horse," *Journal of Abnormal and Social Psychology* 23, no. 4 (1929): 449–66.

63. Milbourne Christopher, *ESP, Seers & Psychics: What the Occult Really Is* (New York: Crowell, 1971).

64. Ray Hyman, "Ouija, Dowsing, and Other Seductions of Ideomotor Action," in *Tall Tales about the Mind and Brain: Separating Fact from Fiction*, ed. Sergio Della Sala (Oxford: Oxford University Press, 2007), pp. 411–24.

65. Evon Z. Vogt and Ray Hyman, *Water Witching USA* (Chicago: University of Chicago Press, 1959).

66. Hyman, "Ouija, Dowsing, and Other Seductions of Ideomotor Action.""

67. J. T. Enright, "Testing Dowsing: The Failure of the Munich Experiments," *Skeptical Inquirer* 23, no. 1 (January/February 1999): 39–46.

68. Daniel M. Wegner, Valerie A. Fuller, and Betsy Sparrow, "Clever Hands: Uncontrolled Intelligence in Facilitated Communication," *Journal of Personality and Social Psychology* 85, no. 1 (July 2003): 5–19.

69. Scott O. Lilienfeld, Julia Marshall, James T. Todd, and Howard C. Shane, "The Persistence of Fad Interventions in the Face of Negative Scientific Evidence: Facilitated Communication for Autism as a Case Example," *Evidence-Based Communication Assessment and Intervention* 8, no. 2 (2014): 62–101.

70. Daniel Garber, "Understanding Interaction: What Descartes Should Have Told Elisabeth," in *Debates in Modern Philosophy: Essential Readings and Contemporary Responses*, ed. Stewart Duncan and Antonia Lolordo (London: Routledge, 2013), p 38.

71. Daniel M. Wegner, "Self Is Magic," in *Are We Free? Psychology and Free Will*, ed. John Baer, James C. Kaufman, and Roy F. Baumeister (Oxford: Oxford University Press, 2008), p 226.

72. Michael S. Gazzaniga, *The Social Brain: Discovering the Networks of the Mind* (New York: Basic Books, 1985).

73. Benjamin Libet et al., "Time of Conscious Intention to Act in Relation to Onset of Cerebral Activity (Readiness-Potential): The Unconscious Initiation of a Freely Voluntary Act," *Brain* 106, no. 3 (September 1983): 623–42.

74. Bargh and Morsella, "The Unconscious Mind."

75. Daniel M. Wegner and Thalia Wheatley, "Apparent Mental Causation: Sources of the Experience of Will," *American Psychologist* 54, no. 7 (July 1999): 480–92.

76. Daniel M. Wegner, "The Mind's Best Trick: How We Experience Conscious Will," *Trends in Cognitive Sciences* 7, no. 2 (February 2003): 65–69.

77. Chun Siong Soon et al., "Unconscious Determinants of Free Decisions in the Human Brain," *Nature Neuroscience* 11, no. 5 (May 2008): 543–45.

78. Sean Müller, Bruce Abernethy, and Damian Farrow, "How Do World-Class Cricket Batsmen Anticipate a Bowler's Intention?" *Quarterly Journal of Experimental Psychology* 59, no. 12 (December 2006): 2162–86.

79. Jonah Lehrer, *How We Decide* (Boston: Houghton Mifflin Harcourt, 2009), p. 25.

80. Müller, Abernethy, and Farrow, "How Do World–Class Cricket Batsmen Anticipate a Bowler's Intention?"

81. Graziano and Cooke, "Parieto-Frontal Interactions, Personal Space, and Defensive Behavior."

82. Dionne S. Coker-Appiah et al., "Looming Animate and Inanimate Threats: The Response of the Amygdala and Periaqueductal Gray," *Social Neuroscience* 8, no. 6 (2013): 621–30.

Chapter 11: Not Quite in Our Right Minds

1 Teresa of Avila, *The Life of Saint Teresa of Avila*, trans. J. M. Cohen (1562; London: Penguin, 1988), ch. 8.

2. Andrew M. Greeley, *Ecstasy: A Way of Knowing* (Englewood Cliffs, NJ: Prentice-Hall, 1974).

3. Evelyn Underhill, *The Mystics of the Church* (Cambridge: James Clarke, 1975).

4. Jeff Levin and Lea Steele, "The Transcendent Experience: Conceptual, Theoretical, and Epidemiologic Perspectives," *Explore* 1, no. 2 (March 2005): 89–101.

5. William James, *The Varieties of Religious Experience* (1902; New York: Mentor, 1958).

6. Abraham H. Maslow, *Religions, Values, and Peak Experiences* (London: Penguin 1964).

7. Ibid., p 59.

8. Levin and Steele, "Transcendent Experience."

9. Walter N. Pahnke, *Drugs and Mysticism: An Analysis of the Relationship between Psychedelic Drugs and the Mystical Consciousness* (thesis presented to the Committee on Higher Degrees in History and Philosophy of Religion, Harvard University, 1963).

10. Rick Doblin, "Pahnke's 'Good Friday Experiment': A Long Term Follow-Up and Methodological Critique" *Journal of Transpersonal Psychology* 23, no. 1 (1991): 1–25.

11. R. R. Griffiths et al., "Psilocybin Can Occasion Mystical-Type Experiences Having Substantial and Sustained Personal Meaning and Spiritual Significance," *Psychopharmacology* 187, no. 3 (2006): 268–83.

12. Evan D. Murray, Miles G. Cunningham, and Bruce H. Price, "The Role of Psychotic Disorders in Religious History Considered," *Journal of Neuropsychiatry and Clinical Neuroscience* 24, no. 4 (Fall 2012): 410–26.

13. Adair de Menezes Júnior and Alexander Moreira-Almeida, "Differential Diagnosis between Spiritual Experiences and Mental Disorders of Religious Content," *Revista de Psiquiatria Clínica / Archives of Clinical Psychiatry* 36, no. 2 (2009): 69–76.

14. Barry L. Beyerstein, "Anomalous Perceptual Experiences: Believing Is Seeing Is Believing," *Scientific Review of Alternative Medicine* 6, no. 2 (2002): 73–82.

15. Antti Revonsuo, Sakari Kallio, and Pilleriin Sikka, "What Is an Altered State of Consciousness?" *Philosophical Psychology* 22, no. 2 (2009): 187–204.

16. A. J. F. Brière de Boismont, *The Rational History of Apparitions, Visions, Dreams, Ecstasy, Magnetism, and Somnambulism* (Philadelphia: Lindsay & Blakiston, 1853).

Available online at https://archive.org/details/hallucinationso00boisgoog (accessed June 17, 2017); See also R. R. Madden, *Phantasmata or Illusion and Fanaticisms of Protean Forms, Productive of Great Evils* (London: T. C. Newby, 1857), https://archive.org/stream/phantasmataoril01maddgoog/phantasmataoril01maddgoog_djvu (accessed June 17, 2017).

17. Dieter Vaitl et al., "Psychobiology of Altered State of Consciousness," *Psychological Bulletin* 131, no. 1 (2005): 98–127.

18. Beyerstein, "Anomalous Perceptual Experiences."

19. Vaitl et al., "Psychobiology of Altered States of Consciousness."

20. Beyerstein, "Anomalous Perceptual Experiences.'"

21. Revonsuo, Kallio, and Sikka, "What Is an Altered State of Consciousness?"

22. Robert E. Ornstein, *The Psychology of Consciousness* (New York: Penguin, 1976).

23. Richard P. Bentall, "The Illusion of Reality: A Review and Integration of Psychological Research on Hallucination," *Psychological Bulletin* 107, no. 1 (January 1990): 82–95.

24. David S. Loverock and Vito Modigliani, "Visual Imagery and the Brain: A Review," *Journal of Mental Imagery* 19, no. 1 & 2 (January 1995): 91–132.

25. Barry L. Beyerstein, "The Neurology of the Weird: Brain States and Anomalous Experience," in *Tall Tales about the Mind and Brain: Separating Fact from Fiction*, ed. Sergio Della Sala (Oxford: Oxford University Press, 2007), pp. 314–35.

26. Bentall, "The Illusion of Reality."

27. Chris D. Frith and Karl J. Friston, "False Perceptions & False Beliefs: Understanding Schizophrenia," in *Neurosciences and the Human Person: New Perspectives on Human Activities*, ed. Antonio Battro, Stanislas. Dehaene, and Wolf Singer (Vatican City: Pontifical Academy of Sciences, 2014).

28. Ornstein, *Psychology of Consciousness*.

29. Olaf Blanke et al., "Stimulating Illusory Own-Body Perceptions," *Nature* 419, no. 6904 (September 19, 2002): 269–70.

30. Revonsuo, Kallio, and Sikka, "What Is an Altered State of Consciousness?"

31. Barry L. Beyerstein, "Neuropathology and the Legacy of Spiritual Possession," *Skeptical Inquirer* 12, no. 3 (1988): 248–62.

32. Oliver Sacks, *Hallucinations* (New York: Knopf, 1995).

33. Beyerstein, "Anomalous Perceptual Experiences.'"

34. Arnold M. Ludwig, "Altered States of Consciousness," *Archives of General Psychiatry* 15, no. 3 (1966): 225–34.

35. Aldous Huxley, *The Doors of Perception, Heaven, and Hell* (Harmondsworth: Penguin, 1959).

36. Beyerstein, "Anomalous Perceptual Experiences."

37. William Chambers and Robert Chambers, "The Story of a Gas," *Chambers's Journal of Popular Literature, Science And Arts* 545 (Edinburgh: W. & R. Chambers, 1874): 357.

38. Huxley, *Doors of Perception*.

39. Ronald K. Siegel, *Fire in the Brain: Clinical Tales of Hallucination* (New York: Penguin, 1992).

40. Lotfi B. Merabet et al., "Visual Hallucinations during Prolonged Blindfolding in Sighted Subjects," *Journal of Neuro-Ophthalmology* 24, no. 2 (June 2004): 109.

41. Revonsuo, Kallio, and Sikka, "What Is an Altered State of Consciousness?"

42. Shoshana Shapiro and Paul M. Lehrer, "Psychophysiological Effects of Autogenic Training and Progressive Relaxation," *Biofeedback and Self-Regulation* 5, no. 2 (1980): 249–55.

43. Herbert Benson, *The Relaxation Response* (New York: William Morrow, 1975).

44. Jonathan C. Smith et al., "Relaxation: Mapping an Uncharted World," *Biofeedback and Self-Regulation* 21, no. 1 (March 1996): 63–90.

45. William Sargant, *The Mind Possessed: A Physiology of Possession, Mysticism, and Faith Healing* (London: Heineman, 1973), p. 194.

46. Albrecht H. K. Wobst, "Hypnosis and Surgery: Past, Present, and Future," *Anesthesia & Analgesia* 104, no. 5 (May 2007): 1199–208.

47. Ormond McGill, *New Encyclopedia of Genuine Stage Hypnotism* (Bancyfelin, Wales: Crown House, 1996).

48. Scott O. Lilienfeld and Hal Arkowitz, "Is Hypnosis a Distinct Form of Consciousness?" *Scientific American Nature*, December 1, 2008, https://www.scientificamerican.com/article/is-hypnosis-a-distinct-form/ (accessed November 16, 2017).

49. Martin T. Orne et al., "'Memories' of Anomalous and Traumatic Autobiographical Experiences: Validation and Consolidation of Fantasy through Hypnosis," *Journal of Psychological Inquiry* 7, no. 2 (1996): 168–72; M. T. Orne, "The Use and Misuse of Hypnosis in Court," *International Journal of Clinical and Experimental Hypnosis* 27, no. 4 (1979): 311–41.

50. Peter W. Sheehan and Kevin M. McConkey, *Hypnosis and Experience* (Hillsdale, NJ: Erlbaum, 1982).

51. Etzel Cardeña, Steven Jay Lynn, and Stanley Krippner, eds., *Varieties of Anomalous Experience: Examining the Scientific Evidence* (Washington, DC: American Psychological Association, 2014).

52. Revonsuo, Kallio, and Sikka, "What Is an Altered State of Consciousness?"

53. Nicholas P. Spanos and John F. Chaves, eds., *Hypnosis: The Cognitive-Behavioral Perspective* (Amherst, NY: Prometheus Books, 1989).

54. Benjamin A. Parris, "The Prefrontal Cortex and Suggestion: Hypnosis vs. Placebo," *Frontiers in Psychology* 7 (2016): 415.

55. Kenneth S. Bowers, "The Relevance of Hypnosis for Cognitive-Behavioral Therapy," *Clinical Psychological Review* 2, no. 1 (1982): 67–78.

56. Irving Kirsch and Wayne Braffman, "Imaginative Suggestibility and Hypnotizability," *Current Directions in Psychological Science* 10, no. 2 (2001): 57–61.

57. Martin T. Orne and Frederick J. Evans, "Social Control in the Psychological Experiment: Antisocial Behavior and Hypnosis," *Journal of Personality and Social Psychology* 1, no. 3 (1965): 189–200.

58. Sheryl C. Wilson and Theodore X. Barber, "The Fantasy-Prone Personality: Implications for Understanding Imagery, Hypnosis, and Parapsychological Phenomena," in *Imagery: Current Theory, Research, and Application*, ed. Anees Sheikh (New York: Wiley, 1983), pp. 340–87.

59. Nicholas P. Spanos et al., "Close Encounters: An Examination of UFO Experiences," *Journal of Abnormal Psychology* 102, no. 4 (1993): 624–32.

60. Dale Purves et al., eds., *Neuroscience*, 2nd ed. (Sunderland, MA: Sinauer Associates, 2001).

61. Allan Rechtschaffen, "The Control of Sleep," in *Human Behavior and Its Control*, ed. William A. Hunt (Cambridge, MA: Schenkman, 1971), pp. 75–92, 88.

62. Emmanuel Mignot, "Why We Sleep: The Temporal Organization of Recovery," *PLoS Biology* 6, no. 4 (April 2008): e106.

63. Purves et al., eds., *Neuroscience*.

64. K. Adam and J. Oswald, "Sleep Is for Tissue Restoration," *Journal of the Royal College of Physicians of London* 11, no. 4 (July 1977): 376–88.

65. Philipp Mergenthaler et al., "Sugar for the Brain: The Role of Glucose in Physiological and Pathological Brain Function," *Trends in Neuroscience* 36, no. 10 (October 2013): 587–97.

66. Lulu Xie et al., "Sleep Drives Metabolite Clearance from the Adult Brain," *Science* 342, no. 6156 (October 18, 2013): 373–77.

67. Eugene Aserinsky and Nathaniel Kleitman, "Regularly Occurring Periods of Eye Motility, and Concomitant Phenomena, during Sleep," *Science* 118, no. 3062 (September 4, 1953): 273–74.

68. Mark Solms, "Dreaming and REM Sleep Are Controlled by Different Brain Mechanisms," *Behavioral and Brain Sciences* 23, no. 6 (December 2000): 793–1121.

69. Aserinsky and Kleitman, "Regularly Occurring Periods of Eye Motility."

70. Mark Shein-Idelson et al., "Slow Waves, Sharp Waves, Ripples, and REM in Sleeping Dragons," *Science* 352, no. 6285 (April 29, 2016): 590–95.

71. Purves et al., eds., *Neuroscience*.

72. Michael K. Scullin and Donald L. Bliwise, "Sleep, Cognition, and Normal Aging: Integrating a Half Century of Multidisciplinary Research," *Perspectives on Psychological Science* 10, no. 1 (January 2015): 97–137.

73. Mary A. Carskadon and William C. Dement, "Normal Human Sleep: An Overview," in *Principles and Practice of Sleep Medicine*, 4th ed., ed. Meir H. Kryger, Thomas Roth, and William C. Dement (Philadelphia: Elsevier Saunders, 2005), pp.13–23.

74. Harvey R. Colten and Bruce M. Altevogt, *Sleep Disorders and Sleep Deprivation: An Unmet Public Health Problem* (Washington, DC: National Academies Press, 2006).

75. David Shulman and Guy G. Stroumsa, eds., *Dream Cultures: Explorations in the Comparative History of Dreaming* (New York: Oxford University Press, 1999).

76. Revonsuo, Kallio, and Sikka, "What Is an Altered State of Consciousness?"

77. Vaitl et al., "Psychobiology of Altered States of Consciousness."

78. Antti Revonsuo, Jarno Tuominen, and Katja Valli, "The Avatars in the Machine: Dreaming as a Simulation of Social Reality," in *Open MIND*, ed. Thomas K. Metzinger and Jennifer M. Windt (Frankfurt am Main: MIND Group, 2015), pp. 1–28, 2.

79. Vaitl et al., "Psychobiology of Altered States of Consciousness."

80. M. Solms, "Dreaming and REM Sleep Are Controlled by Different Brain Mechanisms," *Behavioral and Brain Sciences* 23 (2000): 793–1121.

81. J. Allan Hobson, *The Dreaming Brain: How the Brain Creates Both the Sense and the Nonsense of Dreams* (New York: Basic Books, 1988).

82. Solms, "Dreaming and REM Sleep Are Controlled by Different Brain Mechanisms."

83. J. Allan Hobson, "REM Sleep and Dreaming: Towards a Theory Protoconsciousness," *Nature Reviews Neuroscience* 10, no. 11 (November 2009): 803–13.

84. Revonsuo, Tuominen, and Valli, "Avatars in the Machine."

85. Caroline L. Horton and Josie E. Malinkowski, "Autobiographical Memory and Hyperassociativity in the Dreaming Brain: Implications for Memory Consolidation in Sleep," *Frontiers in Psychology* 6 (2015): 874.

86. Terrence J. Sejnowski and Alain Destexhe, "Why Do We Sleep?" *Brain Research* 886, no. 1-2 (December 2000): 208–23.

87. Richard Boyce et al., "Causal Evidence for the Role of REM Sleep Theta Rhythm in Contextual Memory Consolidation," *Science* 352, no. 6287 (May 13, 2016): 812.

88. Ernest Hartmann, *The Nature and Functions of Dreaming* (New York: Oxford University Press, 2011).

89. J. N. Berry, "Sir Frederick Banting's Dream," *Canadian Notes and Queries* 23, no. 7 (1980): I–00961.

90. Vaitl et al., "Psychobiology of Altered States of Consciousness."

91. Maurice M. Ohayon et al., "Hypnagogic and Hypnopompic Hallucinations: Pathological Phenomena?" *British Journal of Psychiatry* 169, no. 4 (October 1996): 459–67.

92. Graham Reed, *The Psychology of Anomalous Experience: A Cognitive Approach* (Amherst, NY: Prometheus Books, 1988).

93. Guy de Maupassant, cited by James Allan Cheyne, "Nightmares from the Id," University of Waterloo, 2013, http://www.gambassa.com/public/collaborations/2073/1377/8873/Cheyne%202013.html (accessed June 17, 2017).

94. Ibid.

95. Ibid.

96. Robert C. Ness, "The *Old Hag* Phenomenon as Sleep Paralysis: A Biocultural Interpretation," in *The Culture-Bound Syndromes: Folk Illnesses of Psychiatric and Anthropological Interest*, ed. Ronald C. Simons and Charles C. Hughes (Boston: D. Reidel, 1985), pp. 123–45.

97. Melvin C. Firestone, "The 'Old Hag': Sleep Paralysis in Newfoundland," *Psychoanalytic Anthropology* 8, no. 1 (1985): 47–66.

98. Brian A. Sharpless and Jacques P. Barber, "Lifetime Prevalence Rates of Sleep Paralysis: A Systematic Review," *Sleep Medicine Review* 15, no. 5 (October 2011): 311–15.

99. Susan Blackmore, "Lucid Dreaming: Awake in Your Sleep?," *Skeptical Inquirer* 15 (1991): 362–70.

100. Hobson, "REM Sleep and Dreaming."

101. Robert James Broughton et al., "Homicidal Somnambulism: A Case Report," *Sleep* 17, no. 3 (May 1994): 259.

Chapter 12: Belief and Well-Being

1. Tomasz Witkowski, *Psychology Led Astray: Cargo Cult in Science and Therapy* (Boca Raton, FL: Brown Walker, 2016).

2. Abiola Keller et al., "Does the Perception That Stress Affects Health Matter? The Association with Health and Mortality," *Health Psychology* 31, no. 5 (September 2012): 677–84.

3. Hermann Nabi et al., "Increased Risk of Coronary Heart Disease among Individuals

Reporting Adverse Impact of Stress on Their Health: The Whitehall II Prospective Cohort Study," *European Heart Journal* 34, no. 34 (September 2013): 2697–705.

4. Joe Tomaka et al., "Cognitive and Physiological Antecedents of Threat and Challenge Appraisal," *Journal of Personality and Social Psychology* 73, no. 1 (July 1997): 63–72.

5. Kelly McGonigal, *The Upside of Stress: Why Stress Is Good for You, and How to Get Good at It* (New York: Avery, 2015).

6. Suzanne C. Kobasa, "Stressful Life Events, Personality, and Health: An Inquiry into Hardiness," *Journal of Personality and Social Psychology* 37, no. 1 (1979): 1–11.

7. Richard J. Contrada, "Type A Behavior, Personality Hardiness, and Cardiovascular Responses to Stress," *Journal of Personality and Social Psychology* 57, no. 5 (1989): 895–903.

8. Marek J. Celinski and L. M. Allen, "Resilience and Resourcefulness in Predicting Recovery Outcome," in Kathryn M. Gow and Marek J. Celinski, eds., *Mass Trauma: Impact and Recovery Issues* (New York: Nova Science, 2013), pp. 139–52.

9. Mark Antoniazzi, Marek J. Celinski, and James E. Alcock, "Self-Responsibility and Coping with Pain: Disparate Attitudes toward Psychosocial Issues in Recovery from Work Place Injury," *Disability and Rehabilitation* 24, no. 18 (2003): 948–53.

10. Esther M. Sternberg, "Walter B. Cannon and '"Voodoo" Death': A Perspective from 60 Years On," *American Journal of Public Health* 92, no. 10 (October 2002): 1564–66.

11. M. A. Samuels, "'Voodoo' Death Revisited: The Modern Lessons of Neurocardiology," *Cleveland Clinical Journal of Medicine* 74, supplement 1 (2007): 8–16.

12. Marilyn S. Cebelin and Charles S. Hirsch, "Human Stress Cardiomyopathy: Myocardial Lesions in Victims of Homicidal Assaults without Internal Injuries," *Human Pathology* 11, no. 2 (March 1980): 123–31.

13. Saeed Ullah Shah et al., "Heart and Mind: (1) Relationship between Cardiovascular and Psychiatric Conditions," *Postgraduate Medicine Journal* 80, no. 950 (December 2004): 683–89.

14. Laura S. Gold et al., "Disaster Events and the Risk of Sudden Cardiac Death: A Washington State Investigation," *Prehospital and Disaster Medicine* 22, no. 4 (August 2007): 313–17.

15. A. Myers and H. A. Dewar, "Circumstances Attending 100 Sudden Deaths from Coronary Artery Disease with Coroner's Necropsies," *British Heart Journal* 37, no. 11 (November 1975): 1133–43.

16. David P. Phillips et al., "The *Hound of the Baskervilles* Effect: A Natural Experiment on the Influence of Psychological Stress on the Timing of Death," *British Medical Journal* 323, no. 7327 (December 22, 2001): 1443–46.

17. Daniel E. Moerman and Wayne B. Jonas, "Deconstructing the Placebo Effect in Finding the Meaning Response," *Annals of Internal Medicine* 136, no. 6 (2002): 471–76.

18. D. P. Phillips, T. E. Ruth, and L. M. Wagner, "Psychology and Survival," *Lancet* 372, no. 8880 (November 6, 1993): 1142–45.

19. Shelley R. Adler, *Sleep Paralysis: Night-Mares, Nocebos, and the Mind-Body Connection* (New Brunswick, NJ: Rutgers University Press, 2010).

20. Ibid.

21. Ilan S. Wittstein et al., "Neurohumoral Features of Myocardial Stunning Due to

Sudden Emotional Stress," *New England Journal of Medicine* 352, no. 6 (February 10, 2005): 539–48.

22. Arthur Glyn Leonard, *The Lower Niger and Its Tribes* (London: Macmillan, 1906), p. 257. (Cited by Walter B. Cannon, "'Voodoo' Death," *American Anthropologist* 44, no. 2 [April-June 1942]: 169–81).

23. Wade Davis, *The Serpent and the Rainbow: A Harvard Scientist's Astonishing Journey into the Secret Society of Haitian Voodoo, Zombis, and Magic* (New York: Simon and Shuster, 1985), p. 136.

24. Michael S. Pollanen, "Alleged Lethal Sorcery in East Timor," *Forensic Science International* 139, no. 1 (January 6, 2004): 17–19.

25. Cannon, "'Voodoo' Death."

26. Emilio Mira, "Psychiatric Experience in the Spanish War," *British Medical Journal* 1, no. 4093 (June 17, 1939): 1217–20.

27. David Lester, "Voodoo Death: Some New Thoughts on an Old Phenomenon," *American Anthropologist* 74, no. 3 (June 1972): 386–90.

28. Harry D. Eastwell, "Voodoo Death and the Mechanism for Dispatch of the Dying in East Arnhem, Australia," *American Anthropologist* 84, no. 1 (March 1982): 5–18.

29. Horatio Prater, *Lectures on True and False Hypnotism, or Mesmerism* (London: Piper Brothers, 1851).

30. Peter Lamont, *The Rise of the Indian Rope Trick: How a Spectacular Hoax Became History* (New York: Little, Brown, 2004).

31. Janice Reid and Nancy Williams, "'Voodoo Death' in Arnhem Land: Whose Reality?" *American Anthropologist* 86, no. 1 (March 1984): 121–33.

32. Pollanen, "Alleged Lethal Sorcery in East Timor."; Francis J. Clune, "A Comment of Voodoo Deaths," *American Anthropologist* 75, no. 1 (February 1973), p. 312.

33. Stephen D. Glazier and Mary J. Hallin, "Health and Illness," in *21st Century Anthropology: A Reference Handbook*, ed. H. James Birx, vol. 2 (Thousand Oaks, CA: Sage, 2010), pp. 925–37.

34. Plato, *Timaeus*, in *The Dialogues of Plato*, vol. 3, trans. Benjamin Jowett, 3rd ed. (London: Macmillan, 1892), p. 514.

35. Rachel P. Maines, *The Technology of Orgasm: "Hysteria," the Vibrator, and Women's Sexual Satisfaction* (Baltimore: Johns Hopkins University Press, 1999).

36. Davis, *Serpent and the Rainbow*.

37. Valerie Steele, *The Corset: A Cultural History* (New Haven, CT: Yale University Press, 2001), p. 70.

38. George Frederick Shrady, ed. "The Effects of Tight Lacing," *Medical Record* 3 (September 15, 1868): 347; see also "Tight-Lacing," *Lancet* 91, no. 2329 (April 18, 1868): 508; "Death from Tight Lacing," *Lancet* 135, no. 3485 (June 14, 1890): 1316.

39. Robert E. Bartholomew and Jeffrey S. Victor, "A Social-Psychological Theory of Collective Anxiety Attacks: The 'Mad Gasser' Reexamined," *Sociological Quarterly* 45, no. 2 (March 2004): 229–48.

40. Barbara Newman, "Possessed by the Spirit: Devout Women, Demoniacs, and the Apostolic Life in the Thirteenth Century," *Speculum* 73, no. 3 (July 1998): 733–70.

41. Robert E. Bartholomew, "Tarantism, Dancing Mania, and Demonopathy: The Anthro-Political Aspects of 'Mass Psychogenic Illness,'" *Psychological Medicine* 24, no. 2 (May 1994): 281–306.

42. Robert E. Bartholomew, "Rethinking the Dancing Mania," *Skeptical Inquirer* 24, no. 4 (2000): pp. 42–47.

43. Robert E. Bartholomew and Erich Goode, "Mass Delusions and Hysterias: Highlights from the Past Millennium," *Skeptical Inquirer* 24, no. 3 (May/June 2000): 20–28.

44. Robert E. Bartholomew and Benjamin Radford, *The Martians Have Landed: A History of Media-Driven Panics and Hoaxes* (New York: McFarland, 2011).

45. Wen-Shing Tseng, *Handbook of Cultural Psychiatry* (New York: Academic Press, 2001), p. 219.

46. I. Pilowsky, "Dimensions of Hypochondriasis," in *Handbook of Psychiatry*, vol. 4, ed. Gerald F. M. Russell and Lionel Hersov (Cambridge: Cambridge University Press, 1983). See also Zbigniew J. Lipowski, "Somatization: A Borderland between Medicine and Psychiatry," *Canadian Medical Association Journal* 135, no. 6 (September 15, 1986): 609–14.

47. *Online Etymology Dictionary*, s.v. "Hypochondria,", http://www.etymonline.com/index.php?term=hypochondria (accessed May 25, 2017).

48. William Cullen, *First Lines of the Practice of Physic*, 3 vols., vol. 3 (Edinburgh: Bell & Bradfute, 1789), 3: 250. Available online at https://archive.org/details/firstlinesofprac003cull (accessed November 16, 2017).

49. Christina Korownyk et al., "Televised Medical Talk Shows—What They Recommend and the Evidence to Support Their Recommendations: A Prospective Observational Study," *British Medical Journal* 349 (2014): g7346.

50. Adam Lenny, "The Worried Well," College of Family Physicians and Surgeons of Canada, 2009, http://www.cfpc.ca/ProjectAssets/Templates/Resource.aspx?id=4489 (accessed November 16, 2017).

51. Loren Pankratz, "The Power of Belief in the Creation of Symptoms: From Dancing Manias to Multiple Chemical Sensitivity Syndrome," *Scientific Review of Alternative Medicine* 9, no. 1 (Spring/Summer 2005): 35–48.

52. Martin Röösli, "Radiofrequency Electromagnetic Field Exposure and Non-Specific Symptoms of Ill Health: A Systematic Review," *Environmental Research* 107, no. 2 (2008): 277–87.

53. David McGonigal, *Antarctica: Secrets of the Southern Continent* (London: Francis Lincoln, 2009).

54. Meredith Hooper, *The Longest Winter: Scott's Other Heroes* (London: John Murray, 2012).

55. Ed. Diener and Micaela Y. Chan, "Happy People Live Longer: Subjective Well-Being Contributes to Health and Longevity," *Applied Psychology: Health and Well-Being* 3, no. 1 (March 2011): 1–43.

56. Martin. E. P. Seligman, *Learned Optimism: How to Change Your Mind and Your Life* (New York, NY: A. A. Knopf, 1991).

57. Barbara L. Frederickson, "The Role of Positive Emotions in Positive Psychology: The Broaden-and-Build Theory of Positive Emotions," *American Psychologist* 56, no. 3 (2001): 218–26.

58. Melvin J. Lerner and Dale T. Miller, "Just World Research and the Attribution Process: Looking Back and Ahead," *Psychological Bulletin* 85, no. 5 (1978): 1030–51, 1030.

59. Ellen J. Langer, "The Illusion of Control," *Journal of Personality and Social Psychology* 32, no. 2 (1975): 311–28.

60. Shelley E. Taylor et al., "Psychological Resources, Positive Illusions and Health," *American Psychologist* 55, no. 1 (January 2000): 99–109.

61. Shelley E. Taylor, and Jonathon D. Brown, "Positive Illusions and Well-Being Revisited: Separating Fact from Fiction," *Psychological Bulletin* 116 no. 1 (July 1994): 21–27.

Chapter 13: Belief and Healing

1. Howard Spiro, "Clinical Reflections on the Placebo Effect," in *The Placebo Effect: An Interdisciplinary Exploration*, ed. Anne Harrington (Cambridge: Harvard University Press, 1997), pp. 39–55.

2. Franklin G. Miller, Luana Colloca, and Ted J. Kaptchuk, "The Placebo Effect: Illness and Interpersonal Healing," *Perspectives in Biology and Medicine* 52, no. 4 (Autumn 2009): 518.

3. Fabrizio Benedetti, *Placebo Effects: Understanding the Mechanisms in Health and Disease*, 2nd ed. (Oxford: Oxford University Press, 2014).

4. "False Face Society," Historica Canada, http://www.thecanadianencyclopedia.ca/en/article/false-face-society/ (accessed November 16, 2017).

5. Fabrizio Benedetti, *The Patient's Brain: The Neuroscience behind the Doctor-Patient Relationship* (Oxford: Oxford University Press, 2011), p. 18.

6. Lorraine G. Allan and Shepard Siegel, "A Signal Detection Theory Analysis of the Placebo Effect," *Evaluation & the Health Professions. Special Issue: Recent Advances in Placebo Research* 25, no. 4 (2002): 410–20.

7. C. U. M. Smith, "The Brain and Mind in the 'Long' Eighteenth Century," in *Brain, Mind, and Medicine: Neuroscience in the 18th Century*, ed. Harry Whitaker, C. U. M. Smith, and Stanley Finger (New York: Springer, 2007), pp. 15–28, 22.

8. C. U. M. Smith et al., *The Animal Spirit Doctrine and the Origins of Neurophysiology* (Oxford, England: Oxford University Press, 2012).

9. George Cheyne, *The English Malady* (London: G. Strahan, 1733), p. 4, cited by Whitaker, Smith, and Finger, eds., *Brain, Mind and Medicine*.

10. Franz Anton Mesmer, "Letter from M. Mesmer, Doctor of Medicine at Vienna, to A. M. Unzer, Doctor of Medicine, on the Medicinal Usage of the Magnet," in *Mesmerism: A Translation of the Original Scientific and Medical Writings of F. A. Mesmer*, ed. George J. Bloch (1775; Los Altos, CA: William Kaufmann, 1980), p. 26, cited by Douglas J. Lanska and Joseph T. Lanska, "Franz Anton Mesmer and the Rise and Fall of Animal Magnetism: Dramatic Cures, Controversy, and Ultimately a Triumph for the Scientific Method," in Whitaker, Smith, and Finger, eds., *Brain, Mind, and Medicine*, pp. 301–20.

11. Lanska and Lanska, "Franz Anton Mesmer and the Rise and Fall of Animal Magnetism."

12. Ibid.

13. Ibid.

14. Benjamin Franklin, *The Life of Benjamin Franklin, Written by Himself. Now First Edited from Original Manuscripts and from His Printed Correspondence and Other Writings by John Bigelow* (Philadelphia: Lippincott, 1881), pp. 258–59.

15. Benjamin Franklin, *The Life of Benjamin Franklin, Written by Himself. Now First Edited from Original Manuscripts and from His Printed Correspondence and Other Writings by John Bigelow* (Philadelphia: Lippincott, 1881), pp. 258–59.

16. Fabrizio Benedetti, "Placebo and the New Physiology of the Doctor-Patient Relationship," *Physiological Reviews* 93, no. 3 (2013): 1207–46.

17. Lanska and Lanska, "Franz Anton Mesmer and the Rise and Fall of Animal Magnetism," p. 301.

18. Robert A. Hahn and Arthur Kleinman, "Belief as Pathogen, Belief as Medicine: 'Voodoo Death' and the 'Placebo Phenomenon' in Anthropological Perspective," *Medical Anthropology Quarterly* 14, no. 4 (August 1983): 16–19.

19. Daniel E. Moerman and Wayne B. Jonas, "Deconstructing the Placebo Effect in Finding the Meaning Response," *Annals of Internal Medicine* 136, no. 6 (2002): 471.

20. Amir Raz et al., "Placebos in Clinical Practice: Comparing Attitudes, Beliefs, and Patterns of Use Between Academic Psychiatrists and Nonpsychiatrists," *Canadian Journal of Psychiatry* 56, no. 4 (April 2011): 198–208.

21. Jon C. Tilburt et al., "Prescribing 'Placebo Treatments': Results of a National Survey of US Internists and Rheumatologists," *BMJ* 337 (October 23 2008): a1938.

22. Arthur K. Shapiro, "Semantics of the Placebo," *Psychiatric Quarterly* 42, no. 4 (1968): 653–95.

23. Plato, "Charmides," 155–56, in Plato, *Plato in Twelve Volumes*, trans. W. R. M. Lamb, vol. 8 (Cambridge, MA: Harvard University Press; London: William Heinemann Ltd., 1955), available online at http://www.perseus.tufts.edu/hopper/text?doc=Perseus%3Atext%3A1999 .01.0176%3Atext%3DCharm.%3Apage%3D155 (accessed May 25, 2017).

24. Arthur K. Shapiro and Elaine Shapiro, *The Powerful Placebo: From Ancient Priest to Modern Physician* (Baltimore: Johns Hopkins University Press, 1997).

25. Benedetti, *Placebo Effects*, p. 4.

26. Franklin G. Miller et al., "Ethical Issues Concerning Research in Complementary and Alternative Medicine," *Journal of the American Medical Association* 291, no. 5 (February 4, 2004): 599–604.

27. Irving Kirsch et al., "Initial Severity and Antidepressant Benefits: A Meta-Analysis of Data Submitted to the Food and Drug Administration," *PLoS Medicine* 5, no. 2 (February 2008): 260–68.

28. Irving Kirsch, "Antidepressants and the Placebo Effect," *Zeitschrift für Psychologie* 222, no. 3 (2014): 128–34.

29. J. C. Nickel, "Placebo Therapy of Benign Prostatic Hyperplasia: A 25 Month Study," *British Journal of Urology* 81, no. 3 (March 1998): 383–87.

30. Felipe Fregni et al., "Immediate Placebo Effect in Parkinson's Disease—Is the Subjective Relief Accompanied by Objective Improvement?" *European Neurology* 56, no. 4 (2006): 222–29.

31. Mary McClung and Dave Collins, "'Because I Know It Will!' Placebo Effects of an

Ergogenic Aid on Athletic Performance," *Journal of Sport & Exercise Psychology* 29, no. 3 (June 2007): 382–94.

32. Constantinos N. Maganaris, Dave Collins, and Martin Sharp, "Expectancy Effects and Strength Training: Do Steroids Make a Difference?" *Sport Psychologist* 14, no. 3 (September 2000): 272–78.

33. J. Bruce Moseley et al., "A Controlled Trial of Arthroscopic Surgery for Osteoarthritis of the Knee," *New England Journal of Medicine* 347, no. 2 (July 11, 2002): 81–88.

34. Raine Sihvonen et al., "Arthroscopic Partial Meniscectomy Versus Sham Surgery for a Degenerative Meniscal Tear," *New England Journal of Medicine* 369, no. 26 (December 26, 2013): 2515–24.

35. J. B. Thorlund et al., "Arthroscopic Surgery for Degenerative Knee: Systematic Review and Meta-Analysis of Benefits and Harms," *British Medical Journal* 350 (2015): h2747.

36. Henry K. Beecher, "The Powerful Placebo," *Journal of the American Medical Association* 159, no. 17 (December 24, 1955): 1602–606.

37. Benedetti, *Placebo Effects*.

38. Adrian G. Barnett, Jolieke C. van der Pols, and Annette J. Dobson, "Regression to the Mean: What It Is and How to Deal with It," *International Journal of Epidemiology* 34, no. 1 (February 1, 2005): 215–20.

39. Clement J. McDonald, Steven A. Mazzuca, and George P. McCabe Jr., "How Much of the Placebo 'Effect' Is Really Statistical Regression?" *Statistical Medicine* 2, no. 4 (October/December 1983): 417–27.

40. Gunver S. Kienle and Helmut Kiene, "The Powerful Placebo Effect: Fact or Fiction?" *Journal of Clinical Epidemiology* 50, no. 12 (December 1997): 1311–18.

41. Asbjørn Hróbjartsson and Peter C. Gøtzsche, "Is the Placebo Powerless? An Analysis of Clinical Trials Comparing Placebo with No Treatment," *New England Journal of Medicine* 344, no. 21 (May 24, 2001): 1594–602.

42. Asbjørn Hróbjartsson and Peter C. Gøtzsche, "Is the Placebo Powerless? Update of a Systematic Review with 52 New Randomized Trials Comparing Placebo with No Treatment," *Journal of Internal Medicine* 256, no. 2 (August 2004): 91–100.

43. Bruce E. Wampold, Zac E. Imel, and Takuya Minami, "The Story of Placebo Effects in Medicine: Evidence in Context," *Journal of Clinical Psychology* 63, no. 4 (April 2007): 379–90.

44. James E. Alcock, "Chronic Pain and the Injured Worker," *Canadian Psychology* 27, no. 2 (1986): 196–203.

45. Lucretius, *The Complete Works of Lucretius*, trans. H. A. J. Munro (Cambridge: Deighton Bell, 1866), p. 72.

46. Alexander Copland Hutchison, *Some Practical Observations in Surgery* (London: J. Callow, 1816), pp. 6–7.

47. Woods Hutchinson, *The Doctor at War* (New York: Houghton Mifflin Harcourt, 1819), cited by Joanna Bourke, *The Story of Pain: From Prayer to Painkillers* (Oxford: Oxford University Press, 2014), p. 224.

48. Ronald Melzack and Patrick D. Wall, "Pain Mechanisms: A New Theory," *Science* 150, no. 3699 (November 19, 1965): 971–79; A. H. Dickensen, "Editorial 1: Gate Control Theory of Pain Stands the Test of Time," *British Journal of Anaesthesia* 88, no. 6 (June 1, 2002): 755–57.

49. Dickensen, "Gate Control Theory of Pain Stands the Test of Time."

50. Luana Colloca et al., "Placebo Analgesia: Psychological and Neurobiological Mechanisms," *Pain* 154, no. 4 (April 2013): 511–14.

51. Wilbert E. Fordyce, "Behavioral Science and Chronic Pain," *Postgraduate Medical Journal* 60, no. 710 (December 1984): 865–68.

52. Luana Colloca and Fabrizio Benedetti, "How Prior Experience Shapes Placebo Analgesia," *Pain* 124, no. 1-2 (September 2006): 126–33.

53. Lars-Gunnar Lundh, "Placebo, Belief, and Health: A Cognitive-Emotional Model," *Scandinavian Journal of Psychology* 28, no. 2 (June 1987): 128–43.

54. Benedetti, "Placebo and the New Physiology."

55. Fabrizio Benedetti, "How the Doctor's Words Affect the Patient's Brain," in "Recent Advances in Placebo Research," ed. R. Barker Bausell, special issue, *Evaluation & the Health Professions* 25, no. 2 (December 2002): 369–86.

56. Jean Bruxelle, "Placebo et effet placebo dans le traitement de la douleur," *Douleur et Analgésie* 17 (March 2004): 3–7.

57. Benedetti, *Placebo Effects*.

58. Harriet Hall, "The Placebo Effect," *eSkeptic*, May 20, 2009, https://www.skeptic.com/ eskeptic/09-05-20/ (accessed November 18, 2017).

59. Irving Kirsch, "Specifying Nonspecifics: Psychological Mechanisms of Placebo Effects," in Harrington, ed., *Placebo Effect*, pp. 166–86.

60. Anton de Craen et al., "Effect of Colour of Drugs: Systematic Review of Perceived Effect of Drugs and of Their Effectiveness," *British Medical Journal* 313, no. 7072 (December 21–28, 1996): 1624–26.

61. Barry Blackwell, Saul S. Broomfield, and C. Ralph Buncher, "Demonstration to Medical Students of Placebo Responses and Non-Drug Factors," *Lancet* 299, no. 7763 (June 10, 1972): 1279–82.

62. Paolo E. Lucchelli, Angelo D. Cattaneo, and J. Zattoni, "Effect of Capsule Colour and Order of Administration of Hypnotic Treatments," *European Journal of Clinical Pharmacology* 13, no. 2 (March 1978): 153–55.

63. E. C. Huskisson, "Simple Analgesics for Arthritis," *British Medical Journal* 4, no. 5938 (October 26, 1974): 196–200.

64. Fabrizio Benedetti, Elisa Carlino, and Antonello Pollo, "Hidden Administration of Drugs," *Clinical Pharmacology & Therapeutics* 90, no. 5 (November 2011): 651–61.

65. Fabrizio Benedetti et al., "Conscious Expectation and Unconscious Conditioning in Analgesic, Motor, and Hormonal Placebo/Nocebo Responses," *Journal of Neuroscience* 23, no. 10 (May 15, 2003): 4315–23.

66. Ibid.

67. Tom J. Johnsen and Oddgeir Friborg, "The Effects of Cognitive Behavioral Therapy as an Anti-Depressant Treatment Is Falling: A Meta-Analysis," *Psychological Bulletin* 141, no. 4 (July 2015): 747–68.

68. Luana Colloca and Fabrizio Benedetti, "Placebo Analgesia Induced by Social Observational, Learning," *Pain* 144, no. 1-2 (July 2009): 28–34.

69. Sibylle Klosterhalfen and Paul Enck, "Placebos in Clinic and Research: Experimental

Findings and Theoretical Concepts" [in German], *Psychotherapie, Psychosomatik, Medizinische Psychologie* 55 (2005): 433–41; See also Daniel E. Moerman and Wayne B. Jonas, "Deconstructing the Placebo Effect and Finding the Meaning Response," *Annals of Internal Medicine* 136, no. 6 (March 19, 2002): 471–76.

70. Omer van den Bergh, Winnie Winters, Stephan Devriese, and Ilse van Diest, "Learning Subjective Health Complaints," *Scandinavian Journal of Psychology* 43 (2002): 147–52.

71. Ibid.

72. Colloca et al., "Placebo Analgesia."

73. Jon-Kar Zubieta et al., "Belief or Need? Accounting for Individual Variations in the Neurochemistry of the Placebo Effect," *Brain, Behavior, and Immunity* 20, no. 1 (January 2006): 15–26.

74. Colloca et al., "Placebo Analgesia."

75. Martina Amanzio and Fabrizio Benedetti, "Neuropharmacological Dissection of Placebo Analgesia: Expectation-Activated Opioid Systems Versus Conditioning-Activated Specific Subsystems," *Journal of Neuroscience* 19, no. 1 (January 1, 1999): 484–94

76. Jon D. Levine, Newton C. Gordon, and Howard L. Fields, "The Mechanism of Placebo Analgesia," *Lancet* 312, no. 8091 (September 23, 1978): 654–57.

77. Benedetti, "Placebo and the New Physiology."

78. Ibid.

79. Fabrizio Benedetti and Sara Dogue, "Different Placebos, Different Mechanisms, Different Outcomes: Lessons for Clinical Trials," *PLoS One* (November 4, 2015).

80. Kathryn T. Hall, Joseph Loscalzo and, Ted J. Kaptchuk, "Genetics and the Placebo Effect: the Placebome," *Trends in Molecular Medicine* 21, no. 5 (May 2015): 285–94.

81. Tor D. Wager et al., "Placebo-Induced Changes in fMRI in the Anticipation and Experience of Pain," *Science* 303, no. 1162 (February 20, 2004): 1162–67.

82. Donald D. Price et al., "Placebo Analgesia Is Accompanied by Large Reductions in Pain-Related Brain Activity in Irritable Bowel Syndrome Patients," *Pain* 127, no. 1-2 (January 2007): 63–72.

83. Benedetti, *Placebo Effects*, p. 4.

84. Fabrizio Benedetti et al., "Loss of Expectation-Related Mechanisms in Alzheimer's Disease Makes Analgesic Therapies Less Effective," *Pain* 121, no. 1-2 (March 2006): 133–44.

85. Brenda L. Stoelb et al., "The Efficacy of Hypnotic Analgesia in Adults: A Review of the Literature," *Contemporary Hypnosis* 26, no. 1 (March 1, 2009): 24–39.

86. David R. Patterson, "Treating Pain with Hypnosis," *Current Directions in Psychological Science* 13, no. 6 (2004): 252–55.

87. Theodore X. Barber, "The Effect of 'Hypnosis' on Pain: A Critical Review of Clinical and Experimental Findings," *Psychosomatic Medicine* 25, no. 4 (July 1963): 303–33.

88. Nicholas P. Spanos et al., "Hypnotic Suggestion and Placebo for the Treatment of Chronic Headache in a University Volunteer Sample," *Cognitive Therapy and Research* 17, no. 2 (1993): 191.

89. Walter B. Cannon, "'Voodoo' Death," *American Anthropologist* 44, no. 2 (April-June 1942): 169–81; Janice Reid and Nancy Williams, "'Voodoo Death' in Arnhem Land: Whose Reality?" *American Anthropologist* 86, no. 1 (March 1984): 121–33.

90. R. C. Pogge, "The Toxic Placebo, Part 1: Side and Toxic Effects Reported during the Administration of Placebo Medicine," *Medical Times* 91 (1963): 773–78.

91. Benedetti, "Placebo and the New Physiology."

92. Fabrizio Benedetti et al., "Conscious Expectation and Unconscious Conditioning in Analgesic, Motor, and Hormonal Placebo/Nocebo Response," *Journal of Neuroscience* 23, no. 10 (May 15, 2003): 4315–23.

93. Jonathan C. Smith, *Pseudoscience and Extraordinary Claims of the Paranormal: A Critical Thinker's Toolkit* (New York: Wiley-Blackwell, 2011).

94. William A. Nolen, *Healing: A Doctor in Search of a Miracle* (New York: Random House, 1975).

95. James Randi, *The Faith Healers* (Amherst, NY: Prometheus Books, 1989).

Chapter 14: Folk Remedies and Alternative Medicine

1. Rufus Blakeman, *A Philosophical Essay on Credulity and Superstition; and Also on Animal Fascination, or Charming* (New York: D. Appleton, 1849), pp. 119–20.

2. Gunnar Almgren and Taryn Lindhorst, *The Safety-Net Health Care System* (New York: Springer, 2012).

3. John M. Barry, *The Great Influenza: The Story of the Deadliest Pandemic in History* (New York: Penguin, 2004).

4. Franklin G. Miller, Luana Colloca, and Ted J. Kaptchuk, "The Placebo Effect: Illness and Interpersonal Healing," *Perspectives in Biology and Medicine* 52, no. 4 (Autumn 2009): 532.

5. Thomas R. Egnew, "The Meaning of Healing: Transcending Suffering," *Annals of Family Medicine* 3, no. 3 (May 1, 2005): 255–62.

6. David. H. Gorski and Steven P. Novella, "Clinical Trials of Integrative Medicine: Testing Whether Magic Works?" *Trends in Molecular Medicine* 20, no. 9 (September 2014): 473–76.

7. David Bell, "David Stephan Gets Jail Time, Collet Stephan Gets House Arrest in Son's Meningitis Death," CBC News, June 24, 2016, http://www.cbc.ca/news/canada/calgary/lethbridge-meningitis-trial-sentence-parents-toddler-died-1.3650653 (accessed November 18, 2017).

8. "Tim Minchin's Storm the Animated Movie," YouTube video, 10:38, posted by stormmovie, April 7, 2011, https://www.youtube.com/watch?v=HhGuXCuDb1U, at 3:05–3:20.

9. Floyd H. Ross and Tynette Hills, *The Great Religions by Which Men Live* (New York: Fawcett, 1956).

10. George J. Shen, "Study of Mind-Body Effects and Qigong in China," *Advances, Institute for the Advancement of Health* 3, no. 4 (1986): 134–42.

11. David Ownby, *Falun Gong and the Future of China* (Oxford: Oxford University Press, 2008).

12. David A. Palmer, *Qigong Fever: Body, Science, and Utopia in China* (New York: Columbia University Press, 2007).

13. Eric Karchmer, "Magic, Science, and Qigong in Contemporary China," in *China Off Center: Mapping the Margins of the Middle Kingdom*, ed. Susan D. Blum and Lionel M. Jensen (Honolulu: University of Hawaii Press, 2002), pp. 311–22.

14. Andrew J. Vickers et al., "Acupuncture for Chronic Pain: Individual Patient Data Meta-Analysis," *Archives of Internal Medicine* 172, no. 19 (2012): 1444–53.

15. "Expert Reaction to Meta-Analysis of Studies into Acupuncture and Chronic Pain," Science Media Centre, October 9, 2012, http://www.sciencemediacentre.org/expert-reaction-to -meta-analysis-of-studies-into-acupuncture-and-chronic-pain-2/ (accessed November 19, 2017).

16. Edzard Ernst, Myeong Soo Lee, and Tae-Young Choi, "Acupuncture: Does It Alleviate Pain and Are There Serious Risks? A Review of Reviews," *Pain* 152, no. 4 (April 2011): 755–64.

17. David W. Ramey and Wallace Sampson, "Review of the Evidence for the Clinical Efficacy of Human Acupuncture," *Scientific Review of Alternative Medicine* 5, no. 4 (2001): 195–201.

18. Laura Donnelly, "Homeopathy Is Witchcraft, Say Doctors," *Telegraph*, May 15, 2010, http://www.telegraph.co.uk/news/health/alternative-medicine/7728281/Homeopathy-is -witchcraft-say-doctors.html (accessed November 19, 2017).

19. Sarah Knapton, "Queen's Physician Calls for More Homeopathy on NHS," *Telegraph*, July 17, 2015, http://www.telegraph.co.uk/news/health/news/11739270/Queens-physician -calls-for-more-homeopathy-on-NHS.html (accessed November 19, 2017).

20. Robert L. Park, "Alternative Medicine and the Laws of Physics," *Skeptical Inquirer* 21, no. 5 (September/October 1997).

21. Kees Dam, "Berlin Wall," *Interhomeopathy*, April 2006, http://www.interhomeopathy .org/berlin_wall (accessed November 19, 2017).

22. David D. Palmer, *The Science, Art, and Philosophy of Chiropractic* (Portland, Oregon: Portland Printing House, 1910).

23. Harriet Hall, "The End of Chiropractic," *Science-Based Medicine: Exploring Issues & Controversies in Science & Medicine*, December 11, 2009, https://www.sciencebasedmedicine .org/the-end-of-chiropractic/ (accessed November 19, 2017).

24. Ibid.

25. William P. McDonald, Keith F. Durkin, and Mark Pfefer, "How Chiropractors Think and Practice: The Survey of North American Chiropractors," *Seminars in Integrative Medicine* 2, no. 3 (2004): 92–98.

26. Samuel Homola and Stephen Barrett, *Inside Chiropractic: A Patient's Guide* (Amherst, NY: Prometheus Books, 1999).

27. Timothy A. Mirtz et al., "An Epidemiological Examination of the Subluxation Construct Using Hill's Criteria of Causation," *Chiropractic & Osteopathy* 17 (2009), http://chiromt .biomedcentral.com/articles/10.1186/1746-1340-17-13 (accessed November 19, 2017).

28. Hall, "End of Chiropractic."

29. "Aromatherapy: All about the Art and Science of Aromatherapy," Canadian Federation of Aromatherapists, http://cfacanada.com/aromatherapy/ (accessed November 19, 2017).

30. "The Father of Aromatherapy & the Miracles of Lavender," Bio Source Naturals, http://biosourcenaturals.com/blog/2013/11/gattefosse-lavender-essential-oil-aromatherapy/ (accessed November 19, 2017).

31. "Aromatherapy," Canadian Federation of Aromatherapists.

32. Roberta Wilson, *Aromatherapy: Essential Oils for Vibrant Health and Beauty* (New York: Avery, 2002).

33. Jean Mercer, *Alternative Psychotherapies* (London: Rowman & Littlefield, 2014).

34. Ibid.

35. Roger J. Callahan, "The Impact of Thought Field Therapy on Heart Rate Variability," *Journal of Clinical Psychology* 57, no. 10 (October 2001): 1153–70.

36. "Craniosacral Therapy," Team Rehabilitation, https://team-rehab.com/specialties/craniosacral-therapy/ (accessed November 19, 2017).

37. Andrew J. Wakefield et al., "Evidence of Persistent Measles Virus Infection in Crohn's Disease," *Journal of Medical Virology* 39, no. 4 (April 1993): 345–53.

38. N. P. Thompson et al., "Is Measles Vaccination a Risk Factor for Inflammatory Bowel Disease?" *Lancet* 345, no. 8957 (April 29, 1995): 1071–74.

39. Andrew J. Wakefield et al., "Ileal Lymphoid Nodular Hyperplasia, Non-Specific Colitis, and Pervasive Developmental Disorder in Children," *Lancet* 351, no. 9103 (February 28, 1998): 637–41 [retracted].

40. Editors of the *Lancet*, Retraction: "Ileal-Lymphoid-Nodular Hyperplasia, Non-Specific Colitis, and Pervasive Developmental Disorder in Children," *Lancet* 375, no. 9713 (2010), p. 445.

41. Fiona Godlee, Jane Smith, and Harvey Marcovitch, "Wakefield's Article Linking MMR Vaccine and Autism Was Fraudulent," *BMJ* 342 (2011): c7452

42. Patrick Cain, "Deadly Measles Outbreak Spreads in Europe as Vaccinations Fall," *Global News*, March 30, 2017, http://globalnews.ca/news/3345439/deadly-measles-outbreak-spreads-in-europe-as-vaccinations-fall/ (accessed November 19, 2017).

43. Kumanan Wilson et al., "A Survey of Attitudes towards Paediatric Vaccinations Amongst Canadian Naturopathic Students," *Vaccine* 22, no. 3-4 (January 2, 2004): 329–34.

44. Jason W. Busse et al., "Attitudes toward Vaccination: A Survey of Canadian Chiropractic Students," *CMAJ* 166, no. 12 (July 11, 2002): 1531–34.

45. Lois Downey et al., "Pediatric Vaccination and Vaccine-Preventable Disease Acquisition: Associations with Care by Complementary and Alternative Medicine Providers," *Maternal Child Health* 14, no. 6 (November 2010): 922–30.

46. Jason W. Busse, Rishma Walji, and Kumanan Wilson, "Parents' Experiences Discussing Pediatric Vaccination with Healthcare Providers: A Survey of Canadian Naturopathic Patients," *PLoS One*, August 2, 2011, http://dx.doi.org/10.1371/journal.pone.0022737 (accessed November 19, 2017).

47. Miller et al., "Placebo Effect," p. 532.

48. Angus Rae, "Osler Vindicated: The Ghost of Flexner Laid to Rest," *Canadian Medical Association Journal* 164, no. 13 (June 26, 2001): 1860–61.

49. James Le Fanu, *The Rise and Fall of Modern Medicine* (New York: Basic Books, 2002).

50. Walter Isaacson, "Biographer: Jobs Refused Early and Potentially Life-Saving Surgery," CBS News, October 21, 2011, http://www.cbsnews.com/news/biographer-jobs-refused-early-and-potentially-life-saving-surgery/ (accessed November 19, 2017).

51. George Malkmus, Peter Shockey, and Stowe Shockey, *The Hallelujah Diet* (Shippensburg, PA: Destiny Image, 2006).

52. William A. Nolen, *Healing: A Doctor in Search of a Miracle* (New York: Random House, 1974).

53. Barry L. Beyerstein, "Why Bogus Therapies Seem to Work," *Skeptical Inquirer* 21, no. 5 (September/October 1997): 29–34.

54. Paul Kurtz et al., "Testing Psi Claims in China: Visit of CSICOP Delegation," *Skeptical Inquirer* 12, no. 4 (Summer 1988): 365–75.

55. Ronald B. Turner et al., "An Evaluation of *Echinacea angustifolia* in Experimental Rhinovirus Infections," *New England Journal of Medicine* 353 (2005): 341–48.

56. Scott O. Lilienfeld, Steven Jay Lynn, and Jeffrey M. Lohr, eds., *Science and Pseudoscience in Clinical Psychology* (New York: Guilford, 2012).

57. Loren Pankratz, "Persistent Problems with the Munchausen Syndrome by Proxy Label," *Journal of the American Academy of Psychiatry and Law* 34, no. 1 (2006): 90–95.

58. Ibid.

59. James D. Herbert and Kim T. Mueser, "Eye Movement Desensitization: A Critique of the Evidence," *Journal of Behavior Therapy and Experimental Psychiatry* 23, no. 3 (September 1992): 169–74.

60. Francine Shapiro, "Efficacy of the Eye Movement Desensitization Procedure in the Treatment of Traumatic Memories," *Journal of Traumatic Stress* 2, no. 2 (April 1989): 199–223.

61. Jeffrey M. Lohr et al., "Eye Movement Desensitization and Reprocessing: An Analysis of Specific Versus Nonspecific Treatment Factors," *Journal of Anxiety Disorders* 13, no. 1-2 (January-April 1999): 185–207.

62. James D. Herbert et al., "Science and Pseudoscience in the Development of Eye Movement Desensitization and Reprocessing: Implications for Clinical Psychology," *Clinical Psychological Review* 20, no. 8 (November 2000): 945–71.

63. Jeffrey M. Lohr, David F. Tolin, and Scott O. Lilienfeld, "Efficacy of Eye Movement Desensitization and Reprocessing: Implications for Behavior Therapy," *Behavior Therapy* 29, no. 1 (Winter 1998): 123–56.

64. Hal Arkowitz and Scott O. Lilienfeld, "EMDR: Taking a Closer Look," *Scientific American*, August 1, 2012, https://www.scientificamerican.com/article/emdr-taking-a-closer-look/ (accessed November 19, 2017).

65. Scott O. Lilienfeld, "EMDR Treatment: Less than Meets the Eye?" Quackwatch, last updated April 17, 2011, https://www.quackwatch.org/01QuackeryRelatedTopics/emdr.html (accessed November 19, 2017).

66. Megan K. Traffanstedt, Sheila Mehta, and Steven G. LoBella, "Major Depression with Seasonal Variation: Is It a Valid Construct?" *Clinical Psychological Science* 4, no. 5 (2016): 825–34.

67. Ibid., p. 8.

68. Tomasz Witkowski, *Psychology Led Astray: Cargo Cult in Science and Therapy* (Boca Raton, FL: Brown Walker, 2016). See also Tomasz Witkowski and Maciej Zatonski, *Psychology Gone Wrong: The Dark Sides of Science and Therapy* (Boca Raton, FL: Brown Walker, 2015).

69. Arkowitz and Lilienfeld, "EMDR: Taking a Closer Look."

70. Scott O. Lilienfeld et al., "Why Ineffective Psychotherapies Appear to Work: A Taxonomy of Causes of Spurious Therapeutic Effectiveness," *Perspectives on Psychological Science* 9, no. 4 (2014): 355.

Chapter 15: Magic and Superstition

1. Dorothy Hammond, "Magic: A Problem in Semantics," *American Anthropologist* 72, no. 6 (December 1970): 1349–56.

2. Jean Eugène Robert-Houdin, *Secrets of Conjuring and Magic: Or How to Become a Wizard*, trans. and ed. Louis Hoffman (1868; Cambridge, UK: Cambridge University Press, 2011), p. 43.

3. Exodus 7:10–11 (New King James Version).

4. Walter B. Gibson, *Secrets of Magic* (New York: Penguin, 1973).

5. Kyle Butt, "Egyptian Magicians, Snakes, and Rods," Apologetics Press, 2005, http://apologeticspress.org/apcontent.aspx?category=11&article=1704 (accessed November 19, 2017).

6. Michael D. Bailey, "The Age of Magicians: Periodization in the History of European Magic," *Magic, Ritual, and Witchcraft* 3, no. 1 (Summer 2008): 1–28.

7. Ibid.

8. Michael Mangan, *Performing Dark Arts: A Cultural History of Conjuring* (Bristol, UK: Intellect, 2007), p. 195.

9. Edward Peters, *The Magician, the Witch, and the Law* (Philadelphia: University of Pennsylvania Press, 1982).

10. Mangan, *Performing Dark Arts*, p.195.

11. Rufus Blakeman, *A Philosophical Essay on Credulity and Superstition; and Also on Animal Fascination, or Charming* (New York: D. Appleton, 1849), pp. 25–26.

12. Mangan, *Performing Dark Arts.*, p.195.

13. Ronald A. Rensink and Gustav Kuhn, "A Framework for Using Magic to Study the Mind," *Frontiers in Psychology* 5 (2014): 1508.

14. Michael Mangan, "Conjuring, Consciousness, and Magical Thinking," in *Consciousness, Theater, Literature and the Arts 2007*, ed. Daniel Meyer-Dinkgräfe (Newcastle, UK: Cambridge Scholars, 2007), pp. 17–18.

15. James George Frazer, *The Golden Bough* (New York: Macmillan, 1922).

16. Bronislaw Malinowski, *Magic, Science and Religion* (1954).

17. Richard A. Shweder et al., "Likeness and Likelihood in Everyday Thought: Magical Thinking in Judgments about Personality," *Current Anthropology* 18, no. 4 (December 1977): 637–58.

18. Karl S. Rosengren and Jason A. French, "Magical Thinking," in the *Oxford Handbook of the Development of Imagination*, ed. Marjorie Taylor (Oxford, England: Oxford University Press, 2013), pp. 42–60.

19. Shweder et al., "Likeness and Likelihood in Everyday Thought."

20. Michael R. Waldmann, York Hagmayer, and Aaron P. Blaisdell, "Beyond the Information Given: Causal Models in Learning and Reasoning," *Current Directions in Psychological Science* 15, no. 6 (December 2006): 307–11.

21. Jean Piaget, *The Construction of Reality in the Child* (New York: Basic Books, 1954).

22. Rosengren and French, "Magical Thinking."

23. Jacqueline D. Woolley, "Thinking about Fantasy: Are Children Fundamentally Different Thinkers and Believers from Adults?" *Child Development* 68, no. 6 (December 1997): 991–1011.

24. Ibid.

25. Ibid.

26. Eugene Subbotsky, *Magic and the Mind: Mechanisms, Functions, and Development of Magical Thinking and Behavior* (Oxford, UK: Oxford University Press, 2010).

27. Jane E. Cottrell, Gerald A. Winer, and Mary C. Smith, "Beliefs of Children and Adults about Feeling Stares of Unseen Others," *Developmental Psychology* 32, no. 1 (1996): 50–61.

28. Subbotsky, *Magic and the Mind.*

29. Laura R. Kim, and Nancy S. Kim, "A Proximity Effect in Adults' Contamination Intuitions," *Judgment and Decision -Making* 6, no. 3 (April 2011): 227.

30. Woolley, "Thinking about Fantasy."

31. Jane L. Risen and Thomas D. Gilovich, "Why People Are Reluctant to Tempt Fate," *Journal of Personality and Social Psychology* 95, no. 2 (2008): 293–307.

32. George E. Newman et al., "Early Understandings of the Link between Agents and Order," *Proceedings of the National Academy of Sciences* 107, no. 40 (October 5, 2010) : 17140–45.

33. Jesse Bering, *The Belief Instinct: The Psychology of Souls, Destiny, and the Meaning of Life* (New York: W. W. Norton, 2011).

34. Daniel C. Dennett, *The Intentional Stance* (Cambridge, MA: MIT Press, 1987).

35. Paul Bloom and Csaba Veres, "The Perceived Intentionality of Groups," *Cognition* 71, no. 1 (May 3, 1999): B1–B9.

36. Deborah Kelemen, "Are Children 'Intuitive Theists'"? Reasoning about Purpose and Design in Nature," *Psychological Science* 15, no. 5 (2004): 295–31.

37. Justin L. Barrett, *Why Would Anyone Believe in God?* (Lanham, MD: Altamira, 2004).

38. Jan van der Tempel and James E. Alcock, "Relationships between Conspiracy Mentality, Hyperactive Agency Detection, and Schizotypy: Supernatural Force at Work?" *Personality and Individual Differences* 82 (August 2015): 136–41.

39. Ibid.

40. Daniel M. Wegner and Thalia Wheatley, "Apparent Mental Causation: Sources of the Experience of Will," *American Psychologist* 54, no. 7 (July 1999): 480–92.

41. Cited by Benedict Carey, "Do You Believe in Magic?" *New York Times,* January 23, 2007, http://www.nytimes.com/2007/01/23/health/psychology/23magic.html?pagewanted=print&_r=0 (accessed November 19, 2017).

42. Emily Pronin et al., "Everyday Magical Powers: The Role of Apparent Mental Causation in the Overestimation of Personal Influence," *Journal of Personality and Social Psychology* 91, no. 2 (2006): 218–31.

43. Laura A. King et al., "Ghosts, UFOs, and Magic: Positive Affect and the Experiential System," *Journal of Personality and Social Psychology* 92, no. 5 (2007): 905–19.

44. Jonathan Haidt, *The Righteous Mind: Why Good People Are Divided by Politics and Religion* (New York: Vintage, 2012).

45. Paul Rozin, Linda Millman, and Carol Nemeroff, "Operation of the Laws of Sympathetic Magic in Disgust and Other Domains," *Journal of Personality and Social Psychology* 50, no. 4 (April 1986): 703–12.

46. Paul Rozin and Carol Nemeroff, "Sympathetic Magical Thinking: The Contagion and Similarity 'Heuristics,'" in *Heuristics and Biases: The Psychology of Intuitive Judgment*, ed. Thomas Gilovich, Dale Griffin, and Daniel Kahneman (Cambridge, UK: Cambridge University Press, 2002), pp. 201–16.

47. Rozin et al., "Operation of the Sympathetic Magical Law."

48. Paul Rozin, Maureen Markwith, and Carol Nemeroff, "Magical Contagion Beliefs and Fear of AIDS," *Journal of Applied Social Psychology* 22, no. 14 (July 1992): 1081–92.

49. Paul Rozin, Linda Millman, and Carol Nemeroff, "Operation of the Laws of Sympathetic Magic in Disgust and Other Domains," *Journal of Personality and Social Psychology* 50, no. 4 (1986): 703–12.

50. Ibid.

51. Kim and Kim, "Proximity Effect in Adults' Contamination Intuitions."

52. Paul Rozin et al., "Operation of the Sympathetic Magical Law of Contagion in Interpersonal Attitudes among Americans," *Bulletin of the Psychonomic Society* 27, no. 4 (April 1989): 369.

53. Bruce M. Hood and Paul Bloom, "Children Prefer Certain Individuals over Perfect Duplicates," *Cognition* 106, no. 1 (January 2008): 455–62.

54. This probably apocryphal story is from Clifton Fadiman and André Bernard, eds., *Bartlett's Book of Anecdotes* (New York: Little, Brown, 2000), p. 68.

55. Rosengren and French, "Magical Thinking," pp. 42–60.

56. Lysann Damisch, Barbara Stoberock, and Thomas Mussweiler, "Keep Your Fingers Crossed! How Superstition Improves Performance," *Psychological Science* 21, no. 7 (July 2010): 1014–20.

57. "Superstition: Do You Believe the Following or Not?" *Statista: The Statistics Portal*, 2017, http://www.statista.com/statistics/297156/united-states-common-superstitions-believe/ (accessed November 19, 2017).

58. Richard Wiseman, "UK Superstition Survey" (Hertfordshire: University of Hertfordshire, Psychology Department, 2003), http://www.richardwiseman.com/resources/superstition_report.pdf (accessed November 19, 2017).

59. Stuart A. Vyse, *Believing in Magic: The Psychology of Superstition* (New York: Oxford University Press, 1999), p. 19.

60. Martin E. P. Seligman and Joanne L. Hager, "Biological Boundaries of Learning: The Sauce-Béarnaise Syndrome," *Psychology Today* 6 (August 1972): 59–61, 84–87.

61. Koichi Ono, "Superstitious Behavior in Humans," *Journal of the Experimental Analysis of Behavior* 47, no. 3 (1987): 261–71.

62. Gregory A. Wagner and Edward K. Morris, "'Superstitious' Behavior in Children," *Psychological Record* 37, no. 4 (October 1987): 471–88.

63. Vyse, *Believing in Magic*.

64. Jan Beck and Wolfgang Forstmeier, "Superstition and Belief as Inevitable By-Products of an Adaptive Learning Strategy," *Human Nature* 18, no. 1 (March 2007): 35–46.

65. Hans G. Buhrmann and Maxwell K. Zaugg, "Superstitions among Basketball Players: An Investigation of Various Forms of Superstitious Belief and Behavior among Competitive Basketballers at the Junior High School to University Level," *Journal of Sport Behavior* 4, no. 4 (December 1, 1981): 163–74.

66. Damisch, Stoberock, and Mussweiler, "Keep Your Fingers Crossed!"

67. Ibid.

68. Judy L. Van Raalte, Britton W. Brewer, Carol J. Nemeroff, and Darwyn E. Linder, "Chance Orientation and Superstitious Behavior on the Putting Green," *Journal of Sport Behavior* 14, no. 1 (1991): 41–50.

69. Michaéla C. Schippers and Paul A. van Lange, "The Psychological Benefits of Superstitious Rituals in Top Sport: A Study among Top Sportspersons," *Journal of Applied Social Psychology* 36, no. 10 (October 2006): 2532–53.

70. Vyse, *Believing in Magic*.

71. Blaise Pascal, *Pensées* (New York: E. P. Dutton, 1958), p. 67.

72. Vyse, *Believing in Magic*, p. 239.

73. Patrick Clark, "Why Are We Still Making Buildings without a 13th Floor?" MoneyWeb, February 15, 2015, https://www.moneyweb.co.za/news/why-are-we-still-making -buildings-without-a-13th-f/ (accessed November 19, 2017).

74. Monica-Maria Stapelberg, *Strange but True: A Historical Background to Popular Beliefs and Traditions* (UK: Crux, 2014).

Chapter 16: The God Engine

1. Ara Norenzayan, *Big Gods: How Religion Transformed Cooperation and Conflict* (Princeton, NJ: Princeton University Press, 2013).

2. "The Global Religious Landscape," Pew Research Center, Washington, DC, December 18, 2012, http://www.pewforum.org/2012/12/18/global-religious-landscape-exec/ (accessed November 19, 2017).

3. "Losing Our Religion? Two Thirds of People Still Claim to Be Religious," Worldwide Independent Network of Market Research, Zurich, Switzerland, April 13, 2015, http://www .wingia.com/web/files/news/290/file/290.pdf (accessed November 19, 2017).

4. Ibid.

5. Ibid.

6. Ibid.

7. Robert A. Hinde, *Why Gods Persist: A Scientific Approach to Religion*, 2nd ed. (New York: Routledge, 2010).

8. "America's Changing Religious Landscape," Pew Research Center, Washington, DC, May 12, 2015, http://www.pewforum.org/2015/05/12/americas-changing-religious-landscape/ (accessed November 19, 2017).

9. "Religion and Faith in Canada Today: Strong Belief, Ambivalence, and Rejection Define Our Views," Angus Reid Institute: Public Interest Research, March 26, 2015, http:// angusreid.org/faith-in-canada/ (accessed November 19, 2017).

10. "US Public Becoming Less Religious," Pew Research Center, Washington, DC, November 3, 2015, http://www.pewforum.org/2015/11/03/u-s-public-becoming-less -religious/ (accessed November 19, 2017).

11. Sarah Eekhoff Zylstra, "Pew: Evangelicals Stay Strong as Christianity Crumbles in America," *Christianity Today*, May 11, 2015, http://www.christianitytoday.com/ gleanings/2015/may/pew-evangelicals-stay-strong-us-religious-landscape-study.html (accessed November 19, 2017).

12. James H. Leuba, *The Belief in God and Immortality: A Psychological, Anthropological, and Statistical Study* (Boston: Sherman, French, 1916).

13. James H. Leuba, "Religious Beliefs of American Scientists," *Harper's Magazine* 169 (1934): 291–300.

14. Edward J. Larson and Larry Witham, "Scientists Are Still Keeping the Faith," *Nature* 386 (April 3, 1997): 435–36.

15. Edward J. Larson and Larry Witham, "Leading Scientists Still Reject God," *Nature* 394 (July 23, 1998): 313.

16. Michael Stirrat and R Elisabeth Cornwell, "Eminent Scientists Reject the Supernatural: A Survey of the Fellows of the Royal Society," *Evolution: Education and Outreach* 6, no. 1 (December 2013): 33.

17. Fenggang Yang, "What about China? Religious Vitality in the Most Secular and Rapidly Modernizing Society," *Sociology of Religion* 75, no. 4 (December 1, 2014): 564–78.

18. Hinde, *Why Gods Persist*.

19. Eugene Subbotsky, *Magic and the Mind: Mechanisms, Functions, and Development of Magical Thinking and Behavior* (Oxford, UK: Oxford University Press, 2010).

20. See for example Karen Armstrong, *Fields of Blood: Religion and the History of Violence* (New York: Anchor, 2014).

21. Richard Sosis, "The Adaptationist-Byproduct Debate on the Evolution of Religion: Five Misunderstandings of the Adaptationist Program," *Journal of Cognition and Culture* 9, no. 3-4 (2009): 315–32.

22. Scott Atran and Ara Norenzayan, "Religion's Evolutionary Landscape: Counterintuition, Commitment, Compassion, Communion," *Behavioral and Brain Sciences* 27, no. 6 (2004): 713–70.

23. Edward B. Tylor, *Primitive Culture: Researches into the Development of Mythology, Philosophy, Religion, Language, Art, and Custom* (1871; New York: Putnam's, 1920).

24. Kelly Bulkeley, "Future Research in Cognitive Science and Religion," *Behavioral and Brain Sciences* 27, no. 6 (December 2004): 733–34.

25. Emile Durkheim, *The Elementary Forms of the Religious Life* (1912; Oxford: Oxford University Press, 2008).

26. Patrick Boyer, *Religion Explained: The Evolutionary Origins of Religious Thought* (New York: Basic Books, 2001).

27. Sigmund Freud, *Moses and Monotheism* (New York: Vintage, 1967).

28. Albert Ellis, "Religious Belief in the United States Today," *Humanist* 37, no. 2 (1977): 38–41, 39.

29. Subbotsky, *Magic and the Mind*, p. 145.

30. Richard Sosis and Candace Alcorta, "Signaling, Solidarity, and the Sacred: The Evolution of Religious Behavior," *Evolutionary Anthropology* 12, no. 6 (2003): 264–74.

31. Norenzayan, *Big Gods*.

32. Robert Hogan, "The Superstitions of Everyday Life," *Behavioral and Brain Sciences* 27, no. 6 (December 2004): 738–39.

33. Jesse M. Bering, "The Cognitive Psychology of Belief in the Supernatural," *American Scientist* 94 (March-April 2006): 142.

34. Raffaele Pettazzoni, *The All-Knowing God: Researches into Early Religion and Culture*, trans. H. J. Rose (London: Methuen, 1956).

35. Norenzayan, *Big Gods*.

36. Ibid.

37. Pelet de la Lozère and Joseph Claramond, *Opinions de Napoléon sur Divers Sujets de Politique et d'Administration, Recueillies par un Membre de son Conseil d'État; et Récit de Quelques Événements de l'Époque* (Paris: Firmin Didot Frères, 1833), https://archive.org/details/opinionsdenapolo00pel (accessed June 3, 2017).

38. Hogan, "Superstitions of Everyday Life."

39. Norenzayan, *Big Gods*.

40. Daniel N. Finkel, Paul Swartwout, and Richard Sosis, "The Socio-Religious Brain: A Developmental Model," *Proceedings of the British Academy* 158 (2009): 287–312, p. 291.

41. Norenzayan, *Big Gods*.

42. James E. Alcock and Stan Sadava, *An Introduction to Social Psychology: Global Perspectives* (London: Sage, 2014).

43. Lee A. Kirkpatrick, "The Evolutionary Social Psychology of Religious Beliefs," *Behavioral and Brain Sciences* 27, no. 6 (December 2004): 741.

44. Peter J. Richerson and Robert Boyd, *Not by Genes Alone: How Culture Transformed Human Evolution* (Chicago: University of Chicago Press, 2005).

45. Ibid.

46. Sosis, "Adaptationist-Byproduct Debate."

47. Deborah Kelemen, "Counterintuition, Existential Anxiety, and Religion as a By-Product of the Designing Mind," *Behavioral and Brain Sciences* 27, no. 6 (December 2004): 739–40.

48. David Cohen, "Founding Fathers of the Psyche," *New Scientist*, December 17, 1994, http://www.newscientist.com/article/mg14419564.600-founding-fathers-of-the-psyche.html (accessed November 19, 2017).

49. Francis Galton, *Memories of My Life* (London: Methuen, 1908), p. 277.

50. Hogan, "The Superstitions of Everyday Life."

51. Robert N. McCauley, *Why Religion Is Natural and Science Is Not* (New York: Oxford University Press, 2011).

52. Scott Atran, *In Gods We Trust: The Evolutionary Landscape of Religion* (Oxford: Oxford University Press, 2002), p. 267.

53. Henry Morris and Martin Clark, "Is the AIDS Epidemic God's Judgement on the 'Gay Liberation' Movement?" in *The Bible Has the Answer* (Green Forest, AR: Master Books, 1987), online at Christian Answers, http://christiananswers.net/q-eden/edn-f020.html (accessed November 19, 2017).

54. McCauley, *Why Religion Is Natural and Science Is Not.*

55. Boyer, *Religion Explained.*

56. Paul Bloom, *Descartes' Baby: How the Science of Child Development Explains What Makes Us Human* (New York: Basic Books, 2004).

57. Norenzayan, *Big Gods.*

58. Bloom, *Descartes' Baby.*

59. Justin L. Barrett, Rebekah A. Richert, and Amanda Driesenga, "God's Beliefs versus Mother's: The Development of Nonhuman Agent Concepts," *Child Development* 72, no. 1 (January-February 2001): 50–65.

60. Ibid.

61. Ibid.

62. Nicola Knight, Paulo Sousa, Justin L. Barrett, and Scott Atran, "Children's Attributions of Belief to Humans and God: Cross-Cultural Evidence," *Cognitive Science* 28, no. 1 (2004): 117–26.

63. Deborah Kelemen, "Are Children 'Intuitive Theists'? Reasoning about Purpose and Design in Nature," *Psychological Science* 15, no. 5 (2004): 295–31.

64. Jacqueline D. Woolley, "The Development of Beliefs about Direct Mental-Physical Causality in Imagination, Magi0c, and Religion," in *Imagining the Impossible: Magical, Scientific, and Religious Thinking in Children*, ed. Karl S. Rosengren, Carl N. Johnson, and Paul L. Harris (Cambridge, UK: Cambridge University Press, 2000), pp. 99–129.

65. Jacqueline D. Woolley and Katrina E. Phelps, "The Development of Children's Beliefs about Prayer," *Journal of Cognition and Culture* 1, no. 2 (2001): 139–66.

66. Paul L. Harris and Melissa A. Koenig, "Trust in Testimony: How Children Learn about Science and Religion," *Child Development* 77, no. 3 (May-June 2006): 505–24.

67. Karl S. Rosengren and Jason A. French, "Magical Thinking," in *The Oxford Handbook of the Development of Imagination*, ed. Marjorie Taylor (Oxford, England: Oxford University Press, 2013), pp. 42–60.

68. Boyer, *Religion Explained.*

69. Harris and Koenig, "Trust in Testimony."

70. Ibid.

71. Pascal Boyer, "Religious Ontologies and the Bounds of Sense: A Cognitive Catalog of the Supernatural," (Stanford, CA: Center for Advanced Studies in the Behavioral Sciences, 2002), http://ontology.buffalo.edu/smith/courses01/rrtw/Boyer.htm (accessed November 20, 2017).

72. Pascal Boyer and Charles Ramble, "Cognitive Templates for Religious Concepts: Cross-Cultural Evidence for Recall of Counter-Intuitive Representations," *Cognitive Science* 25, no. 4 (July 2001): 535–64.

73. Boyer, *Religion Explained.*

74. Michaela Porubanova-Norquist, Daniel Joel Shaw, and Dimitris Xygalatas, "Minimal-Counterintuitiveness Revisited: Effects of Cultural and Ontological Violations on Concept Memorability," *Journal for the Cognitive Science of Religion* 1, no. 2 (2013): 181–92.

75. Atran and Norenzayan, "Religion's Evolutionary Landscape."

76. Boyer, *Religion Explained*, p. 31.

77. Kelly Bulkeley, "Future Research in Cognitive Science and Religion," *Behavioral and Brain Sciences* 27, no. 6 (December 2004): 733–34.

78. Roland B. Dixon, "Achomawi and Atsugewi Tales," *Journal of American Folklore* 21, no. 81 (April-September 1908): 159–77.

79. Atran and Norenzayan, "Religion's Evolutionary Landscape."

80. Ian McGregor et al., "Anxious Uncertainty and Reactive Approach Motivation (RAM)," *Journal of Personality and Social Psychology* 99, no. 1 (2010): 133–471.

81. Michael Inzlicht, Ian McGregor, Jacob B. Hirsch, and Kyle Nash, "Neural Markers of Religious Conviction," *Psychological Science* 20, no. 3 (2009): 385–92.

82. Ibid.

83. Jennifer A. Whitson and Adam D. Galinsky, "Lacking Control Increases Illusory Pattern Perception," *Science* 322, no. 5898 (October 3, 2008): 115–17.

84. Aaron C. Kay, Danielle Gaucher, Ian McGregor, and Kyle Nash, "Religious Belief as Compensatory Control," *Personality and Social Psychology Review* 14, no. 1 (2010): 37–48.

85. Robert Browning, "Pippa's Song," in *The Oxford Book of English Verse*, ed. Arthur Quiller-Couch (Oxford: Clarendon, 1919).

86. Aaron C. Kay, Steven Shepherd, Craig W. Blatz, et al., "For God (or) Country: The Hydraulic Relation between Government Instability and Belief in Religious Sources of Control," *Journal of Personality and Social Psychology* 99, no. 5 (2010): 725–39.

87. Pehr Granqvist, Mario Mikulincer, and Phillip R. Shaver, "Religion as Attachment: Normative Processes and Individual Differences," *Personality and Social Psychology Review* 14, no. 1 (2010): 49–59.

88. Constantine Sedikides and Jochen E. Gebauer, "Religiosity as Self-Enhancement: A Meta-Analysis of the Relation between Socially Desirable Responding and Religiosity," *Personality and Social Psychology Review* 14, no. 1 (2010): 17–36.

89. Maria Straub, "God Sees the Little Sparrow Fall," in *Bright Light: A Collection of New and Selected Songs for Sunday School and Young People's Meetings*, by Solomon W. Straub (Chicago: S. W. Straub, 1893), p. 183.

90. Jesse Graham and Jonathan Haidt, "Beyond Beliefs: Religions Bind Individuals into Moral Communities," *Personality and Social Psychology Review* 14, no. 1 (2010): 140–50.

91. Renate Ysseldyk, Kimberly Matheson, and Hymie Anisman, "Religiosity as Identity: Toward an Understanding of Religion from a Social Identity Perspective," *Personality and Social Psychology Review* 14, no. 1 (2010): 60–71.

92. James E. Alcock, "Religion and Rationality," in *Religion and Mental Health*, ed. John F. Schumaker (Oxford: Oxford University Press, 1992), pp. 122–31.

93. Sander L. Koole et al. "Why Religion's Burdens Are Light: From Religiosity to Implicit Self-Regulation," *Personality and Social Psychology Review* 14, no. 1 (2010): 95–107.

94. David Carrasco, *City of Sacrifice: The Aztec Empire and the Role of Violence in Civilization* (Boston: Beacon, 1999).

95. Plutarch, *Moralia II* (171 BCE), cited by Jeffrey H. Schwartz, *What the Bones Tell Us* (New York: H. Holt, 1993), p. 33.

96. Alcock, "Religion and Rationality."

97. Scott O. Lilienfeld and Rachel Ammirati, "Would the World Be Better Off Without

Religion? A Skeptic's Guide to the Debate," *Skeptical Inquirer* 38, no. 4 (July/August 2014): 30–37.

98. Harold G. Koenig, "Religion, Spirituality, and Health: The Research and Clinical Implications," *ISRN Psychiatry*, article ID 278730 (2012), published online: http://dx.doi .org/10.5402/2012/278730 (accessed November 20, 2017).

Chapter 17: Things That Go Bump in the Night

1. James Hardy, ed., *The Denham Tracts: A Collection of Folklore* (London: London Folklore Society, 1895), pp. 2, 76–80.

2. Suzana Herculano-Houzel, "The Human Brain in Numbers: A Linearly Scaled-Up Primate Brain," *Frontiers in Human Neuroscience* 3, no. 31 (2009).

3. Bruce Goldman, "Stunning Details of Brain Connections Revealed," *ScienceDaily*, November 17, 2010, http://www.sciencedaily.com/releases/2010/11/101117121803.htm (accessed November 20, 2017).

4. Graham F. Reed, *The Psychology of Anomalous Experience: A Cognitive Approach* (Amherst, NY: Prometheus Books, 1988)

5. Christopher French, "Why I Study Anomalistic Psychology," *Psychologist* 14 (July 2001): 356.

6. Wilhelm Wundt, *Hypnotismus und Suggestion* (Leipzig: Engelmann, 1892), pp. 9–10.

7. John J. Cerullo, *The Secularization of the Soul: Psychical Research in Modern Britain* (Philadelphia: Institute for the Study of Human Issues, 1982).

8. R. Laurence Moore, *In Search of White Crows: Spiritualism, Parapsychology, and American Culture* (New York: Oxford University Press, 1977), p. 7.

9. James E. Alcock. "Parapsychology as a 'Spiritual' Science," in *A Skeptic's Handbook of Parapsychology*, ed. Paul Kurtz (Amherst, NY: Prometheus Books, 1985), pp. 537–65.

10. Daniel Cohen, *ESP: The Search Beyond the Senses* (New York: Harcourt Brace Jovanovich, 1973).

11. Moore, *In Search of White Crows*.

12. Ibid.

13. Edmund Gurney, Frederic W. H. Myers, and Frank Podmore, *Phantasms of the Living* (London: Society for Psychical Research, 1886).

14. Henry Sidgwick et al., "Report on the Census of Hallucinations," in *Proceedings of the Society for Psychical Research*, vol. 10 (London: Kegan Paul, Trench, Trübner, 1894), pp. 25–422.

15. Seymour H. Mauskopf and Michael R. McVaugh, *The Elusive Science: Origins of Experimental Psychical Research* (1974; Baltimore, MD: Johns Hopkins University Press, 1980).

16. James E. Alcock, *Parapsychology: Science or Magic?* (Oxford, UK: Pergamon, 1981). See also Brian Mackenzie and S. Lynne Mackenzie, "Whence the Enchanted Boundary? Sources and Significance of the Parapsychological Tradition," *Journal of Parapsychology* 44, no. 2 (1980): 125–66.

17. James E. Alcock, "Parapsychology: Science of the Anomalous or Search for the Sole," *Behavioral and Brain Sciences* 10, no. 4 (1987): 553–65.

18. James E. Alcock, "Attributions about Impossible Things," in *Debating Psychic Experience: Human Potential or Human Illusion?* ed. Stanley Krippner and Harris L. Friedman (Santa Barbara, CA: Praeger, 2010), pp. 29–42.

19. James E. Alcock, "The Propensity to Believe,'" in *The Flight from Science and Reason*, ed. Paul R. Gross, Norman Levitt, and Martin W. Lewis (New York: New York Academy of Sciences, 1996), pp. 64–78.

20. James E. Alcock, "A Comprehensive Review of Major Empirical Studies in Parapsychology Involving Random Event Generators and Remote Viewing," in *Enhancing Human Performance: Issues, Theories, and Techniques*, vol. 2., ed. Daniel Druckman and John A. Swets (Washington, DC: National Academy Press, 1987).

21. Donald O. Hebb, personal communication with the author, 1978.

22. Kyle Kirkland, "Paraneuroscience?" *Skeptical Inquirer* 24, no. 3 (2000): 40–43.

23. Barry L. Beyerstein, "Neuroscience and Psi-ence," *Behavioral and Brain Sciences* 10, no. 4 (December 1987): 571–72.

24. C. Scott and P. Haskell, "'Normal' Explanation of the Soal-Goldney Experiments in Extrasensory Perception," *Nature* 245, no. 5419 (September 7, 1973): 52–54.

25. Charles Cooper, "Belief in the Paranormal Remains Deep," CBS News, June 30, 2010, http://www.cbsnews.com/news/belief-in-the-paranormal-remains-deep/ (accessed November 20, 2017).

26. Dave Clarke, "Belief in the Paranormal: A New Zealand Survey," *Journal of the Society for Psychical Research* 57, no. 823 (1991): 412–25.

27. Laura P. Otis and James E. Alcock, "Factors Affecting Extraordinary Belief," *Journal of Social Psychology* 118, no. 1 (1982): 77–85. See also James E Alcock, *Parapsychology: Science or Magic?* (Oxford: Pergamon, 1981), p. 25; and Laura Otis, "A Survey of Extraordinary Beliefs," (thesis; Toronto: York University, Master of Arts, 1979).

28. Bronislaw Malinowski, *Magic, Science, Religion, and Other Essays* (New York: Free Press, 1948).

29. Vernon R. Padgett and Dale O. Jorgenson. "Superstition and Economic Threat: Germany, 1918–1940," *Personality and Social Psychology Bulletin* 8, no. 4 (1982): 736–41.

30. Jean M. Twenge and W. Keith Campbell, *The Narcissism Epidemic: Living in the Age of Entitlement* (New York: Free Press, 2009).

31. Dave Clarke, "Experience and Other Reasons Given for Belief and Disbelief in Paranormal and Religious Phenomena," *Journal of the Society for Psychical Research* 60, no. 841 (1995): 371–84. See also James E. Alcock and Laura Otis, "Critical Thinking and Belief in the Paranormal," *Psychological Reports* 46, no. 2 (1980): 479–82; Otis and Alcock, "Factors Affecting Extraordinary Belief," pp. 77–85; Alcock, *Parapsychology*; Christopher French and Krissy Wilson, "Cognitive Factors Underlying Paranormal Beliefs and Experiences," in *Tall Tales about the Mind & Brain: Separating Fact from Fiction*, ed. Sergio Della Sala (New York: Oxford, 2007), pp. 3–22.

32. Gordon Pennycook et al., "Analytic Cognitive Style Predicts Religious and Paranormal Belief," *Cognition* 123, no. 3 (June 2012): 335–46.

33. Keith E. Stanovich, *Rationality and the Reflective Mind* (Oxford: Oxford University Press, 2011).

34. Kia Aarnio and Marjaana Lindeman, "Paranormal Beliefs, Education, and Thinking Styles," *Personality and Individual Differences* 39, no. 7 (November 2005): 1227–36.

35. Robert M. Ross, Bjoern Hartig, and Ryan McKay, "Analytic Cognitive Style Predicts Paranormal Explanations of Anomalous Experiences but Not the Experiences Themselves: Implications for Cognitive Theories of Delusions," *Journal of Behavior Therapy and Experimental Psychiatry*, 56, September 17, 2016, available online at http://www.sciencedirect.com/science/article/pii/S0005791616301057?via%3Dihub (accessed November 20, 2017).

36. Romaine Bouvet and Jean-François Bonnefon, "Non-Reflective Thinkers Are Predisposed to Attribute Supernatural Causation to Uncanny Experiences," *Personality and Social Psychology Bulletin* 41, no. 7 (2015): 955–61. See also Andreas Hergovich and Martin Arenday, "Critical Thinking Ability and Belief in the Paranormal," *Personality and Individual Differences* 38, no. 8 (2005): 1805–12.

37. Laura A. King et al., "Ghosts, UFOs, and Magic: Positive Affect and the Experiential System," *Journal of Personality and Social Psychology* 92, no. 5 (2007): 905–19.

38. Kathy Frankovic, "Many Americans Are Scientific Skeptics," YouGov, February 20, 2014, https://today.yougov.com/news/2014/02/20/many-americans-are-scientific-skeptics/ (accessed November 20, 2017); and Peter Moore, "Poll Results: Science," YouGov, February 21, 2014, https://today.yougov.com/news/2014/02/21/poll-results-science/ (accessed November 20, 2017).

39. Harvey J. Irwin, "Fantasy Proneness and Paranormal Beliefs," *Psychological Reports* 66, no. 2 (1990): 655–58.

40. Nicholas P. Spanos et al., "Close Encounters: An Examination of UFO Experiences," *Journal of Abnormal Psychology* 102, no. 4 (1993): 624–32.

41. Kathryn Gow, Tracy Lang, and David Chant, "Fantasy Proneness, Paranormal Beliefs, and Personality Features in Out-of-Body Experiences," *Contemporary Hypnosis* 21, no. 3 (2004): 107–25.

42. Michael A. Thalbourne and Christopher C. French, "Paranormal Belief, Manic-Depressants, and Magical Radiation: A Replication," *Personality and Individual Differences* 18, no. 2 (1995): 291–92.

43. Carla L. Smith, "Personality Contributions to Belief in Paranormal Phenomena," *Individual Differences Research* 7, no. 2 (2009): 85–96.

44. J. E. Kennedy, "Personality and Motivations to Believe, Misbelieve, and Disbelieve in Paranormal Phenomena," *Journal of Parapsychology* 69, no. 2 (Fall 2005): 263–92.

45. Richard Wiseman and Caroline A. Watt, "Belief in Psychic Ability and the Misattribution Hypothesis: A Qualitative Review," *British Journal of Psychology* 97, no. 3 (August 2006): 323–38.

46. Neil Dagnall, Andrew Parker, and Gary Munley, "Paranormal Belief and Reasoning," *Personality and Individual Differences* 43, no. 6 (2007): 1406–15.

47. Krissy Wilson and Christopher C. French, "The Relationship between Susceptibility to False Memories, Dissociativity, and Paranormal Belief and Experience," *Personality and Individual Differences* 41, no. 8 (2006): 1493–502.

48. Peter Fenwick et al., "'Psychic Sensitivity,' Mystical Experience, Head Injury, and Brain Pathology," *British Journal of Medical Psychology* 58, no. 1 (March 1985): 35–44.

Chapter 18: Illusory Experience

1. John Webster, *The White Devil* (1612; London: Bloomsbury, 2008).

2. James E. Alcock, "Extra-Sensory Perception," in *The Encyclopedia of the Paranormal*, ed. Gorden Stein (Amherst, NY: Prometheus Books, 1996), pp. 241–54.

3. Olivier Collignon et al., "Women Process Multisensory Emotion Expressions More Efficiently than Men," *Neuropsychologia* 48, no. 1 (January 2010): 220–25.

4. Douglas L. Hintzman, S. J. Asher, and L. D. Stern. "Incidental Retrieval and Memory for Coincidences," in *Practical Aspects of Memory*, ed. Michael M. Gruneberg, Peter E. Morris, and Robert N. Sykes (New York: Academic Press, 1978), pp. 61–68.

5. Graham F. Reed, *The Psychology of Anomalous Experience: A Cognitive Approach* (Amherst, NY: Prometheus Books, 1988).

6. Caroline Watt et al., "Psychological Factors in Precognitive Dream Experiences: The Role of Paranormal Belief, Selective Recall, and Propensity to Find Correspondences," *International Journal of Dream Research* 7, no. 1 (2014): 1–8.

7. Ibid.

8. Persi Diaconis and Frederick Mosteller, "Methods for Studying Coincidences." *Journal of the American Statistical Association* 84, no. 408 (1989): 853–61.

9. Jane E. Cottrell, Gerald A. Winer, and Mary C. Smith, "Beliefs of Children and Adults about Feeling Stares of Unseen Others," *Developmental Psychology* 32, no. 1 (1996): 50–61.

10. Charles G. Gross, "The Fire That Comes from the Eye," *Neuroscientist* 5, no. 1 (1999): 58–64.

11. Gerald A. Winer, Jane E. Cottrell, Virginia Gregg, Jody S. Fournier, and Lori A. Bica, "Fundamentally Misunderstanding Visual Perception," *American Psychologist* 57, no. 6/7 (2002): 417–24.

12. Jane E. Cottrell and Gerald A. Winer, "Development in the Understanding of Perception: The Decline of Extramission Perception Beliefs," *Developmental Psychology* 30, no. 2 (March 1994): 218–28.

13. "The World's Muslims: Unity and Diversity," Pew Research Center, Washington, DC, August 9, 2012, http://www.pewforum.org/2012/08/09/the-worlds-muslims-unity-and-diversity-executive-summary/ (accessed June 30, 2017).

14. Rupert Sheldrake, "Experiments on the Sense of Being Stared At: The Elimination of Possible Artefacts," *Journal of the Society for Psychical Research* 65 (2001): 122–37.

15. David F. Marks and John Colwell, "The Psychic Staring Effect: An Artifact of Pseudo Randomization," *Skeptical Inquirer* 24, no. 5 (September/October 2000): 41–44.

16. Sarah Chalmers, "The Third Man Factor: How Those in Dire Peril Have Felt a Sudden Presence at Their Side, Inspiring Them to Survive," *Daily Mail Online*, July 3, 2009, http://www.dailymail.co.uk/news/article-1197394/The-Third-Man-Factor-How-dire-peril-felt-sudden-presence-inspiring-survive.html (accessed November 20, 2017).

17. John Geiger, *The Third Man Factor: The Secret to Survival in Extreme Environments* (Toronto: Viking Canada, 2009).

18. Chalmers, "Third Man Factor."

19. Olaf Blanke et al., "Stimulating Illusory Own-Body Experiences," *Nature* 419, no. 6904 (September 19, 2002): 269–70.

20. Shahar Arzy et al., "Induction of an Illusory Shadow Person," *Nature* 443, no. 7109 (September 21, 2006): p. 287.

21. J. Palmer, "The Out of Body Experience: A Psychological Theory," *Parapsychology Review* 9, no. 5 (1978): 19–22, 21.

22. Susan J. Blackmore, *Beyond the Body: An Investigation of Out-of-the-Body Experiences* (Chicago: Academy Chicago, 2005).

23. J. Allan Cheyne and Todd A. Girard, "The Body Unbound: Vestibular-Motor Hallucinations and Out-of-Body Experiences," *Cortex* 45, no. 2 (February 2009): 201–15.

24. Blanke et al., "Stimulating Illusory Own-Body Perceptions."

25. Susan Blackmore, "Near-Death Experiences: In or Out of the Body?" in *Aspects of Consciousness: Essays on Physics, Death, and the Mind*, ed. Ingrid Fredriksson (Jefferson, NC: McFarland, 2012), pp. 104–18.

26. Olaf Blanke and Shahar Arzy, "The Out-of-Body Experience: Disturbed Self-Processing at the Temporo-Parietal Junction," *Neuroscientist* 11, no. 1 (2005): 16–24.

27. H. Henrik Ehrsson, "The Experimental Induction of Out-of-Body Experiences," *Science* 317, no. 5841 (August 24, 2007): 1048.

28. Valeria I. Petkova and H. Henrik Ehrsson, "If I Were You: Perceptual Illusion of Body Swapping," *PLoS ONE* 3, no. 12 (2008): e3832.

29. Arvid Guterstam and H. Henrik Ehrsson, "Disowning One's Seen Real Body during an Out-of-Body Illusion," *Consciousness and Cognition* 21, no. 2 (June 2012): 1037–42.

30. Plato, *The Republic*, cited by Justine Elizabeth Owens, Emily Williams Cook, and Ian Stevenson, "Features of 'Near-Death Experience' in Relation to Whether or Not Patients Were Near Death," *Lancet* 336, no. 8724 (November 10, 1990): 1175–77.

31. Dean Mobbs and Caroline Watts, "There Is Nothing Paranormal about Near-Death Experiences: How Neuroscience Can Explain Seeing Bright Lights, Meeting the Dead, or Being Convinced You Are One of Them," *Trends in Cognitive Sciences* 15, no. 10 (October 2011): 447–49.

32. Pirn van Lommel, Ruud van Wees, Vincent Myers, and Ingrid Elfferich, "Near-Death Experience in Survivors of Cardiac Arrest: A Prospective Study in the Netherlands," *Lancet* 358, no. 9298 (December 15, 2001): 2039–45.

33. Raymond A. Moody, *Life After Life* (1975; San Francisco: Harper Collins, 2001).

34. Christopher C. French, "Near-Death Experiences in Cardiac Arrest Survivors," *Progress in Brain Research* 150 (2005): 351–67.

35. Kenneth Ring, *Life at Death: A Scientific Investigation of the Near-Death Experience* (New York: Coward, McCann, Goeghagan, 1980).

36. Melvin Morse, Doug Conner, and Donald Tyler, "Near Death Experiences in a Pediatric Population," *American Journal of Diseases of Children* 139, no. 6 (June 1985): 595–63.

37. Maurice Rawlings, *Beyond Death's Door* (Nashville: Nelson, 1978).

38. James E. Alcock, "Psychology and Near-Death Experiences," *Skeptical Inquirer* 111, no. 3 (1979): 25–41.

39. Eben Alexander, *Proof of Heaven: A Neurosurgeon's Journey into the Afterlife* (New York: Simon & Schuster, 2012).

40. Eben Alexander, "Proof of Heaven: A Doctor's Experience with the After," *Newsweek*, October 18, 2012, http://www.newsweek.com/proof-heaven-doctors-experience -afterlife-65327 (accessed November 20, 2017).

41. Ibid.

42. Jeff Bercovici, "Esquire Unearths 'Proof of Heaven' Author's Credibility Problems," *Forbes*, July 2, 2013, https://www.forbes.com/sites/jeffbercovici/2013/07/02/esquire-unearths -proof-of-heaven-authors-credibility-problems/#35598fc51fd6 (accessed November 20, 2017).

43. Ernst A. Rodin, "The Reality of Death Experiences: A Personal Perspective," *Journal of Nervous and Mental Disease* 168, no. 5 (May 1980): 259–63, 262.

44. French, "Near-Death Experiences in Cardiac Arrest Survivors."

45. Adriana Sleutjes, Alexander Moreira-Almeida, and Bruce Greyson, "Almost 40 Years Investigating Near-Death Experiences: An Overview of Mainstream Scientific Journals," *Journal of Nervous and Mental Diseases* 202, no. 11 (November 2014): 833–36.

46. Karl L. R. Jansen, "Neuroscience, Ketamine, and the Near-Death Experience: The Role of Glutamate and the NMDA Receptor," in *The Near-Death Experience: A Reader*, ed. Lee W. Bailey and Jenny Yates (New York: Routledge, 1996), pp. 265–82.

47. French, "Near-Death Experiences in Cardiac Arrest Survivors."

48. Zalika Klemenc-Ketis, Janko Kersnik, and Stefek Grmec, "The Effect of Carbon Dioxide on Near-Death Experiences in Out-of-Hospital Cardiac Arrest Survivors: A Prospective Observational Study," *Critical Care* 14, no. 2 (2010): R56.

49. Mobbs and Watts, "There Is Nothing Paranormal about Near–Death Experiences."

50. Susan J. Blackmore and Tom S. Troscianko, "The Physiology of the Tunnel," *Journal of Near-Death Studies* 8, no. 1 (September 1989): 15–28.

51. Mobbs and Watts, "There Is Nothing Paranormal about Near–Death Experiences."

52. Ibid.

53. Ibid.

54. Ronald K. Siegel, "Hallucinations," *Scientific American* 237, no. 4 (October 1977): 132–40.

55. Wilder Penfield and Herbert Jasper, *Epilepsy and the Functional Anatomy of the Human Brain* (Boston: Little, Brown, 1954).

56. Ronald K. Siegel, "The Psychology of Life after Death," *American Psychologist* 35, no. 10 (1980): 911–31.

57. Jansen, "Neuroscience, Ketamine, and the Near-Death Experience."

58. Karl L. R. Jansen, "The Ketamine Model of the Near-Death Experience: A Central Role for the N-Methyl-D-Aspartate Receptor," *Journal of Near-Death Studies* 16, no. 1 (March 1997): 5–26.

59. Mobbs and Watts, "There Is Nothing Paranormal About Near–Death Experiences."

60. Vanessa Charland-Verville et al., "Near-Death Experiences in Non-Life-Threatening Events and Coma of Different Etiologies," *Frontiers in Human Neuroscience*, May 27, 2014, doi: 10.3389/fnhum.2014.00203.

61. Ian Stevenson, Emily Williams Cook, and Nicholas McClean-Rice, "Are Persons

Reporting 'Near-Death Experiences' Really Near-Death? A Study of Medical Records," *Omega* 20, no. 1 (1990): 45–54.

62. Albert Heim, "Remarks on Fatal Falls," *Yearbook of the Swiss Alpine Club* 27 (1892): 327–37, Russell Noyes and Roy Kletti, trans. *Omega: Journal of Death and Dying* 3, no. 1 (April 1972): 45–52.

63. Russell Noyes and Roy Kletti, "Depersonalization in the Face of Life-Threatening Danger: An Interpretation," *Omega: Journal of Death and Dying* 7, no. 2 July (1976): 103–14.

64. James E. Alcock, "Pseudoscience and the Soul," *Essence* 5, no. 1 (1981): 65–76.

65. Vernon M. Neppe, *The Psychology of Déjà Vu: Have I Been Here Before* (Johannesburg: Witwatersrand University Press, 1983).

66. Alan S. Brown, "The Déjà Vu Illusion," *Current Directions in Psychological Science* 13, no. 6 (2004): 256–59.

67. Neppe, *Psychology of Déjà Vu*.

68. James E. Alcock, "Déjà vu," in *The Encyclopedia of the Paranormal*, ed. Gorden Stein (Amherst, NY: Prometheus Books, 1996), pp. 215–22.

69. Radka Jersakova, Akira R. O'Connor, and Chris J. A. Moulin, "What's New in Déjà Vu?" in *Culture and Cognition: A Collection of Critical Essays*, ed. Shamsul Haque and Elizabeth Sheppard (Peter Lang, 2015), pp. 137–50.

70. Reed, *Psychology of Anomalous Experience*.

71. Leonard Zusne and Warren Jones, *Anomalistic Psychology: A Study of Magical Thinking* (Mahwah, NJ: Erlbaum, 1989).

72. Theodate L. Smith, "Paramnesia in Daily Life," *American Journal of Psychology* 24, no. 1 (1913): 52–65.

73. Neppe, *Psychology of Déjà Vu*.

74. James Randi, *The Truth about Uri Geller* (Buffalo, NY: Prometheus Books, 1982).

Chapter 19: A Caboodle of Strange Beliefs

1. "Tim Minchin's Storm the Animated Movie," YouTube video, 10:38, posted by stormmovie, April 7, 2011, https://www.youtube.com/watch?v=HhGuXCuDb1U, at 7:05–7:13.

2. Ian Stevenson, *Children Who Remember Previous Lives: A Question of Reincarnation* rev. ed. (Jefferson, NC: McFarland, 2001).

3. Larry Dossey, "Birthmarks and Reincarnation," *Explore* 11, no. 1 (January-February 2015): 1–4.

4. Ian Stevenson, *Reincarnation and Biology: A Contribution to the Etiology of Birthmarks and Birth Defects*, vol. 1, *Birthmarks* (Westport, CT: Praeger, 1997).

5. Jim B. Tucker and H. H. Jürgen Keil, "Experimental Birthmarks: New Cases of an Asian Practice," *Journal of Scientific Exploration* 27, no. 2 (Summer 2013): 269–82.

6. Stevenson, *Birthmarks*.

7. Helen Wambach, *Reliving Past Lives: The Evidence under Hypnosis* (New York: Harper & Row, 1978).

8. Theodore Flournoy, *From India to the Planet Mars* (London: Harper Brothers, 1900).

9. Grace Rosher, *Beyond the Horizon* (Greenwood, SC: Attic Press, 1961).

10. Simeon Edmunds, "The Automatic Writing of Miss Grace Rosher," *Tomorrow*, 1964, pp. 64–71, 71, https://www.scribd.com/doc/169931749/Tomorrow-Grace-Rosher-1964-pdf (accessed June 23, 2017).

11. Terrence Hines *Pseudoscience and the Paranormal* (Amherst, NY: Prometheus Books, 2003).

12. Eamonn Walsh et al., "Using Suggestion to Model Different Types of Automatic Writing," *Consciousness and Cognition* 26 (May 2014): 24–36.

13. Dilek Evyapan and Emre Kumral, "Visuospatial Stimulus-Bound Automatic Writing Behavior: A Right Hemispheric Stroke Syndrome," *Neurology* 56, no. 2 (January 23, 2001): 245–47.

14. Thomas A. Edison, *Le Royaume de l'au-delà* (Grenoble: Jérôme Millon, collection "Golgotha," 2015).

15. *Encyclopedia of Occultism and Parapsychology*, s.v. "Raudive Voices," 2001, http://www.encyclopedia.com/science/encyclopedias-almanacs-transcripts-and-maps/raudive-voices (accessed November 20, 2017).

16. Imants Barušs, "Failure to Replicate Electronic Voice Phenomenon," *Journal of Scientific Exploration* 15, no. 3 (2001): 355–67.

17. Larry Shannon-Missal, "Americans' Belief in God, Miracles, and Heaven Declines: Belief in Darwin's Theory of Evolution Rises," Harris Poll 97, December 16, 2013, http://www.theharrispoll.com/health-and-life/Americans__Belief_in_God__Miracles_and_Heaven_Declines.html (accessed November 20, 2017).

18. Will Dahlgren, "'Ghosts Exist,' Say 1 in 3 Brits," YouGov Poll, October 31, 2014, https://yougov.co.uk/news/2014/10/31/ghosts-exist-say-1-3-brits/ (accessed November 20, 2017).

19. Richard Wiseman, "The Haunted Brain," *Skeptical Inquirer* 35, no. 5 (September/October 2011): 46–50.

20. Rense Lange and James Houran, "Context-Induced Paranormal Experiences: Support for Houran and Lange's Model of Haunting Phenomena," *Perceptual and Motor Skills* 84, no. S3 (June 1997): 1455–58.

21. James Houran and Rense Lange, "Diary of Events in a Thoroughly Unhaunted House," *Perceptual and Motor Skills* 83, no. 2 (October 1996): 499–502.

22. Rense Lange and James Houran, "The Role of Fear in Delusions of the Paranormal," *Journal of Nervous and Mental Disease* 187, no. 3 (March 1999): 159–66.

23. Christopher C. French et al., "The 'Haunt' Project: An Attempt to Build a 'Haunted' Room" by Manipulating Complex Electromagnetic Fields and Infrasound," *Cortex* 45, no. 5 (May 2009): 619–29.

24. Richard Wiseman et al., "An Investigation into the Alleged Haunting of Hampton Court Palace: Psychological Variables and Magnetic Fields," *Journal of Parapsychology* 66, no. 4 (2002): 387–408.

25. Wiseman, "Haunted Brain."

26. This particular business advice is the actual horoscope provided by Jean Dixon to her Aquarian readers on May 1, 1992.

27. "Delphi," Ancient-Greece.org, 2017, http://ancient-greece.org/history/delphi.html (accessed November 20, 2017).

28. Guy Murchie, *Music of the Spheres* (Boston: Houghton Mifflin, 1961).

29. Humphrey Taylor, "What People Do and Do Not Believe In," Harris Poll 140, December 15, 2009, http://media.theharrispoll.com/documents/Harris_Poll_2009_12_15.pdf (accessed December 14, 2017).

30. Cited by Jay Pasachoff, "Some Tests of Astrology," *Mercury* 9 (November–December 1980): 137.

31. C. Richard Snyder and Randee J. Shenkel, "Astrologers, Handwriting Analysts, and Sometimes Psychologists Use the P. T. Barnum Effect," *Psychology Today* 8 no. 10 (March 1975): 52–54.

32. Peter Glick, Deborah Gottesman, and Jeffrey Jolton, "The Fault Is Not in the Stars: Susceptibility of Skeptics and Believers in Astrology to the Barnum Effect," *Personality and Social Psychology Bulletin* 15, no. 4 (December 1989): 572–83.

33. Philip Ball, "Count John Dee," *New Scientist* 229, no. 3062 (February 27, 2016): 48–49.

34. Gerald Suster, ed., *John Dee: Essential Readings* (Berkley, CA: North Atlantic, 2003).

35. J. Norman Hansen and Joshua A. Lieberman, "Use of a Torsion Pendulum Balance to Detect and Characterize What May Be a Human Bioenergy Field," *Journal of Scientific Exploration* 27, no. 2 (2013): 205–25.

36. Robert W. Loftin, "Auras: Searching for the Light," *Skeptical Inquirer* 14, no. 4 (Summer 1990): 403–409.

37. Loftur R. Gissuarson and Asgeir Gunnarsson, "An Experiment with the Alleged Human Aura," *Journal of the American Society for Psychical Research* 91, no. 1 (January 1997): 33–49.

38. Mayne Reid Coe Jr., "Fire-Walking and Related Behaviors," *Psychological Record* 7, no. 4 (October 1957): 101–10.

39. Bernard J. Leikand and William J. McCarthy, "An Investigation of Firewalking," *Skeptical Inquirer* 10, no. 1 (Fall 1985): 23–34.

40. Matt Nisbet, "The Physics Instructor Who Walks on Fire," *Generation sXeptic*, October 25, 2000, https://www.csicop.org/specialarticles/show/physics_instructor_who _walks_on_fire (accessed December 20, 2017).

41. Tim Walker, "Tony Robbins Firewalking Event in Dallas Sees Five Hospitalised after Stepping across Hot Coals," *Independent*, June 24, 2016, http://www.independent.co.uk/news/ world/americas/fire-walk-tony-robbins-hospitalised-walking-hot-coals-texas-self-help -seminar-a7101871.html (accessed November 20, 2017).

42. James E Alcock, "Afterword: An Analysis of Psychic Sleuths' Claims," in *Psychic Sleuths*, ed. Joe Nickell (Amherst, NY: Prometheus Books, 1994), pp. 172–90.

43. Nickell, ed., *Psychic Sleuths*.

44. Richard Wiseman, Donald West, and Roy Stemman, "An Experimental Test of Psychic Detection," *Journal of the Society for Psychical Research* 61, no. 842 (1996): 34–45.

45. Martin Reiser, Louise Ludwig, Susan Saxe, and Clare Wagner, "Evaluation of the Use of Psychics in the Investigation of Major Crimes," *Journal of Police Science and Administration* 7, no. 1 (March 1979): 18–25.

46. Martin Reiser and Nels Klyver, "A Comparison of Psychics, Detectives, and Students in the Investigation of Major Crimes," in *Police Psychology: Collected Papers*, ed. Martin Reiser (Los Angeles: Lehi, 1982), pp. 260–67.

47. Wiseman, West, and Stemman, "Experimental Test of Psychic Detection."

48. Kendrick Frazier, "The Roswell Incident at 70: Facts, Not Myths," *Skeptical Inquirer* 41, no. 6 (November/December 2017): 12–15.

49. Robert Sheaffer, "Do Fairies Exist?" *Skeptical Inquirer* 2, no. 1 (Fall/Winter 1977): 45–52, 50–51.

50. Philip J. Klass, "NASA, the White House, and UFOs," *Skeptical Inquirer* 2, no. 2 (1978): 72–81.

51. Philip C. Plait, *Bad Astronomy: Misconceptions and Misuses Revealed, from Astrology to the Moon Landing "Hoax"* (New York: Wiley, 2002).

52. Roy Craig, *UFOs: An Insider's View of the Official Quest for Evidence* (Denton, TX: University of North Texas Press, 1995).

53. Peter Davenport, "National UFO Reporting Center Statement," National UFO Reporting Center, August 30, 2009, http://www.nuforc.org/Statement090830.html (accessed November 20, 2017).

54. James E. Alcock and Stan Sadava, *An Introduction to Social Psychology: Global Perspectives* (London: Sage, 2014).

55. Matthew Weaver, "Seen a UFO? Don't Call the MoD," *Guardian*, December 4, 2009, https://www.theguardian.com/world/blog/2009/dec/04/ufo-hotline-closes-down-mod (accessed December 20, 2017).

56. Mary Gooderham, "Crop Circles: The Hoax That Wouldn't Die," *Globe and Mail*, May 23, 1992, D2.

57. Ollie Gillman, "Father and Son Crop Circle-Making Team Reveal the Secrets of How They Have Spent the Past 15 Years Leaving Their Intricate Designs across the Countryside," *Mail Online*, September 4, 2015.

58. Suzanne Zwarun, "Of Little Green Men and Mutilated Cows," *Maclean's*, July 21, 1980, pp. 46–47.

59. Kenneth M. Rommel Jr., *Operation Animal Mutilation: Report of the District Attorney, First Judicial District, State of New Mexico* (Washington, DC: Criminal Justice Department, 1980).

60. Joseph Rose, "UFOs, Mutilated Cows, and Oregon: What's the Link?" *Oregonian*, February 17, 2016, http://www.oregonlive.com/entertainment/index.ssf/2016/02/ufo_cow _mutilations_oregon_no.html (accessed November 20, 2017).

61. "Case of the Mutilated Cows Raises Questions, Udder Chaos," *Globe and Mail*, March 4, 1993, A15.

62. Patricia Kinne, "I've Been Abducted by Aliens," *Current Psychiatry* 7, no. 7 (July 2008): 81–92.

63. John G. Fuller, *The Interrupted Journey: Two Lost Hours "Aboard a Flying Saucer"* (New York: Dial, 1966).

64. Budd Hopkins, *Missing Time: A Documented Study of UFO Abductions* (New York: Richard Marek, 1981).

65. Budd Hopkins, *Intruders: The Incredible Visitations at Copley Woods* (New York: Ballantine, 1987).

66. Whitley Strieber, *Communion: A True Story* (New York: Avon, 1987).

67. Susan Blackmore and Marcus Cox, "Alien Abductions, Sleep Paralysis, and the Temporal Lobe," *European Journal of UFO and Abduction Studies* 1, no. 2 (September 2000): 113–18. Also, Mahzarin R. Banaji and John F. Kihlstrom, "The Ordinary Nature of Alien Abduction Memories," *Psychological Inquiry* 7, no. 2 (1996): 132–35.

68. Caroline McLeod, Barbara Corbisier, and John E. Mack, "A More Parsimonious Explanation for UFO Abduction," *Psychological Inquiry* 7, no. 2 (1996): 156–68.

69. Leonard S. Newman and Roy F. Baumeister, "Toward an Explanation of the UFO Abduction Phenomenon: Hypnotic Elaboration, Extraterrestrial Sadomasochism, and Spurious Memories," *Psychological Inquiry* 7, no. 2 (1996): 99–126.

70. Richard J. McNally, "Explaining 'Memories' of Space Alien Abduction and Past Lives: An Experimental Psychopathology Approach," *Journal of Experimental Psychopathology* 3, no. 1 (2012): 2–16.

71. John Mack, *Abduction: Human Encounters with Aliens* (New York: Simon and Schuster, 1995).

72. Ibid., p. 434.

73. Christopher C. French et al., "Psychological Aspects of the Alien Contact Experience," *Cortex* 44, no. 10 (November-December 2008): 1387–95.

74. Nicholas P. Spanos et al., "Close Encounters: An Examination of UFO Experiences," *Journal of Abnormal Psychology* 102, no. 4 (November 1993): 624–32.

75. Ibid.

76. Ibid. See also Irving I. Kirsch and Steven Jay Lynn, "Alleged Alien Abductions: False Memories, Hypnosis, and Fantasy Proneness," *Psychological Inquiry* 7, no. 2 (1996): 151–55.

77. Spanos et al., "Close Encounters."

78. Blackmore and Cox, "Alien Abductions, Sleep Paralysis, and the Temporal Lobe."

79. Mark Rodeghier, Jeff Goodpaster, and Sandy Blatterbauer, "Psychosocial Characteristics of Abductees: Results from the CUFOS Abduction Project," *Journal of UFO Studies* 3 (1991): 59–90.

80. Carl Sagan, "Alien Abduction," *Nova*, February, 27, 1996, http://www.pbs.org/wgbh/nova/space/sagan-alien-abduction.html (accessed November 20, 2017).

81. Seema L. Clifasefi, Maryanne Garry, and Elizabeth Loftus, "Setting the Record (or Video Camera) Straight on Memory: The Video Camera Model of Memory and Other Memory Myths," in Sergio Della Sala, ed., *Tall Talks about the Mind and Brain* (Oxford: Oxford University Press, 2007), pp. 60–75.

82. Sun Shi Li, "UFO Researchers & People," Extraterrestrial Contact, http://www.ufoevidence.org/researchers/detail57.htm (accessed November 20, 2017).

83. Charles Dickens. *Bleak House* (1853; London: Penguin, 2006)

84. Joe Nickell, "Not-So-Spontaneous Human Combustion," *Skeptical Inquirer* 20, no. 6 (1996): 17–20.

85. Joe Nickell, *Secrets of the Supernatural: Investigating the World's Occult Mysteries* (Amherst, NY: Prometheus Books, 1991). See also Florica Mekereş and Camelia Liana Buhaş,

"Spontaneous Human Combustion, Homicide, Suicide, or Household Accident," *Romanian Journal of Legal Medicine* 24, no. 1 (2016): 11–13.

86. Lawrence Kusche, *The Bermuda Triangle Mystery: Solved* (1975; Amherst, NY: Prometheus Books, 1995).

Chapter 20: A Firewall to Folly

1. Eric Hoffer, *The Passionate State of Mind: And Other Aphorisms* (New York: Harper & Row, 1954).

2. Gary Bauslaugh, personal communication with the author, July 10, 2017.

3. Cited by Stephen A. Di Biase, *Applied Innovation: A Handbook* (Chicago: Premier Insights, 2014), p. 372

4. Ibid.

5. Cited by Gina Hagler, *Modeling Ships and Spacecraft: The Science and Art of Mastering the Oceans and Sky* (New York: Springer, 2013), p. 179.

6. K. E. Boulding, "Science: Our Common Heritage," *Science* 207, no. 4433 (February 22, 1980): 832.

7. Laura J. Snyder, *The Philosophical Breakfast Club* (New York: Broadway, 2011).

8. Francis Bacon, *The New Organon or True Directions Concerning the Interpretation of Nature*, Book 1, XCV (1620; CreateSpace, 2016).

9. George Smith, *Stanford Encyclopedia of Philosophy*, s.v. "Newton's *Philosophiae Naturalis Principia Mathematica*," December 20, 2007, https://plato.stanford.edu/entries/newton-principia/ (accessed July 3, 2017).

10. Keith Thomas, *Religion and the Decline of Magic* (Harmondsworth: Penguin, 1971).

11. Snyder, *Philosophical Breakfast Club*.

12. Ibid.

13. "Sharp Partisan Divisions in Views of National Institutions," Pew Research Center Poll, Washington, DC, July 10, 2017, http://www.people-press.org/2017/07/10/sharp-partisan-divisions-in-views-of-national-institutions/ (accessed July 3, 2017).

14. Marcel Proust, *In Search of Lost Time*: *Swann's Way*, trans. C. K. S. Moncrief and Terrence Kilmartin (1910; London: Vintage, 2005).

15. James E. Alcock, "Thinking Critically," *Humanist in Canada* 150 (Autumn 2004): 25.

16. Davina Mill, Thomas Gray, and David R. Mandel "Influence of Research Methods and Statistics Courses on Everyday Reasoning, Critical Abilities, and Belief in Unsubstantiated Phenomena," *Canadian Journal of Behavioral Science* 26, no. 2 (1994): 246–58.

17. Scott O. Lilienfeld, Jeffrey M. Lohr, and Dean Morier, "The Teaching of Courses in the Science and Pseudoscience of Psychology: Useful Resources," *Teaching of Psychology* 28, no. 3 (2001): 182–91.

18. Rodney Schmaltz and Scott O. Lilienfeld, "Hauntings, Homeopathy, and the Hopkinsville Goblins: Using Pseudoscience to Teach Scientific Thinking," *Frontiers in Psychology*, April 17 2014, https://doi.org/10.3389/fpsyg.2014.00336 (accessed November 20, 2017).

19. "Sharp Partisan Divisions," Pew Research.

20. Daniel Semakula et al., "Effects of the Informed Health Choices Podcast on the Ability of Parents of Primary School Children in Uganda to Assess Claims about Treatment Effects: A Randomised Controlled Trial," *Lancet* 390, no. 10092 (2017): 389–98.

21. Allen Nsangi et al., "Effects of the Informed Health Choices Primary School Intervention on the Ability of Children in Uganda to Assess the Reliability of Claims about Treatment Effects: A Cluster-Randomised Controlled Trial," *Lancet* 390, no. 10092 (2017): 374–88.

22. Scott O. Lilienfeld, Steven Jay Lynn, and Jeffrey M. Lohr, eds., *Science and Pseudoscience in Clinical Psychology* (New York: Guilford, 2004).

23. Jochen Schuld et al., "Popular Belief Meets Surgical Reality: Impact of Lunar Phases, Friday the 13th, and Zodiac Signs on Emergency Operations and Intraoperative Blood Loss," *World Journal of Surgery* 35, no. 9 (September 2011): 1945–49.

24. Geneviève Belleville et al., "Impact of Seasonal and Lunar Cycles on Psychological Symptoms in the ED: An Empirical Investigation of Widely Spread Beliefs," *General Hospital Psychiatry* 35, no. 2 (March-April 2013): 192–94.

25. I. W. Kelly, James Rotton, and Roger Culver, "The Moon Was Full and Nothing Happened," *Skeptical Inquirer* 10, no. 2 (Winter 1985): 129–42. See also Moosa Zargar et al., "The Full Moon and Admission to Emergency Rooms," *Indian Journal of Medical Science* 58, no. 5 (May 2004): 191–95; Simon Kung and David A. Mrazek, "Psychiatric Emergency Department Visits on Full-Moon Nights," *Psychiatric Services* 56, no. 2 (February 2005): 221–22.; Belleville et al., "Impact of Seasonal and Lunar Cycles on Psychological Symptoms in the ED."

26. "Tests Show Wines Contain a Bouquet of Asbestos Fibres," *Ottawa Citizen*, June 14, 1977, p. 15, https://www.newspapers.com/newspage/50129392/ (accessed July 22, 2017). See also A. Gaudichet, Pommier Sebastien, Guillaume Dufour, and Gerard Bonnaud, "Asbestos Fibers in Wines: Relation to Filtration Process," *Journal of Toxicology and Environmental Health* 4, no. 5-6 (November-December 1978): 853–60.

27. Trudy Dehue, "Psychology and the Gradual Origination of the Random Group Design," *Isis* 88, no. 4 (December 1997): 653–73.

28. Thomas Gray, "Changing Unsubstantiated Belief: Testing the Ignorance Hypothesis," *Canadian Journal of Behavioral Science* 17, no. 3 (1985): 263–70.

29. Alex B. Berezow, "The Most Important Question in Science," American Council on Science and Health, November 28, 2017, https://www.acsh.org/news/2017/11/28/most-important-question-science-12210 (accessed December 20, 2017).

INDEX